WORLD STUDY GUIDE
FREE INFORMATION SERVICE

www.babeltech.ac.uk

If you would like more information about Babel Technical College

(details page 388), fill in your name and address below, detach and send off this card.

Name: _____

Address: _____

_____

_____

_____

- -

WORLD STUDY GUIDE
READER INFORMATION SERVICE

L o n d o n

If you would like more information about The Cambridge School of English

(details page 204), fill in your name and address below, detach and send off this card.

Name: _____

Address: _____

_____

_____

_____

D1628960

Affix
stamp
here

Babel Technical College
David Game House
69 Notting Hill Gate
London
W11 3JS
United Kingdom

Affix
stamp
here

The Cambridge School of English
3 Stukeley Street
Covent Garden
London
WC2B 5LB
United Kingdom

WORLD STUDY GUIDE
READER INFORMATION SERVICE

If you would like more information about Queen's University Belfast
(details page 542), fill in your name and address below, detach and send off this card.

Name: _____

Address: _____

_____

_____

_____

Please indicate areas of interest:

Undergraduate ☐   Postgraduate ☐

Subject(s)

WORLD STUDY GUIDE
READER INFORMATION SERVICE

The University of Reading

If you would like more information about The University of Reading
(details page 544), fill in your name and address below, detach and send off this card.

Name: _____

Address: _____

_____

_____

_____

P/G ☐   U/G ☐

Affix
stamp
here

The Admissions Office
Queen's University Belfast
Belfast
Northern Ireland
BT7 1NN
United Kingdom

Affix
stamp
here

International and Study
Abroad Office OC
The University of Reading
PO Box 217
Reading
RG6 6AH
United Kingdom

WORLD STUDY GUIDE
READER INFORMATION SERVICE

City & Guilds of
London Art School

If you would like more information about the City & Guilds of London Art School (details page 103), fill in your name and address below, detach and send off this card.

Name: _____

Address: _____

_____

_____

_____

WORLD STUDY GUIDE
READER INFORMATION SERVICE

UNIVERSITY OF
STIRLING

If you would like more information about The University of Stirling (details page 566), fill in your name and address below, detach and send off this card.

Name: _____

Address: _____

_____

_____

_____

City & Guilds of London Art School
124 Kennington Park Road
London
SE11 4DJ
United Kingdon

Student Recruitment and Admissions
The University of Stirling
Stirling
FK9 4LA
United Kingdom

TOP ⑤ MODERN UNIVERSITIES

- Academic excellence in teaching and research

- 1600 international students from over 100 countries

- International Student Orientation Programme

- London airport collection service for Orientation in September

- Free English Language support classes

- International Foundation Programme

- Dedicated Support Unit for international students

- Immigration and Visa Advice

International Office
University of Plymouth
Drake Circus
Plymouth PL4 8AA
United Kingdom

Tel: +44 (0)1752 233345
Fax: +44 (0)1752 232014
e-mail: intoff@plymouth.ac.uk
http://www.plymouth.ac.uk/international

At studentUK.com you can check out Uni's and Colleges, without setting foot outside your front door.

With virtual open days, campus guides and local info all in one handy place, the search won't tire you out.

studentUK.com ★ ★

Bournemouth University

your future starts here

A dynamic, modern institution, dedicated to providing a world class, professionally-based education

- One of Britain's top Universities for graduate employment

- Courses designed in association with industry professionals to reflect the needs of modern business

- Located in Bournemouth, a stunning seaside location with sandy beaches, a clean, safe environment and a mild climate, only two hours from London

- Guaranteed accommodation to international students applying before mid August deadline

- Free residential Orientation Programme for all new international students

Our University has seven Schools of study:

- The Business School

- Conservation Sciences

- Design, Engineering & Computing

- Finance & Law

- Institute of Health & Community Studies

- Bournemouth Media School

- Service Industries

www.bournemouth.ac.uk

EDUCATION
the best you can be

For more information:
Telephone: +44 (0) 1202 595470
Facsimile: +44 (0) 1202 595287
e-mail: inta@bournemouth.ac.uk

'A' LEVELS/GCSE

Choose from over 25 subjects:
Sciences,
Maths/Further Maths,
Computing,
Business Studies,
Economics,
Communication & Media.

UNIVERSITY FOUNDATION YEAR

This is available to overseas students who wish to combine English,
Business English with a specialist area;
Business, Information Technology, Computing,
Travel & Tourism Management, Art & Design.

UNIVERSITY DIPLOMA (HND)

The Higher National Diploma is available in over 20 subject areas including:
Business/Management/Marketing.
Computing/Software Engineering/IT
Fashion Design/Technology/Graphics
Hospitality Management/Travel & Tourism
Furniture Studies

CREATIVE STUDIES

Web & Graphic Design
Floristry
Beauty & Holistic Therapies
Drama & Music Technology
Fashion
Furniture Making

EFL

EFL – English as a foreign language full-time course. All-year round flexible
enrolment with eight levels throughout the year and four additional levels in
the summer months
EFL-plus – to improve exam skills, grammar, conversation and Business English,
English for Tourism, English with career and leisure options. There are thousands of
choices at **ncn**
IELTS Preparation
Teacher Training (CELTA/Culture Matters)

Sue Griffin HC, The International Office, New College Nottingham,
The Adams Building, Stoney Street, Nottingham NG1 lLJ, England
Tel: +44 115 910 4610/12/15 Fax: +44 115 910 4611
www.ncn.ac.uk email: internat@ncn.ac.uk

ncn offers both the traditional academic route to university as well as more flexible learning choices that include vocational and career focused courses. Students receive tutorial support and key skills on all courses.

These successful one year courses provide international students with the skills and learning styles to study with confidence at degree level at British universities and colleges.

The HND is equivalent to a first year degree course. It can lead to direct entry to the second or in some cases third year of a university degree.

This Diploma course is designed to equip students with the knowledge, understanding and skills needed for success in current and future business employment, or to progress to full degree-level study.

Nottingham is a centre for cultural and creative activities, and New College offers an outstanding range of innovative and creative study courses. These are ideal for international students who wish to pursue their natural talents, develop their English skills and succeed in their career aspirations. The college has won awards for its Floristry course which has flexible start dates, and has a superb **ncn** Arts Centre which is a nationally recognised centre of excellence for music, dance, drama and stagecrafts/ technical theatre. Several famous actors launched their career with us.

We have over 30 years' experience of teaching English to overseas students and our English Language courses have been inspected and accredited by the British Council for 14 years. There is a truly friendly and cosmopolitan atmosphere at **ncn** with nearly 1,000 adult students from over 50 countries studying with us every year.

accredited by
The British Council

New College Nottingham

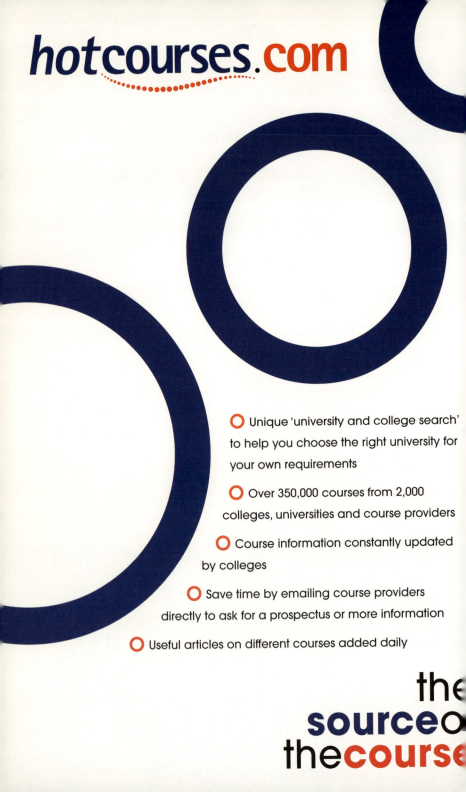

COVENTRY TECHNICAL COLLEGE

Tile Hill College COVENTRY

RECEPTION

Construction - Fabrication & Welding

A Levels

Business, Administration & IT

Art & Design

Construction & Built Environment

English Language

Mechanical Engineering

Hairdressing, Beauty & Holistic Therapies

Automobile Engineering & PSV

Electronics & Telecommunications

...sic Technology

Computing - IT

Multimedia

...ience & ...th Studies

Fashion

Leisure & Tourism

Coventry Technical College working in partnership with Tile Hill College, ...on University (Birmingham), Coventry University and the University of Warwick.

Coventry Technical College: is a major British Council Accredited further education institution located in the centre of the United Kingdom. Offering excellent facilities and tuition all supported by modern equipment and an approved IELTS **English Language Centre**

The College offers International students a wide choice of courses designed to enhance your qualifications, preparing you for University or employment.

INVESTOR IN PEOPLE

Publishers

Mike Elms, Jeremy Hunt

EDITORIAL

Editor

Yolande Taylor

Production Manager

Louise Hadden

Graphic Design

Tim Nolan

Layout

James Clarkson, Jo Flood

Sub-editor

Lisa McFarlane

Assistant Editor

Natalie Bloom

Editorial Assistants

Chris Batty, Louisa Edwards,
Eifion Heap, Jennifer Shiels

ADVERTISING SALES

Commercial Director

Amanda Gregory

Account Managers

Steve Billows, Christian Boesen, Michaela Deegan,
Robert Eagles, Simon Emmett, Danica Hill

ISBN 1 898730 63 6
© Hotcourses Ltd 2002

Hotcourses
121 King Street, London W6 9JG
Tel: +44 (0)20 8600 5300 Fax: +44 (0)20 8741 7716
Email: jeremy.hunt@hotcourses.com
Web: www.hotcourses.com

Using the guide

Welcome to the *World Study Guide Study in Britain Handbook 2002*. Compiled in association with the Universities and Colleges Admissions Service (UCAS) and the Independent Schools Council (ISC), the guide is designed to provide you with all the information you need to make the right choices on where and what to study in the UK. Whatever you are looking for, from GCSEs and A levels to a BSc, MSc or MBA the following pages should have all the details.

UCAS is the UK's central organisation through which applications are processed for entry on to full-time undergraduate courses, HNDs and university diplomas.

ISC provides a single, unified organisation to speak and act on behalf of the eight independent schools' associations which comprise it. It promotes independent schools' common interests.

Structure of the guide

As with all Hotcourses guides, the *World Study Guide* is set out for easy, accessible referencing. If you do not know about matters such as qualifications and the types of colleges in the UK, the early section from pages 25 to 35 explains 'The British education system'. 'Applying to study' (pages 37 to 48) includes useful information on applying for the course of your choice and 'Arriving in Britain' (pages 49 to 54) covers useful visa and immigration information.

A to Z of subjects

The 'A to Z of subjects' starts on page 66 with chapters covering all the main subject areas, from accountancy to veterinary science. This section provides general information on further and higher education programmes, covering Higher National Diplomas and Certificates,

The Hotcourses International Student Festival 2001

bachelor degrees and master's qualifications in the UK. We have chosen a large number of courses which have stood out in quality assessments and a selection of those offered by well-known specialist institutions. It is not, however, a comprehensive list. Given that there are thousands of courses in the UK, it would be impossible to cover them all in a book of this size. However, all the main subject areas at each UCAS institution are listed in the course directory from page 623 to 628.

Teaching and research assessments

The 'A to Z of subjects' also contains results tables from independent inspections of higher education establishments. These assessments appraise the quality of teaching and research. Bear in mind that not all institutions have been assessed for all subjects and, as a result, some tables may be incomplete.

We are delighted to include the results of the most recent Research Assessment Exercise (RAE). Released in December 2001, the tables are primarily of interest to postgraduate research students. The RAEs give an indication of a department's international standing with regard to research.

The teaching quality (TQA) in university departments is tested every four years on a rolling programme. Some are about to be inspected for a second time, whereas some are still awaiting inspection for the first time. Therefore, there may be a number of universities and colleges of higher education providing excellent courses which haven't been visited.

The research and teaching rankings are for higher education only. For vocational and further education, there are no independent assessments available, and it is advisable to visit a college before enrolling to check that it suits your requirements.

Profiles

The 'A to Z of subjects' is followed by detailed profiles of a number of independent schools, specialist and vocational colleges, further education colleges, and higher education colleges and universities in the UK. These are divided into three sections: independent schools, specialist and vocational and further education, and higher education. Further education colleges offer courses that are both academic and vocational to school-leavers, adults who want to train for a new career or improve their qualifications, and people wishing to learn new skills. Higher education institutions provide academic qualifications such as Higher National Diplomas, degrees and diplomas. The profiles contain key information, for example location, fees, which subject areas are particularly strong, and the provision of facilities.

Contact details

Contact details for all UCAS institutions and for those institutions which have a short profile in the 'A to Z of chapters' are included at the back of the book. You can find further information at www.hotcourses.com, at the UCAS website www.ucas.com or at the ISC website www.iscis.uk.net. If you want a prospectus for any of the universities or colleges listed in the guide to be sent to you free of charge, just fill in the Reader Information Service postcard at the front of the guide.

Throughout the guide, for reasons of consistency and brevity, certain conventions are observed. All internet addresses omit 'http://' and start with 'www'.

All telephone numbers are written as if dialled from outside the UK; don't forget to drop the 0 in brackets. If you are dialling from within the UK, you need to omit the international code +44 before the number written and must remember to include the 0 in brackets.

If you have any suggestions for the next issue of this guide, please contact us on +44 (0)20 8600 5300 or email jeremy.hunt@hotcourses.com

Britain and the British

With an area of 240,000 square kilometres, 960 kilometres from south to north and under 480 kilometres at its widest point, Britain has a population of almost 60 million people with an average of 240 inhabitants per square kilometre, making the island one of the most densely populated in the world.

Multicultural Britain

From the Bronze Age 5,000 years ago when neolithic migrants started entering the country, Britain has been evolving into a multicultural nation. In more recent years, this trend has accelerated and there is no longer such a thing as the typical Brit. Forget the stereotypes of bowler-hatted businessmen, fish and chips and stiff upper lips. Britain is one of the most ethnically diverse countries in the world.

The country has benefited in all areas of its culture, from industry and commerce to music, art, sport, science and literature. Multiculturalism has brought fresh ideas, new skills, labour, capital and cultural diversity, making the country richer and more varied.

It is for these very reasons that, as an international student in the UK, you will be made to feel very welcome.

A tour of the country

So, should you tell people you're off to study in Great Britain, the United Kingdom (UK) or the British Isles? Well, it depends on what you mean. Great Britain comprises England, Wales and Scotland; the United Kingdom is Northern Ireland, England, Wales and Scotland, and the British Isles refers to Northern Ireland, the

The Royal Academy of Art, London

ATLANTIC
OCEAN

John o'Groats

Inverness

Aberdeen

SCOTLAND

Dundee

Glasgow   St Andrews

Edinburgh

Newcastle   NORTH
SEA

Belfast

Leeds   York

Galway   Dublin   Manchester

IRISH SEA

 IRELAND   Liverpool   Sheffield

Limerick   Nottingham

Stafford   Norwich

Aberystwyth   Birmingham   **MIDLANDS**

Cheltenham   Cambridge

WALES

Cardiff   Oxford

Swansea   Bristol

CELTIC SEA   London   Dover

Exeter   Brighton   Calais

Plymouth   Portsmouth   Hastings

Land's End

ENGLISH CHANNEL

Le Havre

Brest

Paris

FRANCE

Southeast England

miles of heritage coastline, or thousands of historic buildings and gardens.

South and southeast England

This area encompasses the country's capital, London, the surrounding counties referred to as the Home Counties, and some coastal towns and ports. The Home Counties offer peaceful green landscapes whilst being within reach of the capital. Many universities in this area are located in beautiful countryside, such as Buckinghamshire Chilterns University College and The University of Surrey. Further east and en route to the rest of Europe, Kent is traditionally known as the Garden of England, but other areas along the south coast could claim this title. There are several universities in the coastal towns and ports of the south of England in Brighton, Portsmouth, and Southampton. Here, picturesque villages merge with small towns.

The South Downs Way, running between Eastbourne and Winchester, is one of the UK's ancient long distance footpaths and has great views of the coast. Along the seafront, tourists can enjoy attractions such as chalky cliffs, amusement parks, shingle beaches and Victorian piers.

London

With a population of nearly eight million, London is Europe's largest city and arguably one of the most cosmopolitan places in the world. Its main geographical feature is the River Thames, which divides the city into northern and southern halves. Many people are attracted to London as a place to study, particularly if they have visited the capital before and seen its beautiful old buildings, elegant streets and spacious parks, and returned home long enough to forget its pollution and high

Republic of Ireland, Wales, Scotland and England. In this guide, we have generally used the UK, or Britain where we are not including Northern Ireland.

With the establishment of the Welsh Assembly and the Scottish Parliament, there has been much debate over regional identity and each of the four countries making up the UK has its own flag, identity, traditions and ancient languages. Though there are disagreements over the political roles of England, Scotland, Wales and Northern Ireland, they all have fixed political boundaries.

Wherever you decide to study, whether it is St Andrews in Scotland like Prince William, Cardiff in Wales, Manchester in England or Queen's in Belfast, you will be in easy reach of cities, countryside and coastline. And you'll only be a train ride away from the rest of Europe.

England

As a newcomer, you might find England easier to understand if you divide it into broad areas, as the maps on the following pages illustrate. If the stress of city life gets all to much, you can retreat to one of England's nine national parks, six forest parks, 200 country parks, more than 600

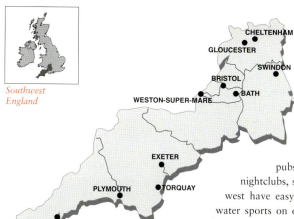

Southwest England

CHELTENHAM
GLOUCESTER
SWINDON
BRISTOL
BATH
WESTON-SUPER-MARE
EXETER
PLYMOUTH
TORQUAY
FALMOUTH

from the fermented juice of apples).

The scenery here is rich and varied, with upland moors, steep river valleys and a magnificent, rocky coastline with sandy coves. As well as the requisite pubs, college bars, and nightclubs, students in the southwest have easy access to the many water sports on offer, such as sailing, surfing, windsurfing and diving. With relatively high unemployment in the southwest, many people depend entirely on the summer tourist trade to make a living. Consequently, the region has some of the cheapest accommodation in the UK. Cornwall is approximately five hours' drive from London.

The Midlands

The Midlands is a term used to describe central England. This region was once the centre of England's manufacturing industry. Although industry now has less prominence in the region, Birmingham (the second largest city in Britain) is still a major manufacturing centre. Along with Bradford and Leicester, it is one of the best places in Britain to eat curry (it even has its own dish – the Balti). Other large cities in the area like Nottingham and Coventry have at least two, sometimes three universities. The rest of the Midlands has plenty of tourist attractions, with historic villages and towns including Stratford-upon-Avon, birthplace of English playwright and poet, William Shakespeare.

North England

The North is a mixture of mountainous scenery and farmland, and industrial towns and cities. The east and west sides of northern England are divided by the Pennines – a range of hills and valleys

prices. London offers a huge number of education opportunities. 40 per cent of university students in Britain study in London, and there are hundreds of private language and specialist colleges.

If you are ever feeling homesick you are guaranteed to find a sample of your home country in London, be it food, cinema, newspapers, books or drama. But, on the downside, if you are looking to improve your English, you may find it hard to escape the international community. Meeting people from all over the world is certainly one of the benefits of studying in the capital but you may not talk to as many native English speakers as you would like, particularly if you are studying in a language school.

Southwest England

The region can be divided between Devon and Cornwall in the far west, Dorset, Wiltshire and Somerset in the east, and Gloucestershire to the north. The south-westerly tip of England is washed by the Gulf Stream, so it tends to be warmer than the rest of the country and is a popular holiday destination.

Devon and nearby Somerset are known for their traditional cream teas (tea served with scones, jam and clotted cream) and scrumpy (a strong alcoholic drink made

The North and The Midlands

Scotland

Scotland's landscape varies from the rolling hills of the Borders – the lowlands roughly to the southwest of Edinburgh – to the wild and uninhabitable crags of the Cairngorms. The countryside has an unrivalled variety of wildlife, with some species not found anywhere else in Britain. It's an often underrated country; few English realise what an extraordinary neighbour they have. There has been a long history of conflict and rivalry between the two countries but fortunately these days this is limited to good-natured banter.

The Scottish are justifiably proud of their rich, Celtic cultural heritage which is alive and thriving. And although Scotland's best known poet, Robert 'Rabbie' Burns, wrote an ode to it, there is much more to Scottish culture than the haggis (and bagpipes and kilts for that matter). The Gaelic language, Celtic in origin, is spoken by over 60,000 people, most of whom reside in the Western Isles. Although this may seem like a fraction of the total population of Scotland, government support for Gaelic education and Gaelic organisations demonstrate that it is an important part of Scottish culture and heritage. Scotland has its own currency but all notes and coins are legal tender in the rest of the UK. The education system is different to England and is covered in detail in 'The British education system' from page 25.

Scotland is also home to one of the world's leading cultural events – the annual Edinburgh International Festival. This is the largest arts festival in Britain and a must if you are interested in seeing fringe theatre, music and poetry being performed to audiences from all over the world. If you are interested in science, you will be pleased to hear Edinburgh also hosts the

which extend from Derbyshire towards the Scottish border. The Yorkshire Moors and the Yorkshire Dales offer plenty of hilly terrain for walkers. The region used to be heavily industrialised. Liverpool, Sheffield and Newcastle all have a history of industry whether it be a busy dock or steel or coal production.

Northern cities are now undergoing major regeneration projects, striving to be major centres of communication and commerce. Most offer a whole host of theatres, concert halls, sports venues, art galleries and museums. Northerners have a reputation for being open and friendly and the cost of living tends to be quite a bit lower than in the South.

Manchester

With a population of about 2.6 million, Manchester is often regarded as Britain's second city. Hosting the Commonwealth Games in 2002, it is a commercial, educational and cultural capital of the northwest of England. There is also a vast student population.

Scotland

Wales

The principality of Wales has some exciting cities. Cardiff, for example, has some fantastic architecture, Victorian arcades and elegant public buildings. Wales is also home to some of the most stunning scenery in the British Isles. Rugged and imposing mountains, rolling hills, moorlands, forests and valleys are major attractions for visitors from all over the world. To protect this beauty, Snowdonia, the Pembrokeshire Coast and the Brecon Beacons have been designated as national parks.

Until recent decades, coal and steel production were the centre of the Welsh economy. The coal industry has now largely died out due to competition in prices from abroad and the switch to other methods of supplying power. While steelmaking remains significant, the largest area of growth has been in the service industries and the development of technology.

England and Wales were united by the half-Welsh king, Henry VII, in 1485 so Wales shares many of England's political and cultural systems including its currency and legal system. Nevertheless, like Scotland, Wales has a strong independent identity and its own parliament, the Welsh Assembly.

The Welsh language is believed to be one of the oldest in Europe (the Celts crossed from Europe to Wales in about 600 BC). It is still widely spoken by those living around Lampeter and Aberystwyth on the mountainous west side of the country, and in pockets in the north and centre. Until 1942, the Welsh language was suppressed but the Welsh have since become more and more determined to keep their language alive. There are Welsh television and radio

world's biggest single-city science festival. Scientists in Scotland are at the forefront of research into the human equivalent of BSE and Aids.

Edinburgh

Scotland's capital, Edinburgh, is an ancient city built on crags and cliffs with serpentine streets that rise and dip. During the late 18th and early 19th centuries, Edinburgh was the focus of an age of Scottish cultural brilliance which produced philosophers such as David Hume. Today, its castles and palaces, its Great Kirk, its streets and galleries, not to mention its public parks and golf courses, are major attractions for tourists and for the students who attend its universities and colleges.

Glasgow

Scotland's largest city is home to over 667,540 people. The 1990 European City of Culture, Glasgow has several large theatres, great art galleries and major collections of fine and applied arts. Its many fine buildings earned Glasgow the title of UK City of Architecture and Design (1999).

Wales

Cardiff

Cardiff, the Welsh capital since 1955, is in south Glamorgan. Its rich maritime heritage comes from its 19th-century growth as a port whose primary function was to ship coal produced in the Welsh valleys. At its centre is its castle, originally built in the 11th century but largely rebuilt in neo-Gothic style in the 19th century.

As well as being a thriving cultural centre with excellent museums, such as the Welsh Folk Museum and the Maritime Museum, Cardiff is also the headquarters of Welsh rugby. Cardiff hosted the 1999 Rugby World Cup at its sports venue, the Millennium Stadium – the focus of many international events. The city's cultural status is enhanced by the fact that it has the largest concentration of film and TV production companies outside London, resulting in plenty of media-related industries. In addition, you will find numerous cafés, restaurants, pubs and bars in which to relax.

stations and all Welsh schools teach Welsh up to the age of 16. At Welsh universities where there is no separate Celtic or Welsh department, the language is offered as an optional modern language which all students can learn free of charge alongside their major studies. All Welsh college and university courses are taught in English.

Every town and village has its own special local traditions and events. Wales is home to 'Town of Books' Hay-on-Wye which comes alive every year when its literary festival attracts internationally-renowned poets, writers and celebrities. The country's strong literary tradition is matched by its musical history. Both are celebrated at some of the most respected arts festivals in Britain. Eisteddfods, literally meaning 'a sitting', are cultural gatherings at which artists compete in music and literature, and only Welsh is spoken. The Llangollen International Music Eisteddfod takes place annually with music and dance from all over the world. The Royal National Eisteddfod, celebrating arts, crafts, literature, dance and drama, is held in a different location in Wales every year.

Northern Ireland

The northeastern corner of Ireland is part of the United Kingdom and its official name is Northern Ireland.

Ireland was an independent state until, in 1171, when the English kings made the first of a series of encroachments into Irish territory. Subsequently, English monarchs of the late 15th and 16th centuries waged a campaign against Irish dissidents. Since then, the history of Ireland has been rife with political upheaval, fluctuating between uneasy peace and violent rebellions. In 1801, Ireland was officially united, under the Act of Union, with England and Scotland as the United Kingdom of Great

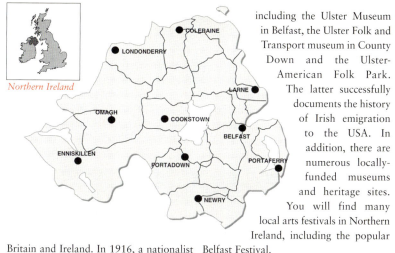

Northern Ireland

including the Ulster Museum in Belfast, the Ulster Folk and Transport museum in County Down and the Ulster-American Folk Park. The latter successfully documents the history of Irish emigration to the USA. In addition, there are numerous locally-funded museums and heritage sites. You will find many local arts festivals in Northern Ireland, including the popular Belfast Festival.

Britain and Ireland. In 1916, a nationalist rising was quelled and its leaders executed. Sinn Fein, the Irish Nationalist Party, declared Ireland a republic and, in 1922, the country was given dominion status. The six northern counties of the ancient province of Ulster were given the right to opt out. When Ireland became independent in 1921, the Protestant majority in the northern counties opted to stay as part of the United Kingdom, with a separate parliament (Stormont) and limited self-government. From the beginning, Northern Ireland's parliament had a unionist majority from which ministers were drawn for government. Nationalists resented this domination and their marginalisation from political life. After a sophisticated civil rights movement developed in the region during the 1960s, a series of sectarian insurrections erupted. This has been the root cause of the 'Troubles', as the province's civil and political problems are known. The Good Friday Agreement, signed in 1998, was meant to mark an end to sectarian violence and signal the beginning of peace talks involving all parties. Its success remains to be seen. The next stage is for unionists and republicans to decommission illegal weapons.

Northern Ireland's cultural heritage is rich and varied. It has several museums

Belfast

The city of Belfast is home to a third of Northern Ireland's population, nearly half a million people. The city grew rapidly in the 19th century with the expansion of industries such as linen, rope making and shipbuilding. Industry has played an enormous part in developing the region. The city has been at the heart of the Troubles but has more recently transformed itself into a city of culture and tourism. There are numerous museums chronicling Irish heritage. Queen's University Belfast is half a mile away from the city itself.

The weather

One of the only things that you can count on with British weather is its unreliability. British people also love talking about the weather. Despite the changeable nature of British weather, there are four distinct seasons: winter, spring, summer and autumn. On the whole it is fairly temperate – temperatures rarely fall below -5°c or rise above 32°c. One of the most noticeable climactic features in Britain is long summer days and short winter ones – getting dark at 10 pm in July and 4 pm in December.

International weather comparisons

Place	Month	Average temp max c	min c	Extreme temp max c	min c	Month	Average temp max c	min c	Extreme temp max c	min c	Rainfall
London	Jun-Jul-Aug	21	13	33	6	Dec-Jan-Feb	7	3	15	-9	611mm
Belfast	Jun-Jul-Aug	18	10	28	3	Dec-Jan-Feb	4	2	14	-12	951mm
Birmingham	Jun-Jul-Aug	20	12	32	5	Dec-Jan-Feb	7	3	14	-8.9	622mm
Cardiff	Jun-Jul-Aug	20	12	32	6	Dec-Jan-Feb	7	2	15	-11	1061mm
Edinburgh	Jun-Jul-Aug	18	11	28	4	Dec-Jan-Feb	6	2	14	-8	638mm
Plymouth	Jun-Jul-Aug	19	12	29	4	Dec-Jan-Feb	8	4	14	-7.3	982mm
York	Jun-Jul-Aug	20.3	15	32.2	3.7	Dec-Jan-Feb	6.6	1	16.5	-13	588mm
Buenos Aires	Jun-Jul-Aug	15	6	28	-5	Dec-Jan-Feb	28	17	39	5	950mm
Rio de Janeiro	Jun-Jul-Aug	24	18	33	11	Dec-Jan-Feb	29	23	38	15	1086mm
Hong Kong	Jun-Jul-Aug	30	26	35	21	Dec-Jan-Feb	18	14	27	3	2208mm
Beijing	Jun-Jul-Aug	31	20	41	12	Dec-Jan-Feb	3	-8	15	-20	624mm
Bombay	Jun-Jul-Aug	30	25	35	22	Dec-Jan-Feb	29	20	35	12	1811mm
Tokyo	Jun-Jul-Aug	27	20	36	12	Dec-Jan-Feb	9	-1	36	-12	1565mm
Kuala Lumpur	Jun-Jul-Aug	32	23	36	20	Dec-Jan-Feb	40	22	36	19	2448mm
Mexico City	Jun-Jul-Aug	20	6	29	9	Dec-Jan-Feb	39	12	24	-2	749mm
Lisbon	Jun-Jul-Aug	27	16	40	12	Dec-Jan-Feb	18	8	22	-1	708mm
Singapore	Jun-Jul-Aug	31	24	34	21	Dec-Jan-Feb	31	23	34	20	2415mm
Madrid	Jun-Jul-Aug	29	16	38	7	Dec-Jan-Feb	10	2	19	-9	682mm
Washington	Jun-Jul-Aug	29	19	40	9	Dec-Jan-Feb	7	-2	26	-26	1064mm

The British education system

Education in Britain enjoys a long and distinguished history. From the 14th century onwards, schools of many different kinds began to spring up; from small, informal schools run in parish churches and schools attached to religious foundations such as cathedrals and monasteries, to craft guilds that were set up to educate apprentices in a chosen skill.

Most of the early schools offered elementary education to the children of ordinary parents. The humblest taught their pupils to read, learn prayers and psalms, the Ten Commandments, the seven deadly sins and seven sacraments. At grammar schools, such as the one at Stratford-on-Avon which Shakespeare attended, the pupils, drawn from the wealthier sections of town society, were expected to be able to read and write before they were admitted. They then went on to learn Latin grammar and compose Latin verse.

Schooling was not free nor was it easy. The holidays were short and the school days were long, often beginning at 6 am and continuing until 6 pm with short breaks for food. The classes were also large with up to a hundred pupils being taught in one room. The masters believed wholeheartedly in corporal punishment.

Just before the end of the Second World War, the Education Act of 1944 was passed. This act established many aspects of British schools which are familiar now, such as the separate primary and secondary school system, local autonomy under the guidance of central government, social and games facilities, and the provision of school meals at a very low cost. More importantly, it established a pattern of different types of schools

Picture courtesy of the Teacher Training Agency

providing different types of education for different types of pupils.

The thinking behind the 1944 Education Act was that all children should have an equal opportunity to participate in secondary schooling and that the education they received should be suited to their age, aptitude and ability. This essentially meant a division into different schools according to academic ability, and resulted in the tripartite system. Grammar schools continued to provide an academic education, secondary modern schools were set up to provide a more vocational training and secondary technical schools were meant to provide the kind of education that a modern, industrial society would need its citizens to have.

Much of what has been passed down in terms of today's education system has remained; from the importance of religion to the provision of sport or social facilities.

The British education system today

Education in Britain is broadly divided into three categories: primary (five to 11 years), secondary (11 to 18 years), and tertiary (higher education). This is the same for England, Wales and Northern Ireland. Scotland has its own system (the main difference is in the qualifications awarded, which is explained later in this chapter). School is compulsory for children between five and 16 years and there are two sets of official exams. Only the first, at 16, is compulsory. Most 17 year-olds then go on to some kind of further education or work-related training. Adult education has also become more popular and most universities and colleges of higher education now have a growing number of mature students.

Independent and state schools

Education can also be divided into state-funded and privately-funded (independent) sectors. Independent schools charge fees and are said to be 'independent' of state control. There are independent schools of all kinds up and down the country, charging a range of fees and catering for all ages and religious beliefs. Around six per cent of school children attend Britain's 2,400 independent schools. The majority of schools are state-funded and free. In England and Wales there are around 8.5 million pupils in 30,000 state schools. Some are selective and have such good reputations that competition for entrance is fierce. Most state schools are co-educational (mixed sex) and some have a religious bias, usually either Church of England or Roman Catholic, although a number of state-funded Muslim schools have recently opened.

The National Curriculum

Since 1988, there has been a National Curriculum in England, Wales and Northern Ireland, which lays down exactly what is to be taught in school and at what level, from the age of five to 16. It determines the subjects to be taught, sets targets and standards for assessment, and thereby standardises the education experience of pupils across the country.

All state and some independent schools follow the National Curriculum. Pupils are tested at the end of each of four 'key stages' and the results (for each school not for each individual pupil) are published. In this way, there is a measure of the success of each state school available to parents and other interested groups in the form of league tables. With both schools and higher education establishments subject to league tables and rankings, the whole education system has become much more accountable.

From September 2002, the curriculum will include education in citizenship and democracy, helping pupils to develop an understanding of their roles and responsibilities as citizens in a modern democracy.

GCSE and post-16 qualifications

When pupils reach the age of 16, they sit GCSEs (General Certificate of Secondary Education) in six to 10 subjects. These are graded from A* to G. There is also an International GCSE (IGSCSE) which has the same grading system, and is an intenationally-recognised qualification, accepted as a requirement for entry to British universities and institutes of higher education.

Those students who have five or more GCSEs at grades A* to C can go on to study a selection of post-16 qualifications for two years. Post-16 qualifications include A level (Advanced level), AS level (Advanced Subsidiary level) and Vocational A level. A levels are graded between A and E, and recently, the 'super-A grade' has been introduced to recognise outstanding candidates.

In the past, most students took between two and four subjects at A level, and the subjects chosen often reflected what a student would like to study at degree level. Recently, however, the government has introduced a number of reforms, piloted in September 2000 to address undue narrowness and lack of flexibility in the previous post-16 curriculum. The developments were designed to lead to a broader A level programme and improved vocational qualifications, underpinned by rigorous standards and key skills.

Students following A level programmes are now able to broaden their study by taking additional subjects using the new AS level, or by adding a vocational dimension and studying one or more of the new, smaller, six-unit Vocational A level qualifications. Students on vocational programmes can broaden their studies by taking one or more of the smaller Vocational A levels and the new AS level.

Advanced and the Advanced Subsidiary level (A/AS level)

For courses that started in September 2000, A levels normally consist of six assessment units of approximately equal size. Three of these make up an AS level qualification, representing the first half of an advanced level course of study. The additional three are known as A2, representing the second half. A levels and AS levels are graded A to E for pass grades, with U (unclassified) for fail. Achievement on the Advanced Subsidiary with the A2, contributes equally to the full A level.

Vocational A level

Vocational A levels are more concerned with skills needed for an occupation, trade or profession compared with GCSEs and A levels. Based on the old GNVQ (General National Vocational Qualification), the Vocational A level has been designed to meet progression needs in different vocational areas, and to offer choice and flexibility to schools and colleges. Students studying Vocational A levels at post-16 qualification level can apply to universities and colleges of higher education.

Higher National Diploma (HND) and Higher National Certificate (HNC)

HNDs and HNCs are taken at further education colleges or universities and are available in subjects related to work and are the equivalent to four GCSEs, grades A* to C. An HND is a higher education qualification which combines career preparation with opportunities for further study. Students may convert an HND into an undergraduate course, ususally missing out at least the first year of the degree. HNCs tend to be taken part time by people in work, whereas HNDs are usually full-time courses which can be converted into degrees with two additional years of study.

The British education system

National Vocational Qualification (NVQ)

NVQs are work-related, industry practical qualifications relevant to particular occupations. Standards are set by employers, trade unions and professional bodies. Each level is competence based and there is no time restriction to reach the appropriate level.

Qualifications – Scotland

SCE and Highers (the new Higher Still)

Although unique in the UK, the Scottish education system has similarities to countries such as the USA, Australia and Japan. The Scottish Certificate of Education (Standard Grade) is taken at 16 (fourth year), and has three levels – Foundation, General and Credit – awarded by the Scottish Qualifications Agency. At 17, pupils take the Higher Still, of which there are five levels – Access, Intermediate 1, Intermediate 2, Higher and Advanced Higher. The Higher Still (known as 'Highers') fulfills the university or college entrance requirement. Students who wish to begin university or college at 18 years – the same age as in the rest of the UK – stay on to take the Certificate of Sixth Year Studies in relevant subjects, or retake Highers to get better grades.

Scottish Vocational Qualification

Assessment is now done mainly by the Scottish Qualifications Authority (SQA). The new qualification system introduced in 1999 applies to further education colleges as well as secondary schools. Awards include Scottish Vocational Qualifications (SVQ); Higher National Certificate (HNC); and Higher National Diploma (HND). SVQs were designed to be delivered in the workplace and are based on national standards, developed by industry for industry. For detailed information on education in Scotland contact:

Scottish Qualifications Authority
Hanover House
24 Douglas Street
Glasgow G2 7NQ
Helpdesk: +44 (0)141 242 2214
Fax: +44 (0)141 242 2244
Email: helpdesk@sqa.org.uk
Website: www.sqa.org.uk

The International Baccalaureate

This is a two-year course for pupils aged between 16 and 19, and is an equivalent to the A level. It provides a broad curriculum, recognised for entry to higher education in many countries including the UK. It was originally created to suit the needs of children attending international schools across the world and is now offered by some educational institutions in the UK such as independent schools, specialist sixth-forms and tertiary colleges.

Alternative places of study

Specialist and vocational colleges

There are a number of schools and colleges that specialise in particular subjects. Whether it is Blake College or the London Centre for Fashion Studies, there are plenty to choose from in a number of areas. Many, such as the Vidal Sassoon School of Hairdressing offer vocationally-based skills. Some offer degree courses and some do not. Many colleges and universities offer a one-year diploma or foundation course which can be a good way to learn about your chosen subject, prepare for higher education and get used to the British way of life.

There can be confusion over certificates and qualifications awarded at private colleges. Some offer nationally-recognised qualifications, as explained on page 31, and others offer foundation courses that can be a good stepping stone onto degree courses. Those colleges offering diplomas bearing their own name as the accrediting body should be considered with caution. If they are genuinely well-known, and you should do some research to find out if this is the case, then the diploma will be useful to you when you finish. But you need to check very carefully that the qualification you will be awarded is respected. If you are planning to take your studies to a higher level, you should also check whether the diploma satisfies entrance requirements.

Language schools

Many students come to Britain solely to study English; others plan to study something else later but want to brush up on their English first. You should take care when researching prospective schools to ensure that they meet your criteria. Outlined opposite are some accrediting bodies that are useful for ensuring high standards.

Accreditation for language schools

There are various accreditation and membership schemes for English language schools but the best known is run by the British Council. Schools have to meet strict criteria in order to receive British Council accreditation, and undergo a thorough inspection of teaching facilities, teacher qualifications and management. For schools that have received British Council accreditation, there are two further associations. The British Association of State English Language Teaching (BASELT) is an association of state-sector English language teaching institutions. ARELS, the Association of Recognised English Language Schools, is for schools in the private sector. Courses in the state sector are often run in further education colleges. Class sizes may be larger than at private schools but courses are often cheaper. Universities and higher education colleges also run English language programmes (also accredited by the British Council).

Awarding bodies

Business and Technology Education Council (BTEC)

BTEC is now part of Edexcel but its name is still used to describe courses. It covers areas such as technology, business, health and social care, and leisure and tourism. For more information contact Edexcel on +44 (0)870 240 9800 or see their website at www.edexcel.org.uk

City & Guilds of London Institute (C&G)

City & Guilds is a major provider of vocational qualifications in the UK. There are more than 8,500 approved City & Guilds centres throughout the world offering more than 400 qualifications in almost all sectors – from agriculture to hairdressing and from IT to vehicle maintenance. There is also a range of qualifications in essential skills such as numeracy, communication and literacy. For more information contact City & Guilds of London Institute on +44 (0)20 7294 2468 or see their website at www.city-and-guilds.co.uk

The Royal Society for the Encouragement of Arts, Manufactures & Commerce (RSA)

RSA offer similar courses to both BTEC and City & Guilds but also specialise in office skills, English teaching and English as a foreign language. The RSA Examinations Board is now part of OCR (Oxford, Cambridge and RSA exams) a new awarding body. For more information, contact either the RSA on +44 (0)20 7930 5115 or the OCR on +44 (0)1223 553998 or, alternatively, visit their website at www.rsa.org.uk/www.ocr.org.uk

Colleges of further education

Many non-degree courses can be taken at colleges of further education. 'Further education' is the title given to any non-degree level qualification taken after the minimum school-leaving age in Britain, which is 16. Further education colleges tend to offer more vocational courses. Until recently they did not recruit international students and were not accustomed to arranging and validating student visas. This situation is changing quickly, as demand from international students increases.

Adult education colleges

Adult education courses are often run at further education colleges but tend to be run part time in the evening, at lunchtime or at the weekend. Subjects range from cookery to salsa and last anything from a day to a year. Students pay fees for a set number of sessions. Classes tend to be informal and friendly because they are mostly made up of people who are keen to learn and experience something new. Taking an adult education course in a large city is often a way of meeting people and making new friends. Publications like *Hotcourses* magazine will give you information on these courses in London or, alternatively, try the comprehensive search facility at www.hotcourses.com for courses right across the UK.

Colleges of higher education

Higher education refers to academic and professional courses which range from diplomas to undergraduate degrees and postgraduate study. Higher education colleges offer full-time degrees, HNDs and Diplomas of Higher Education (DipHE). Some colleges of higher

education have a validation arrangement with a university.

Getting on to your chosen degree course

A levels, AS levels, Vocational A levels, HNDs and Scottish Highers are the traditional route of entry into British universities for British students. International qualifications are recognised by universities and colleges of higher education but it is always best to check with the institution to which you are applying that your qualifications are appropriate. You will be expected to demonstrate your English language skills with the appropriate TOEFL, IELTS or equivalent score. For full-time undergraduate courses, you must apply through UCAS, the Universities and Colleges Admissions Service.

Access and foundation courses

(also see the Access chapter on page 68)
One-year foundation courses are generally tailored for international students (apart from foundation years in art and nursing which can be studied by anyone) and they are a way of gaining entrance to university or college degree courses. Although you may have completed your secondary education in your home country, your qualifications may not be recognised by admissions tutors, and you may need to bring your qualifications up to the standard required for degree-level courses. Foundation courses serve as an alternative route into British universities or colleges and as a bridge between

English language examinations

Examining board	Examination
University of Cambridge Local Examination Syndicate (UCLES) Syndicate Buildings 1 Hills Road Cambridge CB1 2EU Tel: +44 (0)1223 553311 Website: www.ucles.org.uk	Preliminary English Test (PET) First Certificate in English (FCE) Certificate in Advanced English (CAE) *Some UK universities and colleges accept this level of English* Certificate of Proficiency in English (CPE) *Acceptable level of English for most UK colleges and universities* International English Language Testing System (IELTS) *Most UK universities expect students to reach between 5.5 and 6.5*
TOEFL Educational Testing Service PO Box 6151 Princeton NJ 08541-6151 USA Tel: 001 609 921 9000 Website: www.toefl.org	Test of English as a Foreign Language (TOEFL) *Popular with US universities and colleges. Currently most UK universities accept a score between 550 and 600 for paper-based tests and between 213 and 250 for computer-based tests. The paper-based TOEFL is being phased out*
Northern Examinations and Assessment Board Devas Street Manchester M15 6EX Tel: +44 (0)161 953 1180	University Entrance Test in English for Speakers of Other Languages (UETESOL) *Acceptable at most UK universities*
English Speaking Board (International) Ltd 26a Princes Street Southport PR8 1EQ Tel: +44 (0)1704 501730 Website: www.esbuk.demon.uk	English Speaking Board, English as an Acquired Language (ESB, EAL) *Oral assessments on several levels from pre-foundation through intermediate to advanced*
Oxford – ARELS University of Cambridge Local Examination Syndicate 1 Hills Road Cambridge CB1 2EI Tel: +44 (0)1223 553538	ARELS Oral Exams: Preliminary Certificate Diploma Higher Certificate Oxford Written Exams: Preliminary Level Higher Level
Trinity College Exams 89 Albert Embankment London SE1 7TP Tel: +44 (0)20 7820 6100	Spoken English 12 levels *Oral assessment at all levels, beginners to advanced*

your own qualifications and entry onto a degree course.

Access programmes are another well-established route into higher education. These are specifically designed for mature students and for those who have been disadvantaged in terms of their educational opportunities for whatever reason. There are over 30,000 Access students in Britain and over 1,000 recognised Access courses throughout England, Northern Ireland and Wales.

Degrees

Undergraduate degrees

In England, Wales and Northern Ireland, the undergraduate degree is generally studied over a three-year period, leading to the award of an honours degree. In Scotland, students study for three years to qualify for an ordinary degree and four years to gain an honours qualification. An increasing number of institutions are running four-year courses that result in a master's degree.

There is no standardisation of degrees in Britain and the approach to teaching may differ between one university or college and another. Most universities and colleges, however, employ a combination of teaching styles that includes tutorials, lectures and seminars.

Lectures are given to a large group of students, usually in an auditorium or lecture theatre, and students are expected to listen and take notes. Seminars are taken by one or more staff members with a smaller group of students. Students are asked to prepare presentations for the group to debate. Tutorials often involve a much smaller group – usually one member of staff with four or five students. Oxford and Cambridge universities, however, are renowned for their unique tutorial system, whereby students attend regular one-to-one discussions with a personal tutor.

Degree structure

At some universities and colleges of higher education, your results in the first-year exams do not count towards your final degree classification. The second and third year exam results, combined with a mark awarded for your undergraduate dissertation (if you have to do one), will make up your final degree result. Other universities and colleges have a modular structure. Here, courses are made up of units and a credit rating derived from the number of hours of tuition and private study given to each module.

The grade you are awarded for your degree may be made up of points you have collected under a modular system, or will be awarded on the basis of your final examinations (usually called 'finals'). The top grade is a first class (Honours) degree. The upper second (Honours), or 'two-one', is awarded more frequently than a first, followed by a lower second (Honours), or 'two-two'. There is also the third class (Honours) degree and a pass or ordinary degree.

Combined and joint honours degrees

Many universities and colleges offer students the chance to combine two or more subjects in a combined or a joint honours degree. A combined degree will involve different subjects which will not necessarily have equal weighting. A joint honours degree will have two subject areas with equal weighting. It may involve two closely related subjects such as economics and mathematics or more distant, but still connected, subjects such as computing and psychology.

Sandwich courses

Sandwich courses are made up of a combination of periods of study and time spent in industry, commerce or administration relating to your course. This usually means that the course extends to four years instead of the usual three. Work experience can be carried out in a single block, lasting a year, or two blocks, each lasting about six months. In either case, you return to university or college in your final year to complete your studies. Sandwich courses are often seen as a good way for students to gain valuable experience during their degree so that they graduate not only with academic qualifications but also with relevant work experience. The year in industry is known to develop an individual's maturity, confidence and work-related skills. This makes it easier to get a job on graduation, perhaps even with the company you spent your work placement with. Another bonus is that you receive a salary during the sandwich year.

As an international student, you either have a restriction or prohibition on your right to work in this country. This is stamped into your passport on arrival. Rules introduced by the UK government make it much easier for international students to get permission to work on a sandwich course. You should talk to your chosen college or university for further information.

Degrees with study abroad programmes

These days it is common for British universities and colleges to offer students the opportunity to study abroad, anything from a term to a year . In the latter case, degrees usually last for four years with students returning to university for their final year. This is often an option with language degrees but is also a feature of many other courses such as engineering, nursing, business studies and law.

If your course entails studying in another country you will need to check which documents are necessary for departure and re-entry. You should also check the visa requirements of the country in which you intend to study or visit. It may be wise to seek the advice of your head of department or the international officer.

Postgraduate degrees

There are generally three levels of postgraduate study in Britain – postgraduate certificate and diploma, master's and PhD. One of the most attractive things about UK universities and colleges for international students is the fact that you can study for a master's degree in one year instead of the usual two. All postgraduate applications should be made directly to the relevant institution and should not go through UCAS.

Postgraduate certificate and diploma

Many international students choose the UK to study for postgraduate diplomas or certificates, which are available in many subjects, from education to management. These qualifications act as bridging courses to provide access for students who do not qualify for direct entry onto master's courses. They are often accepted as

Typical undergraduate qualifications

BA	Bachelor of Arts
BBA	Bachelor of Business Administration
BEd	Bachelor of Education
BSc	Bachelor of Science
BD	Bachelor of Divinity
BTh	Bachelor of Theology Licence in Theology
LLB	Bachelor of Law
BMus	Bachelor of Music
BVSc	Bachelor of Veterinary Science

professional qualifications in the relevant field. In fact, the postgraduate diploma is usually the same as a master's but without a dissertation. For a postgraduate certificate or diploma, you will usually need a first degree in a relevant subject from a UK institution or an international equivalent. Some institutions may ask you to register initially for a postgraduate diploma as the first stage of a master's programme. Those that progress at a satisfactory level can then transfer to the master's course.

Master's

There are two kinds of master's you can choose – taught or by research.

Taught master's

A taught master's course consists of two elements: completing a number of modules and writing a dissertation. During the first part of the course, you attend lectures and take part in seminars. You then have to write an essay for each module and may also be required to sit exams in the subject, the grades from which count towards your degree. You will probably attend sessions on research methodology and academic writing skills. The second part of the course involves researching and writing a dissertation under the guidance of a supervisor who is normally a specialist in the field.

For most master's degrees you either pass or fail. Outstanding candidates graduate with a distinction. Four-year undergraduate courses which culminate in a master's are graded in the same way as other undergraduate degrees (see page 32).

Research master's (MRes)

A master's by research does not typically involve lectures and students devote the whole year to research. Some do allow you to take a taught element but your final mark will be primarily determined by the quality of your dissertation.

The PhD

People usually progress to a PhD after completing a master's but it is possible to go in directly with a first-class degree or a significant amount of relevant work experience. You usually enrol on an MPhil and then need to satisfy your department that you are capable of transferring to a PhD. It takes at least three or four years to complete.

For the first couple of years, you engage primarily in research. You then have to write up your thesis which is a massive undertaking of around 100,000 words and has to be based on an original idea. Students are assigned a supervisor with whom they agree the project title or research area. The choice of supervisor is crucial to the success of your doctorate and you should thoroughly investigate their track record and standing with previous students. Bear in mind that university lecturers and professors tend to disappear, either on sabbatical to write books or to other universities for a year. You may wish to confirm whether your supervisor intends to do this during your research.

Master of Business Administration (MBA)

In Britain, postgraduate management education began to develop in the 1960s and the MBA title was adopted in the 1980s. Content has developed considerably since its inception and continues to do so in response to an ever-changing and evolving commercial sphere.

You can choose between different programme structures, for example, part time, modular or joint honours, and there are various specialist pathways catering for people in different sectors, such as financial management, information management, strategic marketing or e-business. Courses vary enormously in what they offer, the type of experience they provide, their cost, accessibility and duration, and how highly they are regarded.

Distance learning/ external programmes

These programmes are available at most higher and further education institutions and are ideal for students who are not able to physically attend the institution at which they are studying. As such, they may appeal to international students seeking a British qualification whose financial, family, work or other commitments prevent them from studying in the UK for three or four years. Tuition fees are considerably less and you don't have the expense of moving to and settling in the UK. In addition, you can carry on earning money as you study, because the programmes are flexible to suit your needs and fit your schedule.

There are a number of institutions which offer distance learning programmes, from the traditional higher education institutions such as the University of London External Programme, to further education colleges and professional bodies, such as the Association of Certified Accountants. Qualifications range from GCSEs, A levels and Scottish Highers to diplomas and degrees.

Whilst you will receive written materials and be expected to study alone, you may also have to attend local seminars and study groups at certain times of the year when academics from the home institution visit. Some courses may require students to attend summer schools and revision courses for a short period of time in the UK. Work is mostly assessed by examination at the end of the course but you may also be given written assignments to complete as assessed coursework.

Applications for distance learning courses should be made directly to the institution and not through UCAS. For more details look at the distance learning web page, where all the UK institutions offering distance-learning programmes are listed, along with all the application details: www.distance-learning.co.uk

Typical postgraduate qualifications

MA	Master of Arts
MBA	Master of Business Administration
MEd	Master of Education
MSc	Master of Science
MPhil	Master of Philosophy
MChem	Master of Chemistry
LLM	Master of Laws
MEng	Master of Engineering
PhD	Doctor of Philosophy

Futher sources of information

Many libraries and careers offices in Britain have prospectuses and, if you live outside Britain, the British Council is a good source of information. They publish the *British Education* guides which are usually available free of charge or a very reasonable price. You can visit their website at www.britishcouncil.org or at www.educationUK.org. We have also listed the addresses of most British Council offices around the world on pages 592 to 595.

The easiest way to get information about universities or colleges in this guide is to use the reader information service postcard at the front of this book. Just fill in the institutions in which you are interested, send the card to us, and we will arrange for the information to be sent to you free of charge.

You can also call or fax the Hotcourses Hotline and we will make arrangements for a prospectus to be sent to you; please call +44 (0)20 8600 5300 or fax on +44 (0)20 8741 7716.

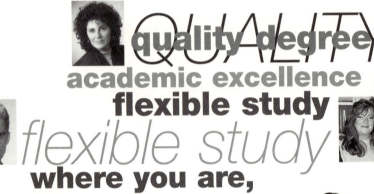

Applying to study

For many courses in the UK, including English language, vocational and postgraduate courses, you need to apply directly to the institution. Each involves a slightly different process. You will not usually be required to come to Britain for an interview (although the institution may interview you by phone) – a correctly filled-in application form plus deposit is usually enough. For full-time undergraduate courses, you must apply through UCAS, the Universities and Colleges Admissions Service. It is important to fill in the UCAS application form correctly and ensure that it is fully completed.

Specialist, vocational and language schools

The application process depends on the type of college in question. If you are applying to a specialist college to do a non-degree course, you simply need to write, call, fax or email the college and ask for an application form. They will also tell you the submission deadline for applications. You may be asked to send a deposit to secure your place when you return the completed application form. Deposits are often non-refundable but you should ask if the amount will be deducted from your fee if you decide to take your place. For art courses, you may have to produce proof of your ability, such as a portfolio or photos of your work. Admission to dance/music courses may require a video.

University degree programmes

There are a number of things to consider when choosing whether you want to study for an undergraduate degree. The two major decisions are what you want to study, and where.

Choosing a course

Choosing the right course can be difficult. The guidelines below offer some help:

○ get a good idea of the courses available. Read through course descriptions in prospectuses and get an idea of entrance requirements. Refer to the UCAS *Big Guide* (available from UCAS on +44 (0)1242 544610 or online at www.ucas.com) which has information on all undergraduate courses in the UK.

○ narrow your choice down to a list of your top subjects or combinations.

○ assess your criteria: what are your reasons for wanting to study the subject at the top of your list? Do you have the qualifications you need to be accepted? Is your English fluent enough to allow you to study in English? What would you like to do after you have finished your degree? Will the degree be accepted in the country in which you want to work? How long are you prepared to study to achieve your aim for?

○ Estimate the total costs, taking the following into consideration: travel to and from your country, fees for the duration of the course, books and equipment, termtime and vacation accommodation, living expenses, and how you will finance your studies.

Choosing a university or college

There are a number of things to consider when choosing a university or college. If at all possible, you should visit a number of institutions as often you will get a gut feeling as to which one will be right for you. Alternatively, it may be a particular course or professor which is more important to you that the institution itself.

UCAS/*The Guardian* higher education conventions

In collaboration with *The Guardian*, UCAS organise a series of over 50 higher education conventions each year. They are held across the UK and are attended by most of the UCAS-approved universitites and colleges who are there to give information and guidance face to face to prospective students. Also present are organisations such as careers services, gap-year companies, student support services, travel firms and financial services.

The conventions are held between March and July in England and Wales, and between August and October in Scotland and Northern Ireland. Visit the UCAS website for information on exact dates and locations (www.ucas.com).

For those not already in the UK, UCAS sends representatives to several education events in other countries, mainly in Southeast Asia. Check the international student section of their website for details.

British Council Education Counselling Service

As well as British Council offices around the world which have a mine of useful information on studying in the UK, its Education Counselling Service organises more than 60 education exhibitions worldwide each year. Representatives from many UK colleges and universities attend these events, giving you the chance to make detailed enquiries about institutions and their courses.

Hotcourses International Student Festival

Each summer, Hotcourses hosts the International Student Festival in central London. The one-day event gives international students the chance to meet and talk with admissions officers and staff from UK universities and colleges. The 2002 International Student Festival will be held on Saturday 27 July at the New Connaught Rooms near Covent Garden.

Last year's festival attracted over 60 universities, colleges and language schools and 1,500 international students. If you would like more information, call the Hotcourses Hotline on +44 (0)20 8600 5300, Fax: +44 (0)20 8846 9775, or go to www.hotcourses.com/isf/

Other opportunities outside the UK to find out about courses and institutions

A growing number of higher education institutions have offices and representatives around the world. If they don't have their own offices, they may arrange for you to attend orientation sessions at local British Council offices.

Undergraduate courses

UCAS processes applications for all full-time Higher National Diploma (HND), Diploma of Higher Education (DipHE), and first degree courses at UK universities and colleges of higher education, except the Open University. They handle more than 450,000 applications a year, including over 50,000 from international students.

Before you apply

Before applying, make sure you have the necessary qualifications. These are normally shown in prospectuses. If you are not sure if your qualifications are acceptable, speak to staff in the relevant department. See page 31 for further information and the Access, Diploma and Foundation chapter (page 68) for university and college foundation programmes.

When to apply
(for 2003 entry UK/EU)

If you are applying from within the UK/European Union (EU), whatever your nationality, your application form must arrive at UCAS between 1 September 2002 and 15 January 2003 except for the following exceptions:

You must apply to UCAS by 15 October 2002 for courses at Oxford or Cambridge universities, or for courses in medicine (courses codes A100, A101, A103, A104 or A106), dentistry (course codes A200, A203, A204, A205 or A206) or veterinary medicine/science (course codes D100 or D101).

For Route B art and design courses, we recommend that you apply by 8 March 2003, if possible.

The universities and colleges guarantee to consider your application if UCAS receives your form by the appropriate deadline. If you send in your form after the deadline date they may consider it at their discretion but are under no obligation to do so.

When to apply
(for 2003 entry non UK/EU)

If you are a student of any nationality applying from outside the EU you can apply at any time between 1 September 2002 and 30 June 2003, unless you are applying for Oxford or Cambridge, medicine, dentistry, veterinary medicine/science or Route B art and design courses (see above). You must read the next paragraphs carefully before you decide when to apply.

Most applicants will apply well before 15 January 2003 and, if you want to be sure that a place is available on your chosen course, you should not wait until then to apply. UCAS cannot guarantee that applications for places on popular courses at some universities and colleges will be considered if they receive the applications after 15 January 2003. You should check with individual universities and colleges if you are not sure.

If you think that you may be assessed as a 'home' student (UK or EU) for fee purposes, you should apply by 15 January 2003, exactly the same as if you are applying from an EU country. If you apply early, this will give you enough time to make immigration, travel and accommodation arrangements. This preparation may take a lot of time, particularly during the summer when immigration departments are extremely busy. If you are a student from a non-EU country wishing to apply to one choice only and you already have the necessary qualifications, you may apply at any time. Before completing an application form, however, you should contact UCAS or your chosen university or college for advice.

How to apply

For full-time undergraduate courses, you need to apply through UCAS and the process is the same for both UK and international students. The UCAS system has the following benefits:

- ❑ you can apply for up to six different universities or colleges on one application form. When you receive offers of a place, you can then choose which one to accept.

- ❑ All UCAS institutions are recognised by the British government or they offer courses which are validated by government-recognised universities.

- ❑ UCAS makes sure that applicants receive fair treatment and detailed impartial advice.

- ❑ UCAS can also provide advice on the admissions system including how to provide the information that selectors are looking for.

You may apply for up to six universities or colleges by completing a single UCAS application form (but you should not complete more than one form). Six is the maximum for all courses except medicine, veterinary science and dentistry, for which you may only enter four choices (plus two other non-medicine, veterinary science or dentistry courses if you wish). You can apply for just one course, and add further choices at a later stage up to the maximum of six, provided you have not accepted an offer.

UCAS forms are distributed across the world, so non-UK applicants can pick them up in schools or from their local British Council office (look in the useful addresses section on pages 592 to 595 for the location and contact details of your nearest office.) Alternatively, you can order an application form online.

Enter the institutions you have chosen in the order they appear in the UCAS Directory, not in your order of preference. You only declare your preference after you have received offers from the institutions you list. There is a £15 fee which must be sent with your application. If you initially make a single application, there is a £5 fee and if you wish to add other choices later, you will be asked to pay an additional fee of £10 (for 2003 entry).

Electronic Application System (EAS)

The Electronic Application System (EAS) provides a fast and user-friendly alternative to the paper application. The EAS allows prospective students to fill in their application forms on a personal computer at their school, college, local careers service, or even at home. The EAS is not available to applicants on an individual basis and applications must be submitted to UCAS through a teacher or careers adviser, either via the internet, email or by floppy disk. Benefits of using the EAS include:

○ automatic checking ensuring accurate applications.

○ common mistakes, such as an invalid date of birth or an invalid course code, are eliminated.

○ corrections may be made at any time prior to sending the application to the administrator.

○ 'Print Preview' lets you see what your application form will look like when UCAS sends it to the universities and colleges you have chosen.

○ electronic forms are processed in three days, compared with up to three weeks for paper forms during busy periods.

Online applications

UCAS have introduced a new online service designed to make the application process even easier. The online system will enable applicants to fill out the form on the UCAS website. Once your school, college, careers office or British Council office has signed up to use this service, you will be able to complete your UCAS application form anywhere that has access to the internet.

How to pay (UK applicants)

You can pay by cheque, postal order, credit or debit card. If you pay by cheque, make it payable to 'UCAS Applications Account' and cross it 'account payee only'. On the back, you should write the applicant's full name and the seven-digit number from the top right corner of the front page of the application form.

Some schools and colleges prefer to collect individual fees themselves and send UCAS one payment to cover all their applicants.

If you are using EAS (the Electronic Application System), consult the on-screen help section for details of how to pay.

How to pay (non-UK applicants)

You can pay by credit/debit card, or by sending one of the following:

- evidence that you have arranged payment by an international money order.

- evidence that your bank has arranged payment by a bank draft payable at a UK bank.

- a sterling cheque payable at a UK bank.

- evidence of direct payment such as Economy International Money mover to the following bank account: 'UCAS International Account' at Lloyds Bank plc, Montpellier Branch, sort code 30-95-72, account number 0188578.

On the back, write your name, address and seven-digit number from the top right corner of the front page of the application form.

Art and design courses
Selection for courses in art and design is normally by interview or inspection of a portfolio of work. You should contact any institution to which you are considering applying before completing the application form. This will establish the arrangements to be made regarding submitting a portfolio and whether an interview is necessary. You can apply through 'Route A' (the closing date is 15 January 2003 for entry the following September) or 'Route B' (closing date 24 March 2003 for entry in September of the same year).

Route A
Applicants may enter up to six choices on the UCAS application form but may, if they wish, reserve up to three choices for later application through Route B. The choices must be listed in the order in which they appear in the UCAS Directory. Copies of the application form will be sent simultaneously to each institution listed.

Route A timetable
15 January 2003: closing date for all applications.

Early May 2003: last date for decisions by institutions.
End May 2003: last date for replies by applicants.

Late applications received up to 30 June 2003 will be sent to the universities and colleges of higher education for consideration at their discretion. Applications received after the June 30 2003 will be entered in clearing.

Route B
Applicants may enter up to three choices in the order in which they appear in the UCAS Directory. Applicants should indicate on a separate form, supplied with the UCAS application form, the order in which they wish to be interviewed or to have their portfolios considered by the institutions. Copies of the form will be sent to the institutions in that order.

Route B timetable
24 March 2003: closing date for applications.
15 April 2003: first round of interviews and portfolio inspection commences.
23 May 2003: second round of interviews and portfolio inspection commences.
12 June 2003: third round of interviews and portfolio inspections commences.

Late applications received between 25 March 2003 and 12 June 2003 will be referred to institutions in the next available round. Applications received after June 12 2003 will be entered in Clearing.

Filling in the UCAS form
The UCAS form is four pages long and looks rather complicated, especially if English is not your first language. However, each form is supplied with a booklet called *How to Apply* which contains detailed instructions on how to complete the form. On the next few pages are a few hints and tips on how to fill in the form.

- Fill in the form completely. Do not leave any unanswered questions or leave out any information.

- Fill in the form in black ink. The form has to be photocopied and red or blue ink does not photocopy well.

- Fill in the form neatly. Bear in mind that there are many thousands of forms passing through UCAS and the offices of each college and university – a messy, illegible or grammatically incomprehensible form will not do you any favours. Photocopy the blank form and practise filling in the copies before you fill in the real form.

UCAS will not accept:

- a photocopy or faxed copy of the completed form. You must send the original.

- separated pages. You must keep the original form intact.

- extra sheets. You must write everything you have to say in the boxes. However, you can write to the admissions offices of the colleges or universities to which you are applying and give them any extra information once you have your application number.

You must:

- keep a photocopy of your completed application form.

- write your name and address on the back of the small reply card you will have received with the application form and send it to UCAS with your completed application form. It will be posted to you when UCAS has received your application.

- send the original form by registered or express post.

After you have applied, UCAS will send a copy of your application form to the institutions you have named. Each institution will consider your application and tell UCAS whether they wish to make you an offer of a place.

If you have already achieved the entrance qualifications for the course, the institution may make an unconditional offer.. If you still have to take qualifying examinations, any offer you receive will be conditional on passing those examinations at specific grades. UCAS will pass this decision on to you, although the institutions may also write to you directly. You should not reply to any offers you receive until you are asked by UCAS which offers you wish to accept. You may hold no more than two choices: your first choice/firm acceptance and your second choice/insurance acceptance. Your reply should be sent to UCAS who will then send it on to the institutions.

Accepting an offer

You must think very carefully about your replies to any offers as you will be expected to keep to them and not change your mind later. When your examination results come out, you must send a copy of your results slip to the university or college at which you are holding conditional offers.

If you have met the conditions of any offer you are holding, the institution will make the place unconditional. If your first choice institution confirms your place, your insurance offer is automatically cancelled. If you didn't quite achieve the required grades, you must still send a copy of your results to the universities and colleges. One of them may still confirm your place through UCAS.

UCAS will notify you of the final decision. If you receive a confirmed offer of a place you must immediately return the enclosed slip directly to the institution, to confirm

Filling out the UCAS form

Below we have set out an example of how to complete the UCAS application form

Photocopy your UCAS form several times before you begin. This will allow you to write out some trial copies before you complete the real thing. It also means you can gauge spaces, cut down on crossings out and generally make the final version that you send to UCAS tidy and legible. UCAS will reduce it in size, photocopy it and then send it to the relevant universities and colleges so it is very important that you fill it out as neatly and clearly as possible in black pen or type only. Once you have finished writing it out, re-read your answers very carefully. No matter how irrelevant a box or section may appear, double check to make sure whether it applies to you. Get someone to look over it before you send it to UCAS.

Do not forget to sign and date the form, and to include the appropriate payment. Keep a photocopy (or a draft) so that you can remind yourself what you wrote before any interviews.

The instructions are in a pamphlet UCAS sent to you with your application form entitled *How to Apply*

SECTION 1

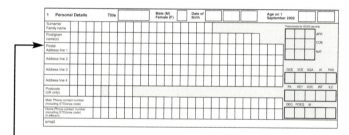

Make sure that you, or someone reliable, is resident at your correspondence address throughout the application procedure

SECTION 2

If you are taking or have taken Scottish qualifications, write your Scottish Candidate Number (SCN)

If you are taking a BTEC qualification, write your registration number in this box

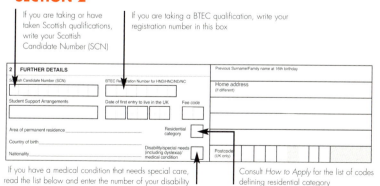

If you have a medical condition that needs special care, read the list below and enter the number of your disability

Consult *How to Apply* for the list of codes defining residential category

0   None
1   You have dyslexia
2   You are blind or partially sighted
3   You are deaf or hard of hearing
4   You are a wheelchair user or have mobility difficulties
5   You need personal care or assistance

6   You have mental health difficulties
7   You have a disability that cannot be seen, for example diabetes, epilepsy, a heart condition
8   You have two or more of the above
9   You have a disability, special needs or a medical condition not listed above

SECTION 3

List the institutions and courses you want to apply for in this section, one college or course per line, in the order in which they appear in the *UCAS Directory*

If you intend to defer any course for a year (eg to take a gap year), write a 'D' in the box in this column

If the institution has agreed to let you miss the first year, write 2 or 3 etc here. If you are going straight into the first year, do not enter anything

Only tick this column if you are going to live with friends or relatives whilst studying

SECTION 4

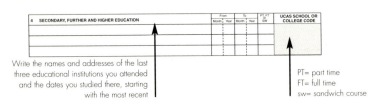

Write the names and addresses of the last three educational institutions you attended and the dates you studied there, starting with the most recent

PT= part time
FT= full time
sw= sandwich course

SECTION 6

6	ADDITIONAL INFORMATION (not used for selection purposes)																B	Ethnic Origin
A	Occupational Background																	(UK applicants only)
C	UCAS may send you information from other organisations about products and services directly relevant to higher education applicants. Please tick the box if you *do not* want to receive it.																	

If you are under 21, please give the occupation of your parent, step-parent or guardian who earns the most. If he or she is retired or unemployed, give their most recent occupation. If you are 21 or over, please give your own occupation

Ethnic origin codes – this box only applies to UK residents

White		Asian or Asian British		Mixed	
British	11	Indian	31	White and Black	
Irish	12	Pakistani	32	Caribbean	41
Other white	19	Bangladeshi	33	White and Black	
		Chinese	34	African	42
Black or Black British		Other Asian	39	White and Asian	43
Caribbean	21			Other mixed	49
African	22				
Other black	29			Other ethnic	80

SECTION 7a

7A QUALIFICATIONS COMPLETED (Examinations or assessments (including key/core skills) for which results are known, including those failed)											
Examination/Assessment centre number(s) and name(s)											
Examination(s)/Award(s)			Subject/unit/module/component	Level/qual	Result Grade Mark or Band	Examination(s)/Award(s)			Subject/unit/module/component	Level/qual	Result Grade Mark or Band
Month	Year	Awarding body				Month	Year	Awarding body			

In this box write a list of all the examinations you have taken.
You have to put all academic qualifications down, even if you failed or received a bad grade. They all count. You may have to dig out past certificates to find the correct name of the awarding body

SECTION 7b

Find out the centre number and address of your school or college

Applicants who have already taken their A levels write nothing here and fill their results in section 7a

7B QUALIFICATIONS NOT YET COMPLETED (Examinations or assessments (including key/core skills) to be completed, or results not yet published)											
Examination/Assessment centre number(s), name(s) and address(es)											
Examination(s)/Award(s)			Subject/unit/module/component	Level/qual	Result	Examination(s)/Award(s)			Subject/unit/module/component	Level/qual	Result
Month	Year	Awarding body				Month	Year	Awarding body			

What is the name of the exam?
(For example, A level is abbreviated to A)
See How to Apply

What is the abbreviated name of the academic institution or professional body that awards the qualification for the exam?
See How to Apply

When will you be taking your exam?

Applying to study

45

SECTIONS 8, 9 and 10

Have you ever had a job or spent some time in work experience? Write down the details here

If you put a number in the disability/special needs square in section 2 (see page 43), you should explain here what your disability is and which special needs you have

USE BLACK BALLPOINT OR BLACK TYPE

8	SPECIAL NEEDS or **support** required as a consequence of any disability or medical condition stated in Section 2.						

9	DETAILS OF PAID EMPLOYMENT TO DATE Names and addresses of recent employers	Nature of work	From Month	Year	To Month	Year	PT/ FT

10 PERSONAL STATEMENT

Name of applicant (block capitals or type)

I've been fascinated by the sea since I was small. As part of my examination course, I'm studying the effects of pollution on marine life in Tokyo Bay. I've had to analyse water samples continually over a period of six months, write up the results and come to conclusions based upon my findings. Biology has always been my best subject at school and I feel that there's such a comprehensive range of courses on offer in the UK for someone with my interests. I have thoroughly researched the courses and institutions of my choice to ensure that I get the most from the subject and my time in the UK.

My English exchange partner works for the Environment Agency in Bangor and specialises in hydrology. I have learnt a great deal from accompanying her on field trips on two recent visits to Wales. Through my time in Bangor, I have also found out more about oceanography which is an area I would like to develop further. I have organised a three-month period helping a PhD student with their research in this field over the summer. The level of expertise, the dedicated approach towards learning and the encouraging atmosphere in the UK are the main reasons I would like to study here.

In order to help me make the most of my studies, I have recently successfully completed an advanced Excel course for scientists in Cambridge. This has increased my technical confidence and also gave me the chance to meet interesting people from all around the world. The course was taught in English which allowed me to enhance my listening and speaking skills.

For the past two years, I have been a student representative on the staff/student council. This position has mainly entailed voicing concerns on many issues from a student perspective. This has meant strong communication skills and the need for tact and diplomacy. I have learnt how to strike the balance between standing firm and remaining true to those whom I represent yet, at the same time, maintaining a flexible and deferential attitude towards other council members.

Out of college, I really enjoy playing tennis and am a member of my local club. I like singles but get most satisfaction from playing doubles and helping with the training of more junior players. I also swim regularly, go to the theatre and am an avid reader of 20th-century French literature which I read in the original language.

11 Tick (✓) if you have a National Record of Achievement or Progress File (UK applicants only)	pre-16		post-16	

12 DECLARATION:
I confirm that the information given on this form is true, complete and accurate and no information requested or other material information has been omitted. I have read *How to Apply*. I undertake to be bound by the terms set out in it and I give my consent to the processing of my data by UCAS and educational establishments. I accept that, if I do not fully comply with these requirements, UCAS shall have the right to cancel my application and I shall have no claim against UCAS or any higher education institution or college in relation thereto.

	tick one
I have attached payment to the value of £15.00/£5.00	
or	
I have attached a completed credit/debit card payment coupon	

Applicant's Signature... *Kazumi Saito* .... Date .August 20 2001.......

REMEMBER TO KEEP A PHOTOCOPY - SEE APPLICANT CHECKLIST ON BACK OF *HOW TO APPLY*

Page 3

Don't forget to sign and put the date

Remember to attach your cheque or bank draft to the form before you give it to the referee for the reference

Checklist
Information to include in the personal statement

- Why have you chosen the course(s) listed in section 3?

- What do you already know about the subject(s) you wish to study?

- How did you acquire that knowledge?

- Are you currently involved in any work or activity that relates to the subject(s) you wish to study?

- What particular aspects of your current studies do you enjoy most?

- Why do you want to study in the UK?

- What do you plan to do with your higher education qualification?

- What other interests (for example cultural, sporting) do you have?

- Are there any non-examined subjects which you are studying?

- Have you been involved in any activities where you have been in a position of authority or have had to demonstrate communication skills?

- Have you obtained or applied for any industrial or professional sponsorship or placement? If so give details.

- Are you planning to defer entry to the year 2004? If so, give your reasons for doing so.

- Apart from any English language test results you have included in section 7, what other evidence can you give of your ability to successfully complete a higher education course taught in English? For example, if all or part of your studies have been conducted in English it is important to mention it.

finally whether or not you are accepting the offer. If you do not get accepted because you have missed the required grades, you will be eligible to join the Clearing process.

Clearing

Each year, UCAS operates a service known as Clearing from mid-July to mid-September. This is to help candidates who have been unsuccessful in finding a place at their preferred institution, or who have applied late. You are eligible for Clearing if you fall into one of the following categories:

- having applied to UCAS in the normal way, you receive no offers from any of your chosen institutions.

- you receive offers from some of your choices but your subsequent exam results are not good enough for you to be accepted.

- if you have applied through UCAS for the first time after 30 June 2003 (or 12 June 2003 for Art and Design Route B courses) you will automatically be sent a Clearing Entry Form (CEF) by UCAS with the necessary details and information on how to proceed.

Finances

As an international student, you will be responsible for paying fees to cover registration, tuition, accommodation and other expenses such as books and travel. Although tuition fees and living expenses vary from institution to institution and region to region, there are approximate standard rates per year throughout the UK: arts courses are in the region of £6,000, science courses cost around £8,000, and clinical courses cost around £14,000. If you are an EU student, then you pay the same as English and Welsh students, namely around £1,075 a year. Bear in mind that these fees only cover your tuition costs.

When you arrive in the UK, you will have to prove your intention to study and that you can fund your studies. You must organise adequate sponsorship from individuals or organisations at home before you leave. Immigration restrictions prevent you from working to fund your studies whilst you are in the UK.

To be eligible for a mandatory award (local education authority grant) or a student loan, you have to have been 'ordinarily resident' in the UK for three years before the day you start your course. You may be entitled to an award or a student loan if you are on a full-time course and you are from a European Economic Area country or if you can show that your husband/wife or either of your parents has migrant worker status.

You may be able to apply for funding through your own government. Or, you might find help from other sources: the British Council awards bursaries, and the Foreign and Commonwealth Office and Overseas Development Administration both run scholarship and awards schemes.

Applying for postgraduate courses

Unless you are applying for postgraduate studies in teaching or social work (see Education and Health chapters), there is no central admissions body like UCAS which deals specifically with postgraduate applications. You will have to contact the relevant institutions directly. Some have a separate office that deals with postgraduate admissions, others expect you to apply directly to the relevant department.

Application procedures differ from one institution to the next. Generally, however, you will be asked to complete a detailed application form in which you are asked about academic qualifications, work experience and your reasons for wanting to study the course. If you are applying for a research place, you may be asked to outline a proposal.

If and when you decide you want to come to Britain to study, you will need to make a number of arrangements before leaving for the UK. Otherwise, you may be refused entry into the country or have to leave your course for some other reason. You may have military service obligations, for example, or need permission to leave your country. The British High Commission, British Embassy, British Consulate (General), or the British Council may be able to help by providing supporting documents. Remember too that your government may impose restrictions on the transfer of currency to the UK.

Visas and immigration

The basic division is between European Economic Area (EEA) citizens (European Union plus Iceland and Norway); people from other countries who do not need a visa to enter Britain ('non-visa nationals'); and people from countries who do need a visa before entering Britain ('visa nationals'). The Home Office divides the categories as follows:

European Economic Area

If you are a national of a European Union country or are from Norway or Iceland, you are free to enter the UK to study, live and work and you do not need a visa. European Union citizens face fierce competition for places from British students and also have to contribute towards the cost of their course. Icelandic and Norwegian students have to pay full fees as international students but do not need work visas, so can fund their course by finding a job.

Non-visa nationals

Non-visa nationals are from non-EEA countries and don't require a visa to enter Britain. You can arrive with the necessary documentation and be issued the visa when you arrive. You need:

- proof that you have been accepted onto a full-time course of at least 15 hours a week) at a publically-funded institution of further or higher education, a private education institution or an independent fee-paying school.

- a letter from the school, college or university on their official headed paper to state that you have paid your deposit and/or your tuition fees.

- proof that you have the funds to pay for your study and living expenses. This could be in the form of traveller's cheques in sufficient quantity to cover your expenses, a bank draft drawn on a UK bank, letters or bank documents from sponsors, or a combination of all these things. You will have to show that you will not have 'recourse to public funds' and that you can support yourself financially without relying on the British welfare state or by working to fund your studies.

If you are staying for longer than six months, your finances will be inspected much more rigorously. It is advisable to submit your documentation to the British Embassy/High Commission in your own country and get entry clearance (a visa) prior to arrival. Your status can still be challenged but you have the right to lodge an appeal and remain in Britain while your case is heard. If you were intending to be issued with a visa on arrival, you could be sent back at your own expense. There are plenty of scare stories around but this is unlikely to happen in practice, unless you have done something to arouse suspicion, for example travelling back and forth from Britain a number of times over a short period, appearing to have little money, or enrolling at a school with a reputation as a 'visa factory'.

You can bring your partner/husband/wife or children with you. However, they will require a separate 'student dependent visa', which they must obtain before they arrive (even though your own visa can be issued on arrival). To obtain this, you will have to show that you can support them out of your own pocket, without help from public funds. It can be difficult to find accommodation for families, and it tends to be expensive, so try and make arrangements before you arrive.

Most universities and colleges offer family accommodation but space is limited. Be as organised in your arrangements as possible, as this will make you look more credible in the eyes of the immigration officials.

You could also enter Britain as a tourist. In theory, non-visa nationals can then apply to have it changed to a student visa without leaving the country as an 'in-country application'. In practice, this is not advisable as the immigration department is suspicious of people who change the purpose of their stay while they are in Britain. You may succeed in getting your visa changed this way but you will get a grilling in the process. Many people come to Britain on a tourist visa, and then look around for a school to enrol with. Be careful, because you could end up being deported if you are thought to have deliberately deceived the immigration department. The best thing

European Economic Area

Austria, Belgium, Denmark, Finland, France, Germany, Greece, Holland, Iceland, Ireland, Italy, Liechtenstein, Luxembourg, Norway, Portugal, Spain, Sweden, United Kingdom

Non-visa nationals

Andorra, Anguilla, Antigua and Barbuda, Argentina, Australia, Bahamas, Barbados, Belize, Bermuda, Bolivia, Botswana, Brazil, Brunei, Canada, Chile, Costa Rica, Czech Republic, Commonwealth of Dominica, El Salvador, Estonia, Grenada, Guatemala, Honduras, Hong Kong, Hungary, Jamaica, Japan, Korea (South), Latvia, Lesotho, Lithuania, Israel, Kiribati, Malawi, Malaysia, Malta, Marshall Islands, Mexico, Micronesia, Monaco, Montserrat, Namibia, Nauru, Netherlands Antilles, New Zealand, Nicaragua, Palau, Panama, Paraguay, Poland, Samoa, San Marino, Seychelles, Singapore, Slovenia, Solomon Islands, South Africa, St Helen, St Kitts and Nevis, St Lucia, St Vincent, Swaziland, Switzerland, Tonga, Trinidad and Tobago, Turks and Caicos Islands, Tuvalu, Uruguay, USA, Vanatu, Vatican City, Venezuela, Zimbabwe

www.educationuk.org

to do is to apply for a 'prospective student visa' in your home country. You will need to show that you have the finances to support your course and will be allowed to stay in the UK for a maximum of six months.

Visa nationals

Visa nationals need to get a student visa from their nearest British Embassy, Consulate or High Commission before arriving in Britain. In order to get this, you will need to show the following:

- proof that you have been accepted onto a full-time course (of at least 15 hours a week) at a publically-funded institution of further or higher education, a private education institution or an independent fee-paying school. If it is at a language school, it should preferably be an ARELS or British Council accredited school.

- a letter from the school, college or university, on their official headed paper, to state that you have paid your deposit and/or tuition fees.

- proof that you have the funds to pay for your study and living expenses. This could be in the form of traveller's cheques in sufficient quantity to cover your expenses, a bank draft drawn on a UK bank, letters or bank documents from sponsors, or a combination of all these things. Immigration officials prefer a bank draft as this is the most difficult to forge and can be checked with the issuing bank. You will have to show that you will not have 'recourse to public funds'.

The longer your proposed stay, the more convincing your financial credentials will need to be.

You will need to get your visa and bring it along with all the above documentation

Visa nationals

Afghanistan, Albania, Algeria, Angola, Armenia, Azerbaijan, Bahrain, Bangladesh, Belarus, Benin, Bhutan, Bosnia-Herzegovina, Bulgaria, Burkina- Faso, Burundi, Cambodia, Cameroon, Cape Verde, Central African Republic, Chad, China, Colombia, Comoros, Croatia, Cuba, Cyprus, the Democratic Republic of the Congo, Djibouti, the Dominican Republic, Ecuador, Egypt, Equatorial Guinea, Eritrea, Ethiopia, Fiji, Gabon, the Gambia, Georgia, Ghana, Guinea, Guinea-Bissau, Guyana, Haiti, India, Indonesia, Iran, Iraq, Israel, the Ivory Coast, Jordan, Kazakhstan, Kenya, Kyrgyzstan, Korea (North), Kuwait, Laos, the Lebanon, Liberia, Libya, Macao, Macedonia, Madagascar, the Maldives, Mali, Mauritania, Mauritius, Moldova, Mongolia, Morocco, Mozambique, Myanmar, Nepal, Niger, Nigeria, Oman, Pakistan, Palestinian Authority, Papua New Guinea, Peru, Philippines, Qatar, Romania, Russia, Rwanda, São Tomé e Principe, Saudi Arabia, Senegal, Sierra Leone, Slovakia, Somalia, Sri Lanka, Sudan, Surinam, Syria, Taiwan, Tajikistan, Tanzania, Thailand, Togo, Tunisia, Turkey, Turkish Republic of Northern Cyprus, Turkmenistan, Uganda, the Ukraine, United Arab Emirates, Uzbekistan, Vatican City, Vietnam, Yemen, Yugoslavia, Zambia

when you enter Britain, as immigration officials may wish to see it on arrival. If you have been given entry clearance in your home country, this is usually sufficient. However, your right of entry may be challenged if immigration officials believe that there has been a change of circumstances or you have not disclosed, or have hidden, some relevant information. In this situation, you have the right to remain in Britain while lodging an appeal.

If you entered the UK as a tourist, you will not be able to get your tourist visa changed to a student visa in Britain. You will have to leave the country, and re-apply for a student visa before re-entering.

If you have problems

You should not be afraid of the immigration desk but you should be prepared to be questioned quite closely. Immigration officials will try to establish whether you are a genuine student, and not coming to the UK for the purpose of work or permanent residence. They also want to be sure you will go home when you have finished your studies.

If, for any reason, the officials are dissatisfied with your answers and decide to hold you at the immigration stage, airport officials will provide you with an interpreter if necessary. It can be a scary experience and the best thing to do is ask officials to contact the college or university where you have a place, or anyone else who can help you by supporting your case. You should also be honest and direct. Immigration officials become more suspicious if they detect even the smallest half-truth or lie.

If you have entry clearance and choose to appeal, you can then contact an immigration solicitor. It is important that you use a reputable firm. There is an organisation called UKCOSA, specifically set up to help students in such situations. They can recommend a solicitor or take on your case.

UKCOSA Council for
International Education
9-17 St Albans Place
London N1 0NX
Advice Line: (Monday to Friday
1 pm to 4 pm) +44 (0)20 7354 5210
Email: enquiries@ukcosa.org.uk
Website: www.ukcosa.org.uk

Another organisation that may be of use if you are experiencing difficulties is the Joint Council for the Welfare of Immigrants (JCWI). They do, however, mainly deal with those people who are coming to settle rather than study in the UK.

Joint Council for the Welfare of
Immigrants (JCWI)
115 Old Street
London EC1V 9RT
Advice Line: (open Tuesday and
Thursday 2 pm to 5 pm)
+44 (0)20 7251 8708
Email: info@jcwi.org.uk
Website: www.jcwi.org.uk

If you use a solicitor and have problems with the firm, you can contact the Law Society on +44 (0)20 7242 1222. Or, contact the Immigration Law Practitioners Association on +44 (0)20 7251 8383. They can give you the names and addresses of immigration solicitors and advisers. You can get further information on general immigration issues by writing to the Foreign and Commonwealth Office at:

The Visa Correspondance Unit
Joint Entry Clearance Unit
89 Albert Embankment
London SE1 7TP
Tel: +44 (0)20 7238 3838

Registration and visa obligations

If you are from a visa-national country that is not a member of the Commonwealth, and you are going to be in Britain for more than six months, you will be required to register with a local police station. If you are in London, you should visit the Overseas Visitors Records Office at Ground Floor, Brandon House, 180 Borough High Street, London SE1 1LH (Monday to Friday 9 am to 4.30 pm), Tel: +44 (0)20 7230 1208. Residents outside London should register at the local central police station. You must take your passport, travel documents, any appropriate home office documents, two passport-size photos and a £34 registration fee. If you later change address, course or any aspect of your registration details, you must return to the same office and alter your record.

Registration with your embassy

You should also register with your national embassy in London in case you lose your passport and other travel documents, or are involved in an incident of any kind. If you are living outside London, you will have to contact the embassy by telephone and request the appropriate registration forms. Otherwise, it is always possible to go there and register in person. It may be sensible to phone first in case you need to make an appointment. You can check with Yellow Pages or directory enquiries (Tel: 192) for the correct telephone number.

Extending your student visa

This is best done by post as the queues at immigration offices tend to be painfully long. You need to write to the Application Forms Unit at the Immigration and Nationality Directorate (address below), and send the original copies of relevant documents by registered or recorded delivery. You must provide original documents. Photocopies will lead to your application being instantly dismissed. You need to include proof of your school or college registration and, if you are trying to get an extension of your student visa, proof of an 80 per cent or better attendance

record to date. If you have attended fewer than 80 per cent of your lectures, seminars and other course requirements, you will have to present a medical certificate or similar evidence to justify your absence. Again, this should be the original document and not a photocopy. If you are applying in person, you can go to any one of the Immigration and Nationality Directorate offices up and down the UK. Application forms may be obtained by writing to:

Immigration and Nationality
Directorate
Lunar House, Wellesley Road
Croydon, Surrey CR9 2BY

For immigration application forms
Tel: +44 (0)870 241 0645
For general enquiries
Tel: +44 (0)870 606 7766
For individual case enquiries
Tel: +44 (0)870 608 1592

This is the nearest office to London and it is also the busiest; queues regularly form from 6 am. For this reason, use one of the non-London offices if you can.

Other offices:

Belfast
Immigration Office, Olive Tree House
Fountain Street, Belfast BT1 5EA
Tel: +44 (0)1232 322547

Birmingham
Immigration office, Dominion Court
41 Station Road, Solihull
Birmingham B91 3RT
Tel: +44 (0)121 606 7345

Glasgow
Immigration Office, Admin Block D
Dumbarton Court, Argyll Avenue
Glasgow Airport
Paisley PA3 2TD
Tel: +44 (0)141 887 2255

Liverpool

Immigration Office, Graeme House
Derby Square, Liverpool L2 7SF
Tel: +44 (0)151 236 4909

You can also look on the Immigration and Nationality Directorate website: www.ind.homeoffice.gov.uk

Travel

Britain may be a relatively small country but it can still be complicated to get around when you are not familiar with the system. When you first arrive you will have to get from the airport, port or railway station to your destination. If you are enrolling at a university or college of higher education, its international officer should have sent you a map and instructions on how to travel. They may even have arranged to meet you at your point of entry. Heathrow, Gatwick, Stansted and Luton airports are all on the outskirts of London and you have to take a train, tube or bus to get into town. There are major international airports all over the British Isles including Edinburgh, Glasgow, Derry, Prestwick, Birmingham, Cardiff and Bournemouth.

Travel to and from Heathrow

If you are travelling between Heathrow airport and central London, you can either take the Heathrow Express service to Paddington station (£12 for a 15-minute, one-way journey), or the tube (underground). Heathrow is on the Piccadilly line and a one-way ticket to or from central London will cost £3.60 for the one-hour journey. The underground is safe and relatively cheap, although you will have to negotiate escalators with all your luggage. You can use the Airbus service, which leaves every 30 minutes and costs around £7. The A2 Airbus goes to Russell Square via Holland Park tube, Baker Street tube and Euston station. By taxi, the journey will cost you about £45. It may take longer than the tube if the traffic is bad.

Travel to and from Gatwick

You can travel easily to and from Gatwick airport via the Gatwick Express, which runs in and out of Victoria station. Trains leave every 15 minutes and cost £10.50 for a one-way journey. Trains run through the night. Coaches run regularly between Gatwick and Victoria and cost about £5 for a one-way journey. The last coach leaves Gatwick at 10 pm and the last to leave Victoria is at 11.30 pm.

Travel to and from Stansted

Stansted is further out of London than Heathrow and Gatwick and is usually quiet. Trains from Stansted to Liverpool Street Station, central London, take about 40 minutes and cost £13 one way.

Regional airports

If you are going to a college or university outside London, you may be able to fly directly to the nearest big airport from your home country. If you land at Aberdeen, Edinburgh or Glasgow, the best option for getting to your destination may be to take a taxi from the taxi rank at the airport (costing between £8 and £15).

You may find there is a long queue at the taxi rank. It is considered rude and unfair for people to 'jump' the queue or push in front of others, so be warned! There may be a bus that serves the airport from the station on a circular route, which will be cheaper than a taxi.

Accommodation

Once you have been accepted on to the course of your choice the next step is to find out whether the institution provides accommodation or if it expects you to arrange it yourself. The options include university or college accommodation, flat or houseshare arrangements, bedsit or lodgings, or 'homestay' (living with a British family). Unless your university or college is arranging accommodation for you, it is advisable to view the place before making a commitment or, more importantly, before paying a deposit.

Student accommodation may attract dishonest types who are tempted by computers, CD players, mountain bikes and musical instruments. It is highly recommended that you arrange some room or contents insurance and that you read the small print carefully. Endsleigh (www.endsleigh.co.uk) specialises in insurance for students but you may wish to shop around to get the best deal.

College and university accommodation

As an undergraduate, you are usually guaranteed accommodation in your first year at least. It is best to accept any offers of accommodation as early as possible. Few universities and colleges have enough room to accommodate all of their students, therefore they need to know as early as possible if rooms are going to be free.

International students at higher education institutes are often guaranteed accommodation at least for their first year. Living arrangements vary from old-style single, double and triple study-bedrooms which have a shared bathroom in a hall of residence, to new apartments in a 'student village', with single rooms for about eight students with a shared kitchen, bathroom and living room. Some universities have also purchased houses which they have adapted for student use. There are also some schemes whereby private landlords allow their houses to be managed and let by universities for their students.

Halls of residence

The more traditional halls of residence are usually supervised by university staff. Security is often provided in the form of porters who are on duty 24 hours a day.

Some halls provide two meals a day, and others provide facilities for students to cater for themselves. Although self-catering halls tend to be cheaper, you may prefer to pay extra to have meals cooked for you. Meal times can be a good opportunity to meet people and make new friends. Most halls of residence have laundry facilities as well as cleaning staff who change bedsheets and empty dustbins.

Though some halls are stricter than others, permission can usually be obtained to allow guests to stay. Generally, few people bother to seek this permission. Spare rooms can sometimes be booked in advance for visiting parents or friends. Living in student halls of residence is a great way to meet new people and make lasting friendships. The stresses that can sometimes be associated with living out, such as bills and landlords, are avoided in halls where you have the benefit of being part of a large group, but you also have privacy if you need it.

Living in halls of residence also means that you can take part in organised activities. Each hall usually has an elected student body who have a say in the running of the hall and who organise a lively social programme. Many halls have their own bar, café, TV lounge, music practice room and even sports facilities.

Bearing all this in mind, it is worth noting that the rules can be restricting. There is also the risk that you might not get on with your fellow students and prefer a noisier/quieter environment. The predominant culture, be it partying or studying, does not suit everyone. However, as they are owned and run by universities, halls can provide a supportive environment.

Not all halls provide accommodation for the whole year, and will require you to clear your room during the holidays. Check with your international officer whether this is the case. Most universities will make exceptions for international students and allow you to stay in halls during vacations. Some may charge extra. In any case it will probably be possible for you to store luggage in secure storage space if you are going home for the holidays.

House and flatshare

In most instances, a place in hall is only guaranteed for one or two years of a three-year course; usually the first and/or third years. It is for this reason that flat and house sharing tends to be popular.

Flats and houses for rent are advertised in local papers and in accommodation offices at universities and colleges. In London, the papers to look in are *Loot* and *The Evening Standard*. Loot also has a good website: www.loot.co.uk. Prices vary widely, depending on the location and standard of accommodation required. Generally, the best time to look for accommodation is before the end of the summer term in June and July. Bear in mind that if you find a flat or house at this time of year, you will need to pay for it over the summer. Some landlords will, however, reduce the amount if you are not going to be living there straight away. If you enjoy independence and cooking for yourself (and occasionally others!) then sharing a flat or house is a great option.

Homestays

This is a popular option for language school students. You live in the home of a host family, where you have your own study bedroom and a certain number of meals with the family. Arrangements are flexible according to the needs and wants of the student, although it is usually seen as a kind of cultural exchange. The host family may be interested in getting to know you in the same way that you may be interested in their culture and traditions. Complete immersion in British life is often the best way to develop your language skills and understanding of the culture and customs of a British family.

You will be expected to respect and abide by basic rules that the family may impose. However, you are paying, so services, such as baby-sitting, are entirely at your discretion and not part of the deal.

Homestays can work very well for students who value security and prefer a home environment. However, if the host family has young children, you may not find it the best atmosphere for study. The real advantage is that you have to speak English daily.

Homestays can be arranged for the duration of your course, either privately or through the institution you are going to attend. Some international offices arrange a short, one-off weekend homestay as a way of introducing you to British culture and home life. They can also be arranged through organisations such as local churches, temples, mosques or synagogues, and charitable organisations with international links. You may prefer to get in contact with people who you know through family or friends.

Bedsits

Short for 'bedroom/sitting room', a bedsit is a one-room apartment in a larger building. A single or double bed with a washing area, cooker and bathroom are usually common in all bedsits. They can be any size from reasonably spacious to extremely cramped. Although very cheap, bedsits can be lonely unless you are in a building with lots of other students. Noisy neighbours can also make it difficult to study and you will have a landlord or agency to contend with but bedsits can be a good way of assuring your freedom.

Lodgings

This is a room in a family house – just like a homestay – but the relationship is purely commercial. You will have fairly little to do with the family and will be treated as a tenant rather than as a paying guest.

As a paying lodger, you are entitled to privacy, respect and a decent standard of living, although the family may have rules about bringing guests and friends into the house. Lodgings are usually advertised locally in shops and supermarkets, or through student accommodation offices and religious and charitable organisations.

Working in the UK

If you have a student visa, immigration laws will not permit you to work as a means of financing your studies. You can, however, work for up to 20 hours a week, on a part-time basis. You are allowed to work full time in the holidays. The UK government has recently simplified the rules to make it easier to work. One of the useful changes is that a spouse is now allowed to work full time, provided his or her partner is in full-time study.

You will need to present your passport and a local police registration certificate so your temporary student resident status can be checked. Job centres are listed in the local telephone book under 'Employment Services and Job Centres'. It is also worth checking shop/café/bar windows for vacancies and local newspapers.

Working without a permit is illegal and means that you will not be protected by employment laws. Companies caught employing illegal workers are fined when found out, and illegal employees are instantly deported.

Bank accounts

As a student on a full-time course of two years or more, you are entitled to open a student bank account. These usually have interest-free overdrafts, and other attractive offers such as rail tickets, mobile phones, record tokens, and sometimes cash gifts.

As a student, you are normally offered a current or student account that entitles you to a cheque book, and a cheque guarantee and cashpoint card. You can also use it as a debit card (used like a credit card in shops but the money is automatically deducted from your account about three working days from making the purchase).

Cheques are commonly used as a method of payment in Britain; a few important points should be remembered when filling them in:

- do not leave any gaps.

- sign your name in a way that is difficult to imitate. Keep your cheque book separate from your cheque guarantee card at all times.

You will be asked if you require an overdraft when you open an account. This is a good idea, as becoming overdrawn without authorisation can be costly incurring a charge as well as interest. Most pre-agreed student overdrafts are interest free, although some banks may charge extra fees for handling cheques. Read all the relevant literature available before you choose where to bank. Banks tend to range from the large, nationwide operations (eg HSBC, Royal Bank of Scotland, Barclays,

instalments over five years, or seven if the student has taken out loans for more than five academic years. Repayments include interest. Contact the Student Loans Administrator in the Student Finance Department at your university or college for details. Although loans are arranged through your university, you can ask questions about eligibility at:

The Student Loans Company Ltd
100 Bothwell Street
Glasgow G2 7JD
Tel: +44 (0)800 405010
Website: www.slc.co.uk

Postgraduate research students are not eligible for loans, partly because graduates can more easily obtain loans from banks and partly because they can apply for research grants (although the latter are limited in number).

Health and welfare

If your course is longer than six months you are entitled to free treatment within the National Health Service (NHS). There may be a surgery attached to your college or university, and it is a good idea to register here. Staff are used to student patients and the location is likely to be convenient. If not, you should apply to a local surgery and ask if you can register. You can find the nearest one in the Yellow Pages or by asking your local chemist. Take proof of your student status with you. Once you have registered, you will be sent an NHS medical card with an individual identity code. Do not lose this card, as you will also need it to register with a dentist. Students are entitled to free dental treatment on the NHS although this is not available from all dentists.

NHS prescriptions for medicines in the UK (except for Wales) cost £6.10 per item. You are exempt from this charge if you are under 19 years of age and in full-time education, or if you are pregnant or have

Lloyds TSB, NatWest) to smaller regional banks (for example Clydesdale) and building societies (Nationwide, Halifax) which offer very competitive terms for students. It is worth joining a bank or building society near your college or university as staff are more likely to be used to dealing with students.

Student loans

Student loans are offered as part of the financial support package for higher education students. Although essential to students in the UK, they are unlikely to apply to international students. Student loans are arranged with the Student Loans Company Ltd, based in Glasgow, and offer more competitive rates than high street banks. To qualify, you need to have been a resident in the UK for the three years immediately before the first day of your course, and need to be attending a full-time course of higher education (15 or more hours a week), or a Postgraduate Certificate in Education (PGCE).

Loans must be repaid in monthly

had a baby within the last year. There is no charge for prescriptions for the contraceptive pill. In Wales, the charge is £6 and everybody under 25 gets free prescriptions. Prepayment certificates are available if you are likely to need medicines frequently, which may mean an overall saving. For example, it is worth it if you are an asthmatic who needs more than one kind of inhaler at all times, because each inhaler and each cylinder of medication incurs a separate prescription charge.

Food

Britain has an excellent range of shops selling food for all tastes and diets. You can usually buy a wide variety of foods even in smaller towns. Larger cities, in particular, have shops selling authentic ingredients from all over the world and will stock kosher and halal products. There are Chinatowns in most big cities such as London, Manchester, Birmingham and Liverpool. Local shops tend to be more expensive than large supermarkets but fresh fruit and vegetables may be of better quality. Markets are a great source of cheap food. Food will cost you at least £25 per week, depending on your dietary requirements. Vegetarianism and veganism are common in Britain, and organically-grown produce is widely available .

In most towns and cities you will find excellent restaurants from many different countries serving food such as European, Indian, Thai, Chinese, Greek and Turkish food. Although fish and chips is a famous stereotypical English dish, chicken tikka masala is the most widely eaten – an indication of the international flavour that British food is now enjoying. A 'greasy spoon' café is the best place to try a traditional British breakfast. This typically consists of sausages, bacon, fried tomatoes, fried bread, fried eggs, fried mushrooms, fried potatoes, baked beans, black pudding, and a hot cup of tea. Not for the faint-hearted or for those on a low-cholesterol diet. Fastfood – burgers, kebabs and pizzas – is everywhere, much of which can be delivered to your door.

Entertainment

With very few exceptions, all universities in the UK have unions that are affiliated to the National Union of Students (NUS). When you register at university, you will be issued with an NUS card and a student identity card. You can also apply to your school or university for an International Student Identity Card (ISIC). Both are proof of your student status and entitle you to concessions. Your NUS card will get you discounts on most things from nightclubs, shopping and going to the cinema, to bungee jumps and health centres.

You will probably be attracted to at least one society connected to your college or university. This may be the best way to take part in and organise events that relate to your specific interest.

Cities such as London and Manchester are well known for their clubbing scene. In reality, the best clubs are dotted all over the UK and it is common for DJs to tour the country. Clubbing can be expensive – drinks may be double the price that they are in pubs. Some clubs have a reputation for drugs. Drug-related deaths and subsequent media attention have resulted in there being increased police interest in clubs.

You will find music of all types all around the country: orchestras and choirs, classical music, rock, jazz and folk bands playing in clubs and pubs.

Pubs are the best known social centres in Britain. They sell alcohol and soft drinks and sometimes have live music and stand-up comedy acts. People may spend the whole evening playing darts or pool, taking part in quizzes, or karaoke, or simply chatting and listening to a band. Pubs are equally inviting during cold winters when you can often find a burning log fire, or during the summer when you can sit outside in the pub garden.

Most pubs will expect you to go up to the bar to get your drinks although some do offer waiter/waitress service. Drinks are bought in 'rounds' where each person takes it in turn to buy the drinks for the group. If the group is very large or individuals are short of money, people might opt out of the round, preferring to buy their own drinks. It is considered very poor form if it is your round and you disappear.

Most colleges and universities have at least one bar, usually in the students' union. The bar is often the focus of student life, a place where people gather between lectures or at the end of the day. Groups of friends often meet at a pub before going off somewhere else for the rest of the evening. English licensing laws forbid the sale of alcohol after 11 pm, but plenty of bars and clubs have extended licensing hours and sell alcohol into the small hours of the morning.

Sightseeing

The UK is relatively small, yet a great deal is crammed in. It offers outstandingly beautiful landscapes, historic buildings and vibrant cities and, because of its size, it is easy to travel between places of particular interest. Don't be fooled into thinking you can 'do' the major sights in a long weekend; there are so many places worthy of a visit it is important to allow enough time for each one.

You should take advantage of any opportunity to get off campus, and make sightseeing a regular feature of your stay. Whether you prefer the many attractions of London, the ancient mystery of Stonehenge, the tranquil beauty of the Lake District or the stunning coasts of Cornwall and west Wales, you will be sure to find something of interest.

Getting around London

To get around London it is sensible to invest in a tourist map and a one-day, four-zone travel card that will allow you to use most public transport in the London area.

Stations and trains

Travelling by train in the UK is, at times, frustrating, for example buying a ticket in a busy station may involve a long wait. Try to find out the time of the train that you want to catch, and the name of your destination station before you buy your ticket. Stations are often very noisy places, and customers are separated from ticket vendors by thick glass screens. You will need bionic ears and a clear loud voice to get what you want. Another way to buy them is to go online:www.thetrainline.com

As a student, you can apply for a Young Person's Railcard if you are under 26 years old or in full-time education. This enables you to get a third off all rail tickets at a cost of £18 for one year. If you are planning to travel a lot by train, the railcard is a worthwhile investment. You must carry it on all rail journeys.

Trains which travel between cities ('Inter-City' trains) usually have a buffet carriage or trolley, depending on length of the journey. Trains running along short local routes rarely have anything but a toilet.

Services are not known for reliability and can be prone to delays and cancellations so allow plenty of time for the journey if you have an important engagement.

The following rules tend to operate on public transport:

- don't get on a train without a ticket that is valid for your entire journey. There will be an inspector checking every ticket, possibly more than once, on every mainline train and usually on the tubes. Immediate fines apply (£10 on the London Underground), even if you profess ignorance.

- there is a no-smoking rule on most public transport – although Inter-City trains usually have one carriage reserved for smokers. The London Underground is strictly non-smoking.

Buses and coaches

In London, you can catch coaches from Victoria Coach Station (near Victoria Railway Station) to most parts of Britain and to many other European destinations. Coach journeys usually take a lot longer than by train, seating is more cramped, and facilities are minimal – if they exist at all. However, the fares are a lot cheaper, and if you get a journey scheduled at night, you can try and sleep all the way.

Most towns and cities have coach stops, and some coach services form transport links for small towns with no railway station. Buses usually operate local routes in rural areas and small towns, and district routes in cities. London has its famous red London buses, and most cities have a multicoloured range of buses all owned by different companies. Fares vary according to where you start your journey and how far you travel. City bus routes are much more frequently served than rural routes, which often take in every village in an area.

Similar to the Young Person's Railcard, a coachcard, which costs £9, also entitles you to a third off.

Studying in English

If English is not your first language then you may find yourself struggling through the first few weeks of your chosen course. Whether you are studying mechanical engineering or dance and drama, you will find yourself having to study in the English language very intensively. You will be expected to understand what is being said at normal speed in classes; take notes; understand classmates when they talk to you and each other; and read and write reasonably quickly. However familiar you are with the English language, you may need time to adjust.

If you are having serious difficulties there will always be people who are willing to help you in your period of adjustment, however long. If you are at university or a college of higher education, the international officer in particular will understand the difficulties you may be facing. If, as sometimes happens, one of your teachers or lecturers speaks too fast or with an accent you have trouble understanding, you should not be afraid to let them know. They should take your needs into consideration, and speak more clearly and slowly if necessary. Above all, don't be afraid to ask for help.

One way to overcome these problems is to arrive a few weeks before your course starts and enrol on a language course. Most colleges, universities and English language schools offer summer courses at all levels. Some also offer courses in 'study skills' which prepare you for things like essay writing and planning workloads. Learning in this environment before you start a university or college course may be useful as you will become familiar with learning in English, and hearing it in an academic environment. Don't panic if you find things difficult. Ask for written notes from your teachers to supplement your own notes if it helps. They should be more than happy to help.

The main thing to remember is that you will find that things should become easier as time passes. Most international students say they start to feel much more confident after a month to six weeks.

National Rail network

▬▬▬	Principal routes
●━━●	Other selected routes
⊗	Airport interchange
✈	Railair coach link with Heathrow Airport
🚢	Ferry interchange

London Terminals

C	Charing Cross
E	Euston
F	Fenchurch Street
K	Kings Cross
L	Liverpool Street
M	Marylebone
P	Paddington
S	St Pancras
V	Victoria
W	Waterloo

National Rail Enquiries
08457 48 49 50
www.nationalrail.co.uk

Channel Tunnel Services
LILLE, BRUSSELS, PARIS

Useful information

Transport

London Black Cabs (24-hour bookings)
Tel: 020 7272 0272

Underground enquiries
Tel: 020 7222 1234   **Website:** www.thetube.com

National Rail
Tel: 08457 48 49 50   **Website:** www.nationalrail.co.uk

Brittany Ferries
Tel: 08705 360360   **Website:** www.brittany-ferries.com

P&O Ferries
Tel: 08701 296002   **Website:** www.poferries.com

Gatwick Airport
Tel: 0870 0000123   **Website:** www.baa.co.uk/main/airports/gatwick

Heathrow Airport
Tel: 08700 000123   **Website:** www.baa.co.uk/main/airports/heathrow

Eurostar
Tel: 0870 1606600   **Website:** www.eurostar.com

Health services

Emergency services
999

Drug, Alcohol Help Advice Line
020 8200 9575

Family Planning Association
0845 310 1334

Rape Crises Centre (24 hours)
020 7837 1600

Samaritan's Helpline
08457 90 90 90

Telephone

Operator
100

Directory enquiries
192

International operator
155

International directory enquiries
153

Living and studying in Britain

63

How to make the most of studying in the UK

Choose a great university town to study in

Your choice of university town will affect how much you enjoy your stay, the friends you meet and how much you spend. That is why so many students make a cheap visit to the UK to visit university towns before choosing to stay in the university town they'll enjoy the most. Many book accommodation for their stay on TravelStay.com. By booking on TravelStay.com, you may qualify for an exclusive international student discount and may even be able to stay in university accommodation during your visit.

Settle in before your course starts

You might choose to arrive in the UK a few weeks before your course starts. This will allow you to improve your English, find your way around, settle into the culture, travel around the UK and find a place to live before you start your course. While in the UK, you can stay in cheap hostels, budget hotels and short-stay university accommodation, all of which can be booked quickly and easily on TravelStay.com

Discover the UK and Europe during your stay

You'll have plenty of chances to discover world famous cities such as Edinburgh, Dublin, Cambridge, Bath, Paris, Amsterdam and the rest of Europe during weekends, vacations, and before or after your term. Travel from the UK is quick, cheap, and easy. By logging on to TravelStay.com and selecting 'tours', you can choose from a range of tours across the UK and Europe designed especially for international students. If you prefer the freedom of independent travel, the TravelStay.com transport page also makes it easy to find cheap flights, train and coach travel. You can then book a cheap and friendly place to stay with an international student discount directly from TravelStay.com

Travel with friends after your course

The ending of your course could provide your last chance to tour the UK and Europe. Some international students travel with friends they've met on your course. Others invite friends from home to travel with them before returning home together. You can find cheap tours, transport and can book accommodation on TravelStay.com in your own time.

Win a free holiday courtesy of TravelStay.com

Don't miss out on the chance to travel! For the chance to win a free holiday to a European city with a friend, visit TravelStay.com and select 'competition'. If you tell your friends about the TravelStay.com competition you may also win a digital camera to use during your travels!

TravelStay.com features exclusive international student discounts and new travel offers to help international students travel, save money and meet other travellers. If you can't find the travel or short-term accommodation you're looking for on TravelStay.com, simply email Info@TravelStay.com and we'll do our best to help!

Short-term accommodation

For students taking one of almost 5,000 short full time courses listed in hotcourses.com, the following types of accommodation are available:

University vacation accommodation is offered by most universities. It is available during the summer and Easter only and offers private rooms in a hall of residence or a shared self-catering apartment. Rooms with and without bathrooms are available.

Benefits include living with other students, often the cheapest form of accommodation, plenty of extra student facilities are often available such as a gym, restaurant, kitchens, laundry facilities and a bar.

Budget hotels offer private rooms ranging from single rooms to rooms for groups of six. Rooms both with and without bathrooms are available.

Benefits: inexpensive, you can check in and out whenever you please, easy to invite friends to stay with you, can enjoy a quiet nights sleep, hotel staff are always available to give you the information you need and help you enjoy your stay.

Hostels offer a bed in a shared room of between four and twelve people.

Benefits: meeting other student travellers, some have a party atmosphere, hostel staff are available to give you the information you need and help you enjoy your stay

All can be found and booked on
www.TravelStay.com
with exclusive long-term and international student discounts.

Student profile

Dionne Lee,
Malaysia

"While I was studying English in London, I heard about TravelStay.com from friends. It's a great website; it's quick and easy to use and it lists some great places to stay which you can book online. I used it to book university accommodation in Edinburgh during the Edinburgh Festival, which was fantastic! I've also used TravelStay.com to find cheap flights and accommodation for my weekend trips all over the UK and Europe. It has also given me lots of ideas on how and where to travel on my budget. I've had a great time travelling and I've made some really nice friends!"

A to Z of subjects

The first thing you will need to decide is which subject you would like to study, and this section will give you an outline of what is on offer. It is designed to cover not just the traditional academic disciplines such as physics, law and economics but also more vocational areas such as graphic design, fashion and media studies. This is not a comprehensive list of subjects but we have tried to include the main ones.

Each of the following chapters are divided into three parts. The first part gives an introduction to the general subject area, explaining such details as the history of a subject, the various branches it has (the difference between civil engineering and chemical engineering, for example) and it will describe how it is studied in Britain.

The second section of each chapter concentrates on specialist and vocational courses which are offered both by public and private institutions. These courses can last anything from one week to three years. Featured in this section are a number of independent colleges that specialise in courses for international students.

The third section of each chapter profiles undergraduate and postgraduate degree courses. This contains a selection of courses available at various institutions, including some of those which scored highly in the 2001 research assessment exercise, or alternatively in recent teaching quality assessments.

For reasons of space, many institutions with excellent ratings in the teaching quality assessments or level 5/5* ratings in the research assessment exercises are not featured, and should be given equal consideration. Each profile finishes with a reference to a page containing further information and/or contact details of institutions.

Research ratings and teaching quality assessments

The chapters also include tables showing the results of independent assessments of standards at universities and colleges of higher education. These assessments are carried out on a subject-by-subject basis. One assessment is carried out for the quality of research in a particular subject. This is known as the research assessment exercise (RAE), and these were carried out in 2001. Assessors look principally at the number of papers published nationally and internationally in a particular field. These tables are probably more relevant to postgraduate students. Scores range from 5* for departments recognised as having the highest standards of research to 1 for departments with weak research capabilities. This, however, does not necessarily mean that the teaching standards are any worse. On the contrary, it could be possible that lecturers at a university with less research capabilities have more time to devote to undergraduate students. The research assessment exercise is carried out every five years.

The second assessment is for the quality of teaching, known as the teaching quality assessment (TQA). These are probably more significant to undergraduate courses but also include taught master's programmes. The TQAs are performed by separate organisations in England, Scotland and Wales. Because it can take up to three years to assess a subject and the process is still in its early days, many are not yet complete. As the TQAs are performed separately for England, Scotland and Wales, there are some subjects that have been completed for Scotland and Wales but not for England. The Scottish TQAs also have an extra category, 'highly satisfactory', which can make it difficult to make comparisons.

Another complication is that the system of scoring has changed for TQAs in England. Departments used to be given an excellent, satisfactory or unsatisfactory rating but are now given a score out of a maximum of 24. This score is based on curriculum design, teaching, student progress, student support and guidance, learning resources and quality control.

So, you will find some tables that are incomplete, use conflicting systems and apply to one part of Britain but not another. But despite this, we believe that it is important information, and that it is better to include the tables in order to help you in making an informed choice. Do be careful, however, not to see these as the whole picture.

Sample table from the research assessment exercise

RESEARCH RANKINGS

Clinical Dentistry

rae

Institution	Grade	Institution	Grade
University of Bristol	5*	The University of Birmingham	4
King's College London (University of London)	5*	University of Leeds	4
University of Newcastle upon Tyne	5	The University of Liverpool	4
Queen Mary, University of London	5	The University of Manchester	4
The University of Sheffield	5	University of Wales College of Medicine	4
University College London (University of London)	5	Queen's University Belfast	3a
University of Dundee	5	University of Glasgow	3a

Source: RAE 2001

Sample table from the teaching quality assessments

TEACHING QUALITY ASSESSMENTS

Medicine
(England and Northern Ireland) 1998/99/2000

tqa

Institution	Grade	Institution	Grade
The University of Liverpool	24	Queen's University Belfast	22
University of Newcastle upon Tyne	24	Imperial College of Science, Technology and Medicine (University of London)	21
University of Southampton	24		
Institute of Child Health, Institute of Opthalmology	23	Institute of Psychiatry, King's College London (University of London)	21
University of Leicester	23	University College London (University of London)	21
St George's Hospital Medical School (University of London)	23	The University of Birmingham	20
King's College London (University of London)	22	University of Bristol	20
Queen Mary, University of London	22	The University of Sheffield	19

Source: HEFCE, SHEFC, HEFCW latest available ratings
For a more complete list of institutions offering these courses at undergraduate level refer to the Course Directory

Access, foundation and diploma

Although British universities and colleges of higher education do recognise many international qualifications, it may be the case that they do not accept the awards that you hold. It may also be the case that your level of education or knowledge of the English language is not of the necessary standard for you gain entry on to the course you want to study. Don't worry if you are in this situation, as there are a number of alternative routes available that can provide a recognised step into higher education. International students can follow a number of courses ranging from foundation and access programmes to diploma courses. These may be taken at universities and higher education institutions, as well as at a range of further education colleges.

Access courses tend to be recognised by universities as an alternative to A levels and are specifically designed for mature students and those who may have been disadvantaged in terms of their education. For many people, access courses can provide a second chance to pursue academic opportunities and, in general, they have no formal entry requirements. Programmes vary considerably and can be broad based in nature and aimed solely at university entrance, or discipline-related and geared towards certain subjects or vocations such as business or teacher training. Access courses usually cover a variety of topics, including study skills, and will provide students with guidance and support.

Foundation courses usually last one year and aim to provide students with a solid basis from which to progress. In addition to covering core subjects, programmes often provide classes in IT and English language skills. The advantage of taking a course associated with a higher education institution is that successful students are normally guaranteed a place on a degree course at that institution. The advantage of an independent foundation course, on the other hand, is that it can offer both impartial advice on degrees and universities and greater flexibility if you are not sure what you want to study. If you choose the latter option, you should ensure that the qualification will be recognised by universities before you enrol.

An alternative route is a diploma course, and these can be taken in many subjects, from film-making to conservation. Courses vary in length and are available at higher and further education institutions as well as a number of independent schools and colleges around the country. Unlike foundation and access courses, diplomas are not specifically designed for entry to higher education, concentrating instead on a certain subject and the skills required to succeed in a relevant profession. Completion of a diploma course may not necessarily guarantee a place at a higher education institution but it could be the key qualification for entering a profession that does not currently have an equivalent degree programme.

Bell International

Bell International, a leading provider of English courses for nearly 50 years, offers courses in general English, English for further education, professional English and teacher development. Courses for young learners are also available, for students aged eight to 17. Bell's curriculum is equalled by its programme of student services, ensuring high levels of personal student care, accommodation and excellent social programmes. Contact the centre on +44 (0)1223 212333 or alternatively visit the website at www.bell-centres.com for more information.

Contact details, see page 611

Bromley College of Further & Higher Education
Cambridge Business Skills

This one-year, full-time foundation course run by the business school is designed to prepare students for undergraduate study. It emphasises the skills required for successful study at degree level such as independent work and research. Modules covered include meeting and presentation skills, the world of business, business communication, marketing and finance. English as a foreign language (EFL) tuition is also offered where appropriate. Teaching takes place at the college's Rookery Lane site. There are currently around 20 international students enrolled on the course.

For further information, see page 458

Cavendish College

Established in 1985 and set in central London, this private college specialises in courses such as art and design, business, hospitality and computing. The college offers modern and spacious facilities including specialist creative studios, a

lecture theatre and five different computer laboratories, and it has also established its own cyber café. Due to the vocational nature of a lot of the courses, the college updates the content regularly to keep abreast of contemporary developments in particular fields. The college has a large international community with students coming from over 80 countries around the world. The creative department offers a variety of courses at different levels which cater for both the beginner and the advanced student. In addition, the creative department offers diplomas in fashion design or marketing, interior design and graphic design. Diploma programmes run for the whole academic year and students can take additional subjects to further their skills and interests.

For further information, see page 410

Chichester College of Arts, Science and Technology
Academic Foundation Course

The academic foundation courses have been specifically designed for those students who are intending to follow undergraduate or postgraduate study in the UK. The college runs a number of English language courses that are designed to develop language, communication and IT skills with qualifications available in Cambridge Proficiency, NVQ English and RSA CLAIT, amongst others. There is an English language summer school that is popular with international students. The two-year Foundation in Medical, Dental and Veterinary Science provides an academic programme of A level subjects which is accepted by universities. The course is also complemented by work experience. Music courses are available including a pre-professional music course, a BTEC National Diploma in Popular

Bell International

International contact:
Bell UK, Hillscross, Red Cross Lane, Cambridge CB2 2QX
Tel: +44 (0)1223 212333
Email: info@bell-centres.com
Website: www.bell-centres.com

The University Foundation Course prepares international students for a wide range of degree courses and provides help with successful application to a UK university. Bell has firm academic links with five university partners.

Why choose Bell?

Bell has nearly 50 years' experience of English language teaching. Bell's university partners have approved the University Foundation Course. The course includes:

- 21 hours a week of tuition in small groups with individual care and attention
- one-to-one weekly tutorials to review your progress
- an independent educational consultant to provide advice for your choice of university and courses
- a programme of visits to universities
- use of a well-equipped multimedia centre
- weekly lectures by visiting speakers
- internet access and word processing facilities after classes
- IELTS materials and practice tests

Entrance requirements

The course is for students who have IELTS level 4.5 or equivalent and have graduated from secondary school and want to enter university in the UK.

Course objectives

The University Foundation Course will help you to:

- enter university in the UK
- build up your knowledge in the subject modules – economics, geography, politics and business studies
- develop your listening and speaking skills through a guest speaker programme
- practise for IELTS and improve your exam technique
- gain greater confidence in analysing and manipulating data
- extend your research and academic skills

- develop confidence in communication skills for academic and social life
- get used to campus life and living in the UK

Course structure
The course lasts 36 weeks over three terms of an academic year.

Term one core modules (compulsory):
General English
Academic Skills
Information Technology
IELTS
Self Study
Life in Britain

Terms two and three core modules (compulsory):
Academic Skills
Quantitative Analysis
Information Technology
IELTS
Life in Britain
Language Skills

Subject modules (choose three):
Economics
Geography
Politics
Business Studies

Assessment
Progress is assessed throughout the course by regular assignments, exams, project work, essays, reports and presentations.

Application to university
An independent educational consultant advises you on the best degree courses and universities and on the application process. On successful completion of the Foundation course, you will then have a place at one of Bell's university partners (at their discretion), which are:

- Oxford Brookes University
- The University of Essex
- University of East Anglia
- University of North London
- Roehampton University of Surrey

Bell has been very successful in placing students on courses at a reputable range of British universities.

Term one is spent at either Saffron Walden, Essex, in a residential campus or in Norwich in a private homestay. Terms two and three are spent in either Cambridge or Oxford in a private homestay.

Art and Design Access Course
This course was designed with the Surrey Institute of Art and Design. It provides a strong visual arts focus in addition to English language development for students who want to go on to complete a foundation course in art and design.

Student profile

Daniel Ganz,
Switzerland,
Foundation
Course

"I want to study a degree in economics in Britain to help my career. After my degree I plan to work in a bank again in international relations where I will use English a lot. The course develops all aspects of language and academic skills such as note taking, listening and report writing and this enables me to study the subject modules such as Life in Britain and Economics. I have never met such good teachers. They offer personal tuition when I have questions. I also have weekly one-to-one tutorials with the teacher where I can talk about my progress, tests and university application. The British university placement representative visits every month to advise us on university application. The partner universities have also visited us. I have really enjoyed my experience at Bell and have met an interesting mix of very nice people and learnt about a new culture."

Music and a Foundation in Music lasting two years. Chichester College was the 1999 Beacon Award winner for international student support.
Contact details, see page 614

City College, Birmingham
Access to Higher Education

The Access to Higher Education is designed for mature students, lasting one year on a full-time basis. It prepares students for entry into university or higher education and leads to the award of the access certificate for successful candidates. City College offers students an extensive range of such courses which may lead on to degree and diploma courses in social work, nursing and related areas in healthcare, science, primary teaching, computing, law, English and history. Students enjoy a friendly and positive atmosphere and a teaching team who provide substantial assistance. City College, Birmingham's success rate is one of the best in the Midlands with numbers of international students going on to study at degree level each year. Students must be 21 years or over. No formal qualifications are required but there is an entry assessment test. A pre-access course is available for those who do not succeed with this test.
For further information, see page 412

City College Manchester
Science and Engineering Foundation

In conjunction with The University of Manchester, this one-year, full-time programme is aimed at international students wishing to progress on to a first degree course in science or engineering. It consists of compulsory units in maths and IT and an investigative project, plus a range of options in physics, chemistry and biology. An intensive English language course is integral to the programme, leading to an internationally-recognised English test (for example IELTS). Successful completion of the programme at the appropriate level will gain students access to one of the following degree subjects at The University of Manchester: engineering (aerospace, civil, electrical, electronic and mechanical), chemistry, earth sciences, materials science, maths, physics, and biological sciences. Students can also apply for computer science studies at a number of other universities. A foundation certificate is awarded by The University of Manchester and City College Manchester.
For further information, see page 466

Dudley College of Technology
Access Courses

Dudley College of Technology is set in the West Midlands, in the centre of England. It offers access courses in various subjects including computing, teacher training and business. The courses are designed to allow people with non-typical qualifications to enter higher education and degree-level programmes. This transition is helped by the college's guidance service, which gives students assistance in making university choices. Students benefit from the college's libraries and study centres. The library contains over 38,000 books, some 200 specialist periodicals, up-to-date reference books and useful services such as computer access. More than 200 study places offer both group and individual work areas while quiet room facilities are ideal for completing assignments or concentrating on exam revision.

Contact details, see page 615

Hopwood Hall College

Hopwood Hall College runs foundation and access courses which last for one year. In 2000, 70 per cent of enrolled students progressed to higher education. The level of success at access level 2 is also very high with 81 per cent achieving the equivalent of A/C pass at GCSE. Subject areas for foundation and access courses include business, IT, art and design, science and humanities. Also available is a foundation degree course in science, computing and engineering, leading to direct entry to The Manchester Metropolitan University. New developments include a pre-MBA/master's leading to entry on to an MBA or master's in business at a local university. Annual tuition fees range from £3,800 for foundation and access courses to £5,610 and £6,000 for foundation degree courses. The pre-MBA/pre-master's is £5,000. The access courses attract over 100 students a year, many of whom have subsequently succeeded at university.

For further information, see page 624

University of Luton

International Foundation Course (Science, Technology and Design)

This course combines the study of English language with that of science, technology, computing or design. The aim is to develop communication skills in English to the level required for entry on to a degree or HND, while providing the necessary background knowledge and technical skills. In order to apply for this course, the student's first language must not be English and they must hold a qualification which is suitable for entry to UK higher education. Entry is for those of 18 years and over. To complete each part of the course, four core modules must be passed. These modules include English language for academic purposes, contemporary English language and IT.

Contact details, see page 618

New College Nottingham

New College Nottingham offers university foundation courses in business, computing, information technology, travel and tourism management. These courses run on a one-year, full-time basis, providing international students with the skills and learning styles to study at degree level with confidence at British universities and colleges. English language and essential study skills are combined with one main subject chosen from your area of interest. Also inclusive is an NCN Diploma in the main subject, with a Business English Certificate and an IELTS qualification. These foundation courses have been formally recognised as a degree entry qualification by The Nottingham Trent University, Loughborough University, De Montfort University and University of Lincoln. Students can also choose to continue their studies at New College

Nottingham which offers over 30 Higher National Diplomas and other qualifications. *For further information, see page 518*

Northbrook College

Access programmes

Access and Foundation courses at Northbrook College provide an opportunity to study in an environment with students on Northbrook's higher education courses. Northbrook is a large college and has five campuses. Class sizes are small (usually of 15 to 20 people) and the college offers individual tuition to students. The college is based on the south coast of England in Worthing, a traditional town of just under 100,000 people. It is a holiday resort with a reputation for being clean and friendly. Worthing is 75 kilometres from London and its airports. Subjects which can be taken include engineering, business studies and IT, hospitality and tourism, visual arts, media, music and performing arts and

also various English language courses. *For further information, see page 524*

The Women's Academy

The Women's Academy was specially established to provide study opportunities for women whose cultural or personal preference was to study in an all-female environment. Housed in a purpose-built facility, it offers an excellent learning environment and resources. The academy provides a range of full-time programmes suitable for international students. Within easy reach of the city centre, this modern campus has on-site catering for students and is served by several bus routes. A full student tutorial service is provided, including careers advice and guidance. Additional support in English, numeracy and information technology is available. Information is available through City College, Birmingham's international office. *For further information, see page 412*

Accountancy and finance

Despite its reputation for being a rather dull profession, accountancy of the 21st century is, in fact, far from boring. It is considered a key social discipline, a central factor to the decisions made by a huge spectrum of people, from investors and company managers to housekeepers and students. Essentially, everyone has money issues and everyone needs to keep track of their finances. Demand for newly-qualified accountants, therefore, is high.

This is particularly true of the UK, where many of the largest accountancy firms in the world are based. In fact, four out of the 'Big Five' professional services firms (PricewaterhouseCoopers, Ernst & Young, KPMG, Arthur Andersen and Deloitte & Touche) are listed in the millennium edition of *The 100 Best Companies to Work for in the UK*. Many young graduates choose accountancy or finance-related careers because they provide financial security as well as intellectual stimulation.

An accountancy qualification is highly regarded and is considered a good grounding in any area of business. To qualify as an accountant in Britain, you must sit the exams set by one of six institutions. Students are expected to have gained a first or upper second class degree or equivalent before taking these exams, though not necessarily in a related subject.

As an accountant, you may be involved in audit, tax, corporate finance, insolvency, financial consultancy or management accounting. Since accountancy, on the whole, deals with processing financial information and giving detailed business advice to clients, those thinking of pursuing it as a career need to think logically and show proficiency in all business areas. Good oral and written communication skills are essential as you will interact with clients on a day-to-day basis. Students do not necessarily have to be highly numerate to be an accountant but for certain business areas, such as auditing, it is beneficial to be comfortable with numbers.

Accounting and finance degrees tend to concentrate on disciplines like economics, elementary statistics, behavioural studies and law. Students are taught through lectures, tutorials and workshops or seminars. Most courses have some practical element, familiarising students with spreadsheets and basic computer skills at an early stage.

It is possible to study finance as a whole, usually with reference to the constantly changing global economy. Students develop an understanding of finance theory, stock markets, financial instruments and treasury management. It is often studied as a joint honours, linked with such subjects as accountancy or computer science, or specialisms like sports or hotel management.

Some courses involve an element of practical work experience, so students from outside the European Union should be aware that they may be restricted by visa requirements.

Specialist and vocational

City of London College
Accountancy

Established in 1979 and situated in close proximity to the financial heart of the capital, this private college specialises in providing training courses for adults on a full-time basis. Courses on offer can lead to master's level qualifications awarded by UK universities or directly to the employment market. In accountancy, the college offers the ACCA professional course. Also on offer are two accounting technician courses leading to the technician qualification by ACCA and by the Association of Accounting Technicians (AAT). Students completing the Certified Accounting Technician (CAT) are automatically transferred to the ACCA professional students register and exempted from part one of the ACCA qualification. Students completing the technician qualification offered by the Association of Accounting Technicians (AAT) are awarded the NVQ level four in accountancy and earn exemptions from two of the ACCA papers. The college has an experienced team delivering lectures in well-furnished classrooms at a convenient location.

Contact details, see page 611

Undergraduate

The University of Aberdeen
MA (Hons) Accountancy

The single honours degree in accountancy at The University of Aberdeen lasts for four years and covers all areas of financial accounting, management accounting, accounting for business, taxation, business finance, accounting systems and audit. Students intending to complete an accountancy degree are also required to take courses in economics, law, statistics and management during their first two years. The development of IT skills is encouraged and web-based learning is very much part of the course. All of the accountancy degrees at Aberdeen are fully accredited by the accountancy professional bodies. Students are given the opportunity to study accountancy with a number of other subjects such as finance, French, anthropology, economic science, geography, German, Hispanic studies, legal studies, management studies, philosophy, political economy, sociology and statistics, either as joint honours programmes or as major-minor programmes.

For further information, see page 613

Bournemouth University
BA (Hons) Accounting with Law

An innovative course combining legal,

TEACHING QUALITY ASSESSMENTS
Accountancy and Finance
(Scotland) 1995/96

tqa

Institution	Grade	Institution	Grade
University of Dundee	Excellent	Heriot-Watt University	Highly Satisfactory
The University of Edinburgh	Excellent	The University of Stirling	Highly Satisfactory
The University of Aberdeen	Highly Satisfactory	University of Abertay Dundee	Satisfactory
University of Glasgow	Highly Satisfactory	Napier University	Satisfactory
Glasgow Caledonian University	Highly Satisfactory	University of Paisley	Satisfactory
		The University of Strathclyde	Satisfactory

Source: HEFCE, SHEFC, HEFCW latest available ratings
For a more complete list of institutions offering these courses at undergraduate level refer to the Course Directory

Institution	Grade	Institution	Grade
London School of Economics and Political Science (University of London)	5*	University of Glasgow	5
		University of Newcastle upon Tyne	5
The University of Manchester	5*	University of Paisley	5
University of Wales, Bangor	5	The University of Stirling	5
University of Bristol	5	The University of Strathclyde	5
University of the West of England, Bristol	5	The University of Aberdeen	4
		University of Dundee	4
The University of Durham	5	Glasgow Caledonian University	4
The University of Edinburgh	5	The University of Liverpool	3a
The University of Essex	5	Sheffield Hallam University	3a
University of Exeter	5	University of Central Lancashire	3b

Source: RAE 2001

accounting and business skills, this new degree combines accounting skills and legal knowledge, allowing graduates the opportunity to follow a career in either profession, or indeed both. The course responds directly to a demand in industry and practice for better-trained accountants and finance managers who are able to apply their knowledge and skills within a legal context. A focus on communication and IT skills also gives students an advantage over others, helping them to build the superior interpersonal and commercial skills needed in any career. Assessment comprises a mixture of traditional examinations, practical assignments and presentations, which draws on the full range of students' developing abilities. Students are totally involved and responsible for the quality of their learning experience.
For further information, see page 448

University of Exeter
BA (Hons) Accounting and Finance
This degree is targeted at those aiming for a career in accountancy with major accounting firms in industry or in the financial sector. It develops useful career skills such as communication and teamwork and looks at the role of accounting

and finance in society. The department has strong links with professional firms and institutes, many of which award prizes for excellence in examinations and give guest lectures each year. The degree gives full exemption from the professional stage of the Institute of Chartered Accountants in England and Wales and is fully recognised by the Scottish Institute. Various exchange programmes provide opportunities to spend the third year studying in an EU country, usually in that country's language.
Contact details, see page 616

University of Glamorgan
BA (Hons) Accounting and Finance
This course covers the four main themes of financial reporting, computerised accounting systems, financial management and management accounting. It is intended to give students a sound foundation in preparation for a career in professional, management or financial accounting. The skills that students develop while on the course are equally appropriate within the manufacturing and service sectors or in the private and public sectors. The University of Glamorgan has a student-centred approach to learning through workshops and seminars. Students also

Accountancy

Institution	Grade	Institution	Grade
The University of Wales, Aberystwyth	Excellent	Cardiff University	Excellent
		University of Glamorgan	Excellent

Source: HEFCE, SHEFC, HEFCW latest available ratings
For a more complete list of institutions offering these courses at undergraduate level refer to the Course Directory

develop their communication skills while the use of relevant computer software enhances their know-how. Modules have been designed to incorporate this and students also have an opportunity to use a variety of relevant computerised accounting software packages.

Contact details, see page 616

The University of Manchester
BA (Economic and Social Studies) (Hons) Accounting, Finance or Accounting and Finance
These are three of the main degrees specialising in accounting and finance at The University of Manchester. You can choose to specialise either in accounting or finance or you can combine the two. The course is suitable for anyone considering a career in accounting and finance, whether in public practice, the public sector or in other areas of the financial world. It can also be studied alongside another social sciences. Combinations with economics, government, econometrics, sociology and other areas are all possible within the course structure.

For further information, see page 514

University of Plymouth
BA (Hons) Accounting and Finance
The first stage of the BA (Hons) Accounting and Finance degree at the University of Plymouth provides students with a foundation in the principles and practices of business and management.

This means that the main areas of study do not only include a strong core in accounting and information technology but also in economics, quantitative methods, a business skills course, personnel and marketing and practical computing. Stage two introduces the areas of law and business modelling for decision making. The final stage of the course provides core specialist elements in advanced financial accounting, business finance and also advanced managerial accounting. Students may also choose to study a language.

For further information, see page 536

The University of Stirling
BA (Hons) Money, Banking and Finance
Financial institutions are playing an increasingly important role in the world economy and are a major employer of graduates. This programme is specifically designed to provide a good understanding of how the financial sector of the economy works. The programme combines the study of core units in economics and finance, taught by the Department of Accounting, Finance and Law, with options in the area of money and banking, taught by the Department of Economics. Career opportunities include posts with major national and international institutions, such as central banks and other companies which are engaged in the buying and selling of stocks and shares in the City of London.

For further information, see page 566

Accountancy

Student Profile

Vivian Musni Guina

United Kingdom

BA (Hons) Accounting

Bournemouth University

"I chose Bournemouth University because their approach is to interact with students and show real interest in students' progress. I found this very useful during my years at Bournemouth and have no doubt that it has motivated me and helped me through my accounting degree. Choosing the accounting degree at Bournemouth University was the smartest move I ever made. It was all up to me to motivate myself to succeed but I had access to support from lecturers whenever I required help in my studies. The course also gave me the experience of interacting with the accounting world, which other universities do not offer (for example, the AFECA conferences in Europe). If you want to succeed in your degree you have to be willing to work at it but the help is there, handed to you on a platter; all you have to do is make the most of it."

Postgraduate

University of Glasgow

MAcc in International Accounting and Financial Management

This course is designed for graduates with a good honours degree or equivalent who would like a career in accounting and international business. It also provides a base from which to do research at doctoral level. The MAcc degree addresses the issues facing international organisations, focusing mainly on accounting and finance related matters. Core and optional courses give you the flexibility to pursue chosen areas of interest. You can study for one year on a full-time basis or part time over two years, though part-time students must

be able to attend daytime courses.

For further information, see page 480

Leeds Metropolitan University

MSc Finance and MSc Accounting

The MSc Finance course is designed for aspiring finance professionals wishing to develop their knowledge of finance in a number of areas. Students develop skills relating to finance and an understanding of developments in and relationships between specific areas of the profession. The MSc Accounting course is designed to provide students with an understanding of accounting and its implications in the broader business environment. The course provides a detailed insight into the concepts involved in accounting and a fundamental grasp of necessary principles. The practical relevance of this course provides students with excellent preparation for a professional qualification.

For further information, see page 500

London School of Economics and Political Science (University of London)

MSc Accounting and Finance

This master's degree is designed for those hoping to enter a career in business, consulting or government. Students need some academic background in subjects such as accounting, finance, economics and quantitative methods for this course, which provide a good preparation for academic research in accounting or finance. Students can choose to focus either on accounting or finance or can opt for an equal combination of the two. The first week involves a refresher course in mathematics and statistics, followed by four examined courses. Everyone must study corporate finance and asset markets and then pick at least one from corporate financial reporting and management accounting. To make up the required four courses, options include international accounting and finance, securities and investment analysis and topics in the theory of finance.

For further information, see page 508

University of North London
MA International Finance

This one-year taught course is designed for graduates from accounting, economics, business and related disciplines. Students examine both the developing world of international finance and the management of finance through the examination of such issues as the current state of global finance and economics and the impact of international finance on economic and political activity. Core modules on the course include global financial markets, finance and quantitative analysis, and investment research methods. Options include mergers and acquisitions and strategic management control. Teaching and learning methods involve group discussions, problem analysis and videos, as well as conventional lectures,

seminars and a 12,000 to 15,000 word dissertation. Students may apply to develop their dissertation topic into an MPhil/PhD programme.

For further information, see page 520

Northumbria University
MA Global Financial Management

The dramatic changes in financial systems over the last 30 years have led to their globalisation, with companies and financial institutions now operating on an international basis. This one-year MA is aimed at individuals seeking a career within this industry. The programme examines key aspects such as globalisation of financial markets, strategic investment and risk analysis. This is one of many focused master's programmes offered by Northumbria University's Business School, which has been rated excellent in the most recent Teaching Quality Assessments. Other programmes include business, IT, human resources management, international business, MBA, marketing and risk management.

For further information, see page 526

Useful links

www.accountancyage.com	●	*Accountancy Age* magazine
www.aat.co.uk	●	Association of Accounting Technicians
www.accaglobal.com	●	The Association of Chartered Certified Accountants (ACCA)
www.cipfa.org.uk	●	The Chartered Institute of Public Finance and Accountancy
www.cimaglobal.com	●	The Chartered Institute of Management Accountants (CIMA)
www.tax.org.uk	●	The Chartered Institute of Taxation
www.icaew.co.uk	●	The Institute of Chartered Accountants in England and Wales (ICAEW)
www.ifa.org.uk	●	Institute of Financial Accountants

Agriculture and land management

Since the 18th century, landowners have been constantly experimenting with new crops, new species of animals and more efficient methods of production. The popular view of agriculture is of a simple industry where farmers pass their skills through the generations. Today, continuing developments ensure that the industry is far from basic. In the UK, farming contributes £6.6 billion a year to the national economy. It uses three quarters of Britain's land area and employs over half a million people. This makes Britain an ideal place to study agriculture.

Under the broad heading of agriculture and land management come a number of courses ranging from animal care, agricultural science, tree management, horticulture, forestry and greenkeeping to environmental or estate management. Courses are offered at degree, HND, City & Guilds and Edexcel level. Many of these will have certain core courses and options for specialised study. It may also be possible to gain qualifications which are a legal requirement for operators in the industry (if you wish to work in the UK), for example NPTC crop sprayers.

You should be aware that teaching will probably be based around specific UK practices or those of other countries with similar methods. If you are particularly interested in use of the land in other countries, you will need to check courses very carefully to ensure they contain the elements that will be most relevant to you.

Agriculture

Studying agriculture involves farming methods, crop and livestock production and, increasingly, the relationship between farming and protecting our environment. Common elements include accounting for agricultural businesses, farm planning, animal production and animal nutrition.

Arboriculture

This is the science and practice of cultivating trees and shrubs. It is similar to forestry but less concerned with timber production, concentrating more on conservation. Subjects include plantations, landscape design, tree plant science, timber harvesting and establishing countryside management. Practical skills such as chainsaw use may also be covered.

Horticulture

This is the production and use of plants both for eating and for creating an attractive environment. Course content may include plant growth, development, protection and selection, preparing sports areas, alternative ways of growing plants, propagation and garden centre skills.

Countryside skills/conservation

This kind of course provides you with the skills and knowledge to carry out practical conservation and management work in the countryside. Core modules may include plant science, countryside awareness, ecology and climate and conservation law.

Harper Adams University College

HND Agriculture with Land and Farm Management

Harper Adams has a modular curriculum and each module is assessed at the end of the semester of study. Once students have passed a module they are awarded credit which builds up towards an HND or degree. The HND in Agriculture with Land and Farm Management is a three-year sandwich course, where two semesters are spent on industrial placement. Students are taught about current agricultural practice and principles and take a module in communications and IT, which includes work on information retrieval, presentation and study skills. This is a vocational course with the aim of producing highly employable graduates.

Contact details, see page 616

The University of Wales, Aberystwyth

BSc (Hons) Agriculture with Countryside Management

This course offers students a knowledge of agriculture and an understanding of its increasing role in countryside access, rural enterprise, environmental conservation and recreation. The first two years provide a foundation in crop and animal science, production systems and rural economics, together with core modules in information technology and statistics. Optional modules introduce a range of countryside topics including forestry and woodland, habitat ecology and countryside organisations. The final year provides a choice of optional environmental modules and students also prepare a dissertation on a subject of their own choice. A combination of teaching methods is used, supported by fieldwork and visits in Wales and other parts of the UK. Assessment is continuous, based on projects, essays and seminars in addition to written examinations.

For further information, see page 436

University of Wales, Bangor

The School of Agricultural and Forest Sciences has been involved in the research and teaching of land use studies for over 100 years. BSc courses are available in agriculture, agroforestry, rural resource management, forestry, forest products, environmental science and environmental conservation. There is an extensive portfolio of MSc taught courses including rural resource management, water resource management,

picture courtesy of Capel Manor College

TEACHING QUALITY ASSESSMENTS

Agriculture and Land Management

Land and Property Management (England and Northern Ireland) 1997/98

Institution	Grade	Institution	Grade
Kingston University	24	Leeds Metropolitan University	21
De Montfort University	23	Sheffield Hallam University	21
Harper Adams University College	23	University of Ulster	21
Oxford Brookes University	23	The Nottingham Trent University	20
Cambridge University	22	University of Portsmouth	20
Liverpool John Moores University	22	Anglia Polytechnic University	19
Northumbria University	22	City University	19
University of Plymouth	22	University of Westminster	19
The University of Reading	22	University of Central England	
Southampton Institute	22	in Birmingham	18
University of the West of England, Bristol	22	The University of Salford	18
The University of Manchester Institute		South Bank University	18
of Science and Technology (UMIST)	22	Staffordshire University	17
University of Greenwich	21	NESCOT	15

Source: HEFCE, SHEFC, HEFCW latest available ratings
For a more complete list of institutions offering these courses at undergraduate level refer to the Course Directory

RESEARCH RANKINGS

Agriculture

Institution	Grade	Institution	Grade
The University of Aberdeen (Plant and Soil Science)	5	University of Newcastle upon Tyne	4
The University of Nottingham	5	The University of Aberdeen (Agriculture and Forestry)	3a
The University of Reading	5	University of Greenwich	3a
The University of Reading (Plant Sciences)	5	University of Plymouth	3a
The University of Stirling	5	The University of Wales, Aberystwyth	3a
University of Wales, Bangor	5	Royal Agricultural College	3a
Imperial College of Science, Technology and Medicine	4	De Montfort University	3b
		Harper Adams University College	3b
University Marine Biological Station, Millport	4	University of Wolverhampton	3b
		Writtle College	2

Source: RAE 2001

agroforestry, animal production and environmental forestry. All teaching is underpinned by an active research environment. Areas covered include the effect of climate change upon agriculture and forestry practices, contaminated soil remediation, rural economics, geographical information systems (GIS), tropical forestry, salination of soil and the use of sustainable derived industrial feedstocks. The school has many well-established links including the Centre for Arid Zones Studies, the Centre for Ecology and Hydrology and the Bio-Composites Centre in Bangor.

For further information, see page 440

University of Plymouth

BSc (Hons) Agriculture

The first stage of the BSc (Hons) in Agriculture at the University of Plymouth covers the food production chain, the scientific and business principles which support it and the context within which it operates. Students take modules including agricultural systems, food production, introductory microbiology and the European business environment. The aim of this stage is to give students a solid grounding of knowledge and information-handling skills for later specialisation. In years two and three, students may undertake an optional industrial placement, at home or abroad, on a farm or in related industries. Successful completion leads to a Certificate of Industrial Experience. Students choose to specialise in arable, livestock, food, environment or business, or any appropriate combination choice from a further range of modules. The final stage emphasises the integration of knowledge and skills to analyse and solve real problems.

For further information, see page 536

The University of Reading
BSc Agricultural Botany

This degree provides the scientific and technical skills needed for a career in the arable advisory, plant breeding or crop protection industries. It is a three-year, full-time course that gives you a grounding in core topics such as cell biology and biochemistry, crop disease, plant genetics and soil use and management. Students are encouraged to broaden or specialise their skills by selecting option modules from

within the Faculty of Life Sciences or from other faculties. The BSc in Agricultural Botany with a year in Europe provides an opportunity to study abroad and learn a modern foreign language. In the final year, everyone must produce a research project. *For further information, see page 544*

Postgraduate

University of Newcastle upon Tyne
MSc in International Agricultural and Food Marketing

The taught programme at the University of Newcastle caters for students seeking career opportunities in international agricultural and marketing management, both in developed and developing nations as well as in the transitional economies. It is a transfer degree for those wishing to gain a thorough grounding in marketing and has a strong emphasis on application as well as theory.

Contact details, see page 618

Useful links

www.countryside.gov.uk	◉	The Countryside Agency
www.dardni.gov.uk	◉	Department of Agriculture and Rural Devlopment, Northern Ireland
www.defra.gov.uk	◉	Department for Environment and Rural Affairs
www.scotland.gov.uk/who/dept_rural.asp	◉	Environment and Rural Affairs Department, Scotland
www.farminguk.co.uk	◉	Farming UK
www.nfu.org.uk	◉	National Farmers' Union
www.rhs.org.uk	◉	The Royal Horticultural Society
www.wales.gov.uk/subiagriculture/index.htm	◉	Welsh Argiculture Department

Archaeology and anthropology

Culturally, socially and economically, humankind varies hugely across the globe and has changed dramatically over time. It is this diversity in ways of life that fascinates anthropologists and archaeologists. However, both disciplines are also concerned with the parallels that can be discovered between cultures and consistencies which recur throughout time.

Archaeology

Archaeology, in its simplest terms, is about digging up the past and studying human societies from their material remains. Discovering a coin from 2,000 years ago, for example, goes some way towards revealing the existence of a market economy and the minting technology of the time. Material remains are recovered through archaeological excavations, where objects are removed from the ground and scientifically recorded.

Both science and arts students are well equipped to study archaeology. The first year of an archaeology course is often a general introduction to the subject and the methods surrounding it. Modules may include the biological and social evolution of *Homo sapiens*, the Neolithic revolution and the advent of farming. Over the next couple of years, students are given more choice and specialise in a dissertation or project. There is a practical side to archaeology and some departments demand that students complete a minimum period of fieldwork, helping to bring theory to life.

Britain has a number of museums and exhibitions displaying local and foreign cultural materials. Students in London can participate in seminars, visit national museums and attend public lectures on all aspects of archaeology. In Wales, there are archaeological sites such as prehistoric hill forts, Roman gold mines and medieval castles.

Anthropology

Anthropologists study human societies from many perspectives including culture, religion, economics, politics and biology. The subject can be divided broadly into two strands: biological and physical anthropology on the one hand and social anthropology on the other.

Biological anthropologists look at human evolution and aim to explain the differences in human populations. This branch is more laboratory based, working with bone or blood samples, for instance.

Social anthropologists study the varied lifestyles and community organisations that exist among human populations. This can cover anything from shamanism in the Amazon to artificial insemination in the UK.

A general introduction to the subject in the first year is followed by specialisation in a particular society or topic. A dissertation is a common part of most degrees, and some courses offer students the chance to carry out fieldwork abroad. Universities have specific areas of expertise and it is worth finding out what these are and whether they fit your interests.

Anthropology
(England and Northern Ireland) 1994/95

tqa

Institution	Grade	Institution	Grade
Brunel University	Excellent	Oxford University	Excellent
Cambridge University	Excellent	School of Oriental and African Studies	
The University of Durham	Excellent	(University of London)	Excellent
The University of Kent	Excellent	University of Sussex	Excellent
London School of Economics and Political		University College London	
Science (University of London)	Excellent	(University of London)	Excellent
The University of Manchester	Excellent	Goldsmiths College	
Oxford Brookes University	Excellent	(University of London)	Satisfactory

Archaeology
(Wales) 1995/96

tqa

Cardiff University (Archaeology, Archaeological Conservation and Ancient History)	Excellent	The University of Wales, Lampeter	Excellent

Archaeology
(England) 2000/01

tqa

Institution	Grade	Institution	Grade
Cambridge University	23	The University of Bradford	22
The University of Durham	23	The University of Kent	22
The University of Manchester	23	Oxford University	22
The University of Reading	23	The University of Sheffield	22
Queen's University Belfast	23	University of Newcastle upon Tyne	21
Bournemouth University	22	The University of Nottingham	21

Source: HEFCE, SHEFC, HEFCW latest available ratings
For a more complete list of institutions offering these courses at undergraduate level refer to the Course Directory

Specialist and vocational

University of Sussex

Certificate in Archaeology

This programme aims to introduce students to a broad range of archaeological approaches, methods and theory. It looks to explain the history of how people have attempted to reconstruct and interpret the past from archaeological data. There is a core course, studied by all students, which covers archaeological theory and looks at the historical development of the discipline. This is complemented by a range of optional courses, of which at least three must be taken. These allow students to review the known information about and the current and former understandings of various archaeological periods and topics. Optional courses include maritime archaeology, industrial archaeology, Roman archaeology and people in the landscape.

For further information, see page 572

Undergraduate

Brunel University

BSc (Hons) Social Anthropology

This four-year sandwich degree gives students the opportunity to carry out overseas fieldwork in areas such as South Africa, India, Botswana and Nepal. There is also the possibility of developing practical skills through two, 22-week work experience placements with organisations such as the BBC or the Foreign and Commonwealth Office. Students may also choose to spend one semester at another European university. The degree provides a broad grounding in social anthropology and an introduction to other key areas of the social sciences. Staff have special interests in the anthropology of medicine and of childhood, with regional expertise in the cultural analysis of Britain, Africa, Asia and the Pacific. Assessment is by written exams, coursework and a 10,000-

word dissertation based on research done during students' final work placement. *For further information, see page 460*

London School of Economics and Political Science (University of London)
BSc (Hons) Social Anthropology

The Department of Anthropology at LSE is concerned with the analysis of ritual, cognition, power relations, gender and the way in which non-industrial peoples make a living. Students focus on development studies and the needs of rural people in less developed countries. There are three core courses in the first year. The Introduction to Social Anthropology course discusses the characteristic theories and methods of anthropology, while Ethnography and Theory introduces classic problems in understanding social institutions, as they have appeared in the works of major theorists. The third core course is Reading Other Cultures: The Anthropological Interpretation of Text and Film. Five core courses are then taken over the next two years on subjects including kinship, sex and gender and the anthropology of religion. Students are assessed through formal exams and assessed essays and have the option of writing a dissertation in the final year. *For further information, see page 508*

Queen's University Belfast
BA (Hons) Archaeology and Palaeoecology

In the first year, students take modules in prehistoric archaeology, historic archaeology, the environment of human evolu-

Archaeology and anthropology

RESEARCH RANKINGS

Archaeology

rae

Institution	Grade	Institution	Grade
Cambridge University	5*	Birkbeck College	4
Oxford University	5*	The University of Birmingham	4
The University of Reading	5*	University of Bristol	4
The University of Bradford	5	University of Glasgow	4
Cardiff University	5	The University of Wales, Lampeter	4
The University of Durham	5	The University of Nottingham	4
University of Exeter	5	Bournemouth University	3a
University of Leicester	5	The University of Edinburgh	3a
The University of Liverpool	5	King Alfred's Winchester	3a
Queen's University Belfast	5	University of Newcastle upon Tyne	3a
The University of Sheffield	5	Trinity College Carmarthen	3b
University of Southampton	5	University of Wales College, Newport	3a
University College London (University of London)	5	The University of York	3a

Anthropology

rae

Institution	Grade	Institution	Grade
London School of Economics and Political Science (University of London)	5*	Roehampton University of Surrey	5
University College London (University of London)	5*	School of Oriental and African Studies (University of London)	5
Cambridge University	5	University of St Andrews	5
The University of Durham	5	University of Sussex	5
The University of Edinburgh	5	The University of Aberdeen	4
Goldsmiths College (University of London)	5	Brunel University	4
The University of Kent	5	Oxford Brookes University	4
The University of Manchester	5	The University of Hull	3a
Oxford University	5	University of Wales, Swansea	3a
Queen's University Belfast	5	The University of Wales Lampeter	3a

Source: RAE 2001

tion and the human impact on the environment. These modules present a world view which serves as a background for modules taken in the second and third years. After the first year, the modules concentrate on examining evidence in detail. This includes specialised study of archaeological artefacts and chronological and environmental evidence. The taught modules taken in the second year focus on individual topics which may be linked to the substantial dissertation. Students take part in training and excavations in Ireland, Great Britain and abroad.

For further information, see page 542

Postgraduate

Cardiff University
MA in Archaeology

This course takes students to a higher level of archaeological study by developing a deeper, more critical understanding of specific areas and preparing them for further independent research. Students improve their research skills and these are put to the test in an extended dissertation which counts as part of the assessment. Students can choose between various optional modules such as the archaeology of Celtic Britain, Molluscan analysis in archaeology, post-Roman Britain and Ireland, craft and industry in the Roman world and religions of pre-historic Europe.

Contact details, see page 614

Useful links

www.britarch.ac.uk	⊙	Council for British Archaeology
www.cix.co.uk/~archaeology/	⊙	Current Archaeology
www.rescue-archaeology.freeserve.co.uk	⊙	Rescue: British Archaeological Trust
www.royalarchaeolinst.org	⊙	The Royal Archaeological Institute
www.therai.org.uk	⊙	The Royal Anthropological Institute
www.channel4.com/plus/timeteam	⊙	The Society for the Anthropology of Europe
www.channel4.com/plus/timeteam	⊙	*Time Team* Club
vlib.anthrotech.com	⊙	Virtual Library: Anthropology

Architecture and the built environment

With its recent upsurge in cutting-edge architecture, Britain is an an ideal place to study this discipline. The past few years have seen exciting projects such as The Gateshead Millennium Bridge, The Eden Project in Cornwall, the Tate Modern in London and The Magna Centre in Rotherham; all epitomising Britain's thirst for groundbreaking design.

British architects are critically acclaimed not only today but throughout history. London's first square at Covent Garden was designed by Inigo Jones (1573-1652). Sir Christopher Wren (1632-1723) was responsible for another famous London landmark – St Paul's Cathedral. William Talman (1650-1719), a contemporary of Wren, is most famous for Chatsworth House in Derbyshire.

Architecture

Studying architecture in Britain has several advantages. Teacher to student ratios tend to be lower than in the rest of Europe. Teaching may be less theoretical than in your home country and you are able to specialise in architecture as a first degree, which is not possible in the USA. British architecture degrees lead to professional membership of the Royal Institute of British Architects (RIBA). You need to pass RIBA parts one, two and three to qualify. The traditional route to qualification starts with a three-year undergraduate programme. Depending on the university or college, a degree in architecture may exempt you from the RIBA part one exam. The degree is followed by a year in professional practice, leading to a two-year graduate programme. Part two exams are then taken, followed by another year of professional practice at the end of which you sit part three. As architecture qualifications include work placements, international students should check visa requirements.

The built environment

The complexity of the social, environmental and aesthetic issues involved in building and land usage is reflected in the variety of degrees on offer, the possible combinations of majors, and the range of interdisciplinary modules which make up the course.

Town and country planning, for example, is concerned with using social, economic and ecological knowledge to manage change and development in the built and natural environment. The subject covers elements such as the development process, planning skills, graphics, urban politics and transport planning.

Other significant areas of study include quantity surveying, which is mainly concerned with the organisation and financial management of building and civil engineering work, and also construction management, which aims to produce professional managers who can understand building technology as well as the business aspects which are involved in running a construction company.

Specialist and vocational

University of Greenwich
Architecture Diploma
Students can choose to study for the diploma full time over two years or part time over three years. For those wanting to become architects, the full-time programme makes students eligible for corporate membership of RIBA and election to the Register of the Architects' Registration Board. You need a good honours degree or equivalent and a year of practical experience in an architect's office. The part-time programme is intended for advanced students wishing to gain exemption from ARB/RIBA part two exams. For a place on the part-time course, students must be working full time in an architectural practice. There are nine hours a week in lectures and seminars, usually one day and an evening each week. The main core of the course is architectural design but students also study urban design, computation in design, landscape design, humanities, technology and professional studies.

For further information, see page 486

Undergraduate

Cardiff University
The Bachelor of Architecture Scheme
This two-year course is available to those with an undergraduate degree or equivalent in architectural studies and is a step towards becoming a qualified architect. In the first year, all students have the opportunity to work in architectural practices whilst continuing their academic development. As well as gaining practical experience and completing the RIBA logbook, students compile a descriptive and analytical portfolio of office experience. End-of-module exams are held either at the end of each semester or academic year and project work exams are held at the end of the year. After graduation and two years of practical training, students are eligible to sit the part three examination

TEACHING QUALITY ASSESSMENTS

Town and Country Planning and Landscape
(England and Northern Ireland) 1996/97/98

tqa

Institution	Grade	Institution	Grade
University of Greenwich	24	University of Newcastle upon Tyne	21
Kingston University	24	Northumbria University	21
Oxford Brookes University	24	University of Central England	
The University of Liverpool	23	in Birmingham	20
The University of Nottingham	23	The University of Manchester	20
The University of Sheffield	23	The Manchester	
University of the West of England, Bristol	23	Metropolitan University	20
Queen's University Belfast	22	University of Westminster	20
The University of Reading	22	Anglia Polytechnic University	19
The University of Salford	22	Coventry University	19
Sheffield Hallam University	22	Doncaster College	18
South Bank University	22	Liverpool John Moores University	18
De Montfort University	21	Southampton Institute	18
University of Gloucestershire	21	Edge Hill College of Higher Education	17
Leeds Metropolitan University	21	NESCOT	15

City and Regional Planning
(Wales) 1996/97/98

tqa

Cardiff University	Excellent

Source: HEFCE, SHEFC, HEFCW latest available ratings
For a more complete list of institutions offering these courses at undergraduate level refer to the Course Directory

of the Welsh School of Architecture. Students can apply to the Royal Institute of British Architects for corporate membership and to the Architects' Registration Board for admission to the Register of Architects.

Contact details, see page 614

University of Dundee
BSc (Hons) Architecture

The curriculum for the BSc in Architecture at the University of Dundee is based on the idea of 'learning through doing'. Throughout the course, students carry out design projects, usually related to actual situations using real sites and clients. Students' progress is monitored through a combination of continuous assessment of studio design projects and written examinations and essays for each of the lecture courses. During the first year of the course, students are introduced to the study of architecture through existing examples both in Scotland and further afield. This involves looking at buildings as diverse as mud huts and prestigious construction projects. First-year students usually spend a week to 10 days on a foreign study visit. Students also have the opportunity to test their design skills throughout the year in studio projects. Years two and three are designed to build on the knowledge gained in the first year by the inclusion of more complex design

TEACHING QUALITY ASSESSMENTS

Architecture
(England and Northern Ireland) 1994 — **tqa**

Institution	Grade	Institution	Grade
University of Bath	Excellent	The University of Huddersfield	Satisfactory
Cambridge University	Excellent	Kingston University	Satisfactory
University of East London	Excellent	Leeds Metropolitan University	Satisfactory
University of Greenwich	Excellent	Liverpool John Moores University	Satisfactory
University of Newcastle upon Tyne	Excellent	The University of Liverpool	Satisfactory
The University of Nottingham	Excellent	The University of Manchester	Satisfactory
The University of Sheffield	Excellent	The Manchester	
University College London		Metropolitan University	Satisfactory
(University of London)	Excellent	Oxford Brookes University	Satisfactory
The University of York	Excellent	University of Plymouth	Satisfactory
University of Brighton	Satisfactory	Queen's University Belfast	Satisfactory
De Montfort University	Satisfactory	University of Westminster	Satisfactory

Architecture
(Scotland) 1994/95 — **tqa**

Institution	Grade	Institution	Grade
Glasgow School of Art	Excellent	Edinburgh College of Art	Highly Satisfactory
The University of Strathclyde	Excellent	The Robert Gordon University	Highly Satisfactory
The University of Edinburgh	Highly Satisfactory	University of Dundee	Satisfactory

Architecture and Building
(Wales) 1994/95 — **tqa**

Institution	Grade	Institution	Grade
Cardiff University (Architecture)	Excellent	University of	
Cardiff University		Glamorgan (Surveying)	Satisfactory
(Architectural Engineering)	Satisfactory	The North East Wales	
University of Wales		Institute of Higher Education	Satisfactory
Institute, Cardiff (Building)	Satisfactory	Swansea Institute of Higher	
University of Wales		Education (Built Environments)	Satisfactory
Institute, Cardiff (Housing)	Satisfactory		

Architecture
(England and Northern Ireland) 1997 — **tqa**

University of Central England in Birmingham	20

Source: HEFCE, SHEFC, HEFCW latest available ratings
For a more complete list of institutions offering these courses at undergraduate level refer to the Course Directory

Built Environment

rae

Institution	Grade	Institution	Grade
Loughborough University	5*	Edinburgh College of Art	3a
The University of Salford	5*	The University of Edinburgh	3a
University of Bath	5	Glasgow Caledonian University	3a
Cardiff University	5	University of North London	3a
Heriot-Watt University, Edinburgh	5	The Nottingham Trent University	3a
The University of Reading	5	Sheffield Hallam University	3a
The University of Sheffield	5	University of Wolverhampton	3a
University of Ulster	5	Coventry University	3b
Cambridge University	4	University of Glamorgan	3b
De Montfort University	4	University of Greenwich	3b
The University of Liverpool	4	Leeds Metropolitan University	3b
The University of Manchester Institute of Science and Technology (UMIST)	4	Liverpool John Moores University	3b
		Napier University	3b
University of Newcastle upon Tyne	4	Northumbria University	3b
The University of Nottingham	4	The Robert Gordon University	3b
Oxford Brookes University	4	South Bank University	3b
The University of Strathclyde	4	University of Central England in Birmingham	2
University College London (University of London)	4	Queen's University Belfast	2
University of Central Lancashire	3a	University of Teesside	2

Source: RAE 2001

Architecture

problems and difficulties, for example adapting existing buildings for new use. *Contact details, see page 615*

The University of Edinburgh
MA (Hons) Architectural Design
The MA in Architectural Design is one of three undergraduate courses offered by the Architecture Department at Edinburgh. It is a studio-based design course for those who intend to become architects. Graduates of the course normally proceed to the two-year MArch. As a vocational course, it equips students with the knowledge and skills needed to enter the profession. Full-time study is complemented by periods of practical training in architects' offices and other approved placements. The distribution of placements within the overall programme effectively results in six years of study, followed by a further period of practical training before the final professional examination.

For further information, see page 474

University of North London
BA (Hons) Interior Design
Interior design at the University of North London is taught in an environment combining the excitement of teamwork – in studios, seminars, workshops and on site – with the challenge of individual, conceptual and design development. This course is a blend of academic, creative and practical aspects of interior design. The course develops students' individual creativity and awareness of contemporary design and covers three main areas: philosophy and theory, design development and technology. The balance between academic and professional aspects is maintained throughout the course, which includes a six-month industrial placement. Applicants should have a portfolio of design work or A level art and an appropriate English qualification (IELTS 5.5 or TOEFL 550), plus good results at A level or the local equivalent.

For further information, see page 520

The University of Salford
BSc (Hons) Building

This course focuses on managing and controlling building operations through a combination of academic study and project work. The course teaches transferable skills such as organisation, communication and presentation. Students are taught through lectures and seminars with an emphasis on directed study. Assessment is by coursework, project work, exams and a dissertation. The course can be studied for three years full time, four years with an industrial placement or five years part time. Upon successful completion of the course, students are exempt from the academic requirements of the Chartered Institute of Building and are qualified to work at management level across the building industry.

For further information, see page 552

For further information, see page 552

For further information, see page 490

For further information, see page 552

Postgraduate

Heriot-Watt University, Edinburgh
MPhil and PhD Research Programmes
The School of Architecture

These programmes are designed for students with a background in architecture, urban design, landscape or planning and are dedicated to providing the knowledge and theoretical skills needed to understand the nature and complexity of the built environment. They bring together socio-cultural experiences and culturally-borne symbolic values to develop a people-centred approach to architectural and environmental issues. Students are shown how to obtain a working knowledge of their subject area and to be capable of contributing to it. Overseas students receive support in relation to aspects of language and writing.

For further information, see page 490

Oxford Brookes University
MA/Graduate Diploma
in Built Resources Studies

This design-based course focuses on the regeneration, conservation and management of buildings and urban areas. The first term addresses the problems of area regeneration, building fabric, energy saving retrofits and financing. In the second term, students have the opportunity to develop a project in a chosen direction which may be taken abroad. Full-time students complete the diploma in two terms

Architecture

RESEARCH RANKINGS

Town and Country Planning

Institution	Grade	Institution	Grade
Cardiff University	5*	South Bank University	4
University of Leeds	5*	University of the West of England, Bristol	3a
The University of Aberdeen	5	City University	3a
Cambridge University	5	Heriot-Watt University, Edinburgh	3a
University of Glasgow	5	Leeds Metropolitan University	3a
University of Newcastle upon Tyne	5	Liverpool John Moores University	3a
The University of Reading	5	Loughborough University	3a
The University of Sheffield	5	The University of Strathclyde	3a
Edinburgh College of Art	4	University of Westminster	3a
University of Gloucestershire	4	Queen's University Belfast	3b
The University of Liverpool	4	University of Central England in Birmingham	3b
The University of Manchester	4	University of Dundee	3b
Oxford Brookes University	4	Anglia Polytechnic University	2
Sheffield Hallam University	4	Swansea Institute of Higher Education	1

Source: RAE 2001

The Sydney Harbour Bridge

and can then progress to the MA stage, requiring a further six months' full-time study, involving a dissertation of between 15,000 and 20,000 words. One or both stages can be studied part time. Learning and teaching is based on individual and team project work supported by review seminars, tutorials and lectures. Part-time students attend one day a week and full-time students have 20 hours of teaching time a week. Students are assessed by a combination of project work, coursework and a dissertation.

For further information, see page 532

Useful links

www.arb.org.uk	◉	Architects' Registration Board
www.biat.org.uk	◉	British Institute of Architectural Technologists
www.ciob.org.uk	◉	The Chartered Institute of Building
www.fbe.co.uk	◉	Foundation for the Built Environment
www.l-i.org.uk	◉	The Landscape Institute
www.architecture.com	◉	Royal Institute of British Architects (RIBA)
www.rics.org.uk	◉	Royal Institute of Chartered Surveyors
www.rtpi.org.uk	◉	Royal Town Planning Institute

Art, design and history of art

Britain has a tradition for producing great and often eccentric art. Recently, British art has tended to become lumped together under the banner of 'Young British Art', headed up by Damien Hirst and his Goldsmiths contemporaries. Whilst this small movement has received great media attention over the past decade, the UK is also at the cutting edge of other artistic forms: sculpture, abstract painting, photography and animation, to name a few. While we debate over the artistic value of Tracey Emin's soiled bed, UK artists have steadily produced a stream of original and challenging work.

Britain can boast a vast array of museums and galleries, from the Royal Academy in London, to the Burrell Collection in Glasgow, the Arnolfini in Bristol and the Tate Galleries in St Ives and Liverpool. With the opening of the Tate Modern in London, housing the world's largest collection of international modern art, Britain is now more than ever an exciting place for artists to study.

Art and design

Art schools have been very quick to adapt to the ever-expanding range of media in which artists now work. Instead of being briefed on what to draw, paint or sculpt, students are now encouraged to plan their own schedules allowing for greater individual creativity. Most courses offer the chance to experiment or specialise in areas such as typography, graphic design, interior design, photography, film-making, animation and computer-aided design.

It is possible to study art either at a university or at an art college. Both typically offer specialist courses as well as those covering a whole range of artistic media and skills. Entrance on to degree courses, for British students, will typically depend on an interview at which the student's portfolio of work is shown and discussed. International students may well be expected to submit slides or photos of their work as part of their application.

Degree courses usually last four years, the first year being a foundation year in which students experiment with a wide variety of artistic disciplines. This gives them freedom to choose which subjects they wish to specialise in later on. Some students complete their foundation year at one school and then apply elsewhere. Similarly, if you have studied art in your own country, you can sometimes be admitted directly in to the second year of an art degree. Check with the International Office of a university or college to see if this is possible.

History of art

Whilst all art courses will involve a certain amount of theory, it is also possible to study this side of art as a course in its own right. History of art courses are purely theoretical and can be studied singularly, or combined with subjects such as archaeology, languages, English, arts management and philosophy.

Specialist and vocational

Blake College

This independent art college offers courses which are suited to both beginners and advanced students. Named after the 18th-century painter, William Blake, and set in a converted Victorian warehouse, the college has up-to-date facilities including a print room and fully-equipped darkroom. The college provides scholarships for a small number of talented EU students on a limited budget. Students are multinational and classes are small. Classes are supplemented by visits to galleries, museums, and exhibitions as appropriate. There are national museums and art galleries, internationally-renowned design consultancies and arts organisations, such as the Design Council, in the immediate vicinity of the college. Blake College was the first independent college in the UK to receive full validation from BTEC for its Foundation Diploma in Art and Design. Courses generally last for one academic year although there is flexibility for students who join later in the year or who wish to study for shorter periods. Courses are available in a variety of practical disciplines including life drawing, painting and drawing, sculpture, history of art and design, printmaking, graphics, fashion and interior design as well as photography, video and film.

Contact details, see page 611

Cavendish College

Art and Design Foundation Diploma

This course is ideal for students wishing to develop a portfolio of work to the standard required for entry on to a BA Honours university degree. It is a one-year, full-time course leading to a

Art and Design
(England and Northern Ireland) 1998/99/2000

tqa

Institution	Grade	Institution	Grade
The Central School of Speech and Drama	24	The University of Salford	21
Falmouth College of Arts	24	Stockport College of	
Newcastle College	24	Further & Higher Education	21
Oxford University	24	University of Sunderland	21
City University	23	Surrey Institute of Art and Design,	
City College Manchester	23	University College	21
Lancaster University	23	University of Westminster	21
University of Leeds	23	University of Wolverhampton	21
Loughborough University	23	University College Worcester	21
Oxford Brookes University	23	York St John	
Royal College of Art	23	(A college of the University of Leeds)	21
University College London		Buckinghamshire Chilterns University College	20
(Slade School of Fine Art)	23	Chester (A College of The	
Wimbledon School of Art	23	University of Liverpool)	20
Bath Spa University College	22	Cleveland College of Art and Design	20
University of Brighton	22	University of Derby	20
University of the West of England, Bristol	22	University of Lincoln	20
University of Central England in Birmingham	22	Liverpool Hope	20
Goldsmiths College (University of London)	22	University of Newcastle upon Tyne	20
University of Hertfordshire	22	University of Portsmouth	20
Kent Institute of Art and Design	22	Ryecotewood College	20
The Manchester Metropolitan University	22	St Martins College,	
University of North London	22	Lancaster: Ambleside: Carlisle	20
Northumbria University	22	Blackburn College	19
Sheffield Hallam University	22	Canterbury Christ Church University College	19
University of Southampton	22	Croydon College	19
Staffordshire University	22	Liverpool John Moores University	19
Anglia Polytechnic University	21	University of Ulster	19
Blackpool and The Fylde College	21	Leeds College of Art & Design	18
Bradford and Ilkley Community College	21	NESCOT	18
Bretton Hall	21	North East Worcestershire College	18
Cumbria College of Art and Design	21	Reading College and School	
De Montfort University	21	of Arts and Design	18
The University of Huddersfield	21	North Riding College	17
Leeds Metropolitan University	21	Southampton Institute	17
Northbrook College	21	West Thames College	17
Norwich School of Art and Design	21	Westhill College	17
University of Plymouth	21	Wigan and Leigh College	17
Ravensbourne College of		York College of Further and Higher Education	17
Design and Communication	21	Suffolk College	15

Source: HEFCE, SHEFC, HEFCW latest available ratings
For a more complete list of institutions offering these courses at undergraduate level refer to the Course Directory

foundation diploma qualification. Course modules include visual studies, design communications, life drawing, printmaking, photographic studies and contextual studies. Regular trips to major London galleries and exhibitions support the study programme and raise the student's knowledge of both historic and current developments within the field of art and design.

Students are taught through a balance of practical and theoretical studies via group discussions, presentations and written components.

For further information, see page 410

The Hampstead School of Art

Founded in 1965, The Hampstead School of Art is a registered charity

Art and design

History of Art, Architecture and Design
(England and Northern Ireland) 1996/97/98/99

tqa

Institution	Grade	Institution	Grade
Birkbeck College	24	De Montfort University	21
School of Oriental and African Studies (University of London)	24	The University of Manchester	21
		Northumbria University	21
University College London (University of London)	24	Open University	21
		Staffordshire University	21
Courtauld Institute of Art (University of London)	23	University of Sunderland	21
		The University of Warwick	21
University of Leeds	23	The University of York	21
The University of Nottingham	23	University of Bristol	20
Oxford Brookes University	23	University of Central England in Birmingham	20
The University of Reading	23	Falmouth College of Arts	20
Wimbledon School of Art	23	Kingston University	20
The University of Birmingham	22	Sheffield Hallam University	20
Cambridge University	22	University of Southampton	20
University of East Anglia	22	University of Sussex	20
The University of Essex	22	University of Central Lancashire	19
The University of Kent	22	University of Derby	19
University of Leicester	22	Goldsmiths College (University of London)	19
The Manchester Metropolitan University	22	London Institute	19
Middlesex University	22	Anglia Polytechnic University	18
Royal College of Art	22	Southampton Institute	18
University of Brighton	21		

History of Art
(Scotland) 1995/96

tqa

The University of Aberdeen	Highly Satisfactory	University of Glasgow	Highly Satisfactory
The University of Edinburgh	Highly Satisfactory	University of St Andrews	Highly Satisfactory

Source: HEFCE, SHEFC, HEFCW latest available ratings
For a more complete list of institutions offering these courses at undergraduate level refer to the Course Directory

Art and design

dedicated to the field of art and design. The school is open to applicants of any age or academic background. Most of the classes teach both beginners and more experienced students. It is located at the King's College campus in Hampstead. Courses on offer range from part-time, pre-foundation and A level art to one-week summer courses in pottery and life drawing. The portfolio preparation/pre-foundation art course, for example, prepares students for entry to a BA art and design course. Entry is by interview and candidates are expected to show evidence of previous work. Specialist subjects include mosaics, silk painting and colour theory.

Contact details, see page 611

Heatherley's School of Fine Art

Heatherley's was established more than 150 years ago by a group of students unable to tolerate the academic restrictions imposed on them at the government School of Design. It is now the oldest independent art school in London. Since then, the college has moved to a 19th-century building in Chelsea, within walking distance from the King's Road and Chelsea Harbour. All members of staff are practising artists. Courses are for beginners and experienced artists and include a two-year Diploma in Portraiture, a one-year foundation/portfolio course, a one-year continuing studies course and various short courses. The Diploma in Portraiture aims to prepare students for professional practice as portrait painters. It has external examiners chosen by the Royal Society of Portrait Painters. In addition, the school has recently introduced a two-year Diploma in Figurative Sculpture with an excellent new purpose-built studio. The school's open studio, founded in 1845, is based on the French atelier system and can be joined at any time in the academic year.

Contact details, see page 611

Northbrook College
Art and Design

Northbrook College's art and design faculty was praised in a recent government inspection confirming its status as a quality provider of education in the field. As well as providing 40 courses at undergraduate level, it is one of the largest colleges in the UK for foundation courses in art and design. Northbrook's facilities are purpose built and include fashion and textiles workshops, a 3D workshop, a working theatre and a new state-of-the-art music and media complex. The courses on offer include fashion and textiles, media arts, graphic and communication design, three dimensional and interior design, fine arts, theatre and performing arts, music and music technology. The traditional foundation studies course in art and design is offered, as well as an international foundation year.

For further information, see page 524

Northumbria University
Foundation Diploma
in Arts and Design

Northumbria University has officially been recognised for its high quality courses in art and design. Disciplines at under-

Art and design

Fine Art, Printmaking, Sculpture and Painting
(Scotland) 1995/96/97

tqa

Institution	Grade	Institution	Grade
University of Dundee	Highly Satisfactory	Glasgow School of Art	Highly Satisfactory
Edinburgh College of Art	Highly Satisfactory	The Robert Gordon University	Satisfactory

Source: HEFCE, SHEFC, HEFCW latest available ratings
For a more complete list of institutions offering these courses at undergraduate level refer to the Course Directory

Art and Design and Art History
(Wales) 1995/96

tqa

Institution	Grade	Institution	Grade
University of Wales Institute, Cardiff (Art, Design and Art History)	Excellent	University of Wales Institute, Cardiff (Ceramics, Fine Art, Internal Architecture)	Satisfactory
Swansea Institute of Higher Education	Excellent	Carmarthenshire College	Satisfactory
		University of Wales College, Newport	Satisfactory
The University of Wales, Aberystwyth	Satisfactory	The North East Wales Institute of Higher Education	Satisfactory

Graphic Design and Textile Design
(Scotland) 1995/1999

tqa

Institution	Grade	Institution	Grade
University of Dundee	Excellent	The Robert Gordon University	Highly Satisfactory
Edinburgh College of Art	Highly Satisfactory		
Glasgow School of Art	Highly Satisfactory	Scottish College of Textiles	Highly Satisfactory

Source: HEFCE, SHEFC, HEFCW latest available ratings
For a more complete list of institutions offering these courses at undergraduate level refer to the Course Directory

Art and design

graduate, master's and research level include fine art, photography, media production, dance, performance and many branches of design, such as graphic, transportation, fashion, industrial, 3D and multimedia. The one-year Foundation Diploma provides an ideal preparation for international students who want to take an undergraduate degree in one of the above fields. This course allows students to build up a portfolio of work and improve their English. There are opportunities for study trips to art centres such as London, Florence and Paris.

For further information, see page 526

Telford College of Arts and Technology
Advanced Vocational Certificate of Education in Art and Design

This Advanced GNVQ full award programme is a two-year, full-time course

and is equivalent to two A levels. 12 art and design units, selected from a choice of 'broadening studies' and taken throughout both years achieve key skill units in communication and information tech-nology, among other subjects. Enrichment opportunities include European travel (previous years have included weekends in Paris and Barcelona) and visits to galleries and universities. The main focus within the first year of the course is to complete six art and design units in two-dimensional and three-dimensional language, research historical and contextual referencing, work to set briefs, use visual communication and develop professional practices. Year two develops creative skills through life drawing, studio work and media, while also specialising in choices that will decide the form of the students' final portfolio. Most students graduating from this course have carried on their studies into higher education.

For further information, see page 430

Walsall College of Art and Design
Edexcel Foundation in Art and Design

This course is the long-established route to higher education in art and design for students aged 17 or above and provides a thorough grounding in all areas of the subject. The college has considerable experience in running such courses with a consistent level of success. The aim is to help students develop skills for higher-level education programmes and make an informed decision about their future. It is a one-year course based on continuous assessment and leads to an Edexcel Diploma in Foundation Studies or accreditation of whole units completed. Students study drawing, painting, sculpture, graphic design, fashion and textiles, three-dimensional design, photography and theoretical studies. After Christmas, students have the opportunity to specialise for part of the week in an area of their choice. The college places special emphasis on assisting students wishing to progress to courses at university.

For further information, see page 432

West Thames College
HND Fine Art

This is a two-year, full-time course for students wishing to practise art professionally, either in their own studios, as assistants in established studios or as part of community arts projects. It is also aimed at those who want to progress to the second or final year of a degree. Students study drawing in fine art developing a fine art identity, historical

Art and design

and contextual referencing, critical study and visual arts professional practice while compiling their portfolio. They select one of the following combinations according to their own interests: painting and sculpture, painting and fine art printmaking, or sculpture and fine art ceramics. Additional subjects in drawing include lens-based recording techniques, digital imaging, commissioned artwork and exhibiting art work. In the second year, students undertake a work placement, which may take place in practising artists' studios, with community or other arts projects, in galleries or in allied craft industries.

For further information, see page 408

The Arts Institute at Bournemouth

BA (Hons) Modelmaking for Design and Media

This is a very practical course where students use a variety of media and materials to produce models or visuals for different design and media industries. Employment opportunities therefore exist within a broad range of model-making companies, media and film production companies, architectural practices, design houses, museums and computer-aided art and design companies. Modelmaking particularly appeals to versatile and practical people who have an enthusiasm for three-dimensional physical and digital design and media. The Arts Institute at Bournemouth is recognised as having one of the leading modelmaking courses within the UK. Former students from the Arts Institute have worked in all areas of modelmaking including visual effects modelling for such films as *The Mummy*, *Gladiator* and *Harry Potter* and architectural modelling for such prestigious architects as Sir Norman Foster & Partners and Sir Richard Rogers.

For further information, see page 446

RESEARCH RANKINGS

History of Art, Architecture and Design

Institution	Grade	Institution	Grade
Courtauld Institute of Art (University of London)	5*	The Manchester Metropolitan University	4
The University of Birmingham	5	The University of Reading	4
Cambridge University	5	University of Southampton	4
University of East Anglia	5	University of Bristol	3a
The University of Essex	5	The University of Kent	3a
The University of Glasgow	5	University of Leeds	3a
The University of Manchester	5	Loughborough University	3a
Middlesex University	5	Northumbria University	3a
Open University	5	Oxford Brookes University	3a
University of Plymouth	5	Royal College of Art	3a
University of St Andrews	5	School of Oriental and African Studies	
University of Sussex	5	(University of London)	3a
University College London		De Montfort University	3b
(University of London)	5	Edinburgh College of Art	3b
The University of Warwick	5	Goldsmiths College (University of London)	3b
The University of Aberdeen	4	University of Newcastle upon Tyne	3b
The University of Edinburgh	4	The University of Nottingham	3b
Falmouth College of Arts	4	The University of Huddersfield	2
Kingston University	4	Keele University	2
University of Leicester	4	Southampton Institute	2

Source: RAE 2001

Chelsea College of Art and Design

BA (Hons) Sculpture

Sculpture at Chelsea provides a critically stimulating context in which the concept of sculpture and sculptural space are explored. Students are taught by practising artists, each with an individual approach and an intensive programme of individual tutorials, along with group seminars which will encourage them to explore the sculptural medium. Exhibitions of students' work in the foyer gallery and other venues provide a focus of critical debate. Experienced technical staff run well-equipped workshops and a foundry as well as film, video, photography, computer and printmaking facilities. To gain a place on the course, potential and creative ability in art and design must be demonstrated, along with a portfolio of work, passes in two subjects at A level and three other subjects at GCSE.

Contact details, see page 611

City & Guilds of London Art School

This small, independent school was established in Kennington by the City & Guilds Institute in 1879 as an extension of the Lambeth School of Art. Originally it provided training mainly in carving, modelling and architectural decoration. Over the years, it has expanded its activities and courses and now attracts students from abroad and throughout the UK. The school offers full and part-time courses in architectural stonecarving and ornamental woodcarving and gilding together with a full-time, three-year BA (Hons) Conservation Studies. The department of fine art offers three-year, full-time BA (Hons) courses in Painting and Sculpture, as well as a one-year, full-time or two-year,

Art and design

Herefordshire Colleges
BLACKSMITHING

I f you have an interest in working with metals, welding or blacksmithing, the range of metalwork and forgework courses offered by Herefordshire College of Technology and Herefordshire College of Art and Design could be of interest to you.

Over the years, Herefordshire College of Art and Design and Herefordshire College of Technology have been successfully working together to deliver a number of courses, unique in the higher education sector, in particular the Higher National Diploma in Forged Metals and BA (Hons) Design Crafts. The collaboration between the two colleges gives students on the courses the best technical knowledge from a team of experienced blacksmithing tutors and the artistic environment to develop the skills, concepts and design capacity necessary to become an artist blacksmith. As well as specialist craft lecturers based at Herefordshire College of Art and Design, there are links with the blacksmithing and craft industries who play an important role within the courses in the setting of live projects, offering guidance and real opportunities.

Students are recruited on a national and international basis, coming from the USA, Australia, New Zealand and all over Europe including Denmark, Spain, Germany and Ireland. Retention and achievement are both high, with the majority of students eventually achieving their ambition of running their own business.

Over 300 students train at Herefordshire College of Technology's Centre for Rural Crafts, making it the largest training centre of its kind in England. This £1.5 million development provides a state-of-the-art building for the traditional craft training of blacksmithing and farriery (shoeing of horses). The centre gives a work area of 1,900 square metres. The teaching block contains classrooms, display and conference areas, a library and IT centre. The workshops include a well-equipped fabrication and welding workshop, blacksmithing and farriery workshops housing 60 forges, an indoor shoeing area adjacent to the farriery workstations and a demonstration forge.

The blacksmithing and metalwork courses at Hereford are based on full-time attendance with opportunity to progress from the Edexcel/BTEC First Diploma to degree level, so that no matter what your previous experience, there are opportunities to enter at a level suited to your abilities and then to develop them further. The college also welcomes applications from art and design students who may not have previously studied blacksmithing but possess drawing and design abilities.

A summary of the courses on offer:
- Edexcel/BTEC First Diploma in Blacksmithing and Equine Studies
- Edexcel/BTEC National Certificate in Blacksmithing and Metalwork
- Edexcel/BTEC National Diploma in Blacksmithing and Metalwork
- Edexcel/BTEC HND in Forged Metals
- BA (Hons) Design Crafts validated by the University of Wales

New course under development:
- BA (Hons) Architectural and Ornamental Forged Ironwork
  (subject to validation)

For more information contact:
The Enquiries Office
Herefordshire College of Technology
Folly Lane
Hereford HR1 1LS
England, UK

Tel: +44 (0)1432 365376
Fax: +44 (0)1432 353449
Email: enquiries@hereford-tech.ac.uk
Web: www.hereford-tech.ac.uk or **www.hereford-art-col.ac.uk**

Student profile

Tom left school in Ireland when he was 15 and trained to become a welder. Five years ago, he became interested in blacksmithing and, hearing of the reputation of Herefordshire College of Technology's National School of Blacksmithing based at The Centre for Rural Crafts in Hereford, Tom then embarked on a two-year National Diploma in Blacksmithing. Throughout this course, Tom was able to build up the techniques and disciplines which make up this incredible craft to become a highly skilled maker. Tom then applied to the Higher National Diploma in Blacksmithing (Forged Metals), a unique course for artists who wish to utilise the blacksmithing process, which is run at Herefordshire College of Art and Design. Over the two years, his blacksmithing disciplines developed through further technical studies and refined through the production of design concepts. Tom completed the course in June 2001. He now works at a co-operative forge with other craftspeople, while designing, making and selling his work.

part-time MA Fine Art. The foundation course (one year, full time) has a success rate of over 80 per cent of students gaining entrance to their first choice of subsequent specialist art course. All students are required to study life drawing. Housed in a terrace of 18th-century houses, the facilities include purpose-built fine art studios, a stonecarving studio, printroom, wood workshop, drawing studio and a specialist library to back up the humanities programme – an important component of the full-time courses. Part-time courses include life drawing, printmaking, stone and wood carving and gilding.

Contact details, see page 612

De Montfort University

BA (Hons) Ceramics and Glass

This studio-based degree course begins by introducing students to ceramic and glassmaking techniques and processes, providing them with a toolbox of skills to be employed and developed throughout their projects over the three years. Students are encouraged to develop the ability to be self-critical in order to express an individual style and create confident and professional work. The second and third years offer a flexible structure to enable students to work according to individual interests and requirements. Students write their own design briefs and are encouraged to work with industry whenever possible. All students have the opportunity to participate in the national RSA Student Design Awards each year. In the final year, students develop an understanding of the professional and business context of practice. There are regular visits to exhibitions and manufacturers across the UK and sales of students' own work.

Contact details, see page 615

Falmouth College of Arts

BA (Hons) Illustration

Students of illustration at Falmouth College of Arts develop a distinct, personal style through intensive studio practice, working to realistic briefs and solving visual communication problems. Recent students have secured agency representation with organisations such as Meiklejohn, The Art Collection, Art Market and Folio. Falmouth College of Arts has well-developed contacts with the design industry in London, New York and Amsterdam where there is a substantial market for illustration. Students are supported by a staff of practising professional illustrators and guest lecturers. The programme respects the traditional skills of drawing and composition and embraces new technologies. Students may choose to develop a specific interest during the latter half of the programme. Recent live illustration commissions include work for Reed International, The Body Shop, Nationwide Building Society, The National Trust and the London Transport Museum.

For further information, see page 478

Goldsmiths College (University of London)

BA (Hons) Fine Art and History of Art

This joint degree combines study of the history of art with fine art studio practice, informing students' practice and putting it into context. History of art and theory courses are taught in the Historical and Cultural Studies Department. Fine art studio practice is taught in the Visual Arts Department, where students are encouraged to develop work in their chosen media through experimentation. There is an emphasis on modern art and on the issues affecting artistic practice in

today's world. The course is studied full time over three years and assessment is through formal written exams, an oral exam, essays, studio portfolio, research files, creative journals, a dissertation and final exhibition. Students develop many transferable skills including critical and analytical skills, IT and communications. The degree aims to prepare students for a career as a practising artist or art historian, in arts administration, museums, galleries and art journalism or for postgraduate study.

For further information, see page 482

Kingston University
BA (Hons) Illustration

This course is designed to develop highly individual approaches to the creation of descriptive images, applied to a wide range of contexts. Good draftsmanship and painting skills are encouraged as the basis for all development. There is a strong studio culture on the course, with an emphasis on drawing in the life room and on location. Studio projects provide students with stimulus and challenge. Cultural studies, art history and business studies are included in the curriculum, giving students a cultural framework for their work along with the necessary skills for entering the marketplace. There is access to excellent technical facilities including printmaking, photography, moving image and digital media. The opportunity to specialise in animation (traditional and computer generated) is available. Students working in the moving image area have produced internationally-recognised, award-winning animation. Graduates of Kingston's illustration degree are employed worldwide, mostly as freelance practitioners commissioned by magazine and newspaper editors or by advertising groups and publishers of nonfiction, fiction and children's books. Others pursue careers in animation, games, multimedia or special effects design for film and television.

For further information, see page 496

Leeds Metropolitan University
BA (Hons) Three-dimensional Design

This course interprets three-dimensional design in a very broad sense and is concerned with human interactions with a range of artefacts, products and environments including the consideration of historical, theoretical, cultural, professional, social and environmental contexts of design. The course develops intellectual, critical and practical skills relevant to creativity and the practice of three-dimensional design and related fields. Students have opportunities to focus their studies on particular issues within three-dimensional design through interpretation of project briefs, choices of projects and negotiation of learning contracts. Students are supported by workshops and computer suites and the course is studio based.

For further information, see page 500

University of Lincoln
BA (Hons) Animation

The animation degree at the University of Lincoln is firmly focused on effective communication with an audience through the creative development of mood, atmosphere, narrative and graphic depth. Students have the opportunity to acquire time-based communication skills and use animation as an abstract, narrative or commercial media tool, within a film and television context. Emphasis is on the primary animation skills of movement, 3D spatial design, studio production, film and digital postproduction. These

picture courtesy of Falmouth College of Arts

skills are developed through a series of project-driven works. In the second year, there is the opportunity to specialise in one of the three key areas of animation – 2D, 3D or electronic image animation. This allows for specific skills to be developed in an area of choice. In the final year, the work-load becomes increasingly self-managed and there are various opportunities for students to develop personal production projects.

Contact details, see page 617

Loughborough University

The School of Art and Design offers a pre-degree foundation programme and degree courses in a number of different areas. It also shares the delivery of a Joint Honours BA in English and History of Art with the Department of English and Drama. All degree programmes follow a structure common throughout the university that has been designed to enable specialist study of the chosen subject but with inbuilt opportunities for broadening students' range of interests at key points. The student's chosen programme consists of a combination of compulsory and optional modules. The school is fortunate in being able to offer studio and workshop accommodation, equipment and technical support of a very high order. The school was ranked fifth in the UK in *The Guardian University Guide to Art and Design 2001* and achieved a score of 23 out of a maximum of 24 for teaching and learning in the Quality Assurance Agency for Higher Education external subject review.

For further information, see page 510

School of Oriental and African Studies (University of London)

BA History of Art (Asia, Africa and Europe)

This course is taught jointly by SOAS and the History of Art Department at University College London. Students must take four courses in each year, which in the first year consists of two course units at UCL and two in the SOAS department. Students must take a minimum of one and a half units from either side in the second year and a minimum of one unit a side in the final year. This brings together the study of European, Asian and African art in a flexible manner. The units taken at UCL in the first year are general courses introducing students to the skills needed of the art historian. In the second year, these units focus on western art since 1200 and topics such as current approaches to art history of the methods and materials of artists. Courses taken within SOAS cover diverse topics such as the decorative arts of Islam, Buddhist art, Chinese ceramics and the visual culture of 18th-century Japan.

For further information, see page 554

Swansea Institute of Higher Education

BA (Hons) Fine Art (Combined Media)

This course is for those who want to study fine art on a broad, integrated basis using a number of different media. Students are encouraged to develop an individual response and personal expression within and beyond the boundaries of established art forms. The course allows students to construct a studio practice programme from a range of modules to suit their individual needs and interests through discussions with the programme director. Studio practice workshops in painting, drawing, sculpture and time-based applications of fine art form an essential part of the course as well as the opportunity to work in printmaking, photography and computers. Entry requirements are usually two A levels at grade C and five GCSEs at grade C or above, including English. Students must also demonstrate an ability to work across a spectrum of art and media forms, including drawing.

Contact details see page 621

The Surrey Institute of Art and Design, University College

BA (Hons) Photography

This programme enables students to realise their creative potential, and aims to provide a sound basis for a career in professional photography and related areas. The programme links critical study and creative practice to promote students' imaginative and judgmental powers, their communication, technical and study skills and their understanding of the social and historical context of photographic practices. Practical projects, workshops, lectures and seminars provide the foundation on which students build their individual programmes in the third stage of the course. Engagement with professional and business opportunities is encouraged through work placements and exhibitions.

For further information, see page 570

Postgraduate

Courtauld Institute of Art (University of London)

MA Painting Conservation (Wall Painting)

This three-year MA in the conservation of wall painting is open to graduates in both the humanities and sciences. The training

Art and Design

Institution	Grade	Institution	Grade
Bournemouth University	5	Dartington College of Arts	3a
University of Brighton	5	Falmouth College of Arts	3a
City University	5	University of Gloucestershire	3a
Goldsmiths College (University of London)	5	University of Hertfordshire	3a
The London Institute	5	Kent Institute of Art and Design	3a
University of Wales College, Newport	5	Lancaster University	3a
Open University	5	Leeds Metropolitan University	3a
The University of Reading (Typography)	5	University of Lincoln	3a
Royal College of Art	5	Liverpool John Moores University	3a
Sheffield Hallam University	5	Middlesex University (Electronic Arts)	3a
University College London		Middlesex University (Design Disciplines)	3a
(University of London)	5	Middlesex University (Fine Art)	3a
University of Ulster	5	The Robert Gordon University	3a
University of the West of England, Bristol	4	The Nottingham Trent University	3a
Brunel University	4	University of Plymouth	3a
University of Wales Institute, Cardiff	4	University of Portsmouth	3a
Coventry University (The Design Institute)	4	Napier University	3a
University of Central England in Birmingham	4	Surrey Institute of Art and Design,	
De Montfort University	4	University College	3a
University of Dundee	4	University of Wolverhampton	3a
University of East London	4	The University of Reading (Fine Art)	3a
Edinburgh College of Art	4	Anglia Polytechnic University	3b
Glasgow School of Art	4	University of Central Lancashire	3b
Kingston University	4	Chester (A College of the University of Liverpool)	3b
Loughborough University	4	Cumbria College of Art and Design	3b
The Manchester Metropolitan University	4	University of Derby	3b
University of Newcastle upon Tyne	4	The University of Huddersfield	3b
Northumbria University	4	London Guildhall University	3b
Oxford University	4	Norwich School of Art and Design	3b
University of Southampton	4	Oxford Brookes University	3b
Staffordshire University	4	Southampton Institute	3b
University of Sunderland	4	Swansea Institute of Higher Education	3b
University of Westminster	4	Bolton Institute of Higher Education	2
Wimbledon School of Art	4	University College Chichester	2
Bath Spa University College	3a	Liverpool Hope	2
The University of Wales, Aberystwyth	3a	University College Northampton	2
Bretton Hall	3a	The North East Wales	
Buckinghamshire Chilterns University College	3a	Institute of Higher Education	2
Coventry University (Creative Practice)	3a	Thames Valley University	1

Source: RAE 2001

Art and design

is interdisciplinary and integrates science, art history and the theory and practice of conservation. In the first year, students receive formal teaching in subjects such as basic science, conservation theory and methods and the history of European wall painting. The second year includes specialist courses in the environmental causes of deterioration, scientific examination and cleaning and consolidation linked to departmental programmes and collections, as well as periods of fieldwork in England and abroad. During the final year, students undertake further fieldwork and a three-month research project on an aspect of the examination, deterioration, analysis or conservation of wall paintings.

Contact details, see page 615

University of Southampton

MA European Fine Art

This course encourages students to produce a body of work at master's level and develop subject-specific skills. They will learn to interpret, conceptualise and critically evaluate the work of artists in relation to their own practice and learn to gather information and develop ideas independently. Students improve their contextual awareness and understanding of professional practice, including the handling, transportation and exhibition of art works. The course offers graduates the opportunity to study contrasting cultures from Barcelona to Winchester. The transferable skills of communication, time management, lecturing and teamwork are developed and students are offered an intensive Spanish language course at the beginning of the first phase. To gain a place on the course, students need a fine art or design-related first degree or equivalent.

For further information, see page 562
For further information, see page 562

The University of Sussex

MA in The History of Art: Europe, Asia and America

This course offers global perspectives in the history of art and emphasises cross-cultural approaches. The programme of study includes the core course, Readings in the History of Art, which is taken by all students in the first term and three options courses selected from those on offer in any one year. In addition, a full programme of research skills and methods is provided for all students. The MA programme may be taken as a one-year, full-time course or, for part-time students, it can be taken over two years. It is assessed by four term papers of 5,000 words each and a dissertation of up to 20,000 words. A good honours degree in the history of art or a related discipline, together with a strong commitment to advanced studies in the subject is required for admission.

For further information, see page 572
For further information, see page 572

Useful links

www.artscouncil.org.uk	◗	The Arts Council of England
www.ccc-acw.org.uk	◗	The Arts Council of Wales
www.art-review.co.uk	◗	*Art Review* magazine
www.britcoun.org/arts	◗	The British Council: Arts, Literature and Design
www.clayzee.com	◗	Clayzee: worldwide ceramics and pottery directory
www.craftscouncil.org.uk	◗	The Crafts Council
www.arts.org.uk	◗	Regional Arts Boards Online
www.tate.org.uk	◗	Tate Online

Biology and the biological and food sciences

Biology, with its basis in living and often breathing things, is the science we all feel part of. The broad nature of biology and the biological sciences makes it relevant to much of contemporary life. Some aspects are particularly sensational and raise both political and ethical questions. Who can forget the mouse with the ear genetically grown onto its back? Or Dolly, the cloned sheep; an experiment which has provoked arguments over scientific patents? Biologists need to be sympathetic to public interest and aware of controversies surrounding their subject. There is more to biology, though, than these reports. Biologists understand the mystery that newspapers try to explain.

Biology is referred to as a 'soft science'. This means that the number of variables in any one situation is so great that constructing a formula or an equation is impossible. This sets it apart from 'hard sciences' like chemistry, physics and mathematics.

Biologists study all forms of life, from unicellular organisms to ecological systems and the laws that govern the plant and animal kingdom. There is a broad spectrum of interest within any one biology departments and most degrees allow students to specialise.

Although there are many subdisciplines within the biological sciences, the first year of a three or four-year degree may well share courses. There are core elements such as cell biology, genetics, microbiology, nutrition and the form and function of living organisms.

After the first year, students progress in various directions, depending on their degree title and department. In the second and third years, students are involved in an increasing amount of lab work and will undertake fieldwork, which sometimes takes place in the summer holidays but is not always compulsory. Subjects studied in the final year sometimes diverge and some institutions introduce students to management issues and discuss current biological controversies.

Students can opt for a sandwich course which includes a year spent in industry, sometimes abroad. This usually takes place between the second and third years, with students working for government research stations, museums or large multinational firms such as Shell and GlaxoSmithKline.

Food science

Food science applies pure science disciplines, such as chemistry, nutrition, microbiology and physical sciences, to the nature and composition of foods and the changes they undergo during development, storage and processing. It is concerned with the maintenance and improvement of food quality and safety. The food industry has a shortage of well-qualified experts who possess a technical and scientific base, strong analytical skills and an understanding of the relationship between food manufacturing technologies, management of the production process and the marketing of the product.

TEACHING QUALITY ASSESSMENTS

Applied Sciences
(Wales) 1994/95

tqa

Institution	Grade	Institution	Grade
University of Glamorgan	Satisfactory		

Biochemistry
(Wales) 1997/98

tqa

Cardiff University	Excellent		

Cellular and Molecular Biology
(Scotland) 1996/97

tqa

The University of Aberdeen	Excellent	Heriot-Watt University, Edinburgh	Highly Satisfactory
University of Dundee	Excellent	Napier University	Highly Satisfactory
The University of Edinburgh	Excellent	University of Paisley	Highly Satisfactory
University of Glasgow	Excellent	The University of Stirling	Highly Satisfactory
University of St Andrews	Excellent	The University of Strathclyde	Highly Satisfactory
University of Abertay Dundee	Highly Satisfactory		
Glasgow Caledonian University	Highly Satisfactory		

Organismal Biology
(Scotland) 1996/97

tqa

The University of Aberdeen	Excellent	University of St Andrews	Excellent
University of Dundee	Excellent	Napier University	Highly Satisfactory
The University of Edinburgh	Excellent	University of Paisley	Highly Satisfactory
University of Glasgow	Excellent	The University of Stirling	Highly Satisfactory

Biosciences
(Wales) 1996/97

tqa

The University of Wales, Aberystwyth	Excellent	University of Wales Swansea	Excellent
University of Wales, Bangor	Excellent	The North East Wales Institute of Higher Education	Satisfactory
Cardiff University	Excellent		
University of Wales Institute, Cardiff	Excellent		

Source: HEFCE, SHEFC, HEFCW latest available ratings
For a more complete list of institutions offering these courses at undergraduate level refer to the Course Directory

Specialist and vocational

Birkbeck College
Certificate of Continuing Education in Biology

This is a one-year course providing a foundation in the biological sciences and allowing progression to an honours degree in the subject. All students follow courses in the foundations of biology, molecular cell biology and animal diversity, and develop scientific skills and knowledge of key biological concepts. Students are trained in numeracy, literacy and computer-based skills and are graded by a mixture of continuous assessment and examination. Assessed coursework may include practical reports, problem solving, data analysis, presentations, internet-based exercises, essays and role-play. The entry requirements include evidence of intellectual ability and strong motivation. Relevant work experience is also useful.

Contact details, see page 611

University of Hertfordshire
HND Applied Biology

This programme gives those with one science-based A level or equivalent the opportunity to obtain a nationally-recognised vocational qualification in two years, at the same time as offering the chance to continue on to the university's specialist degrees in biosciences. The course includes courses in biochemistry, microbiology and pharmacology. Many of the HND classes are shared with the BSc. It is then possible to transfer onto an honours degree after the first semester or obtain an HND then continue to work towards a BSc degree within three years or a BSc honours within four years full time. Part-time students work towards an HNC and may continue for a further three years part time for a BSc honours degree.

Contact details, see page 616

Undergraduate

University of Wales, Bangor
BSc Zoology

The aim of this degree is to provide students with a broad zoological training that covers both pure and applied aspects of animal life while introducing them to a diversity of laboratory and field zoology experience. Students receive a thorough grounding in general zoology in exploring the diversity of animal form and function and its evolution and ecology. Immunology and parasitology are also studied and fieldwork is an integral part of the course. Students acquire many transferable skills, including data analysis, group work, writing and professional skills and IT competency. Graduates of this degree should have gained a thorough understanding of theoretical and practical zoology as well as associated practical skills and a comprehensive range of qualities demanded by potential employers.

For further information, see page 440

Kingston University
BSc (Hons) Biology

This degree gives students the opportunity to study a broad-based course in the biological sciences or to specialise in a narrower range of topics. They will gain an understanding of biological processes and an in-depth knowledge of topics selected from life sciences modules. The course is studied for three years full time or six years part time. An extended four-year programme is available for those without traditional science-based qualifications, which includes a preparatory year designed to equip students with the skills and knowledge to continue with the degree. Assessment is through a combination of examinations and coursework, including essays, practical and project reports, presentations and group exercises. Successful graduates have found employment in medical and veterinary laboratories, biological research and the pharmaceutical,

Biology

TEACHING QUALITY ASSESSMENTS

Food Science
(England and Northern Ireland) 1997/99

tqa

Institution	Grade	Institution	Grade
Harper Adams University College	23	University of Lincoln	20
The University of Nottingham	23	Oxford Brookes University	20
University of Plymouth	22	Bournemouth University	19
The University of Reading	22	The Manchester	
Queen's University Belfast	21	Metropolitan University	19
The University of Surrey	21	University of North London	19
The University of Huddersfield	20	South Bank University	18
University of Leeds	20	University of Teesside	17

Food Science
(Wales) 1996/97

tqa

University of Wales Institute, Cardiff	Satisfactory

Source: HEFCE, SHEFC, HEFCW latest available ratings
For a more complete list of institutions offering these courses at undergraduate level refer to the Course Directory

Molecular Biosciences
(England and Northern Ireland) 1998/99/2000

Institution	Grade	Institution	Grade
University of Bath	24	University of Leicester	22
University of Bristol	24	Liverpool John Moores University	22
University of the West of England, Bristol	24	University College London	
Cambridge University	24	(University of London)	22
The University of Durham	24	University of Luton	22
The University of Kent	24	The Manchester	
Kingston University	24	Metropolitan University	22
University of Newcastle upon Tyne	24	University of Plymouth	22
The Nottingham Trent University	24	University of Portsmouth	22
Oxford University	24	Queen Mary, University of London	22
The University of Salford	24	University of Sussex	22
University of Sunderland	24	University of Ulster	22
The University of York	24	Anglia Polytechnic University	21
Aston University	23	De Montfort University	21
The University of Birmingham	23	University of Hertfordshire	21
The University of Essex	23	Keele University	21
The University of Hull	23	Lancaster University	21
University of Leeds	23	Northumbria University	21
The University of Manchester	23	Queen's University Belfast	21
The University of Nottingham	23	The University of Reading	21
University of Southampton	23	The University of Surrey	21
The University of Warwick	23	University of Westminster	21
Birkbeck College	22	University of Greenwich	20
University of East Anglia	22	Halton College	20
University of Exeter	22	South Bank University	20
The University of Huddersfield	22	Coventry University	19
Imperial College of Science, Technology		University of East London	19
and Medicine (University of London)	22	The University of Liverpool	19
King's College London (University of London)	22	University of North London	18

Source: HEFCE, SHEFC, HEFCW latest available ratings
For a more complete list of institutions offering these courses at undergraduate level refer to the Course Directory

forensic, environmental, food and bio-technology industries.

For further information, see page 496

The University of Edinburgh
BSc (Hons) Biological Sciences
Within biological sciences at The University of Edinburgh, there are 17 single honours degree specialisations. In each case, the honours subject occupies the whole of the final year with a research project as a major component. Students are helped to appreciate current research controversies in their subject and, through their own experience of research, they learn to appraise such topics critically. Experience in the laboratory or in the field gives those who do not intend to undertake research as a career the opportunity to learn how their subject has progressed through experiment. Students are encouraged to take a broad curriculum in the first year. In the second year, students take six out of 17 biological courses. It is also possible to take non-biological courses. Increased specialisation is encouraged in the third year. Admission to an honours specialisation depends on performance in the third year and can be competitive but the School of Biology tries to place all students onto a suitable honours course.
For further information, see page 474

University of Leeds
BSc Food Production Processing and Marketing
This three-year course aims to give students

an overview of the entire food chain through teaching modules in agricultural practice and systems of production, food science, food processing, food analysis, biotechnology, nutrition, quality control, management, business studies, marketing and sales. Students are taught through lectures, laboratory classes and tutorials. Taught modules are examined and formal exams will account for 50 to 60 per cent of the final degree classification. Formal laboratory classes are continually assessed whilst research projects, team projects and literature surveys also count towards the final degree classification. Entry requirements are normally three good A levels including one science

subject. The school welcomes applications from mature students and other non-standard applicants.

Contact details, see page 617

The University of Reading

BSc Food Science

This degree programme teaches students to apply technological expertise and knowledge to ensure the manufacture of safe and high quality foods. Students can opt to specialise in food chemistry, human nutrition, food microbiology or biotechnology. The first year develops understanding of basic scientific disciplines involved in food science followed by detailed study in the second year. The degree can be studied

Biology

TEACHING QUALITY ASSESSMENTS

Organismal Biosciences
(England and Northern Ireland) 1998/99/2000

tqa

Institution	Grade	Institution	Grade
University of Bath	24	Imperial College of Science, Technology and Medicine (University of London)	22
Birkbeck College	24	Keele University	22
The University of Birmingham	24	King's College London (University of London)	22
University of the West of England, Bristol	24	University of Leicester	22
Cambridge University	24	University of Luton	22
The University of Kent	24	The Manchester Metropolitan University	22
Kingston University	24	University of Newcastle upon Tyne	22
The Nottingham Trent University	24	University of Plymouth	22
Oxford University	24	University of Portsmouth	22
Royal Holloway, University of London	24	Queen Mary, University of London	22
The University of Salford	24	University of Sussex	22
The University of Sheffield	24	Anglia Polytechnic University	21
University of Sunderland	24	Bath Spa University College	21
University College London (University of London)	24	Chester College	21
The University of York	24	Lancaster University	21
Aston University	23	Liverpool Hope	21
Edge Hill College of Higher Education	23	Queen's University Belfast	21
The University of Essex	23	The University of Reading	21
The University of Hull	23	Suffolk College (An Accredited College of the University of East Anglia)	21
Liverpool John Moores University	23	The University of Surrey	21
The University of Manchester	23	University of Ulster	21
Roehampton University of Surrey	23	Westminster University	21
University of Southampton	23	University of Greenwich	20
St Mary's College	23	Halton College	20
The University of Warwick	23	South Bank University	20
Bolton Institute of Higher Education	22	University College Worcester	20
University of Bristol	22	Coventry University	19
University of Derby	22	University of East London	19
University of East Anglia	22	The University of Liverpool	19
University of Exeter	22		
The University of Huddersfield	22		

Source: HEFCE, SHEFC, HEFCW latest available ratings
For a more complete list of institutions offering these courses at undergraduate level refer to the Course Directory

TEACHING QUALITY ASSESSMENTS

Food Science
(England and Northern Ireland) 1997/99

tqa

Institution	Grade	Institution	Grade
Harper Adams University College	23	University of Lincoln	20
The University of Nottingham	23	Oxford Brookes University	20
University of Plymouth	22	Bournemouth University	19
The University of Reading	22	The Manchester	
Queen's University Belfast	21	Metropolitan University	19
The University of Surrey	21	University of North London	19
The University of Huddersfield	20	South Bank University	18
University of Leeds	20	University of Teesside	17

Food Science
(Wales) 1996/97

tqa

University of Wales Institute, Cardiff	Satisfactory

Source: HEFCE, SHEFC, HEFCW latest available. For a more complete list of institutions offering these courses at undergraduate level refer to the Course Directory

for three years full time or students can choose a four-year option with an industrial placement. Those who opt for the four-year course spend their third year on two, six-month placements in industry. The final year of the course allows students to develop expertise in a selected area of food science by advanced lectures and a research project. Entry requirements are three A levels including at least one core science at A level and a second science at A/S level.

For further information, see page 544

Postgraduate

Cambridge University
MPhil Biological Science

This course is designed to provide further study and training in biological research and is available for candidates working in the departments of anatomy, biochemistry, experimental psychology, genetics, pathology, pharmacology, physiology, plant science and zoology in the Institute of Biotechnology. It is based around an independent research project and is not a taught course. Assessment consists of a thesis on a subject approved by the degree committee for the Faculty of Biology and includes an oral examination on the thesis

and the general field of knowledge in which it falls. The thesis must satisfy examiners that the candidate can design and carry out investigations, assess and interpret the results obtained and place the work in the wider context of the subject.

Contact details, see page 614

The University of Sheffield
MMedSci in Anatomy and Cell Biology

This master's degree course aims to familiarise students with modern methods in anatomy and cell biology and teach them how to apply research to contemporary questions. It aims to develop the attitudes and skills needed for further research into anatomy and cell biology. The course aims to give students detailed knowledge of subjects led by departmental research and teaches them to explain how these relate to their project work. They will also compile a written dissertation and will have to present work orally. The entry requirement is a first or second class honours degree from an approved institution in a suitable subject or equivalent. Assessment is by satisfactory completion of five modules, a year long research project and regular tutorials.

For further information, see page 558

Biological Sciences

Institution	Grade
Cambridge University (Biochemistry)	5*
Cambridge University (Zoology)	5*
University of Bristol (Biochemistry)	5*
Institute of Cancer Research	5*
Imperial College of Science, Technology and Medicine (University of London)	5*
University of Dundee	5*
University of Leicester (Genetics)	5*
The University of Manchester	5*
University of Newcastle upon Tyne	5*
The University of Sheffield (Animal and Plant Sciences)	5*
The University of Sheffield (Molecular and Cellular Biology)	5*
The University of Aberdeen	5
University of Bath	5
The University of Edinburgh	5
Birkbeck College (Crystallography)	5
The University of Birmingham	5
University of Bristol	5
Cambridge University (Biotechnology)	5
Cambridge University (Genetics)	5
Cambridge University (Plant Sciences)	5
Cardiff University (Mammalian and Medical Biology)	5
The University of Durham	5
University of East Anglia	5
University of Glasgow	5
University of Leeds	5
University of Leicester (Biochemistry)	5
University of Leicester (Biology)	5
King's College London, University of London (Biophysics, Randall Centre)	5
The University of Liverpool	5
The University of Manchester Institute of Science and Technology (UMIST)	5
Oxford University (Biochemistry)	5
Oxford University (Zoology)	5
The University of Nottingham (Genetics)	5
Royal Holloway, University of London	5
University of Southampton	5
University of St Andrews	5
University of Sussex	5

Institution	Grade
University College London, University of London (Biochemistry and Molecular Biology)	5
University College London (Biology)	5
The University of Warwick	5
The University of York	5
University of Wales, Bangor	4
Brunel University	4
Cardiff University (Ecological and Environmental Biology)	4
Cranfield University	4
The University of Essex	4
University of Exeter	4
The University of Hull	4
Institute of Zoology	4
Keele University	4
The University of Kent	4
Lancaster University	4
Open University	4
Queen Mary, University of London	4
Queen's University, Belfast	4
Oxford University (Plant Sciences)	4
The University of Reading	4
The University of Stirling	4
The University of Wales, Aberystwyth	3a
Birkbeck College (Biology/Chemistry)	3a
The University of Nottingham (Life and Environmental Science)	3a
Oxford Brookes University	3a
King's College London, University of London (Life Sciences)	3a
University of Plymouth	3a
University of Sunderland	3a
University of Wales Swansea	3a
Bath Spa University College	3b
University of Central Lancashire	3b
Liverpool Hope	3b
University of Westminster	3b
Coventry University	2
University of East London	2
University of Luton	2
The Manchester Metropolitan University	2
Northumbria University	2
University College Worcester	2

Food Science and Technology

Institution	Grade
University of Leeds	5*
The University of Nottingham	5
The University of Reading	5
Heriot-Watt University, Edinburgh	4
Queen's University Belfast	4
South Bank University	3a

Institution	Grade
The University of Strathclyde	3a
University of Wales Institute, Cardiff	3b
University of Lincoln	3b
The Robert Gordon University	3b
University of Teesside	2

Source: RAE 2001

Biology

The Eden Project, Cornwall

Useful links

www.bshg.org.uk	▶	British Society for Human Genetics
www.genetic.com	▶	Genetic Internet Ltd
www.ornl.gov/hgmis	▶	Human Genome Project Information
www.ifst.org	▶	Institute of Food Science and Technology
www.nibsc.ac.uk	▶	National Institute for Biological Standards and Control
www.newscientist.com	▶	*New Scientist*
www.who.int	▶	World Health Organisation

Business, management and marketing

Business-related subjects are becoming increasingly popular as students recognise their value in terms of career potential and financial rewards. Business in the 21st century is a fast moving, competitive environment which is continuously evolving. Technological advances such as the world wide web and video conferencing are breaking down the boundaries that once existed, opening the gateway to international commerce. In general, business courses aim to educate future managers for the business world.

Undergraduate courses in business studies typically last between three and four years. The first year tends to give an overview of the discipline, with modules such as economics, accountancy, finance and computing. These concepts underlie the theory and practice studied in subsequent years. Most courses emphasise the importance of practical experience and include presentations, role-play and work experience. Sandwich courses include a six-month or one-year stint in an appropriate field of industry and commerce, either in the UK or abroad.

At postgraduate level, there is a higher level of specialisation, with the possibility of studying technology or personnel management, for example. The MBA (Master of Business Administration), developed in the USA, is now very popular in the UK. To follow an MBA, you need a minimum of three years' work experience, a good first degree in any subject and often a satisfactory Graduate Management Admissions Test (GMAT) score. Due to their popularity, entry onto courses at some of the internationally-renowned institutions is difficult and expensive. However if you do succeed, you will obtain a qualification which is highly respected worldwide.

Short courses in a number of business-related areas can be taken on a part or full-time basis at private colleges. These provide a good starting point for students considering going into higher education or for those wanting some initial training.

Marketing

The role of marketing is to ensure that consumers look beyond price and function when weighing their consumption options. Marketers create, develop and enhance brands through an understanding of the desires, needs, preferences and constraints which define the consumer target market. They aim to expand a company's market share and keep customers satisfied. In order to achieve this, it is vital that those working in the marketing industry have an extensive knowledge of advertsing, sales packaging and publicity material design, public relations and after-sales service.

Marketing courses usually begin within a general introduction along with study in supporting disciplines such as IT, economics and behavioural science. Second and third-year modules include marketing communications, sales management, advertising, public relations, internet marketing, project management and consultancy.

Business and Management Studies
(England and Northern Ireland) 2000/01

Institution	Grade
Aston University	24
Leeds Metropolitan University	24
London School of Economics and Political Science (University of London)	24
The University of Manchester	24
University of North London	24
Oxford Brookes University	24
University of Ulster	24
Bridgwater College	23
University of the West of England, Bristol	23
University of East Anglia	23
The Manchester Metropolitan University	23
North Warwickshire and Hinckley College	23
University of Southampton	23
Spelthorne College	23
Warrington Collegiate Institute	23
Askham Bryan College	22
Blackburn College	22
Bolton College	22
Burton College	22
The College of St Mark and St John	22
Coventry University	22
Dearne Valley College	22
University of Derby	22
Doncaster College	22
Dudley College of Technology	22
University of Exeter	22
Exeter College	22
King Alfred's Winchester	22
Liverpool John Moores University	22
London Guildhall University	22
The London Institute	22
Loughborough University	22
Halton College	22
Mid-Cheshire College	22
Rugby College of Further Education	22
South Trafford College	22
Stockport College of Further Education	22
Stoke-on-Trent College	22
The University of York	22
Birkbeck College	21
The University of Birmingham	21
Bishop Auckland College	21
Blackpool and The Fylde College	21
Canterbury Christ Church University College	21
Chesterfield College	21
Keele University	21
The University of Kent	21
Knowsley Community College	21
New College Durham	21
North Hertfordshire College	21
North Nottinghamshire College	21
College of North West London	21
The University of Reading	21
Royal Holloway and Bedford New College	21
South Cheshire College	21
South Nottingham College	21
St Helens College	21
Warwickshire College, Royal Leamington Spa and Moreton Morrell	21
University College Worcester	21
York St John College	21
Accrington and Rossendale College	20
Barnfield College	20
Bath Spa University College	20
City of Bristol College	20
City College, Birmingham	20
Crawley College	20
Gateshead College	20
University of Greenwich	20
Hammersmith & West London College	20
North East Surrey College of Technology, Ewell	20
Northbrook College Sussex	20
Rotherham College of Arts and Technology	20
Park Lane College	20
Sandwell College	20
South Bank University	20
Chichester College of Arts, Science and Technology	19
Coventry Technical College	19
Eastleigh College	19
Farnborough College of Technology	19
Henley College Coventry	19
Highbury College	19
Matthew Boulton College of Further and Higher Education	19
Newcastle College	19
Newham College of Further Education	19
North Lincolnshire College	19
North Tyneside College	19
Oxford College of Further Education	19
Reading College and School of Arts and Design	19
Tamworth and Lichfield College	19
West Cumbria College	19
Wirral Metropolitan College	19
Beverley College of Further Education	18
Salford College	18
Somerset College of Arts and Technology	18
West Cheshire College	18
Wigan and Leigh College	18
Brooklands College	17
Mid-Kent College of Further and Higher Education	17
Northumberland College	17
St Mary's College	17
Wakefield College	17
Basingstoke College of Technology	16
Solihull College	16
Walsall College of Arts and Technology	16
Herefordshire College of Technology	14

Source: HEFCE, SHEFC, HEFCW latest available ratings
For a more complete list of institutions offering these courses at undergraduate level refer to the Course Directory

Business, management and marketing

Specialist and vocational

Bromley College of Further & Higher Education
Cambridge Business Skills

This one-year, full-time foundation course run by the Business School is designed to prepare students for undergraduate study. It emphasises the skills required for successful study at degree level, such as independent work and research. Modules covered include business communication, marketing, the world of business, meeting and presentation skills and finance. English as a foreign language (EFL) is also taught where appropriate. Teaching takes place at the college's Rookery Lane site. There are currently about 20 international students enrolled on the course.

For further information, see page 458

Cavendish College
Business Studies

Established in 1985 in central London, this private college specialises in academic and vocational courses. Full and part-time courses can be taken in business studies, hospitality and tourism, secretarial training, creative studies, computer studies, media studies and English language. The college offers modern facilities and has recently established its own cyber café where students can relax and use the internet. Courses are continually updated to reflect the market and therefore meet changing demand. The college has a diverse international student population from over 80 countries around the world. The business studies department offers a variety of courses which aim to prepare students for work in the international business world. Intensive diplomas can be obtained in subjects including marketing, PR, advertising and communications.

Other courses include diplomas in international management, import/export, investment analysis, creative advertising and executive secretarial studies. The college offers specialised computer training in all its business courses.

For further information, see page 410

Computing and Business College

Computing and Business College (CBC) is located 10 minutes away from Liverpool Street station in central London, where some of the major academic and financial institutions are located in the Square Mile. CBC is an independent college providing tuition which leads to examinations for various professional qualifications, particularly in computing, management and the travel industries. Courses offered include the Association of Business Executives (ABE) certificate, diploma and advanced diploma, the Institute for Management of Information Systems (IMIS) diploma and higher diploma and the London Chamber of Commerce and Industry (LCCI) examinations at various levels.

For further information, see page 390

School of Business and Languages Coventry Technical College

The school offers a range of full-time business programmes at advanced level. This includes the Advanced Vocational Certificate in Education (AVCE) in Business. Achievement of good grades can lead directly onto a university degree programme or entry onto the Higher National Diploma (HND) in Business, which is a two-year modular programme covering management, resourcing, marketing and finance. Both the AVCE and HND are popular programmes for over-seas students, as is the International Business Foundation Programme. All overseas

students receive English language lessons and support as well as the opportunity to sit IELTS examinations. The college has a range of facilities and all students are allocated a personal tutor and have access to the internet and email facilities.

For further information, see page 414

Grimsby College
Business Studies

Grimsby College offers several courses in business studies, aiming to provide students with a professional environment and learning resources. Courses on offer range from BA (Hons) and HND Business Studies to professional courses such as the Chartered Institute of Marketing. The college's Business Studies Department has facilities which include specialised business rooms, a secretary room with audio equipment and a main business room with everything students need to complete their chosen course. After finishing their course, students leave the college equipped to work in areas including accountancy, personnel, marketing and administration.

For further information, see page 416

London School of Technology and English (LITE)

The course in international business English is designed for people who need or use English in a business environment. It is important to understand that business English is not a special language, yet, by using a range of business settings and situations, students can become more aware, confident and fluent in the use of the English language and will display confidence in a commercial environment. The courses follow the Cambridge University recognised syllabus which involves all the elements of a business course including reading, writing, speaking and listening. All these elements are taken from real-life situations and prepare students for what to expect in the business world. Other areas covered include ways of marketing, insurance, stocks and shares, corporate strategy and retailing.

For further information, see page 400

University of Luton
HND Business Studies (Marketing)

This course aims to provide a sound theoretical and practical foundation for a successful career in marketing. It covers all areas of the topic and allows for a degree of specialisation in the many different aspects of marketing. A thorough understanding of contemporary business practice is taught to complement marketing skills aquired by students. The course is taught at nearby Barnfield College and many students have progressed to the degree programme at the university and have graduated with first class honours. Employment prospects for graduates are

TEACHING QUALITY ASSESSMENTS
Business and Management Studies
(Scotland) 1994/95

tqa

Institution	Grade	Institution	Grade
The University of Strathclyde	Excellent	University of Abertay Dundee	Satisfactory
The University of Edinburgh	Highly Satisfactory	University of Glasgow	Satisfactory
The Robert Gordon University	Highly Satisfactory	Glasgow Caledonian University	Satisfactory
University of St Andrews	Highly Satisfactory	Heriot-Watt University, Edinburgh	Satisfactory
The University of Stirling	Highly Satisfactory	Napier University	Satisfactory
The University of Aberdeen	Satisfactory	University of Paisley	Satisfactory

Source: HEFCE, SHEFC, HEFCW latest available ratings
For a more complete list of institutions offering these courses at undergraduate level refer to the Course Directory

Business and Management Studies
(Wales) 1993/94

tqa

Institution	Grade	Institution	Grade
University of Glamorgan	Excellent	University of Wales College, Newport	Satisfactory
The University of Wales, Aberystwyth	Satisfactory	The North East Wales Institute of Higher Education	Satisfactory
University of Wales, Bangor (Administrative Studies)		University of Wales Swansea	Satisfactory
Cardiff University	Satisfactory	Swansea Institute of Higher Education	Satisfactory
University of Wales Institute, Cardiff	Satisfactory		

Consumer Studies
(Scotland) 1995

tqa

Institution	Grade	Institution	Grade
Glasgow Caledonian University	Highly Satisfactory	University of Dundee	Satisfactory
Queen Margaret University College, Edinburgh	Highly Satisfactory	The Robert Gordon University	Satisfactory

Source: HEFCE, SHEFC, HEFCW latest available ratings
For a more complete list of institutions offering these courses at undergraduate level refer to the Course Directory

good. Over the past decade, there has been a significant increase in the number of graduates employed by large London-based agencies and smaller regional agencies. Graduates typically go into careers in marketing management, public relations, sales or general management.
Contact details, see page 618

Contact details, see page 618

Northbrook College
Business

The philosophy of the Business Studies Faculty at Northbrook College emphasises the practical, vocational and professional aspects of studying business. The college's teaching staff have a wide range of business experience and teach on college, university

Business, management and marketing

and professional courses. The courses allow students to begin from access or foundation levels and build up to a Higher National Diploma or a degree. Foundation and access courses include subjects such as OCR business and information technology skills, advanced VCE diploma in business, advanced VCE diploma in travel and tourism and an international foundation year in business or travel and tourism. The diploma and BA (Hons) degree courses at the college include marketing with design for business, business administration and business with options in IT, transport, management, finance, marketing, international business management and travel and tourism.

For further information, see page 524

Oxford Media and Business School

Oxford Media and Business School is situated in the centre of this ancient university city. The school runs a range of intensive, modular business and media programmes ranging in length from three months to one year. In the Business School, courses incorporate business theory with an emphasis on practical management ability. This includes training in key skills such as the use of the latest computer office systems and the preparation and delivery of an effective business presentation using audiovisual aids. The Media Department offers a choice of courses using the latest in AppleMac G4 system software. Again there is a strong practical emphasis, involving the theory of marketing, design workshops and the importance of working to copy deadlines. All these courses can be combined with a European language option, as part of an integrated European Business Studies Programme which can be studied to certificate or diploma level. A full time

WHERE STUDENTS COME FIRST

The centre of London is an exciting place for anyone to study. The City College is located close to Old Street tube station in the City and therefore within easy access of all the key areas of interest. Established in 1979, The City College was one of the first colleges to have been accredited by the British Accreditation Council for Independent Further and Higher Education (BAC). During the years, thousands of students have successfully completed their studies at the college and have progressed to higher degrees or have secured employment.

The college has an international environment with over 45 different nationalities being represented among the student body. The college has modern computer facilities and a library. All computers are networked, allowing students to have free access to the internet and email facilities. Other facilities include reprographic equipment, an accommodation service and a cafeteria.

The primary focus of study is on business management and information technology, with courses from certificate, diploma and higher diploma, through to bachelor, master and doctorate degrees. Degrees are awarded by British and American universities. Some courses are available by distance learning, enabling students to complete their studies from their home country.

The City College is a corporate member of the UK Institute of Travel and Tourism and has a very lively Hospitality and Tourism Department. Students can obtain IATA points within the tourism course. The hospitality course is one of the few courses available, where students can actively learn and use the FIDELIO computer reservation system, used by hotels around the world.

Apart from the management and information technology departments there are also secretarial courses for the personal assistants of the future, with much emphasis on using the various software programmes to achieve executive secretary status.

Finally, those who need to improve their English language skills can join one of the English as a foreign language classes, in order to reach an acceptable standard for entry into various college programmes.

Contact details, see page 611

The following is the current list of courses offered

- MBA – Master of Business Administration
- BBA – Bachelor of Business Administration
- DBA – Doctor of Business Administration
- PhD – Doctor of Philosophy in Business Administration
- BA/MA/PhD in Human Behaviour
- Diploma/Higher Diploma in Business Administration
- Foundation Programme for Business
- Diploma/Advanced Diploma in Travel and Tourism Management
- Diploma/Advanced Diploma in Hospitality Management
- BSc/MSc in Computer Science
- Certificate/Diploma/Advanced Diploma in Computing
- Executive Secretary Diploma
- English as a Foreign Language

Student profile

Conchita Bethancourt,
Tenerife

"I am completing my final semester on the Travel and Tourism Advanced Diploma course of study. My home is Tenerife in the Canaries and therefore my life has revolved around tourism – when considering a future career, most islanders find that it usually involves some aspect of tourism. I decided that I wanted to study the subject seriously and therefore made the decision to join The City College. It was a decision that I do not regret. The City College is located in the centre of London and the students are from all over the world. I think that everyone finds it easy to make new friends. My studies have taught me a lot about the tourism industry and have made me aware of the many different tasks that are involved. I have worked during my vacations at the main international airport in Tenerife; a good opportunity to put some of my skills into practice and to help me ensure I have a fulfilling career when I graduate."

Business and Management Studies

rae

Institution	Grade	Institution	Grade
Lancaster University	5*	University of Hertfordshire	3a
London Business School	5*	The University of Kent	3a
The University of Warwick	5*	Kingston University	3a
Aston University	5	University of Leicester	3a
University of Bath	5	University of Luton	3a
Cambridge University	5	The Manchester Metropolitan University	3a
Cardiff University	5	Middlesex University	3a
City University	5	University of Newcastle upon Tyne	3a
Imperial College of Science, Technology		University of North London	
and Medicine (University of London)	5	(Centre for Leisure and Tourism Studies)	3a
University of Leeds	5	Open University	3a
London School of Economics and		The University of Salford	3a
Political Science (University of London)	5	South Bank University	3a
The University of Manchester	5	University of Wales Swansea	3a
The University of Manchester Institute		University of Ulster	3a
of Science and Technology (UMIST)	5	University of Abertay Dundee	3b
The University of Nottingham	5	The University of Wales, Aberystwyth	3b
Oxford University	5	University of Glamorgan	3b
The University of Reading	5	University of Greenwich	3b
Birkbeck College (University of London)	4	The University of Huddersfield	3b
The University of Birmingham	4	University of Lincoln	3b
The University of Bradford	4	Liverpool John Moores University	3b
Brunel University	4	London Guildhall University	3b
Cranfield University	4	University of North London	3b
University of Exeter	4	Napier University	3b
The University of Hull	4	Northumbria University	3b
Keele University	4	The Nottingham Trent University	3b
King's College London (University of London)	4	University of Plymouth	3b
Loughborough University	4	Sheffield Hallam University	3b
University of Luton (Tourism)	4	Staffordshire University	3b
University of Portsmouth	4	University of Westminster	3b
Royal Holloway,		University of Wolverhampton	3b
University of London	4	Anglia Polytechnic University	2
The University of Sheffield	4	Buckinghamshire Chilterns University College	2
The University of Edinburgh	4	University of Central England in Birmingham	2
University of Glasgow	4	Coventry University	2
Heriot-Watt University, Edinburgh	4	University of Derby	2
University of Southampton	4	University of East London	2
The University of Surrey	4	Leeds Metropolitan University	2
University of St Andrews	4	University College Northampton	2
The University of Stirling	4	Oxford Brookes University	
The University of Strathclyde	4	(Hospitality Management)	2
Queen's University Belfast	4	Oxford Brookes University	2
The University of Aberdeen	3a	University of Paisley	2
Bournemouth University	3a	Queen Margaret University College, Edinburgh	2
University of Brighton	3a	The Robert Gordon University	2
University of the West of England, Bristol	3a	Southampton Institute	2
De Montfort University	3a	The University of Sunderland	2
The University of Durham	3a	Bolton Institute of Higher Education	1
University of East Anglia	3a	Dartington College of Arts	1
Glasgow Caledonian University	3a	Trinity and All Saints College	1
University of Gloucestershire	3a		

Source: RAE 2001

accommodation manager helps with living arrangements. Help with English language is available for international students.

Contact details, see page 612

Telford College of Arts and Technology

Advanced Vocational Certificate of Education in Business

Equivalent to two A levels, this two-year

course develops knowledge and skills in business. The programme enables progression to both higher education and employment within business, while developing key skills and building confidence. This course is divided into 12 units (six of which are compulsory) leading to a broad understanding of business from marketing to accounting. Topics include business at work, the competitive business environment, business and finance, human resources and business planning. The six optional units build on the knowledge gained in the above and allow students the opportunity to analyse selected areas in more depth. This programme values the importance of learning in a practical and realistic way. Students undertake up to four weeks' appropriate work experience for complementary research. As well as entering higher education, previous students have progressed to a wide range of careers including banking, the civil service and retail management.

For further information, see page 430

For further information, see page 430

Undergraduate

The University of Aberdeen
MA (Hons) Management Studies

To meet the increasing demand for management skills in the modern world, The University of Aberdeen provides a range of honours degree programmes involving management studies. The pre-honours programme (years one and two) provides an understanding of the key roles of management and the organisational context within which they are performed. In addition, an understanding of the environment in which public and private organisations operate and recognition of the relationship between the external environment and internal operations is covered.

Business, management and marketing

133

At the honours level (years three and four), the management studies element comprises core components in managerial research and analysis and organisational change, together with a range of management electives including strategic marketing, international business, entrepreneurship and information management.

Contact details, see page 613

University of Wales, Bangor
School for Business and Regional Development

The School for Business and Regional Development at Bangor is a multidisciplinary department offering an extensive portfolio of undergraduate and postgraduate degrees. Subject areas include business, marketing, banking, economics, accounting and finance, leisure tourism, heritage management and environmental management. Core studies, topical issues, fieldwork and practical experience characterise the school's degrees. Due to the broad range of disciplines, students have the opportunity to add options chosen from different areas to the core programme of specialised study in the student's main degree discipline. The school also offers opportunities for small group teaching and good pastoral care and has a particular commitment to understanding the community including its people, culture and environment.

For further information, see page 440

The University of Birmingham
BCom (Hons) Commerce

The BCom (Hons) at The University of Birmingham equips students with the expertise needed to understand business and its administration on a global scale. It is structured to reflect the changing world of commerce, providing a firm foundation for the world of work as well as the neces-

Student Profile

Naomi Yoneyama
Japan

Advanced Vocational Certificate in Business Studies

Harrogate College

"I chose business studies because I would like a career with an international company. There are 12 units in different subjects and you have to pass them all to get the qualification. In four of the subjects you have to take examinations but the other eight are continuous assessment which means that you get lots of feedback on how well you are doing. So far I've received distinctions in every subject. I chose to study at Harrogate because it is quiet here but there are still lots of young people and things to do. I like being near to Leeds as much as I love fashion and enjoy shopping there. Although it is possible to go to university after you qualify, I am hoping to get a good job with a Japanese company."

sary academic theory and research skills. The BCom also allows students to tailor parts of the programme to meet their individual preferences. The key areas covered over the three years are marketing, economics, law, accounting and business organisation. Throughout the whole of the BCom programme, teaching is delivered in a variety of ways. Seminars, tutorials and classwork are supported by lectures, giving students an opportunity to learn in groups or as individuals. Work is assessed by examination, coursework, projects, essays and IT exercises. With the BCom, students gain exemptions from professional exams such as those of the Chartered Institute of Marketing and the Institute of Personnel Management.

Contact details, see page 613

Bournemouth University

BSc (Hons) Business Information Systems Management

95.6 per cent of graduates following this programme find jobs within six months of graduating, making it one of the most popular and successful programmes at Bournemouth University. The Business School at Bournemouth is known for its vocational focus with lecturers coming straight from industry and organisations sponsoring student projects. The placement year is critical to graduates' success and many companies sponsor students for the final year and employ them after graduation. This programme equips students to be able to effectively manage information systems and technology in a business environment. There is also an independently-run, real-life IT project which students complete, enabling them to put the theory they have learnt into practice. Graduates typically go on to work as in-house IT consultants or at external management consultancy firms.

For further information, see page 448

Canterbury Christ Church University College

BSc (Hons) Business Information Management

The BSc (Hons) Business Information Management at the Business School of Canterbury Christ Church University College introduces the fundamentals of information technology as a business tool by teaching students to select and use a variety of appropriate software packages. It also broadens knowledge of working in a business environment by studying functional areas in business and through a work placement. The course explores the practical and theoretical concepts of IT and how they can be applied in the

business environment in order to generate a competitive advantage. Modules include marketing, finance, PC skills, systems analysis, design and emerging technologies and their impact on IT.

Contact details, see page 614

University of Glasgow

MA (Hons) Business History

This course can be studied as a joint degree in conjunction with business economics. The business history courses are taught in the Department of Economic and Social History at the University of Glasgow. The aim is to examine the historical development of business in Britain and internationally, and to give students a firm grasp of the changing nature and impact of business. Students taking the course gain an appreciation of the different ways of understanding and analysing firms and enterprises. There is a core module which analyses the main theoretical perspectives on business organisations and their performance, drawing on ideas from economics, management and other disciplines. Further modules examine the nature of business enterprise in the USA, Germany and Japan or deal with topics such as technological change, finance and industrial relations. All students undertake a project-driven training course whichuses primary and secondary sources related to businesses.

For further information, see page 480

University of Gloucestershire

BA (Hons) Business Management

A study of business management helps prepare students for employment and provides them with a fuller perspective of the many social, economic and political constraints shaping society. The aim of this course is to meets students' career and vocational needs by equipping them with transferable business, educational and personal skills required by industry and the community. Undergraduates spend stage one of the course developing their knowledge by examining the nature of organisations in the public and private sector. At stages two and three, students undertake modules which focus on the process of management and the activities of managers. At the same time, they are given opportunities to examine the work of more specialised management activities by studying modules such as the management of human resources, finance and marketing.

Contact details, see page 616

Greenwich School of Management

BSc (Hons) in Business Management

Greenwich School of Management was founded in 1974 and is an affiliated college of The University of Hull, meaning that students study at Greenwich and graduate at The University of Hull at the end of their programme. Start dates are flexible and students can commence courses in February, June or October. The BSc (Hons) degree has specialisations in management, information technology or travel and tourism. The programmes cover such topics as law, statistics and computing, business organisation and policy, economics, marketing, human resources management and strategy. Assessment is by examination, course and project work. The library has a large study area, as well as CD-Rom and internet access. Greenwich offers access courses which lead on to the Hull degrees for students who do not have the traditional entry requirements for direct access on to a BSc course.

For further information, see page 484

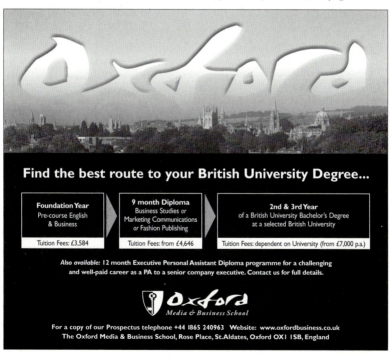

International University of America

BBA (Management)

The rapidity with which new problems challenge modern business management demands that students of business administration understand the historical background of contemporary economic issues. They must have a solid grasp of basic managerial strategies and an understanding of the fundamental principles of marketing, finance, management, computer technology, future trends, threats and business opportunities. IUA faculty members endeavour to involve students in discussions through the use of question and answer sessions, media and forums of debate. In addition to transmitting an understanding of the functional fields of specialisation with business administration, IUA's programmes help develop an appreciation of the dynamic forces that change the focus and an individual commitment to challenge faculty and other fellow students with questions on the readings prepared before each class session. Faculty members expect students to raise issues about course readings and will respond to them while incorporating their own thoughts. Other devices which stimulate discussion and debate include case studies, conferences, guest speakers, films and tutorials.

For further information, see page 394

The University of Kent

BBA (Hons) Business Administration

The Bachelor of Business Administration (BBA) provides the foundation needed to pursue a career in business or management. The programme aims to provide students with knowledge of the key areas essential in managing organisations including accounting, human resource management, management science, marketing, strategic management and operations management. The content and modes of study reflect the increasingly global nature of business and aim to provide the skills needed to succeed in this exciting environment. As part of this global focus, students study business and economic developments in Europe, Asia, Japan and North America. Modules include people and organisations, economics, management accounting, marketing analysis and strategic behaviour. In a typical week, students spend four or five hours in lectures and four or five hours in classes, group discussion and seminars.

Contact details, see page 617

King's College London (University of London)

BSc (Hons) Business Management

The Management Centre at King's College is the principal supplier of undergraduate teaching in business management studies at the University of London. The standard method of teaching is by lecture or tutorial classes where the lecturer and students work together through problem sheets, case studies or discuss in greater detail material covered in the lectures. One special feature of the programme is that the second year is spent in Canada. Students following any of the undergraduate degree courses with a management component take core courses in each of the following four areas: human and behavioural, marketing and strategy, economics and accounting, and finance. Students on the business management programme take core courses in the four main subject areas in the first two years of the degree. In addition, they choose from a selection of skills courses. In the final year, students are free to choose from a range of optional courses, including a project.

Contact details, see page 617

Kingston University
BSc(Hons) Business Information Technology
This is a four-year sandwich programme which develops students' understanding and skills in the areas of business, quantitative methods and information technology. The course is recognised as one of the leading business information technology degrees in the country, with a strong academic record, excellent links with employers and state-of-the-art facilities. The third year of the programme consists of a work placement of between 36 and 48 weeks' duration and will be complemented at level three by a live group consultancy project. This component of the degree has been recognised by a national award. Graduates from this programme find well-paid employment very quickly. Former students are employed worldwide and in a range of business and information technology related positions. They work in multinational companies, specialist consultancies and enterprises across a range of different industry sectors.

For further information, see page 496

Lancaster University
BA (Hons) Marketing
Lancaster University has the longest-established marketing department amongst traditional UK universities. The intensive courses cover market research, new product development, segmentation, product positioning, organisational buying behaviour and advertising. Computers are used for word processing, statistics and market research – the skills acquired being

UNIVERSITY OF
STIRLING

Faculty of Management

The University of Stirling offers a wide range of management degrees which combine academic rigour with professional training. The campus, located in the heart of Scotland is the ideal place to live, study and relax, with extensive leisure facilities, and easy access to the cities of Scotland, and the Highlands.

Programmes available include:

- MBA
- MSc Banking & Finance
- MSc International Business
- MSc Marketing

- BAcc Accountancy
- BA Business Studies
- BA Human Resource Management
- BA Marketing

The International Office
University of Stirling
Stirling FK9 4LA
Scotland UK

Tel: +44 (0) 1785 467046
E-mail: international@stir.ac.uk
www.stir.ac.uk

'Promoting excellence in teaching and research'

Business, management and marketing

combined in a computer-linked market research exercise. Students are also given exemptions by the Chartered Institute of Marketing for their Postgraduate Diploma in Marketing and for membership of the institute. The marketing course is assessed by coursework including tutorial essays, a market research project and exams. In the first year, students must pass all three subjects in order to continue with their degree. In the second and third years, students take eight courses: four or five in marketing, the rest in subjects of their choice.

Contact details, see page 617

London School of Economics and Political Science (University of London)
BSc Management

This course is designed for people who want a broad preparation for management. It has a strong international flavour and places emphasis upon management as an applied social science. Students may also choose to specialise in one of the major social sciences during their studies. They also take courses enabling them to develop their knowledge of essential mathematical and statistical techniques. Examinations on the four courses studied over the year are taken in June. The class of degree attained is based on exam performance, with some emphasis placed on marks gained in the second and third years.

For further information, see page 508

The University of Manchester Institute of Science and Technology (UMIST)
BA (Hons) Management and Information Technology

This joint honours degree was launched in September 1998. Managing IT systems is as much about managing people as it is about managing technology. Organisations require people who possess both technical and management expertise and who must therefore understand the social and behavioural dimensions of management as well as appreciating the changing environment within which modern organisations must operate. The first year involves study of selected aspects of key disciplines such as economics, accounting, psychology, sociology, law, statistics and mathematics. In subsequent stages, the focus shifts to the various classes of management activity such as production, marketing, finance, personnel and strategy. It is also possible to study other approaches to management problems such as operational research, organisational behaviour and industrial relations.

Contact details, see page 618

North Highland College
BA in Golf Management

This degree is designed to produce a new breed of managers who can deal in every area of the golf industry, including golf tourism and event management. The three-year course consists of 24 modules (eight per year, of which 17 are compulsory and the remaining seven optional) selected from a range of 13 golf and business subjects. The programme is taught through a variety of methods, such as formal lectures, videos, case studies and site visits. The course takes place in a listed building, situated a few yards from the Royal Dornoch Golf Club, with which it enjoys a close working relationship. This course prepares students for employment in a wide range of management posts in golf facilities and industry-based scenarios. Successful completion of the ordinary degree may allow students

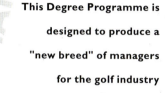

to progress to an honours degree in areas such as business or sports management.
Contact details, see page 619

University of North London
BA Single Honours E-commerce/
BA Combined Honours (Major, Joint, Minor)
The course focuses on the management of e-business, rather than wholly on technical aspects. Included are marketing, finance, management and business strategy, all studied in relation to online business. This programme recognises the growth of e-commerce transactions and the impact of e-commerce on virtually every sector of the international economy. It examines the ways in which developments in communications and information technologies are transforming aspects of the business environment. Particular attention is paid to supply chain relationships and the means whereby business relates to consumers. The single honours programme also focuses on the changes in organisational structures and functions which are taking place in response to these technological developments.
For further information, see page 520

Oxford Brookes University
BA (Hons) Business and
Human Resource Management
This degree is one of several offered by the Oxford Brookes Business School. In the first year, the focus is on developing an overview of business, its environment and management and on familiarisation with some of the skills necessary for effective business operation. In years two and three, students build on the core business competencies, including the knowledge and skills established during

the first year. Study includes an introduction to personnel and human resource management, with other modules such as employment law and organisation development. There is the opportunity to choose further modules such as training and development and employee relations. Students can undertake a one-year business placement after they have completed the second year. In the final year, students work on a dissertation, which incorporates an extended study of a topic from the course.

For further information, see page 532

Richmond, The American International University in London

BA (Hons) Business Administration: E-commerce

This innovative programme aims to put graduates on the fast track for careers in e-commerce and entrepreneurship by providing them with the skills necessary to plan and manage the virtual technology resource requirements of organisations. It covers interactive media, multimedia authoring for the internet, direct and electronic marketing, business-to-business marketing and strategic e-commerce planning and implementation. Richmond offers five different degrees in business administration. All share a common set of courses in the first two years, introducing the different functional areas of business and reflecting the strategic areas in business activity where organisations make decisions and choices about how to allocate and utilise scarce resources to achieve their goals and objectives. The business administration degree subjects offered include business economics, e-commerce, finance, international business and marketing.

For further information, see page 428

The University of Strathclyde

BA (Hons) International Business and Modern Languages

This five-year programme is designed for students who wish to acquire a firm foundation in the essential business subjects, combined with an ability to communicate and conduct business or public affairs internationally. The first three years combine the study of core business subjects such as economics, finance and marketing, along with two modern languages selected from French, German, Italian, Spanish and Russian. Students spend their fourth year at an overseas business school or equivalent, normally in the country of their main European language. In the fifth year, most of the time will be taken up by a dissertation on a business topic with a synopsis of the dissertation written in a foreign language.

For further information, see page 568

Postgraduate

Cardiff University

MA International Public Relations

To public relations professionals, the core responsibility of their job is to assist organisations or clients in the careful management of information flow and their hard won reputations. Increasingly, they have to deal with organisations which operate in an international context, across borders and political, social and cultural divides. This is Europe's first master's degree in the field of international public relations. It is aimed at aspiring global professionals, those who want to work for emerging multicultural corporations, government agencies, non-governmental organisations, single-issue groups and charities.

Courses are designed by a multinational team including some of the world's leading practitioners in the field. Students write a 20,000-word dissertation; a major piece of independent work which allows them to design an authentic public relations strategy for a real world organisation.

Contact details, see page 614

Cranfield University
MBA

This course is suitable for ambitious managers with a good degree and at least three years' full-time work experience. It is designed to help develop management skills to a depth and breadth that could never be attained through work experience alone. Typically, people use an MBA to accelerate or change their career, for example to move from a specialist to a more general management role. During the first two terms, students increase their knowledge of the basic elements of business management. In part two of the programme, there is the opportunity to choose from a wide range of elective courses and project work. Students can concentrate on a particular area such as e-commerce, entrepreneurship, finance, marketing or human resource management or a more broad mix of topics.

Contact details, see page 615

Leeds Metropolitan University
MA Business Studies and
MA International Business

The MA Business Studies is a multidisciplinary programme for students whose first degree is not in business studies. The MA in International Business is aimed at graduates and practising managers who are required to work in internal and global environments, particularly those

Business, management and marketing

not based in the UK. Core modules cover international business strategy, the international business environment and cross-cultural management. The university also runs an MBA programme, which is designed with the needs of aspiring managers in mind. It has been designed to develop more innovative, enterprising and effective managers with the requisite knowledge, skills and managerial competencies to face the opportunities and challenges of the 21st century.

For further information, see page 500

The University of Stirling
MSc in Marketing

This 12-month programme has been developed in response to the need for highly qualified and trained marketers who are well equipped for intellectually-demanding positions in business, academia and the public services. The aim is to provide well-qualified participants with an understanding of the concepts and systems underlying marketing practice and to develop their skills of diagnosis and implementation in marketing management and research processes. Graduates of the MSc can expect to develop a successful career in marketing or general management in a variety of organisations and policy environments. Recent graduates have built careers in product management, marketing research, media planning, account management, logistics, sales planning and control in organisations of various sizes operating internationally in many different sectors. An MSc in Retail Management is also available.

For further information, see page 566

Useful links

www.abeuk.com	▶	The Association of Business Executives
www.the-abs.org.uk	▶	The Association of Business Schools
www.britishchambers.org.uk	▶	The British Chambers of Commerce
www.cim.co.uk	▶	The Chartered Institute of Marketing
www.cipd.co.uk	▶	Chartered Institute of Personnel and Development
www.dti.gov.uk	▶	Department of Trade and Industry
www.inst-mgt.org.uk	▶	The Institute of Management
www.imc.co.uk	▶	Institute of Management Consultancy

Business, management and marketing

Chemistry

Chemistry is perhaps the most creative of all subjects, giving you the scope to create new substances, discover what makes organisms live and think, while allowing you to spend three years at university blowing things up. Its vast spectrum makes it perhaps the most wide-ranging of all sciences, overlapping as it does with so many areas of biology and physics.

The last two centuries have seen rapid expansion in the development of chemistry as a discipline and today it is at a more exciting stage than ever. The over-confidence in the ability of science to tame nature has been replaced by an impetus to work in harmony with the world around us. Chemistry's response to these challenges means that it continues to be at the cutting edge of modern existence.

The study of chemistry involves both exploration and creation. The former through continued discovery of how chemical reactions make humans and their surroundings tick, and the latter by developing processes and materials to help us utilise the energy and resources available from our environment.

Chemistry degrees vary between three-year straight chemistry degrees to four or five-year undergraduate MChem, MSc or MSci degrees, to combined studies courses. Some courses include a sandwich year with an industrial placement. Master's degrees are particularly suitable for students who want to make a career out of chemistry or progress to research. Standard chemistry honours

degrees give broad coverage of the subject and allow you to specialise, to an extent, in your final years. Optional courses allow you to tailor your degree to suit your interests.

Teaching is carried out in a number of ways including lectures, small group tutorials, seminars and practical laboratory classes. Students are usually required to make use of computer-assisted learning materials and project work. They are taught to develop their skills in report writing, presentations, numeracy, IT and information retrieval.

You can combine chemistry with other sciences such as physics or the biological sciences. These joint honours courses enable you to pursue any interests you have in outside areas, while being taught a core of chemistry, allowing you to follow careers or research in various interdisciplinary areas. There are also vocationally-oriented degrees which allow you to become a professionally-qualified chemist with skills to contribute towards a career in business or management.

For those students who chose to enrol on four or five-year MChem, MSci or MSc degrees, the additional year allows you to apply your knowledge to practical problems and develop your skills as a professional scientist. There is also emphasis on private study and on individual and group project work. Laboratory and library-based study, problem solving and essay and report writing are also important features.

TEACHING QUALITY ASSESSMENTS

Chemistry
(England and Northern Ireland) 1993/94

tqa

Institution	Grade	Institution	Grade
University of Bristol	Excellent	Keele University	Satisfactory
Cambridge University	Excellent	King's College London	
The University of Durham	Excellent	(University of London)	Satisfactory
The University of Hull	Excellent	Kingston University	Satisfactory
Imperial College of Science, Technology		Leeds Metropolitan University	Satisfactory
and Medicine (University of London)	Excellent	The University of Liverpool	Satisfactory
University of Leeds	Excellent	Liverpool John Moores University	Satisfactory
University of Leicester	Excellent	The Manchester	
The University of Manchester	Excellent	Metropolitan University	Satisfactory
The University of Nottingham	Excellent	University of North London	Satisfactory
The Nottingham Trent University	Excellent	University of Portsmouth	Satisfactory
Open University	Excellent	The University of Reading	Satisfactory
Oxford University	Excellent	The University of Salford	Satisfactory
University of Southampton	Excellent	Staffordshire University	Satisfactory
Aston University	Satisfactory	University of Sunderland	Satisfactory
University of Bath	Satisfactory	University of Sussex	Satisfactory
The University of Birmingham	Satisfactory	University of Teesside	Satisfactory
De Montfort University	Satisfactory	The University of Manchester Institute	
University of East Anglia	Satisfactory	of Science and Technology (UMIST)	Satisfactory
The University of Essex	Satisfactory	University College London	
University of Exeter	Satisfactory	(University of London)	Satisfactory
University of Greenwich	Satisfactory	The University of Warwick	Satisfactory
The University of Huddersfield	Satisfactory	The University of York	Satisfactory

Chemistry
(England and Northern Ireland) 1998/99

tqa

Canterbury Christ Church University College	21

Chemistry
(Scotland) 1993/94

tqa

Institution	Grade	Institution	Grade
The University of Edinburgh	Excellent	University of	
University of Glasgow	Excellent	Abertay Dundee	Highly Satisfactory
Glasgow Caledonian University	Excellent	Heriot-Watt University,	
The Robert Gordon University	Excellent	Edinburgh	Highly Satisfactory
University of St Andrews	Excellent	Napier University	Highly Satisfactory
The University of Strathclyde	Excellent	University of Paisley	Highly Satisfactory
The University of Aberdeen	Highly Satisfactory	University of Dundee	Satisfactory

Chemistry
(Wales) 1993/94

tqa

Institution	Grade	Institution	Grade
University of Wales, Bangor	Excellent	The North East Wales	
Cardiff University	Excellent	Institute of Higher Education	Satisfactory
University of Glamorgan	Satisfactory	University of Wales Swansea	Satisfactory

Source: HEFCE, SHEFC, HEFCW latest available ratings
For a more complete list of institutions offering these courses at undergraduate level refer to the Course Directory

Specialist and vocational

The Robert Gordon University

HND Applied Chemistry

This course is designed to provide a foundation in a wide range of chemical principles supported by basic study in biology and physics. Highly practical and relevant to the needs of industry, this course combines theory and practice to equip students with a broad range of skills. The emphasis is on analytical chemistry and, along with the laboratory programme, this helps students to develop problem-solving, communication and IT skills.

For further information, see page 546

Chemistry

Institution	Grade	Institution	Grade
University of Bristol	5*	Heriot-Watt University, Edinburgh	4
Cambridge University	5*	The University of Hull	4
The University of Durham	5*	King's College London (University of London)	4
Imperial College of Science, Technology and Medicine (University of London)	5*	University of Leicester	4
		Loughborough University	4
Oxford University	5*	The University of Manchester Institute of Science and Technology (UMIST)	4
University College London (University of London)	5*	University of Newcastle upon Tyne	4
The University of Birmingham	5	Queen's University Belfast	4
University of East Anglia	5	The University of Reading	4
The University of Edinburgh	5	The University of Strathclyde	4
University of Leeds	5	University of Wales, Swansea	4
The University of Liverpool	5	The University of Aberdeen	3a
The University of Manchester	5	University of Wales, Bangor	3a
The University of Nottingham	5	De Montfort University	3a
The University of Sheffield	5	Keele University	3a
University of Southampton	5	The North East Wales	
University of Sussex	5	Institute of Higher Education	3a
University of St Andrews	5	The Nottingham Trent University	3a
The University of Warwick	5	Open University	3a
The University of York	5	Queen Mary, University of London	3a
University of Bath	4	The University of Surrey	3a
Cardiff University	4	The University of Huddersfield	3b
University of Exeter	4	Northumbria University	3b
University of Glasgow	4		

Source: RAE 2001

Undergraduate

University of Bath

BSc Chemistry

The Chemistry Department at the University of Bath has an excellent research facility, influencing the teaching at both undergraduate and postgraduate level. The first two years introduce a broad range of topics to give students a thorough grounding in chemistry. This allows them to discover areas of special interest to study in depth in the final year. They receive training in computer skills and can study a variety of options in the first year, including management or languages. Students get the opportunity to do short research projects in their final year, conducted in the department's fully-equiped research laboratories. Students without satisfactory mathematics must follow an introductory course. For students opting for a four-year course, the third year can be spent studying at an overseas university or, more commonly, as a work placement. Assessment for the degree is via a combination of continuous assessment tasks and end-of-semester exams.

For further information, see page 444

The University of Durham

MChem (Hons) Chemistry

This is a four-year degree in which students cover all aspects of chemistry with the opportunity to pursue specialisms of particular interest or relevance to future careers, especially in scientific research and development. It is also the normal route to a PhD degree. In the first year, students have a broad introduction to inorganic chemistry, organic chemistry, physical chemistry and mathematics or chemistry. The fourth-year research project will, for most students, be based at

Chemistry

147

Student Profile

Purvi Bhatia
Kenya
BSc Chemistry
University of Bath

"As a keen traveller, I thought studying abroad would give me the chance to visit a different place and learn about its culture. I chose Bath because it has a friendly atmosphere. Everything is within walking distance – shops, bars and the university. I feel at home, mainly because of the campus life – people are really friendly and everyone knows each other. I enjoy being independent and the challenge of being away from home. I find that I now know myself better and have become more responsible. In the third year, you go on a placement within a company or another university. In my placement year, I studied at the Simon Fraser University in Canada and really enjoyed meeting new people and experiencing a different style of education. Long-term, I plan to get a job in the UK. The people here are great and very helpful."

course has been developed in consultation with the pharmaceutical industry. This degree concentrates on the medicinal and pharmaceutical aspects of chemistry, preparing students for careers as chemists in the industry. In the first year, students study fundamentals including inorganic, organic, physical and analytical chemistry, as well as essential practical skills including an appropriate level of IT and mathematics. The second year provides a background to medicinal chemistry with modules on pharmacology and analytical chemistry. Optional modules are also available on topics concerned with the pharmaceutical industry. The final year includes a research project on a topic chosen by the student.

For further information, see page 528

Oxford University
BA/MChem (Hons) Chemistry

Chemistry at Oxford is a four-year course. The first three years are conventionally structured, with final exams at the end of the third. The fourth year, consists of a single research project. The first year is spent on chemistry, mathematics and one chosen option, while the second and third years concentrate more exclusively on mainstream chemistry, although there is an opportunity to pursue supplementary courses in related areas. The fourth-year research project is unique to Oxford. A variety of projects are available in both pure and applied chemistry and in related sciences. The year's work results in a thesis, the assessment of which counts towards about one quarter of the MChem degree. While it is possible to leave after three years with an unclassified BA (Hons) degree, this is unusual as students tend to benefit from and enjoy the final year's research.

For further information, see page 534

the university, although there are opportunities to carry out work in industry or at another European university. The programme involves a mixture of lectures, tutorials, workshops, practical work and a dissertation of 3,000 words. Transfer from the three-year programme to the four-year is possible up to the start of year two. A transfer from four years to three may be made as late as the first month of the third year.

Contact details, see page 615

The Nottingham Trent University
BSc (Hons) Medicinal Chemistry

The department at The Nottingham Trent University has close ties with clinical laboratories and the medicinal chemistry

Postgraduate

Aston University
MChem Chemical Product Technology

This is an enhanced chemistry degree which focuses on processes, products and 'designer' chemicals. Designer chemicals are developed to meet individual customer's specific needs and are particularly common in the pharmaceutical, adhesive, packaging, clothing and food industries. The majority of the programme is chemistry based but it can incorporate modules from the chemical engineering strand. Final-year assessments are largely based on a major practical design and research project. The programme caters for the needs of pure chemists while providing the opportunity to explore the industrial, pharmaceutical, technological and commercial dimensions of chemistry and enabling students to develop valuable skills such as management.

Contact details, see page 613

University College London
(University of London)
Chemistry PhD Studentships

Students interested in applying for a postgraduate studentship should have (or expect to have) at least an upper second degree, master's degree or overseas equivalent in a relevant discipline. All higher degrees in chemistry at UCL incorporate a large research component. Thus, students study under the direct supervision of a member of the academic staff who is an expert in his or her particular field. Although working for a higher degree involves considerable specialisation on the part of the student, the department ensures that a student's broader chemical background and general transferable skills are developed. In the final year, students are eligible to enter for the prestigious Ramsay Medal which is awarded to the best PhD student in that graduating year.

Contact details, see page 622

EDUCATI🇺🇰N

www.educationuk.org

Useful links

www.chemsoc.org	▶	The Chemistry Society's Network
www.chemweb.com	▶	Chemweb.com
www.environmentalchemistry.com	▶	Environmental Chemistry
www.nobelprizes.com/nobel /chemistry/	▶	The Nobel Prize Internet Archive: Chemistry
www.rsc.org	▶	Royal Society of Chemistry
www.chemdex.org	▶	The Sheffield Chemdex
www.webelements.com	▶	Web Elements: The Periodic Table on the Net

Classics

It is fair to say that virtually everything we regard as Western culture originated within the Greek and Roman empires. Literature, philosophy, art, theatre and politics all have their origins in the classic civilisations. The prevailing view of classics as a degree subject is one of poring over the *Iliad* in a dusty library and reciting Latin verb declensions. Today, however, the subject is becoming more widely studied and is being recognised for its vibrant, multidisciplinary content. Knowing Greek, said Bernard Shaw, "stamps a man at once as an educated gentleman."

Traditionally, studying classics meant studying the Greek and Latin languages and reading, translating and criticising Greek and Latin texts. Today, however, most university courses still have Greek and Latin at their core but also put considerable emphasis on the teaching of the history, art, architecture, religion and philosophy of Greece and Rome. Each institution will specialise in different areas of interest, so it is worth finding out what each course specifically involves before applying. Classics courses can go under a number of guises, such as ancient history or classical civilisation, which focus more directly on specific areas of study.

Within the classics are four main areas of study: literature, history, philosophy and language. These components can be combined at university and also lend themselves to joint honours degrees. Single honours classics degrees are typically based on Latin and/or Greek literature and language. Modules such as Greek language, Latin love poetry, Greek tragedy and Greek and Latin textual criticism are often taught. Courses entitled classical civilisations or ancient history cover the whole Greco-Roman achievement. This can include the study of the thought, religion and culture of these civilisations. Most ancient history or classics courses involve a dissertation where students focus on a specific area of interest.

Classics is a European discipline; many of the books and articles you read will have been translated into English from French, German or Italian, or written by non-English speaking scholars. While studying, you will meet students from other countries studying classics in Britain and you may have the opportunity to travel to Greece or Italy for research. Prospective students should be able to demonstrate a broad interest in the field.

Because of the decline in popularity of classics as an A level subject, universities and colleges are encouraging applications from students who would not have had the qualifications to apply a few years ago. Most universities accept those with no experience of Greek, provided they start learning it on arrival and reach a certain standard by the time they finish. Command of the language is important, since a significant part of any course involves the translation and close study of Latin and Greek texts.

Classics and Ancient History
(Wales) 1997/98

tqa

Institution	Grade	Institution	Grade
The University of Wales, Lampeter	Excellent	University of Wales, Swansea	Excellent

Classics and Ancient History
(England) 2000/01

tqa

Institution	Grade	Institution	Grade
Cambridge University	24	Royal Holloway and Bedford New College	23
King's College London		The University of Warwick	23
(University of London)	24	University of Exeter	22
The University of Nottingham	24	University of Kent	22
Open University	24	University of Newcastle upon Tyne	22
Oxford University	24	The University of Durham	21
Queen's University Belfast	23	University of Leeds	19

Source: HEFCE, SHEFC, HEFCW latest available ratings
For a more complete list of institutions offering these courses at undergraduate level refer to the Course Directory

Undergraduate

Cambridge University
BA Classics

The aim of this degree is to provide a broad-based study of classical antiquity, with a flexible series of options which allow you to follow either a specialist path or a more general approach. Teaching is divided between lectures, classes and college supervision. Students normally attend 12 lectures a week in the first two years, together with two or more language classes a week. Seminars and lectures are still attended in the final year but a less intensive supervision programme allows in-depth essay research. Potential students must have a competent command of either Latin or Greek. Preferably, candidates should have A level, AS or A2 level or equivalent in Latin or Greek.
Contact details, see page 614

The University of Manchester
BA (Hons) Classical Studies

The BA (Hons) Classical Studies programme offers a broad study of the culture and history of the Greek and Roman worlds. It is available to students who have no previous knowledge of Greek or Latin. It is also open to those who have studied Greek and Latin at A level but who wish to combine the study of classical languages and literature with another course. All students reading classical studies also take a course in Greek or Roman history and it is possible to specialise in this area. In the second and third years, the element of choice increases and students are offered a range of topics which may vary from year to year. Those currently available include comedy at Athens; Greek lyric poetry; Latin, Greek and Indo-European; reading ancient texts today; Vergil; classical Sparta; Rome and Italy 343 BC to AD 14; ancient political thought; and governors and provinces.
For further information, see page 514

Postgraduate

The University of Birmingham
MA Classics

The classics department at Birmingham specialises in Greek and Roman literature, thought and culture. The MA in classics is open to graduates with a good degree in any area of classical studies or related disciplines. There are six taught modules, leading to a 12,000-word dis-

Classics

Institution	Grade	Institution	Grade
Cambridge University	5*	University of St Andrews	5
Institute of Classical Studies	5*	The University of Warwick	5
King's College London (University of London)	5*	The University of Edinburgh	4
Oxford University	5*	University of Glasgow	4
University College London (University of London)	5*	University of Leeds	4
Warburg Institute	5*	The University of Liverpool	4
The University of Birmingham (Centre for Byzantine, Ottoman and Modern Greek Studies)	5	The University of Nottingham	4
		Queen's University Belfast	4
University of Bristol	5	University of Wales Swansea	4
The University of Durham	5	The University of Birmingham (Classics)	3a
University of Exeter	5	The University of Wales, Lampeter	3a
The University of Manchester	5	University of Newcastle upon Tyne	3a
The University of Reading	5	Open University	3a
Royal Holloway, University of London	5		

Source: RAE 2001

sertation. Three of the modules are designed to develop the skills you would need for advanced work in classics, two of which consist of linguistic tuition in Latin and Greek, the other of which gives training in classical research. The remaining modules are chosen from a wide range of options in literature and culture. They draw as fully as possible on the research interests of staff, enabling students to move on smoothly, if they wish, to research projects within the department. Postgraduates in classics take part in regular presentations to the department, as well as to the Midlands Consortium with the universities of Nottingham and Warwick.

Contact details, see page 613

University of Bristol

MA in Classics

The MA in Classics at Bristol is designed to develop students' reading and interpreting skills in many different areas. They receive an overview of different theoretical approaches to the study of the past as well as training in research methods. During the first part of the one-year course, students attend a number of taught units including the compulsory theories and approaches course, of which there are two parts, each assessed by a 5,000-word essay. During the second half of the year, students carry out individual research under the guidance of an academic supervisor, after which they submit a 15,000-word dissertation.

For further information, see page 454

Useful links

www.thebritishmuseum.ac.uk	●	The British Museum
www.gla.ac.uk/library/cas	●	Classical Association of Scotland
www.sas.ac.uk/icls/classass	●	The Classical Association
www.sas.ac.uk/icls	●	Institute of Classical Studies
www.soa.org.uk	●	Society of Ancients

Classics

Computing and IT

Computers and information technology have become as powerful as they have inescapable. Bill Gates is the richest man in the world, his fortune according to *Forbes* standing at $90 billion (£54.3 billion), on the back of his computer empire. Not only do computers play an important part in our working lives, with few businesses able to operate efficiently without them, they are also adopting an increasingly important role in our leisure pursuits. The advent of email and the internet has meant that we can now chat with friends, do our shopping or book a holiday, all at the touch of a button.

Despite much of the technological impetus coming from the USA, with the huge influence of Microsoft and Intel, Britain has made a significant contribution to the research and development of computers, having devised the first working prototypes in the 1940s and 1950s. The UK also has over eight million internet users, the third highest amount in the world behind the USA and Japan.

Computer science is essentially the study of information and computation. Its multidisciplinary nature means that it has ties with a number of other subjects including psychology, maths and engineering. Typical first-year modules include the mathematical foundations of computing, basic programming and the practical aspects of computer systems. Subsequent years allow students to specialise in fields such as computer architecture, system modelling and artificial intelligence. Teaching is through lectures and seminars and most courses involve laboratory work with hands-on computer experience. Courses are likely to involve an industrial placement, either during the summer vacation or through a sandwich year as part of the course.

As the importance of computers in all aspects of our lives continues to grow, so too does the range of courses available. Apart from degrees, there are many postgraduate and research opportunities. Some can be used as conversion courses from another subject. Many institutions also offer HNDs lasting one or two years. For those who want a practical introduction to the basics, such as word processing, spreadsheets or databases, there is a large number of shorter computing and IT courses at private or specialist colleges and adult education centres.

Most people have regular contact with IT yet there are still relatively few people who have an in-depth knowledge of how computers and information systems work. This has meant that over recent years, the computing and information technology sectors have been growing much faster than the supply of skilled workers. Armed with an IT qualification, you should find yourself in hot demand. A computing degree can lead to a number of different jobs, from designing and building complex computer systems, to writing programming languages or designing web pages.

Babel Technical College

This small college was established in 1984 and is based in David Game House in Notting Hill, London. The college provides practical, vocational, professional and academic courses in computing and information technology at levels suitable for the office and at more advanced computing and programming levels. All the courses are certified by external institutions such as City & Guilds, Pitman, Cisco and Cambridge University. City & Guilds diplomas and advanced diplomas are offered in computer applications, business and office technology, data processing and information systems, programming and networking. Diploma courses last for two terms and advanced diplomas for three terms. The Cisco CCNA runs for three terms. Courses can be full time, part time or in the evening. Students are taught in small groups, averaging seven, through lectures and supervised hands-on experience in the college's five computer laboratories.

For further information, see page 388

Cavendish College

Established in 1985 in central London, this private college offers both academic and vocational courses. Both full and part-time courses can be taken in business studies, hospitality and tourism, secretarial training, creative studies, computer studies, media studies and English language. The college offers modern facilities and has recently established its own cybercafé where students can relax and use the internet for recreational purposes. Courses are continually updated to reflect the market and therefore meet changing demand. The college has a diverse international student population from over 80

different countries around the world. The Computer Studies Department offers courses which aim to prepare students for work in a rapidly-changing environment. Facilities include five, well-equipped computer suites offering the latest software packages. Students are encouraged to make full use of these facilities in their own time.

For further information, see page 410

Harrogate College

Advanced Vocational Certificate in Information and Communication Technology

This is a two-year, full-time course although exceptional students can complete it within one year. Students must complete 12 units of study in total. In the first year, they must complete modules including ICT serving organisations, spreadsheet design, multimedia and internet systems. In year two, they study certain core modules and choose three units from a range of modules, allowing them to develop their personal career profile. There are four pathways available incorporating hardware, networking, programming, business applications or a pathway of the student's choice. On completion of the course, many progress to further specialist study and others enter employment in ICT related fields.

For further information, see page 418

Hastings College of Arts and Technology

Hastings College of Arts and Technology was established in 1956 but its origins date back to 1891. It is located just outside the historic seaside town of Hastings, which today is a thriving artistic and cultural centre with a lively music scene. Hastings College has over 12,000 students studying on a full and part-time basis, including many international students. The college has modern facilities and fantastic sea views and Hastings offers a low cost of living. The college has both vocational and academic information technology courses from intermediate to higher levels. The two-year Higher National Diploma in Computing has a second year emphasis on internet programming and the two-year Higher National Diploma in Multimedia Studies focuses on the design and production of CDs and website. There are strong links between the information technology courses and the art and design programmes.

For further information, see page 422

London Institute of Technology and English (LITE)

Computing courses

LITE's computing department offers courses from Microsoft Office skills, programming in Visual Basic object-oriented environ-

ment, Java script or programming, web design in HTML, Flash, Dreamweaver, databases and Photoshop, amongst others. These courses are taught following the City & Guilds syllabus and for which LITE is an accredited centre. LITE's computing facilities are well equipped with the latest technology and its ASDL/ISDL web browsing facilities ensure the quickest possible access to the internet. Thus, beginners in computing who are seeking to gain office skills in information technology are catered for, as well as more proficient users.

For further information, see page 400

Queen's Business and Secretarial College

Queen's was founded in 1924 and caters for international students, school leavers and graduates, running courses of varying lengths which cover business and computing

Computing and IT

155

TEACHING QUALITY ASSESSMENTS

Computer Science
(England and Northern Ireland) 1994/95

Institution	Grade	Institution	Grade
Cambridge University	Excellent	Keele University	Satisfactory
University of Exeter	Excellent	Kingston University	Satisfactory
Imperial College of Science, Technology and Medicine (University of London)	Excellent	Lancaster University	Satisfactory
		University of Leeds	Satisfactory
The University of Kent	Excellent	University of Luton	Satisfactory
The University of Manchester	Excellent	The University of Manchester Institute of Science and Technology (UMIST)	Satisfactory
Oxford University	Excellent	University of Newcastle upon Tyne	Satisfactory
University of Southampton	Excellent	Northumbria University	Satisfactory
University of Teesside	Excellent	The University of Nottingham	Satisfactory
The University of Warwick	Excellent	The Nottingham Trent University	Satisfactory
The University of York	Excellent	Open University	Satisfactory
Blackburn College	Satisfactory	Oxford Brookes University	Satisfactory
Bournemouth University	Satisfactory	University of Plymouth	Satisfactory
University of Brighton	Satisfactory	Queen Mary, University of London	Satisfactory
Buckinghamshire Chilterns University College	Satisfactory	Queen's University Belfast	Satisfactory
		The University of Reading	Satisfactory
Canterbury Christ Church University College	Satisfactory	Royal Holloway, University of London	Satisfactory
Chester (A College of the University of Liverpool)	Satisfactory	Salford College	Satisfactory
		The University of Sheffield	Satisfactory
City University	Satisfactory	Sheffield Hallam University	Satisfactory
De Montfort University	Satisfactory	Suffolk College (An Accredited College of the University of East Anglia)	Satisfactory
University of Derby	Satisfactory	University of Sunderland	Satisfactory
The University of Durham	Satisfactory	Thames Valley University	Satisfactory
The University of Essex	Satisfactory	University of Ulster	Satisfactory
Farnborough College of Technology	Satisfactory	University College London (University of London)	Satisfactory
University of Hertfordshire	Satisfactory		
The University of Huddersfield	Satisfactory		

Computer Studies
(Scotland) 1994

Institution	Grade	Institution	Grade
The University of Edinburgh	Excellent	University of Abertay Dundee	Satisfactory
University of Glasgow	Excellent	University of Dundee	Satisfactory
Heriot-Watt University, Edinburgh	Highly Satisfactory	Glasgow Caledonian University	Satisfactory
		Napier University	Satisfactory
University of St Andrews	Highly Satisfactory	University of Paisley	Satisfactory
The University of Strathclyde	Highly Satisfactory	The Robert Gordon University	Satisfactory
The University of Aberdeen	Satisfactory	The University of Stirling	Satisfactory

Computer Science and Computer Studies
(Wales) 1993/94

Institution	Grade	Institution	Grade
University of Wales Swansea	Excellent	University of Wales College, Newport	Satisfactory
The University of Wales, Aberystwyth	Satisfactory	The North East Wales Institute of Higher Education	Satisfactory
Cardiff University	Satisfactory		
University of Wales Institute, Cardiff	Satisfactory	Swansea Institute of Higher Education	Satisfactory
University of Glamorgan	Satisfactory		

Source: HEFCE, SHEFC, HEFCW latest available ratings
For a more complete list of institutions offering these courses at undergraduate level refer to the Course Directory

skills and business English. There are three courses with a business focus and these require students to have a high level of English language skills. The Diploma in Marketing and Business Skills is completed in three terms. The students take the LCCI level III examinations in PR, marketing and advertising, as well as learning the Microsoft Office packages and business administration skills. The two-term diploma course provides students with the IT and business skills to work as a PA for

Computing and IT

KINGSTON

Computer Science

Institution	Grade	Institution	Grade
Cambridge University	5*	University of Hertfordshire	4
The University of Edinburgh	5*	The University of Kent	4
Imperial College of Science, Technology and Medicine (University of London)	5*	King's College London (University of London)	4
The University of Manchester	5*	University of Leicester	4
University of Southampton	5*	The University of Manchester Institute of Science and Technology (UMIST) (Language Engineering, Computer Science)	4
The University of York	5*		
The University of Birmingham	5		
University of Bristol	5	Queen Mary, University of London	4
Cardiff University	5	Queen's University Belfast	4
University of Glasgow	5	The University of Reading	4
Lancaster University	5	South Bank University	4
University of Leeds	5	University of Ulster	4
The University of Liverpool	5	The University of Huddersfield	3a
University of Newcastle upon Tyne	5	The University of Hull	3a
The University of Nottingham	5	Liverpool John Moores University	3a
Oxford University	5	Loughborough University	3a
University of Plymouth	5	The Manchester Metropolitan University	3a
Royal Holloway, University of London	5	Middlesex University	3a
The University of Sheffield	5	The Nottingham Trent University	3a
University of Sussex	5	Open University	3a
University of St Andrews	5	University of Sunderland	3a
University of Wales Swansea	5	University of the West of England, Bristol	3a
University College London (University of London)	5	University of Westminster	3a
The University of Warwick	5	Napier University	3a
The University of Aberdeen	4	University of Paisley	3a
The University of Wales, Aberystwyth	4	The Robert Gordon University	3a
University of Bath	4	The University of Strathclyde	3a
Birkbeck College (University of London)	4	Goldsmiths College (University of London)	3b
The University of Bradford	4	Keele University	3b
University of Brighton	4	Kingston University	3b
City University	4	London Guildhall University	3b
De Montfort University	4	University of North London	3b
University of Dundee	4	Oxford Brookes University	3b
The University of Durham	4	Sheffield Hallam University	3b
University of East Anglia	4	Glasgow Caledonian University	3b
The University of Essex	4	The University of Stirling	3b
University of Exeter	4	Bournemouth University	2
University of Glamorgan	4	Coventry University	2
University of Greenwich	4	Northumbria University	2
Heriot-Watt University, Edinburgh	4	University of Teesside	2
		University of Wolverhampton	2

Source: RAE 2001

senior management. A one-term course in intensive business skills or business technology is completed in 12 weeks. Students with an intermediate knowledge of English can take a one-term certificate or two-term diploma course especially designed to give them the necessary IT and administrative skills for their career at the same time as developing their business English.

Contact details, see page 612

Undergraduate

University of Abertay Dundee

BSc (Hons) Computer Games Technology

Close collaboration with the interactive industry means that many of the senior students secure work placements with games companies during vacations. Computing facilities at Abertay include a number of digital video, audio and console programming laboratories as well as the International Centre for Computing and Virtual Entertainment (IC-CAVE). This four-year degree focuses heavily on software engineering and mathematical modelling but personal creativity is also encouraged. Students learn about games genres, 2D and 3D game production skills, as well as learning to programme games consoles and PCs. In the fourth year, students are involved in the design of a complete game and the production of a personal research project. There are opportunities to learn Japanese and to spend time studying at Gifu University in Japan. Demand for this course is high and candidates should expect to be interviewed.

Contact details, see page 613

The University of Wales, Aberystwyth

BSc (Hons) Internet Computing

The Department of Computer Science at The University of Wales, Aberystwyth has introduced a new degree scheme in internet computing which has been open to applicants since October 2000. The course combines practical training in building and supporting internet applications to professional standards with study of the commercial, legal and technical context in which the internet operates. On the course, students learn to use the latest available technologies for constructing internet applications including programming languages, scripting and mark-up languages and design methods developed specifically for web usage. The scheme can be taken with or without a sandwich year, although the department strongly encourages students who have no previous industrial experience to take one.

For further information, see page 436

Bournemouth University

BSc (Hons) Software Engineering Management

Successful software entrepreneurs and managers possess both technical skills and business awareness. BSc (Hons) Software Engineering Management is a unique course designed to develop these capabilities through combining a detailed study of software development practices with an appreciation of engineering management approaches. This degree course encourages and promotes a professional approach to the production of high-quality software products and aims to produce graduates capable of effectively managing software projects. Teamwork is an important factor in software design and is emphasised throughout the course. This course also includes a year working in industry, which students find invaluable. Bournemouth is a large town on the south coast of England. Based by the sea, it enjoys a warm climate all year round.

For further information, see page 448

City University

BSc (Hons) Business Computing Systems

This four-year course is concerned with the development and management of computer-based information systems and services in all kinds of organisations. In the first year, students explore the basics of information technology and business systems, and study modules in business, database systems, programming and communication. In the second year, the focus is on the integration of computing technologies and organisations by looking at the design of information systems in general and by studying specific organisational needs. The third year is spent in employment with a professional organisation. The final year involves specialist study and a major individual research project.

Contact details, see page 615

Greenwich School of Management

BSc (Hons) in Business Management and Information Technology

Greenwich School of Management was founded in 1974 and is an affiliated college of The University of Hull. The undergraduate programmes are two-year accelerated courses and start dates are flexible, with students starting courses in February, June or October. The degree in business management and IT is split into three parts, each consisting of two semesters. In part one, students cover modules including statistics, computing, C programming, systems analysis and design, business organisation and policy, management and accounting. Part two includes Visual Basic programming, telecommunications, database systems, organisational behaviour and marketing. Part three covers project management, corporate strategy, information systems and human resources management. Assessment is by exam at the end of each module, as well as by course and project work.

For further information, see page 484

Imperial College of Science, Technology and Medicine (University of London)

MEng Information Systems Engineering

The information era is well and truly with us and has brought with it a rapidly-growing demand for graduates with a balanced education in computing and electrical engineering. The objective of this course is to educate students in the theoretical and practical aspects of the design and implementation of modern information systems. This requires graduates to be fully conversant with state-of-the-art techniques in electronics, communications and computing. As well as a thorough grounding in the subject, students on the MEng course undertake a sizeable individual project in their fourth year. This provides them with the opportunity to demonstrate independence and originality, to plan and organise a large project over a long period and to put into practice the techniques they have learnt.

Contact details, see page 617

The University of Kent

BSc Computer Science

A computer science degree from Kent equips students with programming, modelling and design skills which they will use throughout their careers. Students learn about the basics of computer technology, from architecture and languages to operating systems and networks. The course also covers the software engineering principles which underlie large-scale programme construction. This is explored through project work carried out individually and in groups. There is an optional year in industry, providing valuable experience in applying theoretical principles to day-to-day industrial work. During the course, students are given the opportunity to gain hands-on experience using state-of-the-art equipment in the department's graphics and networks laboratories.

Contact details, see page 617

Kingston University

BSc(Hons) Computer Science and related disciplines

Kingston University has a developing reputation as a centre of excellence for computing-related education. The first year features a common set of modules for all of the associated disciplines offered. This enables students to make a more informed choice as to the particular computing discipline most suited to them. The range of disciplines includes computer science, software engineering and computer information systems design. The course content is rapidly changing as state-of-the-art developments in IT are included year on year. All courses have a compulsory year in industry, providing the opportunity to gain invaluable work experience which enhances career prospects on graduation. For those wishing to continue their studies, there is an extensive MSc and research programme.

For further information, see page 496

The University of Leeds
School of Computing

The school offers four undergraduate degree programmes of three years' duration, leading to a BSc (Hons) in Computing, Computer Science, Information Systems or Cognitive Science. Each programme includes a core of technical computing and emphasis is placed on practical applications in areas of the school's research expertise including artificial intelligence and virtual working environments. Compulsory modules in professional development ensure students are prepared for the challenges of employment. International students are guaranteed accommodation throughout their course. The school also offers taught and research degree programmes of study for graduates. Supported research leads to PhD, MPhil, or MSc (research) programmes. The area of study can be chosen from either computer vision and language, knowledge repre-

Computing and IT

sentation and reasoning, scientific computation or visualisation, theoretical computer science and informatics. The two courses leading to MSc are information systems and distributed multimedia systems, both requiring 12 months' full-time study, assessed by exams, coursework and a project. Scholarships are available for undergraduate and postgraduate study.

Contact details, see page 617

University of North London
BSc (Hons) Computer Networks

This course provides students with a solid background in advanced software development with networking and telecommunications. Both the practical and theoretical skills necessary to produce computing professionals are emphasised. During the first year, students attend lectures and practical sessions in core modules including information technology applications, programming, internet technology and communications. Later on, students specialise in networking, software engineering, mobile telecommunications, WAP and internet technology, data modelling and databases, programming in C++, HTML, ASP and Java and rapid application development. An optional sandwich placement provides students with paid work experience. International applicants should have a background in either mathematics, statistics, computer studies, physics or electronics.

For further information, see page 520

Northumbria University
Computing

At undergraduate and postgraduate level, the university's School of Computing and Mathematics covers a wide range of courses in computing and IT. First degree courses allow students to take the general

BSc (Hons) Computing Studies or to focus on an application of computing such as business, industry, e-computing or multimedia. For students with the right educational background there are opportunities to transfer directly to the second or third year. There is the chance to spend a work placement year in the UK or another country. Master's degrees are offered in e-business, technology and computing software with specialisms in information systems design.

For further information, see page 526

University of Plymouth
BSc (Hons) Computing Informatics

The aim of this programme is to provide students with the technical knowledge and commercial acumen to become an effective link between the business literate and the computer literate. The first stage provides students with an introduction to the workings and applications of computers. The second stage strengthens the student's ability to apply the techniques associated with analysis, design and development of sophisticated information systems. The third year involves a 48-week period of professional training with an organisation in the UK or abroad. The final stage allows students to specialise in areas such as electronic commerce, networking and multimedia.

For further information, see page 536

Richmond, The American University in London
BSc (Hons) Computing: Computer Systems Engineering

Richmond educates computer systems engineers who are able to apply transferable skills to a wide range of computing activities, particularly in an international engineering context. Software engineering, computer architecture, graphic applications, programming languages, functional programming, data communications and operating systems are all included in this programme. Richmond offers three different degrees in computing. All share a common set of courses in the first two years, designed to provide a firm foundation in mathematics and computer application information systems. In the third and fourth years, students specialise and earn a degree in either computer systems engineering, computer graphics and multi-media systems or information systems. Richmond also offers BSc (Hons) degrees in systems engineering and management (BS) with either international management or information technology.

For further information, see page 428

Roehampton University of Surrey
MComp Computer Modelling and Simulation

One of the major uses of computing is to build models, as computer-based models can be used to learn more about some part of the real world. Models can be made to understand more about global warming, financial markets or the human brain, as well as how to control complex systems such as industrial processes or robots, or to create virtual realities. This undergraduate programme adopts a multidisciplinary approach to give students the skills they will need as computing professionals to build reliable models and simulations. The degree includes a broad grounding in mathematical and modelling techniques and core computing modules. A year of professional training in either the public or private sector is an integral part of the programme. In the final year, students choose options in which they learn about specialist areas of computing.

Contact details, see page 621

The University of Strathclyde
BSc (Hons) Computer Science

This course provides a sound foundation in the first two years. Students then select classes which cover programming, software design, business computing, computer networks and communications, artificial intelligence and advanced computer architecture. Before graduating, students work on a major computing project. A choice of specialist subjects in later years enables students to tailor the course to their interests and aspirations. The course is accredited by the British Computer Society (BCS).

For further information, see page 568

University of Wales Swansea
BSc Computer Science

The philosophy of this course is that levels one and two provide foundation knowledge that every computer scientist should know and level three comprises advanced study, including a substantial project and a sizeable range of options. These options are designed so students can specialise in areas which interest them including graphics, artificial intelligence, expert systems, silicon chip design, neural networks, logic, theory and microprocessor architecture. Most modules are taught via lectures but the department has recently started a series of industrial seminars in which visitors from industry help students to develop an awareness of the needs and demands of industry.

Contact details, see page 621

The University of York
BSc Computer Science

Computer science at York is a broad-based subject covering theory and hardware, practice and professional competence as well as intellectual adventure. The design of computer systems involves both hardware and software. The engineering approach of the course does not mean that hardware predominates, since software design is also an engineering activity, but rather that the hardware and software aspects are deliberately integrated into the design of systems. The early part of the course forms a solid foundation in the subject, while the later years allow for a sharpening of the focus and the greater exercise of creativity. Practical and project work receives great emphasis throughout the course.

For further information, see page 590

Postgraduate

University of Glasgow
MSc Information Technology

This challenging MSc in IT provides honours graduates with the intellectual tools and practical experience to enter the IT industry. To proceed to master's level, students must attain a high standard in the core of the course. This requires intensive study of fundamental aspects including Java programming, computer systems and information management. Students choose a further six electives and the university offers a range of application areas. The final part of the course involves a project chosen by the student, often comprising the application of techniques learnt on the course to an area in which they already have experience. This fast-paced course lasts 12 months and an excellent understanding of English is a pre-requisite for overseas students. Graduates are sought after and there is an excellent record of employers recruiting directly from the course.

For further information, see page 480

Leeds Metropolitan University
MSc Mobile and Distributed Computer Networks

This course is designed to meet the needs of people with graduate or equivalent qualifications in a computing discipline who wish to pursue career opportunities as specialists in mobile and distributed computer networking. It covers current developments in the underlying technology and the associated techniques and tools required for developing, maintaining and managing the elements of these complex systems.

For further information, see page 500

Useful links

www.awc-hq.org	▶	Association for Women in Computing
www.bcs.org.uk	▶	The British Computer Society
www.cssa.co.uk	▶	Computing Services and Software Association
www.itsupport.com	▶	IT Support
www.microsoft.com	▶	Microsoft
www.ncc.co.uk	▶	National Computing Centre
www.vnunet.com	▶	UK Technology News, Reviews and Downloads

Computing and IT

Drama and dance

Since Shakespeare and the King's Players worked magic to packed audiences in theatres on London's South Bank, Britain has been at the epicentre of the drama and dance world. Today, the crowds still flock to see a myriad of shows, from Theatre de Complicité's *Mnemonic* to Trevor Nunn's *Starlight Express*. The Royal Opera House is reaching new heights in innovation and aesthetic appeal with its recently-refurbished building in Covent Garden, and Matthew Bourne is leading British choreography proudly into the 21st century with the Royal National Theatre's current production of *South Pacific*.

Drama

For aspiring dramatists, designers, directors, actors, constructors, technicians and dramaturgs, there are two types of institutions in Britain where you can study drama: at university, where you receive a broader academic qualification, or at a specialist school, where you are trained in a more practical environment for work as a professional. Some drama schools have joined with universities to offer degree courses. Other schools, however, have eschewed this association, claiming that it is necessary for a creative institution to remain free to direct its own syllabus, unrestricted by the criteria of university validation.

Certain British drama schools are considered to be of undisputed excellence, with long traditions in the performing arts. Entrance is usually by audition, based on talent and potential to achieve in the chosen profession.

Drama schools aim to train their students in the fundamental skills needed to enter the professional worlds of theatre, television and film. All acting courses at drama schools provide tuition in voice, movement and acting but how these three are studied will differ widely. Students reading performance studies at university are taught about several styles of theatre, including Greek, Shakespearean, Restoration and 20th century. A drama or theatre studies degree, with its more academic approach, will include such areas as the history of theatre, playwrights and the history of directing.

Dance

Dance courses do take place at universities and colleges but are more commonly taken at specialist schools. At university, courses sometimes combine music, drama and dance or include a dance module in a drama course. They develop students' interpretive, creative and critical skills and awareness of dance in its cultural context. Choreography and production skills are key elements so students have the opportunity to perform and stage their own work. Gaining a qualification in dance may lead to a professional career with a dance company, or it may take you into areas such as dance therapy, community dance, or even into acting.

Specialist and vocational

The London Academy of Music and Dramatic Art (LAMDA)
Foundation Course
The one-year foundation course is arranged for people who wish to pursue a career in theatre in any of its many forms: actor, designer or stage manager. It is a useful course to take prior to drama school or university. The one-year course is structured over three terms and is open to all, including those with little or no experience. Practical classes are given in subjects including voice, movement and dance, acting and improvisation, technical aspects of the theatre, the history of English, verse and prose, play analysis, aspects of design and audition technique. Selection is by audition or interview, depending on experience and career intentions. The minimum age is 18 and though there is no upper age limit, those enrolled must be of good health and capable of undertaking the strenuous nature of some facets of the course.

Contact details, see page 612

Undergraduate

The University of Reading
BA (Hons) Film and Drama
The development of cinema and television as institutions has made it increasingly difficult to confine discussion of drama to theatre alone. On this degree, the emphasis is on the close study of films and plays/productions and on the consideration of critical debates and competing theories which have influenced discussion of film, drama and theatrical production over the past 125 years. Although it is critical in its orientation, the single subject course in film and drama places strong emphasis on

the importance of practical work as well. It is also possible to study film and drama as part of a combined subject degree. Students on both the single and combined subject degrees can become involved as performers and technicians in research productions, other students' practical projects and in lively extracurricular drama and film projects.

For further information, see page 544

Rose Bruford College
BA (Hons) Actor Musicianship
Primarily, the actor musician joins a company as an actor but is able to introduce musical skills to performance. These may be musical direction, composition or singing/instrumental work. To this end, the actor musician degree is a thorough and complete actor training, with musical skills encouraged and developed alongside. The degree offers three things: actor training, music-theatre performance and the technical and study skills needed to support both. All students are expected to have already developed musical abilities which the course builds upon and extends as theatre skills. To take this course, you need no previous experience of musical direction, composition or high level of music theory. You will need, however, an ability on keyboards or guitar to approximately grade 4/5 level plus some ability on one other instrument, which could be your singing voice.

For further information, see page 548

Royal Academy of Dramatic Art (RADA)
BA Acting
The acting course trains students who wish to earn a living working not only in the more traditional outlets but in the many alternative areas of theatre, film,

Dance, Drama and Cinematics
(England and Northern Ireland) 1997/98

tqa

Institution	Grade	Institution	Grade
The University of Hull	24	Liverpool Community College	21
The University of Kent	24	Liverpool John Moores University	21
Lancaster University	24	The University of Manchester	21
The University of Reading	24	Queen Mary, University of London	21
The University of Warwick	24	University of Surrey Roehampton	21
University of Bristol	23	The University of Salford	21
Brunel University	23	Southampton Institute	21
The Central School of Speech and Drama	23	University of Sunderland	21
Dartington College of Arts	23	North Riding College	20
Loughborough University	23	Rose Bruford College	20
The Manchester Metropolitan University	23	St Mary's College	20
Northern School of Contemporary Dance	23	The University of Surrey	20
Royal Holloway, University of London	23	University of East London	19
Bournemouth University	22	King Alfred's Winchester	19
Bretton Hall	22	Liverpool Hope	19
Canterbury Christ Church University College	22	Sheffield Hallam University	19
De Montfort University	22	St Martin's College,	
University of Exeter	22	Lancaster: Ambleside: Carlisle	19
Goldsmiths College (University of London)	22	University of Wolverhampton	19
Leeds Metropolitan University	22	University of Derby	18
Middlesex University	22	Suffolk College	18
Newcastle College	22	Chester (A College of	
University of North London	22	the University of Liverpool)	17
Northumbria University	22	The University of Huddersfield	17
University of Ulster	22	City College Manchester	16
The University of Birmingham	21	University of Hertfordshire	15
University College Chichester	21	Edge Hill College of	
University of East Anglia	21	Higher Education	14

Drama
(Scotland) 1998

tqa

University of Glasgow	Highly Satisfactory	Royal Scottish	
Queen Margaret University		Academy of Music	
College, Edinburgh	Highly Satisfactory	and Drama	Highly Satisfactory

Drama
(Wales) 1994/95

tqa

Welsh College of Music and Drama	Satisfactory

Source: HEFCE, SHEFC, HEFCW latest available ratings
For a more complete list of institutions offering these courses at undergraduate level refer to the Course Directory

Drama and dance

television and radio. The course divides itself roughly into two parts: intensive work on individual skills and the application of those skills to group projects, and productions for public performance. Each actor appears in several public, professionally-directed and designed productions. The 'tree performance' of individual speeches and scenes is presented to an invited audience of agents and casting directors. No specific academic qualifications are required but a good education is advantageous. Entry is by audition and interview in Belfast, London, Manchester, Newcastle, Nottingham or New York. *Contact details, see page 613*

The Royal Scottish Academy of Music and Drama (RSAMD)
BA Acting

RSAMD is located in Glasgow, close to the Theatre Royal. The BA Acting course is designed for those intending to pursue a professional career in acting. Performance

Royal Academy of Dance

The Royal Academy of Dance offers a unique range of internationally-recognised dance and dance teaching qualifications with opportunities to study either in your country of residence or at the academy's London headquarters. The degrees, diplomas and certificates on offer enable student teachers, teachers, professional dancers and notators to gain qualifications at times and locations best suited to their needs, interests and career aspirations.

Write to: Academic Registrar
Faculty of Education
Royal Academy of Dance
36 Battersea Square
London SW11 3RA

Tel: +44 (0)20 7326 8000

Email: edunn@rad.org.uk

Website: www.rad.org.uk

Students: 1,500 students on full or part-time teacher education programmes in more than 46 countries. The academy has over 17,000 members including 5,700 RAD-registered teachers teaching over 250,000 children worldwide.

Accommodation: there is a wide range of accommodation available in town. Advice service available.

Entrance requirements: applicants for all Faculty of Education programmes must be at least 18 years of age. Each programme has different requirements.

EFL: for all higher education programmes IELTS 6.5 required. English requirements vary for professional qualifications.

Fees: teaching certificate approx £1,100; other programmes from £3,000 to £8,200 a year. A leaflet detailing fees and funding is available on request.

Academic strengths: The Royal Academy of Dance is internationally-renowned and respected. It has an excellent team of staff who are highly qualified – professionally and academically.

If you decide to study at the Royal Academy of Dance's London headquarters, you can take advantage of its excellent resources: eight spacious dance studios, a music/recording suite, a Pilates gym, lecture and seminar rooms, a multimedia computer room, a physiotherapist treatment room and the Philip Richardson Library.

Study by distance learning from your country of residence:
- BA(Hons) in Dance Education, validated by The University of Durham
- Diploma in Dance Education, validated by The University of Durham
- Certificate of Higher Education: Dance Teaching, validated by The University of Durham*
- Teaching Certificate, leading to RAD Registered Teacher Status

Study at the academy's London headquarters:
- BA(Hons) Art and Teaching of Ballet, validated by The University of Durham*
- Professional Graduate Certificate in Dance Teaching, leading to RAD Registered Teacher Status
- Professional Dancer's Teaching Diploma, leading to RAD Registered Teacher Status
- Professional Diploma in Benesh Movement Notation
  *(may be eligible for RAD Registered Teacher Status)

Graduates from the Faculty of Education's programmes have taken up posts as dance teachers running their dance schools in both the private and state sector and as choreographers, administrators, notators and directors.

Student life
The academy is located in London, in an open courtyard setting in Battersea Square on the banks of the River Thames, within easy reach of the wide-ranging arts attractions in the capital. For dance enthusiasts, venues such as the Barbican Centre, Royal Festival Hall, Sadler's Wells Theatre, The London Coliseum and The Royal Opera House play host to internationally-renowned dance companies.
Contact details, see page 613

Student profile

Casssa Poncho
BA Art and Teaching of Ballet final-year student, United Kingdom

"I didn't want to dance professionally but still wanted to get the best classical training available and felt that the academy's course had the most to offer. I had taught at my previous dance school and had enjoyed the experience and wanted to expand my knowledge and teach professionally. I was also interested in choreography, anatomy and repertoire. The academy has excellent resources: fully-equipped studios, a specialist dance library which is continually updated, a Pilates studio, good IT facilities and a very knowledgeable and supportive staff. Our focused environment also means that we are all very close and there is a friendly atmosphere between staff and students. I particularly like the fact that we get to mix with ex-professional dancers who are also training at the academy and they often teach us, providing valuable experience. I have just started my own company, Ballet Black."

Drama, Dance and Performing Arts

Institution	Grade	Institution	Grade
University of Bristol	5*	Middlesex University	3a
The University of Warwick	5*	Queen Margaret University College Edinburgh	3a
The University of Wales, Aberystwyth	5	Roehampton University of Surrey	
The University of Kent	5	(Drama, Theatre Studies, FTV)	3a
The University of Manchester	5	University of Ulster	3a
The Nottingham Trent University	5	University College Worcester	3a
The University of Reading	5	Bournemouth University	3b
Royal Holloway, University of London	5	Bretton Hall	3b
The University of Birmingham	4	Dartington College of Arts	3b
University of East Anglia	4	King Alfred's Winchester	3b
University of Glasgow	4	University College Northampton	3b
University of Exeter	4	Queen's University Belfast	3b
Goldsmiths College (University of London)	4	York St John College	3b
The University of Hull	4	Brunel University	2
Lancaster University	4	The Central School of Speech and Drama	2
Roehampton University of Surrey (Dance)	4	University of Glamorgan	2
University College Chichester	3a	Liverpool John Moores University	2
De Montfort University	3a	Northumbria University	2
The University of Huddersfield	3a	Rose Bruford College	2
The Manchester Metropolitan University	3a	University of Sunderland	2

Source: RAE 2001

is at the core of the course. Training in television acting, conducted in the academy's TV studio, and training in radio techniques, conducted in the academy's broadcasting studio, form part of the course. Recent productions have been staged in Singapore, Macedonia and Poland. There is no upper age limit and entry is by audition and interview. The School of Drama has a 350-seat theatre adaptable to proscenium, open stage, thrust, promenade and in-the-round as well as a 100-seat, similarly flexible studio theatre, television and radio studios, workshops, paint frame, wardrobe, dressing rooms, rehearsal rooms and voice and movement rooms.

Contact details, see page 612

them with the approaches and techniques needed to create and communicate a diversity of roles. The first year of the course is based on improvisation, building a character (based on the work of Stanislavsky), ensemble work and the exploration of other, non-textual methods of expression. In the second year, students experience a variety of performance styles and genres, with a particular emphasis on the practical approaches to Shakespeare. The final year, with its extensive public performance programme of main stage and studio productions, seeks to prepare students for professional work. The course culminates in showcase presentations in London, Manchester and Cardiff.

Contact details, see page 622

Welsh College of Music and Drama

BA (Hons) Acting

Students on the acting course at the Welsh College of Music and Drama receive an integrated training which seeks to equip

Postgraduate

The Central School of Speech and Drama

PGDip Acting Musical Theatre

This one-year, full-time course is intended

Drama and dance

for graduates and/or professional performers with established skills in singing and dance seeking to develop complementary skills in acting as applied to musical theatre. It is a practical course, involving theories of practice, development of voice, musicianship, a practical exploration of spoken and sung text and the consolidation of learning through performance contexts. Wherever possible, new musical theatre works will be used for public workshop performance.
Contact details, see page 614

Roehampton University of Surrey
Dance MPhil/PhD
The School of Arts at Roehampton is renowned for its academic research. The Dance MPhil and PhD are based in the Centre for Dance Research, which hosts a wide range of projects including historical, analytical and anthropological studies. In the last HEFCE research assessment exercise, the school achieved the highest rating awarded to dance in the UK for the second time running. Research students can take advantage of the excellent library, as well as having easy access to the many research and archive facilities London has to offer. There is also a fully-equipped

professional-standard theatre, dance studio and dance computer facilities. The course offers students a programme of seminars and conferences, including lectures and lecture-demonstrations from eminent dance scholars.
Contact details, see page 621

The University of Warwick
MA Theatre Studies
The School of Theatre Studies at The University of Warwick is one of the leading research-based departments in the UK. It has seven full-time members of staff, as well as a research fellow and research assistant. There are normally between three and five students admitted to pursue research-based degrees a year. Selection is based on the competence of staff to supervise the chosen topic but candidates are usually required to have at least an upper second class degree in a relevant subject. Research is concentrated within several programmes including architecture and space, Renaissance studies, contemporary theatre and performance and cultural policy studies. Graduates have access to the Faculty of Arts and Research methodology training programme.
For further information, see page 578

Useful links

www.cdet.org.uk	◗	Council for Dance Education and Training
www.ballet.org.uk	◗	English National Ballet
www.equity.org.uk	◗	Equity
www.ncdt.co.uk	◗	National Council for Drama Training
www.nsdf.org.uk	◗	National Student Drama Festival
www.thestage.co.uk	◗	*The Stage* Online

Drama and dance

Ecology and environmental science

Every day, millions of people conscientiously separate their paper, cans and plastic to be recycled in response to an ever-increasing need to save the planet. Virtuous though their actions are, few fully understand the theories, processes and reasons behind their trips to the bottle bank, or the wider and more complex issues affecting the environment.

Intense media coverage of controversial topics such as genetically-modified food, environmental activism and the devastating effects of man-made environmental disasters can hinder public understanding and discussion of other environmental issues. Subsequently, the research carried out by scientists in the diverse and rewarding fields of ecology and environmental science can often be neglected or obscured.

Although ecology and environmental science overlap, the two subjects are distinguishable. Ecology is the scientific study of plants and animals in relation to their physical and biological environment, whereas environmental science gives students a thorough grounding in all aspects of the environment as well as helping them understand the way it is influenced by human activity. Environmental science is based on various aspects of pure sciences such as biology and chemistry but also studies aspects of geography, geology, oceanography, mathematics and politics.

Increasingly, universities and colleges also run courses in related subjects such as environmental chemistry and environmental management. Environmental chemistry deals with the behaviour of both natural and man-made substances in relation to their surroundings such as the atmospheric, aquatic and terrestrial environments. You can expect to study all aspects of chemistry and topics such as geology, climatology, ecotoxicology and radioactivity. Environmental management looks at the scientific processes which effect the environment and its management. It also explores the social, legal and political implications of environmental issues.

In most ecology and environmental science courses, fieldwork plays an integral part. Preliminary courses usually involve an introduction to the methods employed by environmentalists in the field. Subsequent courses, normally held at a variety of locations across Britain and sometimes abroad, allow you to gain experience in the analysis and study of ecosystems. Whilst you are initially only introduced to the methodology of field research, you will later be equipped to decide for yourself the most appropriate method of research for a particular area.

Many courses offer students the chance to study abroad. Sandwich courses, incorporating a work experience placement, are also available. A substantial project, usually in the final year, is a feature of many courses. Ecology and environmental science courses are usually taught through a combination of lectures, seminars, fieldwork and laboratory work.

TEACHING QUALITY ASSESSMENTS

Environmental Studies
(England and Northern Ireland) 1994/95/96/97

tqa

Institution	Grade	Institution	Grade
University of Bath	Excellent	King Alfred's Winchester	Satisfactory
University of East Anglia	Excellent	University of Lincolnshire	
University of Greenwich	Excellent	and Humberside	Satisfactory
University of Hertfordshire	Excellent	University of Luton	Satisfactory
Lancaster University	Excellent	The Manchester	
The University of Liverpool	Excellent	Metropolitan University	Satisfactory
Liverpool Institute	Excellent	North Riding College	Satisfactory
University of Plymouth	Excellent	Northumbria University	Satisfactory
The University of Reading	Excellent	York St John College	Satisfactory
University of Southampton	Excellent	Southampton Institute	Satisfactory
University of Ulster	Excellent	Staffordshire University	Satisfactory
Anglia Polytechnic University	Satisfactory	University of Sussex	Satisfactory
University of Central Lancashire	Satisfactory	University of Teesside	Satisfactory
De Montfort University	Satisfactory	University of Wolverhampton	Satisfactory
The University of Kent	Satisfactory	Worcester College of Technology	Satisfactory

Environmental Studies
(England and Northern Ireland) 1997/2000

tqa

The University of Nottingham	23	King's College London (University of London)	22

Environmental Science
(Scotland) 1994

tqa

The University of Edinburgh	Excellent	University of Glasgow	Excellent

Environmental Studies
(Wales) 1994/95

tqa

Cardiff University (Environmental Engineering)	Excellent	The North East Wales Institute of Higher Education (Environmental Sciences)	Satisfactory
University of Wales, Bangor (Environmental Sciences)	Satisfactory	Trinity College Carmarthen (Rural Environment and Health and the Environment)	Satisfactory

Environmental Studies
(Wales) 1996/97

tqa

Cardiff Institute	Excellent

Source: HEFCE, SHEFC, HEFCW latest available ratings
For a more complete list of institutions offering these courses at undergraduate level refer to the Course Directory

Undergraduate

Lancaster University
BSc Environmental Science

Lancaster offers seven different degrees in environmental science, allowing students to specialise in different aspects of the subject, including Earth sciences and geophysics, hydrology and water quality and management or pollution of the environment. A wide range of subjects is available for those who do not wish to specialise. The other option involves spending the middle year of the course in the USA or Canada.

All of the modules involve fieldwork as well as lectures and small tutorial groups. One of the attractions of this course is its flexibility – at the end of the first year, students can change to another major department if they wish. The latter part of the course is taken up with a dissertation; a substantial thesis based on original, independent work.
Contact details, see page 617

University of Southampton
Environment Department

Southampton's international reputation as a leading centre of interdisciplinary envi-

Maritime Studies
(Wales) 1994/95

tqa

Institution	Grade	Institution	Grade
Cardiff University	Excellent		

Earth and/or Ocean Studies
(Wales) 1994/95

tqa

Institution	Grade	Institution	Grade
The University of Wales, Aberystwyth (Earth Studies)	Excellent	Cardiff University (Earth Sciences)	Satisfactory
University of Wales, Bangor (Ocean Sciences)	Excellent	The University of Wales, Lampeter (Geography)	Satisfactory
University of Wales Swansea (Geography)	Excellent		

Source: HEFCE, SHEFC, HEFCW latest available ratings
For a more complete list of institutions offering these courses at undergraduate level refer to the Course Directory

Ecology

ronmental science is underpinned by the university's record for excellence in scientific research and teaching across a range of environmental fields. All students study a core of environmental science subjects in their first year. They then focus on one pathway and specialise in one interdisciplinary science area. Students may focus on a hard science pathway (the physical environment or global change, for example), or they may choose a more human-focused pathway, such as scientific management or human sciences which look at the impact of our activities on the world around us. There are two residential field courses and students can further focus their interests through individual research or work placements.

For further information, see page 562

Postgraduate

University of Wales, Bangor
MSc Applied Physical Oceanography

This 12-month course is intended to introduce students with a relevant first degree to the subject of applied physical oceanography. As well as giving a broad perspective of marine science, it aims to enable students to study those aspects of the subject in which they have a particular interest. The course is con-

cerned with the structure and dynamics of the ocean, dealing with the features of water movements. Individual subject preferences can be expressed in the selection of the research project and in the

Student Profile

Diana Cheng
British/Hong Kong
BSc/MEnvSci
Environmental Sciences

University of Southampton

"When I first started my degree at Southampton, I was struck by the small size and yet the warm and friendly atmosphere. The staff are very approachable and helpful. I have chosen to follow the biodiversity and ecology pathway but there is a broad range of units from other degree courses on offer. This means that I have taken units as diverse as environmental economics, environmental law and geography units. This has been both challenging and interesting. It has allowed me to gain a valuable insight into the practical aspects of the natural environment. I appreciate this knowledge may widen my opportunities when I graduate. I attended two field courses in the first and third years. These were enjoyable and gave me the chance to use my fieldwork skills in designing, planning and executing my own ideas. I look forward to continuing my MEnvSci here in the fourth year".

Earth Sciences

Institution	Grade	Institution	Grade
University of Bristol	5*	University College London (University of London)	5
Cambridge University	5*	The University of Aberdeen	4
Oxford University	5*	The University of Durham	4
Birkbeck College (University of London)	5	University of Glasgow	4
Cardiff University	5	University of Leicester	4
The University of Edinburgh	5	The University of Birmingham	3a
Lancaster University	5	Keele University	3a
University of Leeds	5	The University of Reading	3a
The University of Liverpool	5	The University of Sheffield	3a
The University of Manchester	5	Kingston University	3b
University of Newcastle upon Tyne	5	University of Portsmouth	3b
Open University	5	University of East London	2
Royal Holloway, University of London	5		

Environmental Sciences

Institution	Grade	Institution	Grade
University of East Anglia	5*	The University of Bradford	3b
The University of Reading	5*	Cranfield University	3b
University of Leeds	5	University of Greenwich	3b
University of Southampton	5	Liverpool John Moores University	3b
University of Abertay Dundee	4	Middlesex University	3b
University of Wales, Bangor	4	University of Sunderland	3b
University of Exeter	4	University of Ulster	3b
The University of the Highlands and Islands Project	4	University of the West of England, Bristol	2
Imperial College of Science, Technology and Medicine (University of London)	4	Canterbury Christ Church University College	2
		University of Derby	2
The Manchester Metropolitan University	4	Glasgow Caledonian University	2
University of Newcastle upon Tyne	4	University of Hertfordshire	2
University of Plymouth	4	University of Luton	2
The University of Sheffield	4	Oxford Brookes University	2
The University of York	4	University of Paisley	2
Napier University	3a	Roehampton University of Surrey	2
The University of Stirling	3a	Southampton Institute	2
		Staffordshire University	2

Source: RAE 2001

Ecology

associated literature review. The course applies basic theory, observational methodology and data analysis techniques to the solution of marine environmental problems, particularly in the coastal and estuarine situation. The research project is selected to be of direct relevance to the work in which the student expects to be involved. Five studentships to cover tuition fees and maintenance are available each year until 2005/06.

For further information, see page 440

The University of Stirling

MSc Environmental Management

This course has evolved to meet the needs of employers in the environmental management sector. It has been running for over 13 years and has produced more than 400 environmental managers. The one-year postgraduate programme provides a foundation in the scientific and management principles which underpin environmental management. It also provides the opportunity to specialise in select areas of the subject. It is suited to recent graduates, professionals seeking a career change, personnel who are already in the industry, and governmental workers wishing to further their knowledge of environmental management. The course consists of two taught semesters (nine months), leading to a postgraduate diploma. This is

UNIVERSITY OF STIRLING

Faculty of Natural Sciences

The University of Stirling offers a wide range of degrees within natural sciences. These exciting programmes are designed to enable graduates to address the challenging ecological and environmental decisions affecting society in the 21st century.

- MSc Aquaculture
- MSc Environmental Management
- BSc Ecology

- MSc Aquatic Veterinary Studies
- BSc Conservation Science
- BSc Freshwater Science

The International Office

University of Stirling
Stirling FK9 4LA
Scotland UK

Tel: +44 (0) 1785 467046
E-mail: international@stir.ac.uk
www.stir.ac.uk

'Promoting excellence in teaching and research'

followed by a three-month dissertation which leads to the MSc. Candidates from almost all degree backgrounds are considered, particularly those who show ability in handling scientific and numerical information. The department of environmental science also teaches undergraduate degrees. *For further information, see page 566*

Useful links

www.demon.co.uk/bes	▶	British Ecological Society
www.ceh.ac.uk	▶	Centre for Ecology and Hydrology
www.defra.gov.uk	▶	Department for Environment, Food and Rural Affairs
www.edenproject.com	▶	Eden Project
www.environment-agency.gov.uk	▶	Environment Agency
www.foe.co.uk	▶	Friends of the Earth
www.greenpeace.org.uk	▶	Greenpeace UK
www.ukenvironment.org	▶	UK Environment

Ecology

Economics

The strength of a country's economy determines the success of its government, and nations are often considered 'good' or 'bad' depending on their economic status. Economics and its related issues evoke powerful emotions in people. The riots in Seattle at the time of the World Trade Organisation's talks in November 1999, and the anti-capitalist demonstrations held throughout the world each May show just what an impact economic issues can provoke.

A degree in economics provides the opportunity for students to develop excellent all-round skills, and is one of the few subjects where essay writing is combined with mathematical work. There is evidence to suggest that economics graduates can command higher salaries than some of their counterparts. A survey in 1998 (Blackaby et al) showed that graduates in arts subjects earned 9.4 per cent more than those not educated to degree level, whereas those with economics and related degrees earned an impressive 40.8 per cent more than non-graduates.

A career in the city is one obvious option for an economics graduate but you will also be prepared for a variety of alternative careers, since economics courses combine art and science and teach a wide range of transferable skills.

The discipline aims to find solutions to basic economic problems. Students look at the distribution of resources, supply and demand, income, inflation, unemployment and many other fundamental economic issues. Basic economic models are learned, then applied to the various economies existing in different societies, since any economic model will face social, political and international constraints when applied to a real-life situation.

Economics is broken down into microeconomics, macroeconomics and econometrics. Microeconomics (small economies) deals with particular aspects of economies, such as commodities, firms, individuals and the relationships between them. Marcoeconomics (large economies) studies major themes such as national income, consumption and investment. Econometrics refers to the statistical and mathematical analysis of economic problems.

First-year economics students are introduced to general principles. On microeconomics courses, these include the study of how individuals or companies operate; on macroeconomics courses, the economy is studied as a whole; and on applied economics courses, you look at the practical application of economic theory. Students specialise further in the second and third years. Some institutions offer an industrial placement year allowing you to apply theoretical concepts in a practical working environment.

Assessment is normally through exams, assessed essays and research. Some courses are based solely on research and coursework. Students are taught through lectures, tutorials and seminars.

Undergraduate

The University of Wales, Aberystwyth
BSc Economics

The core of this single honours programme consists of a series of modules which, over the three years of the degree scheme, develop the analytical understanding and quantitative techniques which allow economic ideas to be developed, tested and applied empirically. This provides the foundation of the course and constitutes half of the programme. The other half is devoted to the study of elective modules. In the first year, these can include a wide variety of subjects, allowing students to broaden their education or study subjects complementary to economics. In the second and third years, modules are chosen from lists of specialist economic subjects. While these vary, they usually include industrial, labour, international, environmental and development economics, economics of transitional economies and econometrics.

For further information, see page 436

Lancaster University
BA (Hons) Advertising, Economics and Marketing

The first year courses accommodate both students with an economics background and those who have not studied the subject before. Students are trained to analyse present-day policy issues with the aid of information technology. The scheme draws upon the strengths of the economics and marketing departments, and offers students the opportunity to study the theory and practice of advertising and marketing in the wider context of economic analysis and competitive strategy. The one-year work experience placement in the third year enables students to improve their practical skills in this area. By the end of the degree, students will have developed analytical and vocational skills which will prepare them for a range of careers in business.

Contact details, see page 617

London School of Economics and Political Science (University of London)
BSc Economics

Economics is the systematic study of financially-related questions such as how and why businesses set prices, how the price system in a market economy allocates resources and incomes and how businesses and households interact to determine national output, the balance of payments, inflation and unemployment. The study of economics develops a mental approach suitable for analysing a range of problems, often well outside what is conventionally thought of as the domain of economics. This course aims to provide a well-rounded coverage of the whole area. The first year gives students an essential foundation in the subject, while the second year concentrates on building a firm grasp of core analytical methods and applying them to a range of problems. The third year allows students to specialise and to apply those methods to particular areas. The LSE offers two single honours degrees in economics and econometrics and mathematical economics.

For further information, see page 508

Loughborough University
Department of Economics

Loughborough's range of degree programmes in economics combine contemporary economic analysis of topical issues with a wide range of applications to real world problems. Students' personal skills are developed through a range of modules developing their ability to present projects and analyse data. For undergraduates, Loughborough offers BScs in economics, business economics and finance, international economics and economics with accounting, politics, sociology, social policy or a language. Each undergraduate degree programme offers options in economics to second and final year students. For postgraduates, there are MScs in financial economics, international finance and economics, monetary Economics and Economics with finance. The Economics Department's teaching quality has been recognised by the Quality Assurance Agency for Higher Education as excellent with a score of 23 out of 24. In addition, the committed staff have considerable experiencein postgraduate education, consultancy and research which ensures that teaching draws on the latest principles and applications.

For further information, see page 510

TEACHING QUALITY ASSESSMENTS

Economics
(Scotland) 1993

tqa

Institution	Grade	Institution	Grade
The University of Aberdeen	Excellent	The University of Edinburgh	Satisfactory
University of Dundee Institute of Technology	Excellent	University of Glasgow	Satisfactory
		Heriot-Watt University, Edinburgh	Satisfactory
The University of Stirling	Excellent	Napier University	Satisfactory
University of St Andrews	Excellent	University of Paisley	Satisfactory
University of Dundee	Satisfactory	The University of Strathclyde	Satisfactory

Economics
(Wales) 1997/98

tqa

University of Wales, Bangor (Economics and Financial and Management Studies)	Satisfactory	The University of Wales, Aberystwyth	Excellent
		Cardiff University	Satisfactory
		University of Wales Swansea	Satisfactory

Economics
(England) 2000/01

tqa

Cambridge University	24	School of Slavonic and Eastern Studies, University College London (University of London)	23
Leeds Metropolitan University	24		
University of Leicester	24		
The University of Manchester	24	Brunel University	22
The University of Nottingham	24	City University	22
Oxford Brookes University	24	University of Exeter	22
University of Southampton	24	Goldsmiths College (University of London)	22
Staffordshire University	24	The University of Hull	22
The University of Warwick	24	Northumbria University	22
The University of York	24	The Nottingham Trent University	22
University College London (University of London)	24	Open University	22
		University of Central England in Birmingham	21
The University of Birmingham	23	Kingston University	21
University of Bristol	23	Middlesex University	21
Coventry University	23	University of Portsmouth	21
Keele University	23	The University of Reading	21
London Guildhall University	23	School of Oriental and African Studies (University of London)	21
London School of Economics and Political Science (University of London)	23	University of Sussex	21
		University of East London	20
Loughborough University	23	University of Greenwich	20
Oxford University	23	South Bank University	20

Source: HEFCE, SHEFC, HEFCW latest available ratings
For a more complete list of institutions offering these courses at undergraduate level refer to the Course Directory

The University of Stirling
BSc Economics

What causes inflation? Can we reduce unemployment? How can we decide on the appropriate levels of public expenditure and can we find a system of taxation which is both equitable and efficient? These are some of the questions which economists try to answer. A degree in economics is widely regarded as a worthwhile preparation for many careers in business and governments. This course offers a broad introduction to methods of economical analysis, including microeconomics and macroeconomics. Single honours students take a sequence of core units, including quantitative techniques, using economic data and economic policy in Britain and Europe. In the final year, they write a dissertation on a subject of their choice.

For further information, see page 566

Postgraduate

Northumbria University
MA/MSc Economics

These two courses are designed to equip students with the main tools of the professional economist, whether they intend to work in government, business, teaching or research. They provide students with skills in economic analysis and relevant quantitative techniques. The MA programme allows students to specialise in more discursive aspects of economics, whilst the MSc programme places greater emphasis on the quantitative dimension. Both provide appropriate training in core theory, combined with the opportunity to take specialist options such as development economics, financial economic theory and environmental economics. Applicants should hold a first degree in economics

or a related subject.

For further information, see page 526

University College London (University of London)
MSc Economics

This is a 12-month, full-time programme involving coursework, written examinations and a dissertation. Both this programme and the specialised MSc Environmental and Resource Economics provide the advanced training essential for professional economists in public and private sectors and provide a background for entry into the PhD programme. The MSc Economics offers the full range of concepts and techniques of modern economics with in-depth treatment of six key areas: empirical microeconomics, environmental economics, game theory, industrial organisation and innovation, labour economics and transitional economics. The department is involved with the universities of Barcelona, Brussels, Mannheim, Tilburg and Toulouse in the European Network for Training in Economics Research (ENTER), giving students the chance to interact with some of the best economics departments in Europe.

Contact details, see page 622

The University of York
MSc Econometrics and Economics

York has a strong research background and one of the largest groups of econometricians in the country. The MSc reflects this, emphasising the more quantitative side of economics. Some of the options teach technical skills useful in the analysis of financial markets and can lead to employment in investment firms. Potential employers also include research agencies, consultancy firms and economic and statis-

RESEARCH RANKINGS

Economics and Econometrics

Institution	Grade	Institution	Grade
The University of Essex	5*	The University of Kent	4
London School of Economics and Political Science (University of London)	5*	The University of Liverpool	4
		The University of Manchester	4
University College London (University of London)	5*	University of Newcastle upon Tyne	4
The University of Warwick	5*	Royal Holloway, University of London	4
Birkbeck College (University of London)	5	University of St Andrews	4
Cambridge University	5	The University of Stirling	4
University of Exeter	5	The University of Strathclyde	4
University of Leicester	5	University of Sussex	4
The University of Nottingham	5	University of Wales Swansea	4
Oxford University	5	The University of Aberdeen	3a
Queen Mary, University of London	5	City University	3a
University of Southampton	5	University of Dundee	3a
The University of York	5	University of East London	3a
The University of Birmingham	4	Keele University	3a
University of Bristol	4	London Guildhall University	3a
Brunel University	4	Loughborough University	3a
The University of Durham	4	The Manchester Metropolitan University	3a
University of East Anglia	4	Northumbria University	3b
The University of Edinburgh	4	The University of Sheffield	3a
University of Glasgow	4	The University of Surrey	3a

Source: RAE 2001

tical advisory services for a wide range of industries. The compulsory components of the course are advanced econometrics, advanced microeconomics, macroeconomic theory and a project. Students can then take a number of options, ranging from statistical distribution theory and multivariate analysis to environmental economics and environmental evaluation. *For further information, see page 590*

Economics

Useful links

www.economist.co.uk	●	*The Economist*
www.esrc.ac.uk	●	Economic and Social Research Council
www.actuaries.org	●	International Actuarial Association
www.neweconomics.org	●	New Economics Foundation
www.sbe.co.uk	●	Society of Business Economists
www.iea.org.uk	●	The Institute of Economic Affairs

181

Education

"Education is the passport to the future," wrote Malcolm X, and undeniably it has a huge influence on our aspirations and achievements. Teachers have the opportunity and the responsibility to help shape people; their influence on children being second only to that of parents or guardians. If you study education and become a teacher, you are given the opportunity to put something back into the system and gain enormous personal satisfaction.

To qualify as a primary or secondary school teacher in Britain and gain Qualified Teacher Status (QTS), students can choose between two main routes. There is the specialist teaching degree, the three or four-year Bachelor of Education (BEd), or the one-year Postgraduate Certificate in Education (PGCE), which is taken after completing an undergraduate degree in another subject.

Primary education

Most British primary teachers (nearly 70 per cent) complete an undergraduate teaching degree – normally the BEd. This trains you to teach a range of subjects including maths, science and English accompanied by physical education, religious studies, geography, art and history. Supervised time in the classroom forms an important part of the course. Theoretical elements explore such topics as child development, learning theory, motivation ethics and the history of education.

Secondary education

90 per cent of secondary school teachers in the UK qualify by completing a postgraduate teaching course. The PGCE is the standard, one-year, full-time postgraduate teaching programme. Courses vary but the majority consist of three main areas: practical experience of teaching in a school, study of a main subject area (normally the subject in which the student has graduated), and the theory of teaching. PGCE application forms are available from the Graduate Teacher Training Registry (GTTR) on +44 (0)1242 544788, www.gttr.ac.uk All applications have to go through the GTTR, so do not apply directly to colleges or universities.

As the approach to teaching varies between countries, it is important for international students to consider where they eventually wish to teach. Qualifications gained in the UK may not be recognised outside the European Union or may require a conversion course. Similarly, qualifications from outside Europe may not be sufficient to start a British QTS course.

A further route into British teaching is via the Overseas Trained Teacher Scheme, which leads to QTS and can take between one term and three years. It provides teachers who have a degree in education, or a postgraduate qualification and one year's teaching experience, with a way into the British system by combining teaching experience with training in a school.

RESEARCH RANKINGS

Education

Institution	Grade
University of Bristol	5*
Cardiff University	5*
University of Bath	5
The University of Birmingham	5
Cambridge University	5
The University of Durham	5
Institute of Education (University of London)	5
University of Exeter	5
Homerton College, Cambridge	5
King's College London (University of London)	5
Lancaster University	5
Oxford University	5
The University of Sheffield	5
University of Sussex	5
University of East Anglia	4
The University of Edinburgh	4
University of Glasgow	4
Goldsmiths College (University of London)	4
University of Leeds	4
University of Leicester	4
The University of Manchester	4
The Manchester Metropolitan University	4
University of Newcastle upon Tyne	4
The University of Nottingham	4
Open University (Educational Technology)	4
Open University (Education)	4
Queen's University Belfast	4
University of Southampton	4
The University of Surrey	4
The University of Stirling	4
The University of Strathclyde	4
The University of Warwick	4
The University of York	4
The University of Wales, Aberystwyth	3a
University of Wales, Bangor	3a
University of the West of England, Bristol	3a
Brunel University	3a
Canterbury Christ Church University College	3a
University of Dundee	3a
University of Gloucestershire	3a
University of Greenwich	3a
The University of Hull	3a

Institution	Grade
Keele University	3a
Leeds Metropolitan University	3a
University of Plymouth	3a
Roehampton University of Surrey	3a
The University of Reading	3a
Sheffield Hallam University	3a
University of Sunderland	3a
University of Wales Swansea	3a
University of Ulster	3a
Westhill College	3a
Anglia Polytechnic University	3b
Birkbeck College (University of London)	3b
University of Brighton	3b
University of Central England in Birmingham	3b
City University	3b
Coventry University	3b
University of Derby	3b
University of East London	3b
Edge Hill College of Higher Education	3b
Glasgow Caledonian University	3b
University of Hertfordshire	3b
The University of Huddersfield	3b
King Alfred's Winchester	3b
The University of Liverpool	3b
Liverpool John Moores University	3b
St Martin's College	3b
University College Northampton	3b
University of North London	3b
Northumbria University	3b
The Nottingham Trent University	3b
Oxford Brookes University	3b
University College Worcester	3b
Bath Spa University College	2
University College Chichester	2
Middlesex University	2
North East Wales Institute of Higher Education	2
The College of St Mark and St John	2
Staffordshire University	2
Swansea Institute of Higher Education	2
University of Wolverhampton	2
Queen Mary, University of London	1

Source: RAE 2001

Northumbria University
Education

Two courses popular with international students are the MA Studies in Education and BA (Hons) Primary Education. The MA allows students to start in February or September and is aimed at qualified and experienced teachers. The course allows education professionals to add specialist knowledge to their existing expertise. The BA (Hons) Primary Education equips students with the necessary knowledge and skills for effective primary school teaching. Northumbria was one of only five universities to be awarded a grade one by Her Majesty's Inspectors in all categories of primary teacher training. *For further information, see page 526*

TEACHING QUALITY ASSESSMENTS

Education
(Scotland) 1994/95

tqa

Institution	Grade	Institution	Grade
Moray House Institute of Education, Edinburgh	Highly Satisfactory	The University of Stirling	Highly Satisfactory
University of Paisley	Highly Satisfactory	The University of Strathclyde	Highly Satisfactory
St Andrew's College of Education, Glasgow	Highly Satisfactory	Northern College of Education	Satisfactory

Education
(Wales) 1997/98

tqa

Cardiff University	Excellent

Education
(England) 2000/01

tqa

Institution	Grade	Institution	Grade
Bolton Institute of Higher Education	24	Institute of Education (University of London)	22
University of Bristol	24	University of Newcastle upon Tyne	22
University of the West of England, Bristol	24	The University of Nottingham	22
University of Central Lancashire	24	South East Essex College	22
University of Exeter	24	Middlesex University	22
Keele University	24	The University of Birmingham	21
King Alfred's Winchester	24	University of Brighton	21
University of Southampton	24	Liverpool John Moores University	21
The University of Warwick	24	The Oldham College	21
University of Bath	23	University of Sunderland	21
Cambridge University	23	The City Literary Institute	20
The Central School of Speech and Drama	23	De Montfort University	20
Croydon College	23	University of Greenwich	20
King's College London (University of London)	23	The University of Hull	20
Leeds Metropolitan University	23	New College Durham	20
Queen's University Belfast	23	University of North London	20
Sheffield Hallam University	23	Northbrook College Sussex	20
South Bank University	23	St Mary's College	20
The University of Surrey	23	Warrington Collegiate Institute	20
University of Wolverhampton	23	University of East London	19
University College Worcester	23	Herefordshire College of Technology	16
University of Central England in Birmingham	22	Stockport College of Further & Higher Education	16
The University of Huddersfield	22		

Source: HEFCE, SHEFC, HEFCW latest available ratings
For a more complete list of institutions offering these courses at undergraduate level refer to the Course Directory

Useful links

www.dfes.gov.uk	▸	Department for Education and Skills
www.gttr.ac.uk	▸	Graduate Teacher Training Registry
www.ngfl.gov.uk	▸	National Grid for Learning
www.ofsted.gov.uk	▸	Office for Standards in Education
www.canteach.gov.uk/info.grtp/otts.htm	▸	Overseas Trained Teachers
www.canteach.gov.uk	▸	Teacher Training Agency
www.tes.co.uk	▸	The Times Educational Supplement

Education

Engineering

Engineers are the silent stars behind our everyday lives. Each time we catch a train or a bus we are experiencing a truly remarkable feat of engineering brilliance. Every time we drive across a bridge or plug in our electronic game consoles, engineers are in some way responsible.

Traditionally, Britain's strengths in engineering have lain in inventiveness and innovation rather than manufacturing skills. In recent years, however, there has been a great deal of investment in production facilities. The UK now leads the way in aerospace and automotive research, for example, and many of the world's formula one teams are based in Britain. The standing of British engineering is reflected in the fact that a large proportion of top executives (chief executives, managing directors or chairmen) of FTSE top 100 companies have a degree in engineering. Moreover, those with engineering degrees enjoy one of the highest graduate employment rates.

Engineering degrees in the UK last from three to five years and lead to a Bachelor of Engineering (BEng) or a Master of Engineering (MEng). More often than not, students are expected to spend one year on an industrial placement. Following graduation, a further period of employment allows students to become chartered (CEng) or incorporated (IEng) engineers.

All engineers need technical and managerial skills and the knowledge to understand the design, construction, operation and maintenance of products. As well as these general principles, however, engineers must specialise in a chosen field which can range from aeronautical to software engineering. There are a large number of specialisms under the general heading of engineering but those most commonly studied include chemical, civil, computer, mechanical and electrical engineering. If you are planning to do an engineering course, you need to consider the type of engineering which interests you the most. If you are unsure, then university courses which include an introductory or foundation year might be the answer. These allow you to cover a broad range of topics and to get to know the different parts of the subject before specialising.

Group work and imaginative problem solving are important features of all engineering courses, as are design and research projects. Programmes tend to be demanding and you can usually expect 35 hours a week of lectures, practicals and tutorials. Each engineering degree normally begins with an introduction to the basic principles of engineering. Subjects relevant to the particular specialism are then studied in more depth from the second year onwards. Assessment is by a combination of written examinations, essays, laboratory practicals, design projects and presentations. Work placements of up to one year may also be assessed or may form the basis for an assessed project.

Mechanical Engineering
(England and Northern Ireland) 1993/94/95

Institution	Grade	Institution	Grade
University of Bath	Excellent	Harper Adams University College	Satisfactory
University of Bristol	Excellent	The University of Hull	Satisfactory
Coventry University	Excellent	Lancaster University	Satisfactory
Cranfield University	Excellent	University of Leeds	Satisfactory
The University of Manchester	Excellent	Loughborough University	Satisfactory
The Manchester Metropolitan University	Excellent	University of Luton	Satisfactory
The University of Nottingham	Excellent	The University of Manchester Institute of Science and Technology (UMIST)	Satisfactory
The University of Reading	Excellent	Middlesex University	Satisfactory
The University of Sheffield	Excellent	University of Newcastle upon Tyne	Satisfactory
The University of Birmingham	Satisfactory	University College Northampton	Satisfactory
Bolton Institute of Higher Education	Satisfactory	The Nottingham Trent University	Satisfactory
University of Brighton	Satisfactory	Open University	Satisfactory
University of the West of England, Bristol	Satisfactory	Oxford Brookes University	Satisfactory
Brunel University	Satisfactory	University of Portsmouth	Satisfactory
University of North West London	Satisfactory	Queen's University Belfast	Satisfactory
University of Central England in Birmingham	Satisfactory	South Bank University	Satisfactory
		University of Southampton	Satisfactory
Coventry Technical College	Satisfactory	Southampton Institute	Satisfactory
De Montfort University	Satisfactory	The University of Surrey	Satisfactory
University of Derby	Satisfactory	University of Sussex	Satisfactory
University of Greenwich	Satisfactory	University College London (University of London)	Satisfactory

Mechanical (and Manufacturing) Engineering
(Scotland) 1995

Institution	Grade	Institution	Grade
The University of Strathclyde	Excellent	University of Paisley	Highly Satisfactory
The University of Aberdeen	Highly Satisfactory	The Robert Gordon University	Highly Satisfactory
University of Abertay Dundee	Highly Satisfactory	The University of Edinburgh	Satisfactory
University of Glasgow	Highly Satisfactory	Glasgow Caledonian University	Satisfactory
Heriot Watt University, Edinburgh	Highly Satisfactory	Napier University	Satisfactory

Mechanical Engineering
(Wales) 1993/94

Institution	Grade	Institution	Grade
Cardiff University	Excellent	University of Wales College, Newport	Satisfactory
University of Wales Institute, Cardiff	Satisfactory	The North East Wales Institute of Higher Education	Satisfactory
Carmarthenshire College	Satisfactory	University of Wales Swansea	Satisfactory
University of Glamorgan	Satisfactory	Swansea Institute of Higher Education	Satisfactory

Source: HEFCE, SHEFC, HEFCW latest available ratings
For a more complete list of institutions offering these courses at undergraduate level refer to the Course Directory

Specialist and vocational

Coventry Technical College

The School of Engineering offers students well-managed programmes and organisation which include nationally-recognised assessment procedures, student feedback and external verification. Courses are designed to ensure that, on completion, students are well equipped with the knowledge and transferable skills that will enable them to pursue their chosen career in engineering. The scope of provision offered by the school includes Edexcel, BTEC, GNVQ, City & Guilds and specialist full and part-time training programmes. These include a first diploma in engineering and also higher national, national, diploma or certificate courses in engineering science, telecommunications and computing, mechanical manufacturing, electronics, aerospace, information technology, com-

Engineering

Electrical and Electronic Engineering
(Scotland) 1995

tqa

Institution	Grade	Institution	Grade
The University of Edinburgh	Excellent	University of Glasgow	Satisfactory
Heriot-Watt University, Edinburgh	Excellent	Glasgow Caledonian	
The University of Strathclyde	Excellent	University	Satisfactory
The University of Aberdeen	Satisfactory	Napier University	Satisfactory
University of Dundee	Satisfactory	University of Paisley	Satisfactory
University of Dundee Institute	Satisfactory	The Robert Gordon University	Satisfactory

Electrical and Electronic Engineering
(Wales) 1995/96

tqa

Cardiff University	Excellent	University of Wales	
University of Glamorgan	Excellent	College, Newport	Satisfactory
University of Wales Swansea	Excellent	The North East Wales	
University of Wales, Bangor	Satisfactory	Institute of Higher Education	Satisfactory
University of Wales Institute, Cardiff	Satisfactory	Swansea Institute of Higher Education	Satisfactory

Materials Engineering
(Wales) 1997/98

tqa

University of Wales Swansea	Excellent

Source: HEFCE, SHEFC, HEFCW latest available ratings
For a more complete list of institutions offering these courses at undergraduate level refer to the Course Directory

puting or CAD/CAM. Additional programmes are offered in partnership with Aston and Coventry universities which provide excellent introductions to studying chosen subjects, coaching to improve basic English language skills and a good grounding in the study skills needed to be successful at a high-quality British university. The foundation and partnership programmes include engineering and science, aerospace and electronic technology. Teaching methods on all programmes include lectures, seminars and tutorials. Students are continually assessed through written exams, oral/word-processed assessments, objective testing, computer-based assessments and projects. Every effort is made to ensure international students achieve the maximum social and academic benefit from their stay whilst studying in the UK.

For further information, see page 414

University of Glamorgan
Foundation Year in Civil Engineering
Successful completion of the Foundation Year in Civil Engineering will enable students to progress to the first year of one of the university's degree or HND programmes. The course is ideal for students who wish to pursue a career in civil engineering but do not have the required secondary education qualifications for an engineering degree. It is designed to develop essential skills in mechanics and mathematics but students also learn computing and personal development in order to improve their communication and information technology skills. The flexibility of a foundation course allows them to prepare for a particular degree or tailor their studies to their own interests and career aspirations. *Contact details, see page 616*

Grimsby College
Refrigeration and Air Conditioning
Grimsby College is proud of its reputation for its air conditioning and refrigeration courses. The courses run at the college have a reputation worldwide for the quality of their specialist training.

Engineering

187

Civil Engineering
(England and Northern Ireland) 1996/97/98

Institution	Grade	Institution	Grade
University of Plymouth	23	The University of Bradford	20
University of Bath	22	Liverpool John Moores University	20
University of Bristol	22	University of Newcastle	
Kingston University	22	upon Tyne	20
The University of Liverpool	22	The Nottingham Trent University	20
Loughborough University	22	University of Portsmouth	20
The University of Nottingham	22	South Bank University	20
Queen's University Belfast	22	University of Westminster	20
Southampton Institute	22	University of Wolverhampton	20
The University of Surrey	22	City University	19
The University of Manchester Institute		Coventry University	19
of Science and Technology (UMIST)	22	University of Derby	19
The University of Birmingham	21	University of Leeds	19
University of Brighton	21	University College Northampton	19
University of East London	21	The University of Salford	19
University of Greenwich	21	University of Teesside	19
Imperial College of Science, Technology		University College London	
and Medicine (University of London)	21	(University of London)	19
Leeds Metropolitan University	21	University of Ulster	19
Oxford Brookes University	21	University of Hertfordshire	18
The University of Sheffield	21	The University of Manchester	18
University of Southampton	21	Sheffield Hallam University	18
Anglia Polytechnic University	20	Stockport College of Further	
Aston University	20	& Higher Education	15
Bolton Institute of Higher Education	20	Wigan and Leigh College	15

Civil Engineering
(Scotland) 1993

Institution	Grade	Institution	Grade
The University of Aberdeen	Highly Satisfactory	Napier University	Highly Satisfactory
University of Dundee	Highly Satisfactory	University of Paisley	Highly Satisfactory
University of Dundee Institute	Highly Satisfactory	The University of Strathclyde	Highly Satisfactory
The University of Edinburgh	Highly Satisfactory	Glasgow Caledonian University	Satisfactory
University of Glasgow	Highly Satisfactory		
Heriot-Watt University,			
Edinburgh	Highly Satisfactory		

Source: HEFCE, SHEFC, HEFCW latest available ratings
For a more complete list of institutions offering these courses at
undergraduate level refer to the Course Directory

Students can choose from a broad choice of courses at several different levels which can lead them into an excellent career with wonderful prospects. Students enjoy well-equipped, purpose-built refrigeration workshops and laboratories at the college. A course of this kind is ideal for those wanting to enter a career in service engineering or refrigeration installations, as a refrigeration technician, an applications engineer or alternatively for those wishing to progress to a degree course. A new £3 million engineering centre is to be built at the college which is due to open in time for the 2002 academic year. The new centre will house facilities to train school pupils, students, employees and employers in construction and engineering. *For further information, see page 416*

Liverpool John Moores University

Engineering and Technology Foundation

This programme is designed to prepare students, in one year, for a degree or an HND course by offering a firm foundation in engineering and technology principles, associated mathematics and a range of computing and study management skills. It is open to a wide range of poten-

Civil Engineering
(Wales) 1996/97/98

tqa

Institution	Grade	Institution	Grade
Cardiff University	Excellent	University of Glamorgan	Satisfactory
University of Wales Swansea	Excellent		

Electrical and Electronic Engineering
(England and Northern Ireland) 1996/97/98

tqa

Institution	Grade	Institution	Grade
The University of Birmingham	24	University of Brighton	20
University of Bristol	24	University of Hertfordshire	20
The University of Essex	24	King's College London (University of London)	20
The University of Huddersfield	24	University of Luton	20
The University of Hull	24	The University of Manchester	20
Imperial College of Science, Technology and Medicine (University of London)	24	The Nottingham Trent University	20
		University of Portsmouth	20
Queen's University Belfast	24	Staffordshire University	20
The University of Sheffield	24	University of Ulster	20
University of Southampton	24	Anglia Polytechnic University	19
The University of York	24	Bournemouth University	19
Cambridge University	23	University of Central England in Birmingham	19
University of Leeds	23	De Montfort University	19
The University of Surrey	23	University of Derby	19
Coventry Technical College	22	University of East Anglia	19
Loughborough University	22	Middlesex University	19
University of North London	22	Oxford Brookes University	19
Northumbria University	22	South Bank University	19
The University of Nottingham	22	Southampton Institute	19
The University of Manchester Institute of Science and Technology (UMIST)	22	University of Sunderland	19
		Blackburn College	18
University College London (University of London)	22	Coventry University	18
		Doncaster College	18
Aston University	21	University of Lincoln	18
The University of Bradford	21	Liverpool John Moores University	18
University of the West of England, Bristol	21	Loughborough College	18
Brunel University	21	University College Northampton	18
City University	21	University of Plymouth	18
The University of Kent	21	Sheffield Hallam University	18
Kingston University	21	University of North West London	17
The University of Liverpool	21	University of Greenwich	17
The Manchester Metropolitan University	21	Leeds Metropolitan University	17
University of Newcastle upon Tyne	21	Sandwell College	17
Queen Mary, University of London	21	Liverpool Community College	16
The University of Reading	21	The University of Salford	16
University of Sussex	21	University of Central Lancashire	15
University of Teesside	21	University of East London	15
University of Westminster	21	Stockport College of Further & Higher Education	15
University of Bath	20	Wigan and Leigh College	15
Bolton Institute of Higher Education	20		

Source: HEFCE, SHEFC, HEFCW latest available ratings
For a more complete list of institutions offering these courses at undergraduate level refer to the Course Directory

tial applicants, from those with a GCSE pass in mathematics to those with a National Diploma or a similar vocational qualification in a non-engineering subject. Assessment takes the form of a combination of examination, continuous assessment and project work. Experienced lecturers are available to assist students with any problems they may encounter. Successful completion of the programme guarantees a place studying an engineering-related subject at Liverpool John Moores university.

Contact details, see page 618

Engineering

Materials Technology
(England and Northern Ireland) 1996/97/98

tqa

Institution	Grade	Institution	Grade
Imperial College of Science, Technology and Medicine (University of London)	24	The University of Nottingham	21
		The University of Birmingham	20
Bolton Institute of Higher Education	23	Brunel University	20
Cambridge University	23	University of Leeds	20
Oxford University	23	Liverpool Community College	20
University of Southampton	23	London Guildhall University	20
Cranfield University	22	University of Newcastle	
The London Institute	22	upon Tyne	20
The Manchester Metropolitan University	22	The Nottingham Trent University	20
University College Northampton	22	Queen Mary, University of London	20
Sheffield Hallam University	22	The University of Manchester Institute of	
The University of Sheffield	22	Science and Technology (UMIST)	20
The University of Surrey	22	De Montfort University	19
University of Bath	21	University of North London	19
University of Exeter	21	University of Plymouth	19
The University of Huddersfield	21	Southampton Institute	19
The University of Liverpool	21	Sandwell College	17
Loughborough University	21	Staffordshire University	17
The University of Manchester	21	Bradford College	16

Source: HEFCE, SHEFC, HEFCW latest available ratings
For a more complete list of institutions offering these courses at undergraduate level refer to the Course Directory

The Manchester Metropolitan University

BTEC HND Electronic Engineering

This two-year, full-time course begins with strengthening the fundamentals in the area of mathematics and electrical and electronic principles. Students are also given an understanding of and practical ability in analogue and digital electronics. Both years include practical-based units which incorporate carefully developed and integrated themes progressing through the course. The units fall into the categories of communications and enterprise or design and software techniques. Students also get the chance to develop their skills through a technical project. The course is accredited by the Institution of Incorporated Engineers so those who complete the course satisfy the academic requirements for corporate membership of the institution. Students typically find careers with electrical, electronics and computing companies, among other professions.

For further information, see page 512

Undergraduate

The University of Aberdeen

MEng/BEng (Hons) Mechanical Engineering

The first two years of the mechanical engineering degrees involve a common core covering the basic principles of all branches of engineering. In later years, students specialise in mechanical engineering options. In the second half of the fourth year, BEng students engage in an extended project at home or abroad, leading to the preparation of a dissertation. At this time, MEng students also undertake a project at home or abroad. MEng students in the fifth year follow courses to develop personal skills and technical capabilities, also carrying out a group project. Students do not need to finalise their choice of specialisation until they begin level three, when a final decision between MEng and BEng must be made. Successful BEng students are offered the chance to change programme.

Contact details, see page 613

General Engineering
(England and Northern Ireland) 1996/97

tqa

Institution	Grade	Institution	Grade
Open University	24	University of Ulster	20
Cambridge University	23	University of Wolverhampton	20
Imperial College of Science, Technology and Medicine (University of London)	23	University of Central England in Birmingham	19
		De Montfort University	19
Oxford University	23	Queen Mary, University of London	19
University of Southampton	23	South Tyneside College	19
Brunel University	22	Southampton Institute	19
The University of Durham	22	Bournemouth University	18
Lancaster University	22	Coventry University	18
Sheffield Hallam University	21	Doncaster College	18
The University of Warwick	21	University of Lincoln	18
The University of Bradford	20	University College Northampton	18
University of Central Lancashire	20	Buckinghamshire Chilterns University College	17
Cranfield University	20	University of Greenwich	17
University of Exeter	20	Leeds Metropolitan University	17
University of Hertfordshire	20	South Bank University	17
University of Leicester	20	Bradford College	16
The University of Liverpool	20	Rycotewood College	15

Chemical Engineering
(England and Northern Ireland) 1995/96

tqa

Institution	Grade	Institution	Grade
Cambridge University	23	The University of Sheffield	21
Imperial College of Science, Technology and Medicine (University of London)	22	University of Bath	20
		The University of Bradford	20
Loughborough University	22	University College London (University of London)	20
The University of Manchester Institute of Science and Technology (UMIST)	22	Aston University	19
The University of Birmingham	21	University of Leeds	19
University of Newcastle upon Tyne	21	South Bank University	18
The University of Nottingham	21	The University of Surrey	18
Queen's University Belfast	21	University of Teesside	17

Chemical Engineering
(Scotland) 1997/98

tqa

Institution	Grade	Institution	Grade
The University of Strathclyde	20	Heriot-Watt University, Edinburgh	19
The University of Edinburgh	19		

Chemical Engineering
(Wales) 1997/98

tqa

Institution	Grade
University of Wales Swansea	Excellent

Source: HEFCE, SHEFC, HEFCW latest available ratings
For a more complete list of institutions offering these courses at undergraduate level refer to the Course Directory

Engineering

University of Abertay Dundee
BSc (Hons) Electronics

This course aims to provide students with a broad-based understanding of electronic engineering principles as well as more specialist knowledge of microprocessors, digital and analogue electronics. In the first year of the course, students are introduced to the principles and techniques required in the electronics industry. The second year involves a more in-depth study of these subjects. In the third year, the course covers electronic applications and systems, instrumentation and manufacturing management and the honours year contains higher level studies and a major individual project. Teaching on the course consists of lectures, laboratory work, industrial case studies and project activities. Both group and individual project work are integral parts of the course. The department offers a multidisciplinary approach to the study of mechanical and

Mechanical, Aeronautical and Manufacturing Engineering
(England and Northern Ireland) 1996/97/98

tqa

Institution	Grade	Institution	Grade
Kingston University	24	Anglia Polytechnic University	19
The University of Nottingham	24	University of Central England in Birmingham	19
Cambridge University	23	City University	19
Loughborough University	23	Southampton Institute	19
University of Bristol	22	University of Sunderland	19
Cranfield University	22	Writtle College	19
University of Hertfordshire	22	Bournemouth University	18
Imperial College of Science, Technology and Medicine (University of London)	22	Coventry University	18
		University of East London	18
Queen's University Belfast	21	University of Lincoln	18
Sheffield Hallam University	21	Loughborough College	18
University of Southampton	21	Farnborough College of Technology	17
The University of Birmingham	20	Leeds Metropolitan University	17
Brunel University	20	Sandwell College	17
The University of Liverpool	20	South Bank University	17
The University of Manchester	20	Wigan and Leigh College	15
University of Newcastle upon Tyne	20		
The University of Manchester Institute of Science and Technology (UMIST)	20		

Source: HEFCE, SHEFC, HEFCW latest available ratings
For a more complete list of institutions offering these courses
at undergraduate level refer to the Course Directory

electronic engineering, well-equipped engineering and CAD laboratories and strong links with the electronics industry.

Contact details, see page 613

University of Wales, Bangor
MEng/BEng Electronic Engineering

The MEng/BEng Electronic Engineering course has recently been revised to ensure that it provides the training demanded by a career in electronics in the 21st century. The course follows the general themes of electronic systems, microelectronics, communications and computing. In addition, a fifth engineering practice theme covers business aspects of the electronics industry. Individual study modules build up expertise from a basic level through to the latest technology and practices. Importance is placed on developing intellectual, practical and transferable skills. To promote this, students undertake projects to allow them to gain experience of the electronics and business skills they have been taught. The course makes use of

well-equipped laboratories, networked computers and industry-standard software. The department has close links with the electronics industry and a strong research base. The staff are practising professionals who work with companies to provide research, development consultation, design and training services.

For further information, see page 440

Cardiff University
BEng Environmental Engineering

This course is aimed at students who want to combine an interest in practical solutions in conservation with a particular concern for the environment. Engineering forms the essential core of the scheme, training students to recognise, define and solve environmental problems. Teaching includes the study of the relevant technology as well as legislation, the application of pollution control, occupational health and safety and public health engineering. Relevant elements are built into each year of the course to ensure a broad appreciation of global aspects of the environment.

Engineering

KINGSTON

FACULTY OF TECHNOLOGY

School of Engineering

A TOP QUALITY ENGINEERING EDUCATION

Recent government teaching quality assessments have included a maximum score of 24 points out of 24 for our Mechanica I,/ Aerospace courses and 22 out of 24 for our Civil Engineering courses.

FACILITIES

The School has a well equipped modern laboratory and computing facilities. The recent acquisition of a flight simulator is an example of the commitment to providing a first class teaching environment.

COURSES OFFERED

■ **Chartered Engineer accredited courses:**
  MEng Aerospace and Mechanical Engineering.
  BEng (Hons) Aerospace, Civil and Mechanical Engineering.

■ **Incorporated Engineer accredited courses:**
  BEng (Hons) Aerospace, Automotive, Civil,

Mechanical, and Motorcycle Engineering Design.
BEng (Hons) Construction Management.

■ **Non-accredited courses with bridging to Incorporated accredited courses:**
  BEng (Hons) Aerospace, Automotive Systems, Mechanical, and Motorcycle Engineering Studies.

Also HND and Foundation courses available

CONTACT

Admissions Office, Faculty of Technology, Kingston University, Penrhyn Road, Kingston upon Thames, Surrey KT1 2EE.

Tel: +44 20 8547 8234
Fax: +44 20 8547 7887
Email: eng@king.ac.uk
Web: http://www.kingston.ac.uk

Make
Kingston
your first
choice

T(0280)M

Institution	Grade	Institution	Grade
Cambridge University	5*	University of Hertfordshire	3a
Imperial College of Science, Technology		Kingston University	3a
and Medicine (University of London)	5*	The Manchester Metropolitan University	3a
Oxford University	5*	The University of Salford	3a
Aston University	5	Sheffield Hallam University	3a
Brunel University	5	University of Wolverhampton	3a
The University of Durham	5	Bolton Institute of Higher Education	3b
Keele University	5	Bournemouth University	3b
University of Leeds	5	The University of Bradford	3b
University of Leicester	5	University of Brighton	3b
Liverpool John Moores University	5	University of Central	
University of Sussex	5	England in Birmingham	3b
The University of Strathclyde	5	Leeds Metropolitan University	3b
The University of Warwick	5	Oxford Brookes University	3b
The University of Aberdeen	4	The Robert Gordon University	3b
Cranfield University	4	University of Sunderland	3b
University of Dundee	4	University of Ulster	3b
University of Exeter	4	University of the West of England, Bristol	3b
The University of Hull	4	Anglia Polytechnic University	2
Lancaster University	4	University of East London	2
The University of Nottingham	4	Heriot-Watt University, Edinburgh	2
Napier University	4	Open University	2
University of Abertay Dundee	3a	Southampton Institute	2
University of Central Lancashire	3a	University of Teesside	2
University of Greenwich	3a	University of Paisley	2

Source: RAE 2001

The degree in environmental engineering is accredited by the Institution of Civil Engineers and meets the educational requirements for chartered engineer status (CEng). Corporate membership of a professional institution rests on practical training and professional experience as well as on educational requirements.

Contact details, see page 614

The Technical College
City College, Birmingham
Civil, Mechanical and Motor Vehicle Engineering

The Technical College is a part of City College, Birmingham. Originally built in the early 1990s as a specialist motor vehicle training centre, it was extended in 2000 and now provides training for undergraduate students wishing to study in the fields of

Institution	Grade	Institution	Grade
The University of Birmingham	5*	University of Bath	4
Imperial College of Science, Technology		Heriot-Watt University, Edinburgh	4
and Medicine (University of London)	5*	Loughborough University	4
University College London		Queen's University Belfast	4
(University of London)	5*	The University of Sheffield	4
Cambridge University	5	The University of Surrey	4
The University of Manchester Institute		The University of Edinburgh	4
of Science and Technology (UMIST)	5	The University of Bradford	3a
University of Newcastle upon Tyne	5	South Bank University	3a
The University of Surrey		Glasgow Caledonian University	3b
(Centre for Environmental Strategy)	5		

Source: RAE 2001

Engineering

Mechanical, Aeronautical and Manufacturing Engineering

Institution	Grade	Institution	Grade
University of Bath	5*	City University	4
Imperial College of Science, Technology and Medicine (University of London)	5*	Cranfield University	4
		De Montfort University	4
University of Leeds	5*	The University of Edinburgh	4
The University of Liverpool	5*	University of Glasgow (Aerospace Engineering)	4
Queen's University Belfast	5*	University of Glasgow (Naval Architecture)	4
University of Southampton	5*	Heriot-Watt University, Edinburgh	4
The University of Bradford	5	The University of Huddersfield	4
University of Bristol (Mechanical Engineering)	5	University of Newcastle upon Tyne	4
Brunel University	5	University of Plymouth	4
University of Glasgow (Mechanical Engineering)	5	University of Portsmouth	4
King's College London (University of London)	5	The University of Surrey	4
Loughborough University	5	The University of Strathclyde (Design Manufacture and Engineering Management)	4
The University of Manchester	5		
The University of Manchester Institute of Science and Technology (UMIST)	5	University of Wales Swansea	4
		Coventry University	3a
The University of Nottingham	5	University of Derby	3a
Queen Mary, University of London	5	Glasgow Caledonian University	3a
The University of Sheffield	5	Liverpool John Moores University	3a
The University of Strathclyde (Mechanical Engineering)	5	University of Wales College, Newport	3a
		South Bank University	3a
University College London (University of London)	5	Northumbria University	3b
The University of Birmingham	4	The Nottingham Trent University	3b
University of Bristol (Aeronautical and Manufacturing Engineering)	4	Staffordshire University	3b
		Buckinghamshire Chilterns University College	2
Cardiff University	4	Swansea Institute of Higher Education	2

Source: RAE 2001

Engineering

construction, engineering and motor vehicle engineering. The well-equipped centre has strong links with local industry and ensures that the teaching is of the highest standards. The Technical College already provides programmes for students from the Caribbean and West Africa and international students are welcomed. The following subjects are available: basic motor vehicle servicing and maintenance, repair and maintenance of road vehicles, vehicle mechanical and electronic systems, CITB brick laying levels one and two, CITB site carpentry levels one and two and NVQ levels one and two in performing engineering operations.
For further information, see page 412

The University of Essex
Electronic Systems Engineering
Electronic systems are everywhere. Apart from the obvious electronic hardware, they include the communications infrastructures we all take for granted. Essex offers students the opportunity to study a broad range of topics or to specialise in, for instance, computer, electronic or telecommunication engineering. Graduates will be in an excellent position to find jobs – a recent survey showed that electronics graduates have the lowest rates of unemployment and the highest starting salaries. Students at Essex have access to continually upgraded, state-of-the-art equipment. After the first or second year, students can choose to go on to a BEng or MEng. Both are accredited by the Institution of Electrical Engineers and the Engineering Council.
For further information, see page 476

Heriot-Watt University, Edinburgh
BSc in Engineering and Management
The course is an integrated degree that

Metallurgy and Materials

Institution	Grade	Institution	Grade
The University of Birmingham	5*	University of Leeds	4
Cambridge University	5*	Loughborough University	4
The University of Manchester	5*	The University of Manchester Institute of Science and Technology (UMIST) (Paper Science)	4
The University of Manchester Institute of Science and Technology (UMIST)	5*	The University of Manchester Institute of Science and Technology (UMIST) (Textiles)	4
Oxford University	5*	The Manchester Metropolitan University	4
The University of Sheffield	5*	Open University	4
Imperial College of Science, Technology and Medicine (University of London)	5	The University of Salford	4
The University of Liverpool	5	University of Ulster	4
Queen Mary, University of London	5	Kingston University	3a
Sheffield Hallam University	5	University College Northampton	3a
Bolton Institute of Higher Education	4	The Robert Gordon University	3a
Coventry University	4	Buckinghamshire Chilterns University College	3b
De Montfort University	4	Heriot-Watt University, Edinburgh	3b
University of Greenwich	4	Liverpool John Moores University	3b
The University of Huddersfield	4	University of North London	3b

Source: RAE 2001

Engineering

aims to provide graduates with a qualification covering the essential ingredients of modern industry. It provides the necessary technological, managerial and interpersonal skills and knowledge that enables graduates to progress to effective senior management positions within manufacturing or service industries, or to manage their own business. This is a four-year honours degree with each successive year building skills from a broad foundation of knowledge. Central to the course is practice in real industrial situations. Industrial partners supply many of the case study and assignment materials. Students learn how products are engineered, manufactured and marketed, how new technology is implemented and applied, how businesses are managed and financially controlled and the importance of human factors in modern industry.

For further information, see page 490

RESEARCH RANKINGS

Civil Engineering

Institution	Grade	Institution	Grade
University of Bristol	5*	The University of Manchester Institute of Science and Technology (UMIST)	5
Cardiff University	5*	The University of Bradford	4
Imperial College of Science, Technology and Medicine (University of London)	5*	City University	4
University of Southampton	5*	University of Glasgow	4
University of Wales Swansea	5*	Heriot-Watt University, Edinburgh	4
The University of Birmingham	5	The University of Liverpool	4
University College London (University of London) (Civil and Environmental Engineering)	5	Loughborough University	4
University of Dundee	5	Napier University	4
The University of Edinburgh	5	University of Newcastle upon Tyne (Geomatics)	4
University of Leeds	5	University of Plymouth	4
The University of Manchester	5	The University of Surrey	4
University of Newcastle upon Tyne (Civil Engineering/Marine Technology)	5	The University of Strathclyde	4
The University of Nottingham	5	University College London (University of London) (Geomatic Engineering)	4
Queen's University Belfast	5	University of Paisley	3a
The University of Sheffield	5	University of Portsmouth	3a
		University of Brighton	3b

Source: RAE 2001

Electrical and Electronic Engineering

Institution	Grade	Institution	Grade
The University of Edinburgh	5*	Heriot-Watt University, Edinburgh	4
University of Leeds	5*	The University of Kent	4
The University of Sheffield (Automatic Control and Systems Engineering)	5*	Lancaster University	4
University of Southampton	5*	The University of Manchester Institute of Science and Technology (UMIST) (Instrumentation and Analytical Science)	4
The University of Sheffield	5*	The University of Nottingham	4
The University of Surrey	5*	University of Plymouth	4
The University of Birmingham	5	South Bank University	4
University of Bristol	5	University of Wales Swansea	4
Cardiff University	5	University of Westminster	4
The University of Essex	5	University of Wales, Bangor	4
Imperial College of Science, Technology and Medicine (University of London)	5	City University	3a
King's College London (University of London)	5	Coventry University	3a
The University of Liverpool	5	De Montfort University	3a
Loughborough University	5	Liverpool John Moores University	3a
The University of Manchester Institute of Science and Technology (UMIST)	5	The Nottingham Trent University	3a
University of Newcastle upon Tyne	5	Queen Mary, University of London	3a
The University of Reading	5	The University of York	3a
The University of Strathclyde	5	The University of Huddersfield	3b
University of Glasgow	5	Northumbria University	3b
Queen's University Belfast	5	Staffordshire University	3b
University College London (University of London)	5	The University of Wales, Aberystwyth	2
University of Bath	4	Glasgow Caledonian University	2
		University of Portsmouth	2

Source: RAE 2001

Imperial College of Science, Technology and Medicine (University of London)

MEng Mining Engineering

The broad scope of this four-year course reflects the fact that careers in mining engineering can be varied. The course is suitable for those who wish to pursue a career in mining but who would like to study widely enough to keep alternative career opportunities available. Much of the first year is a foundation with subjects such as mathematics, computing, thermodynamics and fluid dynamics. Students additionally undertake projects in relevant areas, working in small study groups to prepare reports and presentations. There is also laboratory and fieldwork. In the third and fourth years, there are more advanced specialist studies and projects. Students can study geostatistics, environmental and engineering geology, mining and mineral processing, rock mechanics, materials handling, alluvial mining, mine ventilation and open pit mining.

Contact details, see page 617

Kingston University

BEng (Hons) Civil Engineering

The course features a common first year with other engineering disciplines enabling students to have a broad underpinning of engineering before specialising. There are well-equipped laboratories to provide the practical application of more theoretical studies. Courses are accredited by the Institution of Civil Engineers and a strong reputation with industry-enhancing career opportunities has been developed. A growing research culture means that courses are informed by current applied research, particularly in the areas of geotechnics, concrete and masonry design and structural engineering. This also

Engineering

Mineral and Mining Engineering

rae

Institution	Grade	Institution	Grade
Heriot-Watt University, Edinburgh	5*	University of Exeter	4
Imperial College of Science, Technology and Medicine (University of London)	5*	Source: RAE 2001	

provides possibilities for research study on completion of the degree. All undergraduate courses feature residential fieldwork to develop skills in surveying and geotechnics, whilst site visits provide real-life examples of other engineering subjects.

For further information, see page 496

Lancaster University
MEng/BEng Engineering USA or Canada

This engineering degree scheme has been devised to give maximum flexibility – students do not have to specify an area in which to specialise when they apply. Instead, the decision is made after the first year. The purpose of this degree scheme is to develop an all-round engineer. During the first year, students study the three core subjects of electronic engineering, mechanical engineering and engineering mathematics. These provide a firm foundation to allow students to select a degree scheme in mechatronics, electronic engineering or mechanical engineering. All the engineering courses offer the opportunity to spend the second year at a university in the USA or Canada. Lancaster University has exchange agreements with several North American universities including Purdue and the state universities of Iowa, Kentucky, Nebraska and North Carolina. Courses and syllabuses are matched so that students are properly prepared for the third year back in Lancaster.

Contact details, see page 617

Loughborough University

Loughborough University offers the biggest range of engineering degree courses in the UK. They are offered across the aeronautical and automotive engineering, chemical engineering, civil and building engineering, electronic and electrical engineering and mechanical and manu-facturing engineering departments. The undergraduate courses are offered in either MEng, BEng or BSc and most have a sandwich placement option, allowing students to work during their third year of study. There are also one-year MSc and three-year research degrees offered. All MEng and BEng degree courses are accredited by at least one of the UK's major engineering accrediting bodies including the IMechE, IEE, IChemE and ICE. The average teaching quality score is 22 out of 24 and in the recent research assessment exercise, one 5*, three 5s and two 4s were awarded across the faculty. Loughborough is the only engineering faculty to be awarded the Queen's Anniversary Prize for Higher Education three times.

For further information, see page 510

The University of Strathclyde
BEng (Hons) Chemical Engineering

Chemical engineering is vital to a great number of industries for the production of everyday items such as plastics, petrol, textiles and food. The first year of this course provides a foundation in mathe-matics and chemistry, as well as an intro-

Engineering

duction to computer applications and project work. In the second year, students are introduced to fundamental chemical engineering principles. In the third year, these principles begin to be applied to the most important techniques used in the chemical and process industries. At the end of the third year, depending on performance, students can decide whether to opt for the BEng or the MEng, which is designed for high-calibre students. Both include a sizeable research project with the opportunity to work for a year in Europe.

For further information, see page 568

Postgraduate

University of Leeds
MSc (Eng) or PG Diploma in Environmental Engineering and Project Management
This course is broadly based to permit stu-dents to follow particular themes, depend-ent upon their individual career needs and based around the research strengths and expertise in the school. The course itself covers problems of river, estuarine and marine pollution, groundwater contami-nation, contaminated land and its remedi-ation and the problems resulting from dis-charge of solid and liquid industrial wastes. Relevant technologies for treat-ment of polluting wastes and restoration of contaminated environments are covered in detail. The course is intended for those who find themselves in management posi-tions with little knowledge or experience of the management techniques necessary to manage the range of projects for which they have responsibilities. It is appropriate for those people who have a background in management but feel they lack up-to-date technical knowledge.

Contact details, see page 617

The University of Salford

MSc Gas Engineering and Management

This internationally-recognised programme is intended for those working in, or intending to work in, the natural gas industry. It provides a sound basis from which to select an area for specialised study. It is offered jointly with The College of Petroleum and Energy Studies, Oxford. Students spend three to four months at the college covering modules which include the 'gas chain' concept, the international gas business, natural gas marketing in a competitive environment, gas utility management and gas sales contracts. At Salford, students undertake the same modules as for the Diploma in Gas Engineering, together with a dissertation. Graduates pursue a variety of careers in the natural gas industry. The courses cover all aspects of gas technology and associated gas business management and will enable students to increase their technical knowledge.

For further information, see page 552

University of Southampton

MSc Engineering for Development

This course was started in 1993/94 with six students and has grown over the years to its current size of 12 students. The course aims to give graduates who wish to work with poor communities in developing countries the skills they will need for the planning and development of integrated infrastructural facilities. These services include water supply, sanitation, waste disposal, roads, buildings, energy and agricultural development. The course provides an understanding of basic economics and social issues in international development, as well as offering training (both theoretical and practical) in the design, construction, operation and maintenance of these infrastructural facilities. The course is taught by staff of the Institute of Irrigation and Development Studies (IIDS), together with other staff of the Department of Civil and Environmental Engineering and well-qualified external lecturers, all of whom have many years of work experience in developing countries. Ongoing research projects at IIDS also feed into the course, for example through invited lectures or opportunities for overseas work experience.

For further information, see page 562

Useful links

www.engc.org.uk	●	Engineering Council
www.eef.org.uk	●	Engineering Employers Federation
www.engineering-uk.co.uk	●	Engineering UK
www.ice.org.uk	●	The Institution of Civil Engineers
www.imeche.org.uk	●	The Institution of Mechanical Engineers
www.istructe.org.uk	●	The Institution of Structural Engineers
www.raeng.org.uk	●	Royal Academy of Engineering

Engineering

English as a foreign language

English is the second most widely spoken language in the world, after Chinese. Spoken by an estimated 300 million people as a first language, it is the international language of science, medicine, aviation, tourism and navigation. In today's world, it may be vital to learn English for business or professional purposes, or simply for social reasons. The value of being confident in speaking and writing the language is hard to overestimate.

Learning from teachers in your own country is one way to start learning but nothing can compare with going to an anglophone country and soaking up the language and the culture first hand. Choosing to study in the UK means that you will have the opportunity to sample a different culture and way of life in a diverse and historically-rich country.

There are thousands of language schools throughout the UK and choosing one may appear difficult when they all seem to offer similar courses. But do you want general or business English? Or English for a specialism such as law or aviation? Your budget will probably be a major factor in the decision and the school's location may also be important, not to mention the quality of its teaching.

The British Council, sponsored by the government, was established by Royal Charter in 1934. One of its roles is the monitoring of English as a foreign language (EFL) in Great Britain through the British Council Accreditation Scheme. Schools which apply for accreditation are rigorously inspected every three years. Two inspectors spend several days within each school examining the general and academic management, the teaching premises, student accommodation, equipment, books and welfare and social provisions. The British Council also monitors all the teachers, who should hold a recognised teaching qualification from RSA, Trinity College London or the University of Cambridge Local Examinations Syndicate.

Many universities and colleges provide English classes either as summer school schemes or for students who are enrolling on an undergraduate or a graduate course and feel that their English needs improving. This may include English for academic or formal use because writing a 5,000-word essay involves different English to that used when emailing your friends.

Many students like to take examinations as benchmarks of their progress. Those on offer include the Cambridge exams: the Preliminary English Test (PET), Key English Test (KET), First Certificate in English (FCE), Certificate in Advanced English (CAE) and the Certificate of Proficiency in English (CPE). The International English Language Testing System (IELTS) is a certificate often required for entrance to university. Other available qualifications include the Test of English as a Foreign Language (TOEFL) and the University of Cambridge Local Examinations Syndicate (UCLES) exams.

Specialist and vocational

The Cambridge School of English
Business English Course

Globalisation of trade and industry has led to inevitable changes in the way we communicate in business. English has become the international language for business, which is why the Business English course is becoming ever more popular at The Cambridge School of English. The business classes are for students of intermediate level and above and include all the four language skills: speaking (including pronunciation), listening, reading and writing, which are practised using business and professional themes and contexts. Improving fluency in the use of English in business environments will give students more confidence in situations they will encounter throughout their careers. The Business English course can be taken with an intensive learning option to allow students to learn English at speed. Supplement courses teaching English for particular areas of business ranging from banking to presentations and interview skills are also available.

Contact details, see page 611

City College Manchester
English as a Foreign Language

The college offers full-time courses for those wishing to obtain qualifications in English as a foreign language. Qualifications include IELTS, university entrance test and a range of Cambridge examinations from beginners (KET) to advanced (CAE). Students can study for up to 20 hours a week and are free to use the college's facilities including a multi-gym, a leisure centre, music studios and an IT suite. Through one-to-one tutorials, students work with tutors to identify their

needs and design an individual learning programme. Most courses are based at the Fielden Centre, south of the city. There is also limited provision at the city-centre campus. The English language provision at the college is accredited by the British Council and is a part of the BASELT organisation.

For further information, see page 466

London Institute of Technology and English (LITE)
IELTS, TOEIC, TOEFL

LITE is an independent college providing courses designed to develop students' language skills and enable them to sit a variety of Cambridge, IELTS, TOEIC and TOEFL examinations. Students study for 15 hours a week full-time or can alternatively do a range of part-time courses. Students can enrol at any time of the year and the

course can last from one week to one year. Along with the general English courses, LITE runs specialised courses in conversation and writing. The institute

English as a foreign language

The General English Course has been taught at the Cambridge School of English since its establishment in 1969. Throughout this time, the courses have promoted the idea of personal attention in learning as class sizes are kept low averaging eight students in each and only rising to a maximum of 12. This allows students to improve their English at a fast rate, receive help quickly and settle well in a friendly, welcoming environment.

All four language skills are specifically focused on in the course; namely speaking, listening, reading and writing. The syllabus is structured grammatically and functionally following a course book and includes up-to-date communicative methodology as well as more traditional approaches.

The school realises that many people learn English with a particular purpose and the courses available reflect this. Taught as a supplement to the general English course or on their own, a number of programmes with specific purposes are available.

The Business English course is proving more popular as English has become the internationally-accepted language for business. The business classes include all the four language skills practised using business and professional themes and

contexts. Improving fluency in the use of English in business environments gives students more confidence in the real situations they will encounter in their careers.

Different syllabuses for more specialised purposes are also available. This includes industries and employment ranging from law and journalism to catering and au pairs. English for specific areas of business such as marketing, management and computing can also be studied.

The school teaches English to further academic careers as well. As it is a registered UCAS centre, it offers a complete service to students wishing to enter university in the UK by preparing them for examinations.

The students' level of English is assessed upon arrival and a timetable produced upon these results that best suits the individual. Even this is highly personalised as students can decide how intensively they wish to study and at what time of the day.

The school considers itself more than simply the students' teachers and endeavours to help with as many of the practicalities of studying in England as possible. Student insurance, airport transfers, work placements and excursions throughout the country can all be arranged as well welfare assistance once the course has actually started.

Accommodation is of course another vital part of a stay in England and the Cambridge School has a full range of accommodation, all of which meet the British Council's high standards. Hotels and student hostels are available as well as staying with a British host family. The host family is by far the most popular choice among students of all ages as it can provide them with both comfort and security, as well as further chances to improve their English speaking skills.

As the school is situated in central London, a very busy social programme is available which gives students the chance to experience the very best of English culture and London life. Many events are organised by the school such as tourist walks and trips to local museums, theatres and cinemas.

Students are tested every Monday and receive a one-to-one tutorial once a week so that everyone is always in the correct class at the correct level. Students with all levels of English are welcome although certain standards may be required for individual courses.

Contact details, see page 611

Student testimonials

Masumi
Japanese
34

"I extended my course at the Cambridge School because the examination course is very practical and useful. Also, the teacher is both kind and patient. I need to improve my English for university."

Alessandro
Italian
27

"I would recommend the Cambridge School to my friends and family because of the cool teachers, interesting social programme and sociable schoolmates. I need to improve my English as I intend to work in the UK and Scandinavia."

Valeria
Venezuelian
25

"I extended my course here as I found it an excellent school with professional teachers and a nice atmosphere. I need to improve my English for my job and travelling. We read English and always have meetings with English-speaking people."

UNIVERSITY OF STIRLING

Centre for English Language Teaching

Whether you wish to improve your language skills for study, business, teaching or pleasure, the University of Stirling will offer something to suit. Set within a historic 18th century estate in the heart of central Scotland, the university campus is an ideal place to live, study and relax, with easy access to the cities of Scotland, and to the Highlands.

Programmes available include:
- Foundation Programme
- Short Courses

- Undergraduate Bachelors degrees
- Taught Masters degrees
- Postgraduate research degrees

The International Office

University of Stirling
Stirling FK9 4LA
Scotland UK

Tel: +44 (0) 1785 467046
E-mail: international@stir.ac.uk
www.stir.ac.uk

'Promoting excellence in teaching and research'

also runs examination preparation classes, which are available throughout the year. During the course, students enhance their oral, writing, reading and listening skills, by means of the Cambridge syllabus. In order to assess progress, students sit regular in-class tests. With the intensive and exciting social programme, students are also given the opportunity to use their language skills in real-life environments.

For further information, see page 400

or choose a business English pathway. Most students study for three hours a day but it is possible to select a more intensive programme. Extra benefits include 24-hour free internet access, weekly social activities and parties and the opportunity to make new friends from all over the world. Malvern House is right by Trafalgar Square in London (Charing Cross and Embankment underground stations are a few metres away).

Contact details, see page 611

Malvern House

English as a Foreign Language

Malvern House runs English classes taught by fully-qualified, professional young teachers. Students can enrol any day of the week and may choose to study for any period from two weeks up to a full academic year. They have the option to sit either for Cambridge exams or IELTS

Northbrook College

English

Northbrook College is located in the traditional holiday resort of Worthing. While offering both college and under-graduate courses, Northbrook also offers all levels of English language tuition. Students can follow the syllabus for one of the Cambridge Examinations or undertake

IELTS testing. Their general and academic English courses are available all year round where students can attend courses for up to 20 hours each week at any time throughout the year, as well as courses for one to two terms or even a whole year. English language plus courses offer the opportunity to develop English language skills and to study another subject including business studies, information tech-nology, art, design, music and media. Summer and pre-sessional English courses work towards establishing or improving students' English before they go on to study another course in the UK. *For further information, see page 524*

has an excellent success rate in training students in academic English and providing them with the skills they need for study on foundation, undergraduate or postgraduate degree programmes. Classes are taught by experienced and qualified teachers and all students have access to materials and resources in the learning centre. Students study for a total of 25 hours per week, 15 hours in class and 10 hours of independent study in the learning centre. One-month, three-month, six-month and nine-month academic English programmes

University of North London
English Language Programme
Many students need to improve their English language skills before entering the university. The University of North London

English as a foreign language

King Street College

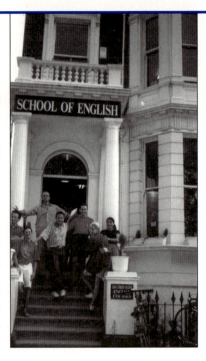

King Street College was founded in 1988 to provide English courses for foreign students. We occupy two buildings in west London and, with nearly 1,000 students from over 40 countries studying with us, we enjoy a busy, cosmopolitan atmosphere. Our courses in general English vary between two weeks and one academic year in length and are available both full and part time. We also provide business English courses and exam training. In addition to these courses, we offer conversation classes in small groups. One-to-one tuition is also available and can be tailored to individual needs.

All our training is delivered by a teaching staff of around 30 qualified and experienced teachers under the guidance of the director of studies. On arrival, all new students undertake a language assessment consisting of a written test and an interview; this allows us to assign them to a class of the correct level and advise them which, if any, exams will be appropriate. We teach all levels of English ranging from beginners' classes through to classes preparing students for the Cambridge Proficiency Exam. For students at the higher level, we have links with an organisation which assists with entry to British universities. Last year we had students go on to university courses ranging from marketing to English literature. Other students have gone on to further study in fields as diverse as pharmacy, translation and IT.

In addition to English courses, we have an accommodation service which arranges host families and operates a student hostel next door to our school in Shepherd's Bush. The KSC hostel provides self-catering accommodation for students in shared rooms. Hostel accommodation is ideal for those students who prefer an independent base from which to explore London. For those who prefer to stay with a host family, the accommodation officer can arrange suitable accommodation for students with local families on either a half-board, bed and breakfast or self-catering basis.

The school employs a staff member to organise extracurricular activities both at weekends and in the evenings. The most popular are European trips such as weekends in Paris and day trips to cultural and historical places of interest in Britain, including Stonehenge, Leeds Castle, Oxford and Cambridge.

We have regular trips to the theatre in the West End of London and frequent parties and discos.

Contact details, see page 611

Student profile

Krisztina Szilagi

Hungary

"My name is Krisztina Szilagyi. I am from Hungary. I came to London a year ago by car on a sunny autumn afternoon. The journey was long – more than 24 hours – and the most memorable part of it was crossing the channel between Calais and Dover. Having studied English before, I knew quite a lot of things about England, and I was very excited about the idea that I was going to study in the seventh biggest capital in the world. I started studying at King Street College immediately because my brother's old friend from Hungary had studied there. At the beginning, I lacked confidence when speaking and was a bit nervous. After taking a test and having an interview, I found myself in a class with students of different nationalities; some of them were very relaxed and confident due to the time they had spent here. Fortunately, I have come across very helpful and devoted teachers, who have helped the students not only in their studies but also to settle in. Looking back from one year's experience, my English has improved considerably and I am now preparing for the Cambridge Proficiency Exam.

Being a student in London gives you special advantages. Owning an international student card, you can get free entry into several museums and exhibitions. And London is never boring from a cultural point of view. Then there are the great opportunities which the school provides for us to take part in many social activities ranging from day trips around London to nights out at the theatre. I feel I spend my time in a useful way and my school plays an important role in this."

are available. A student's level of English may need to be assessed to establish which of the courses is the best for them.

For further information, see page 520

Queen Margaret University College, Edinburgh

English Language Programmes

Queen Margaret University College, Edinburgh offers courses for international students wanting to study for a short time over the summer or spend a year at the university. All-year-round courses are provided to prepare students for degrees at an English-speaking university. Students can also take English as a foreign language as part of a joint BA degree or a pre-MBA course which gives them all they need to enter an MBA programme. Classes cover all aspects of language learning, including general, academic and business English. If students are non-native speakers studying in another department, Queen Margaret can also offer academic English language support. Many modules are now available online. For EFL teachers there is now an MSc in Computer Enhanced Learning. During the summer, the university offers a two-centre, four-week package with the first two weeks of study spent in Bath before going on to Edinburgh.

Contact details, see page 619

SKOLA

English at Work

The Skola Group aims to provide quality education for children and adults. This includes English language courses and the full national curriculum for native and non-native speakers of English. The English at Work course, which is run at Marble Arch Intensive English, helps those who wish to improve their work-related language and job skills. This course

English as a foreign language

enables students to practice job skills in a real office environment including telephone sales and answering techniques, writing a business letter, office culture and vocabulary, writing a resume and individual personalised tutorials. Groups are no larger than eight, ensuring plenty of individual attention. Trainees have a defined role within the small group and learn by hands-on training, role plays and individual tutorials.
Contact details, see page 612

York St John College
International Short Course Centre
The centre offers courses in English language at both intermediate and advanced level throughout the year. Students can study for periods of one to three months on intensive English programmes, staying with specially-selected host families in York. Students can also study for the Foundation Certificate in Marketing and Management which is a one-year programme validated by the University of Leeds to give students the English language, study skills and subject knowledge to progress onto an undergraduate
For further information, see page 588

Undergraduate
The University of Stirling
BA (Hons) English Language and Business (ELaB)
This programme is designed for international students who wish to achieve a high level in English combined with courses in business and management. The programme lasts three years with each academic session lasting two semesters. In the first year, students take four units of intensive study of English language and two units in business. In the second year, the units of study are evenly divided between English language and business and in the third year the units are mainly in the area of business, including options in management, marketing, personnel, retail studies, entrepreneurship and international business. Applicants should have an academic record suitable for university entrance and evidence of ability in English at a level equivalent to IELTS 5.5. For students who do not have the required qualification, there are a range of preparatory courses provided.
For further information, see page 566

Useful links

www.arels.org.uk	◗	Association of Recognised English Language Services
www.baselt.org.uk	◗	British Association of State English Language Teaching
www.bielt.org	◗	British Institute of English Language Teaching
www.cilt.org.uk	◗	Centre for Information on Language Teaching and Research
www.iatefl.org	◗	International Association of Teachers of English as a Foreign Language
www.tefl.org	◗	Teaching English as a Foreign Language
www.toefl.org	◗	Test of English as a Foreign Language

English as a foreign language

English literature

The French philosopher, Descartes, said, "The reading of good books is like a conversation with the finest persons of past centuries." As such, a degree in English literature can be seen as an extended discussion with the likes of William Shakespeare, John Milton and Charles Dickens – an exciting prospect in anyone's book.

Although the British literary tradition goes back hundreds of years, British education was, until the 20th century, pre-occupied with Greek and Latin texts. Turn-of-the-century academics fought long and hard to establish English literature as the respected subject that it is now. As the English language has spread its influence around the globe and Britain has absorbed multicultural influences, so English literature has evolved to represent these changes. Although degrees still require students to study what are known as the 'canonical' texts, including Shakespeare, Chaucer, Pope and Milton, they increasingly include authors as culturally and geographically diverse as Milan Kundera, Arthur Miller and J M Coetzee.

Most universities, colleges and private schools offer English, and many will also offer English as a foreign language (see page 201). The courses are radically different, however, and students should be careful not to confuse the two. A course in English literature will invariably involve a lot of reading but it is also likely to involve discussing subjects and ideas as far reaching as politics, philosophy, art, history and science. A good deal of writing will be required. The ability to do so clearly and concisely and to develop and articulate arguments is essential.

At undergraduate level, a degree in English usually lasts three years. Some courses concentrate primarily on more traditional texts, others allow scope for more modern study including, in some cases, television and film. The first year usually concentrates on canonical texts and provides an introduction to critical theories, as well as important cultural sources which may include Darwin, the *Bible,* Marx and Freud. The following two years then allow students a certain amount of freedom to structure their own course of study. Teaching is generally carried out through a combination of lectures, seminars and tutorials. In seminars and tutorials students may be expected to do presentations or read out their essays, as well as engage in discussion and debate.

At postgraduate level, it is possible to do research in almost any area imaginable. Choices could include critical theory, modern English language or Renaissance literature, and there is often the possibility to branch out into new fields of interest.

At both postgraduate and undergraduate level, the subject helps to cultivate an enquiring mind. It gives you the chance to bring a fresh response to texts which formerly seemed cast in stone.

Undergraduate

The University of Wales, Aberystwyth

BA English

This course encourages students to read widely and to think critically about reading and its contexts. It develops their powers of expression and communication in both speech and writing. Consequently the presentation of seminar papers forms an important part of the coursework. The course starts with a skills and methods module focusing on a range of different approaches to reading and writing about literary texts, a study of different genres of poetry, drama and the novel and an introduction to more recent poetry and fiction. Part two is arranged into four modules organised on a historical basis, with medieval and Renaissance literature, restoration and 18th-century literature, 19th-century and 20th-century literature. Students take two core modules in literary theory and choose four more from a wide-ranging list.

For further information, see page 436

Chester (A College of the University of Liverpool)

BA English Literature

English literature can be studied as a single honours degree or in combination with another subject as part of the combined subjects programme. Students following the latter programme can major in English literature which covers a range of key texts from the Renaissance to the present. The programme proceeds in reverse chronological order, starting with contemporary literature and ending with the age of Shakespeare. In addition, is a series of elective modules allowing students to devise their own individual programme.

Students are taught in a variety of ways; through seminars, lectures, in individual tutorials or through the use of the department's own open-learning materials.

Contact details, see page 614

University of Exeter

BA English and Film Studies

This course aims to develop students' ability to read perceptively and critically a range of primary and secondary material and to foster their capacity for creative thought. The film part of the course teaches students to think about cinema in different ways including the opportunity to explore practical film-making. They will have access to the university's Centre for the History of Cinema and Popular Culture, a collection of over 40,000 artefacts relating to the history and pre-history of cinema. The first year provides an introduction to the concepts of contemporary criticism and theory. Students then take four modules, two from the English course and two from film. Year three involves one film option, one English and one more from either, as well as a dissertation on a topic chosen by the student.

Contact details, see page 616

University of Leeds

BA (Hons) English

Students taking this course follow core modules on English literature and language from the medieval period to the present. These are complemented by a choice of options. In the first year, all single honours students take the same core components. These consist of four modules: strategies of reading, language, text and context, exploring medieval literature and literature, history and difference. In the second year, they choose modules exploring literature between 1350 and 1832 and may develop

TEACHING QUALITY ASSESSMENTS

English
(England and Northern Ireland) 1994/95/96

Institution	Grade	Institution	Grade
Anglia Polytechnic University	Excellent	University of Central	
Bath Spa University College	Excellent	England in Birmingham	Satisfactory
Birkbeck College	Excellent	University College Chichester	Satisfactory
The University of Birmingham	Excellent	University of Central Lancashire	Satisfactory
University of Bristol	Excellent	De Montfort University	Satisfactory
University of the West		University of East Anglia	Satisfactory
of England, Bristol	Excellent	The University of Essex	Satisfactory
Cambridge University	Excellent	University of Greenwich	Satisfactory
Chester College	Excellent	The University of Huddersfield	Satisfactory
The University of Durham	Excellent	The University of Hull	Satisfactory
University of East London	Excellent	Keele University	Satisfactory
University of Exeter	Excellent	The University of Kent	Satisfactory
Kingston University	Excellent	King Alfred's Winchester	Satisfactory
Lancaster University	Excellent	King's College London	
University of Leeds	Excellent	(University of London)	Satisfactory
University of Leicester	Excellent	Leeds, Trinity	
The University of Liverpool	Excellent	and All Saints College	Satisfactory
University of Newcastle upon Tyne	Excellent	University of Luton	Satisfactory
University of North London	Excellent	The University of Manchester	Satisfactory
Northumbria University	Excellent	The Manchester	
The University of Nottingham	Excellent	Metropolitan University	Satisfactory
Oxford University	Excellent	North Riding College	Satisfactory
Oxford Brookes University	Excellent	The Nottingham Trent University	Satisfactory
Queen Mary, University of London	Excellent	University of Portsmouth	Satisfactory
Queen's University Belfast	Excellent	The University of Reading	Satisfactory
The University of Sheffield	Excellent	Royal Holloway,	
Sheffield Hallam University	Excellent	University of London	Satisfactory
University of Southampton	Excellent	The College of St Mark and St John	Satisfactory
University of Sussex	Excellent	St Mary's College	Satisfactory
University College London		Staffordshire University	Satisfactory
(University of London)	Excellent	University of Sunderland	Satisfactory
The University of Warwick	Excellent	University of Teesside	Satisfactory
The University of York	Excellent	University of Westminster	Satisfactory
Aston University	Satisfactory	University of Wolverhampton	Satisfactory
Canterbury Christ Church		University College Worcester	Satisfactory
University College	Satisfactory		

English
(Scotland) 1996/97/98

Institution	Grade	Institution	Grade
University of Dundee	Excellent	The University of Edinburgh	Highly Satisfactory
University of Glasgow	Excellent	University of St Andrews	Highly Satisfactory
The University of Stirling	Excellent	The University	
The University of Aberdeen	Highly Satisfactory	of Strathclyde	Highly Satisfactory

English and Associated Studies
(Wales) 1994/95

Institution	Grade	Institution	Grade
The University of Wales,		University of Wales, Bangor (Literature)	Satisfactory
Aberystwyth	Excellent	Cardiff University (Literature)	Satisfactory
Cardiff University (Language)	Excellent	The University of Wales, Lampeter	
University of Glamorgan (Creative		(English and Victorian Studies)	Satisfactory
Writing, Theatre, Media Drama)	Excellent	University of Wales Swansea	Satisfactory

Source: HEFCE, SHEFC, HEFCW latest available ratings
For a more complete list of institutions offering these courses at undergraduate level refer to the Course Directory

the study of the English language. Students also choose options from 70 topics and may take an elective outside the school. In the third year, core modules explore litera- ture from 1832 to the present day, including North American writing and Post-colonial literature.

Contact details, see page 617

English Language and Literature

Institution	Grade	Institution	Grade
Birkbeck College (University of London)	5*	University of the West of England, Bristol	4
Cambridge University	5*	University of Dundee	4
Cardiff University	5*	The University of Essex	4
The University of Durham	5*	University of Glamorgan	4
The University of Edinburgh	5*	University of Gloucestershire	4
University of Glasgow	5*	King's College London	
University of Leeds	5*	(University of London)	4
The University of Liverpool	5*	Liverpool John Moores University	4
Oxford University	5*	The Manchester Metropolitan University	4
The University of Reading	5*	Middlesex University	4
University of St Andrews	5*	University College Northampton	4
University College London (University of London)	5*	Open University	4
The University of Warwick	5*	Roehampton University of Surrey	4
The University of York	5*	St Mary's College	4
Anglia Polytechnic University	5	Sheffield Hallam University	4
The University of Birmingham	5	South Bank University	4
University of Bristol	5	University of Sunderland	4
De Montfort University	5	University of Wales Swansea	4
University of East Anglia	5	University of Ulster	4
University of Exeter	5	Bolton Institute of Higher Education	3a
Goldsmiths College (University of London)	5	University of Central England in Birmingham	3a
The University of Hull	5	University of Central Lancashire	3a
Keele University	5	University College Chichester	3a
The University of Kent	5	University of Hertfordshire	3a
University of Wales, Lampeter	5	The University of Huddersfield	3a
Lancaster University	5	Kingston University	3a
University of Leicester	5	University of North London	3a
Loughborough University	5	Northumbria University	3a
The University of Manchester	5	University of Plymouth	3a
University of Newcastle upon Tyne	5	The College of St Mark and St John	3a
The University of Nottingham	5	St Martin's College	3a
The Nottingham Trent University	5	Staffordshire University	3a
Oxford Brookes University	5	Bretton Hall	3b
Queen Mary, University of London	5	Edge Hill College of Higher Education	3b
Queen's University Belfast	5	Falmouth College of Arts	3b
Royal Holloway, University of London	5	Liverpool Hope	3b
The University of Sheffield	5	Newman College	3b
University of Southampton	5	Norwich School of Art and Design	3b
University of Sussex	5	Trinity and All Saints	3b
The University of Stirling	5	University of Westminster	3b
The University of Strathclyde	5	University College Worcester	3b
The University of Aberdeen	4	York St John College	3b
The University of Wales, Aberystwyth	4	Chester (A College of the University of Liverpool)	2
University of Wales, Bangor	4	Dartington College of Arts	2
Bath Spa University College	4	Thames Valley University	2

Source: RAE 2001

University of Portsmouth

BA (Hons) English and Creative Studies

This combines the study of English literature with various practical approaches to creative work in performance and writing. The English units span the literary period from the Renaissance to the postmodern era. Each student produces a body of original work which is built on over the three years and much of which will be published or performed. First-year studies introduce notions of authorship and narrative which become prominent themes in students' performances and written pieces. In the second year, students can choose whether to focus on literature or on practical interests. A dissertation is written in the third year, and units are assessed by a variety of essay, project and in-class assignments.

For further information, see page 538

University College London (University of London)

BA English

The Department of English at UCL is the oldest in the country and offers a flexible, distinctive syllabus. Students are encouraged to build their own programmes of study after the first-year foundation course, which covers major narrative texts from the Renaissance to the 20th century and background texts from Homer to Freud and Barthes. In the second and third years, students take two core courses, Chaucer and Shakespeare, as well as choosing six courses from a range of options. There is a fortnightly one-to-one tutorial during which student and teacher agree on essay topics.

Contact details, see page 622

Postgraduate

The Universities of Glasgow and Strathclyde

MLitt Creative Writing

The course aims to provide a stimulating environment in which skills from different genres can be acquired and discussed. It develops a critical understanding of contemporary theories of writing and students go on to produce an extended piece of individual writing or research. Class time and instruction provide a supportive context for individual study. Students learn to research and write with a view to publication. This vocational dimension is reflected in the practical nature of the course and in the acquisition and application of theories of literary production.

For further information, see pages 480 and 568

University of East Anglia

MA Creative Writing

This programme, led by the Poet Laureate, Andrew Motion, is for students who are seriously committed to writing and are practising or prospective authors. It does not claim to teach students to be professional writers, although excellent contacts are maintained with agents, publishers and the professional theatre. The programme involves intensive study of students' own work and also draws on aspects of teaching in 19th and 20th- century literature, literary theory and film and cultural studies. Emphasis is placed on the theoretical and practical aspects of writing, including the possibilities of publication and performance. Each year, UEA publishes an anthology of short stories produced by creative writing students to professional standards which is distributed nationally. The dissertation may be several short stories, a substantial body of poetry, a play, a script or a novel.

For further information, see page 470

Useful links

www.bl.uk	●	The British Library
www.bcla.org/index.htm	●	British Comparative Literature Association
www.le.ac.uk/engassoc	●	The English Association
www.lrb.co.uk	●	London Review of Books
www.poetrysoc.com	●	The Poetry Society

English literature

Fashion and beauty

The UK fashion scene is currently enjoying phenomenal success. With high profile names such as Stella McCartney, Vivienne Westwood, Alexander McQueen, Bruce Oldfield and John Galliano flying the flag, Britain is a major force at an international level. Along with New York, Paris and Milan, London is now a key player on the international fashion circuit. If you want to break into this glamorous industry and mix with the beautiful people, you will need to be prepared for intense competition and hard work.

Fashion and beauty are usually treated separately although there are few schools in the UK where it is possible to study both. Many private and specialist schools offer courses, and frequently their own diplomas, but it is also possible to take university and college courses at an undergraduate or postgraduate level.

Fashion

The term 'fashion' covers a spectrum of activities. From high-street design, the catwalk, fashion buying and marketing to textile design, photography or journalism, there are numerous professions within the industry and this is reflected by the number of different courses available. Design-based courses aim to broaden a student's experience of fashion whilst developing their artistic skills and individual style. Other courses deal primarily with the business side of the industry, teaching similar skills to those taught on general business courses but with a fashion slant, for example setting up a fashion company.

Beauty

There is a vast range of make-up and beauty courses available in the UK. Before enrolling, you should gather information about the course content and what it qualifies you for. Beauty therapy may involve massage, manicure, waxing and facials. Respected qualifications include the International Hair and Beauty Certificate (IHBC), City & Guilds or NVQs. In addition, well known accreditation bodies such as the Comité International d'Esthètique et Cosmétologie (CIDESCO), and its counterpart, the British Confederation of International Beauty Therapy and Cosmetology (CIBTAC), test and inspect establishments before allowing them to display their names.

You may have to decide between fashion-based and special effects make-up courses. Although most will include basic elements of each, they are usually treated as separate subject areas and students are encouraged to specialise. Fashion styling for hair and make-up, for instance, teaches students to prepare models for promotional, catwalk or photographic work. A course in theatrical make-up, on the other hand, teaches various techniques for creating fake wounds, or period looks for the stage or screen.

Harrogate College

BTEC National Diploma in
Fashion and Clothing

This challenging and creative course prepares students for entry into the fashion industry. Combining studio work with lectures and seminars, the course provides students with the opportunity to explore, develop and visualise designs and ideas and acquire the knowledge and skill to make patterns and construct garments from a wide range of related technologies. In addition to exploring materials and craft skills, the course helps students to develop research and presentation skills. It is a two-year, full-time programme covering a total of 12 study modules. Course assessment is continuous and based around a series of project work that aims to allow the student to develop a range of skills. On completion of the course, many students progress onto further specialist study on a degree or Higher National Diploma. Alternatively, students may decide to enter employment in a fashion-related field.

For further information, see page 418

The Ray Cochrane Beauty School

The Ray Cochrane Beauty School, founded in 1954, was the first CIDESCO school in the UK to train students in the CIDESCO international syllabus and to its standard (a worldwide qualification recognised for its consistent high quality training and success rate). The school's principal is Baljeet Suri, who has been an examiner for CIDESCO and CIBTAC. The school aims to train people in health and beauty, enabling them to start a career in the flourishing beauty profession. The college aims to give personal attention and tuition

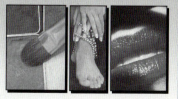

Fashion and beauty

and students undergo both practical and written assessment. Past graduates of the school have gone on to secure employment with luxury cruise liners, health farms, salons, hospitals and beauty schools and others have become freelance therapists. Contact the school on +44 (0)20 7486 6291 for a prospectus and an enrolment form.

Contact details, see page 612

Walsall College of Art and Design

Edexcel National Diploma in Fashion and Textiles

This creative and intensive course is the first step to a career within the world of fashion and textiles. Students study a variety of subjects such as fashion design, textile design, industrial production, fashion history and textiles, CAD and visual studies. The course offers regular visits to trade fairs, exhibitions, galleries and fashion shows and a five-day visit to either Paris or London. There is an opportunity for a work placement within companies such as Red or Dead, Helen Storey or the *Birmingham Post*, and involvement in the student fashion marketing team. The programme is full time. Studying for this course is varied, demanding and highly motivated yet never dull. For graduation, students show their work and collections at the annual fashion show, regularly attended by press and media, industry and the general public.

For further information, see page 432

Undergraduate

Central Saint Martin's College of Art and Design

BA (Hons) Jewellery Design

The course focuses entirely on jewellery design, from concept to realisation.

Although the course is rooted in the acquisition of traditional skills, students are encouraged to experiment with new materials and techniques, since both fine and couture fashion jewellery can be innovative and high quality. Students obtain basic practical and design skills in their first year, and develop and widen these skills in the second year as their personal direction is both defined and refined. In their final year, students prepare for a career through practical design programmes and theoretical studies which are proposed by each student individually. Throughout the course, great importance is given to cultural studies which highlights the social and historical context in which jewellers work and helps to develop essential professional skills. Graduates work in all areas of the jewellery profession.

Contact details, see page 614

De Montfort University
BA (Hons) Contour Fashion

Contour fashion embraces bodywear, swimwear, dancewear, lingerie, structured underwear, active sportswear and leisurewear. The study of these subjects to degree level is a unique feature of this programme which is the only one of its kind in the UK. All study areas are concerned with the development of each individual's creative design ideas. A variety of modules enable students to extend their ideas into reality by underpinning their design innovation with the relevant technical processes. This design can range from an individually-crafted artefact through to mass-produced high street products. The flexible and guided way of study allows students to develop skills and techniques relevant and necessary for a career in contour fashion.

Contact details, see page 615

Fashion and beauty

Liverpool John Moores University
BA (Hons) Fashion and Textiles Design

This degree prepares students for entry into the world of textiles, fashion and related industries or to continue their education through postgraduate study. The route provides a framework for an intellectually-demanding educational experience while aiming to raise visual awareness, critical faculties and aesthetic sensibilities. Technical skills are taught under the major headings of fashion, knitwear, printed textiles and stitch, and students are encouraged to work across these skill areas. Assessment varies according to the modules taken but is usually based on the submission of design portfolios, coursework and assignments.

Contact details, see page 618

The Manchester Metropolitan University
BA (Hons) Textiles

This course aims to produce designers and craftspeople with highly developed creativity, underpinned by technical and interpersonal skills. Offering students the opportunity to work in the areas of knitted, printed and woven textiles, the course also places strong emphasis on drawing and painting. After graduation, students will be well placed to pursue careers in textiles and fashion, as well as other design-related industries. Studio projects concentrating on visual research and the development of ideas, together with practical workshop sessions, form the basis of the first year. The creative and practical aspects are supported by a series of textile history lectures and students are introduced to the wider horizons of art and design through an art history programme in the first two years. In the third year, students undertake an 8,000 to 12,000-word dissertation.

For further information, see page 512

EDUCATI**U**K**N

www.educationuk.org

Useful links

www.beauty-uk.co.uk	◉	Beauty UK
www.cidesco.com	◉	CIDESCO
www.widemedia.com/fashionuk	◉	Fashion UK
www.habia.org	◉	Hair and Beauty Industry Authority
www.londonfashionweek.co.uk	◉	London Fashion Week
www.lucire.com	◉	Lucire: Online Fashion Magazine
www.professionalbeauty.co.uk	◉	Professional Beauty
www.style.com	◉	Style.com

Geography

Geographers are concerned with investigating and analysing the forces that shape our social and physical environments. Geographical, geological and geophysical research, analysis and forecasting are crucial in informing and influencing public attitudes and actions, as well as political decisions and policies. Nowadays there is a huge amount of pressure on the earth's resources and the public needs to be aware of its responsibility to look after the planet. Those studying geography develop the skills and knowledge necessary to work towards a brighter future for the human race and for the environment.

Geography is a broad-based university subject, dividing into two schools – physical and human geography. Physical geography concentrates on the dynamic processes which shape the earth's surface – the actions of rivers, glaciers and other geomorphic agents such as wind. It also focuses on the study of land forms and other physical phenomena created by these agents. Human geographers study various aspects of people in their specific environments. They employ other disciplines such as history, economics and religion to explain, for example, population dynamics or the location of industry. The two schools of thought are interrelated, drawing on the social sciences and economics to formulate theories and provide explanations.

Many institutions offer geography both as a BA and a BSc. Essentially, there is very little difference between the two, although the BSc usually concentrates more on physical geography and the BA on human geography. Those opting for a human geography course study economic, social, political and historical geography, urban and regional geography, population, energy and development studies. Degrees in physical geography cover topics such as soil and water systems, climate studies, land forms and geomorphic and other processes. Students of both types of degree can expect to become familiar with satellite remote sensing, computing for geography and geographical information systems (GIS), all to varying extents, depending on the specific course.

The content of earth science degrees varies hugely, depending on their level of specialisation. Geological science covers areas such as earth history, palaeontology, rocks and minerals, earth chemistry and petrology. Environmental geology focuses on processes occurring at or near the earth's surface. Geophysics covers similar areas but also involves the study of maths and physics-related fields such as electromagnetism and time series analysis.

Geography degrees are highly practical in content with fieldwork playing an important part, often with the opportunity to travel to other countries. Methods of assessment include formal exams, coursework and sometimes a dissertation. Teaching is through lectures, seminars and tutorial sessions, as well as practicals.

Specialist and vocational

University College Worcester
HND Physical Geography

The first year of the HND Physical Geography course allows students to study modules such as introduction to ecology, scientific study skills and diversity of living organisms. The second year is more specialised with students able to take modules such as the Highlands field course, mountains, glaciers and climate and geographical information systems. It is also possible for students to arrange work experience. Teaching methods include lectures, laboratory and field work, directed reading and independent study. A strong emphasis is placed on local field work in Worcester, Birmingham, the Malvern Hills and Herefordshire.
Contact details, see page 622

Undergraduate

Bournemouth University
BSc (Hons) Applied Geography

This vocational degree allows students to apply their geographical skills to live issues in the real world. The programme is taught in Britain's only mainland natural World Heritage Site where the school has exclusive facilities. Recent students have undertaken important project work such as discovering and mapping lava flow caves in Iceland. During year one, students undertake two weeks of fieldwork to develop skills in surveying, recording and identification. Year two includes a six-week placement in a relevant organisation. The programme has been designed for careers as professional geographers, working in landscape science or management, planning, remote sensing and GIS or environmental conservation.

In addition to excellent support facilities, students benefit from close links with professionals in agencies, local government and business.
For further information, see page 448

Canterbury Christ Church University College
BSc (Hons) Geography and Science (Environmental)

The aim of this joint honours programme is to introduce students to the skills and knowledge needed to understand the environment. The emphasis is on understanding physical processes based on sound scientific principles and the influence of socio-economic and political processes. The degree aims to provide stimulating fieldwork experiences in a variety of settings. In the first year, students take four broad-based courses designed to provide basic background material across the disciplines necessary for the second year. Second and third-year options allow students to build a degree to suit their interests and career plans. In the first year, there are one-day field visits, an integral part of the programme serving as a basis for residential field courses in the second and third-years in places such as Portugal and Malta. Links have been established with universities in 10 European countries and also in Africa and Canada.
Contact details, see page 614

The University of Durham
BSc (Hons) Geography

Geography students acquire a range of skills – theoretical and practical – which are relevant to natural and social systems. The department recognises the importance of regional studies in light of the complexity of the natural world.

TEACHING QUALITY ASSESSMENTS

Geography
(England and Northern Ireland) 1994/95/96

tqa

Institution	Grade	Institution	Grade
The University of Birmingham	Excellent	University of Southampton	Excellent
University of Bristol	Excellent	University College London	
Cambridge University	Excellent	(University of London)	Excellent
Canterbury Christ Church		Birkbeck College	Satisfactory
University College	Excellent	University of Central Lancashire	Satisfactory
Coventry University	Excellent	The University of Hull	Satisfactory
The University of Durham	Excellent	The University of Kent	Satisfactory
University of East Anglia	Excellent	King Alfred's Winchester	Satisfactory
University of Exeter	Excellent	Kingston University	Satisfactory
University of Gloucestershire	Excellent	University of Leicester	Satisfactory
King's College London		The University of Liverpool	Satisfactory
(University of London)	Excellent	London School of Economics	
Lancaster University	Excellent	and Political Science	
University of Leeds	Excellent	(University of London)	Satisfactory
Liverpool Institute	Excellent	Loughborough University	Satisfactory
The University of Manchester	Excellent	The Manchester	
The University of Nottingham	Excellent	Metropolitan University	Satisfactory
Open University	Excellent	University of Newcastle upon Tyne	Satisfactory
Oxford Brookes University	Excellent	Northumbria University	Satisfactory
Oxford University	Excellent	The University of Salford	Satisfactory
University of Plymouth	Excellent	School of Oriental and African	
University of Portsmouth	Excellent	Studies (University of London)	Satisfactory
Queen Mary, University of London	Excellent	University of Sunderland	Satisfactory
The University of Reading	Excellent	University of Ulster	Satisfactory
The University of Sheffield	Excellent	University College Worcester	Satisfactory

Geography
(Scotland) 1994/95

tqa

Institution	Grade	Institution	Grade
The University of Aberdeen	Excellent	The University of Strathclyde	Excellent
University of Glasgow	Excellent	The University of Edinburgh	Highly Satisfactory
University of St Andrews	Excellent	University of Dundee	Satisfactory

Geology
(England and Northern Ireland) 1994/95/96

tqa

Institution	Grade	Institution	Grade
The University of Birmingham	Excellent	Oxford University	Excellent
Cambridge University	Excellent	University of Plymouth	Excellent
University of Derby	Excellent	Queen's University Belfast	Excellent
The University of Durham	Excellent	The University of Reading	Excellent
Imperial College of Science, Technology		Royal Holloway,	
and Medicine (University of London)	Excellent	University of London	Excellent
Kingston University	Excellent	University of Southampton	Excellent
University of Leeds	Excellent	University College London	Excellent
The University of Liverpool	Excellent	University of Bristol	Satisfactory
The University of Manchester	Excellent	University of Exeter	Satisfactory
University of Newcastle upon Tyne	Excellent	University of Leicester	Satisfactory
Open University	Excellent	Oxford Brookes University	Satisfactory

Geology
(Scotland) 1993/94

tqa

Institution	Grade	Institution	Grade
The University of Edinburgh	Excellent	The University of Aberdeen	Highly Satisfactory
University of Glasgow	Excellent	University of St Andrews	Highly Satisfactory

Source: HEFCE, SHEFC, HEFCW latest available ratings
For a more complete list of institutions offering these courses at undergraduate level refer to the Course Directory

Students are trained in a range of appropriate geographical skills and develop their ability to think critically about the world through informed opinion. The department has a new suite of teaching laboratories and a microscope room, enabling students to learn a range of laboratory-based skills. There are opportunities for undertaking fieldwork in every year of the degree. Field classes provide an ideal opportunity to collect samples and data for further analysis. The geographical resources centre provides a workspace for students. It offers a range of facilities from aerial photograph interpretation to map collections and useful video resources.

Contact details, see page 615

The University of Edinburgh
BSc (Hons) Geology

Geology comprises one third of the curriculum in each of the first two years of study. The remaining two thirds can be made up from combinations of full and half courses in many science disciplines, for example biology, chemistry, physics, mathematics, geography, geophysics, meteorology, archaeology and computer science. Other options include economics, languages, law and industrial management. The third and fourth years are devoted to geology and include independent project work. There are field excursions in all years; typically

RESEARCH RANKINGS

Geography

rae

Institution	Grade	Institution	Grade
University of Bristol	5*	University of Plymouth	4
The University of Durham	5*	Queen's University Belfast	4
The University of Edinburgh	5*	The University of Reading	4
Open University	5*	School of Oriental and African Studies	
Royal Holloway, University of London	5*	(University of London)	4
University College London (University of London)	5*	University of St Andrews	4
Cambridge University	5	University of Sussex	4
The University of Hull	5	University of Wales Swansea	4
London School of Economics		Birkbeck College (University of London)	3a
and Political Science (University of London)	5	Brunel University	3a
Loughborough University	5	Coventry University	3a
University of Newcastle upon Tyne	5	University of Gloucestershire	3a
University of Leeds	5	Open University	
The University of Nottingham	5	(Geography: Development Studies)	3a
Queen Mary, University of London	5	University of Portsmouth	3a
The University of Sheffield	5	The University of Salford	3a
University of Southampton	5	Anglia Polytechnic University	3b
The University of Aberdeen	4	The University of Bradford	3b
The University of Wales, Aberystwyth	4	University of Brighton	3b
University of Bath	4	University of Greenwich	3b
The University of Birmingham	4	Liverpool Hope	3b
University of Dundee	4	Northumbria University	3b
University of East Anglia	4	The University of Reading (Development)	3b
University of Exeter	4	Staffordshire University	3b
University of Glasgow	4	University of Ulster	3b
King's College London		Bath Spa University College	2
(University of London)	4	Bournemouth University	2
Lancaster University	4	University of the West of England, Bristol	2
University of Leicester	4	University of East London	2
The University of Liverpool	4	The University of Huddersfield	2
The University of Manchester	4	University College Northampton	2
Middlesex University	4	University College Worcester	2
Oxford University	4	York St John College	2

Source: RAE 2001

Geography

students participate in residential courses as well as exploring local geology. Independent fieldwork for an honours thesis is carried out between the third and fourth years.

For further information, see page 474

Royal Holloway, University of London
BSc (Hons) Geography

Geography has a key role to play in framing and answering environmental, economic, social and political questions. The focus of Royal Holloway's department is on the relationship between people and their environments. The course stresses the breadth and relevance of geography and encourages detailed study of topical issues in a range of specialist courses. Students learn the basis of practical research and policy formation, and acquire vital career-related skills involving problem analysis, information management and communication. The course focuses on four major fields of interest: quaternary environments from Ice Age Britain to global warming, the developing world from shanty towns to sustainable development, ecosystem management from wetlands to tropical forests and, finally, social and cultural geographies from urban regeneration to imaginative geographies. Over the three years, students come into contact with issues of policy and decision-making at local, regional, national and global levels.

For further information, see page 550

University of Southampton
BA and BSc Single Honours
Degree Programmes

The Department of Geography was awarded grade 5A in the most recent research assessment exercise and an excellent grading in the most recent teaching quality assessment. There are only five other geography departments in the UK that offer such a potent mix of excellence in both the advancement and communication of geographical knowledge. The two single honours degree programmes offer a strong system of tutorial support which enables students to realise their full intellectual potential. The programmes cover an extensive range of subjects, including theoretically-based units and others that emphasise the applied aspects of geography in the contemporary world. Fieldwork, both in the UK and overseas, helps to reinforce this practical dimension. Constraints on the selection of the units which comprise a student's chosen degree are kept to a minimum. This flexibility, together with the wide range of units on offer, allows students to build up a flexible degree programme, tailored to their specific needs and interests.

For further information, see page 562

Postgraduate

The University of Wales, Aberystwyth
MA Practising Human Geography

The aim of this programme is to provide a unique master's degree which concentrates exclusively on the practice of human geography, giving students a comprehensive research training and preparing them either for postgraduate research or for a career utilising social science research skills. The course explores a number of relevant methodological and philosophical debates in contemporary human geography and looks at how these have been used to develop the research practice of the discipline. It draws on a range of expertise in social sciences across the university in order to deliver research training in research design and in the analysis of quantitative and qualitative research data. *For further information, see page 436*

Queen Mary, University of London
MSc Geography

The MSc course begins in September of each year and is completed 12 (full time) or 24 (part time) months later. The MSc is a modular course and allows the combination not only of specialist modules of a student's own choice but also a choice between variable ratios of taught and research-based modules. All participants undertake the compulsory core methodology course. Beyond that it is possible to opt for primarily research-based modules, an equal balance between taught and research modules, or primarily taught modules from the core methodology course with two optional courses and a 10,000-word thesis. The core methodology course will cover both qualitative and quantitative approaches to geographical research (including GIS techniques).
Contact details, see page 619

The Matterhorn, courtesy of Joanne Cullen

Useful links

www.bgs.ac.uk	◉	The British Geological Survey
www.earth-pages.com	◉	Earth Pages
www.econgeog.org.uk	◉	Economic Geography Research Group
www.environment-agency.gov.uk	◉	Environment Agency
www.geography.org.uk	◉	The Geographical Association
www.geolsoc.org.uk	◉	The Geological Society
www.nationalgeographic.com	◉	*National Geographic* Online
www.rgs.org	◉	Royal Geographical Society

Geography

Health-related sciences

With a degree in a health-related science, one thing is certain, you will always be in demand. Many people regard health as the key to happiness, above money, material goods and job satisfaction. It is not just doctors, nurses and dentists who spend their working lives maintaining the health of the nation. When was the last time you picked up a prescription from a pharmacist, had an eye test or an x-ray? There are a whole host of health-related scientists who play a vital role in our continued well-being.

Health covers a range of professions, from nursing to optometry, pharmacology and speech therapy. The following are brief descriptions of some of the health-related subjects you may want to consider.

Pharmacology and pharmacy

Pharmacists dispense drugs for the treatment of illness and disease. A Master of Pharmacy (MPharm) usually lasts four years and, along with a year of supervised employment after graduation, allows graduates to register as members of a professional body, such as the Royal Pharmaceutical Society, and dispense drugs.

Optometry

Students of optometry learn to examine the eye, to diagnose defects and diseases and treat them with therapy or lenses. A BSc usually lasts three years and will include studying the anatomy and physiology of the eye, visual optics and clinical practice. Students can register with the General Optical Council by completing a postgraduate year of training under the supervision of a qualified optometrist and by passing professional examinations.

Radiography

Radiography has two main branches. One is primarily diagnostic and involves using x-rays and other electromagnetic radiation to produce images of the body's internal structures, and is an important process in the diagnosis of abnormalities and diseases. The other is therapeutic and uses ionising radiation to treat diseases. BSc courses last between three and four years and include a clinical placement.

Nutrition

Nutritionists study foods, what they contain, what happens to them in the body and how they affect health. Dieticians apply nutritional science in the aim of promoting better health, preventing nutritional problems and treating diseases through diet. BSc degrees usually combine both aspects and last between three and four years.

Physiotherapy

Students need high grades to study physiotherapy in the UK. The three to four-year BSc is accepted all over the world. Courses include options such as care of the spine, sports medicine or care of the elderly, and clinical placements are integrated into the study programme.

TEACHING QUALITY ASSESSMENTS

Social Work
(Scotland) 1995/96

tqa

Institution	Grade	Institution	Grade
The University of Edinburgh	Excellent	The Robert Gordon	
University of Dundee	Highly Satisfactory	University	Highly Satisfactory
University of Glasgow	Highly Satisfactory	The University of Stirling	Highly Satisfactory
Glasgow Caledonian University	Highly Satisfactory	The University of Strathclyde	Highly Satisfactory
Northern College of Education	Highly Satisfactory	Moray House Institute of	
University of Paisley	Highly Satisfactory	Education, Edinburgh	Satisfactory

Applied Social Work
(England) 1994/95

tqa

Institution	Grade	Institution	Grade
Anglia Polytechnic University	Excellent	De Montfort University	Satisfactory
Bradford College	Excellent	University of Derby	Satisfactory
University of Bristol	Excellent	University of East London	Satisfactory
The University of Durham	Excellent	University of Exeter	Satisfactory
University of East Anglia	Excellent	University of Hertfordshire	Satisfactory
The University of Huddersfield	Excellent	University of Leicester	Satisfactory
The University of Hull	Excellent	Liverpool John	
Keele University	Excellent	Moores University	Satisfactory
Lancaster University	Excellent	The Manchester	
London School of Economics and		Metropolitan University	Satisfactory
Political Science (University of London)	Excellent	Middlesex University	Satisfactory
Oxford University	Excellent	University College Northampton	Satisfactory
Queen's University Belfast	Excellent	Northumbria University	Satisfactory
The University of Sheffield	Excellent	The University of Nottingham	Satisfactory
University of Southampton	Excellent	Open University	Satisfactory
West London Institute		University of Portsmouth	Satisfactory
of Higher Education	Excellent	The University of Reading	Satisfactory
The University of York	Excellent	South Bank University	Satisfactory
University of Bath	Satisfactory	Stockport College of	
Buckinghamshire Chilterns		Further & Higher Education	Satisfactory
University College	Satisfactory	University of Sussex	Satisfactory
University of Central Lancashire	Satisfactory	University of Ulster	Satisfactory
Croydon College	Satisfactory	The University of Warwick	Satisfactory

Applied Social Work
(Wales) 1993/94

tqa

Institution	Grade	Institution	Grade
University of Wales, Bangor	Satisfactory	The North East Wales Institute	
Cardiff University	Satisfactory	of Higher Education	Satisfactory
University of Wales Institute, Cardiff	Satisfactory	University of Wales Swansea	Satisfactory
University of Wales College, Newport	Satisfactory		

Source: HEFCE, SHEFC, HEFCW latest available ratings
For a more complete list of institutions offering these courses at undergraduate level refer to the Course Directory

Undergraduate

Brunel University

BSc Occupational Therapy

Occupational therapists enable people with disabilities or disadvantages to attain their goals and lead independent lives. They believe that occupational performance is integral to health and well-being. The course provides an educational programme which ensures that graduates are competent and safe to practise in the wide variety of health and social care settings where therapists work. The degree is validated by Brunel University, The College of Occupational Therapists and the Council for the Professions Supplementary to Medicine. Successful graduates gain a licence to practise as occupational therapists. The course integrates theory and practice with academic study, preparing students for fieldwork placements. Occupational therapy students share some modules with physiotherapy students, preparing them for multidisciplinary teamwork care settings. Some students undertake part of their studies in Europe. *For further information, see page 460*

Cardiff University
BSc (Hons) Optometry

Optometry is a varied profession centred round the clinical areas of ocular disease, refraction, binocular vision and contact lenses. This three-year course is designed to unite both the scientific and clinical components of the discipline. In the first year, the basics of the subject are taught and no prior knowledge of the eye or visual system is expected. In the second year, subjects are expanded to prepare students for the patient clinics and 'front-line' projects they meet in the third year. The clinical aspects of the course are spread over all three years and are designed to be as diverse as possible. In the final year, direct clinical experience is enhanced by visits to ophthalmic and orthoptic hospital departments where students encounter first hand ocular disease and the surgical or medical treatment of these conditions. *Contact details, see page 614*

Student Profile

Sally Edmonds
BSc (Hons) Radiography

City University

"The radiography course at City University gave me tremendous confidence in all aspects of radiographic training and healthcare. The knowledge and experience this course gave me allowed me to enter my radiographic career with the ease and assurance that I had been given the best start possible. This was reflected by an immediate job offer on qualification. I was keen to return to the university for my postgraduate training, which is already underway. The support I knew I would receive from my lecturers helped me decide to return to City University."

City University
Department of Radiography

The department offers an undergraduate programme, postgraduate courses and research degrees. Students study the theory of radiographic practice and clinical modules in their chosen area. The three-year, full-time undergraduate courses lead to a bachelor of science honours

Health-related sciences

TEACHING QUALITY ASSESSMENTS

Anatomy and Physiology
(England and Northern Ireland) 1998/99/2000

tqa

Institution	Grade	Institution	Grade
Loughborough University	24	University of Luton	22
University of Newcastle upon Tyne	24	The Manchester Metropolitan University	22
The University of Sheffield	24	University College Northampton	22
Cambridge University	23	Queen's University Belfast	22
The University of Liverpool	23	University College London	
The University of Manchester	23	(University of London)	22
University of Sunderland	23	The University of Reading	21
King's College London		University of Westminster	21
(University of London)	22	South Bank University	20

Anatomy and Physiology
(Wales) 1997/98

tqa

University of Wales Institute, Cardiff	Excellent

Source: HEFCE, SHEFC, HEFCW latest available ratings
For a more complete list of institutions offering these courses at undergraduate level refer to the Course Directory

TEACHING QUALITY ASSESSMENTS

Occupational Therapy
(Scotland) 1997/98

tqa

Institution	Grade	Institution	Grade
Glasgow Caledonian University	Highly Satisfactory	The Robert Gordon University	Satisfactory
Queen Margaret University College, Edinburgh	Highly Satisfactory		

Pharmacology and Pharmacy
(England and Northern Ireland) 1999/2000

tqa

Institution	Grade	Institution	Grade
Aston University	24	The University of Nottingham	23
University of the West of England, Bristol	24	The School of Pharmacy (University of London)	23
University of Derby	24	King's College London	
The University of Manchester	24	(University of London)	22
University of Newcastle upon Tyne	24	The University of Liverpool	22
University of Portsmouth	24	University of Luton	22
Queen's University Belfast	24	University of Sunderland	22
University of Bath	23	The University of Sheffield	21
University of Brighton	23	University College London	
University of Bristol	23	(University of London)	20
University of Leeds	23	University of East London	19
Liverpool John Moores University	23		

Pharmacy
(Scotland) 1997

tqa

The University of Strathclyde	Excellent	The Robert Gordon University	Highly Satisfactory

Pharmacy
(Wales) 1995/96

tqa

Cardiff University	Excellent

Source: HEFCE, SHEFC, HEFCW latest available ratings
For a more complete list of institutions offering these courses at undergraduate level refer to the Course Directory

degree and recognition by the Society of Radiographers. This is essential for registration with the Council for Professions Supplementary to Medicine which is required in order to gain a licence to practise radiography in the UK. BSc students spend 50 per cent of their time at the university with the remaining 50 per cent in a variety of hospital settings. Students have access to a fully-equipped imaging suite, radiotherapy planning suite, a radionuclide imaging ultrasound site, a specialist library and a computer assisted learning (CAL) laboratory. The undergraduate and postgraduate courses were recently assessed by the Quality Assurance Agency and were awarded 23 out of 24 points.

Contact details, see page 615

University of Lincoln
BSc Health Studies

The study of health involves the comprehensive understanding of personal, social,

TEACHING QUALITY ASSESSMENTS

Dietetics and Nutrition
(Scotland) 1997/98

tqa

Institution	Grade	Institution	Grade
Queen Margaret University College, Edinburgh	Excellent	The Robert Gordon University	Excellent
		Glasgow Caledonian University	Highly Satisfactory

Source: HEFCE, SHEFC, HEFCW latest available ratings
For a more complete list of institutions offering these courses at undergraduate level refer to the Course Directory

TEACHING QUALITY ASSESSMENTS

Physiotherapy
(Scotland) 1997/98

tqa

Institution	Grade	Institution	Grade
Glasgow Caledonian University	Excellent	The Robert Gordon University	Highly Satisfactory
Queen Margaret University College, Edinburgh	Excellent		

Radiography
(Scotland) 1998

tqa

Institution	Grade	Institution	Grade
Glasgow Caledonian University	Highly Satisfactory	The Robert Gordon University	Satisfactory
Queen Margaret University College, Edinburgh	Satisfactory		

Speech and Language Therapy, Podiatry, Applied Human Nutrition
(Wales) 1996/97

tqa

Institution	Grade
University of Wales Institute, Cardiff	Excellent

Other Subjects Allied to Medicine
(England and Northern Ireland) 1999/2000

tqa

Institution	Grade	Institution	Grade
The University of Birmingham	24	Queen Mary, University of London	22
Bolton Institute of Higher Education	24	The College of St Mark and St John	22
University of Leeds	24	The University of Salford	22
Liverpool John Moores University	24	University of Teesside	22
Loughborough University	24	University of Wolverhampton	22
University College London (University of London)	24	York St John (a college of the University of Leeds)	22
Aston University	23	Cranfield University	21
The University of Bradford	23	The University of Kent	21
City University	23	University of Lincoln	21
Coventry University	23	University of North London	21
The University of Durham	23	The University of Nottingham	21
University of East Anglia	23	The University of Sheffield	21
King's College London (University of London)	23	South Bank University	21
Kingston University	23	St Martin's College, Lancaster: Ambleside: Carlisle	21
St George's Hospital Medical School (University of London)	23	Suffolk College (An Accredited College of the University of East Anglia)	21
University of Luton	23	The University of Surrey	21
The University of Manchester Institute of Science and Technology (UMIST)	23	Anglia Polytechnic University	20
Northumbria University	23	Bournemouth University	20
University of Portsmouth	23	University College Chichester	20
Sheffield Hallam University	23	De Montfort University	20
University of Brighton	22	University of East London	20
Brunel University	22	Keele University	20
Canterbury Christ Church University College	22	The University of Liverpool	20
University of Central England in Birmingham	22	New College Durham	20
University of Central Lancashire	22	University of Plymouth	20
The University of Huddersfield	22	University of Southampton	20
The University of Manchester	22	Thames Valley University	20
The Manchester Metropolitan University	22	University College Worcester	19
University College Northampton	22	University of Greenwich	18

Source: HEFCE, SHEFC, HEFCW latest available ratings
For a more complete list of institutions offering these courses at undergraduate level refer to the Course Directory

Health-related sciences

political and economical perspectives relating to the delivery of efficient and effective healthcare to all sections of the population. Through a variety of teaching and learning experiences, the undergraduate comes to understand the complex framework of healthcare provision locally and nationally. Modules also cover the theoretical and philosophical basis of modern healthcare management and delivery, research methodologies employed to investigate healthcare practice, multicultural perspectives on healthcare and essential physical sciences. Health studies can be

Anatomy

rae

Institution	Grade	Institution	Grade
The University of Birmingham	5*	Oxford University	5
University of Bristol	5*	University College London	
King's College London (University of London)	5*	(University of London)	5
Cambridge University	5	The University of Liverpool	4

Clinical Laboratory Sciences

rae

Institution	Grade	Institution	Grade
The University of Birmingham	5*	University of Leeds	5
Cambridge University	5*	The University of Liverpool	5
University of Dundee	5*	London School of Hygiene and Tropical Medicine	5
Institute of Cancer Research	5*	University of Southampton	5
Imperial College of Science, Technology		University of Wales College of Medicine	5
and Medicine (University of London)	5*	The University of Aberdeen	4
University of Newcastle upon Tyne	5*	University of Leicester	4
Oxford University	5*	The University of Manchester	4
Oxford University (Dunn School of Pathology)	5*	Queen's University Belfast	4
University of Bristol	5	St George's Hospital Medical School	4
University of Glasgow	5	The University of Nottingham	3a
Institute of Cancer Research (Medical Physics)	5	Queen Mary, University of London	3a
King's College London (University of London)	5	University of East London	3b

Source: RAE 2001

taken as a single subject or in combination with another subject leading to a joint degree. On the joint degree, students follow a more prescribed programme of study geared towards achieving a significant understanding within each subject area. The programme of study is enhanced by visiting lecturers and visits to organisations charged with the delivery of primary and secondary healthcare.

Contact details, see page 617

Queen Margaret University College, Edinburgh

BSc (Hons) Human Nutrition

The course provides core knowledge of nutrition and related biological sciences. It also allows for expertise in areas such as sports nutrition, health promotion and research. In the first year, students take courses in human nutrition and food, biological chemistry, human physiology, cell biology, microbiology and sociology or psychology. Students also develop skills in computing, IT and data collection and analysis. In the second year, students develop their understanding of health and nutrition and begin to integrate biological and social sciences. The third year focuses on acquiring the specialist knowledge and skills needed by the nutritionist while the fourth year covers key areas in current issues of health and nutrition in greater depth and challenges present-day theory and practice. The course culminates in the submission of a research-based thesis.

Contact details, see page 619

University College London (University of London)

BSc Pharmacology

The UCL Pharmacology Department was the top-ranked department in the 2001 research assessment. In 2001, 90 per cent of UCL pharmacology students achieved a first or upper second class degree. In the first year, students learn essential background subjects such as chemistry, physiology, pharmacology and statistics. Practical work concentrates on experimental design, presentation and interpretation of results. Second-year students build on these basics

Pharmacology

rae

Institution	Grade	Institution	Grade
Oxford University	5*	The University of Liverpool	5
University College London		University of Bristol	4
(University of London)	5*	Queen Mary, University of London	4
Cambridge University	5	The University of Edinburgh	4
University of Leicester	5	University of Hertfordshire	3a

Pharmacy

rae

Institution	Grade	Institution	Grade
University of Bath	5*	School of Pharmacy	5
The University of Manchester	5*	The University of Strathclyde	5
Cardiff University	5	The University of Bradford	4
Institute of Cancer Research	5	Queen's University Belfast	4
King's College London (University of London)	5	Aston University	3a
The University of Nottingham	5	University of Sunderland	3a

Source: RAE 2001

with courses in biochemistry and neurobiology, immunology and systematic pharmacology. They also choose one or two courses from other departments throughout the college. In the final year, emphasis is on critical reading of the scientific literature and gaining an understanding of the process of scientific discovery.

Contact details, see page 622

University of Southampton
BSc (Hons) Physiotherapy

Physiotherapy is the health profession which emphasises the use of physical approaches in the prevention and treatment of disease and disability. This course, at the School of Health Professions and Rehabilitation Sciences, aims to equip students with the skills to practice as competent physiotherapists in an ever-changing healthcare system. Students learn some parts of the curriculum together with occupational therapy students. The course is organised around the four main aspects of the occupation: skilled practitioner, educator, evaluator and manager. One third of the course is allocated for clinical placements and the rest for academic and practical skills. The university encourages all applicants to demonstrate an insight into physiotherapy in their personal statement.

For further information, see page 562

Health-related sciences

Physiology

rae

Institution	Grade	Institution	Grade
The University of Liverpool	5*	Cambridge University	4
The University of Aberdeen	5	The University of Edinburgh	4
University of Leeds	5	University College London	
University of Newcastle upon Tyne	5	(University of London)	4
Oxford University	5	St George's Hospital Medical School	3a
University of Bristol	4	University of Hertfordshire	2

Pre-Clinical Studies

rae

Institution	Grade	Institution	Grade
The University of Manchester	5*	Imperial College of Science, Technology and	
The University of Sheffield	5*	Medicine (University of London)	5
The University of Birmingham	5	King's College London (University of London)	5
		St George's Hospital Medical School	5

Source: RAE 2001

Community-based Clinical Subjects

rae

Institution	Grade	Institution	Grade
University of Bristol	5*	University of Dundee	4
Cambridge University	5*	The University of Edinburgh	4
King's College London (University of London) (Institute of Psychiatry)	5*	University of Glasgow	4
		Keele University	4
King's College London (University of London) (School Of Medicine)	5*	University of Leeds	4
		The University of Liverpool	4
Oxford University	5*	The University of Sheffield	4
The University of Aberdeen	5	St George's Hospital Medical School	4
Institute of Cancer Research	5	University College London (University of London)	4
Imperial College of Science, Technology and Medicine (University of London)	5	University of Wales College of Medicine	4
London School of Hygiene and Tropical Medicine	5	Brunel University	3a
		City University	3a
The University of Manchester	5	University of Exeter	3a
University of Newcastle upon Tyne	5	University of Leicester	3a
Queen's University Belfast	5	The University of Nottingham	3a
The University of York	5	Queen Mary, University of London	3a
The University of Birmingham	4	University of Southampton	3a

Hospital-based Clinical Subjects

rae

Institution	Grade	Institution	Grade
Cambridge University	5*	University of Southampton	5
The University of Edinburgh	5*	The University of Aberdeen	4
Imperial College of Science, Technology and Medicine (University of London)	5*	King's College London (University of London)	4
		University of Leeds	4
Oxford University	5*	University of Leicester	4
University College London (University of London) (Institute of Child Health, Institute of Neurology, Institute of Ophthalmology)	5*	The University of Liverpool	4
		The University of Nottingham	4
		Queen Mary, University of London	4
The University of Birmingham	5	St George's Hospital Medical School	4
University of Dundee	5	University of Wales College of Medicine	4
University of Exeter	5	University of Bristol	3a
University of Glasgow	5	The University of Hull	3a
University College London (University of London) (Royal Free and University College Medical School)	5	Keele University	3a
		University of Plymouth	3a
The University of Manchester	5	Queen's University Belfast	3a
University of Newcastle upon Tyne	5	University of Teesside	3b
The University of Sheffield	5		

Source: RAE 2001

Useful links

www.cot.co.uk	●	British Association of Occupational Therapists
www.nutrition.org.uk	●	British Nutrition Foundation
www.csphysio.org.uk	●	The Chartered Society of Physiotherapy
www.cpsm.org.uk	●	Council for Professions Supplementary to Medicine
www.ioo.org.uk	●	The Institute of Optometry
www.rpsgb.org.uk	●	Royal Pharmaceutical Society

Health-related sciences

History

If we do not study history, we are destined to repeat the mistakes of the past. It is only by studying these mistakes that we can learn from them. The words are often quoted but more often misunderstood. When we speak of repeating the errors of the past, some would cite terrible wars, others will bring up economic crises but as any student or enthusiast of history knows, events spiral from the smallest beginnings.

Some people are inclined to dismiss history as a degree which can only lead you into teaching or academia but this is a vast misconception. Of the 1,011 directors in the top 100 UK companies, history is the fourth most common degree subject. Historians are trained to be analytical, organised and objective – all important, transferable skills.

Studying history at university revolves mainly around interpretation. Reading lists are long, reflecting the diversity of approaches and opinions generated by any one issue. When writing essays, a significant part of the history student's time involves examining these different ideas, considering the opinions of various historians, checking to see if there are any gaps in their arguments and working towards a final conclusion. Studying history at university or college is very different to learning history at school. There is a lot more choice in which eras and areas you can study. These depend largely on the specific interests of the department so it is

a good idea to find out what these are before you apply.

History students tend to have fewer contact hours than their scientist counterparts. This is because history is based on private study more than on formal teaching and you will be expected to spend a significant part of your day in the library, even if you only have one lecture. Lectures are often the starting points for essays, offering a foundation of facts and leaving the research up to you. Teaching also occurs through seminars and tutorials.

Most history degrees last for three years, although if you attend a Scottish university or opt to study a language in combination, you will probably study for four years. First-year modules are broad and tend to concentrate on a specific geographic or chronological area such as world history 1500 to 1800 or the Middle Ages. In the second and third years, modules are more focused and, depending on the institution, can include anything from Weimar Germany 1918 to 1933 to the history of philosophy.

The final year involves a specialist subject, along with a range of optional and core modules. This usually takes the form of a dissertation, ranging from 8,000 to 16,000 words in length, written on a subject of the student's choice. This can count towards the final degree classification for between 10 per cent to one third. Assessment is through formal exams and coursework as well as the dissertation.

History
(England and Northern Ireland) 1993/94

tqa

Institution	Grade	Institution	Grade
The University of Birmingham	Excellent	University of the West	
Cambridge University	Excellent	of England, Bristol	Satisfactory
Canterbury Christ Church		University of Derby	Satisfactory
University College	Excellent	University of East Anglia	Satisfactory
The University of Durham	Excellent	The University of Essex	Satisfactory
The University of Hull	Excellent	Goldsmiths College	
King's College London		(University of London)	Satisfactory
(University of London)	Excellent	Keele University	Satisfactory
Lancaster University	Excellent	King Alfred's Winchester	Satisfactory
University of Leicester	Excellent	La Sainte Union College of	
The University of Liverpool	Excellent	Higher Education	Satisfactory
London School of Economics and Political		University of Leeds	Satisfactory
Science (University of London)	Excellent	Leeds, Trinity and	
Oxford University	Excellent	All Saints College	Satisfactory
Queen's University Belfast	Excellent	The University of Manchester	Satisfactory
Royal Holloway,		University of Newcastle upon Tyne	Satisfactory
University of London	Excellent	University of North London	Satisfactory
The University of Sheffield	Excellent	Northumbria University	Satisfactory
University College London,		St Martins College, Lancaster:	
(University of London)	Excellent	Ambleside: Carlisle	Satisfactory
Warburg Institute	Excellent	Sheffield Hallam University	Satisfactory
The University of Warwick	Excellent	University of Southampton	Satisfactory
The University of York	Excellent	Staffordshire University	Satisfactory
Anglia Polytechnic University	Satisfactory	University of Sussex	Satisfactory
Bath Spa University College	Satisfactory	University College Chichester	Satisfactory
University of Bristol	Satisfactory	University of Wolverhampton	Satisfactory

History
(Scotland) 1995/96

tqa

Institution	Grade	Institution	Grade
The University of Edinburgh	Excellent	University of Glasgow	Highly Satisfactory
University of St Andrews	Excellent	The University of Stirling	Highly Satisfactory
The University of Aberdeen	Highly Satisfactory	The University of	
University of Dundee	Highly Satisfactory	Strathclyde	Highly Satisfactory

History
(Wales) 1993/94

tqa

Institution	Grade	Institution	Grade
University of Wales Swansea	Excellent	Cardiff University	Satisfactory
The University of Wales, Aberystwyth	Satisfactory	University of Glamorgan	Satisfactory
University of Wales, Bangor	Satisfactory	The University of Wales, Lampeter	Satisfactory

Source: HEFCE, SHEFC, HEFCW latest available ratings
For a more complete list of institutions offering these courses at undergraduate level refer to the Course Directory

Undergraduate

The University of Birmingham

BA (Hons) History, Ancient and Medieval
The study of ancient and medieval history draws on expertise in the Departments of Ancient History and Archaeology, Classics, Medieval History and the Centre for Byzantine, Ottoman and Modern Greek. At some point during the degree, students cover cultural and intellectual history, broad themes and periods and also research the details of more specialised topics. This degree also gives students the opportunity for travel and to experience practical field archaeology. All students are required to complete a training excavation in their first year. At present, excavations range from prehistoric to late medieval periods and are situated in various parts of the British Isles but there are also continuing projects in Italy, France, Germany and Crete.

History

Institution	Grade
Birkbeck College (University of London)	5*
Cambridge University	5*
The University of Durham	5*
University of East Anglia	5*
King's College London (University of London)	5*
London School of Economics and Political Science (University of London) (International History)	5*
Oxford Brookes University	5*
School of Oriental and African Studies (University of London)	5*
The University of Birmingham	5
Cardiff University	5
University of Dundee	5
The University of Edinburgh	5
The University of Essex	5
University of Exeter	5
University of Glasgow	5
University of Hertfordshire	5
The University of Huddersfield	5
The University of Hull	5
Imperial College of Science, Technology and Medicine (University of London)	5
Keele University	5
The University of Liverpool	5
University of Leeds	5
University of Leicester	5
London School of Economics and Political Science (University of London) (Economic History)	5
The University of Manchester	5
Oxford University	5
Queen's University Belfast	5
Queen Mary, University of London	5
Roehampton University of Surrey	5
Royal Holloway, University of London	5
The University of Sheffield	5
Sheffield Hallam University	5
University of Southampton	5
University of St Andrews	5
The University of Stirling	5
University of Teesside	5
University College London (University of London)	5
The University of Warwick	5
The University of York	5
The University of Aberdeen	4
The University of Wales, Aberystwyth	4
University of Wales, Bangor	4
University of Bristol	4
University of the West of England, Bristol	4
University of Central Lancashire	4
De Montfort University	4

Institution	Grade
Glasgow Caledonian University	4
Goldsmiths College (University of London)	4
Institute of Commonwealth Studies	4
Institute of Historical Research	4
The University of Kent	4
King Alfred's Winchester	4
Kingston University	4
Lancaster University	4
University of Leicester (Economic and Social History)	4
Leeds, Trinity and All Saints College	4
Liverpool John Moores University	4
The University of Wales, Lampeter	4
University of Luton	4
University of Newcastle upon Tyne	4
University College Northampton	4
The University of Nottingham	4
Open University	4
University of Portsmouth	4
The University of Reading	4
The University of Strathclyde	4
University of Sunderland	4
University of Sussex	4
University of Wales Swansea	4
University of Ulster	4
University of Wolverhampton	4
Anglia Polytechnic University	3a
Canterbury Christ Church University College	3a
University College Chichester	3a
University of Glamorgan	3a
University of Gloucestershire	3a
University of Greenwich	3a
London Guildhall University	3a
The Manchester Metropolitan University	3a
University of North London	3a
Northumbria University	3a
The Nottingham Trent University	3a
St Martin's College	3a
St Mary's College	3a
University of Westminster	3a
University College Worcester	3a
York St John College	3a
Bath Spa University College	3b
Bolton Institute of Higher Education	3b
Chester (A College of the University of Liverpool)	3b
Edge Hill College of Higher Education	3b
Liverpool Hope	3b
Middlesex University	3b
Staffordshire University	3b
Thames Valley University	3b

Source: RAE 2001

A funded study tour in the second year, usually in the Mediterranean, lasts three weeks and counts as a course in finals. In the third year, students write a dissertation on a detailed theme, chosen individually. *Contact details, see page 613*

The University of Edinburgh

MA (Hons) History

Edinburgh's remarkable collection of libraries makes it one of the best provided cities in Britain for the study of history, while its archival resources and architectural heritage leave it unrivalled for the pursuit of Scottish history. This course falls into two parts with the division coming at the end of the second year. Part of the first year is devoted either to British and European History since the mid-16th century or to one of those courses and another chosen from economic, social, ecclesiastical, ancient or Scottish history. In the second year, students choose two courses from a wide range of subjects. The third and fourth years consist of seven chosen courses and students write two pieces of independent work related to their individual interests. In the fourth year they also write a specialised dissertation.

For further information, see page 474

University of Wales Swansea
BA (Hons) History

The 18 academic staff who make up the history department represent most major periods and civilisations from the Middle to cover recent trends as well as established approaches to the study of history. The department therefore offers many modules, enabling students to widen their historical knowledge and increase their understanding. Teaching is carried out via lectures, seminars and tutorials, in which four or five students meet with their tutor to discuss historical issues. Students' powers of analysis, argument and expression are developed through regular essay writing and assessment is based upon a combination of coursework, examinations and dissertations. The Higher Education Funding Councils for England and Wales rated the department as excellent – the highest possible grading – in the most recent teaching assessment exercise.

Contact details, see page 621

London School of Economics and Political Science (University of London)
MSc Global History

The Department of Economic History at LSE has received the highest Economic and Social Research Council recognition as a research training programme. This course concentrates on global history, specifically on economic change considered in its social and political contexts. It is intended for graduates of history and of related disciplines including economics, politics and sociology. The programme comprises two core courses that provide a general grounding in major processes and debates in global history over the last millennium, a compulsory unit introducing central debates and key analytical tools and a specialist subject. Students also write a 10,000-word dissertation which may be a critical survey of a well-defined problem in the literature or an empirical case study within a global history framework.

For further information, see page 508

The University of Warwick
MA 18th-century Studies

On this course, students work with Warwick staff researching aspects of the 18th century on major new themes such as consumption, gender, the middling classes, industrialisation and literature. They develop a core historical base in the subject and take optional specialisms in subjects taught inside and outside the department, seeking where possible interdisciplinary links. Candidates will have, or expect to attain, a good honours degree or equivalent in history or related fields. Students choose two options from a list of specialist subjects including politics and opinion in Hanoverian Britain, theories of self in 18th-century Europe and the social history of poetry from 1780 to 1900. The course is unexamined but students submit two 2,500-word assignments, two 5,000-word essays and a 15,000-word dissertation.

For further information, see page 578

History

Useful links

www.bbc.co.uk/history	○	BBC History
www.britannia.com/history	○	Britannia History
www.historybookshop.com	○	History Bookshop
www.history.org.uk	○	The Historical Association
www.history.about.com	○	The History Net
www.historytoday.com	○	History Today
www.local-history.co.uk	○	Local History

Hotel management and catering

The hospitality industry has changed considerably since Cesar Ritz, the celebrated hotelier, first opened his hotels in London and Paris at the beginning of the 20th century. In the UK alone, there are over 260,000 hotels, restaurants, cafés, pubs and clubs, and an estimated 100,000 catering outlets, employing 10 per cent of the country's workforce.

In the last few years, the food industry in Britain has experienced a boom. We have become a nation of latté drinkers, olive oil connoisseurs and sun-dried tomato enthusiasts. No longer do we stick to roast beef and fish and chips. Our supermarkets now stock products like Thai curry paste and artichoke hearts. The fame and wealth of celebrity chefs such as Jamie Oliver, Nigella Lawson and Anthony Worrall-Thompson show just how trendy food is in Britain today.

The hospitality, food and drink industries offer a huge range of jobs so before choosing a course, it is worth considering exactly which career you wish to pursue. Some courses focus on the business and management side of hotel and catering, preparing students for such roles as catering supervisor, publican, or hotel manager. Others concentrate on the cooking and serving of food and drink, training those wishing to become chefs or wine waiters.

Whereas hotel management and catering is more focused upon customer service, food studies is concerned with what makes up the food we eat, how it affects us and what happens to it during processing, storage and distribution. This can encompass a number of subjects from product development, manufacturing and retail to food policies and nutrition. These are generally more science-based disciplines and are covered more thoroughly in the biological sciences chapter (see page 113). If you want to develop a new diet or tackle the problem of genetically-modified food you will need to have the relevant scientific background.

Cookery courses are available to anyone from the amateur hoping to impress dinner guests to those wishing to become professional chefs. Many are offered by colleges and private schools rather than universities. Courses last anything from a day to several years, covering everything from sugarcraft, bread baking, cordon bleu, food hygiene and vegetarian cookery.

There are three main routes into the hospitality or food and drink industries: attending a college or university, joining a training programme or going straight into employment. At college and university level, teaching will usually involves a combination of lectures and seminars with practical sessions in the kitchen. Most courses also involve some sort of work placement in a hotel, restaurant or within the food and drinks industry. Practical experience is an important learning aid, providing students with a useful introduction to their chosen field, and it is invaluable for helping to place that first foot on the rung of the career ladder.

Specialist and vocational

Leith's School of Food and Wine
Cookery and Wine Appreciation

Leith's School of Food and Wine was set up in 1975 with the aim of providing both professional training for career cooks and short courses for amateurs. The school teaches classical techniques and methods but with a fresh, modern approach in a professional but informal atmosphere. Leith's School of Food and Wine is an independent company owned by Christopher Bland and Caroline Waldegrave. The company is made up of

TEACHING QUALITY ASSESSMENTS

Food and Hospitality Management
(Wales) 1996/97

tqa

Institution	Grade	Institution	Grade
Llandrillo College, North Wales	Satisfactory		

Hospitality Studies
(Scotland) 1995

tqa

Institution	Grade	Institution	Grade
University of Dundee	Highly Satisfactory	The University of Strathclyde	Highly Satisfactory
Napier University	Highly Satisfactory	Glasgow Caledonian University	Satisfactory
Queen Margaret University College, Edinburgh	Highly Satisfactory	The Robert Gordon University	Satisfactory

Hotel, Tourism and Leisure
(Wales) 1996/97

tqa

Institution	Grade
University of Wales Institute, Cardiff	Satisfactory

Source: HEFCE, SHEFC, HEFCW latest available ratings
For a more complete list of institutions offering these courses at undergraduate level refer to the Course Directory

Leith's School of Food and Wine and Leith's List – an agency for cooks. The course for those with professional ambitions is the Diploma in Food and Wine. Students attend daily demonstrations and practical classes, each about two and a half hours long. Diploma students study menu planning, budgeting and wine appreciation. There are opportunities to do work experience in London restaurants, visit Smithfield, Billingsgate and Covent Garden markets, and hear lectures from gastronomic celebrities, head chefs and famous food writers. There are also visits from chefs specialising in international cuisine. The diploma can be achieved in three terms (starting in October) or two terms starting in January (if students possess enough basic knowledge of cookery). Other food and wine courses offered by the school include holiday, evening and part-time courses for the enthusiastic amateur.

Contact details, see page 611

Contact details, see page 611

Undergraduate

Sheffield Hallam University

BSc (Hons) International Hotel and Catering Management

This course is designed to produce graduates with all the necessary management, technological and operational skills needed to run hotel and catering facilities successfully. The third year of the four-year sandwich course is spent working in a hotel or catering establishment in Britain or abroad, enabling students to gain practical experience in industry – an element highly valued by prospective employers. The three-year, full-time route is designed for those with work experience. Mature students (over 21 on enrolment) who do not meet course entry requirements, but can demonstrate equivalent work experience relevant to the course, will be considered.

Contact details, see page 620

Contact details, see page 620

Postgraduate

University of Wales Institute, Cardiff

MSc/PGDip/PGCert
Hospitality Management

This one-year full-time or two-year part-time programme is aimed at providing continuing professional development for hospitality graduates/professionals. It is possible to gain a postgraduate certificate on completion of three taught modules and a postgraduate diploma after six. Master's students are required to complete six taught modules plus a 20,000-word dissertation. There are compulsory modules (learning for competitive advantage, contextualising tourism, leisure and hospitality, managing in a changing environment, strategic management of human resources) and a double module focusing on hospitality management.

Each taught module is assessed through exams, written assignments and seminar presentations.

For further information, see page 462

Leeds Metropolitan University

MSc Hospitality Management

This course provides an opportunity for students to develop and expand their knowledge and understanding of the management of hospitality organisations within an international context. The course is divided into two phases: phase one involves taking modules and phase two involves research in hospitality management leading to a dissertation. There is an opportunity for students to take part in a work placement for up to one year. The course is suited for those students who have no previous experience of hospitality management.

For further information, see page 500

Food and Hospitality Management
(Wales) 1996/97

tqa

Institution	Grade	Institution	Grade
Llandrillo College, North Wales	Satisfactory		

Hospitality Studies
(Scotland) 1995

tqa

Institution	Grade	Institution	Grade
University of Dundee	Highly Satisfactory	The University of Strathclyde	Highly Satisfactory
Napier University	Highly Satisfactory	Glasgow Caledonian University	Satisfactory
Queen Margaret University College, Edinburgh	Highly Satisfactory	The Robert Gordon University	Satisfactory

Hospitality, Leisure, Recreation, Sport and Tourism
(England and Northern Ireland) 2000/01

tqa

Institution	Grade	Institution	Grade
The University of Essex	24	Roehampton University of Surrey	21
University of Leicester	24	South Cheshire College	21
Liverpool John Moores University	24	Southampton Institute	21
University of Bath	23	St Mary's College	21
Bridgwater College	23	Suffolk College	21
Chester College of Higher Education	23	Trinity and All Saints College	21
Loughborough University	23	University College Worcester	21
Sheffield Hallam University	23	Blackpool and The Fylde College	20
University of Ulster	23	Croydon College	20
The University of Birmingham	22	North East Surrey College of Technology, Ewell	20
Blackburn College	22	Warrington Collegiate Institute	20
De Montfort University	22	Bradford College	19
Highbury College	22	University of Sunderland	19
The University of Huddersfield	22	West Cumbria College	19
Leeds Metropolitan University	22	Anglia Polytechnic University	18
The University of Manchester	22	Henley College Coventry	18
The Manchester Metropolitan University	22	Liverpool Community College	18
Newcastle College	22	St Helens College	18
St Martin's College, Lancaster:		Worcester College of Technology	18
Ambleside: Carlisle	22	Brooklands College	17
Staffordshire University	22	Guildford College of Further and Higher Education	17
Thames Valley University	22	North East Worcestershire College	17
Bolton Institute of Higher Education	21	Wakefield College	17
Buckinghamshire Chilterns University College	21	Westminster Kingsway College	17
Canterbury Christ Church University College	21	Wirral Metropolitan College	17
University College Chichester	21	Basingstoke College of Technology	16
Dearne Valley College	21	Walsall College of Art and Technology	16
University of Derby	21	Wigan and Leigh College	16
Farnborough College of Technology	21	Barnsley College	14
King Alfred's Winchester	21	Solihull College	14
University of Lincoln	21		
University of Portsmouth	21		

Source: HEFCE, SHEFC, HEFCW latest available ratings
For a more complete list of institutions offering these courses at undergraduate level refer to the Course Directory

Useful links

www.catering-uk.co.uk	●	Catering UK
www.eufic.org	●	The European Food Information Council
www.hcima.org.uk	●	Hotel and Catering International Management Association
www.sofht.co.uk	●	The Society of Food Hygiene Technology

Hotel management and catering

Law

There are laws controlling nearly every human activity, providing the guidelines upon which society is based. A country's legal system reflects the political, cultural, economic and religious forces which have shaped its history. The laws in Scotland and many other European countries are based on statute, or written law, which was derived from the system first codified by Roman legal theorists in the 6th century. England, on the other hand, as well as former Commonwealth countries and the USA, use a common law that is based on precedent which means, in theory, that the law could change from week to week.

The areas covered on law courses vary between institutions but most will include the seven foundation subjects currently required by the UK legal authorities for practising lawyers. These are constitutional and administrative law, criminal law, law of tort, law of contract, land law, law of trusts and European Community law. Apart from these subjects, students can specialise in any range of topics, from patent law to taxation or medical ethics. While British law schools tend to focus mainly on English or Scottish law, there is a growing interest in international law. Many colleges now offer whole courses or elements of courses on foreign legal systems, especially European law.

Most students taking a law course will hope either to become barristers, qualified to practice in higher courts, or solicitors, advising clients and preparing cases for barristers. The salaries for trainee solicitors have risen dramatically over the past two years and graduates working for the larger London law firms can expect a starting salary of at least £40,000. However, studying law does not tie you to one of these two professions and law graduates can find employment in private practice as well as in the legal departments of the civil service, local government, industrial and commercial firms, banks and international organisations. Skills such as the ability to think clearly and logically and to analyse complex problems acquired by law graduates are highly attractive to prospective employers.

There are two routes to becoming a professionally-qualified lawyer. One is to take the three-year undergraduate law degree which exempts them from the first part of the professional qualifications. Alternatively, postgraduates deciding to convert to the legal profession after obtaining a first degree in another subject must first take the one-year Common Professional Examination (CPE) course set by the Bar and Law Society. Following this, students may choose to take either the Bar Vocational course for prospective barristers or the Legal Practice Course (LPC) for prospective solicitors. It is also possible to study law at master's level, with the LLM course. This allows specialisation in a particular subject, or to gain a wider knowledge of the legal system.

Specialist and vocational

Bell College of Technology
Diploma of Higher Education
Legal Studies

This two-year, full-time course is suitable for those who wish to pursue career opportunities in paralegal practice, criminal justice and in business law. Paralegals work in solicitors' offices, carrying out administrative duties requiring a background knowledge of law. Employment opportunities in the criminal justice system include administration in the police force, employment in the prison service and positions in court administration. Knowledge of law is also attractive to employers in the business sector. The course provides a foundation in accounting and research methods before going on in the second year to specialise in one of the following options: law for paralegals, law for criminal justice and law for business. Successful students may be eligible to enter the third year of the BA Legal Studies course at Bell College.

Contact details, see page 613

Southampton Institute
HND Law

This two-year course, taught within the Southampton Business School, aims to provide students with a broad approach to the legal world, with some degree of specialism, and to cater for individual preferences. Law and legal systems are taught in a skills-based system, utilising legal, business and transferable skills. The course takes a foundational and contextual approach to the appreciation of law and legal issues within society. On completion of the programme, students with a good profile of achievement may gain direct entry to the second year of an

Student Profile

Youngjin Shin
Korea
LLM Media Law and Practice
Bournemouth University

"I am on the staff of the Press Arbitration Commission in Korea. As I was interested in the content regulation of new electronic media, I chose this course without hesitation. I was lucky to review simultaneously the traditional English legal system, including that of the EU and modern global communication policy through this course. This course especially is one of the innovative courses linked to The Centre for Intellectual Property Policy and Management, which is based at the university. Anyone who wants to go further in the intellectual property rights of media industry will be supported by the specialty of the CIPPM. I think the important thing is to have a wide and balanced view of society, so I recommend this course as a combination of the academic and the professional."

appropriate law degree course. The knowledge and skills gained on the course will open up a wide range of possible career paths, both within and outside the legal profession.

For further information, see page 560

Undergraduate

University of the West of England, Bristol
LLB (Hons) Law

This LLB degree gives students an understanding of legal concepts, their practical application and the role of law in society. Emphasis is placed upon legal method and research skills and students are given the opportunity to study an extensive range of legal and complementary subjects. Graduates of the three-year

TEACHING QUALITY ASSESSMENTS

Legal Studies
(Scotland) 1995/96

tqa

Institution	Grade	Institution	Grade
University of Abertay Dundee	Satisfactory	Napier University	Satisfactory
Glasgow Caledonian University	Satisfactory	The Robert Gordon University	Satisfactory

Law
(England and Northern Ireland) 1993/94

tqa

Institution	Grade	Institution	Grade
University of Bristol	Excellent	University College London	
University of the West of England, Bristol	Excellent	(University of London)	Excellent
Cambridge University	Excellent	The University of Warwick	Excellent
The University of Durham	Excellent	The University of Birmingham	Satisfactory
University of East Anglia	Excellent	Bournemouth University	Satisfactory
The University of Essex	Excellent	De Montfort University	Satisfactory
King's College London		University of Derby	Satisfactory
(University of London)	Excellent	University of Exeter	Satisfactory
University of Leicester	Excellent	University of Hertfordshire	Satisfactory
The University of Liverpool	Excellent	The University of Hull	Satisfactory
London School of Economics and		University of Leeds	Satisfactory
Political Science (University of London)	Excellent	Middlesex University	Satisfactory
The University of Manchester	Excellent	University of North London	Satisfactory
Northumbria University	Excellent	University College Northampton	Satisfactory
The University of Nottingham	Excellent	Queen Mary,	
Oxford University	Excellent	University of London	Satisfactory
Oxford Brookes University	Excellent	Southampton Institute	Satisfactory
Queen's University Belfast	Excellent	University of Sussex	Satisfactory
The University of Sheffield	Excellent	University of Ulster	Satisfactory
School of Oriental and African		University of Westminster	Satisfactory
Studies (University of London)	Excellent	University of Wolverhampton	Satisfactory

Law
(Scotland) 1995/96

tqa

Institution	Grade	Institution	Grade
The University of Aberdeen	Highly Satisfactory	University of Glasgow	Highly Satisfactory
University of Dundee	Highly Satisfactory	The University of	
The University of Edinburgh	Highly Satisfactory	Strathclyde	Highly Satisfactory

Law
(Wales) 1993/94

tqa

Institution	Grade	Institution	Grade
The University of Wales, Aberystwyth	Satisfactory	University of Wales Swansea	Satisfactory
Cardiff University	Satisfactory	Swansea Institute of	
University of Glamorgan	Satisfactory	Higher Education	Satisfactory

Source: HEFCE, SHEFC, HEFCW latest available ratings
For a more complete list of institutions offering these courses at undergraduate level refer to the Course Directory

Law

full-time degree are exempted from the first stage of academic training in relation to both the Bar and the Law Society's requirements. In addition to lectures and seminars, specific computer and library training exercises are included in the curriculum. Students have access to specially designed video-equipped court-rooms. Each year, the department arranges visits to European institutions in Brussels, Luxembourg and Strasbourg.

For further information, see page 456

For further information, see page 456

Coventry University
BA (Hons) Criminology and Law

Criminology is concerned with the study of crime in society. The key questions that a criminologist may pose include: do prisons work? Who commits which crimes? Are the police and the courts impartial? Criminologists are also inter-ested in broader questions, for example, what processes are involved in certain acts being criminalised or decriminalised? The course aims to develop students'

rae

Institution	Grade	Institution	Grade
Cambridge University	5*	Queen's University Belfast	5
The University of Durham	5*	The University of Reading	5
Keele University	5*	School of Oriental and African	
London School of Economics and		Studies (University of London)	5
Political Science (University of London)	5*	The University of Sheffield	5
Oxford University	5*	The University of Strathclyde	5
Queen Mary, University of London	5*	University of Ulster	5
University of Southampton	5*	University of Westminster	5
University College London		The University of Warwick	5
(University of London)	5*	The University of Wales, Aberystwyth	4
University of Aberdeen	5	University of the West of England, Bristol	4
Birkbeck College	5	University of Central Lancashire	4
The University of Birmingham	5	De Montfort University	4
University of Bristol	5	Institute of Advanced Legal Studies	4
Brunel University	5	The University of Liverpool	4
Cardiff University	5	The Nottingham Trent University	4
City University	5	Oxford Brookes University	4
University of Dundee	5	University of Sussex	4
University of East Anglia	5	Bournemouth University	3a
The University of Edinburgh	5	University of East London	3a
The University of Essex	5	Leeds Metropolitan University	3a
University of Exeter	5	The Robert Gordon University	3a
University of Glasgow	5	Sheffield Hallam University	3a
The University of Hull	5	Southampton Institute	3a
The University of Kent	5	Staffordshire University	3a
King's College London (University of London)	5	University of Wales Swansea	3a
Lancaster University	5	University of Wolverhampton	3a
University of Leeds	5	Napier University	3a
University of Leicester	5	Glasgow Caledonian University	3b
The University of Manchester	5	University of Greenwich	3b
University of Newcastle upon Tyne	5	Thames Valley University	2
The University of Nottingham	5		

Source: RAE 2001

knowledge and understanding of the law and legal skills. Students learn principles and technical rules of law and how to use this to analyse problems, construct arguments and form reasoned conclusions. Depending on the options chosen, graduates can go on to qualify as solicitors or barristers. Students can also look to a career in business, industry, teaching, journalism, politics, the police force and other criminal justice services, management or public administration.

For further information, see page 468

University of Leicester

BA in Economics and Law

Economists study the consequences of dif-ferent choices made by individuals and industry. Legal rules affect the choices they can make. Therefore, an economic analysis of law can help assess the efficiency of the rules and the institutions of a legal system. All rules can be assessed according to their economic effect, from the relative merits of fines and prisons to the economic efficiency of judges' decisions. This degree is unusual in that it concentrates on law and economics separately and in conjunction. It is designed for those who want to see what two substantial academic disciplines can learn from each other. As well as careers in commercial or business law, students may choose accountancy, insurance or general management where knowledge

of economics and law is an advantage.
For further information, see page 502

London Tower College
LLB in Law

This is a four-year, full-time law degree examined by the University of London. Of the 12 papers taken as part of the degree, the following eight are compulsory: criminal law, constitutional law, the English legal system, elements of the law contract, law of tort, law of trusts, land law and jurisprudence and legal theory. Students who need to work on their communication skills can attend extra English classes free of charge, provided they are registered full time. The programme is divided into three terms and enrolment at the college is not rigid. Course fees are £500 per subject, per year and a minimum of three subjects per year must be chosen. The college provides a career advice service

for all registered and potential students. This course is run at the southeast London campus in Southwark.
Contact details, see page 611

London School of Economics and Political Science (University of London)
LLB with French Law

The study of law involves examining and analysing the rules and institutions that society establishes to promote law and order. As well as being a preparation for work in the legal profession, knowledge of law and the analytical and logical reasoning skills it develops are valued by employers. This joint honours course is based around the bachelor of law degree offered at LSE. The first year consists of a general introduction to public law, obligations, law of property and the workings of the legal system. The degree

Law

is stretched to cover four years, however, with the third year spent taking the Diplôme d'Etudes Juridiques Françaises at the University of Strasbourg III (Robert Schuman). This consists of a course in Introduction à l'Etude du Droit et du Droit Civil (Personnes, Famille, Incapacités) and courses from a list of options.

For further information, see page 508

University College Northampton
LLB (Hons) Law

The course gives exemption from the academic stage of qualification for both branches of the profession; the intending solicitor or barrister may move straight on to a course leading to the final exams following graduation. Lectures direct and support students, introducing topics, outlining the basic principles and exploring problem areas or issues. Seminars take place in small groups and utilise a variety of methods to build on the knowledge acquired in lectures. Such methods include problem solving, project work, role play and oral presentations. In addition, there is a skills programme which runs for the first two years of the degree. This involves activities aimed at developing skills such as research, client interviewing, negotiating techniques and advocacy skills.

For further information, see page 522

University of North London
LLB Law

The University of North London's three-year LLB course provides a high quality overview of all relevant areas of law. The course includes contract law, commercial law, international law, family law, the legal system and the law of constitutions and conflict. The course attracts students from a large number of countries, some of whom have studied law before and some of whom have not. The course is taught through a mix of lectures, seminars and tutorials with focus on the practical implementation of legal principles. The university makes sure that students can develop their communication skills, research abilities and are able to make ethical judgements about legal issues. Its students go on to become lawyers, barristers and public administrators, as well as entering a range of other jobs.

For further information, see page 520

Oxford University
BA (Hons) Law

The qualities of mind needed to study law are good logical sense, an ability to make, apply and criticise distinctions and to separate rapidly the relevant from the irrelevant in a large mass of material. From the outset, law students at Oxford are taught these skills and have to apply independent judgement to the raw material of the subject. The course provides academic and critical training in some of the central subjects of English law and the opportunity to study some aspects of other legal systems. It also gives exemption from many barristers' or solicitors' professional exams in England but does not actually confer any professional qualification itself.

For further information, see page 534

School of Oriental and African Studies (University of London)
LLB Law

SOAS offers Law Society exemption subjects and, in addition, offers subjects which reflect the specialist nature of the institution, covering East Asian commercial law, ethnic minority legal issues, human rights law and the study of specific legal

jurisdictions (for example Chinese, Islamic and African law). Law students can also benefit from the comparative approach with courses such as legal systems of Asia and Africa (unique to SOAS), which allows students an overview of the main legal ideas and precepts of other jurisdictions. This is invaluable to anyone considering a career in international law. Graduates are thus well placed for a number of careers, both in law and also within other fields including multi-national business and commerce, develop-ment, governmental and non-governmental organisations and the diplomatic corps.
For further information, see page 554

Postgraduate

The University of Wales, Aberystwyth
Master of Laws (LLM)
Aberystwyth has the oldest law school in Wales and one of the oldest in Britain. The Department of Law is self-contained with lecture halls and a purpose-built law library within a minute's walk of each other. This taught course has been specially designed to allow students the opportunity to study specialist subjects of their choice and to complete a piece of research on a topic of special interest. Subjects include inter-national business law and environmental law and management. The emphasis is on active student participation through presen-tations, discussion and group work. Assessment is by a combination of examina-tion and assessed coursework and students also complete a short dissertation on any topic within their area of specialism.
For further information, see page 436

Bournemouth University
MA/LLM Media Law and Practice
This course has been designed in response to a growing demand for legal and management expertise in the fields of intellectual property rights and media regulation and aims to equip students with the knowledge and skills needed to take advantage of new career opportunities in this field. Students have the opportunity to complete an intensive workshop in media production at the Bournemouth Media School covering the latest production technologies and the practical demands of journalistic and editorial work. The programme is delivered through lectures, seminars and workshops and involves writing a dissertation. The university welcomes overseas students from whom a good standard of written and spoken English is required. This course operates within the School of Finance and Law's master's programme, giving students the opportunity to obtain either an MA or LLM or to widen their field of study.
For further information, see page 448

Cardiff University
PGDip Bar Vocational Course (BVC)
The BVC Western and Wales is a 34-week course starting in early September and concluding the following June. It prepares students for becoming barristers. Students practise and develop essential skills during classes with video-based or written tutor feedback. The intensive advocacy-training programme develops from unopposed submissions through written and oral argument to witness handling in a variety of practice settings. Students also undertake two complete one-day trials – one civil and one criminal – both held in the second term. These give all students the opportunity to be 'on their feet' in practice and assessment exercises prepared by qualified staff and practising members of the local bar. Students have extensive access to high

Law

quality hard copy and IT-based information sources and undertake two full placement weeks in chambers, courts or tribunals.
Contact details, see page 614

City University

Common Professional Examination Course (CPE)

This one-year full-time course is open to graduates who do not hold a qualifying degree in law but who wish to become barristers or solicitors. The course satisfies the requirements of the academic stage of professional legal education in England and Wales. Seven core legal subjects are taught: contract, tort, criminal law, land law, constitutional law, equity and trusts. Students also learn European Community law as well as being given a requisite introduction to an eighth subject, namely jurisprudence and legal

history. A Diploma in Law is available to those completing the CPE. Holders of the Diploma/CPE may fulfil the requirements for an MA in Law by submitting a dissertation.
Contact details, see page 615

The University of Manchester

LLM European Law and Policy

This programme provides a thorough grounding in the legal framework of the European Union and an opportunity for more detailed study of a particular topic through a dissertation. Specifically, students learn how European law is developed through national and supranational mechanisms including law-making institutions and the activities of interest groups. They are made aware of the relationship between policy and law in the emergent European legal order. Where appropriate, students are encouraged to analyse relevant provisions of European law from critical perspectives. Students register for four courses, two of which are usually taken in each semester of the year. Assessment is by examination and essays.
For further information, see page 514

Useful links

www.bailii.org	●	British and Irish Legal Information Institute
www.ials.sas.ac.uk	●	Institute of Advanced Legal Studies
www.ila-hq.org	●	The International Law Association
www.lawsociety.org.uk	●	The Law Society of England and Wales
www.lawsociety.ie	●	The Law Society of Ireland
www.lawscot.org.uk	●	The Law Society of Scotland
www.lawtel.co.uk	●	Lawtel: The Law Online

Librarianship and information science

For hundreds of years, librarians have been developing methods for indexing, abstracting and retrieving information. By creating a controlled system, they organise resources so that others can use them effectively and efficiently. Information specialists are no longer the preserve of libraries and are much in demand in large companies, banking, education, the media, computing and, in fact, anywhere that information systems are used.

There is a great deal of innovation in the UK library environment with projects such as the Electronic Libraries Programme and the New Library People's Network. Other countries have adopted UK models for librarianship and information services. The first BSc in Information Science was introduced in 1967 at the University of Newcastle upon Tyne and, since then, degrees in this field have evolved enormously, in line with the widening job description and latest developments in computer technology. As such, students come from a variety of academic backgrounds with qualifications in any subject from chemistry to English. The ability to speak a language other than English is a great advantage and is becoming increasingly necessary. A high degree of computer literacy is essential.

At undergraduate level, students can study either a BA or BSc degree. On a BA Information and Library Studies, for example, first-year core modules might include information technology and systems, communication methods and research methodology. The second and third years would then allow students to specialise in areas such as business information studies, information and library services or multimedia publishing. A BSc degree, on the other hand, may have a more scientific, management or computing focus and it can often be combined with a computing course.

The majority of library and information courses, however, are studied at postgraduate level. MSc and MA taught courses last for one year. These might include core studies in essential areas such as information technology and information research and modules in business information, health information or information design. It is also possible to do research to PhD level.

Most courses are accredited by the two main professional bodies: The Library Association (LA) and The Institute of Information Scientists (IIS). For full lists of these courses, contact The Library Association on +44 (0)20 7255 0500 or The Institute of Information Scientists on +44 (0)20 7619 0634. Website addresses can be found at the end of the chapter.

Education doesn't end once you graduate, as professional development is important in the fields of librarianship and information science. It's a fast-moving profession and you need to update your skills continually.

Information and Library Studies
(Wales) 1994/95

tqa

Institution	Grade	Institution	Grade
The University of Wales, Aberystwyth	Excellent		

Librarianship and Information Management
(England and Northern Ireland) 2000/01

tqa

Institution	Grade	Institution	Grade
Loughborough University	24	University College London (University of London)	22
University of Brighton	22	City University	21
Northumbria University	22	University of Central England in Birmingham	20
The University of Sheffield	22	University of North London	18

Source: HEFCE, SHEFC, HEFCW latest available ratings
For a more complete list of institutions offering these courses at undergraduate level refer to the Course Directory

Undergraduate

University of Wales, Aberystwyth
Information and Library Studies

Information and its management are central to modern society. Organisations, private and public, national and international, have recognised that information is a key resource and that its management is critical for success. To this end, Information and Library Studies is concerned with all aspects of the production, organisation and communication of information. The department has close links with the growing information industry, making the course academically, practically and vocationally relevant. All courses consist of a series of core and optional modules taught through lectures, seminars, practicals and directed private study. Students are assessed through written examinations and coursework. They also participate in a month-long work placement, further enhancing the vocational relevance of the qualification.

For further information, see page 436

Liverpool Hope
BA (Hons) Business and Information Management

This programme has been designed to give students the opportunity to study the theory and practice of business and IT in a dynamic context. Students completing the course will be versatile graduates, experienced in both areas and strongly positioned to gain employment in a variety of areas. The most effective and successful organisations utilise information and technology proactively in order to keep one step ahead of the competition. This is why the demand is so high for individuals possessing skills in both business and IT. The programme ensures that the business and information technology modules interlink throughout, providing a comprehensive understanding of the role and importance of managing information and communication technology within a business environment. The degree, therefore, meets the needs of both students and potential employers in the 21st century.

For further information, see page 504

Loughborough University
BSc (Hons) Information Management and Business Studies

Offered jointly by the Department of Information Science and the Business School, this programme provides a sound theoretical and practical basis for those aiming for a career in information management. Students are taught core areas that are required for professionals in the information industry together with those needed by business managers. The

256

Institution	Grade	Institution	Grade
The University of Salford	5*	De Montfort University	3a
the University of Sheffield	5*	University of Glasgow	3a
Brunel University	5	Staffordshire University	3a
City University	5	University of Brighton	3b
Loughborough University	5	University of the West of England, Bristol	3b
Leeds Metropolitan University	4	Northumbria University	3b
The Manchester Metropolitan University	4	University of Paisley	3b
Napier University	4	Queen Margaret University College Edinburgh	3b
University of Strathclyde	4	Robert Gordon University	3b
University College London (University of London)	4	South Bank University	3b
The University of Wales, Aberystwyth	3a	Thames Valley University	1
University of Central England in Birmingham	3a		

Source: RAE 2001

first year consists of a general introduction to key areas in each subject, while the second concentrates more on the development of management and business skills, including a series of optional modules from each department. The final-year project gives students the chance to study a topic of their choice in depth with an individual superviser. Students can also opt to take a year out for a suitable, paid work placement, which leads to the additional qualification of the Diploma in Professional Studies.

For further information, see page 510

Thames Valley University

BSc (Hons) Information Systems

With a buoyant demand for IT professionals, graduates of this course can expect to find a range of career opportunities directly in information technology and management and indeed in any organisation using information technology. The course is designed to give you a good understanding of relevant issues and a sound knowledge of which computer-based solutions are appropriate in organisations to meet business objectives. The course's main themes are e-commerce, the internet, information and data management. Systems are studied at a detailed and strategic level with the objective of analysing working situations, thus becoming able to design and develop appropriate information systems. The themes are chosen to give a broader knowledge of the areas that students are likely to come into contact with in the commercial environment.

For further information, see page 576

Postgraduate

City University

MSc Information Science

The course provides the knowledge and opportunity to develop the skills required for responsible work in information science. The core modules are fundamentals of information science, information resources and users, research and communication skills, information law and policy, data representation and management, information-retrieval systems and applications and principles of knowledge organisation. In addition, students take two from of a range of options covering more specialist

Librarianship and information science

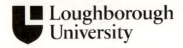

Loughborough University

Department of Information Science

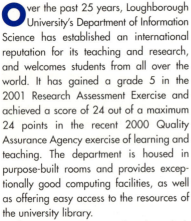

Over the past 25 years, Loughborough University's Department of Information Science has established an international reputation for its teaching and research, and welcomes students from all over the world. It has gained a grade 5 in the 2001 Research Assessment Exercise and achieved a score of 24 out of a maximum 24 points in the recent 2000 Quality Assurance Agency exercise of learning and teaching. The department is housed in purpose-built rooms and provides exceptionally good computing facilities, as well as offering easy access to the resources of the university library.

Information science is a discipline which investigates the characteristics of information and the nature of the information transfer process. Its theoretical and practical components include collection, collation, evaluation and dissemination of information. Areas of study include knowledge management, electronic publishing, document management, web-based applications, and the management of information services.

Accurate information is the key to removing potential barriers to decision-making, such as uncertainty and risk. This information must also get to the right person, in the right place and at the right time. Information science provides the knowledge and skills required for achieving these objectives in an efficient and effective manner.

16 full-time academic staff work in this large and well-resourced department: four professors, supported by eight technical, clerical and administrative staff, with approximately 300 undergraduate students, 100 postgraduates and 30 PhD students, full and part time. The department maintains excellent relations with the information management, computing and library professions; programmes being designed to meet the needs of such vocations. With this objective in mind, the department provides preparation for such careers. Accreditation of relevant programmes by the Institute of Information Scientists, the Library Association and the British Computer Society is given.

While postgraduate programmes promote information management, knowledge management and e-publishing as intellectual disciplines, practical applications are regarded as equally important. Emphasis is placed upon preparing students for their role as information managers, knowledge managers, or indeed as active participants in the wider, information-based management professions or e-publishing. Those already employed as information professionals are invited to pursue part-time research programmes. Through such programmes, staff are actively engaged in contributing to the professional development of information science at local, national and international levels.

Undergraduate admissions
Tel: +44 (0)1509 223080
Email: d.p.stephens@lboro.ac.uk
Postgraduate admissions
Tel: +44 (0)1509 223063
Email: i.a.smith@lboro.ac.uk
Website: www.lboro.ac.uk/departments/dis

areas of information science. As well as the computing facilities provided by the university through its computing services, the department has access to a range of systems through personal computers and network connections and has an experimental retrieval system, Okapi.

Contact details, see page 615

The University of Sheffield
MA Librarianship

The aim of this one-year, full-time course is to introduce students to the principles, disciplines and skills of librarianship. The course prepares graduates for library and information-related careers in academic, government, special, public, voluntary and research employment sectors, as well as the increasing number of posts outside the established library and information sectors. The programme includes core modules in information resources, information storage and retrieval, management, human resource management and public and voluntary sector services. Students also undertake a dissertation project. The department is located in modern, purpose-built rooms and is equipped with computing labs containing a large number of networked PCs and Unix-based workstations.

Contact details, see page 620

The University of Strathclyde
MSc/PGDip Information and Library Studies

This one-year, full-time course is designed to produce professionals who are concerned with the production, organisation and provision of information. This includes the study of information from its generation to its exploitation and its transmission in a variety of forms through a variety of channels. The course is aimed at graduates in any discipline who wish to follow a career in professional information and library work. It incorporates core classes, a placement and elective classes and includes practical exercises in the application of information technologies. Final assessment is based on performance in individual and group project work, written examinations and, if appropriate, in the dissertation.

For further information, see page 568

Librarianship and information science

Useful links

www.bl.uk	◉	The British Library
www.iis.org.uk	◉	The Institute of Information Scientists
www.la-hq.org.uk	◉	The Library Association
www.lic.gov.uk	◉	Library and Information Commission
www.nls.ac.uk	◉	The National Library of Scotland
www.llgc.org.uk	◉	The National Library of Wales
www.rms-gb.org.uk	◉	Records Management Society of Great Britain
www.archives.org.uk	◉	Society of Archivists

Mathematics and statistics

Sir Isaac Newton is recognised as the forefather of mathematics in the UK and his influence still pervades the higher education sector, attracting many international students. It has been suggested that the Newtonian heritage has contributed both to the quality of mathematics research in the UK and to the British emphasis on applied mathematics.

Mathematical studies largely involves the exploration of patterns in the world – it is a way of formalising our understanding of them. It can lead to practical and useful results such as applications of calculus, marginal revenue for accountants, velocity for the physicist or matrix techniques frequently employed in advanced statistics.

Broadly speaking, mathematics can be divided into two main areas: pure and applied. Pure mathematics can be seen as maths for maths sake. Applied mathematics, on the other hand, is the exploration of a problem in the real world such as locating the eyes of a car driver using an in-car camera and then monitoring the blink rate as an indicator of the driver's drowsiness.

Most degrees last for three years and are normally divided into modules. In the first year of both mathematics and statistics degrees, you are likely to cover the basic principles of the subjects. For mathematics, these include calculus, algebra and computing skills; for statistics: probability, foundations in statistics and computational methods. Most three-year modular degrees offer the chance to specialise in the second and third years. Examples of such modules for mathematics may include mechanics, abstract algebra and linear systems; for statistics: distribution theory, theoretical artificial intelligence and techniques of operational research. In the final year, it is often possible for students to undertake a project on a topic of their choice in place of one of these modules, under the supervision of an academic tutor.

Recently, there has been a growth of alternative studies in the mathematical discipline and a shift away from the straight applied and pure mathematical courses. The specialist courses that are available range from mathematical sciences, to numerical analysis, financial mathematics and computational mathematics. Maths can also be combined with other subjects such as management or business to make it a highly vocational pathway, preparing students for various careers such as quantitative analysis in the commercial sector. It is related to so many other things that combining with other subjects proves to be relatively simple.

Teaching methods on a mathematical degree tend to be based around regular lectures as well as seminars, tutorials and practical work. Assessment is usually carried out by examination at the end of the semester although some programmes also include coursework modules and the chance to do an individual project.

Mathematics, Statistics and Operational Research
(England and Northern Ireland) 1998/99

Institution	Grade	Institution	Grade
University of Bath	24	The University of Manchester Institute	
The University of Birmingham	24	of Science and Technology (UMIST)	22
University of Bristol	23	Oxford University	22
Cambridge University	23	Oxford Brookes University	22
City University	23	University of Portsmouth	22
Coventry University	23	The University of Reading	22
University of East Anglia	23	Royal Holloway, University of London	22
Kingston University	23	The University of York	22
The University of Liverpool	23	Birkbeck College	21
University of Newcastle		University of the West of England, Bristol	21
upon Tyne	23	University of Derby	21
The University of Nottingham	23	Goldsmiths College (University of London)	21
Sheffield Hallam University	23	University of Hertfordshire	21
University of Sussex	23	The University of Kent	21
University of Brighton	22	King's College London	
Brunel University	22	(University of London)	21
Canterbury Christ Church		Liverpool John Moores University	21
University College	22	Northumbria University	21
Chester (A College of the		The Nottingham Trent University	21
University of Liverpool)	22	Queen Mary, University of London	21
University of Exeter	22	The University of Sheffield	21
The University of Hull	22	The University of Surrey	21
Imperial College of Science, Technology		Bolton Institute of Higher Education	20
and Medicine (University of London)	22	De Montfort University	20
Keele University	22	The University of Essex	20
Kent Institute of Art and Design	22	The Manchester Metropolitan University	20
Lancaster University	22	University of Southampton	20
University of Leeds	22	University of Wolverhampton	20
University of Leicester	22	Aston University	19
London School of Economics and		University of Central Lancashire	19
Political Science (University of London)	22	University of Greenwich	19
The University of Manchester	22	London Guildhall University	18

Mathematics
(Wales) 1995/96

The University of Wales,		Cardiff University	Satisfactory
Aberystwyth	Satisfactory	University of Glamorgan	Satisfactory
University of Wales, Bangor	Satisfactory	University of Wales Swansea	Satisfactory

Mathematics and Statistics
(Scotland) 1994

Institution	Grade	Institution	Grade
The University of Edinburgh	Excellent	Heriot-Watt University,	
University of St Andrews	Excellent	Edinburgh	Highly Satisfactory
The University of Aberdeen	Highly Satisfactory	Napier University	Highly Satisfactory
University of Abertay Dundee	Highly Satisfactory	University of Paisley	Highly Satisfactory
University of Dundee	Highly Satisfactory	The Robert Gordon	
University of Glasgow	Highly Satisfactory	University	Highly Satisfactory
Glasgow Caledonian		The University of Stirling	Highly Satisfactory
University	Highly Satisfactory	The University of Strathclyde	Highly Satisfactory

Source: HEFCE, SHEFC, HEFCW latest available ratings
For a more complete list of institutions offering these courses at undergraduate level refer to the Course Directory

Specialist and vocational

Middlesex University

Mathematics Foundation Year

This foundation year is an ideal starting point for a mathematics-related career and, as such, provides an entry route to mathematics degree programmes at Middlesex. It is designed for those applicants who have not specialised in A

RESEARCH RANKINGS

Applied Mathematics

Institution	Grade	Institution	Grade
University of Bath	5*	University College London (University of London)	5
University of Bristol	5*	The University of York	5
Cambridge University	5*	The University of Aberdeen	4
University of Durham	5*	The University of Wales, Aberystwyth	4
Imperial College of Science, Technology and Medicine (University of London)	5*	City University	4
The University of Warwick	5*	University of East Anglia	4
The University of Birmingham	5	The University of Hull	4
Brunel University	5	Loughborough University	4
University of Dundee	5	The University of Manchester Institute of Science and Technology (UMIST)	4
The University of Edinburgh	5	University of Newcastle upon Tyne	4
University of Exeter	5	Queen Mary, University of London	4
University of Glasgow	5	The University of Sheffield	4
Heriot-Watt University, Edinburgh	5	University of Abertay Dundee	3a
Keele University	5	University of Brighton	3a
The University of Kent	5	University of the West of England, Bristol	3a
King's College London (University of London)	5	Coventry University	3a
University of Leeds	5	The University of Essex	3a
University of Leicester	5	Northumbria University	3a
The University of Liverpool	5	The Nottingham Trent University	3a
The University of Manchester	5	Oxford Brookes University	3a
The University of Nottingham	5	University of Plymouth	3a
Oxford University	5	The University of Salford	3a
University of Portsmouth	5	University of Westminster	3a
The University of Reading	5	Chester College of Higher Education	3b
University of Southampton	5	De Montfort University	3b
University of St Andrews	5	Glasgow Caledonian University	3b
The University of Strathclyde	5	London Guildhall University	3b
The University of Surrey	5	Staffordshire University	3b
University of Sussex	5	University of Teesside	3b

Pure Mathematics

Institution	Grade	Institution	Grade
Cambridge University	5*	University of Southampton	5
The University of Edinburgh	5*	University College London (University of London)	5
Imperial College of Science, Technology and Medicine (University of London)	5*	The University of Warwick	5
Oxford University	5*	The University of York	5
The University of Aberdeen	5	University of St Andrews	5
University of Bath	5	University of Wales Swansea	5
The University of Birmingham	5	University of Exeter	4
University of Bristol	5	The University of Hull	4
Cardiff University	5	Lancaster University	4
The University of Durham	5	Open University	4
University of East Anglia	5	University of Sussex	4
University of Glasgow	5	University of Wales, Bangor	3a
King's College London (University of London)	5	The University of Essex	3a
University of Leeds	5	Goldsmiths College (University of London)	3a
University of Leicester	5	The University of Kent	3a
The University of Liverpool	5	Middlesex University	3a
The University of Manchester	5	University of North London	3a
The University of Manchester Institute of Science and Technology (UMIST)	5	The University of Reading	3a
University of Newcastle upon Tyne	5	The University of Stirling	3a
The University of Nottingham	5	Queen's University Belfast	3a
Queen Mary, University of London	5	The University of Wales, Aberystwyth	3b
Royal Holloway, University of London	5	University of Plymouth	3b
The University of Sheffield	5	Keele University	2
		Liverpool Hope	1

Source: RAE 2001

Mathematics and statistics

levels for mathematics-related subjects but who do wish to change careers. It is also open to those who have progressed towards mathematics but have not achieved the necessary entry requirements or those students who are over 21, have relevant experience and wish to gain a professional qualification. This course provides the opportunity for students to learn transferable mathematics and problem-solving skills which form the basis for a great number of degrees and careers.
Contact details, see page 618

Undergraduate

The University of Birmingham
BSc/MSci in Mathematical Sciences

Mathematics (known as the 'queen of sciences') is growing in importance in the modern world. To meet these expanding opportunities for mathematicians, this course is designed with four core aims in mind. These are to provide a firm foundation in widely used branches of the subject, to train students to think logically and imaginatively, to afford an insight into recent developments in mathematics and to train students to tackle real problems in engineering, management and scientific research. A recent addition to the course allows students to opt either for a three-year programme leading to a BSc, or four years leading to an MSci. This decision need not be made until the end of second year.
Contact details, see page 613

Imperial College of Science, Technology and Medicine (University of London)
BSc Mathematics with Management

The first two years of this course are spent in the Mathematics Department following the same structure as a mathematics degree. This provides a strong introduction to the fundamentals of the subject. The third year is then spent in the Management School where students take courses ranging from accounting, business economics and cash-flow modelling to international business and operations management. Teaching takes the form of lectures, problem classes and small study groups and students also have a personal tutor available for regular consultation about academic and personal matters. Assessment is by a combination of written examinations and a group project in the third year.
Contact details, see page 617

Postgraduate

Cambridge University
MPhil Statistical Science

This 10-month course provides an introduction to various blends of applied probability, statistical operations research, and theory and practice. Graduates of the Statistical Laboratory have excellent job opportunities in fields such as medical statistics, finance, management consultancy, the Civil Service, the actuarial profession and the pharmaceutical and chemical industries. Applicants should have a good honours

Mathematics and statistics

Statistics and Operational Research

Institution	Grade	Institution	Grade
University of Bristol	5*	The University of Durham	4
Cambridge University	5*	The University of Edinburgh	4
The University of Kent	5*	University of Exeter	4
Lancaster University	5*	The University of Liverpool	4
Oxford University	5*	London School of Economics and	
The University of Warwick	5*	Political Science (University of London)	4
University of Bath	5	The University of Manchester Institute	
University of Glasgow	5	of Science and Technology (UMIST)	4
Heriot-Watt University, Edinburgh	5	The University of Manchester	4
Imperial College of Science, Technology		Open University	4
and Medicine (University of London)	5	The University of Reading	4
University of Leeds	5	University of Sussex	4
University of Newcastle upon Tyne	5	The University of Strathclyde	4
The University of Nottingham	5	City University	3a
Queen Mary, University of London	5	Coventry University	3a
The University of Salford	5	Goldsmiths College (University of London)	3a
The University of Sheffield	5	University of Greenwich	3a
University of Southampton (Statistics)	5	Keele University	3a
University of Southampton (Operational Research)	5	University of North London	3a
The University of Surrey	5	The Nottingham Trent University	3a
University College London (University of London)	5	University of Plymouth	3a
University of St Andrews	5	Napier University	3b
The University of Aberdeen	4	University of Westminster	3b
The University of Birmingham	4	Staffordshire University	2
Brunel University	4		

Source: RAE 2001

degree in mathematics, including some previous knowledge of probability and statistics. Each MPhil candidate is assessed on a written examination and a dissertation that is typically based on practical work arranged with local industry, a research institute or another university department. There are core courses in probability, operations research, and theoretical and applied statistics, as well as optional courses which include biostatistics, actuarial statistics, stochastic networks and also financial mathematics. Candidates receive training in statistical computing and are individually supervised in both their coursework and dissertations.

Contact details, see page 614

Useful links

www.emis.de	●	European Mathematical Information Service
www.ima.org.uk	●	The Institute of Mathematics and its Applications
www.ma.hw.ac.uk/icms	●	International Centre for Mathematical Sciences
www.lms.ac.uk	●	London Mathematical Society
www.rss.org.uk	●	The Royal Statistical Society
www.siam.org	●	Society for Industrial and Applied Mathematics

Mathematics and statistics

Media and communication studies

The 20th century witnessed a boom in media and communications. Newspapers, magazines, television, radio, cinema, advertising and, most recently, the internet all have a massive, daily impact on our social and cultural lives. Part of the reason for this boom is the incredible rate at which new technology has been and is still being developed, and the range of possibilities it has opened up for mass communication.

Courses in media and communications can either be wholly practical, wholly theoretical or a mixture of the two. They can also be highly specialist, providing specific skills in media technology for instance, or can take a broader approach to the subject involving anything from semiotics (the study of signs and symbols) to censorship and the cultural and political influence of media proprietors. It is important to bear in mind that the type of course you study is very important. No degree, no matter how vocational, can ever guarantee a successful career and the media industry is more competitive than most. Where you study is also important. Some universities and colleges are more reputable than others within the industry. Employers looking for journalists, for example, often prefer to recruit from courses associated with the National Council for the Training of Journalists (NCTJ).

For those students aiming to work in a specific area of the media, it may be preferable to take a related training course. Increasingly, these are available through universities but the majority can be found at colleges and specialist institutions. Journalism, for instance, is available as a short course or at NVQ and postgraduate level.

Those wishing to gain a more theoretical understanding of the media may well be interested in degrees in media studies or communication studies, for example. A media studies degree might cover the historical development of mass media, politics and propaganda, photojournalism or media ethics. The communication of information and messages and their effects are also central to a media studies degree.

A degree in communication studies typically revolves around the problems and issues associated with both interpersonal and mass communication. Students may look, for instance, at the role of language in interviews or children's response to television programmes. Other topics include sociolinguistics, the analysis of language and literature and semiotics. Communication studies may also involve project, lab and fieldwork.

Although both degrees involve the discussion and application of theoretical models, they may also feature a certain amount of practical work. Some courses allow students to develop practical interests in areas such as photography, writing or television, others might include a work placement at a communications-related business such as an advertising company or public relations agency.

Undergraduate

University of East Anglia
BA Film and Television Studies

The film and television studies course allows students to study the history, theory and politics of moving images and introduces critical approaches to film and television. There is a strong emphasis on the history of the medium, from silent cinema to the contemporary scene. Some units focus on particular film-makers or genres, others deal with critical issues such as video activism, gender and film or the cinema as an industry. The final year involves researching a dissertation of the student's own devising. They can also choose to engage in some practical work as part of their studies, with units including 16 millimetre film, video, photography and television studio production.

For further information, see page 470

University of Leeds
BA Broadcast Journalism

The communications industry is one of the largest and fastest growing in the modern world. A thorough understanding of communications is also invaluable in a broad range of related occupations from marketing and management to advertising and education. This degree is designed for students who want to be news and current affairs broadcasters in a tri-media (radio, television and internet) environment. It provides the intellectual and practical training required by the broadcasting industry. The curriculum places great emphasis on the legal and ethical responsibilities of journalists and is accredited by the Broadcast Journalism Training Council (BJTC). The course is co-taught by the university, BBC and independent journalists and producers. As well as learning practical reporting and production

UNIVERSITY OF STIRLING

Faculty of Arts

The University of Stirling offers a variety of media related taught Masters degrees as well as the Undergraduate Bachelors degree in Film & Media Studies, most of which are taught in the Department of Film & Media Studies with its Grade 5 research rating.

Programmes available include:

- BA Film & Media Studies
- MSc Public Relations
- MSc Media Management
- MPhil Publishing Studies
- On-line learning media programmes

The International Office

University of Stirling
Stirling FK9 4LA
Scotland UK

Tel: +44 (0) 1785 467046
E-mail: international@stir.ac.uk
www.stir.ac.uk

'Promoting excellence in teaching and research'

Communication and Media Studies
(England and Northern Ireland) 1997/98/99

tqa

Institution	Grade	Institution	Grade
University College Chichester	24	Staffordshire University	20
University of East Anglia	23	York St John College	20
The University of Reading	23	City University	19
The University of Warwick	23	Cumbria College of Art and Design	19
University of Westminster	23	University of Greenwich	19
Bournemouth University	22	Leeds Metropolitan University	19
University of the West of England, Bristol	22	Sheffield Hallam University	19
University of Central Lancashire	22	The College of St Mark and St John	19
Goldsmiths College (University of London)	22	University College Warrington	19
University of Leeds	22	University of Wolverhampton	19
Liverpool John Moores University	22	Anglia Polytechnic University	18
London School of Economics and		Buckinghamshire Chilterns University College	18
Political Science (University of London)	22	Coventry University	18
University of Luton	22	Falmouth College of Arts	18
University of Sunderland	22	The University of Huddersfield	18
University of Central England in Birmingham	21	King Alfred's Winchester	18
University of Leicester	21	Southampton Institute	18
University College Northampton	21	Thames Valley University	18
The Nottingham Trent University	21	University of Derby	17
Oxford Brookes University	21	Farnborough College of Technology	17
Ravensbourne College of		London Guildhall University	17
Design and Communication	21	University of Lincoln	17
University of Sussex	21	University of North London	17
University of Ulster	21	Surrey Institute of Art and	
Bolton Institute of Higher Education	20	Design, University College	17
Brunel University	20	Leeds, Trinity and All Saints College	17
Canterbury Christ Church University College	20	University of East London	16
De Montfort University	20	St Helens College	15
Edge Hill College of Higher Education	20	Suffolk College (An Accredited College	
University of Gloucestershire	20	of the University of East Anglia)	15
The University of Kent	20	Wirral Metropolitan College	15
The London Institute	20	Sandwell College	13
South Bank University	20		

Mass Communications
(Scotland) 1996

tqa

Glasgow Caledonian		The University of Stirling	Highly Satisfactory
University	Highly Satisfactory	Queen Margaret	
Napier University	Highly Satisfactory	University College, Edinburgh	Satisfactory

English and Associated Studies
(Wales) 1994/95

tqa

The University of Wales, Aberystwyth		Trinity College Carmarthen	
(Theatre, Film and Television Studies)	Satisfactory	(Theatre, Music and Media Studies)	Satisfactory
Cardiff University (Journalism)	Satisfactory		
Cardiff University			
(Mass Communication)	Satisfactory		

Source: HEFCE, SHEFC, HEFCW latest available ratings
For a more complete list of institutions offering these courses
at undergraduate level refer to the Course Directory

Media and communication studies

skills, students are taught to research, analyse and execute documentary features. *Contact details, see page 617*

Ravensbourne College of Design and Communication

BSc (Hons) Communication and Technology
This course explores the use of communica-tion technology in both broadcast and non-broadcast environments. In doing so, it provides students with three main tool kits: technology (broadcast video and computer technology), design (especially for screen) and management (marketing, finance and project management). Everyone studies the broadcasting platform during the first year.

Communication, Cultural and Media Studies

rae

Institution	Grade	Institution	Grade
Goldsmiths College (University of London)	5*	University of Leicester	3a
University of East Anglia	5*	University of Luton	3a
Cardiff University	5	Middlesex University	3a
University of East London	5	University of North London	3a
The Nottingham Trent University	5	Sheffield Hallam University	3a
The University of Warwick	5	University of Sunderland	3a
University of Westminster	5	Bath Spa University College	3b
The University of Stirling	5	City University	3b
University of the West of England, Bristol	4	Coventry University	3b
University of Leeds	4	University of Greenwich	3b
The University of Sheffield	4	Liverpool John Moores University	3b
Staffordshire University	4	London Guildhall University	3b
University of Sussex	4	Southampton Institute	2
University of Ulster	4	Trinity and All Saints	2
The University of Birmingham	3a	University of Teesside	2
De Montfort University	3a	University of Wolverhampton	2
Glasgow Caledonian University	3a	Queen Margaret University College Edinburgh	2
King Alfred's, Winchester	3a	University of Hertfordshire	1
Leeds Metropolitan University	3a	Thames Valley University	1

Source: RAE 2001

The emphasis on projects with outside organisations, for example local councils, charities and communications companies, enables students to develop a professional approach towards project management and client presentations and familiarises them with working to deadlines and budgets. The work placement is regarded not only as a form of personal development but an opportunity to evaluate progress in a work situation and to develop links with industry. *Contact details, see page 619*

Richmond, The American International University in London

BA (Hons) Creative Arts and Communications: Communications

With its emphasis on intercultural communication and its balance of theory and practice, this innovative degree draws on interdisciplinary studies to explore globalisation, communication technology and the mass media. Theoretical modules offer a choice of areas of concentration including gender, race, film theory, visual arts and corporate communications. Practical modules cover video production,

photography, graphics, design, journalism and broadcasting. The mix of current communications theory and hands-on practical experience prepares students for graduate study or for careers in international media, international marketing, corporate communications or other creative fields.
For further information, see page 428

York St John College

BA (Hons) Theatre, Film and Television

This programme takes an integrated approach to the study and practice of theatre, film and television. 60 per cent of the degree comprises production activity in well-equipped, purpose-designed studios and workshop areas. The course is vocational with many graduates gaining employment in television, theatre and independent production companies. The degree also considers the aesthetic, cultural, industrial and technological aspects necessary for students in this field. The course has close links with local theatre and television companies and includes a work placement.
For further information, see page 588

Media and communication studies

Postgraduate

University of North London

MA Mass Communications

This course examines the political, techno-logical and economic dynamics of the contemporary sector. The core modules examine both British and international communications developments, while other options enable students to focus on specific sectors such as broadcasting, television, newspapers, music or the internet. Students also consolidate practical skills in computing and media technology such as desktop publishing, video production or developing websites. Students may choose to write their dissertation in any area, working closely with their tutor. International applicants must have a good bachelors degree, prefer-ably in communication studies, English language or literature, film studies, media studies or sociology. Applicants should have an English qualification (IELTS 6.0 or TOEFL 580). The university also provides pre-sessional English courses, an EFL programme and a pre-master's course.

For further information, see page 520

The University of Stirling

MSc in Public Relations/Media

The Department of Film and Media Studies, with its grade five research ranking, offers MSc programmes in public relations and media management. Each can be taken either full time in one year, or part time by online distance learning over two and a half years. The MSc in Public Relations aims to equip its gradu-ates with the necessary practical and analytical skills for a professional career in public relations, while the MSc in Media Management addresses the issues faced by today's media managers and lays emphasis on strategic thinking and analysis for a changing environment. The distance learning versions cover the same core curriculum as the full-time versions but include less in the way of vocational training since students usually have expe-rience in the field. The department also offers an undergraduate degree in film and media studies.

For further information see page 566

Useful links

www.britain-info.org/media_review/	British Press Review
www.bjtc.org.uk	The Broadcast Journalism Training Council
www.mediaguardian.co.uk	*The Guardian*'s Media Website
www.nctj.com	National Council for the Training of Journalists
www.pa.press.net	Press Association
www.publishers.org.uk	The Publishers Association
www.skillset.org	Skillset: The National Training Organisation
www.ecola.com/news/press/eu/uk/	UK Newspapers

Medicine and dentistry

Medicine and dentistry are among the most respected professions. This is not only because of the doctor's power to save lives or the dentist's ability to transform crooked overbites into perfect Hollywood smiles. They are also highly esteemed because of the immense workload involved in the training. Only certain people are cut out to choose these career paths and a strong scientific background will only take you so far. You must be able to deal with people from all backgrounds so communication skills are vital. You must also be prepared to sacrifice the conventional university lifestyle for nine to five lectures, frequent exams and shorter Christmas and Easter breaks. Having said this, medical students do have a reputation for partying harder than anyone else so life can't be too tough.

Britain's teaching hospitals are among the best in the world and attract huge numbers of applicants from Britain and abroad. The government restricts the number of undergraduate places offered to international students and some schools only offer places to those whose countries lack adequate training facilities. Students from outside the UK may find that they have to pass certain tests before being offered a place. Those outside the EEA (though there are exceptions) have to sit the Professional and Linguistic Ability Test (PLAB) which assesses both professional ability and standard of English. Students from some countries may be exempt from this and will only need to take the standard IELTS test, at which a minimum grade of 7.0 is required in all sections.

Both dental and medical courses last five years. Traditionally, the first two were pre-clinical, introducing students to theoretical aspects of anatomy, physiology and dental science. These were followed by three clinical years, which combined study and practical experience on a ward. Nowadays the pre-clinical and clinical divide has all but been removed from medical degrees and students have direct patient contact from day one.

Dental training ends at graduation when students are immediately qualified for practice. There are opportunities to specialise in areas such as orthodontics and though a career in general practice is popular, students can also work in the armed forces, hospitals or academic dentistry.

Medical training, however, does not end at graduation. To be registered as a practitioner with the General Medical Council (GMC), graduates must first spend a year as a house officer. This is a kind of apprenticeship served in a hospital under the supervision of a fully-licensed practitioner. Although hours are not legally supposed to exceed 56 hours a week, many house officers work more than this. Upon registration, doctors can specialise in any number of areas. Many become general practitioners, whereas others undergo further training to become surgeons, anaesthetists or pathologists, for example.

TEACHING QUALITY ASSESSMENTS

Dentistry
(England and Northern Ireland) 1998/99/2000

tqa

Institution	Grade	Institution	Grade
King's College London (University of London)	24	University of Newcastle upon Tyne	23
The University of Manchester	24	The University of Birmingham	22
Queen Mary, University of London	24	The University of Liverpool	21
Queen's University Belfast	24	The Manchester Metropolitan University	21
University of Leeds	23	University of Bristol	19
University College London (University of London) Eastman Dental Institute	23		

Source: HEFCE, SHEFC, HEFCW latest available ratings
For a more complete list of institutions offering these courses at undergraduate level refer to the Course Directory

Medicine

The University of Liverpool
MBChB Medicine and Surgery

Liverpool introduced a completely new medical course in October 1996. It is divided into three phases in which the underlying biomedical sciences are integrated with an increasing proportion of clinical practice. Phase one lasts one year and is concerned with the foundations of medical practice, specifically the sciences which underpin clinical practice. Phase two lasts three years and has an emphasis on increasing clinical experience while continuing to teach the theoretical and scientific side of medicine. The final year,

phase three, is taken up with intensive clinical experience and involves working as part of a clinical team in a peripheral hospital, in a GP surgery or health centre and in a career elective when the student chooses subjects to study in depth.
Contact details, see page 618

Oxford University
BM BCh Medicine with BA (Hons)

The university offers two courses in medicine (one four years and one six), leading to BM BCh. Both courses aim to educate those with intellectual ability and vocational aptitude, regardless of cultural or ethnic background, in order to prepare them for a career as a doctor. Critical

TEACHING QUALITY ASSESSMENTS

Dentistry
(Scotland) 1996

tqa

Institution	Grade	Institution	Grade
University of Dundee	Highly Satisfactory	University of Glasgow	Highly Satisfactory

Dentistry
(Wales) 1996

tqa

Institution	Grade	Institution	Grade
University of Wales Institute, Cardiff	Excellent	University of Wales College of Medicine	Excellent

Medicine
(Scotland) 1996/97

tqa

Institution	Grade	Institution	Grade
The University of Aberdeen	Excellent	The University of Edinburgh	Highly Satisfactory
University of Dundee	Excellent		
University of Glasgow	Excellent	University of St Andrews	Highly Satisfactory

Medicine
(Wales) 1997/98

tqa

Institution	Grade	
Cardiff University	Excellent	
University of Wales College of Medicine	Excellent	

Source: HEFCE, SHEFC, HEFCW latest available ratings
For a more complete list of institutions offering these courses at undergraduate level refer to the Course Directory

thinking and scientifically-patterned enquiry are particularly encouraged by immersion in an environment where basic and clinical research is actively pursued. Students learn to relate sympathetically to patients and to appreciate the factors that affect health in all human societies. The six-year course is taught in two distinct phases; pre-clinical and clinical. The third year, leading to the BA degree, gives students a choice of study areas, together with coherent direction. The four-year course is offered to graduate students with a degree in an appropriate science subject. Students cover basic science teaching in the first two years before joining the last two years of the six-year course.

For further information, see page 534

Queen Mary, University of London
MB BS Medicine

This five-year programme leading to clinical qualifications is divided into three phases. Phase one involves basic medical sciences and lasts for five terms. Understanding the human aspect of medicine is central to the course. Phase two emphasises a holistic approach to medicine, developing communication skills and bringing students into contact with

patients. Modules studied are sociology, psychology, critical appraisal and medical statistics, introduction to patient care, clinical skills, communication skills and medical ethics. Students undertake a major project by carrying out their own research. Phase three is divided into three parts consisting of clinical attachments interspersed with formal teaching. Development involves the supervised study of patients in wards and outpatient departments as well as more formal instruction in clinical and pathological sciences. Students continue to develop their communication skills, practising dealing with difficult situations in small groups using role play.

For further information, see page 540

University College London (University of London)
MB BS Medicine

Students on this six-year course spend five years studying medicine and an additional year pursuing an intercalated BSc. The course is systems based and integrates basic medical science and clinical science with professional skills and competencies throughout the programme. Right from the outset, students have clinical contact with patients, doctors and other health

Medicine and dentistry

TEACHING QUALITY ASSESSMENTS

Medicine
(England and Northern Ireland) 1998/99/2000

tqa

Institution	Grade	Institution	Grade
The University of Liverpool	24	Imperial College of Science, Technology and Medicine (University of London)	21
University of Newcastle upon Tyne	24		
University of Southampton	24	Institute of Psychiatry, King's College London (University of London)	21
Institute of Child Health, Institute of Opthalmology	23	University College London (University of London)	21
University of Leicester	23	The University of Birmingham	20
St George's Hospital Medical School (University of London)	23	University of Bristol	20
King's College London (University of London)	22	The University of Sheffield	19
Queen Mary, University of London	22	University of Leeds	18
Queen's University Belfast	22	University of Derby	16

Source: HEFCE, SHEFC, HEFCW latest available ratings
For a more complete list of institutions offering these courses at undergraduate level refer to the Course Directory

RESEARCH RANKINGS

Clinical Dentistry

rae

Institution	Grade	Institution	Grade
University of Bristol	5*	The University of Birmingham	4
King's College London	5*	University of Leeds	4
University of Newcastle upon Tyne	5	University of Liverpool	4
Queen Mary, University of London	5	The University of Manchester	4
The University of Sheffield	5	University of Wales College of Medicine	4
University College London (University of London)	5	Queen's University Belfast	3a
University of Dundee	5	University of Glasgow	3a

Source: RAE 2001

professionals on the three main clinical sites and in community placements. The course is split into three sections: science and medicine, science and medical practice and preparation for practice. Exceptionally able and highly motivated students may be able to get an intercalated BSc, a PhD and the MB BS in eight years, as opposed to nine.
Contact details, see page 622

University of Wales College of Medicine, Cardiff
MB BCh Medicine

During the last few years, in common with all UK medical schools, Cardiff undertook a review of its medical degree scheme. The course structure has since been modified and improved, aiming to educate students to become competent junior doctors and ensure they are prepared for specialist postgraduate education. They should be able to combine knowledge, skills, judgement and the appropriate attitudes to deliver a high standard of professional care. The internal review was given impetus by a report by the Education Committee of the General Medicine Council. In line with this, students

have direct patient contact from the first year in order to develop clinical skills from the earliest moment. There are two new main elements: a core course representing 60 to 70 per cent of the overall curriculum and the introduction of special study modules providing an extension to the core and further the experiences encountered by students.
Contact details, see page 622

Dentistry

University of Dundee
BDS Dentistry

To become a dentist, you need a high degree of technical skill, accurate clinical judgment and intelligence and a logical mind. You also need to be fit and healthy and have a cheerful and kindly disposition. This five-year course prepares students for a career in dentistry, and as such the BDS is registrable immediately with the General Dental Council. The course takes students through the relevant scientific basics such as anatomy, physiology and first aid, emphasising their practical applications. Second and third years see students gaining clinical experience and knowledge in a broad range of dental topics. The fourth and fifth years, while continuing the teaching of clinical subjects, move steadily towards preparing students for the practice of dentistry.
Contact details, see page 615

274

Other Studies and Professions Allied to Medicine

Institution	Grade	Institution	Grade
Cardiff University	5*	Kingston University	3a
The University of Manchester Institute of Science and Technology (UMIST)	5*	University of Liverpool	3a
		University of North London	3a
The University of Surrey	5*	St George's Hospital Medical School	3a
University of Ulster (Biomedical Sciences)	5*	University of Salford	3a
Aston University	5	University of Sheffield	
The University of Bradford (Biomedical Sciences)	5	(Psychotherapeutic Studies)	3a
University of Brighton (Biomedical Sciences)	5	University of Southampton	3a
City University (Optometry and Visual Science)	5	University of Teesside	3a
King's College London (University of London) (Nutrition and Dietetics)	5	University of Westminster	3a
		University of Wolverhampton	3a
University of Leeds	5	Queen Margaret University College,	
The University of Manchester	5	Edinburgh (Social Sciences in Health)	3a
The Nottingham Trent University	5	Queen Margaret University	
University of Portsmouth (Health Services Research)	5	College, Edinburgh (Nutrition)	3a
		Anglia Polytechnic University	3b
University College London (University of London)	5	University of Brighton	3b
The University of Strathclyde	5	University of Central Lancashire	3b
The University of Bradford (Optometry)	4	University of East Anglia (Occupational Therapy and Physiotherapy)	3b
De Montfort University	4	University of Hertfordshire	
Glasgow Caledonian University (Biological and Biomedical Sciences)	4	(Radiography and Physiotherapy)	3b
		University of Hertfordshire (Arts Therapies)	3b
Glasgow Caledonian University (Vision Sciences)	4	The Manchester Metropolitan University	3b
		University of Portsmouth	3b
King's College London (University of London) (Applied Biomedical Sciences)	4	St Martin's College	3b
		Sheffield Hallam University (Health and Social Care, Evaluation and Practice)	3b
King's College London (University of London) (Gerontology)	4	University of Paisley	3b
Liverpool John Moores University	4	Queen Margaret University College, Edinburgh (Physical Therapy)	3b
Loughborough University	4	The Robert Gordon University (Nutrition)	3b
The University of Sheffield (Human Communication Sciences)	4	The Robert Gordon University (Biomedical Sciences)	3b
Sheffield Hallam University (Biomedical Sciences)	4	University of Wales Institute, Cardiff	3b
Napier University	4	Bath Spa University College	2
Queen Margaret University College, Edinburgh (Speech and Language Disorders)	4	Canterbury Christ Church University College	2
		City University (Radiography)	2
University of Ulster (Rehabilitation Sciences)	4	University of East London	2
University of the West of England, Bristol	3a	University College Northampton	2
Brunel University	3a	Roehampton University of Surrey	2
City University (Measurement and Information in Medicine)	3a	York St John College	2
		The University of the Highlands and Islands Project	2
Coventry University	3a	The Robert Gordon University (Health Services)	2
University of East Anglia (Health Policy and Practice)	3a		
Chester College of Higher Education	3a	Glasgow Caledonian University (Physiology, Podiatry and Radiography)	1
City University (Language and Communication Science)	3a	Leeds, Trinity and All Saints College	1
Goldsmiths College (University of London)	3a	Source: RAE 2001	
University of Greenwich	3a		

King's College London (University of London)

MClinDent Surgical Dentistry

The course is designed for dentists who wish to specialise in surgical dentistry. The programme equips the postgraduate student with a theoretical and practical understanding of surgical dentistry and its relation to other dental specialities. It provides students with academic skills in clinical research and audit. The course encompasses the diagnosis, treatment, planning and management of patients requiring surgical dentistry under local anaesthesia, sedation and day-case general anaesthesia. Trainees undertake specialist clinical modules in those areas of dentistry related to surgical dentistry. Clinical audit and clinical research form a component of the degree and therefore form an integral part of the higher training programme. Trainees are required to maintain an accurate record of all clinical experience in the form of a logbook.

Contact details, see page 617

University of Leeds
BChD Dentistry

This course aims to produce caring and competent dental practitioners with a wide knowledge and considerable practical experience. The undergraduate programme leads to a Bachelor of Dental Surgery (BChD) which allows graduates to become registered dental surgeons. The course lasts five years and is divided into pre-clinical and clinical periods. In the pre-clinical years, students learn general anatomy, physiology, biochemistry and molecular biology, orofacial biology, behavioural science and basic computing. Patient treatment starts early in the second year and students are progressively introduced to different types

of clinics. During the final year, a substantial proportion of students' time is spent in the multidisciplinary restorative dentistry clinic, in which the whole range of treatment necessary for patients is undertaken. The final two years also involve a research project.

Contact details, see page 617

The University of Manchester
BDS Dentistry

Modern dentistry requires specialist knowledge of the mouth, a wide understanding of the whole body and an appreciation of relevant social influences. The BDS degree programme comprises academic and clinical training lasting over five years, designed to provide the knowledge and practical skills necessary for the practice of dentistry. The first two years are taught in the medical schools. Where possible, clinical components are integrated with the theoretical and students attend the Dental School for an introduction to clinical techniques. During the third and fourth years, the basic clinical skills are taught so that, after passing the fourth year exams, students spend the final year working in community dental clinics undertaking whole mouth patient care.

For further information, see page 514

Useful links

www.bda-dentistry.org.uk ⊙	British Dental Association
www.dentalhealth.org.uk ⊙	British Dental Health Foundation
www.bma.org.uk ⊙	British Medical Association
www.bmj.com ⊙	British Medical Journal
www.gdc-uk.org ⊙	General Dental Council
www.gmc-uk.org ⊙	General Medical Council

Modern languages and linguistics

Globalisation has led to increased communication between nations, organisations and individuals across the world. The ability to communicate in another tongue is a highly marketable skill, much sought after by today's increasingly demanding employers. Studying a language other than English in the UK is recommended because of the high quality of teaching, the research opportunities and the range of facilities at British universities and colleges of higher education. Most have good links with other institutions around the world.

Modern language degrees, and the range of subjects with which they can be combined, vary between institutions. Some take a traditional approach, emphasising literature and history, while others have a more contemporary outlook concentrating on business skills and modern culture. All courses, however, include written and spoken language study as their main element, which can include laboratory work and conversation classes with native speakers. Aside from this, most courses offer options covering the literature, culture, history, politics, linguistics, philosophy or society of the relevant countries.

Area studies, such as African or Middle Eastern studies, cover many of these topics as they are multidisciplinary in nature, and focus on nearly every aspect of a particular country, region or culture. Most also include the option to study the relevant language or in the country itself.

Almost all modern language and area study degrees last four years and typically include a period of study in a country of the language studied. This usually takes place in the third year and can involve studying at a university, working as a language assistant or, in some cases, full-time employment. If you are studying one language, it is likely that you will spend a whole academic year in one country; a joint honours will probably mean about five months in each country unless your other subject is not a language, for example business studies.

Many students will have studied the language before but most institutions accept beginners (known as studying a language *ab initio*). If you are starting from scratch, the university or college may reduce your time abroad. If the duration spent in another country is important to you, make sure you check with the department before you apply.

Linguistics

Linguistics is a rapidly-evolving subject which spills over into sociology, economics, psychology and anthropology. At degree level, it usually lasts for three years and courses tend to begin with core subjects such as phonetics, phonology, syntax and semantics. You can then choose options in areas such as sociolinguistics, language and gender, language acquisition and topography. The final year often involves writing a dissertation as well as sitting examinations. Teaching will probably be in the form of lectures, seminars and workshops.

Specialist and vocational

Cardonald College Glasgow

HND Languages and Business for Europe

This two-year course is designed to prepare students for business careers in Europe. They choose two modern languages from French, German, Spanish and Italian. One is studied to intermediate level, the other to advanced level. As well as the languages, students are taught essential business skills, from communication and group skills to marketing and socio-economic issues. There may be an opportunity to take part in an exchange visit to a European country to practise language skills and explore the local business and economy. This is subject to receiving funds from the European Social Fund. Successful graduates can apply for university courses in language and business disciplines, including entry to third-year European students at the University of Paisley.

Contact details, see page 612

Student Profile

Arianna
Italy
Modern Chinese Studies
University of Leeds

"Leeds has so much to offer – the chance to study with native Chinese speakers and tutors who know so much about modern China. We have to work hard, but it is really worth it. After two years I can chat with my Chinese friends, travel around China and understand what's going on! I spent my second year at a university in Beijing. I had fun and became more mature and confident. It's not just knowledge of China and Chinese that I have acquired here. My English has improved and I understand Britain much better than before. When I graduate, I expect to be able to use my written and spoken Chinese professionally. I am using the careers service to find out about companies operating in China and translating and interpreting courses. My teachers say that with good Chinese and a European language I could work for the UN."

Undergraduate

University of Wales, Bangor

Modern European Languages:
BA, MA, and PhD

The School of Modern Languages offers the opportunity to combine the study of English as a foreign language with one or two of the major European languages. Subject areas include language, literature and cultural studies in English, French, German, Italian and Spanish. As well as running BAs in traditional single and joint honours languages, the school offers over 40 combinations of BAs in languages with other subjects. Students have the opportunity to spend at least a semester in the country where the language studied is spoken as a first language. Lectures at the school are taught in small classes which enable students to get to know staff and fellow students. Staff at Bangor have been pioneering the use of satellite TV and computers in language learning since the 1980s. The computerised language centre is open seven days a week. There was zero per cent unemployment amongst 1999 graduates.

For further information, see page 440

The University of Hull

BA (Hons) Southeast Asian Studies

The department emphasises the interdisciplinary nature of Southeast Asian studies, encouraging students both to participate in relevant activities outside the academic

TEACHING QUALITY ASSESSMENTS

American Studies
(England and Northern Ireland) 1996/97/98

tqa

Institution	Grade	Institution	Grade
University of Central Lancashire	24	University of Derby	21
University of East Anglia	24	The University of Kent	21
Keele University	24	Liverpool John	
The University of Hull	23	Moores University	21
University of Leicester	23	The University of Reading	21
The University of Birmingham	22	University of Wolverhampton	21
Middlesex University	22	Liverpool Hope	19
The University of Nottingham	22	King Alfred's Winchester	18
University of Ulster	22	University College	
Brunel University	21	Northampton	18
Canterbury Christ Church		York St John College	17
University College	21	Thames Valley University	15

Dutch
(England and Northern Ireland) 1996

tqa

Institution	Grade	Institution	Grade
University College London (University of London)	22	The University of Hull	20

East and South Asian Studies
(England and Northern Ireland) 1996/97/98

tqa

Institution	Grade	Institution	Grade
Cambridge University	23	Oxford University	22
School of Oriental and African Studies (University of London)	23	The University of Sheffield	22
University of Westminster	23	The University of Durham	21
The University of Hull	22	King Alfred's Winchester	20

English and Associated Studies
(Wales) 1994/95

tqa

Institution	Grade	Institution	Grade
The University of Wales, Aberystwyth (American Studies)	Satisfactory	University of Wales Swansea (American Studies)	Satisfactory

European Languages
(Scotland) 1998

tqa

Institution	Grade	Institution	Grade
The University of Aberdeen	22	Heriot-Watt University, Edinburgh	21
University of Glasgow	22	The University of Stirling	20
University of St Andrews	22	Napier University	19
The University of Strathclyde	22	University of Paisley	19
The University of Edinburgh	21	The Robert Gordon University	19

Source: HEFCE, SHEFC, HEFCW latest available ratings
For a more complete list of institutions offering these courses at undergraduate level refer to the Course Directory

Modern languages

programme and to visit the region whenever possible. The working atmosphere is stimulating and friendly with a beneficial mix of British and international students. This three-year degree also provides the opportunity to explore the region of Southeast Asia in depth. Study is rooted in the major academic disciplines of history, politics, anthropology, geography and socio-economic development. In the first year, the programme involves compulsory core modules on the history, politics,

development, cultures and peoples of Southeast Asia, as well as optional modules from within the centre or from politics, economics, geography, sociology and anthropology.

For further information, see page 492

For further information, see page 492

Lancaster University
BA (Hons) Linguistics

Lancaster University offers a range of degree schemes which suit those interested in descriptive linguistics, applied linguistics, and those who wish to combine linguistics with another field such as a modern language, sociology, psychology, computer science or teaching English as a foreign language (TEFL). The department has an international reputation. Most courses offer the option of a dissertation instead of examination and it is also possible to do independent-study courses. In the first year, students take linguistics and two other options. In the second and third years, all linguistics majors take a core methodology course as well as two full units in theoretical linguistics. The remaining modules are chosen from the range of courses offered by the department. Up to two units of courses may be chosen from another department. The average weekly work-load is about four hours of timetabled lectures plus private study time.

Contact details, see page 617

TEACHING QUALITY ASSESSMENTS

French
(England and Northern Ireland) 1995/96

tqa

Institution	Grade	Institution	Grade
University of Portsmouth	23	The University of Warwick	21
University of Westminster	23	University of Bristol	20
Aston University	22	Keele University	20
The University of Durham	22	Lancaster University	20
University of Exeter	22	Queen's University Belfast	20
University of Leeds	22	University of Ulster	20
The University of Liverpool	22	Birkbeck College	19
Oxford Brookes University	22	University of Leicester	19
University of Sussex	22	The University of Manchester	19
The University of Hull	21	University of Wolverhampton	19
King's College London (University of London)	21	The University of Birmingham	18
The University of Reading	21	The British Institute in Paris (University of London)	18
Royal Holloway, University of London	21	Edge Hill College of Higher Education	17
The University of Sheffield	21	University of Sunderland	17
University College London (University of London)	21	The University of Nottingham	16

French Studies
(Scotland) 1997

tqa

Institution	Grade	Institution	Grade
The University of Aberdeen	Excellent	The University of Edinburgh	Highly Satisfactory
University of Glasgow	Excellent	The University of Stirling	Highly Satisfactory

German
(England and Northern Ireland) 1995/96

tqa

Institution	Grade	Institution	Grade
University of Exeter	24	King's College London (University of London)	20
University College London (University of London)	23	The University of Reading	20
The University of Warwick	23	The University of Sheffield	20
Aston University	22	University of Westminster	20
The University of Durham	22	The University of Birmingham	19
University of Leeds	22	Keele University	19
The University of Nottingham	22	Lancaster University	19
University of Bristol	21	The University of Liverpool	19
The University of Hull	21	Oxford Brookes University	19
University of Leicester	21	Royal Holloway, University of London	19
The University of Manchester	21	University of Ulster	19
University of Portsmouth	21	University of Sunderland	17
Birkbeck College	20	University of Wolverhampton	17

Source: HEFCE, SHEFC, HEFCW latest available ratings
For a more complete list of institutions offering these courses at undergraduate level refer to the Course Directory

University of Leeds
BA Italian

Italy is a country which has profoundly influenced the development of European life, culture and thought. Despite this, Italian is rarely taught in British schools but is a language which can be quickly and enjoyably learned from scratch at university. Students are introduced to selected aspects of Italian history, society and cultural production from the Middle Ages to the present day, with the selection partly determined by the student. The language is taught throughout the degree, with the aim that students graduate with a good level of fluency. The non-linguistic elements of the course offer a popular blend of innovation and tradition. Available topics range from modern Italian history, literature and film to Dante and the varieties of language used in the country.

The third year is spent in Italy attending courses at a local university.

Contact details, see page 617

The University of Liverpool
BA (Hons) Hispanic Studies

This degree aims to develop fluent communication in both Hispanic speech and writing. Core subjects in the first and second years give a solid foundation for an appreciation of Hispanic civilisation. Portuguese language and civilisation is offered throughout the programme with residential stays in Portugal or Brazil. Catalan language, history and culture is offered throughout the programme as an alternative to Portuguese with residential stays in Paisos Catalans. Students spend a year abroad in Spain, Portugal or Latin America, attending a course at university or working as an

Modern languages

TEACHING QUALITY ASSESSMENTS

Russian and Eastern European Languages and Studies
(England and Northern Ireland) 1995/96

tqa

Institution	Grade	Institution	Grade
The University of Sheffield	24	University of Leeds	20
The University of Birmingham	23	The University of Nottingham	19
School of Slavonic and East European Studies (University of London)	23	University of Portsmouth	18
University of Wolverhampton	22	School of Slavonic and East European Studies (University of London) (Eastern European Languages and Studies)	18
University of Bristol	20	University of Westminster	18
The University of Durham	20	The University of Manchester	16
University of Exeter	20		
Keele University	20		

Scandinavian Studies
(England and Northern Ireland) 1996

tqa

University College London (University of London)	23	The University of Hull	19

Welsh
(Wales) 1994/95

tqa

The University of Wales, Aberystwyth	Excellent	The University of Wales, Lampeter	Satisfactory
University of Wales, Bangor	Excellent	University of Wales Swansea	Satisfactory
Cardiff University	Satisfactory		

Celtic Studies
(England) 2000/01

tqa

Cambridge University	23	St Mary's College	21

Source: HEFCE, SHEFC, HEFCW latest available ratings
For a more complete list of institutions offering these courses at undergraduate level refer to the Course Directory

Iberian Languages and Studies
(England and Northern Ireland) 1996

tqa

Institution	Grade	Institution	Grade
The University of Hull	24	Lancaster University	20
King's College London (University of London) (Portuguese)	23	The University of Manchester	20
		University of Wolverhampton	20
The University of Birmingham	22	Birkbeck College	19
University of Bristol	22	University College London (University of London)	19
King's College London (University of London) (Spanish)	22	University of Portsmouth	18
University of Leeds	22	University of Sunderland	18
The University of Liverpool	21	University of Ulster	18
Queen's University Belfast	21	University of Westminster	18
The University of Sheffield	21	The University of Nottingham	17
University of Exeter	20	The University of Durham	16

Italian
(England and Northern Ireland) 1995/96

tqa

Institution	Grade	Institution	Grade
The University of Birmingham	22	University of Leicester	20
University of Exeter	22	University of Portsmouth	20
The University of Hull	22	The University of Reading	20
University of Bristol	21	University College London (University of London)	20
Royal Holloway, University of London	21	University of Leeds	19
The University of Warwick	21	The University of Manchester	19
The University of Durham	20	University of Westminster	19
Lancaster University (with Iberian Studies)	20		

Linguistics
(England and Northern Ireland) 1996

tqa

Institution	Grade	Institution	Grade
Lancaster University	23	The College of St Mark and St John	21
University of Central Lancashire	22	University of Wolverhampton	21
The University of Durham	22	University of Hertfordshire	20
University of Newcastle upon Tyne	22	School of Oriental and African Studies (University of London)	20
Roehampton University of Surrey	22	University of Westminster	20
The University of Sheffield	22	Birkbeck College	19
University of Sussex	22	The University of Reading	19
Thames Valley University	22	York St John College	19
University College London (University of London)	22	University of East London	18
The University of Essex	21	University of Leeds	17
University of Luton	21	University of Exeter	16
The University of Manchester	21		

Source: HEFCE, SHEFC, HEFCW latest available ratings
For a more complete list of institutions offering these courses at undergraduate level refer to the Course Directory

Modern languages

English language teaching assistant. In the final year, students have a choice of options covering the Peninsula and Latin American areas.
Contact details, see page 618

The University of Manchester

BA Linguistics

This course helps students develop skills and ideas in the analysis of language and languages at the same time as encouraging them to learn new languages. In the first year, students learn to look at language in a new way, concentrating on its sounds, meanings and structures. This involves topics ranging from grammar to semantics and from phonetics to discourse analysis. The second year sees the emphasis switch to linguistic theories, with units in syntactic theory, phonology, typology and grammatical semantics as well as others of the students' choice. In the third year,

students are given the freedom to develop interests in particular areas of the subject. The course is taught via many different approaches to teaching and learning.
For further information, see page 514

The University of Nottingham
BA Russian
This is a four-year course with Russian as the main subject. Modules within the department cover Russian language, literature, drama, film and cultural history, as well as study and transferable skills. Students also learn another Slavonic language or take modules in south Slavonic history or literature. The entire third year of this course is spent in Russia and students also go to Russia for a three-week language course in the first long vacation. There are two degree paths in Russian. For one of them, students must have a previous qualification in Russian. Students with no knowledge of Russian can take the single honours Russian (beginners) course, as long as they have shown themselves to be able linguists. For degrees incorporating Serbo-Croat or Slovene no previous knowledge of the

TEACHING QUALITY ASSESSMENTS

Middle Eastern and African Studies
(England and Northern Ireland) 1997/98

tqa

Institution	Grade	Institution	Grade
The University of Birmingham	23	University of Westminster	22
Cambridge University	23	University of Leeds	21
The University of Durham	22	University of Exeter	20
Oxford University	22	The University of Manchester	20
School of Oriental and African Studies (University of London)	22	The University of Salford	20

Modern Languages
(England and Northern Ireland) 1995/96/97

tqa

Institution	Grade	Institution	Grade
Northumbria University	23	La Sainte Union College of Higher Education	19
Queen Mary, University of London	23	Leeds Metropolitan University	19
Cambridge University	22	Liverpool Institute	19
University of Newcastle upon Tyne	22	Liverpool John Moores University	19
Oxford Brookes University	22	London Guildhall University	19
South Bank University	22	Middlesex University	19
The University of York	22	Roehampton University of Surrey	19
Anglia Polytechnic University	21	Sheffield Hallam University	19
University of the West of England, Bristol	21	Queen's University Belfast	19
University of Central Lancashire	21	Bournemouth University	18
Coventry University	21	The University of Bradford	18
Kingston University	21	University of Derby	18
The Manchester Metropolitan University	21	University of East London	18
Oxford University	21	The University of Manchester Institute of Science and Technology (UMIST)	18
Staffordshire University	21	University of Southampton	18
University of Brighton	20	The University of Surrey	18
University of Luton	20	Thames Valley University	18
University of North London	20	De Montfort University	17
The University of Salford	20	Goldsmiths College (University of London)	17
University of Bath	19	The Nottingham Trent University	17
Bolton Institute of Higher Education	19	University of Sussex	17
Chester (A College of The University of Liverpool)	19	Leeds, Trinity and All Saints College	17
De Montfort University	19	University of Hertfordshire	16
University of East Anglia	19	The University of Huddersfield	15
The University of Kent	19		

Source: HEFCE, SHEFC, HEFCW latest available ratings
For a more complete list of institutions offering these courses at undergraduate level refer to the Course Directory

Modern languages

Institution	Grade	Institution	Grade
University of Wales, Bangor (Russian)	Excellent	The University of Wales, Lampeter	Satisfactory
University of Wales Swansea (German, Italian, Spanish)	Excellent	University of Wales Swansea (French, Russian)	Satisfactory
The University of Wales, Aberystwyth	Satisfactory		
University of Wales, Bangor (French, German)	Satisfactory		
Cardiff University	Satisfactory		

Source: HEFCE, SHEFC, HEFCW latest available ratings
For a more complete list of institutions offering these courses at undergraduate level refer to the Course Directory

language is necessary.

For further information, see page 530

University of Portsmouth
BA (Hons) Languages and International Trade

This degree provides a thorough grounding in the theories, techniques and legal framework of international trade and marketing. It also aims to enable students to reach a high level of competence in one or two foreign languages. Students take one or two languages throughout the course and spend an academic year abroad in one or two language areas. Students normally spend at least half their year abroad on a work placement. Language study occupies about one third to one half of the curriculum (depending on whether students take one or two languages), the remainder being made up of the study of business, economics and international trade.

For further information, see page 538

Queen Mary, University of London
BA European Studies
(with a language: French, Spanish, German, Russian or Italian)

This degree is shared equally between a range of language departments. Degree programmes within the European studies framework at Queen Mary enable students with a major interest in European languages and culture to combine their language

study with an extensive range of Europe-related courses. One or two languages are studied in equal measure to honours level and students also take two further courses in linguistics or literature and culture. The third year of the course is spent abroad in the country of the target language. All departments contribute to the already thriving London scene by presenting foreign language films, plays, art and music with seminars and lectures given by staff and guest speakers from abroad.

For further information, see page 540

School of Oriental and African Studies (University of London)
BA (Hons) African Language and Development Studies

This is a combined four-year degree in which the African languages which are normally available are Amharic, Hausa and Swahili. No previous knowledge is expected. Students visit their chosen region and develop their language skills further. Students taking Swahili and development studies, for example, spend the first two terms of their third year studying in Tanzania. The degree

EDUCATI☮N

www.educationuk.org

incorporates the role of language in giving access to a particular culture, as well as the influence that the developing world exerts on the global scene in terms of cultural enrichment expressed through texts, performance, media, orality and music.

For further information, see page 554

Postgraduate

University of Wales, Aberystwyth
MA Medieval Welsh Literature

This one or two-year course is specifically intended for students from outside Wales, or for Welsh students who have not previously studied the Welsh language and its literature. Taught modules account for 120 credits and the dissertation a further 60 credits. The dissertation may be submitted at any time between the September following the examinations and one year thereafter. Candidates study three core modules: the Four Branches of the Mabinogi, Welsh Language I, Welsh Language II and two further modules from a list including the earliest Welsh poetry, Arthurian literature, medieval Welsh law, Dafydd ap Gwilym and comparative celtic literature. Apart from the Welsh and Celtic collections of the university's own Hugh Owen Library, the department benefits from its proximity to the National Library of Wales with its collections of Welsh manuscripts, printed books and journals.

For further information, see page 436

The University of Birmingham
MA European Studies

The school offers this graduate programme based on its range of expertise in European studies with other contributions from across the school. The programme covers Western, Central and Eastern Europe. Students can follow the general programme or can opt

Modern languages

American Studies

Institution	Grade	Institution	Grade
Institute of Latin American Studies	5*	University of North London	4
The University of Nottingham	5*	Brunel University	3a
Keele University	5	University of Derby	3a
University of Liverpool	5	University of Wales Swansea	3a
University of Sussex	5	University of Central Lancashire	3b
The University of Birmingham	4	Institute of United States Studies	3b
University of East Anglia	4		

Source: RAE 2001

for one of the more specialised pathways, including European Union/integration, European political economy, Central and Eastern Europe, contemporary German studies, Western European political thought, Europe and Asia, and modern history. The general programme offers a broad-based, multidisciplinary approach to European studies. There is the opportunity to select from a large number of more specialised modules in a wide range of different areas within European studies. All master's degrees are available as one-year, full-time or two-year, part-time programmes. The degree may also be awarded for the submission of a 40,000-word thesis, researched

Iberian and Latin American Languages

Institution	Grade	Institution	Grade
Birkbeck College	5*	University of Bristol	4
Cambridge University	5*	University of Durham	4
King''s College London (University of London) (Portuguese)	5*	University of Exeter	4
King's College London (University of London) (Spanish)	5*	The University of Hull	4
The University of Manchester	5*	University of Leeds	4
The University of Nottingham	5*	University of Liverpool	4
Queen Mary, University of London	5*	Queen's University Belfast	4
The University of Birmingham	5	Royal Holloway, University of London	4
The University of Edinburgh	5	The University of Strathclyde	4
University of Newcastle upon Tyne	5	University College London (University of London)	4
Oxford University	5	University of Wolverhampton	4
The University of Sheffield	5	Oxford Brookes University	3a
University of St Andrews	5	Roehampton University of Surrey	3a
University of Wales Swansea	5	University of Glasgow	3a
The University of Aberdeen	4	The University of Wales, Aberystwyth	3a
		University of Westminster	3b
		London Guildhall University	2

Italian

Institution	Grade	Institution	Grade
The University of Birmingham	5*	University of Exeter	4
Cambridge University	5*	University of Leicester	4
University of Leeds	5*	Royal Holloway, University of London	4
Oxford University	5*	The University of Strathclyde	4
University College London (University of London)	5*	University of Sussex	4
The University of Reading	5*	University of Wales Swansea	4
University of Bristol	5	University of Westminster	4
The University of Manchester	5	The University of Hull	3a
The University of Warwick	5	University of Glasgow	3b
The University of Edinburgh	4		

Source: RAE 2001

Modern languages

286

Asian Studies

Institution	Grade	Institution	Grade
Cambridge University	5*	University of Westminster	5
Oxford University	5*	De Montfort University	4
The University of Edinburgh	5	The University of Durham	4
The University of Hull	5	The University of Sheffield	4
University of Leeds	5	University College Northampton	3a
School of Oriental		The University of Stirling	3a
and African Studies	5	Liverpool Hope	3b

Celtic Studies

The University of Wales, Aberystwyth	5*	University of Wales Swansea	5
University of Wales, Bangor	5*	University of Wales Centre for	
Cambridge University	5*	Advanced Welsh and Celtic Studies	5
University of Ulster	5*	The University of Aberdeen	4
Queen's University Belfast	5	University of Glasgow	4
Cardiff University	5	University of Exeter	3a
The University of Edinburgh	5	The University of Wales, Lampeter	3b
Oxford University	5	Falmouth College of Arts	1

European Studies

The University of Birmingham (Centre for Russian and East European Studies)	5*	Kingston University	4
The University of Bradford	5*	The University of Manchester Institute of Science and Technology (UMIST)	4
University of Glasgow	5*	Heriot-Watt University, Edinburgh	4
University of Southampton	5*	University of Paisley	4
Aston University	5	University of Central Lancashire	3b
University of Bath	5	University of Lincoln	3b
The University of Birmingham (Institute for German Studies)	5	University of Newcastle upon Tyne	3b
University of Brighton	5	Northumbria University	3b
Cardiff University	5	University of Plymouth	3b
Lancaster University	5	The University of Strathclyde	3b
Loughborough University	5	The Manchester Metropolitan University	3a
University of Portsmouth	5	University of North London	3a
Queen's University Belfast	5	St Mary's College	3a
Queen's University Belfast (Celtic Studies)	5	South Bank University	3a
The University of Salford	5	University of Sunderland	3a
The University of Surrey	5	University of the West of England, Bristol	3a
University College London (University of London)	5	University of Wolverhampton	3a
The University of Bradford (Modern Languages)	4	The University of Edinburgh	3a
Goldsmiths College (University of London)	4	Anglia Polytechnic University	2
The University of Kent	4	Oxford Brookes University	2
		Southampton Institute	2

Source: RAE 2001

Modern languages

and written over one year.

Contact details, see page 613

King's College London (University of London)

MA German

There are two strands to this postgraduate programme, depending on the needs of the student. They can choose either modern German literature: writers and theory or the German language: structure and development. The first is designed for students requiring an intensive grounding in literary studies before going on to a higher degree or for teachers looking for a higher qualification in their discipline. The second is for students wishing to study the historical development of the language as preparation for research in German linguistics. Both are taught through a combination of seminars, tutorials and personal dissertation supervision. Assessment is by a supervised 10,000-word dissertation, written either in English or German, and four term papers of 3,000 to 4,000 words. *Contact details, see page 617*

Lancaster University
New Route PhD in Applied Linguistics
This is a four-year full-time PhD programme in which students spend the first two years on coursework and their research project and the second two years on their research project alone. Each student has an individual superviser for their research project right from the start. Students are required to take 12 courses: six applied linguistics courses and six research methods for applied linguistics courses, and to be assessed on four from

each group (total eight). All courses are taught by staff members from the department. The Department of Linguistics and Modern English Language has over 100 research students (part-time and full-time), and a thriving research culture. Several research groups (for example Classroom Language Learning Research Group, Pragmatics and Stylistics Research Group) meet weekly, and all research students are welcome at these.
Contact details, see page 617

The University of Salford
MA in Translating and Interpreting
This course is designed to meet the international demand for highly-trained translators, interpreters and linguists, as well as meeting the needs of students who are planning a career in international and government departments, regional organisations or the freelance sector.

RESEARCH RANKINGS
German, Dutch and Scandinavian Languages

rae

Institution	Grade	Institution	Grade
The University of Birmingham	5*	The University of Durham	4
Cambridge University	5*	University of Greenwich	4
University of Exeter	5*	University of Glasgow	4
King's College London (University of London)	5*	University of Leeds	4
Institute of Germanic Studies	5*	London Guildhall University	4
The University of Manchester	5*	University of Newcastle upon Tyne	4
The University of Nottingham	5*	Oxford Brookes University	4
Royal Holloway, University of London	5*	The University of Reading	4
The University of Edinburgh	5*	The University of Sheffield	4
University College London (University of London) (German)	5*	University of Sussex	4
Birkbeck College	5	University of St Andrews	4
University of Bristol	5	The University of Stirling	4
University of Liverpool	5	The University of Wales, Aberystwyth	4
Oxford University	5	Queen's University Belfast	4
Queen Mary, University of London	5	The University of Hull	3a
University of Wales Swansea	5	Keele University	3a
University College London (University of London) (Dutch)	5	University of Leicester	3b
		The Nottingham Trent University	3a
University College London (Scandinavian Studies)	5	The Robert Gordon University	3b
The University of Warwick	5	The University of Strathclyde	3b
The University of Aberdeen	4	University of Wales, Bangor	3a
		University of Ulster	3a

Source: RAE 2001

RESEARCH RANKINGS

French

Institution	Grade	Institution	Grade
The University of Birmingham	5*	Birkbeck College	4
Cambridge University	5*	University of Exeter	4
The University of Manchester	5*	The University of Hull	4
Oxford University	5*	The University of Kent	4
Royal Holloway, University of London	5*	University of Leeds	4
		University of Newcastle upon Tyne	4
The University of Aberdeen	5*	The Nottingham Trent University	4
University of Bristol	5	University of Sussex	4
The University of Durham	5	University of St Andrews	4
The University of Edinburgh	5	The University of Strathclyde	4
University of Glasgow	5	University of Wales Swansea	4
King's College London (University of London)	5	Queen's University Belfast	4
The University of Liverpool	5	University of Ulster	4
The University of Nottingham	5	The University of Wales, Aberystwyth	3a
Oxford Brookes University	5	British Institute in Paris	3a
Queen Mary, University of London	5	University of Leicester	3a
The University of Reading	5	London Guildhall University	3a
The University of Sheffield	5	Middlesex University	3a
University College London (University of London)	5	Roehampton University of Surrey	3a
The University of Warwick	5	University of Westminster	3a
The University of Stirling	5	The University of Huddersfield	3b
University of Wales, Bangor	4	The University of Wales, Lampeter	3b

Source: RAE 2001

RESEARCH RANKINGS

Linguistics

Institution	Grade	Institution	Grade
Cambridge University	5*	University of Sussex	4
Oxford University	5*	University of Hertfordshire	3a
Queen Mary, University of London	5*	University of Leeds	3a
University College London (University of London)	5*	University of Luton	3a
The University of Durham	5	School of Oriental and African Studies (University of London)	3a
The University of Edinburgh	5	The University of Reading	3a
The University of Essex	5	University of Ulster	3a
Lancaster University	5	University of Wolverhampton	3a
The University of Manchester	5	Birkbeck College	3b
University of Newcastle upon Tyne	5	University of East Anglia	3b
University of Westminster	5	University of Wales, Bangor	3b
The University of York	5	University of Greenwich	2

Source: RAE 2001

Modern languages

289

RESEARCH RANKINGS

Middle Eastern and African Studies *rae*

Institution	Grade	Institution	Grade
The University of Birmingham	5*	School of Oriental and African Studies (University of London)	5
The University of Edinburgh	5*	The University of Durham	4
Cambridge University	5	University of Leeds	4
University of Exeter	5	University College London (University of London)	3a
The University of Manchester	5	The University of Wales, Lampeter	3a
Oxford University	5		

Russian, Slavonic and East European Languages *rae*

Institution	Grade	Institution	Grade
University of Bristol	5*	The University of Edinburgh	4
Oxford University	5*	University of Glasgow	4
The University of Sheffield	5*	Keele University	4
Cambridge University	5	University of Leeds	4
University of Exeter	5	The University of Manchester	4
The University of Nottingham	5	University of St Andrews	4
University of Portsmouth	5	University of Sussex	4
Queen Mary, University of London	5	The University of Strathclyde	3a
The University of Surrey	5		

Source: RAE 2001

Students come from all over the world. The school normally expects all students to undertake a short work placement in an interpreting environment. Graduates of the course often go on to work in these companies, as well as becoming freelance translators or interpreters. Students take modules in lexicography, terminology, the principles of translation and information technology in consecutive and simultaneous interpreting. It is possible to specialise in either translation or interpreting. Teaching methods are varied and include a mixture of laboratory exercises, seminars and lectures.

For further information, see page 552

Useful links

www.languagelearn.co.uk	⊙	Association for Language Learning
www.cilt.org.uk	⊙	Centre for Information on Language Teaching and Research
www.iol.org.uk	⊙	Institute of Linguists
www.iti.org.uk	⊙	Institute of Translation and Interpreting
www.qub.ac.uk/edu/nicilt	⊙	Northern Ireland Centre for Information on Language Teaching and Research
www.stir.ac.uk/scilt	⊙	Scottish Centre for Information on Language Teaching and Research
www.linguanet.org.uk	⊙	Virtual Language Centre
www.well.ac.uk	⊙	Web Enhanced Language Learning

Modern languages

From Mozart to M People, music today spans the entirety of what it is possible to express in sound. "Music creates order out of chaos," said the musician, Sir Yehudi Menuhin. There was a time when the subject, as taught at university, was thought of as the audible manifestation of mathematics; a science allied to geometry and astronomy. Although music will always embody the mathematical disciplines of acoustics and tempo, the subject has become much more diverse than this as the freedom of what musical expression means has expanded.

Britain has contributed a startling number of famous musicians and composers. Purcell, Elgar, The Beatles, The Spice Girls and Fatboy Slim have all taken the world by storm in their own inimitable styles. For years, the UK has been a place of musical innovation, most recently with the British invasion of the world's pop charts in the 1960s and the birth of 'Britpop' in the 1990s, led by the likes of Oasis and Radiohead. The UK is home to some of the finest orchestras in the world such as the London Symphony Orchestra and the Royal Philharmonic. In terms of musical training, top musicians from all over the world such as Dame Joan Sutherland, have come to London to study at the Royal College of Music and London is host to one of the most exciting events in the musical calendar – The Proms.

A degree in music can be studied in a number of ways leading to a BA, BMus or even a BEng – the latter, for example, in music technology. Generally speaking, there is no significant advantage in studying a BA or a BMus given that the nature and emphasis of a course differs from one university or college to another. Many universities and colleges also provide combined studies degrees with arts, humanities and social science subjects. Although music studies are traditionally associated with the classical, popular music has been introduced to many higher education portfolios. Other specialist degrees include commercial music, composition, jazz, contemporary music, electronic music, ethnomusicology, music technology and performance studies.

The majority of academic music courses aim to give students an understanding of European traditions, from medieval times to the present day, and enable them to develop individual interests. Courses introduce students to various different areas of study – history, criticism, analysis, composition and performance. The ratio between theory and performance varies. Conservatoires such as the Royal Northern College of Music are more than likely to concentrate on performance instead of on the more theoretical approach.

It is advisable to find out exactly what each course entails and to talk to staff in the department before you apply. Entrance requirements vary but performance-based courses will demand a high standard of instrumental skill from all applicants.

Specialist and vocational

Leeds College of Music
BTEC National Diploma in
Music Technology

This two-year, full-time course is likely to be most appropriate for students who intend to continue their studies in higher education or seek employment in the music industry. Students are given an introduction to a wide range of musical topics, from the history of popular music and sound recording techniques to DJ skills and technologies and events management. In addition, they are given a thorough grounding in music theory and harmony and in the techniques of live sound editing, as well as being taught to improve their sense of pitch, rhythm and harmonic awareness. The usual qualifications required are four GCSEs at grade A to C, and students are

TEACHING QUALITY ASSESSMENTS

Music
(England and Northern Ireland) 1994/95 **tqa**

Institution	Grade	Institution	Grade
Anglia Polytechnic University	Excellent	University of Southampton	Excellent
The University of Birmingham	Excellent	The University of Surrey	Excellent
Cambridge University	Excellent	University of Sussex	Excellent
University of Central England in Birmingham		Trinity College Carmarthen	Excellent
City University	Excellent	University of Ulster	Excellent
Goldsmiths College (University of London)	Excellent	The University of York	Excellent
The University of Huddersfield	Excellent	Bretton Hall	Satisfactory
Keele University	Excellent	University of Bristol	Satisfactory
King's College London (University of London)	Excellent	Canterbury Christ Church University College	Satisfactory
Lancaster University	Excellent	The University of Durham	Satisfactory
University of Leeds	Excellent	University of East Anglia	Satisfactory
The University of Manchester	Excellent	University of Exeter	Satisfactory
The University of Nottingham	Excellent	University of Hertfordshire	Satisfactory
Open University	Excellent	The University of Hull	Satisfactory
Queen's University Belfast	Excellent	Kingston University	Satisfactory
Royal Academy of Music	Excellent	The University of Liverpool	Satisfactory
Royal College of Music	Excellent	The Liverpool Institute for Performing Arts	Satisfactory
Royal Northern College	Excellent	Middlesex University	Satisfactory
Salford College	Excellent	University of Newcastle upon Tyne	Satisfactory
Sheffield College	Excellent	Oxford University	Satisfactory
School of Oriental and African Studies (University of London)	Excellent	The University of Reading	Satisfactory
		Royal Holloway, University of London	Satisfactory

Music
(England and Northern Ireland) 2000 **tqa**

University of Sunderland	21

Music
(Scotland) 1994 **tqa**

Royal Scottish Academy of Music and Drama	Excellent	University of Glasgow	Highly Satisfactory
The University of Edinburgh	Highly Satisfactory	Napier University	Satisfactory

Music
(Wales) 1994/95 **tqa**

University of Wales, Bangor	Excellent	Welsh College of Music and Drama	Satisfactory
Cardiff University	Satisfactory	Trinity College Carmarthen (Theatre, Music and Media Studies)	Satisfactory

Source: HEFCE, SHEFC, HEFCW latest available ratings
For a more complete list of institutions offering these courses at undergraduate level refer to the Course Directory

Music

rae

Institution	Grade	Institution	Grade
The University of Birmingham	5*	Open University	4
Cambridge University	5*	Royal Academy of Music	4
City University	5*	Royal College of Music	4
The University of Manchester	5*	Royal Northern College of Music	4
University of Newcastle upon Tyne	5*	The University of Salford	4
The University of Nottingham	5*	The University of Edinburgh	4
Oxford University	5*	University of Glasgow	4
Royal Holloway, University of London	5*	Bath Spa University College	3a
University of Southampton	5*	Bretton Hall	3a
University of Wales, Bangor	5	University of Central England in Birmingham	3a
University of Bristol	5	Oxford Brookes University	3a
Cardiff University	5	The University of Reading	3a
Goldsmiths College (University of London)	5	The University of Surrey	3a
King's College London (University of London)	5	Roehampton University of Surrey	3a
The University of Huddersfield	5	The University of Aberdeen	3a
The University of Hull	5	University of Ulster	3a
School of Oriental and African Studies (University of London)	5	Anglia Polytechnic University	3b
The University of Sheffield	5	Canterbury Christ Church University College	3b
University of Sussex	5	University of Hertfordshire	3b
The University of York	5	Kingston University	3b
Queen's University Belfast	5	Liverpool Hope	3b
Dartington College of Arts	4	London Guildhall University	3b
De Montfort University	4	Royal Scottish Academy of Music and Drama	3b
The University of Durham	4	University College Northampton	3b
University of East Anglia	4	Napier University	2
University of Exeter	4	Liverpool John Moores University	2
Keele University	4	St Martin's College	2
Lancaster University	4	Thames Valley University	2
University of Leeds	4	University College Chichester	1
The University of Liverpool	4		

Source: RAE 2001

Music

expected to show an interest in and understanding of music technology. Admission is by interview.

Contact details, see page 617

Contact details, see page 617

Undergraduate

Birmingham Conservatoire, University of Central England in Birmingham

BMus (Hons) Music

This degree is designed to meet the needs of those students who are excellent performers or composers and who wish to prepare themselves realistically for the challenges of a career in 21st-century music. Support studies are tailored to the specific needs of the modern performer or composer and include an integrated approach to the study of harmony and aural appreciation. The course is designed to provide specialisation together with opportunity for diversification. A number of optional activities provide opportunities for everyone to develop their skills. Optional studies can include work experience and the course has strong links with the City of Birmingham Symphony Orchestra, the Royal Ballet and D'Oyly Carte, the BBC and festival promoters. All years include principal study plus workshops, master classes, ensemble work in orchestras, choirs or bands and optional studies. Students receive one-to-one tuition on their principal study area throughout the course.

For further information, see page 464

For further information, see page 464

Royal College of Music

BMus Music

Famous alumni of the Royal College of Music (RCM) include Sir Benjamin Britten, Dame Joan Sutherland and Anne Dudley – the Oscar-winning composer of the music for *The Full Monty*. The degree involves practical training with a strong emphasis on performance and opportunities to perform in public. More than 250 concerts are given each year. Application involves an audition at which set works are played and a range of general music skills are tested. First-year undergraduates can expect a principal study, aural lessons, stylistic and historical studies and academic seminars. A significant number of graduates find employment with major international orchestras, opera companies, choirs and chamber ensembles. There are many opportunities for RCM students to gain experience within the UK and other countries. The facilities available include the Museum of Instruments, the Department of Portraits and Performance History, a library and computers.

Contact details, see page 613

Contact details, see page 613

King's College London (University of London)

MMus Music

The music department offers a modular syllabus which is flexible and encourages students to select course units according to their particular interests. These may include courses from other departments. Students may specialise in historical musicology, theory and analysis or composition. Each field has its own course units but these may be mixed according to the needs and experience of individual students. The course is designed for students intending to go on to do research or composition at doctoral level or wishing to enhance their existing skills. The course is composed of two semesters of taught courses plus individually supervised special study. Students select six half-units (or equivalent) of coursework, up to a third of which may be chosen from suitable master's-level courses in another humanities department. A dissertation, analysis or portfolio of compositions is submitted at the end.

Contact details, see page 617

Contact details, see page 617

Useful links

www.bmic.co.uk	▶	British Music Information Centre
www.classicalmusic.co.uk	▶	Classical Music UK
www.music-media.co.uk	▶	Music Media
www.musicweb.uk.net	▶	Music Web
www.musicians-union.org.uk	▶	Musician's Union
www.musicians.co.uk	▶	UK Musician's Database

Music

Nursing and midwifery

Where would we all be without nurses and midwives? For a start, we probably wouldn't have made it into the world. Nurses and midwives command respect within society because they are so important to healthcare. If you're in hospital, the doctor may breeze in with checks every few hours but it's the nurse who will give you seemingly undivided attention. Nowadays, nurses are increasingly taking on more responsibility and decision-making power within the health system.

Nursing

Nursing courses combine the study of physiology, biology, social sciences and psychology, developing the skills of nursing practice and health promotion. Courses are available either in the form of a degree course (often lasting four years) or as a diploma (usually lasting either two or three years). Both qualifications lead to professional registration. All pre-registration students study the Common Foundation Programme (CFP) for the first half of their course, then choose to specialise in adult, child or mental health nursing. As the course progresses, students spend an increasing amount of time in a clinical environment, developing their skills through practical experience. This culminates in a period spent working as a nurse with full duties. All courses include an elective, during which students may gain experience in a specialist area.

They then focus on research, assessment and therapy in their chosen area and spend time working in hospitals and other healthcare settings. This training culminates in a lengthy period of rostered service, working as part of a healthcare team.

Midwifery

Midwifery students are often, but not always, qualified nurses. Those who are already nurses can usually bypass the initial training; in fact, many institutions offer separate courses for those who are already qualified. As with nursing degrees, course content combines theory and practice. Clinical experience becomes increasingly prominent and students are supported by experienced midwives.

In the first year, students study principles, practice and the profession in general, as well as developing a knowledge of the social and biological sciences, general health issues and illnesses. Second-year studies focus on procedures and techniques in normal and abnormal childbearing, as well as mental health issues in women. In the second year, the emphasis on clinical training becomes more prominent and students see how theory is translated into practice. The third year is heavily based on clinical training and students will, by the end of the year, be capable of practising independently as a midwife.

Throughout the course, students are supported by experienced midwives.

Nursing
(Scotland) 1996/97

tqa

Institution	Grade	Institution	Grade
The University of Edinburgh	Highly Satisfactory	Queen Margaret University	
Glasgow Caledonian University	Highly Satisfactory	College, Edinburgh	Highly Satisfactory
University of Glasgow	Highly Satisfactory	University of Abertay Dundee	Satisfactory

Nursing
(Wales) 1996/97

tqa

University of Wales		The North East Wales Institute	
College of Medicine	Satisfactory	of Higher Education	Satisfactory

Source: HEFCE, SHEFC, HEFCW latest available ratings
For a more complete list of institutions offering these courses at undergraduate level refer to the Course Directory

Specialist and vocational

City University
Nursing Studies Diploma

This three-year modular course leads to professional registration as a nurse in one of three specialist areas: adult, children or mental health nursing. Regardless of the student's specialism, they combine academic study with practical work in a range of clinical placements in hospitals and the community. The course develops proficient and caring nurses who have the practical skills and intellectual capabilities to work independently and in multidisciplinary teams. The first part of the course concentrates on acquiring practical skills and knowledge related to health and caring for people. The second part focuses strongly on clinical practice and enables the student to apply their skills within their chosen specialist area. This programme is only available to students from the European Union who are exempt from tuition fees.

Contact details, see page 615

Middlesex University
Diploma in Higher Education
Pre-registration Midwifery

This three-year programme prepares students to be a lead professional for women with uncomplicated pregnancies, necessitating both a breadth and depth of knowledge in theory and practice. Students on this course gain a professional qualification in midwifery and learn the application of biological and social sciences in the subject. They also have the opportunity to gain clinical experience in a variety of settings, primarily working with mothers and their babies. On completion of the programme, successful students are eligible to apply for registration as a midwife with the United Kingdom Central Council (UKCC). The NHS Trust maternity units involved in the course are particularly keen to receive applications from Middlesex University.

Contact details, see page 618

Northumbria University
Diploma in Nursing Studies
BSc (Hons) Nursing Studies/
Registered Nurse

The newly developed pre-registration curriculum meets with the government's 'Making a Difference' initiative to provide health and social care centred around the needs of patients. All pre-registration programmes therefore aim to produce highly motivated and knowledgeable nurses who can respond effectively to healthcare needs in a range of different

TEACHING QUALITY ASSESSMENTS

Nursing
(England and Northern Ireland) 1998/98

Institution	Grade	Institution	Grade
Bolton Institute of Higher Education	24	King's College London	
University of Central Lancashire	24	(University of London)	21
Northumbria University	24	Leeds Metropolitan University	21
The University of Reading	24	Liverpool John Moores University	21
Buckinghamshire Chilterns		The Manchester Metropolitan University	21
University College	23	The University of Sheffield	21
The University of Bradford	23	University of North London	21
University of Greenwich	23	Sheffield Hallam University	21
University of Hertfordshire	23	St Martin's College, Lancaster:	
University of Luton	23	Ambleside: Carlisle	21
The University of Manchester	23	University of Wolverhampton	21
University of Plymouth	23	The University of York	21
University of Teesside	23	University of Central England	
Bournemouth University	22	in Birmingham	20
The University of Birmingham	22	City University	20
University of Brighton	22	University of Leeds	20
Brunel University	22	South Bank University	20
Canterbury Christ Church University College	22	Suffolk College (An Accredited College	
Edge Hill College of Higher Education	22	of the University of East Anglia)	20
The University of Huddersfield	22	Thames Valley University	20
University College Northampton	22	University of Derby	19
The University of Nottingham	22	Institute of Cancer Research	19
The University of Salford	22	The University of Liverpool	19
Staffordshire University	22	New College Durham	19
University of Ulster	22	The University of Surrey	19
Homerton College	21	University of East Anglia	18
Keele University	21	The University of Hull	17

Source: HEFCE, SHEFC, HEFCW latest available ratings
For a more complete list of institutions offering these courses at undergraduate level refer to the Course Directory

RESEARCH RANKINGS

Nursing

Institution	Grade	Institution	Grade
The University of Manchester	5	South Bank University	3a
University of Newcastle upon Tyne	5	The University of Birmingham	3b
The University of Sheffield	5	Bournemouth University	3b
The University of York	5	The University of Bradford	3b
City University	4	University of the West of England, Bristol	3b
University of Hertfordshire	4	University of Central Lancashire	3b
King's College London (University of London)	4	University of Glamorgan	3b
University of Leeds	4	Leeds Metropolitan University	3b
University of Ulster	4	Oxford Brookes University	3b
University of Wales College of Medicine	4	University of Plymouth	3b
The University of Edinburgh	3a	University of Southampton	3b
University of Glasgow	3a	Thames Valley University	3b
Glasgow Caledonian University	3a	The University of Stirling	3b
The University of Hull	3a	University of Wales Swansea	3b
Kingston University	3a	University of Brighton	2
Institute of Cancer Research	3a	University of Central England	
The University of Liverpool	3a	in Birmingham	2
Liverpool John Moores University	3a	Keele University	2
Middlesex University	3a	RCN Institute	2
Northumbria University	3a	The Robert Gordon University	2
The University of Nottingham	3a	St Martin's College	2
St George's Hospital Medical School	3a	Swansea Institute of Higher Education	1

Source: RAE 2001

nursing settings. The course prepares students for taking on the responsibilities involved with registration with the United Kingdom Central Council (UKCC) and also for any one of the four specialist branches: adult, child learning, disabilities or mental health. A particular strength of these nursing programmes is the integration of theory and practice. All clinical experience undertaken by nursing students is supervised and supported by clinical mentors and academic tutors.

For further information, see page 526

University of Teesside
Diploma in Nursing Studies

This course prepares students for admission to the United Kingdom Central Council for Nursing, Midwifery and Health Visiting (UKCC). The course comprises 50 per cent theory and 50 per cent practice, enabling students to develop the knowledge they will need as qualified nurses in a demanding and rapidly changing health service. This programme differs from a BSc in Nursing Studies in terms of the academic level at which students undertake their work and the qualifications necessary for entry. During the first year, students explore a range of areas including nursing theory, human physiology and health promotion. Practice placements begin early in the first year. Students follow some core modules but the majority are specific to their chosen pathway.

For further information, see page 574

Undergraduate

Bolton Institute of Higher Education
Community Healthcare Nursing BS/BSc(Hons)

This course is for first level nurses who are registered with the UK Central Council

and who have normally completed two years post-registration experience, preferably with consolidation in the UK. It provides specialist practitioner training in public health nursing or health visiting, community nursing in the home or district nursing, general practice nursing or school nursing. Application is made for one of these pathways. The 43-week course completes study to BSc or BSc (Hons) level, dependent upon the level of previous study undertaken in an institution of higher education. The course consists of college and practice-based learning so readiness to work within the NHS setting is essential. On successful completion of the course, names are registered on the UKCC professional register.

Contact details, see page 613

Canterbury Christ Church University College
BSc (Hons) Adult Nursing Studies

During this course, trainee nurses gain practical work experience through clinical placements in hospitals and in the community, beginning as observers and gradually moving towards participation. The learning programme is shared with the degrees in midwifery, radiography and occupational therapy and leads to registered nurse status. Assessment takes the form of written assignments, exams and practice assessments. The theoretical and practical components carry equal weighting, both contributing to the award.

Contact details, see page 614

King's College London
BSc Midwifery Professional Studies, incorporating DipHE Midwifery Practice and registration as a midwife

This course is taught in the Florence Nightingale School of Nursing and

Midwifery which dates back to the first ever school of nursing opened by Florence Nightingale. The first year of this three-year course introduces students to mid-wifery studies, the biological basis of midwifery assessment, the foundations of practice and the psycho-social context of midwifery. At the end of the first year, criteria are used to make the decision as to whether a student follows the degree pathway or continues on the diploma route. The second and third years build upon this knowledge and introduce other topics, after which students become registered midwives and must then continue for a further six months on a part-time basis in order to complete a research project. A large component of the course is spent in hospital and community settings as clinical competence at registration is mandatory.

Contact details, see page 617

Postgraduate

University of Central Lancashire
MA (Hons) Midwifery Studies

The MA in Midwifery Studies is a taught modular course offered in the Department of Midwifery Studies at the University of Central Lancashire. It aims to encourage qualified midwives to take the profession forward by providing a forum which enables them to explore and further develop a critical understanding of midwifery, critically evaluate the context within which midwifery care is given and develop a strategic perspective to midwifery. The course is structured to allow students to undertake specific strands, namely education, management and clinical practice.

Contact details, see page 614

University of Wolverhampton
MSc Nursing Studies

To join this programme you need to be a registered nurse. It is studied on a part-time basis and topics addressed include developing effective practice, professional development issues, empowerment management and ethics and research methods. Those studying for the MSc research and write a dissertation. The School of Nursing and Midwifery is commissioned by local healthcare providers to recruit pre-registration staff and once they qualify, the school continues to provide for their continuing professional development needs.

For further information, see page 584

Useful links

www.britishjournalofnursing.com	▶	British Journal of Nursing
www.enb.org.uk	▶	English National Board for Nursing, Midwifery and Health Visiting
www.inam.bton.ac.uk	▶	Institute of Nursing and Midwifery
www.nhs.uk	▶	National Health Service
www.nmas.ac.uk	▶	Nursing and Midwifery Admissions Service
www.ukcc.org.uk	▶	United Kingdom Central Council for Nursing and Midwifery and Health Visiting

Nursing

Philosophy, theology and religious studies

For over 3,000 years, from Plato and Aristotle to Wittgenstein and Nietzsche, philosophers have tried to answer some of the most fundamental questions about humankind and the world in which we live. Literally meaning 'love of wisdom', philosophy thrives on discussion about human existence, the mind, free will and determinism. It investigates the causes and laws underlying reality. Studying philosophy is a matter of learning how to use your own mind; to reason and argue rather than to simply assert things dogmatically or take what other people say for granted. These are important skills that will be called upon time and again in future careers or in continuing education.

Ever since the Middle Ages, thinkers from the British Isles have been at the forefront of Western philosophy. Writing in Church Latin, figures such as Roger Bacon and Duns Scotus were admired across Latin Christendom. Later, John Locke and David Hume became giants of the Enlightenment. Karl Marx and Friedrich Engels spent much of their working lives in Britain.

The study of philosophy at university is normally centred on five main areas, namely logic, epistemology (the theory of knowledge), metaphysics (the study of the nature of reality), moral philosophy, and also social and political philosophy. Other options could include political philosophy, symbolic logic, aesthetics or philosophy of religion.

Theology and religion

Theology can be traced back as one of the core subjects taught in Britain's oldest universities. Today, subjects such as religious studies have replaced many theology courses, perhaps reflecting the multicultural climate of British society. Theology comes from two Greek words, 'theos', meaning God, and 'logos', meaning word or reason. In its narrow sense, theology means the doctrine of God and His works but on a broader scale it points to the sum of Christian doctrine. Religious studies, by contrast, compares various faiths and their impact on culture and history.

Both subjects deal with issues in anthropology, sociology, language, history, art and philosophy. It is important to remember that university and college courses are both secular and academic, and that studying theology or religious studies does not mean that you have to be religious, although many students are.

Most theology and religious studies degrees last for three years. In the first year, religious studies is likely to comprise introductory modules, such as religion in contemporary Britain, and may go on to include modules such as religion and working classes in 19th-century England. Studying theology normally involves looking at the texts of both the Old and New Testaments, investigating theologians such as Augustine and Bultmann, church history, and possibly biblical languages such as Greek and Hebrew.

Cardiff University

BA History of Ideas and Philosophy

This is an integrated degree scheme combining study of philosophy with the history of philosophical thought and related developments in other areas such as science, morality, politics and religion. This includes close study of the writings of some of the main contributors to European thought. Important non-European thinkers are also studied. In addition to this integrated degree scheme, there are further programmes in single honours philosophy and joint honours, in which philosophy or history of ideas may be combined with a variety of other subjects. Different methods of teaching are used including lectures, discussion groups, seminars and one-to-one contact with tutors. Assessment takes place at the end of every semester, although some double modules may be assessed at the end of the year. Some modules are examined by formal examinations, others on essays submitted. There is the option to offer a short dissertation on a topic of the student's own choice.

Contact details, see page 614

Heythrop College, (University of London)

BA Philosophy, Religion and Ethics

Heythrop has recently launched a new degree specially designed for those who have taken philosophy of religion or ethics at A level, or for those who are interested in questions about God, meaning and morality in today's world. There are 10 courses, six of which must be chosen from a list of compulsory units, and four which can be chosen from a list of options. In addition, students write a long essay on a subject of their choice. Compulsory units include concept of God, religious language and experience, contemporary moral problems, applied ethics, Aquinas, Kierkegaard, Wittgenstein, Levinas and the human person in the Christian tradition. Optional units include phenomenology, political philosophy, aesthetics, environmental philosophy and feminist ethics.

Contact details, see page 616

Lancaster University

BA (Hons) Religious Studies

Lancaster University offers courses on all the major traditions and methods appropriate to religious studies including history, philosophy, theology, sociology, text, anthropology and psychology. As well as encouraging a sound grasp of traditions, issues and methods, it is the basic aim of the department that students should come to understand beliefs and practices different from their own. In the first year, a core course in religion in the modern world introduces students to some of the world's major religious traditions as they exist in the early 21st century. First-year students also have the choice of specialist courses including representations of Christ in modern art and film, mysticism and modernity, the quest for Eastern wisdom and hippies, new agers and witches. Students are assigned a personal tutor who helps introduce them into the life and activities of the department and guides them through their course of study.

Contact details, see page 617

The University of Birmingham

MPhil in Philosophy

This is a research degree but includes taught components such as a course in a chosen area and structured training in

Philosophy, theology and religious studies

Philosophy
(Scotland) 1995/96

tqa

Institution	Grade	Institution	Grade
Glasgow University	Excellent	University of St Andrews	Highly Satisfactory
The University of Aberdeen	Highly Satisfactory	The University of Stirling	Highly Satisfactory
The University of Edinburgh	Highly Satisfactory	University of Dundee	Satisfactory

Philosophy
(Wales) 1995/96

tqa

Cardiff University	Excellent	The University of Wales, Lampeter	Satisfactory

Philosophy
(England and Northern Ireland) 2000/01

tqa

Institution	Grade	Institution	Grade
The University of Bradford	24	University of Sussex	24
University of Brighton	24	University of Wolverhampton	24
The University of Durham	24	The University of York	24
The University of Essex	24	Bolton Institute of	
Keele University	24	Higher Education	23
The University of Kent	24	The College of St Mark and St John	23
Lancaster University	24	Staffordshire University	23
University of Leeds	24	University of Ulster	23
The University of Liverpool	24	Middlesex University	23
The University of Manchester	24	The University of Hull	22
Oxford University	24	London School of Economics and	
The University of Reading	24	Political Science (University of London)	22
The University of Sheffield	24	University of North London	22
University of Southampton	24	University of Bristol	21

Theology and Religious Studies
(England and Northern Ireland) 2000/01

tqa

Institution	Grade	Institution	Grade
Lancaster University	24	Chester College of	
Anglia Polytechnic University	23	Higher Education	22
Bath Spa University College	23	University of Derby	22
The College of St		University of Newcastle upon Tyne	22
Mark and St John	23	Queen's University Belfast	22
University of Gloucestershire	23	Open University	22
The University of Durham	23	School of Oriental and African Studies	
University of Exeter	23	(University of London)	22
The University of Hull	23	Newman College of Higher Education	21
King Alfred's Winchester	23	University of Wolverhampton	21
University of Leeds	23	The University of Kent	20
Liverpool Hope	23	St Martin's College, Lancaster:	
Canterbury Christ Church University College	22	Ambleside; Carlisle	19

Theology and Religious Studies
(Scotland) 1995/96

tqa

Institution	Grade	Institution	Grade
The University of Stirling	Excellent	University of Glasgow	Highly Satisfactory
The University of Aberdeen	Highly Satisfactory	University	
The University of Edinburgh	Highly Satisfactory	of St Andrews	Highly Satisfactory

Theology and Religious Studies
(Wales) 1995/96

tqa

Institution	Grade	Institution	Grade
University of Wales, Bangor	Excellent	University of Wales Swansea	
Cardiff University (Theology)	Satisfactory	(Philosophy and Theology)	Satisfactory
The University of Wales, Lampeter			
(Theology, Religious Studies			
and Islamic Studies)	Satisfactory		

Source: HEFCE, SHEFC, HEFCW latest available ratings
For a more complete list of institutions offering these courses
at undergraduate level refer to the Course Directory

Institution	Grade	Institution	Grade
Cambridge University (History and Philosophy of Science)	5*	The University of York	5
Cambridge University	5*	The University of Birmingham	4
The University of Edinburgh	5*	The University of Bradford	4
King's College London (University of London)	5*	University of Glasgow	4
London School of Economics and Political Science (University of London)	5*	University of Hertfordshire	4
		The University of Hull	4
Oxford University	5*	The University of Kent	4
Birkbeck College	5	University of Liverpool	4
University of Bristol	5	The University of Manchester	4
The University of Durham	5	Open University	4
University of East Anglia	5	University of Southampton	4
The University of Essex	5	The University of Aberdeen	3a
University of Leeds	5	Bolton Institute of Higher Education	3a
Middlesex University	5	Cardiff University	3a
The University of Nottingham	5	University of Dundee	3a
The University of Reading	5	Keele University	3a
The University of Sheffield	5	The University of Wales, Lampeter	3a
University of St Andrews	5	Lancaster University	3a
The University of Stirling	5	The Manchester Metropolitan University	3a
University of Sussex	5	Queen's University Belfast	3a
University College London	5	Staffordshire University	3a
The University of Warwick	5	University of Sunderland	3a
		University of Greenwich	3b

Source: RAE 2001

research methods. The dissertation is 20,000 words in length. Areas of specialisation are the philosophy of mind and language, metaphysics and the theory of value. The department has established an exchange programme with the philosophy department of the University of Texas in Austin, USA. This is a large department with a number of internationally-recognised scholars. Research students in Birmingham may have the opportunity to spend one or more semesters in Austin, teaching and continuing their research.
Contact details, see page 613

London School of Economics and Political Science (University of London)
MSc Philosophy of the Social Sciences,
The Department of Philosophy, Logic and Scientific Method at LSE is one of the major centres for the discipline of the philosophy of social science in the country. It regularly attracts visiting lecturers and is

well connected with other philosophy departments in the University of London, meaning that students can attend lecture courses within other colleges. The master's course involves one compulsory core seminar and the choice of three courses in topics such as the philosophy of economics, philosophy, morals and politics, logic, the history of science and the philosophy of the biological and cognitive sciences. Teaching takes place through formal lectures and discussion seminars as well as tutorials. Students are assessed by exams, coursework and a 10,000-word dissertation on a topic of their choice.
For further information, see page 508

Roehampton University of Surrey
MPhil Theology and Religious Studies
The university has a number of humanist and Christian-providing bodies and this is reflected in the research opportunities which focus upon the study of Christianity. The university aims to develop the

Philosophy, theology and religious studies

Institution	Grade	Institution	Grade
Cardiff University	5*	Bath Spa University College	4
The University of Manchester	5*	University of Gloucestershire	4
The University of Nottingham	5*	Goldsmiths College (University of London)	4
Oxford University	5*	King Alfred's, Winchester	4
The University of Aberdeen	5	University of Leeds	4
The University of Birmingham	5	Liverpool Hope	4
University of Bristol	5	Roehampton University of Surrey	4
Cambridge University	5	Canterbury Christ Church University College	3a
The University of Durham	5	Chester College of Higher Education	3a
The University of Edinburgh	5	University of Derby	3a
University of Exeter	5	The University of Hull	3a
University of Glasgow	5	The University of Kent	3a
King's College London (University of London)	5	Open University	3a
The University of Wales, Lampeter	5	College of St Mark & St John	3a
Lancaster University	5	University College Chichester	3b
University of Newcastle upon Tyne	5	St Martin's College	3b
School of Oriental and African Studies (University of London)	5	St Mary's College	3b
		University of Sunderland	3b
University of Sheffield (Biblical Studies)	5	Westhill College	3b
University of St Andrews	5	Trinity College Carmarthen	2
The University of Stirling	5	Oxford Brookes University	1
University of Wales, Bangor	4	York St John College	1

Source: RAE 2001

research and related skills needed for a career in biblical, theological, philosophical and religious studies disciplines. The department promotes research projects in which staff and students are actively involved. There are two 'research clusters' that students are encouraged to take part in and these groups run research seminars. Cluster meetings provide an opportunity for students' research to be discussed and critically assessed. Research opportunities are split into biblical studies, philosophy and theology, while the topics that can be studied include Greek language, gospels, hermeneutical methods, feminist theology, world religions and liberation theology.

Contact details, see page 621

Useful links

www.philosophers.co.uk	▶	*The Philosopher's Magazine* on the Internet
www.philsoc.freeserve.co.uk	▶	The Philosophical Society
www.religion-online.org	▶	Religion Online
emuseum.mnsu.edu/cultural/religion/	▶	Religions of the World
www.royalinstitutephilosophy.org	▶	The Royal Institute of Philosophy
www.leeds.ac.uk/trs/sst	▶	Society for the Study of Theology

Philosophy, theology and religious studies

Physics

Physics is the study of the universe, of the way things work and of why things are the way they are. These questions are applied to every working mechanism in existence, using the language of mathematics to solve complex problems and advance scientific thought. Physics is at the very heart of all high technology and engineering. Can you imagine life without electricity, television, radio or computers? As a subject, it is extremely broad, covering disciplines as varied as mechanics, electromagnetic theory, thermodynamics, statistical mechanics, optics, quantum theory, relativity, chaos theory, low dimensional structures, laser physics and the origins of the universe.

Physicists try to understand basic physical processes such as the influence of thermal motion on the properties of solids or the diffuse scattering of x-rays. They also study applied areas such as the biophysics of muscle and bone, the physics of car crashes, applications of lasers and the atomic structure of new materials. Some students keep their options open by combining physics with another subject. Popular combinations include astronomy, computing and mathematics.

In the first year of a physics degree, you are likely to cover the basic principles of physics and mathematics. These include mechanics, nuclear physics, dynamics and quantum physics. In the second year, a more in-depth approach is taken. Among other subjects, students can study optics, thermodynamics and electromagnetism. They will also be allowed to take optional modules which might include electronics, environmental physics or nuclear physics. In the third year, some choose to specialise in advanced topics such as particle or laser physics. Others concentrate on applied areas including nuclear energy, or opt for complementary topics such as geophysics, biomedical physics or materials science.

Research and projects form a significant part of third-year work, allowing students to develop the skills necessary in industry and academia. Many physicists are employed by multinational companies and as a result many courses include a sandwich year allowing you to take up an industrial placement.

There is a normally a fair balance between formal exams, continuously-assessed laboratory work, coursework and essays. The final degree result usually depends on work assessed in the second and third years with the greatest weighting on examination results. Teaching methods include lectures, laboratory work and tutorials.

Many physics degrees have a specific focus. The most common are applied, chemical, computational, mathematical, computer aided, engineering, planetary, environmental, laser, medical, technological, and theoretical physics, as well as astro-physics, biophysics and geophysics. Physics also has natural links with other disciplines including laser science, quantum science, astronomy and philosophy.

Physics

Institution	Grade	Institution	Grade
Cambridge University	5*	University of Wales Swansea	5
Imperial College of Science, Technology and Medicine (University of London)	5*	University College London (University of London)	5
Lancaster University	5*	The University of Warwick	5
Oxford University	5*	The University of Wales, Aberystwyth	4
University of Southampton	5*	Armagh Observatory	4
The University of Birmingham	5	University of Bath	4
University of Bristol	5	University of Central Lancashire	4
Cardiff University	5	City University	4
The University of Durham	5	University of Hertfordshire	4
The University of Edinburgh	5	King's College London (University of London)	4
University of Exeter	5	Liverpool John Moores University	4
University of Glasgow	5	Loughborough University	4
University of Leeds	5	The University of Manchester Institute of Science and Technology (UMIST)	4
University of Leicester	5	University of Newcastle upon Tyne	4
The University of Liverpool	5	The University of Reading	4
The University of Manchester	5	The University of York	4
The University of Nottingham	5	Heriot-Watt University, Edinburgh	4
Queen Mary, University of London	5	The University of Strathclyde	4
Queen's University Belfast	5	University of Brighton	3a
Royal Holloway, University of London	5	Keele University	3a
The University of Sheffield (Physics and Astronomy)	5	The University of Kent	3a
		Open University	3a
The University of Sheffield (Medical Physics and Clinical Engineering)	5	University of Paisley	3a
University of St Andrews	5	University of Plymouth	3a
The University of Surrey	5	Sheffield Hallam University	3a
University of Sussex	5		

Source: RAE 2001

Undergraduate

Imperial College of Science, Technology and Medicine (University of London)
MSci (Hons) Physics

Teaching of the MSci in Physics is by lecture, tutorials in groups of four students, problem-solving classes, laboratory and computing work, and project work. Active participation by students in their learning is strongly encouraged. Each student has, in addition to an academic tutor, a personal tutor who gives individual help and advice throughout the time spent in the department. The core courses during the first two years cover the main themes of modern and classical physics, experimental methods and mathematics. These ensure that all graduates have a thorough grounding in the fundamental aspects of physics and its modern applications, irrespective of specialisation during the third or fourth years. The MSci programme is designed for students who wish to pursue their studies in greater depth before embarking on professional or PhD research work.

Contact details, see page 617

The University of Liverpool
BSc (Hons) Physics with Astronomy

This course is taught in collaboration with the Astrophysics Research Institute of Liverpool John Moores University (JMU). Topics studied throughout the three years of the degree include stellar astrophysics, cosmology, observational astronomy, mathematics, mechanics, quantum and atomic physics, relativity and an astro-

Physics

Physics and Astronomy
(England and Northern Ireland) 1998/99/2000

Institution	Grade	Institution	Grade
University of Bath	24	The University of Salford	23
The University of Durham	24	The University of Surrey	23
University of Leeds	24	University of Exeter	22
The University of Liverpool	24	Imperial College of Science, Technology	
The University of Manchester	24	and Medicine (University of London)	22
The University of Reading	24	Keele University	22
Sheffield Hallam University	24	King's College London	
The University of Warwick	24	(University of London)	22
The University of York	24	The University of Sheffield	22
The University of Birmingham	23	University of Southampton	22
University of Bristol	23	Staffordshire University	22
Cambridge University	23	University of Sussex	22
The University of Hull	23	Canterbury Christ Church	
Lancaster University	23	University College	21
University of Leicester	23	University of Hertfordshire	21
University College London		The University of Kent	21
(University of London)	23	The University of Manchester Institute of	
Loughborough University	23	Science and Technology (UMIST)	21
Northumbria University	23	Queen Mary,	
The University of Nottingham	23	University of London	21
Oxford University	23	University of Portsmouth	20
Royal Holloway, University of London	23	University of Central Lancashire	19

Physics
(Scotland) 1994/95

The University of Edinburgh	Excellent	Glasgow Caledonian University	Highly Satisfactory
University of Glasgow	Excellent	Heriot-Watt University,	
University of St Andrews	Excellent	Edinburgh	Highly Satisfactory
The University of		The Robert Gordon University	Highly Satisfactory
Strathclyde	Excellent	Napier University	Satisfactory
University of Dundee	Highly Satisfactory	University of Paisley	Satisfactory

Physics
(Wales) 1995/96

University of Wales Swansea	Excellent	Cardiff University	
The University of Wales, Aberystwyth	Satisfactory	(Physics and Astronomy)	Satisfactory

Source: HEFCE, SHEFC, HEFCW latest available ratings
For a more complete list of institutions offering these courses at undergraduate level refer to the Course Directory

Physics

physics project in the final year. The programme makes use of the robotic Liverpool telescope situated in the Canary Islands and operated remotely from Liverpool. It is the largest of its kind in the world and provides students with access to observations from a major research-grade telescope using the latest engineering and detector technology. In the second year of the course, there is a field trip to work at the Izana Observatory in Tenerife. Students on this course are members of The University of Liverpool as well as JMU and have access to relevant facilities at both universities.

Contact details, see page 618

University of Newcastle upon Tyne
BSc (Hons) Physics

Students following the degree in physics at the University of Newcastle upon Tyne are offered a modular programme which includes both theoretical and practical aspects of the subject. In the first year, there is an introduction to university-level physics and mathematics. In the second year, compulsory modules are in optics and electronics, atomic physics, statistical

physics, quantum mechanics, solid-state physics and thermodynamics. Skills are enhanced in mathematics, experimental physics and computing. In the third year, compulsory modules are in nuclear physics, particle physics, statistical physics, experimental physics and cosmology. A review project is also mandatory. Optional modules are selected from a list which may include laser physics, quantum mechanics and the physics of the interstellar medium.
Contact details, see page 618

University of Wales Swansea
BSc Physics
Physics students at Swansea look at a huge variety of topics within the discipline, from sub-nuclear particles to the structure and origins of the universe. They are taught through lectures, laboratory work, examples, classes and weekly tutorials. Each student is assigned a personal tutor to follow academic and personal progress. There is a student/staff consultative committee where students can informally discuss views on the teaching and social sides of the department. The department houses undergraduate and research labs, electronic and mechanical workshops, as well as an extensive computer network.
Contact details, see page 621

Postgraduate

The University of Durham
MSc Elementary Particle Theory
This one-year advanced course is intended for students who have already obtained a good first degree in either physics or mathematics including, in the latter case, courses in quantum mechanics and relativity. Each student follows a programme of lecture courses and planned reading, and prepares a dissertation on a topic of current research. The student will be able to choose the topic of special interest from a wide variety of subjects and will be assigned a superviser with expertise in the chosen area. Students lacking background knowledge may be encouraged to attend relevant undergraduate courses. The degree is awarded following satisfactory performances in the examinations taken in January and March and on successful completion of a dissertation. The dissertation must be submitted by September 30, the end of the 12-month course period.
Contact details, see page 615

Useful links

www.cclrc.ac.uk	◉	Central Laboratory of the Research Councils
www.iop.org	◉	Institute of Physics
www.iquest.ucsb.edu	◉	The Institute for Quantum Engineering, Science and Technology
www.npl.co.uk	◉	National Physical Laboratory
www.pparc.ac.uk	◉	The Particle Physics and Astronomy Research Council
www.aip.org/pt	◉	Physics Today

I n order to understand how countries are governed and how they interact, a knowledge of politics is essential. Politics is about power and ideas and it has an impact on every member of the public in any nation. It encompasses a broad spectrum of activities relating to public affairs, from the competition between political parties to the operations of public bureaucracies. In the past, politics was the domain of a relatively small elite but modern democracy ensures that the whole population is involved. Lying at the junction of power and morality, politics has always attracted the attention of philosophers and historians. Its study, originating in Athens in the 4th century BC, is at the root of all the social sciences.

Politics undergraduates (politics may also be known as political science, political theory or government, depending on the department) study the exercise of governmental power within and between nation states. Beyond that, they are concerned with how power is acquired and used, as well as the ethical and material restraints which may be placed on it. From this basic outline, politics divides into a number of strands. Political thought examines the ideas of prominent thinkers and their significance in their own and subsequent times. The big names in politics that are studied as part of political thought include Aristotle, Machiavelli, Hobbes, Rousseau and Burke. Students examine the whole spectrum of players in the political field, from political parties and pressure groups to ethnic and religious groups. They will also study history, since politicians make use of historical analysis to inform their approach to the future in aiming to meet the needs of a changing world.

Comparative politics, the methodical study of several political systems, is an area of politics that has developed in recent years. The comparison of different systems takes students into international politics or international relations. This looks at the political interaction between countries and at the workings of such bodies as the United Nations and the European Union, which are forms of international government. International relations examines the underlying mechanisms which bring countries together. It also focuses on the perceived interests of different societies and the way in which each nation promotes its interests.

Most politics and international relations courses last three years. The first year involves introductory modules looking at how government works and how power is distributed. The second year builds on this foundation and core modules are supplemented by optional ones. The third year is made up of specialised topics reflecting the interests that students have developed and the research areas of the staff. Many students write a dissertation as part of their politics course, allowing them to focus on an area of interest.

TEACHING QUALITY ASSESSMENTS

Politics
(Scotland) 1996

tqa

Institution	Grade	Institution	Grade
The University of Strathclyde	Excellent	The University of Edinburgh	Highly Satisfactory
The University of Aberdeen	Highly Satisfactory	University of Glasgow	Highly Satisfactory
University of Dundee	Highly Satisfactory	The University of Stirling	Highly Satisfactory

Politics
(Wales) 1995/96

tqa

The University of Wales, Aberystwyth	Excellent	University of Wales	
Cardiff University	Satisfactory	Swansea	Satisfactory

Politics
(England and Northern Ireland) 2000/01

tqa

Birkbeck College (University of London)	24	School of Slavonic and Eastern European Studies, University College London (University of London)	23
The University of Bradford	24	University of Sussex	23
De Montfort University	24	University of Central Lancashire	22
The University of Essex	24	Goldsmiths College (University of London)	22
The University of Manchester	24	University of Lincoln	22
Oxford University	24	Liverpool John Moores University	22
The University of Salford	24	London School of Economics and Political Science (University of London)	22
The University of Sheffield	24	Middlesex University	22
The University of York	24	Northumbria University	22
University of Bristol	23	Open University	22
Coventry University	23	Oxford Brookes University	22
University of Exeter	23	University of Plymouth	22
The University of Hull	23	University College London (University of London)	22
Kingston University	23	University of Westminster	22
Lancaster University	23	South Bank University	21
University of Leeds	23	Anglia Polytechnic University	20
University of Leicester	23	University of Sunderland	20
The University of Liverpool	23		
Loughborough University	23		
University of Portsmouth	23		
Queen Mary, University of London	23		
Queen's University Belfast	23		

Source: HEFCE, SHEFC, HEFCW latest available ratings
For a more complete list of institutions offering these courses at undergraduate level refer to the Course Directory

Undergraduate

The University of Wales, Aberystwyth
BSc International Politics

Students look at the ideas and philosophies which shape politics at domestic and international levels and, through the study of international history, present-day developments are placed in an historical context. Teaching is through a combination of lectures and seminars, in which students are often required to prepare short presentations as starting points for discussion. Some modules are assessed purely by written examination, whereas others involve continuous assessment through coursework. There is the opportunity to apply for a place on the Parliamentary Placement Scheme whereby students work as research assistants for MPs or Welsh Assembly members during the summer of the second year. There are also regular trips to the institutions of the European Union and of Nato.
For further information, see page 436

London School of Economics and Political Science (University of London)
BSc Government

At LSE, students approach government

Politics

RESEARCH RANKINGS

Politics and International Studies

Institution	Grade
The University of Wales, Aberystwyth	5*
The University of Essex	5*
King's College London (War Studies)	5*
Oxford University	5*
The University of Sheffield	5*
Birkbeck College	5
The University of Birmingham	5
The University of Bradford	5
University of Bristol	5
De Montfort University	5
The University of Hull	5
Keele University	5
University of Exeter	5
London School of Economics and Political Science (University of London)	5
The University of Manchester	5
University of Newcastle upon Tyne	5
The University of Reading	5
University of Glasgow	5
Queen's University Belfast	5
University of Sussex (Science and Technology Policy Research)	5
The University of Strathclyde	5
University of St Andrews	5
The University of Warwick	5
The University of York	5
The University of Aberdeen	4
Brunel University	4
Cambridge University	4
Coventry University	4
The University of Durham	4
University of Dundee	4
University of East Anglia	4
The University of Edinburgh	4
Lancaster University	4
University of Leeds	4
The University of Liverpool	4
The University of Nottingham	4

Institution	Grade
Queen Mary, University of London	4
School of Oriental and African Studies (University of London)	4
University of Southampton	4
University of Sussex (Politics and International Studies)	4
University of the West of England, Bristol	4
University of Westminster	4
University of Central England in Birmingham	3a
The University of Huddersfield	3a
The University of Kent	3a
King's College London (University of London) (Defence Studies)	3a
Leeds Metropolitan University	3a
University of Leicester	3a
Liverpool John Moores University	3a
London Guildhall University	3a
The Manchester Metropolitan University	3a
University of North London	3a
Northumbria University	3a
The Nottingham Trent University (International Relations)	3a
The Nottingham Trent University (Politics and International Studies)	3a
Open University	3a
Oxford Brookes University	3a
University of Plymouth	3a
The Robert Gordon University	3a
Staffordshire University	3a
University of Stirling	3a
University of Wales Swansea	3a
University of Sunderland	3a
University of Ulster	3a
University College London (University of London)	3a
University of Wolverhampton	3a
University of Derby	3b
Middlesex University	3b
Southampton Institute	2

Source: RAE 2001

Politics

from scientific, historical and philosophic viewpoints. The aim is to form an understanding of how policy is made and implemented through a study of public administration and public policy in social and economic contexts. Ideas such as justice, democracy, liberty and rights are considered in the study of how politics is understood and policy is justified. A comparative approach is taken, by which the governments of different cultures and countries are analysed. The degree involves 12 courses over three years including compulsory modules covering topics such as political thought and the politics and government of another country. Teaching involves lectures, followed up by classes in which lecture topics are discussed. Students meet with personal tutors regularly. Assessment is by formal exams and extended essays.

For further information, see page 508

University of Newcastle upon Tyne

BA (Hons) Government and European Union Studies

During this four-year degree programme, students study the politics, law, economics and culture of the European Union and its member states. They also learn either French, German, Spanish or Portuguese. Between the second and third stages, students travel to a European university for one year. Optional modules are chosen from a range of topics including the politics of countries such as Japan and America, regions such as the Middle East and Africa, environmental politics, political psychology, terrorism and international politics and electoral behaviour. In stage three, students write a dissertation and participate in a role-playing simulation of the European Union, building on knowledge learnt in the second stage and experience gained from the year abroad.

Contact details, see page 618

Contact details, see page 618

Postgraduate

University of Dundee
MA (Hons) Politics

This course covers most aspects of politics with opportunities for the study of political theory, public policy, comparative politics and international relations. Many courses have a strong sociological content and aim to help students acquire an understanding of the political and social environment. In the first two years, students can combine politics with any other subjects in the Faculty of Arts and Social Sciences. Teaching is by lecture and small seminar groups. Assessment is by coursework and written examination. Normally, students take the first MA course in the first year and the second MA course in the second year. However, it is possible for well-qualified applicants to enter directly into the second year.

Contact details, see page 615

Queen's University Belfast
MA in Irish Politics

The Centre for Irish Politics at Queen's University Belfast is a world leader on Irish politics and is particularly concerned with the conflict in Northern Ireland. Research conducted by the department covers both parts of the island and covers political history, theory, intellectual biography, electoral politics and the impact of the EU, amongst other areas of academic interest. The centre organises conferences and memorial lectures, as well as welcoming visiting lecturers and advising politicians. The MA in Irish Politics includes six modules which address various issues and questions relevant to the Irish political climate.

For further information, see page 542

Useful links

www.britpolitics.com	▶	Britpolitics.com
www.europa.eu.int	▶	European Union
www.theonion.com	▶	The Onion
www.parliament.uk	▶	United Kingdom Parliament
www.un.org	▶	United Nations
www.una-uk.org	▶	United Nations of Great Britain and Northern Ireland

Psychology

Studying psychology can involve anything from testing the effects of caffeine to studying non-verbal communication in humans. If you thought vodka and Red Bull was the ultimate high, try the first-year psychology practical, where students have to drink up to 300 mg of caffeine (some six cups of coffee in concentrated form). The scientific side of the subject is an important element and tends to get lost behind popular misconceptions. Psychology is the study of human behaviour and mental processes. Whilst you can never really read someone's mind, with careful observation you can form an educated diagnosis of what is going on.

The most conclusive answers that can be reached come from experiments and observation, analysis of the results and the formulation of theories to interpret the evidence. Practical experiments such as these form the core of most psychology courses. There is often confusion between psychology and psychiatry. Psychologists and psychiatrists work closely in the diagnosis, treatment and care of people with mental problems but their initial training is different. Clinical psychologists graduate with an honours degree in psychology and complete postgraduate training in psychology. Psychiatrists, on the other hand, are medical graduates who then go on to focus on psychiatric medicine.

Undergraduate psychology courses equip students with research skills and problem-solving techniques. Course modules address questions such as the effects of genetic influences on development and behaviour and the processes of learning, memory, thinking and perception. Practicals are a major component of psychology courses, aiming to test theories and replicate previous experiments. Students investigate through experiments, surveys, interviews, observation and diary techniques. Much work is conducted in the laboratory but there is also scope for fieldwork. Studying psychology may have you testing at any number of locations including clinics, factories, schools or even football matches. There are also some standard tests of intelligence, aptitude and ability that you will use as a psychologist and the information learnt in practicals forms some of the evidence used in essays and report writing.

Some institutions have a four-year degree in applied psychology. This involves spending your third year on a related placement, usually as an assistant psychologist, for instance in a forensic setting or with a community mental health team. Such experience can be useful for both your research in the final year and also for a career in psychology.

Psychology is sometimes broken down into more specific subjects such as applied psychology, community psychology, social psychology, cognitive science and experimental psychology. Similarly, degrees are available in particular areas of psychology such as sports psychology, business psychology and consumer science.

Undergraduate

University of Dundee
BSc Psychology

The Psychology Department at Dundee specialises in four main areas: cognitive, social, developmental and biological psychology. The university has laboratories equipped for the specialised study of infant behaviour, language and literacy, vision and brain function. In the first year of the BSc, students are introduced to the core themes of the discipline and gain experience in psychological research, preparing them for more advanced study in the second and third years. At the end of the second year, students must decide whether to study for a non-honours degree, graduating after three years or to continue onto honours or joint honours, requiring four years of study. Assessment is through exams, coursework and a research project.

Contact details, see page 615

University of Hertfordshire
BSc (Hons) Cognitive Science

Cognitive science is a rapidly-developing field, integrating the study of the human mind with the study of artificial intelligence. Students on this programme are introduced to concepts and skills in psychology, computer science, linguistics, philosophy and neuroscience and no previous knowledge of these areas is necessary. They then go on to explore interdisciplinary topics such as speech and language, memory, problem solving, discovery and invention and human computer interaction. The course aims to develop in students both theoretical and practical skills to enable them to contribute to fields of research and industrial application, as well as to pursue more general employment opportunities. Assessment is roughly 70 per cent exam and 30 per cent coursework.

Contact details, see page 616

Roehampton University of Surrey
BSc (Hons) Psychology

During the first year, students cover areas such as social psychology, child development and cognitive processes. In the second and third years, they study these and other topics in greater depth. There is also a wide range of optional courses to choose from including courses on adult development, health psychology, abnormal psychology, intervention and counselling, criminal psychology and neuropsychology. In the final year, students are given the option to work towards a personally-supervised research project.

Contact details, see page 621

Postgraduate

The University of Birmingham
MRes courses in Psychology and Cognitive Science

These year-long MRes courses provide the practical skills and theoretical knowledge needed to undertake psychological or interdisciplinary research in contemporary, commercial or academic settings. One third of the course is taught and provides a background in such general topics as research design, statistical analysis, communication skills and computer use. The remainder of the course allows the student to undertake a flexible programme of laboratory placements and a research project, acquiring experience and skills in any area of psychology, or in an interdisciplinary combination of cognition, computing and neuroscience.

Contact details, see page 613

TEACHING QUALITY ASSESSMENTS

Psychology
(England and Northern Ireland) 1998/99/2000

tqa

Institution	Grade	Institution	Grade
Bolton Institute of Higher Education	24	The University of Liverpool	22
University of Central Lancashire	24	Liverpool Hope	22
Lancaster University	24	London Guildhall University	22
University of Leicester	24	The University of Manchester	22
Loughborough University	24	The Manchester Metropolitan University	22
University of Newcastle upon Tyne	24	Northumbria University	22
The University of Nottingham	24	The Nottingham Trent University	22
Queen's University Belfast	24	Roehampton University of Surrey	22
The University of Reading	24	The University of Surrey	22
Royal Holloway, University of London	24	Bath Spa University College	21
Sheffield Hallam University	24	Buckingham Chilterns University College	21
University of Westminster	24	Cambridge University	21
The University of York	24	City University	21
Birkbeck College	23	King Alfred's Winchester	21
The University of Birmingham	23	Leeds, Trinity and All Saints College	21
University of Bristol	23	University of Lincoln	21
The University of Durham	23	Middlesex University	21
University of East London	23	University of Southampton	21
University of Exeter	23	Suffolk College	21
University of Hertfordshire	23	University of Sussex	21
London School of Economics and Political Science (University of London)	23	The University of Warwick	21
		University of Wolverhampton	21
Oxford Brookes University	23	Canterbury Christ Church University College	20
University of Portsmouth	23	Chester (A College of the University of Liverpool)	20
University of Plymouth	23		
Staffordshire University	23	University of Derby	20
Aston University	22	The University of Huddersfield	20
University of the West of England, Bristol	22	University College Worcester	20
De Montfort University	22	Liverpool John Moores University	19
Edge Hill College of Higher Education	22	University of North London	19
The University of Essex	22	University College Northampton	19
Goldsmiths College (University of London)	22	Southampton Institute	19
University of Greenwich	22	Tavistock and Portman NHS Trust	19
The University of Kent	22		

Psychology
(Scotland) 1995/96

tqa

Institution	Grade	Institution	Grade
University of Dundee	Excellent	The University of Edinburgh	Highly Satisfactory
University of Glasgow	Excellent	Glasgow Caledonian University	Highly Satisfactory
University of St Andrews	Excellent	University of Paisley	Highly Satisfactory
The University of Stirling	Excellent	The University of Strathclyde	Highly Satisfactory
The University of Aberdeen	Highly Satisfactory		
University of Abertay Dundee	Highly Satisfactory		

Psychology
(Wales) 1995/96

tqa

Institution	Grade	Institution	Grade
University of Wales, Bangor	Excellent	University of Wales Institute, Cardiff	Excellent
Cardiff University	Excellent	University of Wales Swansea	Excellent

Source: HEFCE, SHEFC, HEFCW latest available ratings
For a more complete list of institutions offering these courses at undergraduate level refer to the Course Directory

Cardiff University

MSc in Educational Psychology

This one-year course aims to train students in the theory and practice of educational psychology, enabling them to practice within educational psychology services (EPS) and in other contexts. It is based on the British Psychological Society's core curriculum and covers professional practice, intervention methods, special educational provision and research. A minimum of 75 days is spent in practical sessions, taking the

Psychology

rae

Institution	Grade	Institution	Grade
University of Wales, Bangor	5*	The University of Kent	4
The University of Birmingham	5*	University of Leicester	4
University of Bristol	5*	The University of Liverpool	4
Cambridge University	5*	Loughborough University	4
Cardiff University	5*	Northumbria University	4
University of Glasgow	5*	Open University	4
University of Newcastle upon Tyne	5*	Queen's University Belfast	4
Oxford University	5*	The University of Strathclyde	4
The University of Reading	5*	University of Wales Swansea	4
University of St Andrews	5*	University of Central Lancashire	3a
University College London (University of London)	5*	University of Derby	3a
The University of York	5*	University of East London	3a
Birkbeck College	5	The University of Hull	3a
The University of Durham	5	The Manchester Metropolitan University	3a
The University of Edinburgh	5	Middlesex University	3a
The University of Essex	5	The Nottingham Trent University	3a
University of Exeter	5	Oxford Brookes University	3a
Lancaster University	5	University of Portsmouth	3a
University of Leeds	5	Staffordshire University	3a
The University of Manchester	5	Roehampton University of Surrey	3a
The University of Nottingham	5	University of Ulster	3a
University of Plymouth	5	University of Westminster	3a
Royal Holloway, University of London	5	University of Abertay Dundee	3b
The University of Sheffield	5	Bolton Institute of Higher Education	3b
University of Southampton	5	University of Greenwich	3b
The University of Stirling	5	London Guildhall University	3b
The University of Surrey	5	Sheffield Hallam University	3b
University of Sussex	5	University of Sunderland	3b
The University of Warwick	5	University of Wolverhampton	3b
The University of Aberdeen	4	Coventry University	2
Brunel University	4	King Alfred's Winchester	2
City University	4	University of Lincoln	2
University of Dundee	4	Liverpool Hope	2
Glasgow Caledonian University	4	University of Luton	2
Goldsmiths College (University of London)	4	University College Worcester	2
University of Hertfordshire	4	Thames Valley University	1
Keele University	4		

Source: RAE 2001

form of one or two-day placements a week in the autumn and spring terms and a six-week block in the summer term. Students undertake research which they then use to write a dissertation. Each student has two tutors, one for the dissertation and another to supervise practical work. The assessment is continual, by written assignments and through the dissertation.

Contact details, see page 614

Useful links

www.bps.org.uk	●	The British Psychological Society
www.psychology.org	●	Encyclopedia of Psychology
www.iop.kcl.ac.uk/IoP/index.stm	●	Institute of Psychiatry (UK)
www.sagepub.co.uk/journals/details/j0454.html	●	International Journal of Social Psychiatry
www.psychologypsychiatry.com	●	Psychology and Psychiatry

Psychology

Sociology

The study of sociology began in the 19th century when academics tried to make sense of the dramatic social changes initiated by the Industrial and French Revolutions. The fundamental theory of sociology is that people do not act independently but are influenced by history, culture and other people.

Rather than focusing on the actions of individuals, sociologists study human interaction and look at recurring patterns of behaviour. They build conceptual models of social status, social role and social class and more general societal features such as organisation, change and conflict. These concepts help to build larger models which explain the operation of, and the differences between, various societies.

Sociologists ask questions such as what makes organisations, classes or groups tick? Why are some people regarded as heroes and others as villains? Why is some behaviour said to be normal but other practices perceived as strange?

Social sciences are concerned with the collection, analysis and presentation of data, statistics and information, the formulation of theories and models and the constant checking of such theories against the data. Students at undergraduate level are taught a variety of techniques of social investigation and data analysis including survey methods, statistical analysis using specialised computer software, analysis of documents and observational and experimental methods.

An important ancillary subject to sociology is social policy. This is the study of contemporary social problems and society's response to them. It is an applied subject, examining a range of social issues from a variety of perspectives, including economics, sociology and psychology. Some departments offer it both as a feature of the general sociology course and as a subject in its own right. Students wishing to follow a highly applied course may wish to consider studying social policy with or instead of sociology.

Most degrees last three years. In the first and second years of a sociology course, students are likely to study core introductory modules to the subject, and will be allowed to specialise more in the second and third years. In the final year, students undertake a research project or dissertation, under the guidance of a superviser. Having learnt about research methodology during their studies, this is the point at which students put their skills into practice; both an exciting and a daunting prospect. Some institutions offer sociology with a foreign language.

Students are taught through lectures and tutorials and some institutions also hold practical workshops in order to teach sociological methodology. There is a fair balance between formal exams, essays and research. The final degree result is calculated from performance in the second and third-year exams, coursework and the final-year research project.

Social Policy and Administration
(England and Northern Ireland) 1994/95

tqa

Institution	Grade	Institution	Grade
University of Bath	Excellent	Open University	Excellent
Brunel University	Excellent	The University of Sheffield	Excellent
Edge Hill College of Higher Education	Excellent	University of Ulster	Excellent
The University of Hull	Excellent	The University of York	Excellent
The University of Kent	Excellent	The University of Birmingham	Satisfactory
Lancaster University	Excellent	De Montfort University	Satisfactory
London Guildhall University	Excellent	University of East London	Satisfactory
London School of Economics and Political Science (University of London)	Excellent	Leeds Metropolitan University	Satisfactory
The University of Manchester	Excellent	University of Luton	Satisfactory
University of Newcastle upon Tyne	Excellent	University of North London	Satisfactory

Social Policy and Administration
(Scotland) 1997/98

tqa

The University of Edinburgh	Excellent	University of Glasgow	Excellent

Source: HEFCE, SHEFC, HEFCW latest available ratings
For a more complete list of institutions offering these courses at undergraduate level refer to the Course Directory

Undergraduate

Anglia Polytechnic University
BA (Hons) Sociology

The sociology programme at Anglia Polytechnic University aims to demonstrate sociology's applicability and relevance to understanding the social world and to encourage students to examine real-world issues systematically and critically. Candidates initially register for either single or combined honours. The modules are designed to provide students with a firm grounding in the fundamentals of sociology and offer stimulating and challenging exposure to a diversity of specialist areas. They draw on the academic strengths and particular expertise of teaching staff, accommodating and reflecting changing developments within sociology. Students are encouraged to develop specialist interests and are able to construct integrated clusters of modules. As well as the taught modules, it is also possible for students to pursue their individual interests through a dissertation in sociology and through taking independent learning modules.
For further information, see page 438

The University of Birmingham
BA (Hons) Sociology

This courses focuses on the growing importance of cultural forms and practices in contemporary life. The changes underway in Birmingham itself exemplify many of the key issues of the degree: economic restructuring, urban regeneration, multiculturalism and the influence of global forces on localities. There are compulsory elements, along with a range of optional choices which reflect the department's interests in media, information and emerging cultural and social practices. The degree culminates in a dissertation on a topic of the student's choice. The department was ranked first in a survey of British universities in *The Guardian* newspaper in October 1999 and all the staff are active researchers.
Contact details, see page 613

The University of Edinburgh
BSc/MA Sociology

Sociology at Edinburgh starts with an introduction to key ideas within the discipline through an examination of the

Sociology

Sociology
(England and Northern Ireland) 1996

tqa

Institution	Grade	Institution	Grade
The University of Birmingham	24	Northumbria University	20
Open University	24	University of Plymouth	20
University of Sussex	24	University of Portsmouth	20
University of Greenwich	23	Roehampton University of Surrey	20
The University of York	23	The University of Salford	20
Bath Spa University College	22	St Mary's College	20
Brunel University	22	University of Wolverhampton	20
The University of Essex	22	University of Bath	19
Keele University	22	City University	19
Liverpool Hope	22	University of East London	19
The University of Reading	22	University of Leicester	19
The College of St Mark and St John	22	The Nottingham Trent University	19
Thames Valley University	22	South Bank University	19
University of Bristol	21	Southampton Institute	19
University of Exeter	21	University of Teesside	19
Goldsmiths College		University of Central England	
(University of London)	21	in Birmingham	18
The University of Kent	21	University of Central Lancashire	18
Kingston University	21	University of Derby	18
Lancaster University	21	La Sainte Union College	
The University of Liverpool	21	of Higher Education	18
The University of Manchester	21	Liverpool John	
The Manchester Metropolitan University	21	Moores University	18
Oxford Brookes University	21	University of Luton	18
University of Sunderland	21	The University of Bradford	17
The University of Surrey	21	De Montfort University	17
University College Worcester	21	London Guildhall University	17
Anglia Polytechnic University	20	Staffordshire University	17
University of Gloucestershire	20	University of Ulster	17
The University of Huddersfield	20	York St John College	17
Leeds, Trinity and All Saints College	20	Buckinghamshire Chilterns	
London School of Economics and		University College	16
Political Science (University of London)	20	University of East Anglia	16
University College Northampton	20	University of Lincoln	16

Sociolology
(Scotland) 1996

tqa

The University of Aberdeen	Excellent	Glasgow Caledonian	
The University of Edinburgh	Excellent	University	Highly Satisfactory
University of Glasgow	Excellent	University of Paisley	Highly Satisfactory
The University of Stirling	Excellent	The University of Strathclyde	Highly Satisfactory

Sociology and Social Policy
(Wales) 1994/95

tqa

University of Wales, Bangor	Satisfactory
Cardiff University	Satisfactory
University of Wales Swansea	Satisfactory

Source: HEFCE, SHEFC, HEFCW latest available ratings
For a more complete list of institutions offering these courses at undergraduate level refer to the Course Directory

Sociology

relationship between the individual and society. The course addresses situations ranging from 'micro' interpersonal situations to 'macro' international conflict and explores how our lives are shaped by wider social processes. In the second year, students expand upon this knowledge and are introduced to a comparative and more theoretical approach focusing on five major themes: gender, family and childhood, nationalism, ethnicity and culture. After the second year, students

Social Policy and Administration

Institution	Grade	Institution	Grade
The University of Kent	5*	Royal Holloway, University of London	4
London School of Economics and Political Science (University of London)	5*	South Bank University	4
		University of Ulster	4
University of Bath	5	University of Wales, Bangor	3a
University of Bristol	5	City University	3a
Keele University	5	University of Glamorgan	3a
University of Leeds	5	University of Leicester	3a
The University of Manchester	5	University of Lincoln	3a
The University of Sheffield	5	University of North London	3a
University of Southampton	5	Northumbria University	3a
The University of York	5	The Nottingham Trent University	3a
The University of Birmingham (Public Policy)	4	Open University	3a
The University of Birmingham (Social Policy and Social Work)	4	University of Paisley	3a
		Sheffield Hallam University	3a
University of Bradford	4	University of Sunderland	3a
The University of Edinburgh	4	University of Wales Swansea	3a
University of Glasgow	4	Thames Valley University	3a
Goldsmiths College (University of London)	4	University of Westminster	3a
The University of Hull	4	University of Brighton	3b
The University of Liverpool	4	Buckinghamshire Chilterns University College	3b
Middlesex University	4	Edge Hill College of Higher Education	3b
University of Newcastle upon Tyne	4	Liverpool John Moores University	3b
The University of Nottingham	4	Bolton Institute of Higher Education	2
Oxford University	4	University College Chichester	2
University of Plymouth	4		

Source: RAE 2001

must decide whether to opt for a four-year honours programme or finish after three years with a BSc. Students are taught in large lectures and smaller tutorial groups and are assessed through coursework and end-of-year exams.

For further information, see page 474

Goldsmiths College (University of London)
BA (Hons) Sociology
This degree is made up of course units, providing students with a choice of options around a structured core on the foundations of sociology. The main aim of the first year is to introduce students to sociological and critical thought. It looks at the ways in which sociological knowledge has been shaped by disputes about theories and methods. Compulsory courses in the second and third years cover the main approaches to sociological

thought, and their implications for understanding contemporary societies. In the first year, teaching is through lectures, small classes and research workshops. Core courses provide students with a basis for exploring specialist areas in the second and third years.

For further information, see page 482

Postgraduate

University of Bristol
School for Policy Studies
The school aims to link policy and practice, theory and action, via research disseminated through undergraduate, postgraduate (MSc, MPhil and PhD) and professional programmes. The BSc in Social Policy offers the critical study of welfare systems. Introductory social policy units are offered to first-year students. In the second and third years, students take mandatory units

Sociology

Institution	Grade	Institution	Grade
University of Bristol	5*	De Montfort University	3a
University of East Anglia	5	The University of Hull	3a
The University of Huddersfield	5	University of Luton	3a
Lancaster University	5	The Manchester Metropolitan University	3a
The University of Stirling	5	University of Southampton	3a
University of Wales Swansea	5	Coventry University	3b
The University of Warwick	5	University of East London	3b
The University of York	5	University of Hertfordshire	3b
University of Dundee	4	Liverpool John Moores University	3b
The University of Durham	4	The University of Nottingham	3b
University of Exeter	4	The University of Reading	3b
The University of Kent	4	Staffordshire University	3b
Queen's University Belfast	4	University of Ulster	3b
Anglia Polytechnic University	3a	The North East Wales	
Brunel University	3a	Institute of Higher Education	2
University of Central Lancashire	3a		

Source: RAE 2001

of theorising welfare, research methods, welfare in international perspectives along with some options including family policy, violence against women and criminology. The school also offers well-established and highly successful MSc programmes including MSc in Policy Studies, MSc in European Policy Studies and MSc in Society and Space. Many overseas students are working towards a postgraduate degree. For more information, visit www.bristol.ac.uk/depts/SPS
For further information, see page 454

Lancaster University

MA in Contemporary Sociology

This one-year programme draws on numerous areas of current research from the disciplines of anthropology, philosophy, political economy, feminist theory, history and geography. Bodies such as the Institute for Women's Studies, the Institute for Cultural Research and the Centre for the Study of Environmental Change provide much of the research upon which the course is based, making for an interdisciplinary approach. Issues addressed include globalisation, gender,

contemporary capitalism and social inequality. Students are assessed through exams, coursework and a dissertation of between 15,000 and 20,000 words.
Contact details, see page 617

London School of Economics and Political Science (University of London)

MSc Social Policy and Planning

This programme allows students to study in a comparative, international and multidisciplinary environment. Students study a core course in social policy and administration, and explore the key factors determining the formation of social policy.

Sociology

Institution	Grade	Institution	Grade
The University of Essex	5*	Oxford Brookes University	4
Goldsmiths College (University of London)	5*	University of Plymouth	4
Lancaster University	5*	The University of Salford	4
Loughborough University	5*	University of Sussex	4
The University of Manchester	5*	Birkbeck College	3a
The University of Surrey	5*	University of the West of England, Bristol	3a
The University of Aberdeen	5	University of Greenwich	3a
University of Bristol	5	London Guildhall University	3a
Brunel University	5	The Manchester Metropolitan University	3a
Cardiff University	5	University of Portsmouth	3a
Cambridge University	5	The University of Reading	3a
The University of Edinburgh	5	The University of Strathclyde	3a
University of Exeter	5	Staffordshire University	3a
London School of Economics and Political Science (University of London)	5	Roehampton University of Surrey	3a
		University of Teesside	3a
Oxford University	5	Glasgow Caledonian University	3a
Queen's University Belfast	5	University of Central Lancashire	3b
The University of Warwick	5	University College Northampton	3b
The University of York	5	University of North London	3b
City University	4	University of Ulster	3b
The University of Durham	4	University of Derby	2
University of East London	4	The University of Huddersfield	2
University of Glasgow	4	Liverpool Hope	2
University of Leicester	4	University College Worcester	2
Open University	4		

Source: RAE 2001

This includes study of demography, economics and political forces and the legal context for social policy. The implementation of policy is explored, drawing on experience in a number of service areas to illustrate general points. Students can select two subjects from a list of optional courses including social services planning, foundations of health policy, criminal justice policy, social policy research, social exclusion and urban policy and planning. Students also complete a 10,000-word dissertation.

For further information, see page 508

Useful links

www.lse.ac.uk/serials/bjs	●	The British Journal of Sociology
www.britsoc.org.uk	●	British Sociological Association
www.sociology.org	●	Electronic Journal of Sociology
www.valt.helsinki.fi/esa	●	The European Sociological Association
www.ucm.es/info/isa	●	International Sociological Association
www.ssin.org.uk	●	Social Services Information Network
www.socresonline.org.uk	●	Sociological Research Online

Over the past few years, people have become increasingly aware of the need to maintain an active, healthy lifestyle. Obsession with physical fitness for the sake of an aesthetic ideal has existed in the past, largely encouraged by glamorous stereotypes such as models and pop stars. Then, the emphasis was on the result of physical perfection and not on the means, namely exercise and healthy living.

Today, attitudes are changing. It has been shown that lack of exercise is the major cause of many fatal illnesses. The Sports Council and the Health Education Authority have enlisted the help of the media to launch campaigns to increase awareness on the importance of health and fitness. Children are now encouraged to participate in regular exercise to promote healthy living in later life. The public and private sectors have responded to this increased interest by providing specialised facilities which require management, promotion and marketing. This has prompted a growth in the sports and leisure industries, making sport science and related degrees very popular.

Sports science is the study of the physiological, biomechanical and sociological influences on performance during the preparation for, participation in and recovery from sport and exercise. Courses available in recreation management are concerned with the meaning and nature of leisure activity in people's lives. They are also concerned with the planning and management of physical, environmental, human and financial resources needed to meet the demands which have recently arisen in this field.

Sports science courses focus on the theoretical and practical study of sport and recreation. Some of the areas covered include biochemistry, biology, nutrition, physiology and psychology. Another popular course is leisure and sports management which investigates the sociological, political and historical role of sport and leisure in society, while looking at ways to manage the growing sports industry.

Some courses involve an industrial placement, which lasts from 12 weeks on a three-year course to one year on a four-year course. Placements are often industry based, helping students develop knowledge of financial information, marketing, treatment of client groups, strategic planning and decision-making. These placements are usually in sports-related organisations and industries in the UK or abroad.

Students attend lectures, seminars and practical sessions in addition to completing projects and placements. They are assessed through formal examinations, coursework and individual or group presentations. Admissions tutors look for academic qualifications and evidence of sporting, recreational and other interests. To study sports science at degree level, it takes more than just a passion for the playing fields; students must demonstrate academic commitment to the subject.

Specialist and vocational

City of Westminster College
National Diploma in Sport Science

This two-year course aims to equip students to move onto related degrees and has links with Loughborough and Oxford Brookes universities. Alternatively, it can be used to access directly the sport and recreation industry. Course units studied include biological and physical sciences, anatomy and physiology, exercise physiology and sport psychology.

Contact details, see page 611

Undergraduate

The University of Birmingham
BSc Sport and Exercise Sciences

Students learn the science behind our knowledge of how the body works during exercise, the role of exercise in promoting health and how to maximise performance in sport. They have access to specialist laboratories for physiology, biomechanics, biochemistry, psychology and motor control, as well as to numerous sporting facilities including a sports centre with an eight-lane, all-weather track, two all-weather hockey pitches and an active five-a-side football league. There is also an outdoor pursuits centre running courses in water sports instruction and mountain leadership and there are over 60 student-led sports clubs at the university. A sports scholarship scheme exists to help with training, coaching, travel and medical expenses for which students with outstanding sports ability or potential are invited to apply.

Contact details, see page 613

Brunel University
BSc Sport Sciences (Coaching)

Brunel University's Sports Department has an excellent international reputation, producing many of the country's promising young sports professionals. Specialist areas within the department include biomechanics, coaching, research and sociology, psychology and physiology. The course aims to provide students with an understanding of the scientific basis of sports performance and factors influencing behaviour. Students are able to select specific sports on which to concentrate and carry out research in these areas. In the second year, students are able to specialise. One option is to prepare for a PGCE in Physical Education Teaching. A range of assessment methods are used including coursework, individual and group projects, oral presentations, written examinations and practicals.

For further information, see page 460

Liverpool John Moores University
BSc (Hons) Science and Football

This course centres on the application of science to association football and encourages students to develop theoretical knowledge and practical performance skills. Core modules cover physiology, skill acquisition, football violence,

TEACHING QUALITY ASSESSMENTS			
Sports Science (Wales) 1996/97			*tqa*
Institution	**Grade**	**Institution**	**Grade**
University of Wales Institute, Cardiff	Satisfactory		

Source: HEFCE, SHEFC, HEFCW latest available ratings
For a more complete list of institutions offering these courses at undergraduate level refer to the Course Directory

Sport

Sports-related subjects

Institution	Grade	Institution	Grade
The University of Birmingham	5*	University of Wales Institute, Cardiff	3a
University of Glasgow	5*	University College Chichester	3a
Liverpool John Moores University	5*	The University of Edinburgh	3a
Loughborough University	5*	University of Leeds	3a
The Manchester Metropolitan University	5*	Leeds Metropolitan University	3a
University of Wales, Bangor	5	South Bank University	3a
University of Exeter	5	Staffordshire University	3a
The University of Aberdeen	4	University of Wolverhampton	3a
University of Brighton	4	Buckinghamshire Chilterns University College	3b
University of Bristol	4	Canterbury Christ Church University College	3b
De Montfort University	4	University of Glamorgan	3b
The University of Sheffield	4	University of Gloucestershire	3b
Sheffield Hallam University	4	University of Luton	3b
The University of Stirling	4	Roehampton University of Surrey	3b
The University of Strathclyde	4	University of Sunderland	3b
University of Ulster	4	Anglia Polytechnic University	2
University of Bath	3a	University of Liverpool	2

Source: RAE 2001

performance assessment, ergonomics and mental training. This is backed up by modules on IT, psychology, health, sports mechanics, biomechanics and applied social research amongst others. The department has links to professional clubs and previous students have undertaken work experience with Everton, Manchester City and Liverpool football clubs. Many have gone on to work for the Football Association and professional clubs. Assessment is by a combination of essays, lab-based practicals, report writing and exams.

Contact details, see page 618

Contact details, see page 618

Postgraduate

University of Glasgow

Master's in Sport and Exercise Science

The Centre for Exercise Science and Medicine at Glasgow conducts research into the broad area of exercise, sport and health for a range of populations and disease states and this course is designed for those with a background in medicine or science. Students choose six out of nine modules which include skill acquisition, psychology, physiology, children in sport, biomechanics, nutrition and sports medicine. They also take two further modules as a research exercise.

For further information, see page 480

Loughborough University

MSc/DipHE, PGCert in Physical Education

This course has been set up for the continuing professional development (CPD) of physical education teachers and others working in the field such as coaches in schools. The flexible structure of the CPD scheme allows students to study full time or part time, accumulate credits to work towards a master's, a Diploma in Higher Education or a Postgraduate Certificate in Education and to take some modules at a distance and in weekend or summer-school blocks. Areas of study include innovation and change, exercise and children's health, policy and curriculum development and also research methods.

For further information, see page 510

Sport

Northumbria University

Sports Science

Northumbria's degree courses in this field allow students to focus on the exercise, management or coaching aspects of sports science. Graduates are well placed for careers in the sport, recreation and leisure industries. At master's level, the MSc Sport Management covers such topics as sports organisations and facilities. Academic staff have a variety of international contacts and graduates have gone on to work for the International Olympic Committee, the Commonwealth Games and other high profile employers.

For further information, see page 526

Sport

Useful links

www.youthsport.net/iys/	Institute of Youth Sport
www.issaonline.com	International Sport Sciences Association
www.sportscoachuk.org	Sports Coach UK
www.sports.com	Sports.com
www.sportsci.org	Sportscience
www.thetimes.co.uk/sport	*Times* Online Sport
www.uksport.gov.uk	UK Sport
www.wsf.org.uk	Women's Sport Foundation

Travel, tourism and leisure

From the days of Marco Polo to the discovery of the New World by Christopher Columbus in 1492, travel has been a source of excitement, anticipation and discovery. These days, due to a significant increase in leisure time and disposable income over the past 50 years, the leisure and tourism industry has become big business. In the UK alone, the travel and tourism industry is set to become one of the biggest sources of foreign income. It is the country's fourth largest sector in employment terms and, according to the English Tourist Board, is now worth more than £33 billion a year.

Travel and tourism courses in the UK are geared towards producing graduates for a specific industry, so they are often more vocational than other subjects offered at colleges and universities. Tourism courses at degree level tend to last three or four years and lead to BA/BSc honours. Some concentrate on the management side of the industry and may be related to hotel and catering courses. Others focus more on analysing the sociological aspects of the tourist industry. A general degree in tourism could include such subjects as tourism and mass communication, entertainment and event management, travel and tourism law and marketing. Some courses also offer students the opportunity to spend a year within the industry, whether working for an airline, hotel or as a tour operator. An overseas placement may be possible.

As well as higher education courses, many colleges and private schools run programmes which tend to have a more vocational bias. Courses are available that teach students the skills needed to work in various areas of the travel business, including air fares and ticketing, cabin crew and travel agencies. These can be studied in conjunction with language courses in English. It is worth checking whether courses are accredited by associations such as the Association of British Travel Agents (ABTA), the International Air Transport Association (IATA) or by internationally-recognised companies such as British Airways or Galileo.

There are several subject areas closely related to travel and tourism, one of which is transport. This is generally a three or four-year BSc (Hons) degree and covers a variety of areas including transport law, logistics and distribution, transport research methods, passenger transport and freight transport. Other closely-related subjects include languages, entertainment industry management, sport and leisure, hospitality management, business studies, marketing and PR, geography, sociology and landscape or environment management; aspects of which are often included in a tourism course. It may also be possible to do more unusual courses such as international travel law and rural or countryside tourism, or combinations with subjects like mathematics, psychology, radio, film and television studies or IT.

Travel, tourism and leisure

Specialist and vocational

Bromley College of Further & Higher Education
HND in Leisure Management
The course lasts two years, each consisting of two semesters. The first year focuses on the management of business resources. Year two concentrates on business policy and decision making and covers work-based learning, event management, sports development and outdoor recreation. Students are required to complete a professional project at the end of the second year. Assessment is through a combination of coursework and assignments, including course studies, projects, group problem solving, computer exercises and the compilation of a portfolio of work.

For further information, see page 458

Greenwich School of Management
Diploma in Travel and Tourism Management
The diploma acts as a degree access course and aims to provide students with the technical proficiency needed to work in today's travel industry, whilst also instructing them in entrepreneurial and management skills. Areas covered include marketing, accounting, business law, business communications and management for

tourism, and completion of the diploma allows them to go on to The University of Hull BSc (Hons) in Business Management (Tourism Pathway).

For further information, see page 484

Grimsby College
Travel and Tourism
Grimsby College offers several courses in travel and tourism. In this rapidly-growing industry, the college offers BA (Hons) courses in Tourism Operations and Marketing and an HND in Tourism Operations Management. With a wide range of learning resources and several opportunities to travel abroad, Grimsby College is a strong centre to study this popular subject. The tourism department travels to Gambia once a year to study the effect of tourism on a developing country and organises a fundraising event to help local schools and nurseries with building repairs and buying text books. The courses provide an insight into the industry both at home and abroad, looking at subjects such as marketing, finance and customer care and the management of tourist attractions. These courses are aimed at people looking for a career in management, tourism and marketing.

For further information, see page 416

TEACHING QUALITY ASSESSMENTS

Hospitality Studies
(Scotland) 1994/95

tqa

Institution	Grade	Institution	Grade
University of Dundee	Highly Satisfactory	The University of Strathclyde	Highly Satisfactory
Napier University	Highly Satisfactory	Glasgow Caledonian University	Satisfactory
Queen Margaret University College, Edinburgh	Highly Satisfactory	The Robert Gordon University	Satisfactory

Hotel Tourism and Leisure
(Wales) 1996/97

tqa

University of Wales Institute, Cardiff	Satisfactory

Source: HEFCE, SHEFC, HEFCW latest available ratings
For a more complete list of institutions offering these courses at undergraduate level refer to the Course Directory

Train in London for a career in Travel

•

TRAVEL AGENCY MANAGEMENT DIPLOMA

including IATA accredited British Airways airline Fares & Ticketing plus Galileo Computerised Reservations

•

Other courses available include:
**Business Administration
Computer Science
Hotel Management
Tour Operation**

•

Call or write for full Prospectus:
**West London College
Parliament House, 35 North Row
Mayfair, London W1K 6DB
Tel: +44 20 7491 1841
Fax: +44 20 7499 5853
Web: http://www.w-l-c.co.uk**

Courses run by West London College

Undergraduate

Bournemouth University

BA (Hons) International Hospitality Management

Hospitality is a fast-moving, diverse, international industry. Successful managers in this field need business flair as well as technical knowledge and skills. Bournemouth University, where the undergraduate catering and hospitality programmes were ranked first in the UK in 2001 by *The Guardian* newspaper, offers a programme combining a comprehensive curriculum with valuable work experience to develop highly qualified managers. The programme has strong links with key players in international hospitality through industrial placements, live case studies, workshops and projects, supported by extensive kitchen, restaurant, laboratory and computing facilities. The third year of this four-year programme is spent on placement in industry. Recent placement companies include Roux Restaurants, Marriott International and Virgin Airline Catering. Graduates have management skills recognised by industry which, along with the international dimension of the programme, ensure excellent career opportunities.

For further information, see page 448

University of Brighton

BA (Hons) International Tourism Management

This course focuses on the management of tourism in terms of visitor attractions, heritage, cultural aspects and destinations. Students on the international route begin certificate or diploma-level study in French, German or Spanish (optional on the non-international route). A one-year industry placement (optional on the non-interna-

Travel, tourism and leisure

329

St Rémy de Provence, France

Travel, tourism and leisure

tional degree) must be taken. This may be spent with major tour operators or at visitor attractions in the UK or abroad. Students on the international route must spend at least six months of the placement outside their home country. The degree also develops operational management expertise through modules in the social anthropology of tourism, attractions management and heritage tourism and focuses on public sector tourism, planning and development.

Contact details, see page 614

University of Gloucestershire
BA (Hons) Tourism Management with Business Management

This combined degree aims to develop a strong foundation of business knowledge and managerial skills applicable to today's tourism industry. A variety of topics also allows for specialisation in a particular area of interest. Students are given the opportunity to study and work abroad and can take part in a field trip to another European country. It is also possible to undertake a year's industrial placement abroad, either in Europe or North America. The minor in business management helps prepare students for employment and provides a broader perspective of the many social, economic and political forces which shape society. The aim is to meet career and vocational needs by equipping students with the transferable business, educational and personal skills required by industry.

Contact details, see page 616

Liverpool John Moores University
Tourism and Leisure and a Modern Foreign Language (French, German, Italian, Spanish or Mandarin Chinese)

In response to the dynamic growth of the tourism and leisure industry, JMU has

developed a four-year course integrating a tourism and leisure programme with small-group language learning. The language component focuses on communication within the context of tourism and leisure in one of five languages: French, German, Italian, Spanish or Mandarin Chinese. The first year introduces students to the tourism and leisure environment and the second year builds on this information, offering more advanced modules in areas such as people and marketing management. The third year is spend abroad in a partner institution learning the language. Students are expected to establish a relationship with an organisation in the field of leisure and tourism, research-

ing a final-year dissertation. The final year focuses on individual research and tourism human resource management, and on language skills in areas such as translation and liaison interpreting.

Contact details, see page 618

York St John College
BA (Hons) Leisure and Tourism Management

This course is designed for future managers in the tourism and leisure industries. Emphasis is placed on the acquisition of both the theoretical knowledge of business and the practical skills in managing people and resources. The curriculum covers management disciplines such as marketing, economics, financial accounting, organisational behaviour and information systems. These are explored in relation to various organisations within the leisure and tourism industries. The course includes an industrial placement and a major research assignment.

For further information, see page 588

Useful links

www.abtanet.com	●	The Association of British Travel Agents
www.britishtouristauthority.org	●	The British Tourist Authority
www.galileo.com	●	Galileo
www.englishtourism.org.uk	●	English Tourism Council
www.lonelyplanet.com	●	Lonely Planet
www.roughguides.com	●	Rough Guides
www.visitscotland.com	●	Scottish Tourist Board
www.tmi.org.uk	●	Tourism Management Institute

Travel, tourism and leisure

Veterinary medicine

If you have a love for animals and a fascination for medicine, then veterinary medicine may be the degree for you. However, entrance is fiercely competitive at the six veterinary schools and faculties in the UK. In general, there are about three applicants to every place on veterinary medicine courses, which means that the six universities in the UK which offer veterinary degrees can afford to keep their entrance requirements high. A level (or equivalent) chemistry is compulsory whilst the other two subjects can be offered in biology, physics or mathematics. Some, but not all, universities will accept one non-science subject. Veterinary medicine courses are also very expensive – about £13,500 a year, making them even more costly than medicine. It is essential for students to have good English and the communication skills to deal not only with animals but with their owners as well.

Anyone seriously considering studying veterinary medicine should gain practical experience of working with animals. A good place to start is by shadowing a qualified vet during holidays or at weekends. It is also advisable that candidates spend time working in a variety of environments such as a dairy farm, kennels or stables.

Like medicine or dentistry, a Bachelor of Veterinary Science (BVSc) degree is intensive – working a minimum of 9 am to 5 pm every day – and very long – five years at most universities. On top of that you will also have to do vacation work with licensed veterinary surgeons amounting to a total of 38 weeks' unpaid work during the degree. In the first two or three pre-clinical years (depending on the university), students get a general grounding in the subject, studying topics such as cells, anatomy, pathology, genetics and animal husbandry. Students might then have the option of taking a break from their veterinary course to study for an intercalated BSc degree in a specialist area of research such as neuroscience, virology or pathological sciences. The last two or three years combine continued study with clinical practice. The academic side covers areas such as anaesthesia, obstetrics and diseases of reproduction. Clinical rotations are divided into various areas: equine, farm animal and small animal.

What distinguishes the study of veterinary medicine in the UK from many of the other countries in the world is that undergraduates do not specialise early on in the course. Students have to be equally knowledgeable about every type of animal, from the largest to the smallest. The advantage of this approach is that UK graduates are generally more employable than those from other countries. Upon graduation, students gain membership of the Royal College of Veterinary Surgeons (RCVS), which accredits all veterinary science degrees in the UK. This also entitles graduates to practise in former Commonwealth countries or anywhere in the EU.

Institution	Grade	Institution	Grade
University of Bristol	24	Royal Veterinary College (University of London)	24
The University of Liverpool	24	Cambridge University	23

Veterinary Medicine
(Scotland) 1996

tqa

The University of Edinburgh	Excellent	University of Glasgow	Excellent

Source: HEFCE, SHEFC, HEFCW latest available ratings
For a more complete list of institutions offering these courses at undergraduate level refer to the Course Directory

Undergraduate

University of Bristol
BSc (Hons) Veterinary Nursing and Practice Administration

The veterinary nursing degree provides students with the scientific principles and practical skills needed to achieve an honours degree, while also obtaining the Royal College of Veterinary Surgeons Diploma in Veterinary Nursing. In addition, they become qualified NVQ assessors for veterinary nursing and accumulate credit points towards achieving membership of the Veterinary Practice Management Association. In the first year, students work towards the RCVS Part I examination and spend a large proportion of time in veterinary practice. The second year is spent preparing for the RCVS Part II examination and subsequent qualification as a veterinary nurse. In the third year, the student builds upon the basic nursing experience gained in the first two years by studying other species and commencing the practice administration modules. The final year consolidates the previous three years.

For further information, see page 454 *For further information, see page 454*

Cambridge University
BAVetMB Veterinary Medicine

Most vets aspire to some area of private practice and this course is designed to equip students with the essential clinical knowledge and skill to do so. It has also been designed to give students the necessary scientific background to go into any area of veterinary medicine and to be able to respond to change and advances in veterinary science. This programme extends over six years. The first two cover the main biological sciences which underlie the practice of veterinary medicine. In the third year, a wide choice of courses is available, at the end of which students gain the BA degree. In the final three years, students receive clinical instruction leading to the VetMB degree. This degree qualifies the holder for membership of the Royal College of Veterinary Surgeons.

Contact details, see page 614 *Contact details, see page 614*

The University of Edinburgh
BVM&S Degree

The first two years provide a general grounding in the natural sciences, the structure and function of healthy cells and animals, and a series of exercises which examine the biological system in live animals. Students are given theoretical and practical tuition in animal husbandry and are introduced to the processes of disease. The third and fourth years cover paraclinical subjects, providing students with an understanding of the pathogenesis and control of infection. Simultaneous

Veterinary medicine

courses integrate pathological, medical, surgical and pharmacological aspects of disease processes, and their treatment in both individual animals and the flock or herd. The final year consists of clinical rotations, involving large and small animals, and is lecture free, allowing students to integrate into the healthcare team. The emphasis is placed on diagnosis and treatment, by medical or surgical means, and the measures available for the prevention and control of disease.

For further information, see page 474

University of Glasgow
Bachelor of Veterinary Medicine and Surgery

This five-year course combines study with practical experience, involving long hours of work with little free time during the term. Students undertake an additional 12 weeks' extramural studies during vacations in their first and second years. During the third, fourth and final years, students must also spend vacation time gaining experience of general veterinary practice. In the first and second years, students are taught biomolecular sciences, anatomy, physiology and animal husbandry. During the third year, undergraduates study pathology, bacteriology, virology, parasitology and pharmacology and are also introduced to the skills of clinical examination. An intensive lecture course in medicine, surgery, pathology and public health follows in the fourth year. In the final year, there are no formal lectures and the emphasis is on

small-group clinical teaching covering the common species of domestic animals.

For further information, see page 480

The University of Liverpool
BVSc Veterinary Science

The BVSc course extends over five years (or six years, with intercalated honours degree BSc). Different styles of learning are used for different parts of the course, which make use of the university's veterinary teaching hospital and practices. The final year is lecture free and case based. Electives, in which students choose an area or speciality to study in greater depth, are run in the second and final years. The Liverpool BVSc enables registration with the Royal College of Veterinary Surgeons and allows graduates to work as recognised veterinary surgeons throughout the EU. Intercalating students suspend their studies for one year to undertake the honours year of an appropriate course and also gain a BSc or equivalent. The university also offers a BSc in Bioveterinary Science, a three-year course providing a combination of basic science and practical awareness.

Contact details, see page 618

Royal Veterinary College (University of London)
Bachelor of Veterinary Medicine

This is a five-year course. Successful completion entitles graduates to register as a member of the Royal College of Veterinary Surgeons. The pre-clinical

Veterinary medicine

RESEARCH RANKINGS
Veterinary Science

rae

Institution	Grade	Institution	Grade
University of Bristol	5	University of Glasgow	5
Cambridge University	5	University of Liverpool	5
The University of Edinburgh	5	Royal Veterinary College	5

Source: RAE 2001

phase occupies the first two years of the course. This provides an understanding of the healthy animal, together with principles of pathology. From the beginning, the undergraduate is introduced to the subject of animal husbandry and classes are devoted to learning the basic skills of examining farm and companion animals. Students are required to undertake five weeks' animal husbandry in each of their first two years, the first being a three-week period on a sheep farm at Easter. At the start of the third year, students transfer to the Hawkshead campus. Pathology and infectious diseases, pharmacology, animal health, veterinary medicine, surgery and obstetrics are taught through lectures, small group learning, demonstrations and practical work.

Contact details, see page 620

Useful links

www.ahis.org	▶	Animal Health Information Specialists
www.bsava.com	▶	British Small Animal Veterinary Association
www.bvna.org.uk	▶	British Veterinary Nursing Association
www.iah.bbsrc.ac.uk	▶	Institute for Animal Health
www.rcvs.org.uk	▶	Royal College of Veterinary Surgeons
www.vin.com	▶	Veterinary Information Network
www.vetsonline.com/vpma	▶	Veterinary Practice Management Association
www.oie.int	▶	World Organisation for Animal Health

Independent schools

INDEPENDENT SCHOOLS COUNCIL
information service

An independent school is one that is free from local or central government control and must therefore charge fees. It is autonomous in that it appoints its own board of governors to whom the head is responsible, and it has a bursar to control the finances. Roughly six per cent of British children are educated in the country's 2,400 independent schools. This is becoming an increasingly popular option for those from outside Britain, and many independent schools are welcoming an evermore international student population.

For parents considering independent education for their children, there is a large and varied selection from which to choose. There are both day and boarding schools which are either single sex or co-educational, and these cater for pupils from two to 18 years old.

In the past, the independent school was largely the preserve of the wealthy elite but nowadays, this is not the case. Many more people from different sectors of society are recognising the benefits of fee-paying education and are choosing it for their children. This, along with an increasing overseas intake, has ensured that there is no longer such a thing as the typical public school pupil. They have become a far more cosmopolitan population, and there can be no doubt that mixing with people from diverse backgrounds is a valuable experience, especially early in life.

The structure

Preparatory school

Preparatory or 'prep' schools cater for five to 13 year olds and the five to eight age group is often known as 'pre-prep'. These schools are either free standing or joined to a larger, all-age school and some have a nursery section for the under fives. Pupils are prepared for entry into senior schools which can take place at 11, 12 or 13 years old, and this flexibility allows pupils to progress at a suitable rate for each individual. Nowadays, prep schools tend to be co-educational day schools but there are also plenty which provide boarding facilities, and there are some single sex.

Independent prep schools are not obliged to follow the National Curriculum, but many choose to and the tendency to do so is increasing. However, it is seen as a basic guideline and most teachers will go beyond the National Curriculum, teaching French at an earlier age, often Latin and sometimes a second modern or classical language. Facilities in these schools are currently improving and many can now boast design technology centres, libraries, theatres, music schools and specialist sports facilities, much time being devoted to physical education. Fees range from around £600 to £1,100 a term for two to seven year olds, from £950 to £2,500 for day pupils aged seven to 13 and from £2,300 to £3,500 a term for boarders.

Senior independent schools

Pupils take the Common Entrance Exam to enter senior school at the age of 11, 12 or 13. Again, these can be co-educational or single sex, catering for boarding or day pupils, or both. Here, students are prepared for GCSEs, which they sit at 16, then A levels in the final year at 18.

A small number of schools use alternative examination systems such as the International Baccalaureate (IB) or General National Vocational Qualifications (GNVQ). Whilst studying for A levels, sixth formers are being prepared for university entrance and will often receive one-to-one guidance on UCAS applications and on careers. It is increasingly common for people to enter senior independent schools at sixth form level and acceptance is largely dependent on GCSE grades or equivalent.

Fees for senior schools range from £1,300 to £2,700 a term for girls' day schools, £2,700 to £4,400 for boarding girls, £1,300 to £3,200 for day boys and £2,800 to £4,600 for male boarders.

Academic advantages

There are numerous advantages to a British independent school education. Perhaps the most important of these is high academic achievement. Of the 500 schools listed by *The Times* newspaper as achieving the highest GCSE results in 2000, 380 were independent schools. At A level, over 85 per cent of independent school pupils achieve passes, an impressive figure in comparison to the national average of 63 per cent. The proportion of A level candidates achieving A grades was 36 per cent in 2001, an improvement of 1.7 per cent on the previous year and almost twice the national average of 18.6 per cent. High standards in national exam performance ensure that nine out of 10 independent school-leavers progress to higher education.

It is not only the brightest pupils who succeed. It has been shown that pupils of all abilities perform better at independent schools, largely the result of smaller-than-average class sizes, at between 20 and 25 pupils per class. This ensures that each pupil receives plenty of individual attention.

An all-round education

Another advantage of independent schools is the range of extracurricular activities. There is ample opportunity for pupils to develop numerous skills and hobbies from sport to drama and music, and most schools offer sports fields and halls, theatres, rehearsal rooms and even television studios in which to practise. Great value is placed on the contribution each pupil makes by representing the school in sporting events, debating and public speaking competitions. With such a broad-ranging education, pupils are ideally prepared for university entrance, where admissions tutors look beyond academic grades and towards a range of skills and interests.

Pastoral care

Staff at independent schools provide continuous support and care for every pupil. This is particularly the case in boarding schools where students must be made to feel at home. Boarding houses are headed by staff and their families who are there to ensure that boarders are looked after. The homely atmosphere they create is vital for international students whilst they adapt to living away from home and from their parents. It is usually obligatory for parents of overseas students to arrange guardians for their children. These are often recommended by individual schools and they live locally, ready to be contacted by staff at any time. There is often special provision for overseas students who will have access to personal tutors, welfare officers and student councils. The general aim is to develop students' moral characters and teach them personal and social skills as well as to accept and embrace cultural diversity.

Learning the language

Overseas students are able to improve on their spoken and written English through specially-arranged lessons. Perhaps the most valuable method of improving verbal fluency, however, is through regular interaction with the British pupils, teachers and house staff. Some schools have an international study centre which provides foundation programmes for overseas students preparing to enter UK schools. They provide an opportunity for prospective pupils to brush up on their language.

Independent Schools' Council

This section of the guide contains 45 profiles of boarding schools from all over Britain, all of which are accredited by the Independent Schools' Council (ISC). ISC has overall responsibility for the Independent Schools Inspectorate (ISI), which ensures high standards among ISC schools. Schools are evaluated on their educational standards (including attainment, learning and behaviour), quality of teaching, assessment and recording, curriculum, staffing, premises and resources, links with parents and the community, pupils'

personal development and pastoral care, management, efficiency, aims and ethos.

We have exclusively covered boarding schools, as overseas families usually need accommodation for their children. The profiles give you information on the location, history, strengths, boarding facilities, fees and much more. If you like the look of some of these, the next step is to contact the schools to arrange a visit and request a prospectus. You can also find information on the ISC website at www.iscis.net.uk

Constituent associations of the ISC

Governing Bodies' Association (GBA)
Includes the governing bodies of boys' and co-educational schools whose heads belong to HMC and SHMIS (see below).

Governing Bodies of Girls' Schools Association (GBGSA) and the Girls' Schools Association (GSA)
These are the main associations to which the girls' senior independent schools belong.

Headmasters' & Headmistresses' Conference (HMC)
Boys' and co-educational senior schools whose heads belong to the Conference.

Incorporated Association of Preparatory Schools (IAPS)
Includes the heads of more than 500 boys', girls' and mixed preparatory schools for children aged usually from seven to eight and 12 to 13.

Independent Schools Association (ISA)
Members include the heads of some 300 preparatory and senior schools, and schools for children of all ages.

Society of Headmasters' & Headmistresses of Independent Schools (SHMIS)
Comprising heads of 90 boys' and co-educational senior schools with a long tradition of boarding.

Independent schools

Uttoxeter

Abbotsholme School

Contact: Headmaster's Secretary, Abbotsholme School, Rocester, Uttoxeter, Staffordshire ST14 5BS

Tel: +44 (0)1889 590217

Fax: +44 (0)1889 591749

Email: headabbotsholme@btconnect.com

Website: www.abbotsholme.com

Headteacher: Dr Stephen Tommis

Junior school: Miss Carol Orme

Pupils: 164 day, 83 boarders, 165 boys, 82 girls.

Termly fees: £2,000 (junior); £2,465 senior school day (years seven, eight, nine); £4,840 boarding; £3,414 senior school day (10, 11, 12, 13); £5,106 boarding. 5 per cent sibling discount.

Entrance: taster days. Scholarship exams for scholarship candidates only.

Exam results: (2001) A level 96 per cent pass rate, over 56 per cent at A or B; GCSE 30 per cent at A or A*, over 50 per cent at B or above.

Abbotsholme School main building

The school

Abbotsholme School was founded in 1889. It is an independent, co-educational, HMC boarding and day school for students aged between seven and 18 years. The school is situated on a superb 140 acre campus on the Derbyshire/Staffordshire border and provides a safe and stimulating environment. Abbotsholme is easily accessible by road, rail and air. The school has its own working farm and a lively equestrian centre.

Academic record

Abbotsholme believes in the education of the whole person. The school offers high quality teaching in small classes, which enables all pupils to reach their full potential. Results at A level and GCSE are excellent. Facilities for art and sport are first class and music and drama are exceptionally strong. In the last three years, 97 per cent of the sixth form have gone on to university, including Oxbridge. Scholarships are available for all round academic ability and for competencies in music, drama, art and sport.

Boarding facilities

Boarding is in small, friendly houses under the care of a resident houseparent. Each pupil will have a tutor to support their pastoral needs and academic welfare. Younger boarders share bright, cheerful dormitories in rooms of three or four. Most sixth formers share a study bedroom with another student although there are also some single bedrooms. All boarding houses have comfortable sitting rooms with television and small kitchen facilities. There is a full programme of weekend activities.

Adcote School for Girls

The school

Adcote is a beautiful grade one listed building set in 27 acres of landscaped parkland. With marvellous views of the gardens and surrounding countryside, Adcote's facilities include language rooms, science laboratories and specialist areas such as the ICT suite, Great Hall, library, and careers room. Outside there is an all-weather sports surface.

Academic record

Adcote School is regularly the top non-selective school in Shropshire. In *The Sunday Times* survey, it is one of the top 50 independent small schools. Adcote offers a broad, balanced curriculum for pupils aged four to 18 years with careful integration between the senior school and junior department. Classes are small and the school aims to help each individual reach her full potential. All major subjects are studied with a choice of 18 subjects at GCSE and 15 at AS/A2 level. At the end of year 11, girls embark on work experience.

Boarding facilities

There are full-time, weekly or occasional boarding facilities for girls aged seven to 18. Younger girls share a room while older girls have their own study bedroom. Responsibility for boarders' personal development, welfare and happiness rests with the housemistress, assisted by two resident matrons. All pupils and teachers are allocated to one of three houses: Glenmore, Haughton and Innage. These are the basis for competition in the school with house points going towards the top house each year.

Contact: Adcote School Education Trust Limited, Little Ness, Shrewsbury, Shropshire SY4 2JY

Tel: +44 (0)1939 260202

Fax: +44 (0)1939 261300

Email: headmistress@adcoteschool.co.uk

Website: www.adcoteschool.co.uk

Pupils: approx 100.

Termly fees: junior department: day pupils four to six years £1,355 a term; seven years and over £1,545 a term; weekly boarding pupils £3,280 a term; full boarding pupils £3,610 a term. Senior department: day pupils 11 and above entry £2,510 a term; weekly boarding pupils £4,065 a term; full boarding pupils £4,455 a term.

Exam results: 100 per cent of GCSE candidates achieved five or more subjects at grade C or above; 36 per cent of all passes were A* or A.
A level: top candidate gained six A levels, five grade A and one grade C.

Independent schools

Pupils at Adcote School

341

Bristol

Badminton School

Contact: Felicity Hazell, Registrar, Badminton School, Westbury-on-Trym, Bristol BS9 3BA

Tel: +44 (0)1179 055200

Fax: +44 (0)1179 628963

Email: registrar@badminton.bristol.sch.uk

Website: www.badminton.bristol.sch.uk

Headteacher: Mrs Jan Scarrow

Pupils: senior school: 300 girls, 176 boarders, 124 day. Junior school: 100 girls.

Termly fees: boarding £3,780 to £5,560; day £1,470 to £3,130. Senior school entrance at 11+, 12+ and 13+ by Badminton's own entrance and scholarship examinations. Sixth form entrance in November.

Exam results: A level: 68.2 per cent A, 82.4 per cent A and B, pass rate 99.2 per cent. GCSE: pass rate A* to C 100 per cent, grades A*, A and B 94.4 per cent.

Northcote House - Badminton School

The school

Badminton is situated on an attractive and secure 20-acre campus on the edge of the university city of Bristol. The style of Badminton is a combination of discipline and warmth where the parameters are firm and there is a welcome absence of pettiness. Constant encouragement is the key to the success of girls in a relaxed yet purposeful environment in which they are well taught, challenged and enabled to achieve success.

Academic record

Badminton has an outstanding record at GCSE and A level and believes in the pursuit of academic excellence without cramming. Girls are expected to produce results according to their ability and to develop their individual talents. The school attaches great importance to the development of musical, creative and athletic talent and to all round development which complements academic achievement.

Boarding facilities

Badminton is essentially a boarding school which takes day girls. Boarders need security, affection and lots to do at weekends and life is geared to keeping them busy and fully occupied. Boarding is organised to match as closely as possible the location of the various houses on the campus to the age and needs of each age group and to achieve a balance between the requirements of senior girls for increasing independence and privilege as they progress through the school, with the needs of younger pupils.

BATTLE ABBEY
SCHOOL

Battle Abbey School

The school
The site occupied by the senior school dates back to the beginning of modern British history; it was at Battle that William the Conqueror defeated Harold in 1066. A substantial part of the main school building originates from that time. The school took over the property in 1922 and has been in continuous occupation since. Following mergers in 1989 and 1995, the school transferred its prep school to a new site in Bexhill, adding a purpose-built junior school, playing fields, six tennis courts and an indoor swimming pool to its facilities.

Academic record
A major strength is the art department. Both two and three dimensional art can be studied, leading to two GCSEs. There are also A levels in art and art history. The National Curriculum is followed and supplemented by specialist teachers who enjoy the use of dedicated rooms for computer studies, art, textiles, music and science. Most sixth formers study three or even four A levels after taking four or occasionally five AS levels in Year 12 . At AS/A level there are 18 subjects to choose from.

Boarding facilities
The Junior Boarding House stands next to the Headmaster's House. Here, children share bedrooms with one or two others and enjoy the family sitting rooms, a garden and small adventure area. House parents and a female student also live in the house. Older children board in Abbot's House with well-furnished bedrooms which they share with two or three others, while some sixth formers have single rooms.

Contact: Headmaster, Battle Abbey School, Battle, East Sussex TN33 0AD

Tel: +44 (0)1424 772385

Fax: +44 (0)1424 773573

Email: office@battleabbeyschool.btinternet.com

Website: www.battleabbeyschool.com

Headteacher: Mr Roger Clark, BA, MA (Ed)

Head of prep: Mrs Judy Clark, BA

Pupils: 212 day (120 girls, 92 boys); 58 boarding (32 girls, 26 boys), 46 sixth form.

Termly fees: £1,458 to £2,657 (day); £3,467 to £4,288 (boarding).

Entrance: CEE exam, scholarship exam, report and interview. Scholarships available for academic, art, music, drama, sport, all rounder, H M Forces, sixth form.

Exam results: GCSE 96.4 per cent (2001); A level 17.5 points (2001); AS level 57.1 per cent pass; Advanced Subsidiary 88.5 per cent (2001).

Battle Abbey School

Independent schools

Bedford

Bedford School

Contact: The Registrar,
Bedford School, De Parys Avenue,
Bedford MK40 2TU

Tel: +44 (0)1234 362200

Fax: +44 (0)1234 362283

Email: registrar@bedfordschool.org.uk

Website: www.bedfordschool.org.uk

Headteacher: Dr Philip Evans OBE

Pupils: 1,100 boys (250 boarders).

Termly fees: from £3,540 to 5,190
boarding; £2,130 to 3,290 day boys.

Exam results: (2001) 97.81
per cent A level pass rate, 65.9
per cent grades A or B. GCSE
pass rate 96.49 per cent (A to C),
50.18 per cent (A* to A).

Bedford School

The school

Bedford boasts a tradition of high
quality education for boys aged seven
to 18. Set in a 40-acre estate, the school
offers an impressive range of academic,
cultural and sporting facilities and
has a reputation for high standards in
music, drama and sport. The school
benefits from a strong sense of
tradition combined with a modern
outlook towards education. A caring
and supportive ethos underpins life
at the school and a dedicated pastoral
network enables boys to get the best
out of their education.

Academic record

Staff work closely with pupils to ensure
that every boy reaches his full potential
and delights in a sense of achievement.
This partnership means that the school
is able to retain its position in the
first division of independent schools
for A level results. This year, the vast
majority of boys went on to university,
including 15 boys who took up places
at Cambridge and Oxford.

Boarding facilities

A distinctive feature of the school is the
way in which day boys and boarders
combine in the house system. Boys are
integrated in all aspects of school life
and in a full range of social activities.
Each of the six boarding houses is
twinned with a day house. Each has its
own character and is a family concern
run by the housemaster and his wife.
All houses are regularly upgraded
and have excellent facilities, including
common rooms, games rooms and
computers.

I54I

Christ College Brecon

The school
Christ College, founded by Henry VIII, occupies an enviable site on the outskirts of Brecon – a safe, small market town in a national park. Extensive playing fields lead to the foothills of the Brecon Beacons. Originally a boys school, it became fully co-educational in 1995. School buildings reflect the school's ancient past as well as its determination to provide the best modern facilities possible for its pupils.

Academic record
The academic record is solid with a particular strength in sciences. 95 per cent of leavers go to university. Extensive playing facilities and the school's national park location permit a wide range of extracurricular activity from traditional strengths in rugby football to individual outdoor sports. The tradition of choral singing is exceptionally strong. Departments offering English as a second language help pupils from overseas settle quickly. There is a long tradition of overseas tours for sport and music.

Boarding facilities
There is co-educational boarding from 11 to 13 years, after which pupils move to separate senior houses. Extensive boarding house refurbishment is ongoing. Sixth form entrants enjoy a four-day induction leadership course before the new year begins. Boarding houses are run by married houseparents and each pupil has an individual tutor responsible for balancing work and play as well as pastoral concerns. Parental visits are always welcomed and all pupils have access to telephones, faxes and personal email facilities.

Contact: Mr Phillip Jones, Christ College, Brecon, Powys LD3 8AG

Tel: +44 (0)1874 623359

Fax: +44 (0)1874 611478

Email: headmaster@christcollegebrecon.com

Website: www.christcollegebrecon.com

Headteacher: Mr Phillip Jones

Pupils: 80 day pupils, 220 boarding.

Termly fees: £2,675 to £3,540 (day); £3,570 to £4,565 (boarding).

Entrance: pupils entering the school at 11 and 13 are expected to take entrance tests in Maths, English and an IQ test. Pupils entering at 16 are expected to gain five GCSEs at grade C or higher. School reports are requested at all levels.

Exam results: GCSE: A* to A 44.5 per cent, A* to C 89.5 per cent. A levels: A to B 47.8 per cent, A to E 97.6 per cent.

Independent schools

Christ College Brecon School

349

Bideford

Edgehill College

Independent schools

Contact: Edgehill College, Bideford, Devon EX39 3LY

Tel: +44 (0)1237 471701

Fax: +44 (0)1237 425981

Email: edgehill@btconnect.com

Website: www.edgecoll.clara.net

Pupils: 440 (prep school 109, senior school 331).

Termly fees: boarding £3,338 to £4,754. Day £1,215 to £2,509.

Entrance: by entrance exam and/or reports. Scholarships available.

Exam results: (2001) GCSE average pass rate 84 per cent. A level average pass rate 96 per cent.

Edgehill College

The school

Edgehill College is in a semi-rural location, within walking distance from Bideford. The school prides itself on its tradition, providing firm but friendly discipline and a keen sense of moral values. Founded in 1884, Edgehill is one of a group of schools run by the Board of Management for Methodist Colleges and Schools. Its Methodist foundation is reflected in the informality of the college's religious life. Students of all denominations and faiths are welcome.

Academic record

The school motto, 'Beyond the best there is a better' sums up the achievements of its students. Having won the Schools Curriculum Award and been chosen as a National Coaching Foundation Centre, Edgehill has established itself as a leading southwest school. Students are encouraged to reach their potential and develop their talents to the full. A reputation for achievement in music and drama is matched by outstanding results in sports. The academic courses typically lead to a place at university.

Boarding facilities

Edgehill has a large campus and sixth form centre. Resident house staff are responsible for care and leisure time activities. There is supervised study and events are arranged. Houses are friendly with bright, comfortable accommodation. Each house has a kitchen, common room, television room, table tennis and snooker tables. The chaplain and his wife keep open house for any pupil to discuss problems. The medical centre is run by a nursing sister and the doctor is on 24-hour call.

Chislehurst

POSSIDE · SAPIENTIAM

Farringtons and Stratford House

The school

Farringtons and Stratford House is a warm, friendly school with a Christian perspective situated within the beautiful location of Kent. Ideally located for travel to and from airports, London can be reached easily by train. There is a wide ability intake and a commitment to stretch every girl to the best of her ability.

Academic record

The school has small classes and a high level of personal support including, where necessary, additional English language support for overseas students. As well as impressive facilities, the school is able to boast an enviable range of extracurricular activities including clubs, weekend outings, visits, drama productions, sporting events and concerts.

Boarding facilities

Warm and friendly surroundings are provided for boarders with different living areas for each age group. When parents are unable to be nearby, the school recognises that it must create and maintain a homely and secure living environment in which the girls feel safe, confident and cared for, whatever their age. Boarders are cared for by house staff who liaise with parents, guardians, form tutors and other staff to ensure the well being of each student. The newly refurbished boarding facilities provide cosy bedrooms for students as well as common rooms, TV and video rooms, games rooms, kitchens and other facilities appropriate to the age group.

Contact: Registrar, Farringtons and Stratford House, Perry Street, Chislehurst, Kent BR7 6LR

Tel: +44 (0)20 8467 0256

Fax: +44 (0)20 8467 5442

Email: admissions@farringtons.kent.sch.uk

Website: www.farringtons.org.uk

Headteacher: Mrs C E James MA

Pupils: girls aged two to 18 (boarding from seven); 40 nursery, 200 junior, 280 senior.

Termly fees: £4,330 to £4,780 (full boarding); £4,150 to £4,620 (weekly); £1,700 to £2,430 (day).

Entrance: assessment in maths and English and report from current school. Some scholarships available.

Exam results: 77 per cent obtained five GCSEs at grade A* to C, 71 per cent obtained eight GCSEs at grade A* to C. A level pass rate 87.5 per cent with 41 per cent of students gaining A and B grades.

Farringtons and Stratford House

Independent schools

High Wycombe

Godstowe Preparatory School

Contact: Headmistress, Godstowe Preparatory School, Shrubbery Road, High Wycombe, Buckinghamshire HP13 6PR

Tel: +44 (0)1494 529273

Fax: +44 (0)1494 429009

Email: headmistress@godstowe.org

Website: www.godstowe.org

Headteacher: Mrs Frances J Henson BA (Hons), PGCE

Pupils: pre-prep 105; main school 332 (day and boarding).

Termly fees: £800 to £2,960 (day), £4,250 (boarders).

Entrance: age range three to 13, non selective. Scholarships available.

Exam results: (2001) 25 per cent achieved scholarships to senior school, 100 per cent achieved entrance to first choice senior school.

Turner – one of the four comfortable and homely boarding houses

The school

Godstowe has been at the forefront of girls education since its foundation in 1900. The first British boarding preparatory school for girls, it has continued to thrive and is a successful and flourishing boarding and day school with over 430 pupils aged three to 13. The school has a nursery and pre-prep department for boys and girls from three to seven years. The preparatory school has girls from seven to 13 years only and has an equal balance of day and boarding pupils.

Academic record

Godstowe enjoys an excellent academic reputation. Whilst the school has a non-selective intake, some 25 per cent achieve scholarships to their senior schools each year. Pupils are prepared for 13+ common entrance level for entry to senior school. Pupils are taught by specialists in all areas. Language teaching includes many European languages and Latin. Tuition is available in Chinese and Japanese. Sport, ICT, art, music and other expressive arts are taught within first rate facilities.

Boarding facilities

Boarding life is focused within four houses, one of which is weekly boarding. Each house of 30 to 36 girls has boarders aged seven to 13, with four resident staff who are highly professional and caring. The level of individual care, quality of life and happiness of the children are hallmarks of the school. The atmosphere is friendly and relaxed with busy activities. The school is conveniently located in the Chiltern Hills, close to London, Windsor and Oxford.

Independent schools

Great Ballard School

The school
The school's intention is that all children should be given the opportunity to fulfil their academic potential. More importantly, all are encouraged to develop as individuals within a school structure based on Christian principles. School days should be fun days and the happiness, safety and welfare of each individual is of paramount importance.

Academic record
Great Ballard School teaches National Curriculum-based lessons, in addition to which pupils also study Latin, art, drama and information technology, among others. Children in forms seven and eight take part in an annual trip to a French chateau where they can improve their language skills while studying the geography of the region. At the end of their time at the school, all pupils participate in a course of further education. This aims to prepare them for senior school while making them aware of life outside the confines of school.

Boarding facilities
The boarding wing of the school is run by the resident housemaster and housemother with assistance from the headmaster. Boarding is a relaxed but suitably structured way of life. Two school doctors visit weekly (more often if required) and emergencies are taken to the nearby Chichester Hospital. There is a range of clubs and activities every evening with regular outings to the theatre and cinema, as well as ten-pin bowling and ice-skating. Treats are vital ingredients in boarding life; a trip to the housemaster's flat for a taste of oriental cuisine comes high on the list.

Contact: Richard Jennings, Headmaster, Great Ballard School, Eartham, near Chichester, Sussex PO18 0LR

Tel: +44 (0)1243 814236

Fax: +44 (0)1243 814586

Email: gbschool@breathemail.net

Pupils: 191; 100 girls, 91 boys, 30 boarders (full and weekly) two to 13 years co-educational.

Fees: nursery £10.99 per half-day session; £1,370 to £2,438 day; £3,263 full and weekly boarders.

Entrance: interview and informal day spent at school, plus school entrance test.

Exam results: all students pass Common Entrance exams and scholarship exams.

Pupils from Great Ballard School

Independent schools

Harrow on the Hill

Harrow on the Hill

Harrow School

Contact: The Admissions Secretary, Harrow School, 1 High Street, Harrow on the Hill, Middlesex HA1 3HW

Tel: +44 (0)20 8872 8007

Fax: +44 (0)20 8872 8012

Email: admissions@harrowschool.org.uk

Website: www.harrowschool.org.uk

Headteacher: Barnaby Lenon

Pupils: 800 boys.

Termly fees: £5,985.

Entrance: common entrance, scholarship tests or Harrow tests. 30 scholarships each year for academic excellence, exceptional ability in music or art or outstanding talent in another field.

Exam results: A level 44 per cent A grade, 90 per cent A to C, 99.6 per cent pass rate. AS level 42 per cent A grade, 87 per cent A to C. GCSE 62.1 per cent A* to A grades, 90 per cent A to B.

Aerial view of Harrow School

The school

Harrow was founded in 1572 and rapidly became one of the greatest schools in the country. Distinguished Old Harrovians include Stanley Baldwin, Winston Churchill (both former UK prime ministers) and King Hussein of Jordan. Harrow is situated in a 400-acre site near London and specialises in providing high quality boarding education for boys, combining academic excellence with a great range of opportunities outside the classroom.

Academic record

In 2001, the A level results were a record. Over 73 per cent achieved grades A or B and the pass rate rose to 99.6 per cent. A majority of boys achieved entry to their first choice universities. At GCSE, 62 per cent of papers were awarded A* or A grades and the pass rate was 98.5 per cent. Every pupil passed maths and English. In The University of Durham's 'value added' League Table, Harrow has been placed consistently in the top 10 schools.

Boarding facilities

Harrow has 11 boarding houses. There are study bedrooms with boys sharing for their first three or four terms. Each house has a resident housemaster, matron and tutor. Every boy has an academic tutor. During the settling-in period, boys are assigned a shepherd (a junior boy) and a mentor (a senior boy) to guide and encourage them.

Independent schools

Headfort School

The school
Headfort is Ireland's predominately boarding co-educational prep school. The house, designed by Robert Adam and one of the finest in Ireland, is set in 65 acres of games fields, gardens and woodlands, 40 miles north of Dublin. The school caters for children aged seven to 13 as boarders or as day pupils and offers a programme of academic, sporting and cultural activities.

Academic record
Children are prepared for Common Entrance or scholarships to English and Irish independent secondary schools. Children play team and individual games as well as learning to ride, cook, dance and participate in many other activities. Class sizes are small, with an average of 12 pupils. Pupils are prepared for admission to the secondary school of their parents' choice, either in the Republic of Ireland or abroad. Many pupils move on to leading schools in England and Ireland.

Boarding facilities
Pastoral care is of extreme importance and, as such, structures are in place to ensure that each child is monitored constantly to ensure his/her welfare. The exuberant atmosphere reflects the amount of time devoted to this. There is accommodation for about 100 children and associated staff. Dormitories sleep between six and 20 children. There is full central heating in the dormitories and there are washing facilities either en-suite or close by. An extensive programme of refurbishment is nearing completion, which will ensure the continued excellence of academic, social and pastoral provision.

Write to: Headfort, Kells, County Meath, Republic of Ireland

Tel: +353 (0)46 40065

Fax: +353 (0)46 41842

Email: headmaster@tinet.ie

Website: www.headfort.com

Headteacher: Cathal Mcosker BSc

Pupils: 120 pupils.

Termly fees: boarding 3,500 euros; day 2,160 euros.

Entrance: former headmaster's report and interview.

Exam results: (2001) all pupils pass Common Entrance Examinations.

Independent schools

Riding at Headfort School

Dorking

Hurtwood House

Contact: K R B Jackson, Hurtwood House, Holmbury St Mary, Dorking, Surrey RH5 6NU

Tel: +44 (0)1483 277416

Fax: +44 (0)1483 267586

Email: hurtwood2@aol.com

Website: www.hurtwood-house.co.uk

Headteacher: Richard Jackson MA Cantab

Pupils: 290 (130 boys and 160 girls) boarding.

Termly fees: £6,700 (boarding) plus 15 per cent EFL.

Entrance: by interview and reference.

Exam results: (2001) of 352 examinations sat, 351 were passed. 43 per cent of all A levels were grade A, 78 per cent were grades A or B.

Hurtwood Theatre

The school

Hurtwood House was founded in 1970 with the clear vision that the needs of the modern sixth-former have changed. After GCSE, many students are ready for the challenge and the fresh impetus which can only be provided by a community specialising exclusively in their own age range. It is widely recognised that Hurtwood House has the best and most professional drama department of any school in England.

Academic record

In order to achieve the best possible A level results, the school gives sixth form students maximum support. Each student receives a grade in each subject every week and has a personal academic tutor to closely monitor progress. The 100 per cent pass rate in 21 A level subjects leads to the college being consistently well placed in league tables. An experienced careers department is dedicated to finding the correct university course for each and every student.

The vast majority of students come from the public school system. They have usually been happy and successful at their former school but are now ready for fresh challenges, new learning methods and a different lifestyle. At Hurtwood House, students discover an intellectual environment closer to that of a university. Indeed, most students and their parents see Hurtwood House as a logical step between the traditional public school and the adult world of higher education.

Ipswich School

The school

Ipswich School was founded in the 14th century and moved to its present site, just north of Ipswich town centre overlooking Christchurch Park, in 1851. The school is easily accessible from Stansted, Gatwick and Heathrow airports. At the heart of the campus is the First XI cricket square and the school owns a further 35 acres of playing fields nearby. Girls and boys can board from age 11 and there is also a junior school for younger day pupils aged three to 10 plus.

Academic record

Ipswich School is well known for its academic and sporting success as well as its high standards in music and drama. There are strong links with leading UK universities of their first choice. There is a wealth of opportunity outside the classroom and the aim is that girls and boys should be able to realise their potential in many different fields within a caring environment.

Boarding facilities

The boarding house, Westwood, is home during term time to about 45 girls and boys aged 11 to 18. The housemaster, Steve Godfrey, his wife Deborah and their children Hannah and Joshua live at Westwood. They are given energetic support by the house tutor and matron, both of whom are resident. The Westwood staff provide guidance and supervision of the boarders' studies as well as a concern for their welfare and individual development. This is complemented by a system of academic and pastoral monitoring and support of pupils' study and welfare during the 'academic' part of the day.

Contact: Registrar, Ipswich School, Henley Road, Ipswich, Suffolk IP1 3SG

Tel: +44 (0)1473 408300

Fax: +44 (0)1473 400058

Email: registrar@ipswich.suffolk.sch.uk

Website: www.ipswich.suffolk.sch.uk

Headteacher: I G Galbraith MA

Pupils: total roll aged 11 to 18: 685 (501 boys, 184 girls), including 46 boarders (32 boys, 14 girls).

Termly fees: day £2,077 to £2,310; boarding: £3,447 to £4,010.

Entrance: main entry points at ages 11, 13 and 16 but entry at other ages is possible if space is available. Limited number of scholarships and assisted places offered. Church of England but all denominations welcome.

Exam results: (2001) GCSE 96.5 per cent grades A* to C; 57.6 per cent grades A*/A. A level 98.2 per cent pass rate; 78 per cent grades A to C.

Independent schools

Ipswich School

357

Canterbury

Junior King's School

Contact: Headmaster, Junior King's School, Milner Court, Sturry, Canterbury, Kent CT2 0AY

Tel: +44 (0)1227 714000

Fax: +44 (0)1227 713171

Email: office@junior-kings.co.uk

Website: www.junior-kings.co.uk

Headteacher: Mr P M Wells, BEd (Hons)

Pupils: 360 (65 boarders).

Termly fees: boarding £3,700 weekly (boarding); day £1,064 to £2,610.

Entrance: by entry test and report.

Exam results: (1990 to 2001) 56 scholarships, five of which were top scholarships. 26 music scholarships, six art, one sport; 63 of these were awarded to King's, Canterbury.

Common Entrance results: (1990 to 2001) this year, all sixth form leavers passed and gained their place at King's, Canterbury. In the past nine years, over 99 per cent passed to their first choice school. Over 85 per cent go on to King's.

The school
The school occupies an attractive 80-acre, semi-rural setting on the edge of the village of Sturry, a short distance from Canterbury. The estate and manor, which once belonged to Lord and Lady Milner, has been tastefully developed, and provides some of the most impressive facilities of any modern preparatory school. The recreational activities offered include sports, dance, computing, games, art, drama, public speaking and many other interests.

Academic record
The Junior King's School has an excellent academic record which is detailed opposite. The majority of the pupils go on to the King's School through scholarship or common entrance. Classes are kept sufficiently small (an average of 16) to ensure plenty of individual attention and pastoral care. The main computer room houses a suite of PCs that allow the children to explore a Windows environment whilst also using quality educational software to support their class lessons.

Boarding facilities
There is a separate house for the girls who board with a resident house mistress. The boys' boarding is currently located on the middle floor of the main school building with newly furnished dormitories. The boarders can take advantage of a wide range of activities offered in the evenings and at weekends. The recreational activities offered include numerous sports and team games, music, art, drama and dance.

Junior King's School

King Edward's School

The school

Founded in 1553 by Royal Charter, King Edward's School is a modern co-educational boarding school, set in extensive grounds, less than an hour from London and its airports. The campus has a mix of traditional and modern buildings with excellent facilities in all areas, particularly science, ICT, design technology and sport.

Academic record

The school aims to achieve the highest standards possible but admits pupils of a broad range of ability. Over 98 per cent of all pupils go on to higher education with two to three each year entering Oxbridge and the same number going to Central Saint Martin's College of Art and Design. 20 GCSE and 26 A level subjects are offered from design to electronics. Work experience is available in the sixth form and foreign exchanges and field trips are regularly taken. In partnership with the Microsoft Anytime Anywhere Learning Project, the school has developed the widespread use of laptops by staff and pupils. Video conferencing facilities bring outside expertise to the classroom.

Boarding facilities

Approximately 70 per cent of the pupils are boarders. Senior pupils from age 13 are housed in unique paired houses. As a boarding school, it aims to endorse family values wholeheartedly and the staff ensure that no pupil need ever feel isolated. A long tradition of co-education means that gender is not an issue in the school, with boys and girls living and working together.

Contact: Gwyn Phillips, King Edward's School, Witley, Surrey GU8 5SG

Tel: +44 (0)1428 682572

Fax: +44 (0)1428 682850

Email: hm@kesw.surrey.sch.uk

Website: www.kesw.surrey.sch.uk

Headteacher: Mr PK Fulton-Peebles

Pupils: 476 (330 boarders, 146 day). Boys and girls 11 to 18 years.

Termly fees: £4,395 (boarders), £3,010 (day).

Entrance: satisfactory report from previous school, own entrance exams. Scholarships awarded in academic studies, art, music, science and mathematics and sixth form.

Exam results: (2001) 94.3 per cent pass rate at A level (77.4 per cent at A to C grades); 88.4 per cent pass at GCSE (61.9 per cent with 10 plus subjects at grades A to C).

Independent schools

King Edward's School main building

Castletown

King William's College

Contact: The Principal,
King William's College, Castletown,
Isle of Man IM9 1TP

Tel: +44 (0)1624 820428

Fax: +44 (0)1624 820401

Email: principal@kwc.sch.im

Website: www.kwc.sch.im

Principal: Philip John BSc

Headteacher:
George Shaw-Twilley (Buchan)

Pupils: 282; 216 day pupils
(118 boys, 98 girls), 66 boarding
pupils (49 boys, 19 girls).

Termly fees: from £4,070 boarding;
£2,635 day. Scholarships are available.

Entrance: no entrance exam.

Exam results: (2001) GCSEs 94 per
cent pass rate for grades A* to C; A
levels 92 per cent passes A to E.

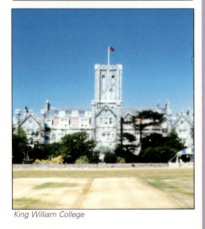

King William College

The school

King William's College was established
in 1833. The school is co-educational
and offers a choice of education
to parents. The broad curriculum
throughout the school aims to provide
the necessary depth of study to ensure
all pupils are well-motivated, can
think critically and are able to
enjoy the experience of learning. The
junior department of the college, The
Buchan, offers kindergarten and primary
education. The college offers formal
education to International Baccalaureate
standard from the age of 11.

Academic record

There is a wide range of activities
on offer, including CCF and the Duke
of Edinburgh's Award Scheme. 26
subjects are offered at GCSE level and
20 for the International Baccalaureate
in the sixth form. There is also a
strong interest in music and termly
drama productions. At 11, children
join Stenning, the junior house. This
provides a transition between primary
and secondary school. The curriculum
provides a broad education and avoids
the temptation to specialise too early.
At 13, pupils move to one of the
five senior houses for their GCSE and
A level studies.

Boarding facilities

There are two boarding houses: School
House for girls within the main college
building; and the boys boarding house,
Colbourne, is situated in its own building
adjacent to the main school building.
Each house has its own housemistress/
housemaster, responsible for the
pastoral and academic welfare of each
pupil in their care.

Kingswood School

The school

Kingswood is a co-educational school for pupils aged three to 18 and is dedicated to providing the best and broadest education within a happy, disciplined environment based on strong Christian principles. It offers excellent facilities in 218 acres of parkland in Lansdown, overlooking the world heritage city of Bath. Within easy reach of major road, rail and air links, the school is only 90 minutes by train from London. The teaching complex has seen a major re-development programme to provide the best possible opportunity for academic study with specialist centres for art, music and design technology. A sports hall complex, indoor swimming pool and astroturf complement the extensive playing fields and provide excellent facilities for all major sports.

Academic record

Music is a key subject attracting scholars across the world. A new music centre opened in May 2000. Drama is also a key subject with the benefit of a drama workshop as well as the 450-seat, state-of-the-art theatre. The sixth form centre has its own study facilities, HE suite and careers office. The library includes the latest computer-integrated desk systems.

Boarding facilities

Boarding accommodation is at hotel standard for both boys and girls. In 2001, there was a 14 per cent increase in the number of boarders. This success is a result of the continuing record of exceptional pastoral care and the upgrading of facilities, particularly in the senior part of the school.

Contact: Ms Angela Carlton-Porter, Registrar, Kingswood School, Lansdown, Bath BA1 5RG

Tel: +44 (0)1225 734210

Fax: +44 (0)1225 734305

Email: registrar@kingswood.bath.sch.uk

Website: www.kingswood.bath.sch.uk

Headteacher: Mr Gary Best MA

Prep school: Miss Anita Gleave MA

Pupils: 871; 686 day (400 boys, 286 girls), 183 boarding (109 boys,74 girls).

Termly fees: £1,343 to £2,163 (day); £3,666 to £5,166 (boarding); £4,499 to 5,499 (boarding with English as a foreign language).

Entrance: all denominations – own entrance exam at years seven, nine and 10 for day and boarding.

Exam results: (2001) GCSE 100 per cent pass rate; 40 per cent at A*/A, 67 per cent A*/B. A level 96 per cent pass rate; 62 per cent at A/B with 90 per cent of pupils achieving three or more passes.

Kingswood School

Independent schools

Norwich

Langley School

Contact: Headmaster, Langley School, Langley Park, Loddon, Norwich, Norfolk NR14 6BJ

Tel: +44 (0)1508 520210

Fax: +44 (0)1508 528058

Email: headmaster@langleyschool.co.uk

Website: www.langleyschool.co.uk

Headteacher: Mr J G Malcolm

Pupils: 325 (80 boarders), boys and girls.

Termly fees: £1,850 to £2,400 (day); £3,800 to £4,600 (boarders).

Entrance: satisfactory report from previous school. Scholarships awarded in drama, sport, music, art, technology and academic studies.

Exam results: 100 per cent pass at A level (66 per cent at top grades); 87 per cent pass at GCSE (60 per cent at top grades); 100 per cent pass in English as a second language.

Langley School grounds

The school

Langley School is one of the most popular, aspiring and forward-looking schools in the region. They offer a blend of traditional high standards and innovative programmes. Each day students can choose from a range of more than 80 different sports and other activities (in art, music, drama, science and technology, amongst others). These allow students to develop their talents to the full. The school is situated in 55 acres of outstanding grounds and sports fields, within easy reach of London and major airports.

Academic record

The school offers an exceptionally broad range of more than 24 GCSE and A level subjects. With a staff to student ratio of less than one to eight, class sizes are small (typically 14 in lower school, 12 at GCSE and eight at A level). There is an excellent department offering English as a second language and students receive support individually or in small groups. 95 per cent of students go on to university including top colleges in the UK and the USA.

Boarding facilities

There are separate houses for boys and girls with no fewer than 14 resident staff to ensure a safe, friendly and purposeful experience. A lot of work has been done recently to upgrade accommodation and facilities to a very high standard. These include a new dining room, Learning Resource Centre, common rooms and internet/email facilities available to students at all times. There are many opportunities for cultural development through the Arts Umbrella programme.

1495

Loughborough Grammar School

The school

Founded in 1495, Loughborough Grammar School is amongst the oldest and most academically successful schools in the UK. The school aims to provide a stimulating environment, a wide range of activities and a family atmosphere. Along with Loughborough High School, a day school for girls between 11 and 18 years of age, and Fairfield, a mixed preparatory school, it is part of Loughborough Endowed Schools.

Academic record

Loughborough prepares young men for post-18 education and careers. Over 95 per cent go on study a wide variety of courses at the most prestigious universities, including an average of 18 boys a year who secure places at Oxford or Cambridge. The school offers a wide range of courses at GCSE and A level and enjoys excellent results at both levels. Every year, a large number achieve top grades in all their A level subjects; in 2001, 50 boys secured three or more A grades. At GCSE, 100 per cent achieved A or A* grades in eight or more subjects.

Boarding facilities

The school has two boarding houses for years six to nine and years 10 to 13, which play an integral part of the school, catering for both weekly and termly boarders. Music and drama are strongly supported, most orchestras and productions being run jointly with the sister girls' high school. Many sports are available, along with a large variety of clubs and societies which cater for most conceivable needs. There is a big emphasis on outdoor pursuits, including a large CCF, scouts and the Duke of Edinburgh Award Scheme.

Contact: Headmaster, Loughborough Grammar School, Burton Walks, Loughborough, Leicestershire LE11 2DU

Tel: +44 (0)1509 233233

Fax: +44 (0)1509 218436

Email: admin@loughgs.leics.sch.uk

Website: www.loughgs.leics.sch.uk

Headteacher: Mr PB Fisher, MA

Junior school: Mr R Outwin-Flinders

Pupils: 990, aged 10 to18 years; boys only.

Termly fees: day boys £2,118; weekly boarding and tuition £3,249; termly boarding and tuition £3,663.

Entrance: by own examination at 10+, 11+ and 13+, by Common Entrance at 13+; sixth form dependant upon GCSE results – at least five A and B grades, preferably with A grades in the subjects to be studied in the sixth form.

Loughborough Grammar School

Independent schools

Marymount International School

Contact: Sister Rosaleen Sheridan, RSHM, School Principal, Marymount International School, George Road, Kingston upon Thames, Surrey KT2 7PE

Tel: +44 (0)20 8949 0571

Fax: +44 (0)20 8336 2485

Email: info@marymount.kingston.sch.uk

Website: www.marymount.kingston.sch.uk

Headteacher: Sister Rosaleen Sheridan RSHM

Pupils: 200 girls (11 to 19).

Termly fees: £3,210 to £3,566 (day); £5,766 to £6,123 (full board); £5,686 to £6,043 (half board).

Entrance: application forms and previous school records are reviewed by the Board of Admissions. Entrance examinations in English are set where necessary. All dominations welcome.

Exam results: 97 per cent of pupils graduated with excellent grades.

The school

Marymount International School was founded in 1955 and is situated on a seven-acre campus in an exclusive residential area in Kingston in north-east Surrey. The school attracts many multinational students and has a separate middle and high school. In the last 20 years, it has been upgrading its facilities, boasting a new science centre, sports hall, computer library and an additional boarding wing.

Academic record

Marymount's syllabus is based on the International Baccalaureate and IB Diploma programme, recognised as university entry around the world. Over 99 per cent of pupils go on to high calibre universities. Creative exploration is encouraged through some 40 subject levels and Marymount hosts international school sports tournaments, riding, golf and cycling along the Thames. A multifaith programme covering major world religions is required for each student.

Boarding facilities

Boarding life fosters a sturdy spirit of self-reliance and helps develop natural social skills. The 100 boarders live in modern, furnished rooms with access to comfortable lounges and kitchenettes. Boarders have access to the gymnasium and tennis courts after school hours. The library and computer centre are open until 6 pm. A registered nurse is in attendance as well as five residential house matrons.

Marymount International School students

London

Mill Hill
SCHOOL

Mill Hill School

The school
Mill Hill was founded in 1807 as a school for the sons of Protestant dissenters. It occupies a magnificent parkland site of 120 acres, 10 miles from central London and within easy reach of transport links. 180 or so boarders form a vibrant, open and cosmopolitan community where the contribution of every child is valued.

Academic record
Mill Hill's primary aim is to provide excellence in education. Pupils are given the opportunity and support to realise their full potential in a range of subjects. Achievement is very high with over 95 per cent of leavers going on to university. Great emphasis is placed on the creative arts, in the context of the curriculum and as part of an extensive activity programme. Music is particularly strong. All pupils are encouraged to participate in competitive and recreational sport.

Boarding facilities
Boarding has always been central to life at Mill Hill. Relationships are easy and informal between house staff, pupils and year groups. Friendships are forged for life. Boarding offers the added attraction of living in the beautiful surroundings of the school estate with open access to all it can offer by way of facilities. A combination of secure country living in close proximity to London is a unique feature of Mill Hill.

Contact: Headmaster, Mill Hill School, The Ridgeway, Mill Hill, London NW7 1QS

Tel: +44 (0)20 8959 1176

Fax: +44 (0)20 8201 0663

Email: registrations@millhill.org.uk

Website: www.millhill.org.uk

Headteacher: William Winfield

Pupils: 610 (462 boys, 148 girls), 430 day, 180 boarding.

Termly fees: £3,488 (day), £5,375 (boarding).

Entrance: at 13 plus and 14 plus is by tests and interviews and a head's confidential reference. Entrance at 16 plus is by interview and school reference and is normally conditional on GCSE performance. Wide range of awards available (particularly music).

Exam results: (2001) GCSE 96 per cent pass rate A* to C, 40 per cent achieved five or more A*/A grades. A level 96 per cent pass rate, top 25 per cent scored equivalent of AAA.

Independent schools

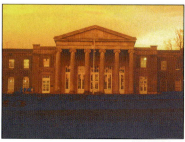

Mill Hill School

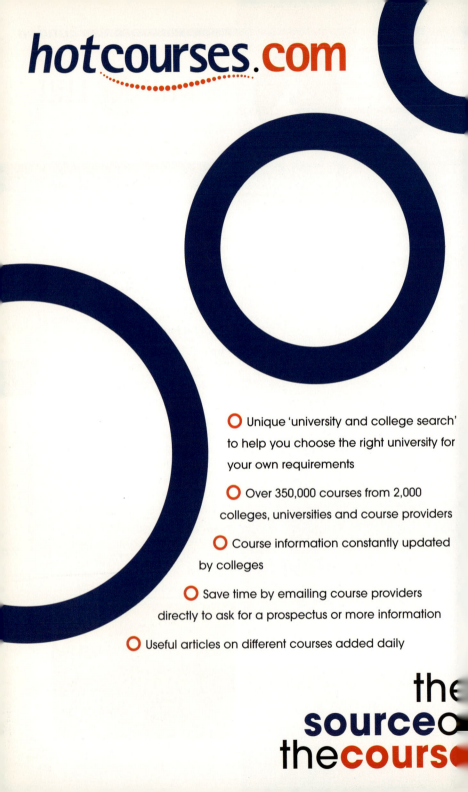

Moira House Girls School

The school

Moira House is situated on the southeast coast, one and a half hours from London. The school enjoys an attractive location overlooking the sea. Moira House was founded in 1875 and has always welcomed girls from across the world. There is a nursery, junior school, senior school and sixth form. Boarders can join from the age of nine. The school pays careful attention to the needs of each individual girl.

Academic record

Although not highly selective, the school has gained excellent results for many years and all girls enter the university of their choice. Increasingly, students are pursuing courses in science, though the school is also known for its strengths in English, drama, languages and excellence in music. The National Curriculum is followed. Teaching groups are small, making for stimulating and inspiring lessons. The school has a wide-ranging activity programme and a well-resourced department to support EFL teaching.

Boarding facilities

Two boarding houses, School House and Boston House, cater for 50 to 60 girls, each in well furnished bedrooms with sitting rooms, computing facilities, kitchens, playing fields and an indoor heated swimming pool. Boston House is the sixth form house where girls enjoy greater independence in preparation for university. School House is home to younger boarders. The girls are looked after by housemistresses, housemothers, nursing sisters, gap-year students and the head of boarding and pastoral care who lives on site with her family.

Contact: Principal, Moira House Girls School, Upper Carlisle Road, Eastbourne, East Sussex BN20 7TE

Tel: +44 (0)1323 644144

Fax: +44 (0)1323 649720

Email: head@moirahouse.co.uk

Website: www.moirahouse.co.uk

Principal: Mrs Ann Harris

Junior school: Mrs Jane Booth-Clibborn

Pupils: 340 girls, 123 boarding (three junior and 120 senior) and 217 day girls.

Termly fees: £1,285 to £3,030 (day); £3,950 to £5,100 (boarding).

Entrance: entrance is dependent on past reports and school decision. Scholarship exams taken with an average of 20 scholarships given per academic year.

Exam results: (2001) AS/A level 94.1 per cent passed, 55.3 per cent with A/B grades, 78.8 per cent A/B/C. GCSE 93.9 per cent achieved A/C grades, 18.6 per cent A* and 50 per cent A.

Moira House Girls School and grounds

Independent schools

Oswestry

Moreton Hall School

Contact: Jonathan Forster,
Moreton Hall School, Oswestry,
Shropshire SY11 3EW

Tel: +44 (0)1691 776020

Fax: +44 (0)1691 778552

Email: forsterj@moretonhall.org

Website: www.moretonhall.org

Pupils: 270 girls; age range eight to 18.

Termly fees: £5,320 (boarding);
£3,655 (day).

Entrance: girls are admitted to the
school at the age of 11, either by
Common Entrance or by the school's
entrance examination, held in January
each year. Sixth-form entrance is
by examination and interview, and
numbers are limited.

Exam results: (2001) A level
grade A 35 per cent, grade A to B 66
per cent, grade A to C 84 per cent,
grade A to E 10 (99 per cent).
GCSE A* and A grades 53 per cent,
A* to C grades 96 per cent.

Moreton Hall School

The school
The new Information Technology
Centre provides internet access both
in classrooms and boarding houses.
There is a well-equipped sports centre
with a sports hall, tennis courts,
nine-hole golf course and playing
fields. The school offers a wide range
of sports including lacrosse, netball,
hockey, cricket, tennis and athletics
as well as a full programme of extra
activities, daily and at weekends. The
girls are given many opportunities to
go on trips such as theatre and concert
visits, adventure programmes and
visits to local towns. The Duke of
Edinburgh Award Scheme is very
popular and Moreton Enterprises, a
sixth-form-managed company, offers
the girls real business experience. A
new radio station and recording studio
were opened in 1997.

Academic record
20 subjects are available at GCSE, from
traditional subjects such as Latin and
the sciences to practical subjects such
as drama and physical education.
Modern languages available include
French, German and Spanish. A levels
in history of art, human biology,
business studies and theatre studies
extend the range of the curriculum.

Boarding facilities
Younger girls are housed under the
supervision of resident housemistresses
and matrons. As pupils progress, the
dormitories are replaced firstly by
double and then by single-study bedrooms. Boarding houses are linked
informally with houses at Shrewsbury
School, pupils meeting regularly for
social and cultural occasions.

Crieff

Morrison's Academy

The school
The school sits in the heart of Scotland in the district of Perthshire. Easily accessible from city airports and rail and bus terminals, the school commands a view of Strathearn to the south and the mountains of the Grampian range to the northwest. Students have a programme of activities and receive membership of the Crieff Hydro Sports Club. Network IT facilities enhance learning and teaching.

Academic record
Morrison's Academy offers art and science courses geared towards university entrance. The school can send students to all British and some American universities, while Scottish Highers provide a one-year course as a fast track to university. Those who prefer to spread their workload over two years can take a combination of Higher Grade with National Units and/or RSA exams. Work experience can be arranged by the school.

Boarding facilities
The school has recently completed a major refurbishment to its residential campus. There are two boarding houses within the Ewanfield campus. Academy House is the home for boys while girls lives with their housemistresses in Dalmhor House. Separate houses provide facilities for private study and relaxation. Boarders share in the social life of the school but also have their own programme of activities. With school and parental permission, senior students make visits to places outside of Crieff.

Contact: Mr I Bendall, Principal, Morrison's Academy, Crieff, Scotland PH7 3AN

Tel: +44 (0)1764 653885

Fax: +44 (0)1764 655411

Email: principal@morrisons.pkc.sch.uk

Website: www.morrions.pkc.sch.uk

Headteacher: Mr I Bendall

Pupils: 520 pupils.

Termly fees: inclusive tuition and accommodation fee £14,520 per annum. Some scholarships available.

Entrance: TOEFL score (500 +) or pass in own test, good school references appropriate to age.

Exam results: Scottish Highers 57 per cent gained three or more passes, 77 per cent secured grades A to C. Standard Grade 96 per cent secured grades 1 to 3. 96 per cent of leavers in 2000 went on to higher education in the UK and abroad.

Independent schools

Morrison's Academy

Oswestry

Oswestry School

Contact: Headmaster, Oswestry School, Upper Brook Street, Oswestry, Shropshire SY11 2TL

Tel: +44 (0)1691 655711

Fax: +44 (0)1691 671194

Email: enquiries@oswestryschool.org.uk

Website: www.oswestryschool.org.uk

Headteacher: Paul Stockdale

Pre-prep department: Mrs Lesley Durham

Pupils: 430; 340 day, 90 boarders (fully co-educational).

Termly fees: from £1,250 to £2,656 (day); £4,454 (boarding).

Entrance: applications to the headmaster. Scholarships, exhibitions and bursaries available.

Oswestry School

The school

Founded in 1407, Oswestry School is Britain's second oldest non-denominational independent school. Set in 50 acres of grounds, the school benefits from a safe, semi-rural position on the edge of the Welsh Marches. The setting allows easy access to the rail system and international airports in Manchester and Birmingham. A modern outlook with respect for old-fashioned values is maintained at the school, which is proud of its warm family atmosphere.

Academic record

The school is non-selective and justifiably proud of its academic record. Its aim is to ensure that each pupil, irrespective of ability, fulfils his or her academic potential. Nearly all sixth formers move on to the university of their choice, including Oxbridge. A wide range of subjects is offered at GCSE and A level. Extracurricular activities include CCF and the Duke of Edinburgh Award Scheme.

Boarding facilities

Boarders are accommodated in one of three houses. School House is for boys aged nine to 16. Holbache House is for boys aged 16 to 18, while Guinevere House is for girls aged nine to 18. There is a separate annexe for sixth formers. Boarders have access to the internet and email facilities. Each house has its own houseparent and assistants or matron. Communication between parents and staff is welcomed and encouraged. A major boarding refurbishment programme has been recently undertaken.

Peterborough

PETERBOROUGH
HIGH SCHOOL

Peterborough High School

The school

Peterborough High School is a GSA day and boarding school for girls aged three to 18 and for boys aged three to 11. The school stands in 10 acres of grounds on the western side of Peterborough, within easy reach of the A1, A47 and the London to Edinburgh mainline railway. It is Peterborough's only independent school. An emphasis is given on individual guidance and target setting and students perform well in the small classes. A wide-ranging curriculum and numerous extracurricular activities lead to high achievement at GCSE in up to 10 subjects and excellent results at A level.

Academic record

Peterborough High School enjoys the reputation of being a centre of excellence for the arts and participation in music, drama and art is strongly encouraged. The school has also achieved considerable success in sporting activities. Senior girls have the opportunity to take part in the Duke of Edinburgh Award Scheme and the Young Enterprise programme.

Boarding facilities

Termly, weekly and flexi-boarding facilities are available. All pupils have access to the excellent facilities which include sports fields, a games hall, library, music rooms, magnificent grounds and a new ICT block. Visitors are always welcome throughout the year and are offered a guided tour of the school. The 2002 open day will be held on 3 October.

Contact: Mrs A Field, Registrar, Peterborough High School, Thorpe Road, Peterborough PE3 6JF

Tel: +44 (0)1733 343357

Fax: +44 (0)1733 355710

Email: phs@peterboroughhigh.peterborough.sch.uk

Website: www.peterboroughhigh.peterborough.sch.uk

Headteacher: Mrs S A Dixon BA (Hons)

Pupils: 345 in total.

Termly fees: September 2001: day £1,186 to £2,050; weekly boarding £3,265 to £3,518; full boarding £3,861 to £4,114; flexi-boarding £17 a night.

Entrance: An entrance examination at year seven must be passed to proceed to the senior school. Academic and music scholarships available for those entering year seven and sixth form.

Exam results: 98.5 per cent at A level, 32 per cent of girls achieving A and A* at GCSE.

Students at Peterborough High School

Independent schools

High Wycombe

Pipers Corner School

Contact: Mrs V M Stattersfield, MA (Oxon), Headmistress, Pipers Corner School, Pipers Lane, Great Kingshill, High Wycombe, Buckinghamshire HP15 6LP

Tel: +44 (0)1494 719800

Fax: +44 (0)1494 719806

Email: pipers@enterprise.net

Website: www.piperscorner.co.uk

Fees: full boarding £10,785 to £12,960; weekly boarding £10,650 to £12,795; day £3,390 to £7,770.

Entrance: sixth form: interview with head, satisfactory GCSE grades. Senior school: examinations in English, mathematics and verbal reasoning, interview, progress report from current school. Prep: assessment of English and mathematics, interview, progress report from current school. Pre-prep: visit with appropriate class.

Exam results: 96 per cent of results at A level were A to E. 99 per cent of results at AS level were A to E. 93 per cent of results at GCSE were A* to C.

Pipers Corner School

The school

Set in 36 acres of the beautiful Chilterns, the spacious campus is only half an hour from Heathrow and less than an hour from London. This independent girls' school caters for 450 girls between the ages of four and 18. Pipers offers both excellent facilities on campus and outstanding opportunities nearby, including the theatres, art galleries and also museums of London, Oxford and Stratford.

Academic record

Pipers is not only for those with academic, artistic or sporting talent who hit the headlines or gain Oxbridge places. It is just as proud of students with average abilities who strive to do their best and achieve more than they had anticipated. There is a wide range of talent and ability amongst the students and each girl is expected to do her best. Every success is valued and, whether a national or purely personal achievement, it is celebrated by other students and staff alike. Pipers offers a combination of personal care with a challenge to every girl to fulfil her potential. Prospective students are welcome to spend a day at the school if requested.

Boarding facilities

Girls may board from the age of eight. Choices include full, weekly and flexible boarding, in which girls move from day to boarding status and back again as their parents' needs change. In boarding, the atmosphere is calm and relaxed, with the emphasis on family values along with friendly, well-ordered supervision. There is also an exciting variety of weekend activities.

York

Queen Ethelburga's College

The school

As soon as you arrive at Queen Ethelburga's College you sense that it is somewhere special, friendly and pleasingly different. The campus is exceptional, with a range and quality of facilities few can equal. Having recently become co-educational, the college is home to girls and boys from age three to 19 years with boarding from age six.

Academic record

Over the last 10 years, £17 million has been invested in new teaching facilities and superb boarding accommodation – probably the best in Europe. Every boarding bedroom has direct dial telephone, voicemail, TV/video (on timer) hot drinks facilities, fridge and much more. Many bedrooms are ensuite. A new £250,000 day centre was recently opened exclusively for day pupils.

Boarding facilities

Boarders can bring their horse or pony to school with free livery. The £3 million Royal Court Equestrian Centre can house 185 horses with an Olympic sized indoor arena, 10 acres of outside all-weather floodlit arenas, three cross country courses and full show facilities.

Each year the College Foundation provides over 100 scholarships, bursaries and riding options worth over £500,000. *The Sunday Times* rates both the junior and the senior school as one of the best in the UK for academic results.

Contact: Head Teacher – Admissions, Queen Ethelburga's College, Thorpe Underwood Hall, York, North Yorkshire YO26 9SS

Tel: +44 (0)8707 423330

Fax: +44 (0)8707 423310

Email: remember@compuserve.com

Website: www.queenethelburga's.edu

Headteacher: Peter Dass

Junior school: Christine Potter

Pupils: junior three to 11 years 150; day 120 (girls 60, boys 60); boarding 30 (girls 15, boys 15); senior 11 to 19 years 250; day 50 (girls 25, boys 25); boarding 200 (girls 150, boys 50).

Termly fees: day £975 to £3,325; boarding £3,695 to £5,425.

Entrance: interview and assessment.

Exam results: junior school: a *Sunday Times* Top UK 100 Preparatory School for Academic Results.

Senior school: a *Sunday Times* Top UK School for GCSE and A level results, 95 per cent of sixth form go on to university.

Independent schools

Queen Ethelberga's College pupils

Newark

Rodney School

Contact: Principal, Rodney School, Kirklington, Newark NG22 8NB

Tel: +44 (0)1636 813281

Fax: +44 (0)1636 813281

Email: rodney@proweb.co.uk

Website: www.rodney-school.co.uk

Principal: Miss G R T Howe

Pupils: day 49 (20 boys, 29 girls); boarding 35 (20 boys, 15 girls).

Termly fees: day prep £1,578; main school £1,872; boarding £3,167; performing arts day prep £1,728; main school £2,022; boarding £3,317.

Entrance: pupils are admitted on the recommendation of their previous school through an interview, a test and school reports. Pupils are accepted in form one (year seven) on the basis of their key stage 2 National Curriculum results, forms two and three (years eight and nine) on their Common Entrance results or key stage levels and into form four (year 10) on their key stage 3 National Curriculum results. For entry into the sixth form, five GCSE passes or equivalent are required.

Kirklington Hall

The school

Rodney School is situated in the village of Kirklington, between Newark and Mansfield on the edge of Sherwood Forest in the north of Nottinghamshire. The M1 and A1 routes are within a short distance and London (Kings Cross Station) is one hour and 20 minutes by train from Newark on the main north/south rail connection. The principal is a member of the Independent Schools Association and the school is accredited by the Independent Schools Council. Rodney is a co-educational boarding and day school for children aged seven plus to 18 years.

Academic record

The academic record is good. At GCSE, 85 per cent of pupils gained five or more subjects graded A* to C in 2001. All those in the sixth form secured the places at university for which they applied. The school is small enough to have a flexible curriculum so that boys and girls may develop their individual talents and interests. A specialist performing arts course is an available option to boys and girls having an interest in this direction.

Boarding facilities

The girls' and boys' dormitories are on different landing levels with an adult on each floor. There is a mixed common room and also separate common rooms for boys and girls where they can relax and watch television. In addition, activities and outings are organised at weekends. Extensive grounds allow for a wide variety of outdoor activities.

London

The Royal School

The school

The school, founded in 1855, is situated in pleasant surroundings 250 metres from Hampstead tube station and Hampstead Village centre. It has modern boarding accommodation and spacious classrooms with views over London. The school has access to excellent sports facilities and its development continues with two newly refurbished science laboratories, upgraded accommodation and a new sixth form study centre with computer work stations and a kitchen. Help with visas is given. The curriculum includes two modern languages plus Latin and three sciences.

Extracurricular activities

There is a wide range of games, sports and activities including the Duke of Edinburgh Award Scheme and Young Enterprise in the sixth form. There is a thriving art and drama department, and over 40 per cent of girls learn a musical instrument. Cultural outings take place regularly to theatres, art galleries and museums. Residential trips are offered to pupils throughout the school, including an annual ski trip for senior pupils.

Boarding facilities

The school offers a homely and friendly environment where boarders thrive. Each new boarder is assigned a 'buddy' who acts as a companion and helper. Communication between parents and staff is welcomed and encouraged. Telephone and email facilities are available. Weekly boarding is a popular option. Flexi-boarding can be arranged when required, as can 'life with local families'.

Contact: Admissions Secretary, The Royal School, 65 Rosslyn Hill, Hampstead, London NW3 5UD

Tel: +44 (0)20 7794 7708

Fax: +44 (0)20 7431 6741

Email: royschham@aol.com

Website: royalschoolhampstead.com

Pupils: 208 (girls only); 158 day, 50 boarders, with low pupil to staff ratios. Age range four to 18 (nursery planned for 2002).

Termly fees: £1,642 to £1,933 (day); £2,553 to £3,195 (weekly board); £3,093 to £3,843 (full board). Flexi-boarding costs dependent on number of nights.

Entrance: junior school: in-class assessment. Senior school: examinations based on National Curriculum (maths and English). Previous school reports required for all pupils. Scholarships/bursaries available.

Caring, happy and friendly

Independent schools

375

ROYAL SCHOOL HASLEMERE

Haslemere

Royal School Haslemere

Contact: Royal School Haslemere, Farnham Lane, Haslemere Surrey GU27 1HQ

Tel: +44 (0)1428 605805

Fax: +44 (0)1428 607451

Email: admissions@royal.surrey.sch.uk

Website: www.royal.surrey.sch.uk

Headteacher: Mrs Lynne Taylor-Gooby BEd, MA

Pupils: three to 18 years, boarding from seven years. Number of pupils enrolled in senior school in 2001: 208. Sixth form: 38. Average class size: 15. Teacher to pupil ratio: 1:8.

Termly fees: September 2001 boarding £3,603 to £4,542; day £1,698 to £2,895.

Entrance: by own entrance papers together with an interview. Academic, PE and performing scholarships are offered.

Royal School Haslemere

The school
Under royal patronage since 1840, the Royal School Haslemere is a registered charity providing high quality education for girls. The school is set in a 30-acre site of beautiful parkland which is only 40 minutes from Heathrow and Gatwick airports and 50 minutes by rail from London.

Academic record
Drawing on a wide ability range, the Royal School Haslemere achieves consistently high grades at GCSE and A level and featured high in the list of top independent schools in London and the southeast. The school has a strong academic tradition and has always believed in enabling all pupils to develop and achieve their potential, as well as placing great emphasis on encouraging girls to become outward looking, independent and considerate to others. Extracurricular activities include dance, music, karate, riding, swimming and the Duke of Edinburgh Award Scheme. Plans are well advanced for the World Challenge Expedition to Peru in 2003.

Boarding facilities
The school offers full, weekly and flexi boarding facilities, with a purpose-built wing. Sensitive pastoral care applies to all girls, both day and boarding, and there is a mentor system for new girls entering the senior school. Private study rooms double as bedrooms, either as single accommodation or shared with one other student. Many sixth formers are boarders, which allows students to take advantage of the extracurricular options.

St Dunstan's Abbey School for Girls

The school

St Dunstan's Abbey School was founded in 1850 by Anglican sisters and was run by religious communities until 1965 when a secular headmistress was appointed. The Christian influence remains evident, both in the buildings and its ethos which lays emphasis on consideration for others. Much of the teaching takes place in buildings which were once the Royal Naval Hospital and at the heart of the school is a chapel with beautiful stained glass.

Academic record

The school prides itself on building self-confidence by emphasising performance. Success in LAMDA examinations supports this ethos. The curriculum reflects traditional subjects and the best of the National Curriculum. Staff are well qualified, pupils motivated and class sizes below those in the maintained sector. There is good support for pupils across the ability spectrum. A sixth form centre attracts a large number of A level students who have a high success rate. As well as getting students to Oxbridge and other respected universities, the school boasts great success with students who are marginal A level candidates.

Boarding facilities

The 40 boarders, from all over the world, form a small family unit enjoying a variety of facilities. The school is within walking distance of Plymouth's shopping and leisure facilities, the historic Plymouth Hoe and Barbican. The picturesque Dartmoor National Park is within close proximity.

Contact: St Dunstan's Abbey School for Girls, The Millfields, Plymouth PL1 3JL

Tel: +44 (0)1752 201350

Fax: +44 (0)1752 201351

Email: info@sda.org.uk

Website: www.sda.org.uk

Pupils: 306.

Termly fees: day £1,253 to £2,099; weekly £2,736 to £3,582; full board £3,230 to 4,076.

Entrance: by school report and interview where appropriate. Scholarship/examinations for senior school and sixth form.

Exam results: (2001) GCSE grades A to C 96.6 per cent; A level grades A to C 88.7 per cent.

St Dunstan's Abbey pupils

Independent schools

377

Chepstow

St John's-on-the-Hill

Contact: St John's-on-the-Hill, Tutshill, Chepstow, Monmouthshire NP16 7LE

Tel: +44 (0)1291 622045

Fax: +44 (0)1291 623932

Email: info@stjohnsonthehill.co.uk

Website: www.stjohnsonthehill.co.uk

Headteacher: I K Etchells BEd

Type of school: co-educational boarding and day.

Pupils: 302 (177 boys, 125 girls). 31 boarding (maximum). Age range two to 13+ years.

Termly fees: £1,406 to £2,350 (day); £3,180 (boarding).

Membership: IAPS, ISCis, BSA.

Building on tradition: creating the future

The school

St John's-on-the-Hill lies in extensive, attractive grounds on the boarder of Monmouthshire and Gloucestershire, overlooking Chepstow Castle and the beautiful Wye Valley. The family atmosphere ensures each child is valued and there is time to cater for the needs of all. A high standard of teaching and small class sizes, combined with first-class facilities, ensure students can develop their academic ability and character to the full. Emphasis is on mutual respect, integrity and the need to discover and develop individual talents, whether they are creative, intellectual or athletic.

Academic record

Children are encouraged to achieve success across the curriculum. Thus sport, music, art and drama are an important part of school life. Scholarships and awards are made for academic, music, sporting and dramatic ability. There is a specialist Learning Support Department and the school welcomes children of all abilities. Children are prepared for entry to a range of leading senior schools. With more than 30 senior scholarships awarded to St John's children in the last two years, the school is proud of its scholarship record and senior school links.

Boarding facilities

Children may board from the age of seven. The family-run boarding house has a friendly, homely atmosphere. A programme of activities and outings is offered to the many boarders who remain at St John's throughout the term. The school is stimulating in its breadth of opportunity, yet personal in its size.

St John's School
Sidmouth Devon UK
Nurturing talent for the future

St John's School

The school

St John's School is one of the very few independent co-education preparatory schools in the southwest. Overlooking the seaside town of Sidmouth, pupils enjoy the safe and invigorating environment of the east Devon coastline as well as a nurturing environment which includes an excellent nursery department offering daycare and holiday sessions.

Academic record

St John's pupils make the most of their abilities in a wide range of areas. Scholarships are regularly won to senior schools and the common entrance record is outstanding. Sporting achievements are excellent with selection to county or district teams at all levels. Pupils are enthusiastic about music and the fine church within the building is an excellent setting for the concerts that pupils give throughout the year.

Boarding facilities

The bright dormitories and bedrooms are situated in the main building. Children share accommodation in small groups and have access to common rooms. The headmaster and his wife live in the school and regard the children as an extension of their own family. They are assisted by an experienced and dedicated team. All children have access to telephone, email and fax. The school is particularly experienced in caring for younger children, many of whom have older brothers and sisters in the school.

Contact: Headmaster, St John's School, Broadway, Sidmouth, Devon EX10 8RG

Tel: +44 (0)1395 513 984

Fax: +44 (0)1395 514 539

Email: nrp@stjohndevon.demon.co.uk

Website: www.st-johns.devon.sch.uk

Headteacher: Neil Pockett
BA DLC CertEd

Pupils: 245; 195 day, (96 boys, 97 girls), 52 boarding (26 girls, 26 boys). Age range from two years (Early Birds daycare nursery) to 13 plus.

Termly fees: £1,244 to £1,890 (day); £3,404 (boarding) with English as a second language and guardianship extra.

Exam results: national curriculum assessments significantly higher than national average over past three years, regular scholarships to senior school. 100 per cent common entrance passes to senior school.

Independent schools

St John's School

Wantage

St Mary's School

Contact: Admissions Registrar, St Mary's School, Wantage, Oxfordshire OX12 8BZ

Tel: +44 (0)1235 773807

Fax: +44 (0)1235 760467

Email: stmarysw@rmplc.co.uk

Website: www.stmarysw.oxon.sch.uk

Headteacher: Mrs Sue Sowden

Pupils: 189 girls, 166 boarding.

Termly fees: £5,475 boarding; £3,650 day.

Entrance: common entrance or own exam. Various scholarships at all age levels. Bursaries for clergy and the forces.

A St Mary's School pupil

School profile

St Mary's School Wantage, was founded in 1873 by William Butler, vicar of Wantage, and run by the sisters of the community of St Mary the Virgin until 1975. Situated in 15 acres of grounds in the centre of this small market town at the foot of the Berkshire Downs, the school is within easy reach of London and major airports via the motorway network. A wireless laptop computer network covers the school. Facilities include an indoor heated pool, tennis courts, a sports hall and a new music school. Major development plans are underway.

Academic record

St Mary's is very proud of its CEM Value Added status. Every subject in recent years has a positive score at GCSE. National results in June 2001 showed that while the average increase of two grades higher than predicted was seven per cent, St Mary's achieved 33 per cent. Only the top five per cent of schools achieved an overall average VA score of 0.6, and St Mary's achieved 1.0 results at A level.

Boarding facilities

Most of the accommodation has been recently refurbished. As girls rise through the school, they progress from shared rooms to single-study bedrooms. The sixth form live in separate houses, where they have their own laundry, kitchens, satellite TV and a new junior common room. This has a coffee bar which serves limited alcohol at week-ends and has a pool table and table soccer. Friends are welcome.

Independent schools

SHERBORNE
SCHOOL
FOR GIRLS

Sherborne School for Girls

The school

Sherborne School for Girls, founded in 1899, is situated in the beautiful Dorset countryside and has always been at the forefront of women's education. It provides a rich environment for the development of confident and committed young women who are determined to make significant, positive contributions to the society in which they live. There is a direct train service from London and a school coach to and from Heathrow at the beginning and end of terms.

Academic record

The school has high academic standards and is particularly famous for its art and music departments. It is also well known for modern languages, mathematics and science and there is a very good ESL department. Over 30 subjects are offered at AS/A level and there are some shared lessons with Sherborne School.

Boarding facilities

Girls who enter the school aged 11 or 12 go into one, mixed-age boarding house. At age 13, girls go into one of eight houses. In their final year, the upper sixth, girls go into Mulliner, a purpose-built house where girls have their own study bedroom. All houses have their own dining facilities. Each girl is issued with her own email address and they are also allowed mobile telephones.

Contact: Registrar, Sherborne School for Girls, Bradford Road, Sherborne, Dorset DT9 3QN

Tel: +44 (0)1935 818287

Fax: +44 (0)1935 389445

Email: enquiry@sherborne.com

Website: www.sherborne.com

Headteacher: Mrs Geraldine Kerton-Johnson BSc, UED

Pupils: 340 (310 boarders, 30 day).

Termly fees: £5,810 (boarding), £4,300 (day).

Entrance: common entrance and own placing papers used.

Exam results: (2001) GCSE 68 per cent gained A*/A grades; 99 per cent A to C. A level 39 per cent gained A grades; 68 per cent A to B.

Sherborne School for Girls

Independent schools

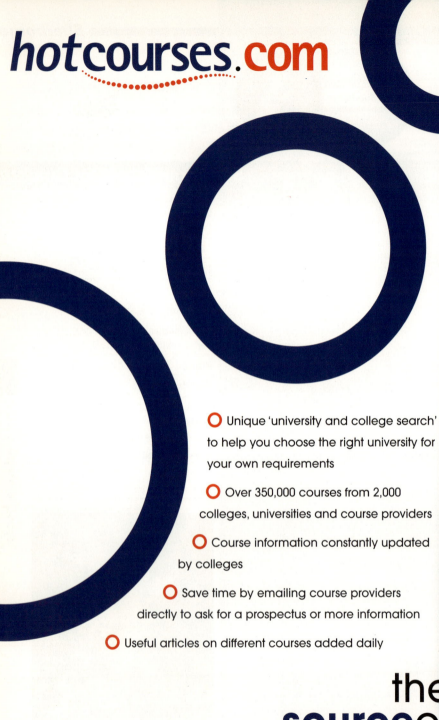

hotcourses.com

○ Unique 'university and college search' to help you choose the right university for your own requirements

○ Over 350,000 courses from 2,000 colleges, universities and course providers

○ Course information constantly updated by colleges

○ Save time by emailing course providers directly to ask for a prospectus or more information

○ Useful articles on different courses added daily

the source of the course

Stamford Endowed School

The school

The school is an integral part of this medieval market town of outstanding beauty. It has excellent road and rail links and first class facilities. The co-educational Junior School, girls from 11 to 18 at Stamford High School and boys from 11 to 18 at Stamford School are all in the same foundation giving continuity of education at the Stamford Endowed Schools for Boys and Girls from two to 18 years. The schools exist to provide quality education for boys and girls.

Academic record

Stamford School offers a wide range of curriculum activities including a full range of GCSE and A level subjects. It has an impressive university entrance, including some pupils going forward to Oxbridge. When students reach sixth form level there is joint class teaching and the average class size throughout the school is 16 to 19 pupils, making the teacher pupil ratio one to 12. The school has exceptionally high standards in the drama and music departments, whilst there is a good range of sporting activities games which includes the Duke of Edinburgh Award Scheme and the large voluntary CCF.

Boarding facilities

There are five boarding houses. The junior pupils are in a co-educational house run on the extended family principle. At senior level, there are two boys houses and two girls houses split by age. Stamford School offers a full weekend programme of activities and so can cater for full, weekly or flexible boarding requirements.

Contact: Stamford Endowed School, St Paul's Street, Stamford, Lincolnshire PE9 2BS

Tel: +44 (0)1780 750310

Fax: +44 (0)1780 750397

Email: ses@stamfordschool.lincs.sch.uk

Website: www.ses.lincs.sch.uk

Principal: Dr P R Mason BSc, PhD, FRSA

Pupils: Stamford Junior School (two to 11 co-educational): 315 (including nursery two to four). Stamford High School (girls): 650. Sixth form: 175. Stamford School (Boys): 650. Sixth form: 175.

Termly fees: day £5,112 to £6,396. Boarding: £10,860 to £12,444.

Entrance: own entrance examination.

Exam results: (2001) girls GCSE pass rate A* to C 99 per cent; A level pass rate 50 per cent A, B grades. Boys GCSE pass rate A* to C 95 per cent; A level pass rate 63 per cent A, B grades.

Stamford Endowed School

Atworth

Stonar School

Contact: Admissions,
Stonar School, Cottles Park,
Atworth, Wiltshire SN12 8NT

Tel: +44 (0)1225 702795/702309

Fax: +44 (0)1225 790830

Email: admissions@stonar.wilts.sch.uk

Website: www.stonar.wilts.sch.uk

Headteacher: Mrs Sue Hopkinson
BA (Oxon)

Junior school: Mrs Barbara Brookes

Pupils: day 224, boarding 176.

Termly fees: day £2,332;
boarding £4,198.

Exam results: GCSE 84 per cent
pass rate A* to C, 33 per cent A* to A;
A levels 99 per cent pass rate A to E,
76 per cent A to C and 37.7 per cent
achieved grade A.

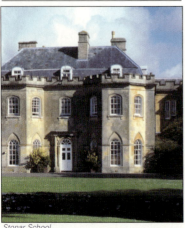

Stonar School

Independent schools

School profile
Stonar is a cheerful, purposeful and
progressive centre of learning for girls,
set in 80 acres of parkland, close to
the heritage city of Bath. The school
develops the abilities of every individual,
providing a breadth of opportunity
to achieve their potential across and
beyond the formal curriculum, while
offering a positive work ethos and quality
pastoral care. Stonar is home to
an internationally-renowned equestrian
centre with opportunities for all, from the
beginner to the ambitious competitor.

Academic record
2001 has seen a 99 per cent pass rate at
A level and 84 per cent pass rate at GCSE.
A talented and committed staff offer
students a broad and flexible curriculum,
offering a wide range of options. Popular
A level courses include psychology,
photography, geology, business studies,
PE and IT. Students go on to university
courses ranging from medicine to
music. Girls of any religion and all
nationalities are welcomed and can
work towards GCSE if English is not their
first language.

Boarding facilities
Girls may board from the age of eight.
Close contact with home through phone,
fax and email and a family atmosphere
at school give the best of both worlds.
Junior and middle school boarders live in
comfortable family style houses and are
guided by the resident housemistress.
Sixth formers enjoy their own purpose-
built college style campus in preparation
for university. A well-equipped medical
centre is staffed by qualified nursing
sisters and doctors.

Tetbury

Westonbirt School

The school

Westonbirt offers academic excellence for all abilities in a happy caring community within a beautiful 250-acre Cotswold setting. Its philosophy is to provide a rounded education. On-site sports facilities include a nine-hole golf course and a heated pool. Music lessons and rehearsals take place in the self-contained Music School while drama is based in the Orangery Theatre. The school is a Church of England foundation with its own historic chapel but also welcomes those of other faiths.

Academic record

Whether academic work comes naturally or needs encouragement, Westonbirt's personal approach will ensure that all girls fulfil their potential. The typical Westonbirt girl passes at least nine GCSEs and three A levels before going on to study for a degree. There is extensive careers advice (Westonbirt is an accredited Investor in Careers) and valuable key skills programmes prepare girls for the world of work.

Boarding facilities

From years seven to 11, pupils share small dormitories in the grade one listed Westonbirt House. In the sixth form house, each girl has a single study bedroom and is encouraged to develop the independence she will require at university. Boarders are cared for by housemistresses and a nurse is always in residence. A lively activity programme ensures boarders are entertained during leisure time. The school provides an escorted travel service to and from airports and major railway stations.

Contact: Mrs Belinda Holley, Registrar, Westonbirt School, Tetbury, Gloucestershire GL8 8QG

Tel: +44 (0)1666 880333

Fax: +44 (0)1666 880364

Email: office@westonbirt.gloucs.sch.uk

Website: www.westonbirt.gloucs.sch.uk

Headteacher: Mrs Mary Henderson MA, PGCE

Pupils: 202 girls aged 11 to 18; full, weekly and flexi-boarding and day.

Termly fees: £3,652 (day), £5,240 (boarding).

Entrance: for 11+ and 13+ entry, Common Entrance or Westonbirt's own entrance examinations; for 16+ entry, a minimum of five GCSEs at A* to C.

Exam results: at A level the pass rate was 97 per cent, with 59 per cent of exams graded A or B. At GCSE the pass rate was 100 per cent, with 93.2 per cent of exams graded A* to C.

Westonbirt School

Independent schools

385

Stonehouse

Wycliffe College

Contact: The Headmaster, Wycliffe College, Stonehouse, Gloucestershire GL10 2JQ

Tel: +44 (0)1453 822432

Fax: +44 (0)1453 827634

Email: senior@wycliffe.co.uk

Website: www.wycliffe.co.uk

Headteacher: Dr R A (Tony)Collins MA, DPhil

Pupils: 425; 144 day (84 boys, 60 girls), 279 boarders (187 boys, 92 girls).

Termly fees: £3,585 to £3,720 (day); £5,100 to £5,505 (boarding); £6,200 (boarding with English as a foreign language).

Entrance: Common Entrance and own exam. Scholarships available for art, academic, music, drama, design and technology and sport. For English development courses, a current school report together with a headteacher's reference is required.

Exam results: (2001) GCSE 37 per cent A*/A grades, 91 per cent A to C grades; at A level 48 per cent A/B grades and 96 per cent pass A to E.

Wycliffe College

The school

Wycliffe aims to educate and develop young people who are confident and capable of dealing with the challenges that lie ahead of them in a fast-changing world. The excellent sports facilities include a new astroturf pitch and plans for the near future include a sports hall and swimming pool. The ICT facilities are superb with interactive white boards and online learning available.

Academic record

With a focus on individual learning, the excellent facilities and enthusiasm of the staff inspire academic achievement and a commitment to lifelong learning. In 2001, the A level pass was over 96 per cent, with 48 per cent at grades A and B; at GCSE the pass rate was over 90 per cent with 38 per cent of A* and A grades. At the junior school, results at key stages 1 and 2 are well above the national average. A varied range of subjects is available at A level; all the traditional disciplines are offered as well as more modern subjects such as sports studies, theatre studies and psychology.

There is a strong musical tradition at Wycliffe with an outstanding team of 18 visiting instrumental teachers. The drama department is also very active. As well as staging first-class productions at the college, the department recently performed a cycle of mystery plays in Prague and Ostrov in the Czech Republic.

Boarding facilities

Wycliffe's facilities are excellent and include boarding houses with en-suite study bedrooms for sixth form, a dining hall and conference centre and a state-of-the-art, 300-seat performing arts centre.

Specialist, vocational and further education colleges

This section contains information on a number of colleges of further education in Britain. Further education colleges allow students to choose from a range of non-degree courses, often including more vocational programmes. As well as covering these colleges, we have also included the details of various specialist and vocational institutions. These colleges are those which specialise in particular subjects and, as such, they may or may not offer degree courses. The type of course available largely depends on the institution, so it is worth contacting the colleges themselves to find out whether the courses on offer suit your needs. Should you wish to take your studies to a higher level, it is worth checking that the qualification you will be awarded will be accepted by the relevant institution.

Write to: the contact details given here are generally those of the international office.

Tel: this is written as if dialled from outside the UK.

Website: these omit the prefix 'http://'.

Students: student numbers include both undergraduates and postgraduates followed by a breakdown into postgraduate and international student numbers.

Accommodation: this section refers to types of residence available at the university or college, including the possibility of staying in married or family flats or rooms, or in single-sex accommodation. Single sex is usually taken to mean female only, and this may include instances whereby male and female students occupy different floors in a hall of residence. This section also states whether students can stay in rooms during vacations, whether there is an additional charge on the normal rates and whether there are storage facilities for students' luggage. Prices for university/college/institute residences generally include heating, water, electricity and cleaning costs. Prices for rooms in town generally exclude all additional costs.

Entrance requirements: these are included as an approximate guide only; grades required will vary according to the subject. Applications are assessed individually and those from students with more unusual qualifications/ backgrounds are usually considered.

EFL: this refers to the various qualifications available in English as a foreign language. Only the minimum grade is given, you might need a higher standard of English for particular subjects such as English literature, law or medicine, so check with the institution.

Foundation: foundation courses are available at many institutions and are intended to bring students up to the required entrance level for a degree course. This section includes specific subjects available alongside study skills and English language classes. If completed successfully, some courses guarantee students a place on a degree programme at the university or college. Also see 'The British Education System' section on page 25 and contact the international office.

Fees: all prices given for accommodation and fees are supplied by the institutions at time of publication and may change.

Babel Technical College
www.babeltech.ac.uk

London

Babel Technical College

Write to: The Principal, Babel Technical College, David Game House
69 Notting Hill Gate, London W11 3JS

Tel: +44 (0)20 7221 1483

Fax: +44 (0)20 7243 1730

Email: info@babeltech.ac.uk

Website: www.babeltech.ac.uk

Students: 200 full and part time in 2000/01.

Accommodation: self-catering single rooms from £110 a week, shared from £85 a week.

Entrance requirements: GCSE or equivalent secondary education. Mature students without such qualifications may be admitted on a case-by-case basis. Depending on the course chosen, some previous IT experience may be required.

EFL: a reasonable command of English. EFL classes can be arranged for students on a foundation computing and English course.

Minimum age: 16+. Younger students may be considered on an individual basis.

Fees: full-time, one-year course from £5,410; full-time, six-month from £3,480; full-time, three-month £1,740. A registration fee of £100 is additional.

Babel Technical College in London

Student profile

"About a year ago, I decided I wanted to go to a technical college where I could educate myself in IT. I wanted to stay in Europe and study in English. I found Babel Technical College on the internet and liked what they were offering. I wanted to commit myself to a year of study and get a Diploma in Networking and Programming, which Babel could give me. The school has a great location in London. Babel is cosmopolitan and each class has a small number of people. The tutors are very nice, informative and smart with great teaching skills, so they are always offering help. Until last year,

I was studying drama so computing is quite a challenge. I enjoy living in London and the staff at Babel make my experience truly wonderful."

Monica Kotyzovia, Czech Republic

Specialist and vocational

388

Established in 1984, the college focuses on computing and information technology and offers a range of practical, vocational, professional and academic courses. Babel Technical College is an associate of the David Game College Group and is uniquely placed to offer IT courses in conjunction with a wide range of academic, business and language courses. International students make up 45 per cent of the student population. Babel has delivered training for many company delegates including household names like the BBC and Disney.

Academic strengths

Each student follows a structured course in an informal atmosphere, combining lectures and lab work. The average group size is seven or eight students. At least half of class contact time is devoted to supervised workshops in computer laboratories. Students are encouraged to use lab rooms outside of class to complete coursework assignments. Most individual modules lead to external certifications from UK and industry-recognised bodies, as well as to various diplomas and advanced diplomas.

The main course areas are programming, web design and development, networking, data processing and information systems, and business IT with generic computer applications, which lead to certificates, diplomas and advanced diplomas. Modules offering skills in a wide selection of software packages are available, such as bitmap and vector graphics, two and three-dimensional CAD, 3D modelling or animation, computerised account or payroll, desktop publishing, web authoring and animation.

Programming students learn Windows programming with Visual Basic and object-oriented programming in Java.

Web technology training includes client-side coding and design of graphics and animation, fundamental programming, databases and the use of servers to deliver dynamic content from online databases.

Babel Technical College is a Cisco Networking Academy, offering the Cisco moderated CCNA programme, with a networking laboratory equipped with routers, switches and hubs. This forms the core of the full-time networking advanced diploma course. The ever-growing importance of the internet and its technologies make it essential for IT professionals to understand the technology of TCP/IP and the design and support of TCP/IP networks.

For beginners to IT and computing, there are foundation courses available which may optionally be combined with English language training.

Student life

Babel Technical College is part of the academic community of the David Game College Group at David Game House, with facilities including a student common room and extracurricular activities such as sports. Group activities, for example trips to Europe, are regular features of the social programmes.

David Game House is situated in the centre of Notting Hill, within walking distance of Kensington Gardens, Hyde Park and the shops of High Street Kensington and Portobello Market. Similarly, it is also near to London's main attractions including Knightsbridge, Oxford Street, the Houses of Parliament and Buckingham Palace.

Specialist and vocational

London

Computing and Business College

Write to: Admissions Department, Metropolitan Business Centre, Suite B010, Enfield Road, London N1 5AZ

Tel: +44 (0)20 7923 7466

Fax: +44 (0)20 7249 0500

Email: cbcedu@aol.com

Website: currently under construction, will be provisionally online January 2002. Contact college for further details.

Students: 500 students; 70 per cent international.

Accommodation: the college will provide help and advice in finding accommodation for international students.

Entrance requirements: no formal entrance requirements but students are expected to be proficient in English and must be over 16 years old. Some individual courses will have specific entrance requirements although, at times, work experience can be taken into account.

EFL: students are expected to have O level English.

Fees: vary according to the specific course and the course duration. Please contact the college for more details.

Travel and tourism class in session

Student profile

Irene Ilnytska enrolled with the college in the academic year 1999/2000 where she successfully completed a Secretarial Diploma of the London Chamber of Commerce and Industry (LCCI). She is currently pursuing a Business Administration course with the Association of Business Executives (ABE). Irene admits that her success emanated from the welcoming, friendly educational environment, excellent teaching and learning resources and a student-focused culture at the college. She maintains that the course content was relevant and career orientated and  *that the diversity of courses created an opportunity to enhance career prospects, as did the development of teaching and learning resources.*

Irene Ilnytska, Ukraine

Computing and Business College is an independent institution, specialising in the delivery of vocational, professional and academic education programmes, designed to meet the needs of many people seeking to pursue different careers. The college is relatively small but very friendly and aims to achieve high pass rates in all areas of its varied programmes. Students are encouraged to attend all lessons and to engage in further research to broaden their knowledge in order to cope with the demands of the business world once they have completed their courses. The college provides a career advice service to all students and potential students offering guidance for those who are unsure of which career path to follow.

Academic strengths

The college tries to ensure that programmes are of great value to students and other participants and should lead to the development of the societies in which graduates live and to the enhancement of individual career prospects.

Many of the courses offered stand alone and are terminal qualifications in their own right. However, most professional bodies which students train for have specific arrangements with universities so that those who complete them can continue at university at an undergraduate or postgraduate level. These include the Chartered Institute of Marketing (CIM), the Association of Accounting Technicians (AAT), the Association of Computer Professionals (ACP) and the Chartered Association of Certified Accountants (ACCA). Courses can vary in length from six to 18 months. Short training packages lasting two weeks are also available.

Registered full-time students of the college who need to improve their communication skills are able to attend extra English classes free of charge. The college provides library services which are open to all students. The college's students may also become members of large public libraries within walking distance of the college itself.

The college offers up-to-date computer facilities allowing students to attend workshops on computing operations plus intensive practical classes to enhance their computing knowledge. There are courses which run in the evening and there are also some which run at weekends. Students who have already registered full time can attend these classes at a special discounted fee.

Student life

Computing and Business College is in an ideal location near all the important East End areas of London with easy access to the city and all entertainment centres. The college is situated near Liverpool Street tube station and is a five-minute walk from the Dalston/Kingsland British Rail station. A number of buses run along the Kingsland Road and all stop outside the premises. The college uses Britannia Leisure Centre and various sports are organised in the centre. It has modern sports equipment and is situated roughly five minutes' walk from the college.

Students are allowed to take up part-time employment in the UK and the college will assist students with advice on the best way to go about this process. In the same way, students can gain assistance with the renewal of their visa through the college registrar.

Specialist and vocational

London

Huron University USA in London

Write to: Rob Atkinson,
Director of Admissions,
Huron University USA in London,
58 Princes Gate, London SW7 2PG

Tel: +44 (0)20 7584 9696

Fax: +44 (0)20 7589 9406

Email: admissions@huron.ac.uk

Website: www.huron.ac.uk

Students: 300 from 55 countries.

Accommodation: guaranteed
to all new students. University
residence within walking distance of
campus from £106 a week.

Entrance requirements: American
High School Diploma or equivalent high
school certificate.

Fees: undergraduate and
postgraduate approximately £8,500;
MBA approximately £10,500.
Payment can be made in instalments.
Scholarships available for up to 30 per
cent of the tuition fee.

Students at Huron University USA in London

Student profile

"I am a studio arts major with a desire to concentrate on interior design. Printing has been an excellent course to take. The atmosphere at Huron is great. It is small so everyone knows each other. It is easy to make friends at events like the welcome party each semester. I am on the yearbook committee this year and a member of the African Club. Huron is different to other universities as classes are small so there is a large degree of personal attention. This makes a better learning environment with more opportunities. As an art student, London is a resource of opportunity to study from

the masters and view originals. The number of galleries and exhibitions is amazing. I think these would delight any student, not just those in the fine arts."

Mashael Ali, Bahrain

Specialist and vocational

Huron University USA in London is an American university located in central London. Accredited in the USA, UK and Europe, the university offers a variety of four-year US bachelor degrees, a 12-month master's degree in international relations and an MBA. The campus is located in the prestigious South Kensington district of central London. Currently, there are 300 students from 55 countries. All of the programmes at Huron have start dates in January, May or September and the advanced standing available to International Baccalaureate, Advanced Programs and A level students means that you could graduate from a bachelor degree in three years. Huron class sizes are an average of 14 students and there is a student to professor ratio of only 12 to one.

Academic strengths

Practical skills and experience are necessary to prepare students for the workplace. Opportunities for internships and work experience are available to students on all courses at Huron University. Consequently, all students undertake practical work experience as part of their course with one of nearly 1,000 partner employers in London. Recent internships have been undertaken at Arthur Andersen, BBC, CNN, Coca-Cola, HSBC, United Nations, European Commission and KPMG, amongst many others. Huron graduates are successful in their chosen fields because they gain professional skills and business contacts while studying. The website demonstrates some examples of what Huron graduates are doing today.

Because Huron offers an American style education, the degrees are very flexible and students are able to tailor courses to their own interests. As such, they are also able to study a wide variety of subjects before finally deciding upon their chosen subject specialism.

Since Huron is a small university with small class sizes, students are able to discuss what they have learned in the classroom with their tutors. Every student is allocated an adviser to help them plan their study. Huron teachers make the most of the central London location by using London's museums, galleries, theatres, concert halls, business premises and just about everything else as extensions of the university.

Student life

Accommodation is guaranteed for new students in centrally located halls of residence, all within walking distance of the campus. The halls of residence offer computing facilities including internet access and there is a residence life manager and two assistants in the halls to look after the students' welfare. Through agreements with neighbouring universities and institutions, students can choose to access extensive libraries and social and sporting facilities including many student clubs and societies.

Most classes have at least eight nationalities represented; students live and work alongside their international classmates. This is very important for most students. Once they have joined the Huron family, they become part of an extensive global network.

There is also the opportunity for students to spend a semester at partner universities in one of 20 countries including the USA.

Specialist and vocational

London

International University of America

Write to: Sahil Aashuri, Management Education Resource Centre, International University of America, Temple Chambers, Temple Avenue, City of London EC4Y 0HP

Tel: +44 (0)20 7353 7700

Fax: +44 (0)20 7353 7722

Email: info@merc-iua.ac.uk

Website: www.merc-iua.ac.uk

Students: 130 London campus (postgraduate 70; undergraduate 30; diploma 30), male:female 70:30.

Accommodation: within five-mile radius. Single and double room £65 a head, a week.

Entrance requirements: good high school grades or equivalent for diplomas and undergraduate. Good degree for postgraduate entrance.

EFL: competence level including oral English; TOEFL 550, IELTS 6.0.

Foundation: available.

Fees: diploma £3,000; undergraduate £3,900; postgraduate £4,900; short courses from £350 per semester. Limited partial scholarships available.

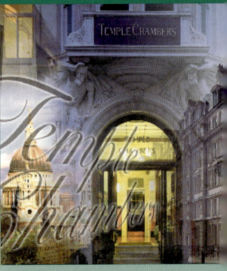

Student profile

"I came to London because I wanted a change of career from being a Russian musicologist to an international lawyer in commercial practice. I decided to study at IUA because of its good track record in business education and legal studies. Its ideal location within the city of London and its close proximity to the Inns of Court is of great appeal to me. Above all, its friendly environment and caring lecturers make you feel like you belong to a family away from home."

Albina Alexandrovna Kostrova, Russi

The International University of America (IUA) in London was founded and incorporated as a degree granting university in California in 1980. For the last seven years in London, IUA has brought international students and faculty together in an effort to promote Anglo-American-style international business management and law in Britain. IUA is an independent, co-educational, business and liberal arts international institution of higher learning. Its sister institution is the Management Education Resource Centre (MERC), incorporated in England and Wales in July 1995 to offer British-style business education. IUA is located in an extraordinary setting in the City of London. Its small campus inhabits one of London's most charming neighbourhoods.

IUA is literally next to the legal profession of the Inns of Court where law students gain a close feel for the legal atmosphere and how the profession works. IUA is surrounded by world-renowned global corporations such as KPMG, J P Morgan, Reuters, Unilever, BP and BAT. Students thus have first-hand experience of the workings of corporate finance and banking in the nation's foremost international nerve centre.

Academic strengths

IUA's mission is to provide its students with a highly professional environment, a strong foundation of knowledge and experience with which to further their careers in the international business arena.

The wide-ranging management programs of IUA are innovative, integrative and flexible. In London, IUA offers degree and diploma programmes focusing specifically on international business in an Anglo-American context. The focus of education is that students should graduate with an ability to be effective and efficient future business leaders. Almost all IUA faculty members have first-hand experience with US and UK higher education and are sympathetic to foreign students. They bring with them a range of experience in both business and academia.

Some IUA students are sponsored by their own governments, such as Gabon and Mongolia, to study at IUA. Such international recognition is largely due to IUA's past students whose performance in the workplace is admirable.

Student life

With a student body representing some 17 countries, IUA students are immersed in a culturally rich and diverse environment. In an effort to create professional and academic contacts to complement studies, students are encouraged to participate in the Associated Students of the International University of America (ASIUA) so as to expand their personal interests. This student government has input on university policy while organising educational and social functions.

Numerous sporting interests can be pursued in the city. IUA also has corporate membership in Espree, a sports club located within the immediate vicinity. Public and private recreational facilities open to students include swimming pools, tennis courts, gymnasiums and parks. Students can also enjoy access to the museums, the Tower of London, river cruises, a floating restaurant and café, Millennium ride and the Houses of Parliament along the River Thames and nearby the university.

Specialist and vocational

LONDON CAPITAL COMPUTER COLLEGE

London Capital College, Registered Office: 38 King Street, Covent Garden,
LONDON WC2E 8JT
Tel: 0171 240 2124   Fax: 0171 240 1991

London

London Capital Computer College

Write to: Mable St Germain,
London Capital Computer College,
38 King Street, Covent Garden,
London WC2E 7BB

Tel: +44 (0)20 7240 2124

Fax: +44 (0)20 7240 1991

Email:
college@lcccollege.freeserve.co.uk

Website:
www.londoncomputercollege.co.uk

Accommodation: the college
has arrangements with a selection
of private landlords who provide
quality residences.

Entrance: three intakes a year.
January, June and September for
certificate and diploma courses.
Advanced diploma courses commence
every September. Intake dependent on
interview and level of education.

Fees: the course fees vary but all
prices include study manuals, practice
equipment and availability of tutors.

London Capital Computer College

Student profile

"Whilst studying my A levels in Uganda,
my tutors recommended me to the
London Capital Computer College in
London. I find the business course
challenging but interesting because
of the wonderful lecturer who I find
so motivating. My aim is to work as a
business administrator in an international
company. Currently, we are completing
our assignments and studying for
our exams. The LCCC is a hospitable
college which has a fantastic study
environment and friendly students. The
college has reasonable fees and a very

central location. LCCC
is also easily accessi-
ble to London's major
museums and enter-
tainment. I am looking
forward to studying
for the two years of
my course."

Lydia Nalugwa, Uganda

London Capital Computer College (LCCC) works strictly to the belief that the student should come first. It has a record of producing good quality, well trained and qualified personnel and is proud of having such a reputation. The excellent relationships between staff and students create an atmosphere which is conducive to good learning – something which is undoubtedly reflected in the examinations pass rate.

Many international students are attracted to the college because of the quality of teaching, small class sizes, personal attention, easy accessibility from public transport, good equipment and for the support offered. All students are given help not only when settling in but also throughout their time at the college and a member of staff meets all international students at the airport upon arrival, if required.

Academic strengths

LCCC is an independent college offering courses in computing and in business administration. Full-time courses are two years in duration while the part-time courses are three to four months. The full-time courses are structured to enable students to start at certificate level and, on completion of an advanced diploma after two years, to allow them to proceed to university for their third year to undertake a conversion course for an MSc. Part-time courses are geared for students who wish to upgrade their computer knowledge in the many different spheres available, for example web designing, networking and programming, giving them a professional qualification to be able to seek good positions in the real world.

Qualifications are obtained from courses with written exams and project work. Students enjoy their studies with the college and most of them continue on to enjoy life at university for their MSc/MBA qualifications.

Corporate training can be arranged at the college or at a company venue.

Student life

The college helps students with opening bank accounts, getting National Insurance numbers to help them get part-time jobs, obtaining international student discount cards and by giving all the information necessary regarding their well-being during their stay in the UK. The college is registered with the London underground and buses for students to obtain photo cards for discounted travel within the Greater London area. All students are encouraged to join the students union where they can become involved in more social activities and entertainment.

Covent Garden, in central London, makes for an excellent location for the college. The balcony overlooks the famous Covent Garden market and thus students have a wealth of opportunity for shopping, eating out, sports clubs, pubs and nightclubs as well as more classic places such as the Royal Opera House, art galleries and museums. The countryside and coastal towns are within easy reach by coach or train if students wish to escape from the bustle of city life for a couple of days. There is an African restaurant and bar in the building as well as numerous bookshops in the vicinity.

London

London Executive Schools (The London Campus of the Irish International University)

Write to: The Administration Officer,
5 Westminster Bridge Road,
London SE1 7XW

Tel: +44 (0)20 7620 0334

Fax: +44 (0)20 7620 0092

Email: info@esbca.co.uk

Website: www.esbca.co.uk

Students: 150 international,
male:female 60:40.

Accommodation: the college helps students to find accommodation through accommodation agencies and private landlords, from £50 a week.

Entrance requirements: application form and curriculum vitae with a letter of recommendation plus two A levels or three years' work experience for those without formal qualifications who may apply on a mature basis for relevant details.

EFL: competence in written and spoken English. Summer pre-sessional English courses available.

Fees: affordable to accommodate all candidates from developing economies; fees range depending on course length from £1,995 bachelor level a year to £4,950 doctorate level a year.

London Executive School

Specialist and vocational

Student profile

"The courses at LESL are designed for busy individuals like myself, who are keen to improve their status with professional qualifications. They are also designed for overseas students to follow postgraduate studies at an affordable course cost. To this effect, my MBA was awarded on the completion of an assignment and an oral examination, which I could not have completed back home. My assignment was assessed and validated by Chris Thomas Consortium London, who are

the validator for the Irish International University. The qualification has enabled me to enrol on to the PhD at the on-campus school."

D K Shahi, Nepal

398

London Executive Schools (LESL), situated in the centre of London, is limited by guarantee as a non-profit educational institution. Its associate school is the London School of Law (LSL) which has been established for over 10 years and is the external tutorial centre for the University of London. LESL is also the London campus for Irish International University (IIU) and is a tutorial and internal examination centre for UK-accredited professional bodies such as The Business Management Association (BMA), the Society of Sales and Marketing (SSM), The Faculty of Certified Business Management Accountants (FCBMA) and the Association of Computer and Operation Management (ACOM). Chris Thomas Consortium London (CCL) is an accrediting educational institution and is the main assessor and examiner for LESL and LSL.

LESL, in association with CCL, conducts management-related seminars and jointly awards certificates and diplomas to successful candidates. These awards form the basis for professional membership and act as credit units towards the professional degree study programme of the IIU. The main aim of LESL and LSL is to provide the opportunity for candidates ranging from school leavers to mature students to obtain professional degree qualification. LESL tries to ensure that its course fees are affordable to all potential students, especially those coming from developing economies. Enrolment takes place three times a year to suit all applicants.

Academic strengths

LESL offers four main courses: Business Management, Sales and Marketing Management, Information Technology Management and Law Management. All courses are available at diploma, bachelor, master and doctorate levels. Syllabus and teaching methodology are structured to assist the integration of theory and practical into related business operations. The school's tutors and professors endeavour to equip students with the skills necessary to meet the demands of today's international business and management challenges and with the tools for resolving learning problems. Continuous assessments are carried out during the study period to monitor progress and development. The study plan is designed to maximise the time available through assignments, locally-held workshops, seminars and work-based projects.

Students are offered advice on their choice of course and guidance in their future career. The school is able to assist in finding suitable accommodation; once students have completed their registration, accommodation can be arranged with private landlords on request. An airport pick-up service from Heathrow and Gatwick airports can be arranged.

Student life

Students are able to take advantage of LESL's close proximity to popular tourist and entertainment attractions such as The London Eye, the Houses of Parliament, The Old Vic theatre and the Imperial War Museum. Waterloo International railway station is also close by with its numerous services to the rest of Europe. The school is part of the Transport for London scheme meaning that students receive a 30 percent discount on buses, the underground and DLR. The school has associate membership of the National Union of Students – the NUS card entitles students to discounts on a wide range of products and cheap entry to various clubs, theatres and museums.

London

The London Institute of Technology and English

Write to: The London Institute of Technology and English, LITE Piccadilly, 1 Sherwood Street, Piccadilly, London W1V 7RA

Tel: +44 (0)20 7439 2226

Fax: +44 (0)20 7439 2240

Email: litepiccadilly@btconnect.com or litecamden@btconnect.com

Website: www.litetraining.co.uk

Accommodation: organised by the international department: Let's Go UK, 74 Wells Street, London W1P Tel: +44 (0)20 7637 0081 Email: letsgo2uk@yahoo.co.uk

Entrance requirements: A level test is taken on enrolment into the large college.

Fees: vary according to course; English 12-month course £700 or nine months £550.

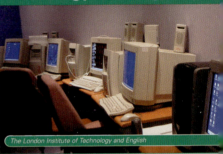

The London Institute of Technology and English

Specialist and vocational

Student profile

"I have been in London for eight months and at first it was difficult for me to adapt. There are many different cultures in London to see and experience – it is quite different to my hometown in the former Yugoslavia. After a few months here I began studying English and computing at LITE in Piccadilly and finding my way around has become much easier. The teachers are enthusiastic and helpful. The English class is great because we learn things that we can use in everyday life. I have found that after only a few months on this course I have obtained the necessary skills to communicate in an  efficient manner with English-speaking people. My experience in London has been constructive and will help me in my future career in journalism."

Margareta Vidic,

The former Yugoslavia

The London Institute of Technology and English (or LITE) is one of the leading schools for foreign learners in London. Throughout its many years of teaching experience, it has developed teaching excellence, building on its young and dynamic staff.

The institute is located in Camden Town in north London, Piccadilly in central London and Prague in the Czech Republic. The Camden campus, situated near the world-renowned market and Camden Lock, is ideal for students who prefer an intimate environment away from the busy London atmosphere. Convenient tube transport is virtually next door.

The Piccadilly Circus campus, housing some 1,500 students, is perfect for those who want to be in the thick of things. The excellent location attracts an international community. As well as LITE's Prague campus, further expansion in other European countries is being considered.

Academic strengths

LITE's experience in offering courses in English from beginners to proficiency, following the Cambridge syllabus is well established. Once mastered to an adequate level, studies can be supplemented by numerous courses which can be combined to achieve the desired skills.

LITE computing courses are taught using the latest technology in a comfortable environment. LITE offers ASDL/ISDN web browsing facilities, which ensure the highest speed when using the internet. The travel and tourism course and hotel and management studies allow students from abroad to return home and work in the tourist industry.

Whichever country a student comes from, or whatever level of English they possess, LITE aims to offer a course to suit their needs in order to help them further their career potential.

Student life

From Brazil to Japan, Korea to Croatia and Colombia to Poland, the cultural mix has helped LITE grow into something of an international centre, where all nationalities feel welcome. As well as this, LITE has professional, fully-trained and friendly staff, who endeavour to make every student's stay the most enjoyable and beneficial experience of their lives.

Although LITE's accomplished approach is one reason for its popularity among foreign learners, the institution maintains that it is the students who have brought something unique to the school, as they have travelled from literally every corner of the globe to further their education with the institution.

LITE's London campuses are all situated in central, easy-to-reach places in the capital. The institution's student services, like the 'Let's Go' department, help students to find accommodation throughout the city. The work placement programme aims to provide students with expert advice. Regular social events are run, from theme nights at world famous nightclubs to popular tourist attractions, day trips to regions outside the capital and educational visits to museums, castles and art galleries.

The institute has recently added a student social centre – an area where students can meet, enjoy themselves and share their experiences. The centre is equipped with free email and internet facilities so that students are able to contact home.

Specialist and vocational

London

London School of Business Administration

Write to: Admissions, London School of Business Administration, 10 Cleveland Way, London E1 4TR

Tel: +44 (0)20 7423 9000

Fax: +44 (0)20 7790 6363

Email: admissions@lsba.org.uk

Website: www.lsba.org.uk

Students: international students.

Accommodation: please contact the school for more information.

Entrance requirements: three GCSE passes and A level passes or equivalent for degree courses; for master's level, a degree pass.

EFL: LSBA proficiency levels 1, 2 and 3.

Fees: £2,745 a year for degree and master's levels.

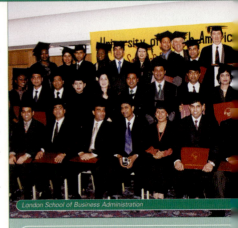

London School of Business Administration

Student profile

"Getting a good degree was very important to me. I have ambition and I always want the best. The decision was not whether to do MBA or not but where to do it and I can safely say that I have chosen the right college. I have found that the LSBA provides the MBA programme in an intellectual and interesting way, the classes are very interactive and stimulating and I am pleased with my choice. The location is also good; it  is very close to the city and the nightlife, which I enjoy. Overall, London is a great place to be."

Gulay Akbas, Turkey

The London School of Business Administration (LSBA) is a private establishment, based near the city of London, one of the world's leading financial centres. The school aims to deliver a highly structured education. The degree programmes have been designed to suit the needs of modern business and industry as well as of the students themselves. The school recognises that international competitiveness now depends on skillful and well-trained managers who can shape the direction and success of an organisation. Its aim is to make and shape the managers and business leaders of tomorrow.

Academic strengths

The LSBA offers an MBA programme to prepare business professionals for the challenges of the rapidly-changing market place. The MBA integrates academic theory with practical experience. It aims to provide students with the knowledge, experience and skills necessary to become leaders in business and industry. The school offers a range of other courses, such as BBA, MSc and BSc programmes which take into consideration the academic background and skills of overseas students. These courses aim to give students the opportunity to enhance their decision-making and problem-solving skills, and to build up an understanding of the way in which companies and organisations operate around the world.

LSBA offers a range of English language courses for international students at various levels. The classes are taught in small, friendly groups by experienced teaching staff. They are designed to help improve students' speaking, listening, reading and writing skills in English, and to assist their ability to study in English.

The school provides research degrees in business, computer science and the social sciences. Students are allocated a supervisor who advises and assists them in their research. In later years, students concentrate on a thesis and are regularly monitored by a thesis committee, interviewing candidates on an annual basis.

LSBA aims to give its students in-depth knowledge of the theory and application of information technology through a bachelor and master's degree in computer science. The information technology diploma is available to students who have a basic knowledge of computers and wish to study these subjects further or to undertake the BSc in Computer Science.

The LSBA Diploma in Business Administration provides students with an inter-disciplinary introduction to the study of management. This programme gives them the opportunity to enhance their knowledge and to develop analytical skills in key areas of management. Students studying this degree are entitled to go on to study for the BSc in Business Administration.

Student life

The school is situated in the East End, a multicultural area of London renowned for its street markets, pubs, restaurants and clubs. The East End also has parks, canalside walks, riding and water sports in the docks on the River Thames. Columbia Road Flower Market attracts visitors from all over London, as do exhibitions at the Chisenhale and Whitechapel art galleries and the Museum of Childhood in Bethnal Green, a branch of the Victoria and Albert Museum.

Specialist and vocational

London

Schiller International University

Write to: Admissions Office, Schiller International University, Royal Waterloo House, 51-55 Waterloo Road, London SE1 8TX

Tel: +44 (0)20 7928 8484

Fax: +44 (0)20 7620 1226

Email: admissions@schillerlondon.ac.uk

Website: www.schillerlondon.ac.uk

Students: 275 students at the London campus.

Accommodation: full board double and single rooms at the university campus. Accommodation officer available to give help and support.

EFL: for undergraduate programmes TOEFL 500 (173 in computer-based tests); graduate programmes TOEFL 550 (213 in computer-based tests).

Entrance requirements: five GCE O levels at grade C or higher or high school/secondary school certificate (showing graduation at 12th grade) or equivalent qualification. For graduate programmes, bachelors degree or equivalent with a major in the graduate area of interest.

Fees: undergraduate courses £8,450 a year (two semesters); graduate courses £10,810 a year (one academic year).

Specialist and vocational

Graduates of Schiller International University

Student profile

"I wanted to pursue a degree in hotel and tourism management and Schiller was recommended by a friend for its wide range of specialisations in this area. In the hotel area, studying in different countries is not only desirable, it is a necessity, so Schiller was the obvious choice for me. I started my degree at the German campus and then transferred to London, as I had always wanted to live in this city. What I value most at Schiller is its international atmosphere with students coming from more than 50 countries. The classroom is where our learning begins but the real education comes  from the interaction with the multicultural student body. Living in London is a very exciting experience and I am making great friends as well!"

Dorothea Schweickert, Germany

Schiller, with its eight campuses in five countries, offers an education where individualised attention and small classes inspire students and help them develop self-confidence for their future careers. Founded in 1964, the university is named after the philosopher and champion of human rights, Friedrich Schiller, whose work exemplifies the highest standards of ethics and multiculturalism. From its inception, the university has offered a truly international education in London, Strasbourg, Paris, Heidelberg, Leysin, Engelberg, Madrid and Florida. Students from some 130 nations currently study at Schiller and enjoy a unique global education.

Schiller London is situated at Royal Waterloo House, an Edwardian building in the centre of the capital. The extensive facilities include classrooms and lecture halls, laboratories, a cafeteria, library, halls of residence and a cybercafé. University students also have access to various other libraries and facilities throughout London.

Academic strengths

Schiller's mission is not only to educate but also to develop the student's ability to think creatively and critically and to communicate well within an international context. Schiller follows the American system of education, which emphasises practical and personalised instruction. The university ensures that its faculty has an outstanding practical background so that its students get the maximum profit from lecturers' experiences in their particular field.

Schiller London offers bachelor degrees, master's and associate degrees in academic areas including international business, hotel and tourism management, pre-medicine, pre-veterinary medicine, computer studies, banking, management, financial management, economics, international relations and diplomacy, psychology, communication, management of IT and art and design. Schiller has designed a flexible programme which allows students to choose their own path of study. Under this system, bachelor degrees, which normally take four years, can be completed in three calendar years.

Student life

It is a common saying among Schiller students that London is their campus, as the university's location in the centre of what is arguably the most exciting city in the world gives access to an array of cultural, historical, and artistic richness. The River Thames and the National Theatre are both near to Schiller, as are the Houses of Parliament, the London Eye and the IMAX cinema. Similarly, Piccadilly Circus, Trafalgar Square, the National Gallery of Art and the theatre district can be reached easily. Across the road is Waterloo Station, the terminal for the Eurostar train, which reaches the centre of Paris in under three hours.

Though London's attractions never end, a busy social calendar is organised by the Cultural Activities Office. Activities include cultural trips, excursions and parties. Schiller has agreements with sports centres in order to offer sporting facilities at affordable prices. The campus offers other facilities, including a library open seven days a week and free computing services open to all students 24 hours a day.

London

Thames Valley College

Write to: Principal, Thames Valley College, 10 Cleveland Way, London E1 4TR

Tel: +44 (0)20 7423 9898

Fax: +44 (0)20 7790 3407

Email: admissions@thamesvalleycollege.org.uk

Website: www.thamesvalleycollege.org.uk

Students: the college recruits students from all over the world.

Accommodation: please contact the college for further details.

Entrance requirements: GCSE and A level passes for degree courses. For master's degrees, a passed degree course is necessary.

EFL: TVC levels I, II and III certificates.

Fees: £2,745 a year for degree and master's levels.

Specialist and vocational

Thames Valley College

Student profile

"London has always attracted me; I have always wanted to come here. It is indeed a dream come true to both live and study in one of the most exciting cities in the world. Studying my MSc in Information Technology at Thames Valley College has been both challenging and interesting and together with the location of this university, which is so close to the city, they have exceeded my expectations. The lecturers are brilliant and helpful and the information they present in

lectures is all up to date and accurate. I'm having the time of my life and there is no place I would rather be or study".

Justyna Kosinska, Poland

Thames Valley College (TVC) was established in London with the aim of providing a comprehensive, varied programme of educational courses to meet the aspirations, demands and expectations of students from both the UK and abroad. The college is a small institution with a varied mix of students originating from the UK as well as from many different parts of the world, creating an international atmosphere.

The teaching programme provides students with a range of options including BBA and MBA programmes which are taught in conjunction with The University of North America. These courses are offered throughout the academic year, which consists of four semesters, and different options are offered in each semester. The lecturing staff are not only academically qualified but are selected for their commercial and industrial experience. Through this mix of academic competence and work experience, the college aims to meet its students' classroom expectations.

Academic strengths

Thames Valley acts as the London campus for The University of North America whose distance learning programmes are internationally recognised. The MBA is one of the most common postgraduate subjects. This programme enables students to have an insight into how organisations and administrations are run. It aims to provide students with the knowledge and skills required to become a manager and is recognised by organisations throughout the world.

The University of North America has a variety of BSc courses which Thames Valley College provides. After completion of the programmes, students should have the required skills to carry out extensive research as well have an eye for problem solving. Students will gain valuable knowledge in their chosen BSc subjects and have a greater understanding of how specific markets and segments operate. Thames Valley College also offers MSc programmes which chart the development of the computer through the 20th century and anticipate the changes that will affect the world in the coming century. The college has a limited number of research degree places available in the business, social science and computer science subject areas. Priority is given to existing TVC postgraduate students for places but ask admission officers for further details.

Thames Valley provides diplomas in fields including IT, business, English, hotel and tourism and e-commerce. Diplomas give a brief introduction (one year) to the subject and prepare students for entry to degree-level programmes.

Student life

The location in the East End proves very convenient for the attractions of central London and the college itself is well served by underground and bus links. London is one of the world's most exciting cities with a large, diverse population – this is reflected in the student community. London as a capital city has many places of interest and every year millions of overseas visitors come to the city, attracted by the historical heritage and the excellent shopping and leisure facilities which includes numerous theatres, cinemas, restaurants and sporting venues. The world-famous Oxford Street and Piccadilly Circus are minutes away from Thames Valley College, where students are able to enjoy shopping, sightseeing and the exciting night life.

London

West Thames College

Write to: Sandra Brodnicki, Admissions Department, West Thames College, Freepost SEA10045, Isleworth, Middlesex TW7 4BR

Tel: +44 (0)20 8326 2020

Fax: +44 (0)20 8569 7787

Email: info@westthames.ac.uk

Website: www.west-thames.ac.uk

Students: 8,000 students, of which 2,500 are part time, 130 international.

Accommodation: the student services department will assist in providing lists of local agencies. No accommodation provided by the college.

Entrance requirements: refer to course listings for specific requirements.

Fees: further education courses £3,840 higher education courses £6,835 EFL £1,750.

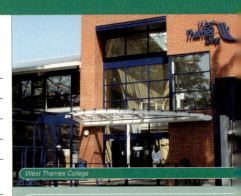

West Thames College

Student profile

"I first heard about West Thames College in Hounslow through the British Council in Tokyo and the internet. I graduated in Japan and worked for five years as a sales representative. I realised I wanted to work with people and I had an enthusiasm in fashion styling for hair and make-up, so made an application to study at West Thames College starting with hairdressing and working my way into fashion hair and make-up. I wanted to study in England, as it is good to gain qualifications and skills in hairdressing and fashion make-up in a country where you can learn from professionals. Trends are set in London

and Paris and I wanted to get experience in London. I find the college to be very friendly and it has great facilities. I'm having a great time."

Eiki Nakajima, Japan

Specialist and vocational

West Thames College is situated in west London, near to Heathrow and other major transport links. West London is a great place to live and study as it is vibrant, diverse and affordable. Many large companies have headquarters in west London so there are business opportunities alongside areas of greenery, historical buildings and landmark features. West Thames College is a single, purpose-built campus with the historical home of Sir Joseph Banks at its heart, and a new modern building to accommodate performing arts and hairdressing facilities. The college's reputation was recognised by the government in both 1996 and 1999 when it became one of the first colleges in London to be awarded the Charter Mark for Excellence.

The mission and purpose of the college is to provide high quality education and training to meet the needs of individuals and organisations within a supportive and challenging learning environment.

Academic strengths

The college is split into nine academic areas with many courses from entry level to higher education and a diverse range of students from 16 years onwards. The college is very proud of its students' achievements and the annual awards ceremony offers a chance to celebrate.

West Thames is heavily committed to offering the best service at all times, from advice and guidance before students join to help and support whilst they are studying. The Student Services Department provides a tutorial system with a personal tutor for each student plus medical, counselling and careers services.

Facilities to help students include a study skills centre and a resources centre which stocks books, journals, papers, videos and CD-Roms. With a network of modern computer facilities, students can use the resource-based learning centre and flexible learning centre to develop skills in IT, communications and maths.

The college's language lab is available for all students to learn a new language or improve their skills, from Arabic to Welsh. Full-time students can use the language lab's self-study materials which include multimedia packages, audio and video programmes for no extra charge.

Student life

On-campus students can benefit from a spacious new cafeteria area and student common rooms where they can play video games, listen to music, use the cybercafé or relax during breaks. The students' union (SU) represents student interests and organises social and recreational events including a wide range of sports activities, street dance, aerobics and kung fu. The SU committee is elected from the student body by the students to represent their views and is affiliated to the National Union of Students.

West London is a great area for students to live in. With central London half an hour away by tube or rail it is easy to experience the activities and opportunities offered by the capital. West London itself may be more affordable but also offers renowned art centres, theatres, clubs and dance venues. The myriad of bars, cafés and restaurants offers food from all around the world. The local area also offers a wide range of leisure services including art centres, sports facilities and many historical houses and parks.

London

Cavendish College

Write to: Cavendish College,
35-37 Alfred Place,
London WC1E 7DP

Tel: +44 (0)20 7580 6043

Fax: +44 (0)20 7255 1591

Email: learn@cavendish.ac.uk

Website: www.cavendish.ac.uk

Students: 350 full time, 150 part time, 80 per cent international.

Accommodation: the college accommodation services will assist students in finding accommodation. Long-term accommodation costs between £60 to £200 a week. Average price is £75 to £90 a week.

Entrance requirements: subject to the course of studies, in general high school diploma.

EFL: all students take an English test on induction day. Tuition available depending on results.

Foundation: access courses available for art and design, digital media, business studies, computing, MBA and postgraduate art.

Fees: £2,000 to £6,000.

Student profile

"Studying the Chartered Institute of Marketing diploma at Cavendish was a rewarding and enjoyable experience. It was hard work but I was constantly encouraged and supported by the teachers who had the knowledge and professional experience to ensure my success. I also benefited from an international study environment. I'm sure I have developed some useful future business contacts and made a number of lifelong friends. Cavendish is a friendly place to be, well resourced and is somewhere I would have no hesitation in recommending to someone considering studying in the

UK. I have now gone on to study for an MBA at a leading British university but I will always recall Cavendish with the fondest of memories."

Lil Bremmermann, Uruguay

Cavendish College has been providing high quality education for all types of students since 1985. It offers a variety of academic and vocational courses designed to equip students for the world of work and enhance their future careers. Students hail from all over the world and thus are able to develop lifelong friendships.

Cavendish continually invests in the latest technology and students have access to comprehensive IT facilities, extensive internet provision and a well-resourced library. The college has collaborative arrangements with other UK universities and gives comprehensive guidance to those wishing to progress to degree and postgraduate courses.

Situated in an ideal central location in London, Cavendish is close to London University Library and several of the capital's most comprehensive bookshops. For those unable to travel to London, Cavendish has introduced online courses where students have the ability to access course material via the internet, meet with classmates through discussion forums and communicate with teachers online.

Academic strengths

Cavendish College is accredited by the British Accreditation Council for Independent Further and Higher Education. Following a successful BAC re-inspection in 2000, Cavendish regards itself as one of the leading educational centres in the private sector, it offers courses that are recognised in academia, commerce and industry alike. Courses are practically oriented but have a sound theoretical content, enabling students to go directly in to employment or continue with higher programmes. Courses lead to internationally-recognised qualifications. Support with English and IELTS exam preparation classes is offered to all full-time students free of charge. These are designed to develop written and spoken English language skills and a more course-specific vocabulary.

Student life

The student population consists of men and women from all over the world. This international flavour is reflected in the courses and stimulating atmosphere. The college strives towards a friendly co-operative environment which will enhance the academic development of students and will ensure an enjoyable stay in London. In addition to substantial classroom space, there are five computer laboratories and eight specialist creative studies studios. There is a well resourced library, numerous internet access points throughout the college and a student cafe.

Cavendish welcomes students of any nationality but pays particular attention to the international students who have made a special effort to come and study in the UK. Adjusting to London life and trying to settle down in a new environment can represent a major step for some students. The college offers the fullest possible support to all students. The college is able to assist in the arrangement of a wide variety of accommodation from homestay, hostels and flats to flat-share and house-share. Students are also assisted with careers guidance and development from their tutors and heads of department and with university applications and advice, including IELTS preparation. If students find that they have queries about their student visa, work permit or Home Office regulations in general, the staff are always on hand and willing to help.

Colleges of further education

Birmingham

City College, Birmingham

Write to: Admissions,
The International Office,
City College, Birmingham,
St George's Post 16 Centre,
Great Hampton Row,
Hockley, Birmingham B19 3JG

Tel: +44 (0)121 233 3275

Fax: +44 (0)121 233 3275

Email: international@citycol.ac.uk

Website: www.citycol.ac.uk

Students: approximately 30,000 home students. 350 international students from outside the EEA.

Accommodation: there is college accommodation and plenty of local student accommodation at rates from £40 a week.

Entrance requirements: varies according to course choice. Some require no previous qualifications. Advice on individual course requirements available from the International Office.

EFL: limited EFL support to students on study programmes can be made available at additional cost.

Fees: vary. Specific information on application. Guideline for 2002/03: £2,600 for further education courses, £4,250 for higher education courses.

City College Birmingham

Student profile

"City College placed me in an excellent position for my future. Not only did I benefit through education but I also gained great experience during my time there, especially when I visited America. My course gave me the opportunity to study for the American Associate Degree, alongside my UK qualification. I visited Chicago twice, the second time to graduate, which was breathtaking. I developed a close relationship with the tutors; they created a very warm and positive environment. They encouraged me to remain focused, helped me through difficult areas of my course and  advised me on my approach. My self-belief and also my determination proved worthwhile when I eventually gained my degree."

Hardip Bhardwaj, United Kingdom

Colleges of further education

City College, Birmingham works on six major campus sites and over 60 other sites across Birmingham – the United Kingdom's second city. At the very centre of England, Birmingham can be reached from London in under two hours by train and has its own international airport just 30 minutes from the city centre. Many of the country's major tourist attractions, such as Stratford, the birthplace of William Shakespeare, Warwick and the Cotswolds are within easy reach. The city itself has three principal theatres and is home to the Birmingham Royal Ballet.

With three universities and many other colleges, there is an active student life and with a further four universities within 30 miles there is great opportunity for progression to higher education for City College's successful graduates.

The college celebrates the wide cultural diversity of all of its students' heritages and provides a facility for worship by all faiths on a number of its sites.

Academic strengths

City College, Birmingham has many years of experience in providing programmes for international students. In the 2001 inspection, the college's Higher National Business course was approved by the Higher Education Funding Council, a grade above that received by many universities.

The college has built lasting relationships with the key institutions in a number of other countries and has even formed partnerships with the Community Colleges Association of Jamaica and The Gambian Department of Technical Training and Vocational Education, as well as agreements with institutions in South Africa, Pakistan and India.

As part of their course, students are involved in study tours to some of City College's European partners such as France, Holland and the countries mentioned above.

In 1998, City College became one of the first colleges in the United Kingdom to provide American Associate Degree courses in partnership with Harold Washington College in Chicago. This means that students study for the American Associate Degree alongside their British qualification. 12 students graduated last year, which allows them to go on to university in either America or the UK with their dual qualification.

Student life

As a city with over 20 institutions providing post-16 education, there is a very active student social life. The pubs and clubs are friendly and many provide concessions for students. The city has one of the widest selections of restaurants in the country, ranging from Balti, Indian, Chinese and Thai to the very best of European food. Student accommodation can be amongst some of the cheapest in the country and there are plenty of food, clothes and other shops that offer lower priced goods.

The International Office at the college offers a support service, including a personal tutor to support you during your course, careers advice, study advice, welfare support and guidance on matters concerning visa difficulties or immigration. City College, Birmingham is a member of UKCOSA, the UK Council for International Education.

In short, Birmingham is an excellent city to study in for international students and City College is an equally stimulating and fun place to study.

Colleges of further education

Coventry

COVENTRY ▪ TECHNICAL ▪ COLLEGE ▪

Coventry

Coventry Technical College

Write to: The International Centre, Coventry Technical College, Butts, Coventry CV1 3GD

Tel: +44 (0)24 7652 6952

Fax: +44 (0)24 7652 6759

Email: info@covcollege.ac.uk

Website: www.covcollege.ac.uk

Students: total number of students 9,500; international students 5 per cent of the student population.

Accommodation: guaranteed accommodation with a homestay £80 a week (bed/breakfast/evening meal), self-catering £40 a week. Guest houses daily rate: single room £23.50 or twin/double room £43.

Entrance requirements: flexible entry requirements for further education courses. For higher education courses, IELTS 5.0 or equivalent is required.

Foundation: foundation course in business and management run in connection with Aston University.

Fees: for further education courses £3,820 a year; for higher education courses £6,900 a year. Please note that these are the course fees for 2001/02, there may be a small increase for 2002/03.

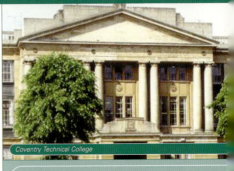

Coventry Technical College

Student profile

"I attended an educational exhibition in the UAE and saw a Coventry Technical College presentation. I was amazed by what they had to offer international students and applied for an Edexel BTEC National Diploma in Engineering. On arrival, I was given an orientation session and received a lot of support from staff and lecturers. The course was very well taught through the help of dedicated lecturers and I was given additional English language support. I am very pleased that I chose to study at Coventry Technical College. I made lots of friends and consider that I have attained some good personal and technical skills and have been given the opportunity to learn all about different cultures and customs."

Abdulla Aballa Abdulla,

United Arab Emirates

Colleges of further education

414

Coventry Technical College is one of the most well-established further education colleges in the Midlands. Situated close to the middle of Coventry city centre, the campus is within short walking distance of the city's many shops, sports facilities and restaurants. There are many local places of interest such as Warwick Castle and Stratford-upon-Avon, the birthplace of William Shakespeare.

Famous for its cathedral and home to the world famous car companies, Jaguar and Peugeot, Coventry is a friendly and modern city. The college is an ideal base for travelling round Britain, with excellent transport links to London and major cities via motorway and rail networks as well as international links via Birmingham International Airport. Established in 1935, the college has offered education and training for over 60 years and now has around 9,500 students enrolled on full and part-time courses.

Academic strengths

The college offers its overseas students a wide choice of courses looking to give the best possible tuition and support. The college aims to improve international students' English language skills and to prepare them for university or employment. There is a full-time student adviser to help with job or university applications.

Courses taught at the college include A levels, National Diplomas, Higher National Diplomas, Access and degree programmes. Subjects include business administration, computing and information technology, construction, engineering, art and design, English language, fashion, hairdressing and beauty, languages, science, open learning programmes, healthcare, teacher training, and university foundation programmes for international students.

The college works in close partnership with The University of Warwick, Coventry University and Aston University (Birmingham) to offer undergraduate study programmes.

Student life

The student union's main role is to represent the views of students and participate in the college's decision-making process. There are clubs and societies which students can join.

The college has an extensive range of facilities to support student learning. The library holds over 17,000 books and periodicals and a wide range of CD-Roms.

The college computer centre has the latest in high technology equipment and is open to students as a drop-in facility.

There is also an English Language Centre where specifically designed teaching programmes are run to meet the varying individual needs of all students. There are many excellent resources designed for classroom and individual use.

The cost of renting property in Coventry is amongst the most reasonable in the UK. The student services team can arrange accommodation. They can also provide support on health, welfare and finance. The college careers co-ordinator and careers library provide a wealth of detailed information regarding further study in higher education and employment opportunities within the UK.

The International Centre serves the needs and interests of all overseas students. Staff will be pleased to give students advice to ensure a happy time while studying at the college.

Colleges of further education

Grimsby

Grimsby College

Write to: The Information Centre, Grimsby College, Nuns Corner, Grimsby, North East Lincolnshire DN34 5BQ

Tel: +44 (0)1472 315002

Fax: +44 (0)1472 879924

Email: infocent@grimsby.ac.uk

Website: www.grimsby.ac.uk

Accommodation: the college offers outstanding accommodation, only a short walk from the college.

Entrance requirements:
A levels, AVCE, BTEC National, European or International Baccalaureate. By interview for mature students over 21 and other qualifications all considered.

EFL: a good level of English required.

Fees: £6,285.

Colleges of further education

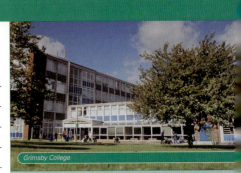
Grimsby College

Student profile

Grimsby College has acted as the springboard for Minna Pisto to launch a career at ITN. Minna (24) is currently employed as a news desk assistant at ITN International News after studying the Higher National Diploma in Media Production at Grimsby College. After strong recommendations about the media centre, Minna joined the course in 1997 and found the college very welcoming. She said,

"Everyone was so friendly and supportive, especially the tutors who all had excellent industry and academic backgrounds. The job at ITN is extremely varied and includes editing programmes, assisting news gathering services and watching raw news coverage unfold."

She is still amazed that she is now sharing office space with ITN's Trevor McDonald!

Minna Pisto, Finland

Grimsby College, centrally situated in Grimsby town, offers students easy access to all local amenities. The majority of accommodation is within safe walking distance of the campus and students find the cheap living costs in Grimsby are a great financial bonus. Over £3 million has been invested in the last year to provide up-to-the-minute learning and social facilities. It is a purpose-built centre for higher education with state-of-the-art lecture and classroom facilities. Grimsby College is one of the largest education providers in the area whose aim is to offer a learning environment which is second to none.

Academic strengths

The college offers more than 30 degree and higher national programmes including business studies, tourism operations and marketing, health and social care to name a few. There are three libraries with full IT access, online archives and group work areas allowing comparable facilities to any national research facility. All of the lecture theatres have video projection and IT displays allowing the use of a range of media to illustrate learning.

Teaching staff have excellent academic and industry backgrounds, many actively engaged in publishing and industry consultation. The college is proud of its links with various industries on a national and international level, in turn providing outstanding work experience opportunities.

It has invested in many departments and has recently launched the East Coast media training centre which offers industry-standard facilities in the TV, film, video, radio, photography and multimedia disciplines. Sponsored by some of the country's biggest media organisations such as Granada Media, Daily Mail Trust Group, Apple computers, Sony Broadcast and the Press Association, students can work alongside media professionals on a range of exciting projects.

There is a large Refrigeration and Air Conditioning Department providing specialist training which is ideal for those looking to go on to degree courses or to move straight into this industry.

Student life

The college has a great student environment which provides facilities such as halls of residence which have individual bedrooms with shared communal facilities. These include a full computer suite, games/common room and fully equipped kitchens. Both Grimsby and the picturesque seaside town Cleethorpes offer an exciting nightlife, with plenty of lively bars and clubs to choose from, along with a range of popular restaurants.

The Hub is the place to meet for great food with a wide range available. Students can unwind in the Drum Bar, award winner of the 1998 RIBA for Design and Innovation, with a relaxing environment in the day, turning into a lively entertainment venue for higher education students in the night. Many students also join the Bargate Fitness Centre. The campus hosts its own hairdressing and beauty facilities, two stationery shops and a campus bakery.

The college's student services department offers orientation tours of the area when international students arrive and, most importantly, offers a full support service for the duration of their time studying at Grimsby College. International airports Humberside and Leeds are both nearby, so home is never too far away for international students.

Harrogate

Harrogate College

Write to: Harrogate College, Hornbeam Park Avenue, Harrogate HG2 8QT

Tel: +44 (0)1423 879466

Fax: +44 (0)1423 879829

Email: oncourse@lmu.ac.uk

Website: www.harrogate.ac.uk

Students: over 1,000 full-time students and 9,000 part-time students in 2000/01.

Accommodation: family home accommodation can be arranged; bed, breakfast and an evening meal costs £80 a week.

Entrance requirements: students need to be at least 16 years of age and must supply proof of an adequate command of English. For General English courses, this should be at least at elementary level.

EFL: IELTS 4.5.

Foundation: General English Programme.

Fees: English, A level and vocational courses £3,790 a year; HND course £6,650 a year.

Harrogate College

Student profile

"For my multimedia course, you have to be very creative and I am really enjoying the work that I am doing, especially the project work at the moment which is about animation. We study at the college and I do work at home on my own PC. There are lectures and tutorials and we have to do a lot of planning and research. It is hard work but it is great to have an idea and see it turned into a finished project. I like the brainstorming sessions we have where we can share ideas with other students. Next year I'm hoping to complete my HND and then transfer to Leeds and do a third year to obtain a BSc

in Media Studies. I am not sure if I want to do further study or get a job after that but I am aware that there are plenty of opportunities in animation."

Siu Kin Chan, Hong Kong

Harrogate College is a government funded general further education college with the unique advantage of operating as a faculty of Leeds Metropolitan University since its merger with the university in 1998. With over 1,000 full-time students and 9,000 part-time students, the college prides itself on being the main provider of further education in the Harrogate area.

The college is located within the centre of Harrogate which lies 16 miles north of Leeds. Harrogate is an attractive, prosperous spa town. Set in the beautiful rolling countryside of the North Yorkshire Dales, it is famed for its green lawns and flower gardens yet also enjoys excellent transport services to the busy city of Leeds. Located nearby is Leeds Bradford Airport where there are daily flights to European destinations and connecting flights to major world destinations.

Academic strengths

Harrogate offers students a broad spectrum of education and training provision with notable specialisms including art and design, multimedia, soccer education and early childhood studies. It is a thriving institution but small enough for a personal teaching approach in lectures and tutorials. All academic staff are highly qualified and experienced, often with industry knowledge. Students have access to advice, guidance and support from their personal tutor, careers and welfare counsellors for both academic and personal issues. English language provision is available and all international students have access to support if required.

Modern facilities at the college include a large IT Learning Centre that houses nearly 80 PC workstations, multimedia rooms, a gym, a student union area, drama and dance studios, hair and beauty salons and a restaurant. All students have access to the facilities at the two university sites in Leeds.

Student life

The students' union plays an active role in the full and varied social life of students at the college. All students are entitled to join the Leeds Metropolitan University student union and have access to all the benefits and facilities that this brings. There is a large recreational student union area within the college including pool tables, televisions and a union shop.

Central to student activity is the college's enrichment programme which provides a full range of activities for students on a Wednesday afternoon including web design, yoga, swimming, football, drama and music.

Harrogate College students live in a pleasant town with few crime problems. Harrogate is also a large conference centre town offering a wide range of excellent local amenities including good sporting facilities, a variety of bars, nightclubs and restaurants, shops, museums and theatres.

Most international students take advantage of homestay accommodation. The college has built up a large network of local families who will provide a room and meals.

The college has over 20 years' experience of offering courses and support to international students. All students are welcomed during the first week of term where a programme of events is arranged including a comprehensive induction to the college and free airport pick-up.

Colleges of further education

Gloucester

Hartpury College

Write to: Hartpury College, Hartpury House, Hartpury, Gloucester GL19 3BE

Tel: +44 (0)1452 702132

Fax: +44 (0)1452 700629

Email: enquire@hartpury.ac.uk

Website: www.hartpury.ac.uk

Students: further education 800; 20 international. Undergraduate 900; 52 international. Postgraduate 12; one international. 50:50 male:female.

Accommodation: approximately 670 places on offer. Mixture of halls of residence on campus and off-site accommodation. Some accommodation specifically for under-18 year olds with single-sex blocks or floors with a warden.

Entrance requirements: vary from course to course. Request a prospectus or discuss with tutor.

EFL: undergraduate IELTS 6.0, TOEFL 570 (or 230 if computer tested). NEAB or Cambridge Proficiency grade C will be acceptable.

Fees: non-EU students, higher education £6,500 per annum, further education £3,595 per annum. Scholarships available to a selection of students; application made directly to the college. EU students higher education £1,075, further education £750.

Hartpury College

Student profile

Ian is a scholarship student who has travelled from Zimbabwe to take part in the Hartpury College/Gloucestershire Rugby Academy. Ian is 18 and studies on the National Diploma in Agriculture course. In 1999 Ian was selected to represent Zimbabwe schools under-19 in the prestigious Danie Craven tournament in South Africa. Ian combines farm duties with the tough academy training. He says, "At the academy, we prepare ourselves well for the game. We train in a variety of ways from skills to weights to team practice – we even train twice a week before*

breakfast which really does concentrate our minds to the task. The squad is close and, as you can imagine, the atmosphere that is generated at a place like Hartpury is great."

Ian Ehrich, Zimbabwe

Colleges of further education

Hartpury College, Gloucestershire is located within a 360-hectare country estate. This, along with exposure to real commercial activities provides the ultimate learning environment for the land-based students.

A major strength lies in the amount of practical involvement students have in estate operations. Hartpury College has spent over £18 million since 1990 on providing first-class teaching resources. At the heart of the college is Home Farm, which is a mixed livestock farm with dairy, sheep, pig and beef enterprises. A newly-completed visitor centre marks the start of current investment at Home Farm, which includes new classrooms, work-shops and a 350-cow dairy unit.

Facilities include woodlands, a com-mercial shoot, a trout lake, conservation zones, a game rearing unit, an arboretum, service workshops, a commercial farm, an equestrian centre, an animal hospital and a rural business centre.

Hartpury College is a Centre of Excellence for equestrian studies with excellent facilities. Studies including animal care, animal science and veterinary nursing science boast similarly good facilities.

The sports facilities are also extensive and the resources available include an impressive range of sports pitches catering for rugby, football, hockey, netball and tennis. A pitch and putt golf course and a swimming pool are also provided at the college. The sports hall provides human performance analysis laboratories as well as a gymnasium and fitness suite. Team sports are an integral part of college life.

Hartpury also has a rugby academy in conjunction with Gloucester Rugby Football Club. Academy students can study a range of courses whist aiming for a professional rugby career. Full-time courses are available in such related subjects as rugby studies and also rugby coaching. Other sports academies are available at Hartpury College, including golf, netball and football.

Academic strengths

The overall winner of the Eqvalan Thesis of the Year Award was Helen Jacks from Hartpury College in Gloucestershire with her thesis entitled, 'The effect of unilateral laterocaudal tungsten-carbide stud nails on equine mediolateral hoof balance'. This examined the effect of using shoe stud nails on both hoof balance and biomechanics, concluding that the use of stud nails does in fact cause imbalance in the horse.

Helen was chosen from a group of five finalists, initially selected from 14 entrants from the UK and Ireland's colleges that run a degree course, who were invited to present their thesis to a panel of three judges at the British Equine Event at the NAC in Stoneleigh, Warwickshire. Helen received a cheque for £500, an Eqvalan memento and a certificate. She was also invited to present her thesis at the National Equine Forum the following year.

Student life

Hartpury provides international students at the college with a comprehensive and helpful wardening service. Other available resources include 650 en-suite bedrooms, a learning resources centre, a wine bar, a coffee shop, the sports centre, students union, restaurant and shop.

The college is located close to cosmopol-itan Cheltenham, which is the home of national hunt racing.

Hastings College
OF ARTS AND TECHNOLOGY

Hastings

Hastings College of Arts and Technology

Write to: Briony Thomson, Student Services, Hastings College of Arts and Technology, Archery Road, St-Leonards-on-Sea, East Sussex TN38 0HX

Tel: +44 (0)1424 442222

Fax: +44 (0)1424 721763

Email: studentadvisers@hastings.ac.uk

Website: www.hastings.ac.uk

Students: 13,906 in 2000/01 (335 postgraduates, 370 international students from 39 countries), 44:56 male:female.

Accommodation: with host families, half board, which includes bed, breakfast and evening meal or private renting approximately £75 a week for 2002/03.

Entrance requirements: specific to course and all applications will be considered on an individual basis.

Fees: (2002/03) UK/EU from £15 to £1,075 a year depending on age and the level of course. Non-EU £3,750 to £5,000 a year depending on the level of course. Contact the college to find out more.

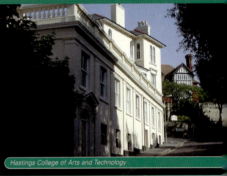

Hastings College of Arts and Technology

Student profile

"The studying environment is nice and lively. The sea views from the classroom windows are wonderful and make you feel relaxed. The teachers treat students like friends. If you have a problem just ask them – they will always be happy to help. As well as having a good time and learning English you can learn many things about other countries. The social organiser offers wonderful trips and there is a good choice of sports. You can go to the self access centre if you want to study by yourself after class. There is always a tutor to help you. In my opinion, there is a big family at Hastings College and everybody is one of the members. I have been here only six months but I would like to stay one or two years because I am very happy here."

Shirley, People's Republic of China

Hastings College of Arts and Technology is just outside the renowned historic town of Hastings on the south coast of the UK, famous for its association with the Battle of 1066. Today, Hastings is a thriving artistic and cultural centre with a lively music scene. Hastings also has a wealth of bars, pubs, clubs and a cinema. It is close to Brighton and London with direct train links. It is easy to get to by air, ferry or train, including Eurostar, and is surrounded by beautiful countryside.

Academic strengths

Hastings College has five specialist schools: Art and Design, Business and Consumer Services, Construction, Health and Social Studies and Technology, as well as a thriving sixth form centre which offers an innovative academic and vocational mix and the prestigious International Baccalaureate Diploma.

The international centre has over 10 years, experience in providing courses for students in English as a foreign language, marketing, IT and management. There are currently over 12,000 students between the ages of 15 and 92 and the college has a large international community with students from 39 countries. Consequently there is a feeling of a rich, diverse, college culture. It aims to be friendly and informal, in two compact campuses, with a creative atmosphere where ideas can flourish.

The college also has strong links with the Pestalozzi village, which itself has been established for over 40 years, educating people in, and promoting an understanding of, different cultures.

The college has modern multimedia resources, with over 160 networked computer stations, a fitness centre, beauty and hair salons, design suites, restaurants, catering kitchens, construction workshops and high quality teaching rooms.

Student life

As well as its lively seaside environment, Hastings offers cheap living costs. As part of National Union of Student membership, there are also substantial discounts available to students and many sporting activities to get involved with. International students have their own social organiser who ensures they can take part in trips and social events such as barbecues, sports games, theatre and cinema.

There is support available through a welfare officer who is experienced in dealing specifically with the problems international students may encounter when coming to study in a foreign country. A range of help and advice is on offer concerning important practical issues. This includes accommodation, registering with doctors and dentists, as well as arranging visas.

Many of the college's international students choose to live with a British family, many of whom have been working with Hastings in this role for a number of years. This is a useful way of continuing to practise English after class and also of learning more about the British culture. In a host family, students receive a single room, breakfast and evening meal from Monday to Friday and all meals at the weekend.

Alternative accommodation is available on request and long-term students have the opportunity to move into self-catering accommodation if they wish.

Colleges of further education

ROCHDALE & MIDDLETON

Manchester

Hopwood Hall College

Contacts: Allan Lawrence, International Business Manager, Yvonne Buckley, International Office Administrator, Hopwood Hall College, Rochdale Road, Middleton, Manchester M24 6XH

Tel: +44 (0)161 654 6661

Fax: +44 (0)161 654 6662

Email: allan.lawrence@hopwood.ac.uk
international@hopwood.ac.uk

Website: www.hopwood.ac.uk

Students: 2,500 full-time students all studying pre-university level two, three and four courses. 45:55 male:female.

Accommodation:
on campus self-catering £60 a week; full board £110 a week; homestay variable £50 to £90 a week.

Entrance requirements: IELTS 4.5 (level 3), IELTS 5 to 5.5 (level 4) plus relevant subject-based qualifications.

EFL: all levels of Cambridge from PET to Proficiency, BEC 1 to 3. IELTS prep, English for special academic purposes £1,100 a term. Summer School £220 a week.

Fees: £3,800 (levels 2 and 3), level 4 £5,000. Foundation £3,800 except MMU foundation year £5,610 and MMU foundation degree at £6,000. All per annum.

Hopwood Hall College computer suite

Student profile

Kate has come to Hopwood Hall College Manchester from Beijing. She is studying the BTEC Edexel foundation year in art and design, which she feels will give her a good practical and theoretical basis from which to move on to her chosen career in fashion design. Kate is one of 50 students from a range of ages, backgrounds and nationalities attending the course and the first from the People's Republic of China. She hopes to pass the course and go on to study fashion design at The Manchester Metropolitan University in

July. Currently, she is living at the Hopwood Hall College halls of residence and enjoying the busy city centre, 30 minutes by bus from her accommodation.

Han Qing Dong (Kate),

People's Republic of China

Colleges of further education

Hopwood Hall College is situated in Middleton, Greater Manchester in the northwest of England. It was formed in 1990 as a result of the amalgamation of three local colleges and a number of local sixth forms. It has two campuses, one situated in the centre of Rochdale and the other on a rural site in Middleton. It is 30 kilometres from Manchester Airport and 30 minutes by direct bus route from Manchester city centre.

The college is organised into six distinct schools which provide a wide range of academic and vocational courses. There are 2,500 full-time and many more part-time students.

Academic strengths

The college offers a broad range of courses including A levels, GCSEs, vocational qualifications (GNVQs), HNDs and other pathways leading to higher education in many vocational and academic subjects. All courses are £3,800 a year, except HNDs which cost £5,000.

There is an access programme for international students in subjects such as social science, science, business and IT. In collaboration with The Manchester Metropolitan University, the college runs a foundation course in science, computing and engineering, which leads directly to university entry. New developments in 2001 included a pre-MBA course leading to entry into a local university and also a foundation degree in new media design. These courses are priced from £5,000 to £6,000 a year.

The college provides English language training including the Cambridge EFL suite of courses from basic to intermediate up to proficiency level. Other available courses include English for academic purposes, the Trinity College Certificate in TESOL and the Cambridge Business English Certificate at three levels. The college hosts the Bobby Charlton Soccer School and there are a range of soccer schools and summer schools, for example football with business, IT and/or English language training. EFL courses cost £1,100 a term (12 weeks). English language summer schools cost £220 a week and football summer schools cost from £380 to £480 a week; these short courses are inclusive of accommodation.

Currently, the college has approximately 90 international students from over 20 different countries. The progress of international students on full-time courses is helped by the provision of English language training and support which is included in the initial tuition fee.

The college has well-stocked libraries with a large number of PCs, journals and books. In a recent government inspection, the college received an excellent report placing it in the top 10 per cent of further education colleges in England and Wales.

Student life

An International Office has staff available to provide support and help with any problems such as visas, accommodation and welfare advice. The college has accommodation which is available for international students on the campus. This is currently undergoing a programme of refurbishment and expansion. The current price for on-campus self-catering accommodation is £60 per week.

The college has sports facilities including a fitness gym. A new sports hall is scheduled for completion in 2002.

Colleges of further education

Huddersfield

Huddersfield College

Write to: International Office Huddersfield College, New North Road, Huddersfield HD1 5NN

Tel: +44 (0)1484 437052

Fax: +44 (0)1484 511885

Email: international@huddcoll.ac.uk

Website: www.huddcoll.ac.uk/international

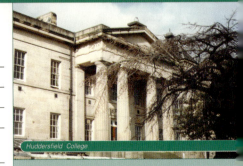

Huddersfield College

Students: 3,000 full-time students, 17,000 part-time students and over 300 international students from across the world.

Accommodation: local host family accommodation on either a full-board or self-catering basis. Private accommodation in the town centre is also available.

Entrance requirements: average English score required; IELTS 4.5 for most academic and vocational programmes. Average entrance exams: five to six passes for most academic and vocational programmes.

EFL: the college can provide EFL programmes for beginners.

Fees: £4,200 for a full-time, one-year academic or vocational programme; £3,960 for a full-time, one-year English language programme.

Student profile

"I came to Britain to study because it's famous for its high standard of education. A friend recommended Huddersfield College. She said it was a great place to study and the quality of teaching was high. She was right! I really like it here. I'm studying an English course because I want to go to The University of Huddersfield to take a Master's in Business Administration. I enjoy the course and my English has really improved since I've been at the college. The tutors are professional. They have a lot of experience and give you individual support. It's nice because the tutors

aren't just teachers but friends too. I'd definitely recommend Huddersfield College. I made a really good decision when I chose to come here."

Li Hengshuo,

People's Republic of China

Colleges of further education

Huddersfield College has been a leader in the field of pre-degree education for over 100 years and welcomes around 300 international students each year from all over the world.

Huddersfield can be found in the centre of England, an area renowned for its magnificent countryside. The town of Huddersfield is an important commercial centre surrounded by the cities of Leeds, Sheffield and Manchester.

Huddersfield is a lively and multicultural town offering excellent leisure and cultural facilities to all, including theatres, shops, markets, restaurants, nightlife, cinemas, museums, sporting facilities and religious venues. The cost of living in Huddersfield is also low, making it a popular location for many students.

Huddersfield College is conveniently located in the centre of town and is therefore easily accessible for all.

Academic strengths

The courses available at Huddersfield College encompass a wide range of pre-degree vocational and academic courses, including hospitality, leisure and tourism, business, computing, engineering and technology, construction and transport, science and communication, art, design, performing arts and caring. The college has close links with The University of Huddersfield and many students progress on to the university after successfully completing a course at the college.

At Huddersfield College, students can complement their studies with access to excellent facilities. Huddersfield College also offers an extensive library and resource area, centres for language learning, English, mathematics and office skills, hairdressing and beauty salons, restaurants and a travel centre are also available on site. The drop-in IT centre offers all students computing, internet and email facilities

BASELT accreditation has helped the English language school at Huddersfield College gain an excellent reputation offering classes at all levels. The school offers a wide range of courses, all accredited by BASELT and the British Council, including general English language courses, business English courses and IELTS preparation courses.

The college also runs a range of English language summer school programmes during July and August.

Student life

Huddersfield College aims to guarantee both a friendly and supportive learning environment to all its students. Its student support service offers advice and guidance on all matters relating to study, finance, accommodation, careers or any other problem, however small. Whilst studying, students are also allocated a course tutor who will attend to their academic needs. The college's students' association also organises social events and sporting activities throughout the year.

Huddersfield College recommends that its international students stay with one of the registered host families where they can be sure of a warm welcome and an enjoyable stay. Alternatively, self-catering accommodation in the town can be organised for students by the accommodation officer.

RICHMOND

Richmond

Richmond, The American International University in London

Write to: Admissions Office, Richmond, The American International University in London, Queens Road, Richmond, Surrey TW10 6JP

Tel: +44 (0)20 8332 9000

Fax: +44 (0)20 8332 1596

Email: enroll@richmond.ac.uk

Website: www.richmond.ac.uk

Accommodation: on-campus accommodation guaranteed for first-year students. Residential options available on both campuses. All meals provided. No self-catering accommodation available.

Students: 1,500 students from over 100 countries. 50:50 male:female.

Entrance requirements: familiar with qualifications from all over the world. Students from all countries are encouraged to apply.

EFL: competence in written and spoken English or IELTS 6.5, TOEFL 550.

Fees: Richmond is independent and receives no funding from the government. All students pay the same undergraduate tuition fee of £5,080 per semester.

Colleges of further education

Richmond, The American International University in London

Student profile

"My brother graduated from Richmond and when I was looking for a university he recommended it to me. I always wanted to study in the UK and at Richmond I have the added advantage of being exposed to different cultures on a daily basis. The faculty staff come from almost as many countries as the students. As well as knowing their subjects and how to teach, they know how to deal with people from different backgrounds and thus they communicate easily with everyone. I also really love the location. You have London with all the excitement it offers right there when

you want it but also Richmond with 2,500 acres of parkland and the River Thames provides a perfect contrast."

Najood Al Feeli, Kuwait

Richmond students come from over 100 countries, from a multitude of ethnic, cultural and linguistic groups and most of the world's religions. No one group dominates or is in the majority. Thus, international, diverse, multicultural and intercultural are just a few of the ways to best describe the university. Understanding and respect are a natural result of students living and studying together. Differences are both recognised and celebrated at Richmond.

The university's main aim is to offer quality undergraduate education in the American liberal arts tradition as well as challenging graduate programmes which emphasise the link between professional achievement and study. Underlying the university's academic programmes, which are taught to a multicultural student body by an internationally-minded faculty, is a commitment to the value of understanding and appreciating human differences.

Academic strengths

The degrees which students gain from Richmond are both British and American. This is because Richmond's undergraduate degrees are accredited and validated in the United States (Middle States) and the United Kingdom (Open University Validation Services). Students receive two degree certificates. One shows students' American degree and the other shows their British degree. Wherever graduates then start a career or go on to graduate study, their dual-validated degree from Richmond will be recognised worldwide.

The foundation of Richmond's academic programme is the American four-year, liberal arts system. A Richmond education enjoys the benefits of flexibility in exploring different subjects. Richmond student organisations, clubs and societies also help students enjoy London with the academic specialisation that characterises British honours degrees. Richmond offers a teaching faculty which is supported by the latest technology and an average class size of 16.

Student life

The university occupies two campuses. The Richmond campus, roughly 30 minutes from central London, is set in seven acres at the top of Richmond Hill. First and second-year students live and study there. Computing students are based at the Richmond campus throughout the duration of their degrees.

Third-year, fourth-year and graduate students take classes at the Kensington campus in central London, only five minutes from Kensington High Street, one of London's liveliest shopping streets.

London is arguably one of the most exciting cities in the world. Richmond students enjoy its museums, libraries, theatres, galleries, concerts and famous historic buildings, while getting to know the other more contemporary and less-known London markets and its street fashion. Students at Richmond, wherever they come from, maintain that London is indeed their second home.

As the university is so international, Richmond staff and faculty are very experienced in dealing with students from all over the world. Their concern is that students enjoy their experience whilst living in London and they offer support and years of experience to ensure that Richmond students, whichever country they are from, feel comfortable.

Colleges of further education

TELFORD COLLEGE
of Arts and Technology

Telford

Telford College of Arts and Technology

Write to: Overseas Admissions,
Student Services,
Telford College of Arts and Technology,
Haybridge Road, Wellington,
Telford, Shropshire TF1 2NP

Tel: +44 (0)1952 642237

Fax: +44 (0)1952 642293

Email: studserve@tcat.ac.uk

Website: www.tcat.ac.uk

Students: 1,200 full time, 12,000 part time, 25 international students.

Accommodation: students would need to organise their own accommodation prior to arrival.

Entrance requirements: depends on level of course required and level of written and spoken English.

EFL: English courses are available to bring students up to entry requirements.

Telford College of Arts and Technology

Student profile

"In the future I want to work for a finance company, which requires qualifications and experience. I have gained both at Telford and have no regrets about coming here. I came for the variety of courses and because it would provide me with the qualifications needed for a British university. As an international student, I was worried about living in Britain but my personal tutor has been helpful and the other students are friendly. Telford has beautiful surroundings and I was lucky to find a house near to Telford Town Park. Because my course is taught in modules we get to  cover a lot of topics, although marketing is my favourite. Studying abroad is the best decision I have made and I am still learning new things every day."

Kevin Shwaga, Kenya

Colleges of further education

430

Telford College of Arts and Technology (TCAT) came into being formally on 1 January 1983. Under its previous name of Walker Technical College it served the area for over 50 years. The college occupies two sites in Telford with the main teaching sites situated at Haybridge Road. The general standards of teaching, learning equipment and buildings are excellent due to a continuous programme of refurbishment. The college is also attracting an increasing number of overseas students. The college has recently constructed a new refectory, library and resource centre and student services unit.

Academic strengths

The college is the major centre for further education in Telford and East Shropshire with over 1,200 full-time students. Telford College of Arts and Technology draws young people from throughout the country on easily the widest range of vocational courses in the area. Telford is a multi-award winning college (the college has won a larger number of Beacon Awards than any other college in England for excellence in curriculum areas) with a well-earned reputation for preparing students over 16 for employment, further training or higher education.

Telford has a number of flexible learning centres where students can study on their own. The Learning Resource Centre (LRC) is the hub of student research and information gathering. As well as having a book and magazine stock of over 50,000 volumes, it houses 70 of TCAT's 500 networked computers linked to the internet and college intranet. The LRC is a constant buzz of activity throughout the week and is also open Saturday from 9 am to 1 pm.

The Bridge Centre can also help with study skills, key skills, writing assignments and so on. Courses combine practical skills with theoretical studies in a way designed to be relevant to work and attractive to university admission tutors.

Where appropriate, students are given the opportunity to spend time in the working world developing the skills employers need and every effort is made to help you obtain a worthwhile placement. The college offers a range of vocational and general education qualifications as well as a large programme of adult non-vocational courses.

Student life

For the last five years, Telford's student population has shown consistent growth in all modes of attendance in the majority of curricular areas. The college has exceeded its growth targets every year since incorporation, recording 60 per cent growth in that period alone.

As well as meeting the needs of full-time students, the college organises and runs over 80 part-time vocational courses, serving more than 8,000 students. All students are assigned a personal tutor who has a special interest in your progress and welfare. Tutors see students on a regular basis to discuss progress and any concerns students may have. Managers, engineers, administrators, secretaries and social care professionals are trained to bring prosperity and also a better quality of life to their organisations. Through understanding the diversity of students, the college provides the opportunity to meet targets and fulfil potential. The college has parking places for disabled students at the front and rear of the college.

WALSALL COLLEGE OF ARTS & TECHNOLOGY

Walsall

Walsall College of Arts & Technology

Write to: Susan Stokes, International Officer, Walsall College of Arts & Technology, St Pauls Street, Walsall WS1 1XN

Tel: +44 (0)1922 657000

Fax: +44 (0)1922 657083

Email: sstokes@walcat.ac.uk

Website: www.walcat.ac.uk

Students: 12,000 students of which 2,500 are full time. There are 70 international from 12 countries.

Accommodation: the college does not have its own halls of residence. Advice and assistance will be available to help students find secure and comfortable accommodation including homestay.

Entrance requirements: vary according to subject. Please contact the International Office for details.

EFL: 4.0 IELTS. Foundation available.

Foundation: foundation courses in vocational subjects with progression opportunities to higher level programmes.

Fees: (2002/03) English or international foundation programme £3,800; AS level, A level, vocational courses £4,000; HND £4,400.

Walsall College of Arts & Technology

Student profile

"I came to Walsall College of Arts & Technology in September 2000 and enrolled on the International Foundation Programme. I wanted to obtain a degree in education which would enable me to work with children with special needs. I worked very hard and I completed the programme in one year. To obtain the place, I needed experience in a primary school and my tutors helped me find a placement. At the start of the foundation programme I was given additional help with English. The programme soon brought results so I became fluent and was able to complete my assign-

ments well. I accepted a place at Bishop Grosseteste College, Lincoln. I then began the degree in special education, which I hope to be able to complete in 2004."

Sawako Ozawa, Japan

Walsall College of Arts & Technology is a friendly local college with an established reputation for academic courses and vocational education. Walsall is a lively, culturally diverse town of over 250,000 people in the Midlands. London is two hours away by train and Britain's second city, Birmingham, is a 20 minute bus or train ride away. The college's main campus is next to the central shopping area, convenient for bus, coach and rail stations and a few minutes' drive from the motorway network.

A new art gallery is part of a major redevelopment of the town centre which will improve public transport facilities and transform a former industrial area next to the town's canal into a vibrant waterfront quarter featuring cafés, restaurants, bistros and small shops. International students arriving via Birmingham International Airport will find it quick, easy and relaxed compared with busier airports elsewhere.

Academic strengths

The college has a growing national and international reputation for its range and quality of provision, friendly staff and modern facilities. Walsall College of Arts & Technology provides educational opportunities for all students across all subject areas in an inclusive environment. Courses lead to university entrance, higher level training or employment. Walsall also offers higher level courses, linked to local universities. English language classes help students gain qualifications such as Cambridge First, Advanced and Proficiency certificates. International students on vocational or academic courses receive support with spoken and written English as required.

The college is constantly upgrading and developing its facilities. It has recently opened the European Design Centre in a brand new building, which has been commended for its exciting and imaginative design. The centre is equipped with learning resources and computers with industry-standard software to meet the needs of students, staff and external clients. There are over 30,000 books, most of which are available for loan, and over 100 journals and periodicals are stocked. There is bookable and drop-in access to 200 networked computers and access to CD-Roms. Walsall offers excellent, free and impartial careers advice to give students the help needed to choose the right course and advise on the important transition into employment or higher education.

Student life

Students are assigned a personal tutor who will offer continuing support, advice and guidance throughout their course. Students thus receive regular feedback on their progress. The Student Services Section is staffed by professional counsellors who provide advice and guidance on any subject and the Health Shop provides free, confidential advice on health-related matters. Walsall has an international officer to assist with any difficulties its international students may face and advice and assistance is available to help them find secure, comfortable accommodation.

The students' union is also based at the college; it arranges events and activities, trips and fund-raising events. Students have the opportunity to participate in all the activities and also in the running of their student union. A nursery is located on site with a dedicated and qualified team of staff.

Universities and colleges of higher education

This section contains details of a selection of universities and colleges in Britain, followed by a list of contact addresses for all UCAS institutions in the UK. It is worth sending for a prospectus before making your final decision and, if possible, making a visit to check whether the university or college meets your requirements.

If you are unable to visit, you could try asking a friend in the UK to go on your behalf. If this is impossible, it is well worth arriving a few days or a week before your course starts as most institutions offer orientation weeks for international students which can help you to get settled in. It also means that you have a chance to sort out any problems that might arise before the course begins (if you want to change accommodation, for example).

Write to: the contact details given here are generally those of the International Office.

Tel: this is written as if dialled from outside the UK.

Website: these omit the prefix 'http://'.

Students: student numbers include both undergraduates and postgraduates followed by a breakdown into postgraduate and international student numbers.

Accommodation: this section refers to types of residence available at the university or college including the possibility of staying in married or family flats or rooms, or in single-sex accommodation. Single sex is usually taken to mean female only, and this may include instances whereby male and female students occupy different floors in a hall of residence. This section also states whether students can stay in rooms during vacations, whether there is an additional charge on the normal rates and whether there are storage facilities for students' luggage. Prices for university/college/institute residences generally include heating, water, electricity and cleaning costs. Prices for rooms in town generally exclude all additional costs.

Entrance requirements: these are included as an approximate guide only; grades required will vary according to the subject. Applications are assessed individually and those from students with more unusual qualifications/backgrounds are usually considered.

EFL: this refers to the various qualifications available in English as a foreign language. Only the minimum grade is given, you might need a higher standard of English for particular subjects such as English literature, law or medicine, so check with the institution.

Foundation: foundation courses are available at many institutions and are intended to bring students up to the required entrance level for a degree course. This section includes specific subjects available alongside study skills and English language classes. If completed successfully, some courses guarantee students a place on a degree programme at the university or college. Also see 'The British Education System' section on page 25 and contact the international office.

Fees: all prices given for accommodation and fees are supplied by the institutions at time of publication and may change.

Aberystwyth

The University of Wales, Aberystwyth

Write to: Catrin James,
Postgraduate Admissions,
The University of Wales
Aberystwyth, Ceredigion SY23 2AX

Tel: +44 (0)1970 622270

Fax: +44 (0)1970 622921

Email:
postgraduate-admissions@aber.ac.uk

Website: www.aber.ac.uk

Students: over 7,000 students including 1,100 postgraduates.

Accommodation: university accommodation is guaranteed for all single international students.

Entrance requirements: the university offers a new international foundation programme that guarantees entry routes to undergraduate study. This combines English language tuition with grounding in the proposed undergraduate programme.

EFL: IELTS 5.5 to 6.0 or TOEFL 550 to 580 at entry.

Fees: flexible arrangements exist for the payment of tuition fees by self-financed students. For current information about funding opportunities for Aberystwyth applicants see the postgraduate pages of the university website.

Aberystwyth

Student profile

"I settled in well to the university and had a lot of help from my tutor. I like the scenic beauty of Aberystwyth and it is great to be beside the ocean. The community here is very nice, friendly and caring. The work is challenging but there's a lot of university staff to help support you. The quality of life is excellent."

Zahid Hussain, Pakistan

"I chose Aberystwyth because it offered me the greatest choice of courses. It is an amazing place, the town is wonderful.

The social life is really hectic. The friendliness of the place helps you to enjoy the nights even more."

Beatrice Ogunsanwo, Nigeria

Established in 1872, Aberystwyth was the first university institution in Wales. The town, built around Edward I's former fortress, is historic and dominated by the vast expanse of Cardigan Bay to the west. The nature of Aberystwyth allows students to study in coastal surroundings without too many distractions in a relaxed, friendly and safe community.

The university considers its information services to be among the best in Britain and the library facilities include the use of one of the six copyright libraries of Britain, the National Library of Wales, adjacent to the university campus. The Language and Learning Unit provides pre-sessional courses to help students prepare for their course. Support is offered to students throughout the academic year.

Academic strengths

There are three main faculties: the Faculty of Arts, the Faculty of Science and the Faculty of Social Studies.

The university's main library has seating for over 1,700 students and houses over one million titles. The National Library of Wales is also situated next to the campus and is one of the six copyright libraries in Great Britain holding over six million books, periodicals, magazines and maps. The university offers postgraduate courses in a range of areas including subjects such as accounting and finance, business studies (in which there is an MBA programme), computer science, economics, film and television studies, equine science, geography and earth science, health information management, heritage studies, library studies and information management.

Aberystwyth has developed a research training programme and in the most recent research assessment exercise a number of subjects were confirmed as producing research of international or national excellence. The university offers a range of methods of studying, developed to suit the needs of modern students. Many postgraduate courses are available on a part-time basis, meaning that while students must maintain regular contact with the university, they do not need to be in residence for lengthy periods.

Student life

The university has plenty to keep students occupied in their spare time, whether it be sport or socialising. There are some 170 clubs and societies in the students' union, covering most of the usual sports and some of the unusual, such as clay pigeon shooting and paintball. As the beach is close to the campus, surfing is also on offer.

Entertainment is both inexpensive and student centred, with excellent facilities offered by the students' union. The sports centre and arts centre, along with the students' union are located on the campus.

The students' union places a great emphasis on campaigns and awareness, ensuring that all students are aware of their rights. It actively supports minorities through activities such as liberation campaigns and support groups.

Aberystwyth takes an approach to student life and learning by encouraging students to be highly motivated, take responsibility for their own studies and to manage time effectively. Full details of postgraduate opportunities are currently available to view on the university website under individual academic departments and it is also possible to download application and reference forms.

Cambridge

ANGLIA POLYTECHNIC UNIVERSITY

Cambridge

Anglia Polytechnic University

Write to: International Office,
Anglia Polytechnic University,
East Road, Cambridge CB1 1PT

Tel: +44 (0)1245 493131

Fax: +44 (0)1245 348772

Email: international@apu.ac.uk

Website: www.apu.ac.uk

Students: 15,000 in 2000
(3,000 international from over 100
countries). 66:33 male:female.

Accommodation: single sex, mixed
and vacation (summer school)
accommodation. University residences
from £50 to £70 a week self-catered,
homestay from £48 to £85 a week.
Room in town from £55 to £65 a week.

Entrance requirements: the
international equivalent to two A level
passes. For postgraduates, the
equivalent to an honours degree.

EFL: for undergraduates, Cambridge First
Certificate, IELTS 5.5, TOEFL 550. For
postgraduates, Certificate of Proficiency,
IELTS 6.5, TOEFL 600.

Foundation: International Foundation
Programme entrance IELTS 4.5, TOEFL
450. Suitable for senior high school
graduates.

Fees: undergraduate and
postgraduate classroom-based £6,858
a year, laboratory-based £7,750 a year.
MBA £8,700 a year. International
foundation programme £5,950 a year.

The Learning Research Centre

Student profile

"It was important for me to go to a
business school which would provide me
with the necessary education that could
not only focus on the job side but also
the entrepreneurial side. International
exposure to business practices, issues,
strategies, effective decision-making and
a broad range of subjects was what I
wanted to learn. Anglia Business School
places an emphasis on small groups
and small class sizes. The MBA at APU
helped me not only to widen my horizons

but to look at issues
differently in order to
approach them strate-
gically. My exposure
at Anglia Business
School has contributed
immensely to my busi-
ness thinking."

Dave Dilkush, India

*Universities and colleges
of higher education*

438

Spread across two campuses, Anglia Polytechnic University's teaching traditions extend back over 100 years. The Cambridge campus is located centrally in the historic city with hidden courtyards and grand architecture. The old city has been an important market and centre of learning for hundreds of years. It is surrounded by fenlands to the north and the rolling chalklands of the Icknield Way to the south. Footpaths, cycleways and bridlepaths decorate the landscape, making it easily accessible to students.

The Chelmsford campus has a range of student facilities. In the last three years, a school of education and a school of nursing have been built. The Ashcroft International Business School is also due to open in 2003, adjacent to the student village which opened in 1995. The campus offers disabled facilities, computer facilities and a medical centre including a dispensary. Chelmsford itself is a quiet market town and has been the county town of Essex for over 700 years. Extensive parks and countryside sit alongside a thriving modern shopping centre and high-tech industry.

Academic strengths

There are several courses here that have been particularly popular with international students. Most notable is the international MBA course which starts in September and February and can be completed in one calendar year, or also English language, computer science, music and optometry. Many courses are even recognised by professional bodies, such as ICSA, ACCA, RCIS and the Law Society.

The university offers a modular system, and with over 8,000 modules on offer, students can enjoy flexibility and diversity in their studies. Both campuses have a range of up-to-date facilities and learning resources. These include art studios, a practice area for music students, a computer facility, a drop-in information centre for international students and a specialist learning technology centre concerned with software development, research and the teaching of information technology. The modern language centre has multimedia language laboratories, with language and machine translation software as well as both television and satellite facilities.

Student life

All students can join the numerous societies according to their cultural, religious, political or recreational interests. Students at the Cambridge site often socialise with students from Cambridge University and get involved in jointly-run societies. Every July in Cambridge, a series of festivals of classical music, art, theatre and film are enjoyed by students and visitors alike. For sporty types, there are plenty of facilities on offer, including tennis courts, a multigym, a sports field for outdoor sports and a swimming pool close by. On the Chelmsford campus, the gym is free and students can take part in most sports from hang-gliding to windsurfing and golf to cricket, usually with a big discount.

The university also offers support services to all of its international students including pre-arrival information and advice, an orientation programme for new students, English language modules as part of studies and a specially assigned personal tutor.

Bangor

University of Wales, Bangor

Write to: Iwan Roberts, International Office, University of Wales, Bangor, Gwynedd LL57 2DG

Tel: +44 (0)1248 382028

Fax: +44 (0)1248 383268

Email: international@bangor.ac.uk

Website:
www.bangor.ac.uk/international.html

Accommodation: family, vacation. All first-year students are guaranteed a room. Catered rooms from £68 to £74 a week, self-catering from £41 to £56 a week.

Students: 8,675 in 2000/01, (2,725 postgraduates, 1,842 international students from 120 countries), 44:56 male:female.

Entrance requirements: A levels, European or International Baccalaureate and other qualifications all considered.

EFL: IELTS 6.0 minimum, TOEFL 560 with a written score of 4, Cambridge Proficiency Higher pass.

Foundation: one-year foundation courses offered in partnership with local college. One, two and three-month pre-sessional courses between June and September. Cambridge exams can be taken in June for those needing a qualification for entry.

Fees: 2001/02 classroom and laboratory courses £7,000; MBAs £8,950; distance learning MBA £7,750.

University of Wales, Bangor campus

Student profile

"I chose to study at Bangor because its ranking is higher than other universities in the UK offering banking and finance. Bangor's coastal setting also appealed to me. I'm very pleased with my course; I can choose from lots of modules so I follow my particular interests. The course has excellent web pages to support the learning. The university is smaller than other city universities, so class sizes are smaller. I've joined trips to different parts of the UK and I've taken part in the HOST programme. I've made friends with students from all over the world. Because it's quiet, it's easier to study but there are plenty of things to do. There is a wide range of clubs and societies. I have joined the photographic society."

Iroda Azizova, Uzbekistan

The University of Wales, Bangor was founded over a century ago in 1884 and prides itself on its long tradition of teaching excellence. More than 250 undergraduate and 100 postgraduate programmes are offered to nearly 9,000 students by 17 academic departments. International students make up 20 per cent of the student population.

The cathedral city of Bangor is situated on the North Wales coast in an area of outstanding natural beauty, and only five miles away from Snowdonia National Park.

Academic strengths

The University of Wales, Bangor has notable specialisms including ocean science, psychology, environmental sciences, education, sports science and electronic engineering, many of which have been recognised for excellence in research. Over half of the departments assessed to date in the teaching quality assessments (conducted on behalf of the government) have achieved the top rating of excellent.

Bangor is a thriving academic institution but is still small enough for a personal teaching approach in lectures and tutorials. The university commitment to small group teaching and the resulting individual approach contributes to the students' positive experiences. The tutorial system provides students with help, advice and support for all matters, whether academic or personal.

Resources include an ocean-going research ship, a natural history museum, botanical gardens and a wealth of natural resources in the surrounding countryside of the area.

Student life

Bangor is compact and convenient; the area around the main university buildings and student housing has become a student village with a new sports centre, supermarket, local shops, restaurants and takeaways (including Chinese, Indian, Italian, Greek), banks and a post office. Bangor has a low crime rate and most university buildings and the city centre are within safe walking distance.

Bangor also offers cheap living costs and a place to live is guaranteed to all first-year students. Many international students choose self-catering accommodation, and food from all over the world can be bought in Bangor.

The international student welfare unit is available to guide, assist and advise on a variety of matters throughout the year. First-year students are allocated their own peer guide; a second or third-year student who is on hand to offer advice and assistance throughout the first year.

Central to student activity is the students' union. During the day, the union building, with its shops, cafés and travel shop, is a bustling meeting place and in the evening is the focal point for club and society activities. International clubs and societies include Pakistan, Hellenic, Islamic, Japanese and Afro-caribbean. Special interest groups include drama, mountain walking, archaeology, the rock society and 45 sports clubs including archery, cycling, windsurfing, jujitsu, tennis, netball, rugby, football and hockey.

Weekend trips are specially organised for international students and visits include the home of Shakespeare in Stratford-on-Avon, the thriving city of Leeds and the historic walled city of Chester.

Universities and colleges of higher education

Bath

Bath Spa University College

Write to: International Activities, Bath Spa University College, Newton Park, Bath BA2 9BN

Tel: +44 (0)1225 875577

Fax: +44 (0)1225 875501

Email: international-enquiries@bathspa.ac.uk

Website: www.bathspa.ac.uk

Students: 3,500 in 2000/01 (500 postgraduate, 200 international from 35 countries), 30:70 male:female.

Accommodation: single sex, vacation, storage facilities – extra charge. University residences from £50 to £75 a week self-catered. Room in town from £50 a week.

Entrance requirements: three A levels or international equivalent.

EFL: from IELTS 6.0; Foundation IELTS 4.0 to 5.0.

Foundation: foundation studies in Art and Design and English £6,450; Music and English £4,680; Foundation in General English £6,760.

Fees: undergraduate £7,460 a year; postgraduate £7,460 to £8,055 a year; UCIS £7,800 a year for 2002/03.

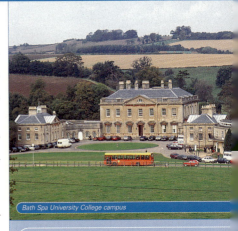
Bath Spa University College campus

Student profile

"Choosing which university to join in the UK wasn't an easy decision for me but I believe that I made the right choice. I am doing my PGDip/MA in Interactive Multimedia at Bath Spa University. What interested me in the programme is the fact that it doesn't only consist of practical modules but also theoretical ones, which I find very challenging. Furthermore, I am enjoying living in Bath, a rather small city with rich history, beautiful nature and busy student life. As well

as this, I feel that I am not only learning at university but learning from experiencing English culture, which I find different from my own."

Samar Yanni, Lebanon

Bath, in the west of England, is a city full of great historical and cultural interest. Being a tourist destination, there are plenty of things to do and see. Amongst the many museums, theatres, galleries, bars and pubs are the world famous Roman Baths, after which the city is named, the Museum of Costume, the Theatre Royal, the Museum of East Asian Art and the Victoria Art Gallery. Classical Georgian terraces line the streets and the distinction of being England's only World Heritage City makes Bath a unique place to study. Nearby, students can enjoy the attractions of Bristol, only 30 minutes away. The Cotswolds to the north and the Mendips and Glastonbury to the south are ideal for visits to the English countryside.

Bath Spa University College is based on two campuses: Sion Hill on the north side of Bath, where the university college's art and design courses are run, and Newton Park four miles west of central Bath, where the other departments are located. Newton Park campus is a Georgian manor house surrounded by landscaped gardens, a nature reserve and lake, woods and farmland. Famous alumni include Anita Roddick, founder of the Body Shop.

Academic strengths

Higher education quality councils noted that Bath Spa is "a close knit institution with a well-developed sense of community and common purpose." The university college now ranks higher than many traditional universities and higher than any new university.

The university college is divided into seven schools, namely Bath School of Art and Design, Science and Environment, Initial Teacher Training, Social Sciences, Historical and Cultural Studies, Music and Performing Arts, and English and Creative Studies. Each offers a diverse range of subjects at both undergraduate and taught postgraduate level.

Courses popular with international students include art and design, business studies, music, health studies, teacher training programmes and the interactive multimedia programme.

The university college specialises in making it easier for international students to enter undergraduate study. The unique support programme for year one of the BA/BSc awards, the Undergraduate Course for International Students (UCIS) allows entry with IELTS 5.5 and direct application to the university college.

Both campuses have well-stocked libraries complete with CD-Rom, multi-media packs and networked computers. The university college provides computer workstations for general use in designated rooms and within some subject areas such as design and technology, education, geography and music.

Student life

The thriving students' union facilities include a bar for each campus, live music venues, a launderette and a store selling stationery, art materials and books, amongst other things. Societies cater for the religious, political, national or cultural tastes of students. The union organises events that have made the university college a major venue of the area.

International students are welcomed with an airport pick-up, an orientation day plus induction week and English language support.

Universities and colleges of higher education

Bath

University of Bath

Write to: University of Bath,
Bath BA2 7AY

Tel: +44 (0)1225 386832

Fax: +44 (0)1225 386366

Email: international-office@bath.ac.uk

Website: www.bath.ac.uk

Students: 8,242 full time in 2000/01
(1,989 full-time postgraduates, 1,196
international students from over 70
countries), 57:43 male:female.

Accommodation: single sex,
some married, vacation. University
residences from £46 to £80 a week.
Room in town from about £50 a week.

Entrance requirements: generally
high: BBC or above at A level. Accept
International or European Baccalaureate
or a range of other international
qualifications.

EFL: IELTS 6.0, TOEFL 580.

Fees: classroom courses £7,660 a year;
laboratory courses £9,800 a year.

The university library

Student profile

"I'm in my second year of an MEng Aerospace Engineering degree. The aerospace department is one of the best in the country. It's got state-of-the-art facilities and the course gives us a lot of exposure to industry. We also do many projects for which we have to go and talk to all sorts of different people. That's helped develop my communication skills which will be useful for my future career. I decided I wanted to come to Bath after visiting on an open day. The university has a very different feel. The city is beautiful and the people are friendly. The cultural atmos-

phere is really good too and there are so many activities to get involved in. The sports facilities are also really excellent."

Bijal Thakore, India

Universities and colleges of higher education

Situated on the outskirts of the city, the university received its Royal Charter in 1966. 30 years on, its 1996 research assessment exercise ratings placed it among the top six universities in the UK. The compact campus is well equipped with shops, cafés, a bank, laboratories, a learning centre and library and a lively students' union.

The city's history stretches back to Roman times and has since grown into one of the most architecturally and culturally renowned destinations in the world. As well as having several major tourist attractions, such as the elegant Pump Rooms and the Roman Baths, Bath has much to offer students in terms of shopping and nightlife. The countryside of the Cotswolds, the Wye Valley and the ancient Forest of Dean are nearby and Bath is only an hour and a half away from London by train.

Academic strengths

The university offers undergraduate, taught postgraduate and research opportunities and comprises a School of Management and the Faculties of Science, Engineering and Design, Humanities and Social Science. The Departments of Mechanical Engineering, Pharmacy and Applied Mathematics have a 5* rating for research (1996), combined with an excellent rating for teaching and learning. International students are attracted to Bath's undergraduate courses because the university aims to emphasise education for the real world, most courses offering a work experience element. Courses that are particularly in demand include engineering, science, architecture, business, education, computer science, pharmacy, sports science and interpreting and translation courses, although the university offers courses in other disciplines. The university year is split into two semesters and programmes are based on modules. The university has a 24-hour library and learning centre and over 1,600 networked computers connected to the campus-wide ethernet.

Student life

Bath is the only UK university to have hosted an Olympic festival, and its 200-acre campus has sports facilities of a high standard. These include an indoor sports centre, two swimming pools (50m and 25m), four indoor and eight outdoor tennis courts and two floodlit all-weather astroturf pitches.

The students' union is active with over 100 clubs and societies. It also runs a newspaper, a magazine, a TV channel and a radio station. There is a predominant sense of participation across campus; social functions usually sell out and music, drama and the arts are flourishing. The university is part of a much larger local student body with another 3,500 students at the City of Bath College and a further 30,000 at universities in Bristol.

The international office at Bath, along with the chaplaincy, medical centre, tutors and student counsellors, provide an information and support network for overseas students. The international office offers advice on most things and contacts overseas students before they leave home, running buses to collect them from the airport. University accommodation on campus or in the city of Bath is guaranteed to all first-year undergraduates and all new first-year graduates from countries outside the European Union. They can also take classes in English and study skills at the English Language Centre.

the arts institute at bournemouth

Bournemouth

The Arts Institute at Bournemouth

Write to: Hilary Colvey, International Office, The Arts Institute at Bournemouth, Wallisdown, Poole, Dorset BH12 5HH

Tel: +44 (0)1202 363233

Fax: +44 (0)1202 537729

Email: h.colvey@arts-inst-bournemouth.ac.uk

Website: www.arts-inst-bournemouth.ac.uk www.lightsource.org.uk

Students: over 1,400 full-time students. 10 per cent of the students are international.

Accommodation: new on-campus halls of residence are being built for September 2002; all rooms will have 24-hour internet access.

Entrance requirements: English level undergraduate minimum of IELTS 6.0. Further education minimum of IELTS 5.5 or equivalent.

Fees: BA degrees or foundation £6,825 a year, foundation and national diploma courses £4,725 a year. Part-time, short courses and one-year options available on request. A number of scholarships, which equate to a £2,000 reduction of tuition fees, available to students in final year. Living in Bournemouth is considerably cheaper than London and students should allow approximately £4,000 to £6,000 a year.

THE QUEEN'S ANNIVERSARY PRIZES 1998

The Arts Institute at Bournemouth

Student profile

"I have almost finished my final year in BA (Hons) Film and Animation, specialising as a director. It was very important to me to go to an institute that could provide me with a broad knowledge of filmmaking; not just academic, but also the practical side. The course gives you the opportunity to produce films, develop your skills and learn from your mistakes. The facilities are extremely good and the reputation of the institute appealed to me – many established professionals took their degree here. The possibility to work with people on fashion, costume design, graphic design and photography courses  has proven extremely satisfying. I have really enjoyed my stay in the UK and got to know interesting people that I will most likely meet in the future."

Jorge Navarro Fica, Chile/Norway

Established in 1883, The Arts Institute at Bournemouth has developed into one of the leading specialist university sector institutions in Europe offering courses in art, design and media.

The institute is located on the beautiful south coast of England, in the county of Dorset. It is within easy reach of London, with regular coach and train services taking under two hours. The institute is committed to providing quality specialist education and is recognised as a Centre of Excellence in many areas including photography, design technologies and new media. Workshops and studios are fully equipped to the latest in industry standards, and all computer equipment is state-of-the-art. There is one computer to every four students.

Academic strengths

With only 1,500 students on full-time courses and a smaller number studying on a part-time basis, the institute can offer a personal and friendly approach to all activities. Class sizes are small (average 35) compared with many other higher education providers. There is a full range of course provision from further to higher education level. These include two-year National Diploma courses in four subject areas, one-year foundation programmes in art or media and specialist BA (Hons) degree courses in areas of study including 3D design, animation, arts and event production, costume, fashion, fine art, film production, graphic design, model making, multimedia and photography. The institute also offers an exciting new two-year higher education qualification called the foundation degree.

Former members of the Arts Institute alumni include Simon Beaufoy (script for *The Full Monty*), the photographer Nick Knight and Wolfgang Tillmans, Turner Prize Winner in 2000 (The UK's most prestigious art award). Students at the institute regularly participate in national competitions and are encouraged to show their work at exhibitions and festivals.

The Arts Institute at Bournemouth has an excellent reputation in the creative industries and many of its specialist courses are considered to be among the best in the country. The value of a reputation cannot be overstated and all students at the institute benefit from this advantage when they seek employment or advanced level education.

Student life

The Arts Institute at Bournemouth prides itself on being able to provide a friendly and supportive environment for all students and especially for those far away from home. In 2002, new on-campus halls of residence with 24-hour internet access will be made available to first-year students.

Bournemouth is an exciting cosmopolitan town with something for everyone, with all the facilities of a large city but still friendly and safe. As one of the Britain's leading seaside resorts there are many theatres, cinemas, museums and art galleries from which to choose as well as an excellent range of pubs, clubs and restaurants. As tourism is a major service industry in the area, there is also a range of part-time and temporary work available for students.

There is also a variety of watersports available including surfing, jet skiing and windsurfing. The coastal environment, in combination with the warmer than average climate, provides the area with an all year round holiday atmosphere.

Bournemouth

Bournemouth

Bournemouth University

Write to: International Office, Bournemouth University, Poole House, PG134, Talbot Campus, Fern Barrow, Poole BH12 5BB

Tel: +44 (0)1202 595470

Fax: +44 (0)1202 595287

Email: inta@bournemouth.ac.uk

Website: www.bournemouth.ac.uk

Students: in 2000/01, 624 international from 63 countries, 51:49 male:female.

Accommodation: mixed, single sex, couples and family. Vacation accommodation and storage facilities. University residences from £53 to £64 a week (self-catered). Room in town from £50 a week.

Entrance requirements: two to three A levels or international equivalent.

EFL: IELTS 6.0, TOEFL 550, 213.

Foundation: one-year courses in applied geography, archaeology, design engineering, computing and electronics, environmental protection, landscape and geographical sciences, heritage conservation.

Fees: for 2002 entry, undergraduate classroom-based £6,500; more resource intensive courses £7,100 a year; postgraduate courses in the region of £7,000.

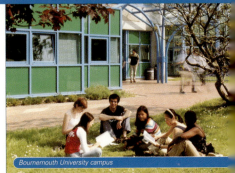
Bournemouth University campus

Student profile

"I liked the way things were taught at Bournemouth University – we weren't spoon fed but exposed to all areas and encouraged to investigate the subjects that interested us and allowed us to experiment to take our careers where we wanted to. My design work-based project really helped me understand what real research is, and has helped me see things differently. It was very useful interacting with students from different disciplines as it helped me look beyond my field and see how work is carried out in other areas. The diverse international background meant that we could discuss

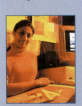

different approaches. Design is essentially a multidisciplinary practice and working in this environment has helped broaden my knowledge."

Komal Sanghavi, India

Universities and colleges of higher education

448

Situated in the middle of the south coast of England, Bournemouth enjoys beautiful local scenery and some of the country's mildest weather. Tourism is a major force and has brought with it a vibrant, cosmopolitan atmosphere and a lively entertainment scene. Bournemouth has all the facilities of a larger city but is still friendly and safe.

Built on heathland several centuries ago, Bournemouth has now matured into an internationally recognised 'garden city by the sea'. Historically, Bournemouth has been the favoured residence of many a writer, poet and artist. Robert Louis Stevenson wrote *Dr Jekyll and Mr Hyde* while living here and JRR Tolkien, author of *The Hobbit*, was a long time resident. Mary Wollstonecraft *(A Vindication of the Rights of Women)*, Mary Shelley *(Frankenstein)* and the heart of her husband, Percy Shelley, are all buried in Bournemouth. Within the wider local area, Dorset was the home of Thomas Hardy and Lawrence of Arabia.

There are many theatres, concert venues and cinemas catering for all tastes within Bournemouth. Poole Harbour, the world's second largest natural harbour, is close by. It is a major centre for all watersports and its historic quayside area dates back to Roman times. Poole also has many bars, cafés and restaurants.

Academic strengths

The university is divided into seven schools of study: business, conservation sciences, design, engineering and computing, finance and law, health and community studies, media and service industries. Most undergraduate courses include an industrial placement. A high graduate employment rate makes Bournemouth one of Britain's best universities for top employment opportunities. The Media School scored 22 out of 24 in the latest teaching quality assessment and the university was also awarded the Queen's Anniversary Prize for Higher and Further Education for its innovative programmes.

Facilities include purpose-built libraries, laboratories and open learning centres. Students have 24-hour access to computer laboratories. The university is also home to specialist research centres, including the National Centre for Computer Animation, the International Centre for Tourism and Hospitality Research and the Centre for Culinary Research.

Student life

Bournemouth University students' union manages the university bars as well as a venue in the centre of town and a series of events throughout the year. Alongside these entertainments are the traditional student balls and discos.

The university has good quality sports facilities which are available to all students and a range of different student societies, from regional and religious to sport and entertainment clubs.

International students are supported through the international office. They run a lively and informative orientation week and offer a month-long, pre-sessional study skills programme. English language support runs throughout the year. All international students who apply before the mid-August deadline are guaranteed university accommodation. The students' union aims to be especially aware of the welfare needs of international students and the chaplaincy embraces all religions.

Bradford

Bradford College

Write to: Howard Clough,
Head of International Centre,
The International Centre, Bradford
College, Great Horton Road,
Bradford, West Yorkshire BD7 1AY

Tel: +44 (0)1274 753348

Fax: +44 (0)1274 736175

Email: international@bilk.ac.uk

Website: www.bilk.ac.uk

Students: 27,000 in 2001/02
(50 postgraduate, 500 international
from 56 countries).

Accommodation: college residences
from £50 to £73 a week self-catered.
Room with family from £53 to £85 a week.
Room in town from £38 to £95 a week.

Entrance requirements: refer to
appropriate course for details.

Foundation: available in all disciplines.

Fees: English, foundation, vocational and
technician courses £3,800 a year; higher
technician and undergraduate courses
£6,450 a year. Postgraduate courses
on application.

Bradford College

Student profile

"After I finished my BA (Hons) Art and
Design course at Bradford College, I
returned to Beijing before coming back to
the college to further my studies. I then
successfully completed the MA in Print
Making. I enjoyed living in Bradford, and
received lots of encouragement and
assistance from the staff. There are many
international students at Bradford
College and I was able to make friends
with people from most parts of the
world. All areas of interest are catered for
at Bradford College, and there
are excellent facilities in all areas of

study which provide
good opportunities for
students. I greatly
enjoyed my time at
Bradford College and
would recommend it
to anyone."

Buri Gude Zhang,

People's Republic of China

Located in the geographical centre of the UK, Bradford is very much a university city that offers students a variety of cultural, historical as well as recreational experiences. The large student community is catered for by Bradford's many restaurants and bars, and the city is home to the National Museum of Photography, Film and Television, housing Britain's first IMAX cinema screen. Historically, Bradford was the centre of Britain's woollen industry. Today, however, engineering, electronics, finance, banking and commerce dominate.

All undergraduate and postgraduate courses are accredited by The University of Bradford, and all other higher education qualifications are awarded by Edexcel (BTEC).

Academic strengths

The college has 11 academic departments: Art and Design, Administrative Studies, Business Studies, Engineering and Construction, Management, Hospitality and Leisure, Information Technology (IT), Science, Teacher Education, Applied Social Science and Applied Human Studies. Degrees and higher education qualifications have been developed through consultation with industrial and commercial sectors in order to prepare students for their careers. Undergraduate courses are modular, allowing students a large degree of flexibility and choice.

The college runs an integrated computer network across the campus as a teaching facility and a shared communication tool. IT courses are available at every level and, as policy, the college has industry-standard equipment and software. The library houses over 200,000 books, 1,200 journal titles and an extensive range of electronic information services, including internet, email and CD-Rom databases. English language courses are available at all levels.

Student life

With both the college and The University of Bradford, the city has a large student population and offers a lively nightlife, from bars and restaurants to theatres and sporting venues. Yorkshire's beautiful countryside is within easy reach and there are a number of opportunities for outdoor pursuits such as climbing, orienteering, fishing, sailing, flying and potholing, as well as the more sedate sports like golf. Most indoor sports are available at Bradford University which houses a 25-metre swimming pool, squash courts, a gymnasium, sauna and solarium. Students can also take advantage of the many varied societies operating through the student union which cater for most cultural, political, sporting, intellectual and social tastes.

The college's international centre is the first point of contact that international students have with the college. The centre aims to provide students with all of the appropriate course materials and to help guide them through the application process. It also ensures that students are given maximum credit for their previous work experience or education and offers information on visas and immigration. Specialist assistance is given to those students who are experiencing difficulties with either financial, medical or academic matters, or any other welfare issues. A meet and greet service is available for international students from the Manchester and Leeds/Bradford airports.

UNIVERSITY OF BRADFORD

Bradford

The University of Bradford

Write to: Enquiries Office,
The University of Bradford,
Bradford BD7 1DP

Tel: +44 (0)1274 233081

Fax: +44 (0)1274 236260

Email: enquiries@bradford.ac.uk

Website: www.bradford.ac.uk

Students: 12,500 of which 11.5 per cent
are international students.

Accommodation: university
residences from £42.50 a week.
Single sex accommodation available.
Private accommodation nearby from
£30 a week.

Entrance requirements: refer to
prospectus for A level requirements.
International and European Baccalaureate
accepted. Advanced standing offered to
students with appropriate qualifications.

EFL: for degree courses, minimum
IELTS 6.0; TOEFL 550; foundation
English available.

Fees: classroom-based courses £6,720
per annum; laboratory courses £8,760
per annum (2001).

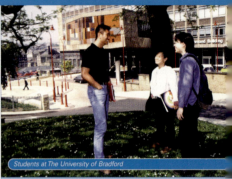

Students at The University of Bradford

Student profile

"I wanted a broader background in communications but I had to be sure that Bradford was a top-quality university before I could get support from Mexico! The computer and microprocessor laboratories are very good and so are the lectures. I find it very helpful that they give out notes so you can concentrate on listening. They prepare seminar and tutorial classes well, so you have the opportunity to practise what you are learning. Bradford isn't a particularly beautiful city but I have been surprised by the people, who are warm and friendly. Soon after I arrived in Britain I needed an

operation in hospital. The Health Service staff were so helpful. In fact, everyone was helpful in making sure I was able to keep up with my work."

Roberto Ramirez-Iniguez, Mexico

Bradford is a city university with its main campus just five minutes' walk from the centre of one of the 10 largest cities in England. The National Museum of Photography, Film and Television, with its five-storey high IMAX cinema screen is even closer, as is the magnificent Alhambra Theatre. Bradford offers a range of cultural, sporting and historic attractions and is an excellent base for trips to the beautiful scenery of the Yorkshire Dales. The historic village of Haworth, home of the Brontë family, lies within the city boundary. Leeds/Bradford International Airport is only 15 kilometres away. Sports facilities on campus include state-of-the-art fitness rooms, a swimming pool and also a sports hall for badminton, basketball and five-a-side football.

Academic strengths

The university has particular strengths in engineering (chemical, civil, structural and environmental, computing, electrical and electronic, mechanical and manufacturing including automotive) in the health-related sciences (such as optometry, radiography, pharmacy and physiotherapy) and in business and management. Bradford School of Management was the first business school to be established in the UK.

Subjects at the University of Bradford have been awarded the highest possible score in six consecutive quality assurance assessments, which is a great accolade. Excellent results have been returned in the assessments for subjects including peace studies, archaeological sciences, nursing and midwifery, interdisciplinary human studies, pharmacy, optometry, physiotherapy and radiography.

The Department of Peace Studies is one of only seven centres worldwide to be selected by Rotary International as a Rotary Centre for International Studies in Peace and Conflict Resolution.

In addition, the university offers a range of innovative courses including electronic imaging and media communications, computer animation and special effects, and cybernetics. The employment record of Bradford graduates is notable, with 94 per cent in employment or further study. This reflects the practical and professional emphasis of the courses offered.

Student life

The university has 2,000 study bedrooms either on campus or within five minutes' walk. These almost all have telephone and computer network links which enable students to access computer facilities and to make and receive international calls from their rooms. Single international students on taught courses are guaranteed accommodation in university residences for their first year at Bradford and it is often possible to extend this to other years if students wish. However, accommodation in Bradford close to the university is cheap and easily available, and many students prefer to rent a house for between four or five people.

The students' union runs a wide range of social activities for students and it has many international student societies. With 7,000 to 8,000 students living in and around the university, there is always something to do for everyone, whatever their interest. On arrival, all students are tested on their English language ability and the university offers a range of English and study skills programmes free of charge to all of its international students.

Bristol

University of Bristol

Write to: Admissions Office, Senate House, University of Bristol, Bristol BS8 1TH

Tel: +44 (0)117 928 7678

Fax: +44 (0)117 925 1424

Email: admissions@bristol.ac.uk

Website: www.bris.ac.uk

Students: 12,867 (2,493 full-time post-graduate, about 1,400 international from over 100 countries), 49:51 male:female.

Accommodation: single sex, some married, vacation. University residences from £45 a week self-catering, from £55 a week catering. Room in town from £50 to £55 a week.

Entrance requirements: generally high: medicine, dentistry, veterinary science As; many subjects As and Bs. European and International Baccalaureate also accepted.

EFL: IELTS 6.5, TOEFL 620.

Fees: 2002/03 (provisional) classroom courses £7,680 a year; laboratory courses £10,100 a year; clinical medicine £18,710 a year.

University of Bristol students

Student profile

"When I was 20, I was studying for a physics degree at Sogang, one of Seoul's top universities. I then started an English course at the British Council and liked the idea of studying in 'the land of physics'. *The Times Higher Education Supplement* listed Bristol among the top universities for physics, so I applied to enter the second year of a BSc. In the first year, all I did was work as I couldn't understand all the lectures. My maths bailed me out and some second-year English students helped me. I passed, and I'm running for election to the students' union. I'm also applying to

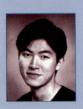

convert my course to a four-year MSc. Then I might do a PhD in Cryogenics. Bristol holds the record for achieving the lowest-ever temperature."

Jisu Kim, Korea

If you like city life, you'll love being at Bristol. Its several sites are spread across a lively, modern city on two rivers. Bristol has been an important commercial port since medieval times. It was from Bristol that John Cabot set sail in 1497 on his voyage to the coasts of Newfoundland and North America. Bristol's most famous sights are its three suspension bridges, one across the Avon Gorge and two across the Severn estuary, which link England with Wales. Just to the east is the historic town of Bath, with its Roman ruins, ancient abbey, Georgian architecture and varied museums. London is just 90 minutes away by train.

Academic strengths

Bristol's respected medical school was founded in 1833, while the university was founded in 1876. Today, there are 36 applicants for every medical school place, and similar pressure for dentistry and veterinary science – the veterinary college, in its rural setting away from the university's main city sites, is strong on farm animals and equine science.

Engineering and computer science are also major strengths; the faculties received excellent ratings in teaching and research and both welcome students from all over the world every year. British Formula 1 racing cars have benefited from Bristol's forward-looking approach to aerospace engineering. Bristol is one of the world leaders in geography; it developed much of the technical equipment, such as night-eyes and other remote-sensing equipment used on geological surveys. Because Bristol is a focus for independent film and TV companies, its media courses receive a high number of applications for places.

International students often study law, economics and accounting, or apply to the arts and social sciences departments, for which the university is also noted. The main library at the university has in excess of one million volumes and subscribes to over 6,000 periodicals. This library forms the focus of the library system and is supported by a further 12 branch libraries throughout the university. Networked computer rooms are located throughout the university precinct and all of the halls of residence. Each room is able to offer personal access to the internet.

Student life

Bristol has entertainment of every kind, from the Old Vic, a leading provincial theatre with its own theatre school, to a rock concert venue and many clubs. The city has good shopping facilities and Clifton's sloping streets are full of antique stores and cafés. There is yachting and water sports at the riverside docks.

The university has a large students' union with facilities including two theatres and a busy entertainments programme. Some of the union's members get involved in social work in the city – helping underprivileged groups. Bristol is a relatively safe city to walk around.

University residence is guaranteed to single international students for the duration of their course. The international office is experienced in welcoming and helping international students. There are events for new arrivals, English classes and a credit transfer system for students on year-abroad schemes. Postgraduate research students often stick around, returning to do more research, or find work in the area.

University of the West of England

Bristol

University of the West of England, Bristol

Write to: Enquiry and Admissions Service, Frenchay Campus, University of the West of England, Bristol, Coldharbour Lane, Bristol BS16 1QY

Tel: +44 (0)117 344 3333

Fax: +44 (0)117 344 2810

Email: admissions@uwe.ac.uk

Website: www.uwe.ac.uk

Students: 24,000 in 2001 (3,158 postgraduate, 1,269 international from over 40 countries), 50:50 male:female.

Accommodation: university residence from £50 a week self-catering. Room in town £46 to £70 a week.

Entrance requirements: minimum two A levels at grade E plus three GCSE subjects at grade C or equivalent. European or International Baccalaureates are accepted.

EFL: Cambridge Proficiency grade C. Undergraduate: IELTS 6.0; TOEFL paper-based 570, computer-based 230. Postgraduate: IELTS 6.5; TOEFL paper-based 600, computer-based 250.

Foundation: English language, art and design, built environment, engineering and science. The Foundation English Language Programme is designed for international students wishing to acquire skills needed to enter higher education in the UK. Running from October to September, the programme has a flexible structure enabling participants to join at the four different entry points.

Fees: Diploma in Foundation Studies in Art and Design £5,130; classroom-based £6,150; laboratory £6,500.

Frenchay Campus, Bristol

Student profile

"I worked on building sites for about five years back in Hong Kong to save the money to study here. I studied part time for an HND in Building Studies so that I could do the BSc in Construction Management in one year instead of three, which I'd have to do in Hong Kong. I've been here for just a couple of weeks and it's challenging. The culture is so different, it's hard to communicate with everyone, especially in class. It's easier in my residence. The library's too good – there's too much information! I feel free here – there's plenty of time to do research and I like the seminars.

What I love most in Britain is the space. What do I hate? Well, the food is different. And I can't believe what they charge in Chinese restaurants!"

David Tze Tung Ngi, Hong Kong

University of the West of England, Bristol (UWE) was established as a university in 1992 and is already in the first division of new universities according to recent league tables. It began life in 1885 as Bristol Merchant Venturers' School, established by the merchants of the time to further the artistic and scholastic life of the city.

The blend of Victorian-to-modern architecture and its mix of traditional and innovative programmes give visitors the impression that UWE is a new university with a traditional slant. The university's programmes are grouped into 11 faculties and one associated faculty. Over 300 different programmes of study are available at degree level and there is also a range of taught professional and master's programmes.

The university's close links with industry and the professions ensure that courses remain relevant and innovative. Many degrees include a period of industrial experience and a large number of students undertake these placements abroad. Research programmes exist in all faculties.

The university is the largest educational institution in the city and is similar in structure and status to an American state university. It is located on four campuses around Bristol, known as the capital of the southwest of England.

Bristol is a city of fine architecture and culture, set in the undulating valley of the River Avon. Excellent road and rail connections let students travel to London, Oxford, and the spectacular scenery of Wales, Devon and the Cotswolds within an hour and a half.

Academic strengths

UWE has scored highly in recent government assessments of teaching quality, reaching 20 or more out of a possible 24 in all the subjects which have so far been assessed. The university has excellent ratings in business and law – subjects with a lasting appeal for international students.

The university aims to develop skilled graduates with real-life experience in their chosen fields of work. Industrial placements in commercial companies are an incredibly important constituent of the business programmes. The law faculty has a replica law court in which its students can stage trials.

Information technology and computer science programmes benefit from high research standards in the Faculty of Computing, Engineering and Mathematical Sciences. British culture and media also won a respectable research rating.

The Art, Media and Design Faculty has programmes in fashion and textile design, ceramics and time-based media (television, video, multimedia, radio and sound). Equine management and sports coaching and rehabilitation are also popular and courses.

Student life

UWE, though large, is a friendly and not impersonal place. Refectories, café bars, shops and banking facilities are on or near all of the campuses along with a full range of student advisory services.

There are fitness facilities and over 40 union sports clubs. Culturally, there is the Centre for Performing Arts, which promotes music and theatre, and there is also an active students' union. There are prayer facilities for all religious groups.

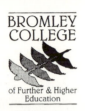

BROMLEY
COLLEGE
of Further & Higher
Education

Bromley

Bromley College of Further & Higher Education

Contact: Peter Reeves or Chantal Milnes, International Office, Bromley College of Further & Higher Education, Rookery Lane, Bromley BR2 8HE

Tel: + 44 (0)20 8295 7031

Fax: + 44 (0)20 8295 7051

Email: international@bromley.ac.uk

Website: www.bromley.ac.uk

Students: 6,000 in 1999/2000 (2,500 full time, 3,500 part time, 200 international from around 30 countries).

Accommodation: no college accommodation. Homestays £90 a week (including meals), vacation.

Entrance requirements: vary according to course of study.

Foundation: one-year access courses in business, law, engineering and science. Successful students are guaranteed entry onto degree programmes at the University of Greenwich.

Fees: foundation £4,000 a year; HND £6,000 a year; undergraduate £6,000 a year.

Universities and colleges of higher education

Bromley College of Further & Higher Education

Student profile

"I decided to come to the UK because public security and welfare are good and it's easy to travel to other EU countries. I also wanted to study at a state college where there are many English people. I'm studying English and business administration with IT. There are many computers, a large library and good English teachers. I like the environment, the student services and the fact that the college is so near to London. The college found my accommodation for me and I live in a house and cook for myself. I enjoy meeting students from other countries as it helps me learn about

different cultures. The countryside is very nice in the UK, though sometimes it can be a bit cold. I find most English people to be friendly."

Chia-Lung Chen, Taiwan

Bromley College of Further & Higher Education is based on three sites in Bromley and Penge and is an Associate College of the University of Greenwich. Bromley is the largest London borough with a population of around 300,000. It is mainly residential in character with large areas of woodland and parks. Just under 20 minutes away from London by train, its students are never far away from the shops and nightlife of the capital. Bromley town centre itself has over 450 shops and stores, as well as restaurants, cafés, bars, a leisure centre, library and cinema.

The college's main site is based at Rookery Lane which is just south of Bromley town centre. The site offers modern laboratories and workshops, a language centre, a library and a number of computer suites, allowing all students free email and internet access. The student union houses a refectory, bistro and student lounge and the site's extensive grounds also offer opportunities for both relaxation and exercise.

The majority of Bromley College's management training and social work courses are held in the college's second site in the Old Town Hall. Situated in the centre of Bromley, the grade two listed building houses a conference hall, seminar rooms, a library, IT suite and bar for both students and staff. The college's third site is the newly-refurbished Hawthorn centre, providing a range of training in areas such as IT, administration and childcare.

Academic strengths

A range of subjects are available at all levels from beginner upwards. Qualifications include GNVQs, NVQs, BTECs, AS levels, A levels, GCSEs, Higher National Diplomas and degrees. The college has approval to offer a number of University of Greenwich awards and students on approved courses are entitled to make use of the university's library and careers service. As well as this, they also receive preferential consideration for progression, or indeed transfer, to other university pathways.

The library at Rookery Lane contains a variety of books, newspapers, journals, videos, audio tapes, computer software and CD-Roms. The library's learning resource centre provides specialist support for maths, English and IT. Along with the learning resource centre at the Old Town Hall, and the information technology facilities available at all sites, students may benefit from modern multimedia resources and the latest computer hardware and software, not to mention a TV-editing suite.

Student life

Many international students who are aiming specifically to improve their English language skills make their first visit to the college by attending its summer school. The summer school provides an excellent opportunity for prospective students to assess the college and its facilities. They may also enquire, first-hand, about their intended course of study and college accommodation.

The college Student Services Department provides advice, information and counselling to all those students who feel they require it. International students also benefit from many college-provided services, including an airport pick-up, an induction week upon arrival and English language support.

BRUNEL
UNIVERSITY
WEST LONDON

London

Brunel University

Write to: Caroline Browne, International Office, Brunel University, Uxbridge, Middlesex UB8 3PH

Tel: +44 (0)1895 203076

Fax: +44 (0)1895 203084

Email: international-office@brunel.ac.uk

Website: www.brunel.ac.uk/admin/registry/international

Students: 13,000 in 2000/01 (1,995 postgraduate, 1,256 international from 110 countries) 53:47 male:female.

Accommodation: single sex, married, vacation, storage facilities. University residence from £50.50 to £62.50 a week self-catered, from £63 to £69 a week catered. Room in town from £60 to £70 a week.

Entrance requirements: 20 points at A level. 26 to 36 at International Baccalaureate with grade five in specified subjects.

EFL: IELTS 6 to 7; TOEFL 570 to 585; or Cambridge Proficiency Level C.

Foundation: programmes available.

Fees: classroom courses £7,075 a year; laboratory courses £9,400 a year (2001/02).

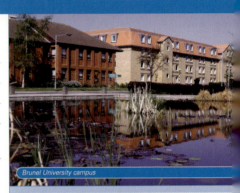

Brunel University campus

Student profile

"I am studying for a postgraduate degree in microelectronics system design. My original choice of programme was based on Brunel's outstanding reputation in engineering. I decided to continue my studies because I have found a sponsor through the department's industrial connections, which will give me the opportunity to gain an insight into the working of an international, broadline manufacturer and supplier of integrated circuits. The department has a good range of facilities. This, together with the enthusiastic and approachable lecturing staff, constitutes an excellent working

environment. Brunel University is a friendly, compact campus with everything close at hand, which makes it a great choice for students."

Christiana Krikis, Greece

Brunel University was first established in 1966 and today it has over 13,000 students. The university is located on the western outskirts of London near Heathrow airport and Windsor. There are four campuses which are based at Uxbridge, Twickenham, Osterley and Runnymede. All of the campuses have on-site halls of residences, social facilities, libraries, computer centres and welfare services.

The university has traditionally taught engineering and sciences but in recent years there has been a significant increase in the number of social sciences and arts courses. Brunel also strongly encourages work experience and offers a number of four-year degrees with either a 'thin' or 'thick' sandwich option.

Academic strengths

Brunel University is divided into three faculties: Arts and Social Sciences, Life Sciences, and Technology and Information Systems. In teaching quality assessments, all departments since 1999 have achieved excellent (at least 22 out of 24), and the last three (education, government and sport) all gained 23 points.

In the 2001 Research Assessment Exercise, there were grade 5s for applied maths, general engineering, law, library and information management, mechanical engineering and sociology, with a 33 per cent rise in overall performance since the last assessment.

Each campus library provides areas for private study, media rooms, video units and computer access. Media facilities include video editing suites and digital image and sound processing. The specialist teaching resources include sports amenities, both engineering and science laboratories, design studios and dance studios. A new art complex and art gallery have recently been added to the list of university facilities.

Student life

Brunel's student union plays an active part at every campus with an office at each one. The union provides a number of services including live entertainment, a free fortnightly magazine and a radio station. The union also supports around 90 different clubs and societies including those representing different ethnic groups. Sports facilities comprise three sports halls, squash courts, a weight room, a fitness suite, tennis courts, playing fields, a running track and a boathouse.

A university counselling service is available to students on all four campuses and the medical centre also looks after student welfare. There is accommodation on campus and the university has a housing office to help those who wish to find somewhere to live off campus.

International students benefit from their own student union representative, and English language tuition is available from the language centre. The international office co-ordinates a meet and greet service from Heathrow and an orientation programme for new students. Meeting houses are available for all faiths and weekly worship is arranged for Christians and Muslims.

Each year, 10 scholarships are offered to international students worth £2,000 for each year of full-time study.

Universities and colleges of higher education

Cardiff

University of Wales Institute, Cardiff

Write to: The International Office, University of Wales Institute, Cardiff, PO Box 377, Western Avenue, Cardiff CF5 2SG

Tel: +44 (0)29 2041 6045

Fax: +44 (0)29 2041 6928

Email: international@uwic.ac.uk

Website: www.uwic.ac.uk

Students: 8,500 in 2000/02 (300 international students from over 50 countries), 50:50 male:female.

Accommodation: mixed university residences from £50 a week. Room in private sector from £40 a week.

Entrance requirements: two A level passes, minimum grade E or equivalent. European or International Baccalaureate pass is accepted.

EFL: Cambridge Advanced grade A, Proficiency grade C; IELTS 6; TOEFL 570.

Fees: International Foundation £5,000; classroom courses £6,600; laboratory courses £7,250; postgraduate and PhD £7,250; MBA £7,750.

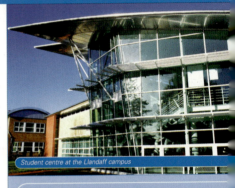

Student centre at the Llandaff campus

Student profile

"I am in my final year having completed a 12-month clinical training placement at the Medical Microbiology Department of the University Hospital of Wales. The year spent in the training laboratory gave me an insight into the professional environment, and boosted my initiative and confidence. I carried out practical work for my final-year dissertation and had invaluable help from people who specialise in the topic area. Not only did it reduce the pressure in my final year, it also made me realise that I definitely want to be part of the growing success of applied research.

I would recommend my course because it is challenging, rewarding and it opens the doors to many career opportunities in the biomedical sciences."

Sissie Wong, Hong Kong

Cardiff, capital of Wales is the location of the University of Wales Institute, Cardiff (UWIC), a constituent university of the federal University of Wales. Cardiff itself is home to the respected Welsh National Opera and the Welsh national rugby team. Cardiff is located in Wales' industrial south but is close to the Brecon Beacons National Park, the dramatic Glamorganshire coastline and historic Welsh castles.

Academic strengths

UWIC has eight faculties, spread over four campuses. The faculties of Product Design and Engineering and Applied Sciences are on a modern campus in the cathedral town of Llandaff, on the city's outskirts. Art, design and engineering are major strengths; UWIC received an excellent rating in the teaching quality assessment for ceramics and interior architecture – courses with a practical and technical focus. Fine art also received an excellent rating. This, along with graphic design, aesthetics and the history and theory of art and design, has a much more theoretical bias.

The Faculty of Art and Design enjoys a city centre location at the Howard Gardens campus. It is linked with engineering and offers courses in design engineering, electronics design, industrial and product design and manufacture. The engineering workshops are equipped with new computer rooms and miniature and factory-sized electronic manufacturing plants. Students take part in industrial experience as part of many UWIC courses, which carry transferable credit points.

The faculties of Business and Hospitality and Tourism and Leisure attract many international students. Students can take a two-year HND in Business and Finance or Computing and go on to a BA Business and Management or a BSc Business Information Systems. Hotel tourism, catering and institution management and food science and technology are also taught in this faculty. All levels are catered for, from the Diploma in Baking Technology to the HND or degree in Food Technology.

The professional emphasis of UWIC is evident in the Faculty of Health and Social Sciences, offering courses in dental technology, biomedical sciences, speech therapy, nutrition, podiatry and environmental risk management. Psychology and communication received an excellent rating in the latest teaching quality assessment. The Education and Sport faculties are centres for teacher training and sports science.

Student life

The university offers some excellent sports facilities. UWIC's £7 million national indoor athletics centre was opened in January 2000 by the Olympic athlete, Colin Jackson OBE. Facilities at the Cyncoed campus are available to all students. Town and gown share the Welsh obsession with rugby, thus UWIC is a strong choice for sports science students. Famous alumni include Olympic medallists such as Lynn Davies and international rugby stars, for example Gareth Edwards.

Modern university accommodation is guaranteed to all international students, who are supported by a specialist welfare programme and free English language tuition and study skill support.

Birmingham

University of Central England in Birmingham

Write to: International Admissions Officer, University of Central England in Birmingham, Perry Barr, Birmingham B42 2SU

Tel: +44 (0)121 331 5389

Fax: +44 (0)121 331 6706

Email: international.admissions@uce.ac.uk

Website: www.uce.ac.uk

Students: 23,744 in 2000/01 (3,616 postgraduate, 1,976 overseas), 9,657:14,087 male:female.

Accommodation: single sex, vacation, family. University residences from £57.50 to £69.50.

Entrance requirements: varies.

EFL: IELTS 6.0 plus, TOEFL 550 plus, Hong Kong Use of English 6 plus, AQA ESOL pass, Cambridge Proficiency/Advanced C or above, or O level English C or above.

Foundation: Foundation programmes available in Art and Design, Business and Computer Technology. Some are run in conjunction with local colleges.

Fees: £6,900 to £8,900.

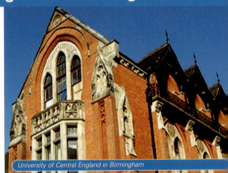
University of Central England in Birmingham

Student profile

"I chose UCE because it is one of only three universities in the UK offering a fast-track course with the Association of Chartered Certified Accountants. Its Business School has a good reputation and the lecturers are all experts in their fields. UCE has good library facilities with electronic journals and internet access so I can email my family back home. Free English classes are on offer to overseas students. I like Birmingham because it has many places of interest. There are also entertainment venues where I can relax, like the Hippodrome Theatre and the Symphony Hall. There are areas of

natural beauty in Birmingham. As the UK's second city, it is centrally placed with good transport. Many places of interest are within easy reach."

May May Ong, Malaysia

The University of Central England in Birmingham (UCE) is located in the centre of the UK, ideal for exploring the country. Birmingham is the country's second largest city and it has its own international airport. With a nightlife to rival that of any major city, a superb arts and cultural scene, world-class sporting facilities, cosmopolitan cuisine and excellent shopping facilities, bold new developments are making Birmingham a city of exciting contrasts. Although it is a modern city, it is equally proud of its history and heritage.

Although UCE is a new university, its lineage can be traced back some 150 years, evolving over this time with the merging of various institutes, schools and colleges. Buildings thus range from the ultra-modern to the historic in locations across the city. Each year, an increasing number of students come from non-European Union countries. At present, there are students from more than 50 countries outside the EU with significant numbers from the Far East, Norway, Africa and the Indian sub-continent.

Academic strengths

UCE is a university of great diversity, offering a broad range of subjects of study and more than 300 courses that cater for over 23,000 students. The courses at UCE are split into nine faculties: Business; Art and Design; Music; Law and Social Sciences; Computing; Information and English; Education; Technology Innovation Centre; Built Environment; and Health and Community Care. The university has subject-focused library facilities and a digital library. All students have access to computer facilities within libraries and faculty resource rooms. Specialist departments have their own resources such as editing suites, art studios and workshops.

The main common factor across the university is the close links it maintains between academic provision and the demands of the real world. Courses enable students to relate theoretical study to real life situations, combining academic and vocational approaches. The experience this provides feeds back in turn into the courses, ensuring that graduates benefit from the most relevant knowledge.

This year has seen the development of the Technology Innovation Centre's new premises at Millennium Point and also the Centre for Defence Medicine under the UCE banner.

Student life

UCE has an active students' union with clubs that cover both sports and general interest. There are also eight bars and an entertainment package at the union club. Throughout the year, there is a calendar of events. The university recently invested £3 million in new sports facilities. Birmingham itself is home to three football clubs and the venue for international cricket.

International students benefit from a meet and greet welcome service, guaranteed accommodation in halls for the duration of their course, fixed fees, free pre-sessional English as well as an orientation programme before they start their course. Throughout the year, there is English language support.

The university has a multifaith chaplaincy team and there are societies for all the major religions.

Manchester

City College Manchester

Write to: Richard Spriggs,
International Admissions Officer,
City College Manchester, Fielden Centre,
141 Barlow Moor Road, West Didsbury,
Manchester M20 2PQ

Tel: +44 (0)161 957 1609

Fax: +44 (0)161 957 8613

Email: rspriggs@ccm.ac.uk

Website: www.ccm.ac.uk

Students: 10,000 in 1997/98
(350 international from 40 countries),
40:60 male:female.

Accommodation: single sex,
married/family, vacation, storage
facilities. Homestay from £75 a
week including bills and meals.
Room in town from £40 a week.

Entrance requirements: vary
according to course, generally
high school certificate or
international equivalent.

EFL: HND programmes IELTS 5.0 to 5.5,
FE courses IELTS 5.0, foundation courses
IELTS 4.5 to 5.0.

Foundation: programmes in
economics, finance, business
studies, IT, art and design,
science and engineering.

Fees: EFL £3,300 a year; FE courses
£3,900 a year; HE courses £5,100 a year;
Foundation £4,900 a year.

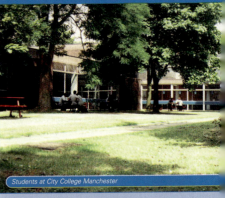
Students at City College Manchester

Student profile

"I came to City College Manchester as
a student and I ended up working in the
international office! I wanted to improve
my English after finishing university in
Spain. I heard about the college from
one of my friends. I really enjoyed my
time at the college. The teaching was
excellent and the staff were very friendly
and eager to help. The college has good
facilities, too. What I enjoyed the most
was the diversity of the students and
the mixture of people from different
cultural backgrounds. The English that I
 learnt enabled me to
enrol on an MA
course and find a
job. Manchester is a
vibrant city – the ideal
place for a young
person to live."

Idoia Garcia, Spain

The city of Manchester, with its 2.5 million inhabitants and student population of over 50,000, is a genuine cosmopolitan blend of tradition and innovation. Two of the most famous football clubs in the world, namely Manchester United and Manchester City, are based here.

Manchester also has an unrivalled reputation for music and entertainment. Some well-known bands that started out in Manchester include M-People, The Smiths, the Bee Gees and Oasis. Students have easy access to the many bars, clubs, theatres, pubs and shopping facilities in the city. The renowned Hallé Orchestra is also based here. Surrounding Manchester are the Pennines, the Peak District National Park and the Cheshire Plains.

City College Manchester is based at five centres across Manchester and is one of the 10 largest further education colleges in England. The college aims for an individual approach to each student and offers education and training in a range of subjects in a full-time, part-time, day release, evening or weekend capacity.

Academic strengths

The college offers flexibility in the mode of and approach to study. Students can choose subjects as diverse as performing arts, computing and IT management and childcare. All students have full access to the facilities on offer.

English language provision is available from beginners to advanced level. International students have previously taken courses at the college to gain a place at a British university. Foundation programmes available are linked to a range of university degrees. Professional training courses are available for those wishing to work in industry and commerce. The vocational qualifications on offer at the college are acceptable throughout Europe. Courses in IT, business management and business administration have been popular with international students in the past.

Modern academic facilities include specialist photographic studios, a fully furnished IT suite, recording studio, business administration suite, theatre, drama and dance studios, fashion and textile studios and technology workshops.

Student life

The students' union plays an active role in the full and varied social life enjoyed at the college. In addition to refectories and common rooms, sporting facilities include several multigyms and a leisure centre. The college has a large performing arts department which has its own record label. Live concerts and plays are a regular feature of college life. The union organises a range of societies that cater to the recreational interests of students. The international society organises social activities throughout the year. Manchester has the largest concentrated student areas in Europe with its three universities and two large colleges, creating a thriving student scene. The college has links with the universities in Manchester.

The college offers international students an accommodation service, free airport pick-up, English language support, counselling and guidance services and a travel agent. There are strong links with the international society and, therefore, local denominations and religious groups.

Coventry

Coventry University

Write to: Ann O'Sullivan,
International Office, Coventry University,
Priory Street, Coventry CV1 5FB

Tel: +44 (0)24 7688 8674

Fax: +44 (0)24 7663 2710

Email: interlink@coventry.ac.uk

Website: www.coventry.ac.uk

Students: 16,000 in 2001/02
(2,267 overseas and EU students from
over 100 countries worldwide).

Accommodation: single sex.
University residences from £35 a
week self-catered. Rooms in city
centre from £30 to £40 a week.

Entrance requirements: generally
two A levels or international equivalent.

EFL: IELTS 6 undergraduate, 6.5 postgraduate; TOEFL 550.

Foundation: art and design, business,
computing, engineering,
environment and sciences for entry to
degree programmes.

Fees: undergraduate £6,500; art
and design foundation £4,500 a year;
postgraduate £6,500 to £7,500 year.
These figures are based on the
2002/03 rate and could change
from one year to the next.

Coventry University

Student profile

"I came to England to do an HND in
Mechanical Engineering in Cheltenham.
I then worked for Minolta in Malaysia.
With an HND I could enter onto the
second year of a degree, so I applied to
the government for a loan. If I get a first,
I don't have to pay it back! I applied to
Coventry because it's a new university. It
used to be a polytechnic, so the courses
are more practical than theoretical and

geared towards work
experience. Facilities
are good here – the
computer centre is
open 24 hours and
the lecturers are
dedicated."

Amir Sharrifuddin, Malaysia

Coventry University is based on a 33-acre campus in the centre of the city. Modern and historical characteristics make Coventry a lively, cosmopolitan centre. The 20th-century cathedral and its cobbled streets are lined with pubs, restaurants and cafés. The university is founded upon moral values and principles of equality, justice and academic freedom.

Academic strengths

All undergraduate courses are in modular form. Students normally take up to eight single modules a year. The university also offers joint programmes to enable students to broaden their study with one or more subjects that are unrelated to their degree. Coventry has gained particular recognition for its courses in transport design. The *Coventry Evening Telegraph* stated in June 2001, "Coventry University is synonymous with car design, spawning creative geniuses who have been snapped up by the likes of Jaguar Cars, Lotus and Land Rover." *Design Focus* magazine commented, "Courses in Transport and Automotive Design are world renowned. Car makers around the world descend on the West Midlands. Head-hunters representing all the major manufacturers and automotive design studios are jetting in to court the 70 students on Coventry University's Transport Design course…"

Most subject areas have scored 21 or more points out of the maximum 24, which has been regarded as a threshold for excellence. The evidence is available in reports from the independent national Quality Assurance Agency. The university focuses on multidisciplinary research of which 10 subject areas have achieved national and international recognition and many subject areas were awarded very good research ratings, such as art and design which received 4 out of 5 in the recent research assessment exercise.

The university's hi-tech environment provides students with access to its virtual campus 24 hours a day, seven days a week through the internet. Its network has recently been updated and refurbished to the extent that Coventry deem it to be one of the best in the UK, while Learn Online and its virtual learning environment is one of the largest and most comprehensive in the world. The award-winning £16 million new library, recently opened by HRH The Princess Royal, is extremely well equipped with computers. It has won awards including The Building of the Year and Best Public Building in the Brick Development Association Awards 2000, as well as the Midland Institution for Civil Engineers' award for energy conservation.

Student life

The most recent HESA statistical return showed that more than 95 per cent of Coventry students gained employment or training immediately after graduation.

The high profile that the university enjoys is reflected in the warm welcome students receive from staff. The international office assists students with their application and provides excellent support services. It has a disability team dedicated to disabled students and to assessing individual student needs. The students' union is at the centre of all student activity. As well as offering a range of welfare, personal development and representation services, the union also organises a busy entertainment programme. Students enjoy the bars, discos, clubs, restaurants and societies run by the union.

There are also opportunities for partial scholarships for overseas students.

Norwich

University of East Anglia

Write to: International Office, University of East Anglia, Norwich NR4 7TJ

Tel: +44 (0)1603 592048

Fax: +44 (0)1603 458596

Email: intl.office@uea.ac.uk

Website: www.uea.ac.uk/international

Students: 9,500 in 1998/99 (2,500 postgraduates, 1,500 international, from over 90 countries), 40:60 male:female.

Accommodation: married/family, vacation extra charge, storage facilities. University residences from £42 to £62 a week self-catered. Room in town from £35 to £45 a week.

Entrance requirements: two or three A level passes or equivalent, European Baccalaureate Diploma pass.

EFL: TOEFL 500, computer-based TOEFL 215, IELTS 6, English language GCE/GCSE.

Foundation: one-year business and English foundation to degree programme, IELTS level 5.5 required.

Fees: classroom courses £7,500 a year (tbc); laboratory courses £9,700 (tbc).

Universities and colleges of higher education

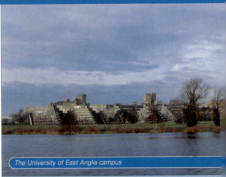

The University of East Anglia campus

Student profile

"I wanted to get to know a different legal system before taking my final exams in Germany, so I decided to spend a term at the University of East Anglia, Norwich. What has impressed me most is the friendly and personal atmosphere and the commitment and open-mindedness of the teachers who seem to have a personal interest in the students' progress. The advantages of a campus university are not to be disregarded: numerous bars, pubs and clubs as well as cultural events of all kinds offer sufficient (often too much!) distraction. Living in close quarters with British and

international students of all subjects provides an opportunity for personal interchange, which is very enriching and helps you make lifelong friends."

Nicolai von Cube, Germany

Set in 320 acres of parks and woodland, the University of East Anglia (UEA) campus was originally designed so that no building was more than five minutes' walk from any other. There are plenty of places to eat and drink, including hot food at the self-service diner, an Italian-style restaurant, snack bars and cafés. Shopping facilities include a food outlet, newsagent, post office, two bookshops and a travel agent. There is also a 24-hour laundrette service and an indoor market on campus.

Norwich city centre is a 15-minute bus ride from the campus, and central London is only two hours away. There is also beautiful unspoilt coastline nearby.

Academic strengths

As well as the traditional humanities, science and social science courses available at UEA, there is a wide range of vocational courses available. The university operates a modular system, whereby students are given a broad introduction to a particular subject and then the opportunity to specialise further, or chose a series of modules to suit their interests. Some courses offer one-year industrial placements and others have study abroad options.

The academic year is divided up into two semesters and students are assessed at the end of each one. This continual assessment removes the pressure of final exams, while the modular programme breaks down the traditional boundaries between arts and science subjects. Students can take business, language and computer modules alongside their degrees. A very wide range of subjects were rated excellent or its equivalent in the most recent teaching quality assessments, including applied social work, business, economics and politics, environmental science, development studies and law. The following departments were awarded 5 ratings in the 2001 research assessment exercise: art history, biological sciences, chemistry, English, environmental sciences, law, philosophy and pure mathematics. History, communication, cultural and film studies were awarded top 5* ratings.

The university has an increasingly well-funded international scholarship programme. There are up to 2,000 international scholarships available this year, between £2,000 to £5,000 per year. Outstanding candidates will be considered for enhanced scholarships.

All students have access to computers. There are 2,000 terminals throughout the university campus with a further 200 available in the Computer Centre, which has trained staff to deal with queries. 150 rooms in halls of residence are connected up to the campus network.

Student life

The students' union organises most of the campus entertainment, from showing films to live concerts, dance nights and live comedy. There are over 100 student-run societies for students, ranging from bell ringing to American football. The Norwich International Club meets weekly for people who wish to widen their knowledge and experience of other cultures. There are religious facilities for students of all faiths – a multifaith chaplaincy. Kosher and halal food is available locally.

The university has an airport pick-up service, an international induction programme, and a dedicated, international student adviser on campus. There is also free English language support throughout the year.

London

University of East London

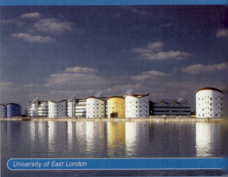

University of East London

Contact: Admissions,
University of East London,
Longbridge Road, Dagenham,
Essex RM8 2AS

Tel: +44 (0)20 8223 3333

Fax: +44 (0)20 8223 2978

Email: admiss@uel.ac.uk

Website: www.uel.ac.uk

Students: 11,500 in 2000/01
(approximately 1,500 international
students from more than 100 countries
worldwide), male:female 1:1.

Accommodation: international
students are guaranteed university
accommodation if you apply in good
time. Halls of residence range from
£40 to £66 a week. Costs for living off
campus range from £45 to £60 a week.

Entrance requirements: A levels,
European or International Baccalaureate
and other qualifications taken in
your own country are all considered.
Some diploma qualifications will
qualify you for entry directly to the
second year of the course.

EFL: IELTS 6.0 minimum, TOEFL 550.

Fees: for 2001/02, £6,500 a year
for full-time undergraduates.
Single unit fee £1,080.

Student profile

"I was introduced to the University of
East London by a friend. I decided to join
UEL because of its engineering facilities
and scholarship scheme for international
students. I was delighted to be accepted
onto the BEng (Hons) in Electrical and
Electronic Engineering. Throughout my
course I was given full guidance and
support to develop my career and my
final-year project led me into industry
and also into postgraduate studies in the
areas of digital signal processing and
control systems. I decided to continue my
postgraduate studies with UEL and I am
working on a research project towards

an MPhil/PhD together
with a motor/drive
manufacturer who is
located in Hampshire.
We have a good social
atmosphere around
the university."

Sujitha Jayasoma, Sri Lanka

The University of East London offers undergraduate and postgraduate programmes across eleven schools, namely Architecture, Biosciences, Art and Design, Cultural and Innovation Studies, East London Business School, Education and Community Studies, Engineering, Health Sciences, Law, Psychology, and Social Sciences. The university has a long tradition of welcoming international students from all over the world and has established links with universities in China, Malaysia, Mexico and many other countries. International students currently make up around 10 per cent of University of East London's student population.

Academic strengths

The University of East London has notable specialisms in subjects including psychology, media studies, history and literature, all of which were awarded an excellent rating by HEFCE in their last teaching assessments. The East London Business School is also well established and offers programmes in accounting, computing and business or management, which prove very popular with international students. The multimedia programmes utilise the state-of-the-art facilities, including specially designed media labs, at the new Docklands campus.

University of East London has three campuses in East London. The first of these is the Docklands campus, which was opened in 2000 and is the first university campus built in London for over 50 years. With student accommodation right on the waterfront, quick travel into central London and a railway station

on campus, this is a very exciting and popular place to study. Barking campus, built in the 1930s has a purpose-built Learning Resource Centre and sports facilities including a swimming pool and netball and tennis courts. Stratford campus is the oldest of all, located in the historic heart of East London, with University House dating back to 1898. A newer building, the Green, was added in the 1980s, with purpose-built teaching facilities. Stratford offers a wealth of cultural opportunities and convenient transport links.

Student life

All three of University of East London's campuses have excellent rail and bus links to central London, and students will find that accommodation and the cost of living is less expensive in this area of London than elsewhere.

East London is a cosmopolitan area with shops and street markets selling foods from all over the world. Local restaurants and take-aways range from Thai, Malaysian, Chinese and Indian, to Italian and Greek, not forgetting the local fish and chip shops.

The students' union is central to student social life and is surrounded by an abundance of bars, restaurants and shops, in an around the campus. The students' union sponsors a huge range of student clubs and societies including the international students' society and sports clubs. The University of East London is renowned for its diversity and great community spirit. Students of all ages and cultural backgrounds learn together in an atmosphere of mutual support and respect.

Edinburgh

The University of Edinburgh

Write to: Craig Mathieson,
The International Office,
The University of Edinburgh,
57 George Square, Edinburgh EH8 9JU

Tel: +44 (0)131 650 4296

Fax: +44 (0)131 668 4565

Email: international@ed.ac.uk

Website: www.ed.ac.uk

Students: 20,333 in 2000/01
(4,383 postgraduates, 3,685
international from 130 countries),
male:female 50:50.

Accommodation: single, married,
family. University residences full board
from £81 to £94 a week, self catered
from £50 to £65 a week. Room in
town from £51 a week.

Entrance requirements: AAB to BBC
in arts, divinity, law, music, medicine,
social sciences and veterinary medicine.
BCC to BDD in education. ABB to CCD in
science and engineering. International
Baccalaureate 34 to 37 points for most
programmes in arts, law, medicine, social
sciences and veterinary medicine. 30
points in divinity, music, science and
engineering.

EFL: IELTS 6.0 to 6.5. TOEFL 550 to 580
or 213 to 237 (computer).

Foundation: contact the
International Office.

Fees: classroom courses £7,460 a
year; laboratory courses £9,810 a year;
clinical courses £17,830 a year; MBA
approximately £11,400 a year.

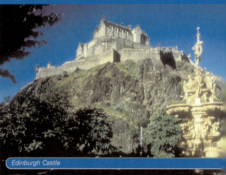

Edinburgh Castle

Student profile

"Before I came to Scotland, I knew that
the University of Edinburgh enjoyed a
worldwide reputation for artificial intelligence. I had always wanted to study IT
so I applied here. It was easy for me to
settle in. People here are very friendly and
my husband (we actually got married in
Edinburgh) had been studying at Edinburgh
for six months before I arrived. Academic
work in artificial intelligence is extremely
intensive. I have had to work overnight to
meet deadlines but I have a great sense of
achievement now that I am finally approach-
ing the completion of my studies. The past

year has been so busy
that I haven't even had
time to look carefully
around Edinburgh. I
really must catch up!
I hope to study for a
PhD here."

Yang (Stella) Xiao,
People's Republic of China

Founded in 1583, The University of Edinburgh is one of the oldest and largest universities in the UK. It is situated right in the centre of Edinburgh – a city of half a million inhabitants but compact enough to provide easy access to cultural, social, shopping and sporting facilities.

The university is firmly rooted in a Scottish educational tradition which places emphasis on breadth as well as depth of study. Notable Edinburgh alumni include the novelists Sir Walter Scott and Robert Louis Stevenson and the senior British ministers, Gordon Brown and Robin Cook.

Academic strengths

The staff at The University of Edinburgh are based in nine faculties. 94 per cent of staff submitted research in the most recent (2001) research assessment exercise and 90 per cent rated 4, 5 or 5*. 34 subjects were assessed for the quality of teaching and 32 gained grades of excellent or highly satisfactory. Accountancy, economic and social history, biological sciences, chemistry, computer science, electrical engineering, geology and geophysics, pure mathematics, physics, astronomy and sociology have been rated excellent for teaching and 5 for research. Edinburgh was recently ranked sixth in a league of European universities and sixth in *The Times Good University Guide 2000*.

Student life

With over 150 student societies, the university's student association is one of the largest in the UK. In addition to providing support services and a student voice in the university's decision-making process, the association hosts social events throughout the year. The sports union runs 50 sport clubs. Facilities include a well-equipped sports centre, playing fields and a field centre in the Scottish Highlands. The university guarantees an offer of university accommodation to all new, first-year students. Approximately 5,700 students are housed in university-owned accommodation.

The university chaplain and his colleagues provide assistance to all students, irrespective of their religious allegiance. The university community includes people from a range of ethnic and religious backgrounds. As a result, there are many opportunities to meet socially or worship with members of the same faith or denomination.

International students are met in Edinburgh by Osprey, which is a support network for students from other countries. The international office co-ordinates an induction day before the beginning of term and provides pastoral support throughout the year. A host programme, which links local families with international students, is active at the beginning of the year and at Christmas.

Throughout the year, the international office continues to support students through the likes of the international student centre and international women's club. The university administers a hardship fund to which international students may apply. The self-funded international students are also protected from economic instability by a mechanism which allows them to defer tuition payments if their currency depreciates by more than 20 per cent during the course of their studies.

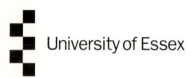

University of Essex

Colchester

The University of Essex

Write to: Professor John Oliver, The University of Essex, Wivenhoe Park, Colchester CO4 3SQ

Tel: +44 (0)1206 873666

Fax: +44 (0)1206 873423

Email: admit@essex.ac.uk

Website: www.essex.ac.uk

Students: 6,250 in 2000/01 (1,500 postgraduate, 2,600 international from 112 countries), 52:48 male:female.

Accommodation: single sex, married, vacation, storage facilities. University residences from £40 a week; £62 a week with en suite facilities self-catered. Room in town from £45 a week.

Entrance requirements: three good A levels or equivalent.

EFL: IELTS 6, TOEFL 540 or 200.

Foundation: nine-month bridging year with English language training if required, success guarantees entry to appropriate degree course at Essex. Teaching is within university and students have access to all its facilities.

Fees: classroom courses £7,090 a year; laboratory courses £9,340 a year; bridging course £7,090 for the year.

The University of Essex campus

Student profile

"I first heard about Essex at an education fair. I was looking for a foundation course and decided on the pre-degree bridging year at Essex. I particularly wanted to go on to study accounting, and Essex has a department devoted to the study of accounting and financial management. In preparation for my degree, I'm taking courses in mathematics and statistics, politics and economics and British institutions and culture. I have made a lot of friends from other different countries and, despite my worries, it was easy to make friends when I first arrived.

Some people do say that English people are rather cold but this is not true. I have found them to be warm and friendly."

Irene Ju-Yung Lai,

People's Republic of China

The University of Essex received its Royal Charter in 1965. It was conceived as a university town rather than a single building which means that the single-site campus incorporates teaching buildings, student accommodation, shops, banks, a gallery, a theatre (Lakeside Theatre), bars, cafés and sports facilities. The campus is set in over 200 acres of parkland, much of which was landscaped in the 18th century. Famous alumni include Dr Oscar Arias, former president of Costa Rica and a Nobel prizewinner, and Dr Rodolfo Neri Vela, Mexico's first and only astronaut.

The university is two miles from the centre of Colchester, which is Britain's oldest recorded town and first capital. Today, it has over 13,500 listed buildings. Amongst its cultural facilities are museums, galleries, a theatre and a multi-screen cinema. Colchester is less than an hour away from London. It has transport links with Stansted Airport and the ferry port at Harwich.

Academic strengths

Essex undergraduate degrees aim to offer flexibility and choice. First-year students can combine core modules of their subject with options in other subjects such as linguistics, philosophy or computing. This allows the possibility of changing to another degree at the end of the year. There are 16 departments which are grouped into four areas of study: the Schools of Humanities and Comparative Studies, Social Sciences, Law and Science and Engineering.

In the teaching quality assessments, The University of Essex achieved an excellent rating for law (1993) and scores of 21 for linguistics (1996), 22 for sociology (1995), 22 for art history (1998), 22 for psychology (1999), 23 for biology and biochemistry (2000), 24 for philosophy (2000), 24 for sports science and 24 for electrical and electronic engineering (1997), out of a possible 24. During the 2001 research assessment exercise, many departments received a rating of 5 or 5*, including accounting, finance and management, economics, electronics, history of art, law, politics and psychology.

Most departments have master's degrees as well as supervising PhD students. 40 scholarships are awarded annually to postgraduate research students.

Students have access to nine computing laboratories which offer IT-based teaching and learning facilities. Three of the computer labs have 24-hour access. The library stocks over 835,000 books, periodical issues and microforms.

Student life

The university has a students' union providing both academic support and entertainment, with over 100 clubs and societies. The sports clubs offer the opportunity to participate in sports including gliding, t'ai chi, subaqua or orienteering. The multifaith centre is used by Anglican, Roman Catholic, Muslim, Buddhist, Hindu and Sikh students.

Support services for the international students begin at the start of the year, with airport pick-ups, pre-sessional English classes and an orientation programme, while year-round facilities include advice and counselling, free in-session language classes for students and their dependents, a campus health centre, travel shop and help with finding part-time jobs.

Falmouth

Falmouth College of Arts

Write to: International Office,
Falmouth College of Arts,
27 Woodlane, Falmouth,
Cornwall TR11 4RH

Tel: +44 (0)1326 211077

Fax: +44 (0)1326 212261

Email: international@falmouth.ac.uk

Website: www.falmouth.ac.uk

Students: 1,700 in 2001 (10 per
cent postgraduate, 10 per cent
international), 50:50 male:female.

Accommodation: college
residences from £61 a week. Room
in town from £40 to £65 a week.

Entrance requirements: normally an
A level pass and three GCSE passes for
foundation course and two or three grade
C passes at A level for BA (Hons)
courses but emphasis is placed on
prior learning and experience.

EFL: evidence of ability to speak and
understand English. Undergraduate
minimum IELTS 6.0, TOEFL 550.

Fees: Foundation £5,500 a year;
BA (Hons), £6,500 to £6,900 a year;
PGDip/MA £6,900 to £8,000 a year;
MPhil/PhD research £6,000 to
£6,500 a year.

Students at Falmouth College of Arts

Student profile

"At an exhibition, I came across
Falmouth's journalism courses. I wanted
to find out what the college was like so I
contacted Norwegian students there
through email. The college heard about
this and thought it was positive, so when
I applied they made me an unconditional
offer. The emphasis is more on analysis
than practical work but we're doing 12
weeks of online journalism which is
useful. The course is very wide ranging,
covering news stories in English, radio,
TV and photography. It's a lot of work but
it's the best of both worlds. I've been
awarded a bursary and I'm looking

forward to studying
in Guatemala for six
weeks. I live in a
house with other
students. I've made
lots of friends. People
here are friendly."

Charlotte Bergloff, Norway

Universities and colleges
of higher education

Falmouth is a coastal seaside town in the picturesque southwest of England. Falmouth College of Arts was established in 1902 and is a specialist college, with just over 1,700 students. Originally founded as an art school, the college now covers various areas of media and cultural studies, as well as art and design.

The college's Woodlane campus is set in eight acres of its own subtropical garden, between the town of Falmouth, the harbour and the beaches. Students work in purpose-designed studios, workshops and other teaching facilities. Nearby annexe studios support those on the Woodlane site. The college's second campus at Tremough comprises an 18th-century house and estate a few kilometres away. Set in 42 acres, the estate includes sports fields, tennis courts, gardens and parkland. Primarily for media and cultural studies students, a new media centre opened in October 2001.

Academic strengths

The one-year Art and Design Foundation course gives students hands-on experience in a wide range of subjects before entering a degree subject. In a teaching quality assessment in 1999, Falmouth College of Arts was awarded 24 out of 24 for art and design provision. In recent years, Falmouth has also developed its media studies courses. The one-year, full-time Postgraduate Diploma in Broadcast Journalism, recognised by the National Council for the Training of Broadcast Journalists, has proved very popular. Several names, now well known, in broadcast media studied at Falmouth, among them Hugh Pym, ITN's political correspondent.

The college library holds about 20,000 volumes, multimedia and computer resources, language materials, career reference information, newspapers and magazines. All of the college's computer suites provide access to the internet, with every student given an email address. Specialist computer studios provide digital video editing, 3D animation, digital cameras, laptops, colour scanning and printing. IT induction sessions and user support services are provided, as is English language tuition by a full-time tutor.

The college operates an international credit accumulation scheme. Apply to the college by the end of January for the foundation year, the end of February for the Postgraduate Diploma in Broadcast Journalism or Creative Advertising and by June for other courses. Late applications will still be considered.

Student life

Falmouth students live in a pleasant town with few crime problems, just a few minutes' walk from the college and beach. A purpose-built student residence is located in Falmouth's town centre, providing accommodation for 156 students. Priority is given to international and first-year students, while other students can choose from good quality accommodation in privately rented houses.

The students' union organises regular entertainment and establishes links with local groups and societies, arranging student rates for many varied events and activities. The students' union organises activities including riding, hang-gliding and climbing.

Being near the sea allows students to take part in watersports such as surfing and sailing.

UNIVERSITY
of
GLASGOW

Glasgow

University of Glasgow

Write to: Student Recruitment and Admissions, University of Glasgow, Glasgow G12 8QQ

Tel: +44 (0)141 330 6150

Fax: +44 (0)141 330 4045

Email: p.wright@admin.gla.ac.uk

Website: www.gla.ac.uk

Students: 21,804 in 2000 (2,681 postgraduates, 1,011 international from over 20 contries) 49:51 male:female.

Accommodation: university rooms from approximately £53 to £66 a week self catering; £77 to £79 catered; room in town approximately £60 a week.

Entrance requirements: good grades at A level or equivalent (As for medicine, veterinary medicine, dentistry, law and accountancy).

EFL: Cambridge certificates, IELTS 6.0 to 6.5, TOEFL 550 to 580.

Fees: classroom courses £7,300 a year; laboratory courses £9,300 a year; medicine £13,980 a year; postgraduate various, check with student recruitment and admissions service.

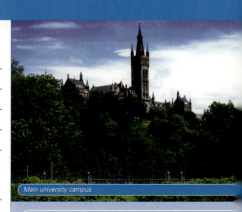
Main university campus

Student profile

"Studying in Britain is a tradition in my family. My father and uncles all studied for a BSc in Mechanical Engineering in London or Scotland. I studied at Singapore Polytechnic for two years so I could enter directly into the third year. Coming here is good for my English and I wanted to live with different people and stand on my own feet. People in Singapore think of Britain as being a rich country and I was shocked at first to see poor people in the street. The hardest thing was learning how to get on with Europeans. It took me three months to understand why they do certain things.

But learning to share other people's views is really good – it makes for success in work as well as in personal relationships."

Kelvin Hui, Singapore

The towers and pinnacles of George Gilbert Scott's neo-Gothic university buildings command wonderful views across a city that vibrates with activity. Glasgow is Scotland's largest city. It stands on the west coast and is known as the gateway to Scotland's lochs, hills and highlands. With its medieval buildings, art galleries, museums and Art Nouveau architecture, the city is itself a tourist attraction – it was recently nominated Britain's third favourite tourist venue.

Glasgow and its oldest university have evolved together. On completion of the city's great medieval cathedral in the mid-1400s, the Pope gave permission for a university to be founded there; the first lectures were held in the new nave. In 1870, the university moved to its present site, high on Gilmorehill.

Today, the Faculty of Veterinary Medicine is out to the north; and Crichton Campus, home of a new MA Liberal Arts degree, is in nearby Dumfries. Glasgow has its own marine biology research station on the Firth of Clyde and a nuclear reactor at East Kilbride.

Academic strengths

The University of Glasgow has many educational firsts to its name. In the 19th century, the town was engulfed by industrial development and in response, the university established the first Chair of Civil Engineering and the first Chair of Naval Architecture.

Today, engineering is one of its major academic strengths and the courses in naval architecture with marine or ocean engineering are respected internationally.

The Faculty of Medicine recently achieved a first among UK universities by directing the emphasis of its clinical training from science to patient care. In addition, accounting, finance and management studies attract students from all over the world. The university won high teaching quality assessment ratings for these subjects and others, including chemistry, computing, geography, astronomy, physics, philosophy and sociology.

The university library holds two million works and has access to the libraries of seven other nearby Scottish universities. Glasgow also has a proportionally large postgraduate intake. In 1998/99, 14 per cent of postgraduate students came from overseas. Postgraduate accommodation and 60 to 70 flats for married students are available.

Student life

Glasgow has a new concert hall, large theatres and several art galleries. The university has two students' unions competing for members, a debating society that has won the World Student Debating Championships five times and sports facilities. Students are guaranteed university accommodation for at least one year.

The Student Recruitment and Admissions Service organises a special orientation programme for international students including talks and tours of the university and surrounding countryside, as well as an opportunity to make friends. An international student adviser is available to provide students from overseas with confidential and practical help with all aspects of living and studying in Glasgow.

Universities and colleges of higher education

London

Goldsmiths, University of London

Write to: Jill Thorn, International Office, Goldsmiths, New Cross, London SE14 6NW

Tel: +44 (0)20 7919 7700

Fax: +44 (0)20 7919 7704

Email: international-office@gold.ac.uk

Website: www.goldsmiths.ac.uk

Students: 8,040 students in 2000/01 (2,708 postgraduates, 1,045 international from 60 countries), 34:66 male:female.

Accommodation: university residences from £63 to £83.50 a week, self-catering.

Entrance requirements: vary according to course applied for; generally two subjects at A level standard or equivalent.

EFL: IELTS 6.5, TOEFL 580 including 4.5 TWE minimum.

Foundation: extension degrees in visual arts, music, art history and fine art, mathematics and textiles allow study for Goldsmiths BA (Hons) degrees. Certificate in English Language for the arts and social sciences is sufficient for application to undergraduate degrees. Postgraduate Diploma in English Language is sufficient for postgraduate study.

Fees: classroom courses £7,470 a year; laboratory courses £9,500 a year.

Goldsmiths, University of London main entrance

Student profile

"The best thing that can happen to a student is to have the chance to study outside their country. When I decided to do a PhD in English Literature, I sought the advice of our embassy in London. They advised me to apply for Goldsmiths because of the outstanding reputation of its English department. After eight months, I am happy to be part of its academic circle. My adviser, Dr Fiona Macintosh, is very helpful and dedicated. I am glad we have mutual respect and understanding. The atmosphere is friendly and warm. Goldsmiths also has the advantage of being in London.

Through living in London and being a research student at Goldsmiths, I have learnt many things and I am, in fact, still learning."

Samia Al-Shayban, Saudi Arabia

Lively, cosmopolitan and innovative, Goldsmiths is a great place to study. The college is part of the renowned University of London and is located in New Cross, southeast London, which is a vibrant, urban setting with excellent public transport connections. Central London is only 20 minutes away by train, and Blackheath's open spaces and the Thames waterfront at Greenwich are even closer.

Goldsmiths is small enough to retain a friendly and welcoming approach yet large enough to provide the facilities needed by its students who come from a rich variety of social and cultural backgrounds.

Academic strengths

Goldsmiths aims to be pre-eminent in the study and practice of creative, cognitive, cultural and social processes. Its combination of disciplines helps it to be at the cutting edge of what it does, as a university renowned for creativity and innovation. Many of the programmes have an interdisciplinary approach, encouraging students to make connections between subjects. As such, most allow students to choose modules suited to their interests. Teaching is through a coherent mix of lectures, group seminars and practical work. Students are assigned a personal tutor to give them academic support, and the quality of degrees is monitored by feedback from the students.

The college is both nationally and internationally known for its academic excellence (the respected *Times Higher Education Supplement* recently called it a "rising star" of research) and its research policy means that students will be in contact with staff who are engaged in their subjects at the highest level through their research activity. The college offers MPhil and PhD research opportunities in most subject areas, and in some the MRes (Master of Research) programmes help bridge the gap between undergraduate study and research.

Students will find most of Goldsmiths' study resources in the Rutherford Information Services Building – winner of an architectural award. The building brings together the library, computer services facilities, the languages resource centre and the media services centre. Many resources elsewhere within the University of London are also available to Goldsmiths' students.

Student life

Goldsmiths has an active students' union with a range of entertainment including comedy, film, bands and DJs, plus societies ranging from aikido to stage musicals. It has bars, a café and a subsidised shop. Students are also free to use the University of London Union with its many societies, swimming pool, gym, bars and shops.

The student newspaper, *Smiths*, has received a huge boost this year in the form of a new editor. As well as this, the student union radio station, *Wired*, has continued to increase its number of listeners, powered by the students.

The international office at Goldsmiths together with the chaplaincy, medical centre, counselling service and student support office, provides an information and support network for overseas students. Goldsmiths also offers an orientation programme to help international students adjust to life in the UK, and can guarantee them accommodation in the college-controlled residence for the duration of their period of study.

Universities and colleges of higher education

London

Greenwich School of Management

Write to: Stephen Fettes, Greenwich School of Management, Meridian House, Royal Hill, Greenwich, London SE10 8RD

Tel: +44 (0)20 8516 7800

Fax: +44 (0)20 8516 7801

Email: enquiry@greenwich-college.ac.uk

Website: www.greenwich-college.ac.uk

Students: 600 in 1999/2000 (300 postgraduate, 250 international from 62 countries), 60:40 male:female.

Accommodation: single sex, married/family, vacation, storage. Room in town from £60 a week.

Entrance requirements: school leaving certificate, or equivalent. For postgraduate courses, any degree.

EFL: competence in written and spoken English.

Foundation: access to BSc (Hons) courses.

Fees: undergraduate courses from £3,000 a year; postgraduate courses from £6,000 a year.

Greenwich School of Management

Student profile

"Before studying at the school, I took an undergraduate degree in business at the University of Virginia and worked in the marketing department of an American company. Whilst at Greenwich School of Management, I followed an MBA, specialising in marketing which taught some of the theory behind the work that I had been doing in practice. Greenwich School of Management was small enough to be friendly and personal. I met people from all over the world and lots of locals. There were good library and computing facilities and I loved being so close to central London.

My time there was brilliant. I like to think it will advance my career. Coming here was one of the best decisions of my life."

Charlotte Hall, USA

Universities and colleges of higher education

484

Greenwich School of Management is located in a historic area of London, close to both Greenwich Park and the River Thames. Greenwich has benefited from the millennium celebrations and has many entertainment and leisure facilities which are popular with both students and tourists from around the world. The West End, London's major centre for the arts and entertainments, and the City, the capital's commercial heartland, are both a bus ride away.

Greenwich is conveniently situated for travel both within the UK and abroad. Both Gatwick and Heathrow airports can be reached relatively easily and Greenwich is the right side of London for crossing the channel to the rest of Europe.

Students from over 60 countries world-wide attend the school each year which helps to create an international atmosphere. The largest single nationality of students attending the school is British, which allows opportunities for those from non-English speaking countries to experience British culture first hand.

Academic strengths

Greenwich School of Management runs a wide range of MBAs, postgraduate diplomas and undergraduate qualifications. Courses are available on a full and part-time basis and last between one and four years.

With the introduction of the BSc (Hons) in Business Management and Information Technology, the school has recently updated its IT resources.

The library at Greenwich School of Management focuses on business and related disciplines, and has resources including periodicals, CD-Roms and computerised online systems. Computers have access to the internet allowing information to be downloaded. There are experienced staff on site to train and give advice to any students who have not used the internet before.

Student life

Greenwich School of Management is affiliated to The University of Hull and it is on occasions such as the degree conferment ceremony that students are strongly reminded of this connection. The programme lists graduates of both institutions alphabetically and full-time students from the Hull campus mix with students from the school. Students on the MBA and BSc programmes are welcome to use any of The University of Hull's facilities, including its career service.

All international students at Greenwich School of Management have the opportunity to take advantage of the school's airport pick-up service which takes them directly to Greenwich. For those with basic English, pre-sessional courses can be arranged which allow students to settle in and make some friends before term begins. The school has a multi-faith feel and most religions can be practised in the locality. Accommodation is comfortable and reasonably priced given the school's London location.

Students are allocated an individual counsellor for any help that they may need. There is also disabled access to most of the college classrooms.

London

University of Greenwich

Write to: The International Office, Room 162 Queen Mary, Maritime Greenwich Campus, University of Greenwich, 30 Park Row, Greenwich, London SE10 9LS

Tel: +44 (0)20 8331 8701

Fax: +44 (0)20 8331 8625

Email: intoffice@gre.ac.uk

Website: www.gre.ac.uk

Students: 17,801 in 2001 (3,905 postgraduates, 3,585 overseas students from over 100 countries), 48:52 male:female.

Accommodation: university residences from £50 to £86 a week self-catering, £77 a week with breakfast and evening meal. Room in town from £50 a week.

Entrance requirements: generally two A levels plus three GCSEs grade C, or equivalent. International Baccalaureate 24 points or international equivalency.

EFL: IELTS 6.0, TOEFL 550 or equivalent.

Fees: (in 2001) undergraduate £6,960 a year; postgraduate from £6,960 to £9,250; MBA £12,500.

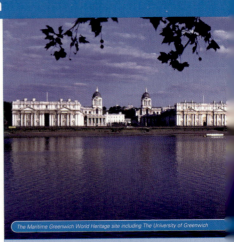

The Maritime Greenwich World Heritage site including The University of Greenwich

Student profile

"I chose the University of Greenwich because of its location and resources. The course has been very interesting, the teaching levels are extremely good and the staff are easily accessible and friendly. The proximity of the rest of Europe made London an easy choice. I am happy at Greenwich. Studying at the University of Greenwich has given me the opportunity to meet people of different backgrounds, nationalities and

ages. On completion of my degree I would like to continue studying a master's degree at the University of Greenwich."

Farah Razzaq, Pakistan

The University of Greenwich was founded as an independent institution in 1890 and has been teaching at degree level since the early part of the last century. From Sir Christopher Wren's baroque masterpiece on the waterfront at Greenwich to a grand mansion and Winter Gardens at Avery Hill and the splendid former naval buildings at Medway, the university is custodian of 17 listed buildings in many spectacular settings. Situated in London and Kent, the university offers easy access to central London, as well as the surrounding countryside and coast.

Academic strengths

Greenwich is the leading new university for research and consultancy income, according to the Higher Education Statistics Agency. You'll find well-equipped laboratories and lecture theatres at Greenwich, with library and computing facilities on every campus. There are also sporting, social and cultural activities for students to enjoy.

The university's framework of combined degrees and programmes allows a wide range of subject options. By choosing to study at the University of Greenwich, students are in turn choosing to concentrate on bettering their employment prospects in order to gain a more fulfilling career. Many students who are applying to university will have an idea of what they want to do when they leave but these ideas need to be developed and planned. Thus, choosing a programme that will suit your employment aspirations is important.

An English language access programme is available for international students whose first language is not English. Also offered are international foundation and international foundation advanced programmes to prepare international students with the skills needed to study at a UK university. The academic year is split into two semesters of 15 weeks starting in September and January each year.

Student life

The university guarantees that all new students will be offered a place to live, either in one of the halls of residence or in university-approved housing. Most rooms have telephone access as well as direct data access for computer connection to the internet. En suite bathroom facilities are available.

International students have the support of a specialist student service counsellor, English language study skills and study skills tuition careers advice and access to a job shop. The jobshop was created to help students find employment. As well as providing money in the short term it also helps with better employment prospects, new skills and an understanding of the world of work and valuable contacts.

Greenwich has facilities for many sports, ranging from football and mixed hockey to scuba diving and sailing. There is also easy access to central London and famous sights such as Piccadilly Circus and the Tower of London. As well as being located near to historic towns, the channel tunnel for Paris and Western Europe is nearby.

Studying at the University of Greenwich provides a rich and diverse cultural experience. Students are from a variety of different backgrounds and countries, which makes the learning experience more enjoyable and interesting.

Reading

Gyosei International College

Write to: Ling Luk, Gyosei International College in the UK, London Road, Reading, Berkshire RG1 5AQ

Tel: +44 (0)118 920 9418

Fax: +44 (0)118 931 0137

Email: ba.admin@gyosei.ac.uk or ma.admin@gyosei.ac.uk

Website: www.gyosei.ac.uk

Students: 350 in 2000/01 (10 postgraduates, 340 international from 5 countries), 40:60 male:female.

Accommodation: vacation and storage. University rooms from £70 a week catered. Room in town from £140 a week.

Entrance requirements: good high school grades, or one A level at grade D (or equivalent).

EFL: IELTS 5.0 (or equivalent).

Foundation: available.

Fees: £1,000 a year (EU students only); £3,000 a year (with Gyosei scholarship); £6,000 a year (with Gyosei bursary).

Gyosei International College

Student profile

"The Gyosei BA degree course is utterly unique. Students get a BA from City University while studying at Gyosei International College at Reading and can also get a Japanese qualification, sometimes in the same time period. The staff are international and courses cover every kind of business and culture subject. When I first came to the college, I had difficulty understanding English but with perseverance, I soon found lectures easier to understand. When I came to the college straight from high school in Japan, I was not used to writing essays but I have since mastered

the art. There is nothing more satisfying, when exams are over, than sharing your thoughts about them (and a beer) with your friends."

Shiro Tamura, Japan

The Gyosei foundation dates back to 1881 when the first Gyosei High School was founded in the centre of Tokyo. The first undergraduates began their studies at Gyosei International College in 1989 at a well-appointed campus in Reading. The city is situated in the county of Berkshire, which lies just to the west of London and is strategically and conveniently placed for much of Britain's road network. Heathrow Airport is a short distance away, and it takes a mere 30 minutes to reach central London by train.

Reading itself has a population of 300,000, and supports a thriving arts community, along with booming commerce and industry.

There are now 300 students at Gyosei International College, which gears its education to non-native English speakers for whom English is a second or third language. The college therefore puts a bicultural and international perspective on all its work. The faculty of 50 staff are mainly Japanese and British academics with international teaching experience. Close links are maintained with universities and businesses in Japan, India, the USA and the UK.

Academic strengths

Gyosei International College is accredited by the British Accreditation Council, institutionally validated by City University and is an associate institution of The University of Reading. Undergraduate courses and degree awards are validated by a UK university. Students take between three and four years to complete their degrees. The degree is arranged in levels one to three (equivalent of years one to three); students pass nine courses a year and complete a dissertation to obtain their degree. The courses are bilingual; subjects may be studied in English or Japanese (so Japanese students are not linguistically disadvantaged). When students arrive at Gyosei, an orientation week gives them a chance to settle in. The degrees equip students to work in both an international field or in Japan and allow mastery of Japanese culture, language and business. Visits to businesses, placements and community projects are provided, some in the UK and some in Japan.

The Gyosei campus has full academic facilities including a library (with English and Japanese textbooks), a resource centre with study materials for each course, a computer centre, language laboratory and careers support service. Students may also take advantage of City and Reading University libraries, computer facilities and clubs.

Student life

Western and Japanese students mix socially as well as on courses, study sessions and observation placements. The college's student union runs a cafeteria, bar and restaurant along with over 22 clubs and societies and a large variety of social events. Students may also join clubs and societies at City and Reading Universities. Vacation and term time trips are arranged for all students, which generally take place around the UK, the rest of Europe and Japan. Gyosei International College's students regularly publish newsletters and journals, and the student-organised Japanese Matsuri festival on campus attracts visitors from far and wide.

Edinburgh

Herriot-Watt University, Edinburgh

Write to: Lorna Halliday, International Recruitment Office, Heriot-Watt University, Riccarton, Edinburgh EH14 4AS

Tel: +44 (0)131 451 3877

Fax: +44 (0)131 451 3630

Email: International@hw.ac.uk

Website: www.hw.ac.uk

Students: 7,602 in 2001/02 (6,199 undergraduate, 1,403 postgraduate, approximately 1,500 international from 80 countries), 60:40 male:female.

Accommodation: single sex, vacation, storage facilities. University residences from £64 a week catered, £32 to £60 a week self-catered. Room in town from £42 to £50 a week.

Entrance requirements: good grades at A level or equivalent.

EFL: IELTS 6.5, TOEFL 213.

Foundation: contact International Office for details.

Fees: classroom courses £6,650 a year; laboratory courses £8,700 a year; MBA £10,485.

Statue of James Watt

Student profile

"After my government granted me a scholarship to go to the UK, I started looking for a place to study. Very few universities offered international degrees that did not include a foreign language, so I chose Heriot-Watt. As a mature student, I thought I would have problems adjusting to university life, as most students are quite young. But, to my surprise, I seem to be getting along well. In fact, I find the students in Heriot-Watt well behaved. The lecturers and tutors are very supportive. I met other students from my country and we have all expressed our admiration for the place.

Its history is written all over the university, even in the names of the buildings. It's amazing! I do look forward to my years of study at Heriot-Watt."

Gaositwe Pusumane, Botswana

Heriot-Watt University, Edinburgh was established by Royal Charter in 1966, yet traces its origins some 150 years earlier to the Edinburgh School of Arts. Today, Heriot-Watt is an integrated campus university. The 380-acre parkland campus at Riccarton is on the greenbelt of western Edinburgh. In the early 1970s, the university relocated here. The purpose-built buildings are located in a natural setting of trees, lawns and a small loch. The university has a second campus, one hour south of Edinburgh. The School of Textiles is located there and some management and IT programmes are also taught there.

Edinburgh is situated on the edge of a large loch, surrounded by volcanic hills. The city has 16,000 buildings that are listed as architecturally or historically important. Socially, there are over 700 pubs and plenty of restaurants. The population almost doubles in August during its international festival. This is one of the largest arts festivals in the world showing a range of theatre, comedy and dance. Edinburgh has an airport and good rail and road links to London.

Academic strengths

Courses at Heriot-Watt University are heavily weighted towards engineering and natural sciences. In the 2001 research assessment exercise, the number of Heriot-Watt research staff working in 5/5* graded subjects has almost doubled since the last assessment. Petroleum engineering retained its 5* rating, built environment and applied mathematics have retained grade 5, and actuarial mathematics and statistics has moved to grade 5. Specialist courses are available in international banking and finance, petroleum engineering, actuarial maths and brewing and distilling.

In the last 10 years, £60 million has been invested into the Riccarton campus and its facilities. Computing is integrated into most courses and students are encouraged to use interactive learning techniques.

Student life

The student welfare services take care of accommodation needs and all new undergraduates are guaranteed a place in halls. The counselling service gives advice on issues such as immigration, money and housing. International students benefit from airport pick-ups, two international student welcome weekends and weekend visits to scenic areas in Scotland.

Students in financial difficulties can apply to the university hardship fund. International students may also apply for an Overseas Scholarship Award. There is an interdenominational chaplaincy which involves leaders from local churches. A special prayer room is provided for Muslim students.

The students' union is at the centre of the Riccarton campus. It has an international students' representative and international societies which organise events. Local culture also features in the Scottish country dancing group and the Christmas ceilidh. There are extensive facilities for sports and exercise at the university, including six football and rugby pitches, a climbing wall, indoor badminton and hockey and an international squash tournament centre.

Students at the Scottish Borders campus have their own student union and facilities but are also free to use those in Edinburgh. A free shuttle bus links the two campuses.

Universities and colleges of higher education

THE UNIVERSITY OF HULL

Hull

The University of Hull

Write to: International Office, The University of Hull, Cottingham Road, Hull HU6 7RX

Tel: +44 (0)1482 466904

Fax: +44 (0)1482 466554

Email: international@admin.hull.ac.uk

Website: www.hull.ac.uk

Students: 12,298 (10,490 undergraduates, 2,108 postgraduates, about 1,230 international from over 100 countries), 49:51 male:female.

Accommodation: guaranteed for unaccompanied international students. University residences £38 to £50 a week self-catering. Private accommodation £35 to £60 a week.

Entrance requirements: generally Bs and Cs at A level or equivalent.

EFL: IELTS 6.0, TOEFL 550 or equivalent.

Foundation: International Foundation Programme to improve qualifications to entrance requirement standards, including English language.

Fees: International Foundation Programme £5,100; classroom courses £7,250 a year; laboratory and MBA courses £8,950 a year.

Students at The University of Hull

Student profile

"My dream of studying overseas became a reality when I was offered the Sir Roy Marshall Scholarship to pursue my BEng Electronic Engineering degree at The University of Hull. The campus is beautiful, with excellent facilities and close, friendly staff. On my course, I am given plenty of opportunities to learn and improve my presentation and design troubleshooting skills. This has equipped me technically for a bright career in industry. My stay in Hull has provided me with valuable exposure and a better understanding of the local Yorkshire culture. Soon after completion of my

degree, I fully intend to further my postgraduate studies in engineering before starting my career as an electronic engineer."

Don Ri Yuen, Malaysia

Universities and colleges of higher education

492

The University of Hull began its life in 1928 and became England's 14th university in 1954. Today there are students from over 102 countries and members of staff from 38 countries on the campus, leading to the cosmopolitan feel. Teaching and research at the university have had an international impact.

The main campus is situated in the city of Hull, with a second in the seaside town of Scarborough. In the 12th century, Hull was an important east coast port. To this day, it remains important as a gateway to the rest of Europe, with regular sailings to Zeebrugge and Rotterdam. Hull has all the usual facilities you would expect of a major city: shopping precincts, galleries, restaurants, museums and opportunities for entertainment of every kind.

Academic strengths

The university was ranked in the top third of UK universities by *The Times*. Several of the university's departments have been awarded excellent ratings in teaching quality assessments including European languages, history and engineering and Southeast Asian studies.

Areas which tend to be popular with international students include business studies, engineering and management and law. The university has research centres such as the Centre for European Studies in which research is carried out into institutions and politics of the European Union. For those students interested in environmental issues, there is an Institute for Environmental Science and Management which provides a focus for interdisciplinary research. The university develops and uses information technology for teaching and learning – the CTI Centre for Modern Languages provides information on computer-assisted language learning. There is a centre for research in virtual environments.

Student life

There are many places around Hull to go for entertainment such as pubs, clubs, theatres and shopping. The city centre is only 10 minutes by bus from the university. It has good sea and air links to the rest of Europe and easy access to other parts of England. Historic cities such as York and Lincoln are within easy reach. The town is safe, combining the bustle of a city with a peaceful environment in which to study.

The university owns and manages a range of accommodation. It guarantees accommodation for unaccompanied international students for the duration of their course. Nearly two thirds of students live in university flats, halls of residence and student houses, many of them close to the campus. Study bedrooms in halls of residence have direct access to campus computer networks and the internet. Students in Hull and Scarborough benefit from the fact that the cost of living is 30 per cent cheaper than elsewhere in the UK.

The students' union has over 120 societies including a range of sporting activities and a fully-equipped sports and fitness centre. The international office has a dedicated team of staff from five different countries who collectively speak more than seven different languages. The university also has an overseas student adviser, religious chaplaincies, careers advisers and supervisors, responsible for the welfare of each individual student.

INSTITUTE OF
EDUCATION
UNIVERSITY OF LONDON

London

Institute of Education, University of London

Write to: The Registry, Institute of Education, University of London, 20 Bedford Way, London WC1H 0AL

Tel: +44 (0)20 7612 6000

Fax: +44 (0)20 7612 6126

Email: info@ioe.ac.uk

Website: www.ioe.ac.uk

Students: 4,342 in 2000/01 (99 per cent postgraduate, 588 international from over 80 countries), 30:70 male:female.

Accommodation: single sex, family, vacation. University residences from £83 a week catered. £59 a week self-catering.

Entrance requirements: normally an approved first degree at second-class honours level, some courses require professional experience.

EFL: foundation courses IELTS 7.0, TOEFL 650.

Foundation: 12-week pre-sessional course in English for academic purposes.

Fees: £7,404 to £16,275 a year (non-EU).

Institute of Education

Student profile

"The institute is the perfect place to learn about other educational systems and societies. You could say that it is London in miniature, with hundreds of students from all over the world with whom you can share your professional experiences. I very much welcomed the fact that throughout the MA in Comparative Education, we were given the opportunity to develop a capacity to think independently and to adopt a critical stance towards the literature in the field. This approach produces an intellectual and international open-

mindedness which is of great benefit not only to students themselves but also to the organisations in which they will work in the future."

Jason Beech, Argentina

The Institute of Education, a graduate college of the University of London, celebrates its 100th anniversary in 2002. Originally called the London Day Training College, the Institute was founded to deliver high quality training for teachers. It remains true to this aim, and every year over 1,000 graduates attend its Postgraduate Certificate in Education courses, offered in partnership with over 500 schools and colleges in the London area.

The Institute of Education is in the heart of Bloomsbury in central London, best known for the writers, artists and philosophers who lived and worked there in the early 20th century. Its main building in Bedford Way was designed by Sir Denys Lasdun, creator of London's Royal National Theatre and the Genoa Opera House. Oxford Street, Regent Street and Covent Garden are nearby, as are numerous restaurants, pubs, cafés, theatres, cinemas, galleries and the British Museum.

Academic strengths

Over the years the institute has expanded its activities and now offers courses leading to higher degrees and advanced diplomas in all areas of education and related aspects of both the social sciences and professional practice. Long recognised as a world centre of educational enquiry, it obtained high rankings in each of the research assessment exercises conducted by the UK university funding bodies.

The scale and excellence of the institute's research attract students from all over the world keen to work with scholars at the forefront of education. It has hosted lectures on educational issues by the leaders of the main UK political parties and by education ministers from around the world, as well as lively debates involving leading figures in the world of education. International links are also fostered through collaborative projects with overseas institutions.

Student life

The students' union is one of the institute's main social centres. Its services include a bar, cafeteria, shop, children's play area and a meeting room used for socials, exercise classes, yoga, religious observances and festivals. Students can stand for union office, vote in elections and gain valuable experience in different fields, including freelance journalism.

A number of student societies provide international students with a welcome break from their studies, including the African, Hellenic, Hong Kong, Japanese, Latin American and multicultural societies. An annual feature of institute life is the lively Multicultural Extravaganza, which features dance, music, poetry and drama from many of the different countries from which the students hail.

A special orientation programme which provides an introduction to studying in English at the institute is offered free of charge each September. Pre-sessional and in-sessional language courses help students with the English appropriate to their studies, help them cope with cultural differences and give them opportunities for practice.

Student accommodation is available at the institute's hall of residence, the nearby John Adams Hall. Students are also entitled to live in any of the University of London's intercollegiate halls and also to use the university's own medical and dental facilities.

Kingston

Kingston University

Contact: Student Enquiry and Applicant Services, Kingston University, Cooper House, 40-46 Surbiton Road, Kingston upon Thames KT1 2HX

Tel: +44 (0)20 8547 7053

Fax: +44 (0)20 8547 7080

Email: int.recruit@kingston.ac.uk

Website: www.kingston.ac.uk

Students: 14,496 in 2000 (2,702 postgraduate, 473 international from 72 countries),52:48 male:female.

Accommodation: single, some en suite, vacation. University residences from £53 to £66 a week self-catering. Room in town from £68 a week.

Entrance requirements: generally C at A level or equivalent (BBC for law and architecture, BCC for business studies). 24 to 30 at International Baccalaureate.

EFL: Cambridge Proficiency grade C, IELTS 6.5, TOEFL 550 plus written test grade 5 (computer-based test 213). Summer pre-sessional English courses available.

Foundation: one-year course includes English language and chosen specialist subjects. Requires IELTS 4.

Fees: art and design foundation £4,200 a year; classroom courses £6,500 a year; studio-based design and some computing and science courses £7,500 a year, laboratory courses £8,000 a year.

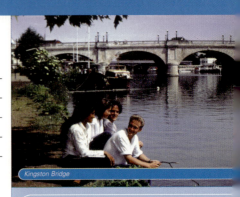

Kingston Bridge

Student profile

"This is my final year on the BEng (Hons) Electronic Engineering with Computing. I am pleased that I chose Kingston as there is a good campus atmosphere and the accommodation is excellent. Kingston is a lively town with plenty to do and it is cleaner and safer than inner London. Adapting to British study methods was challenging but the support services were brilliant. I particularly benefited from PAL – peer-assisted learning whereby new undergraduates are helped by second- year students. The library facilities are excellent and you don't have to wait for computer access

as there are so many of them available. I am working hard but enjoying it and hope eventually to progress to a master's course."

Adeoti Olaiya, Nigeria

The historic town of Kingston upon Thames is a busy retail centre with many shops, restaurants and clubs. The university is close to the town centre, which is now protected as a conservation area. Hampton Court Palace and the open spaces of Richmond Park are nearby. The university's four campuses are served by a free bus and the university is only 25 minutes by train from central London and 30 minutes from Heathrow Airport.

Academic strengths

Several of the courses have received the maximum scores in recent teaching quality assessments including subjects like mechanical, aerospace and production engineering, surveying and landscape architecture. In 2001, *The Financial Times* placed Kingston fifth in the country for teaching standards. The other universities in the top five were Cambridge, York, Loughborough and Oxford. Kingston was shortlisted for University of the Year by *The Sunday Times* in 2000. Many of the staff have considerable industrial experience and most of Kingston's courses are strongly career related. More traditional subjects rated excellent in the recent teaching assessment exercise include geology and English literature.

The Faculty of Business undergraduate courses include business studies, business with French, German or Spanish, business information technology, accountancy and finance, business management, LLB and law with business. The faculty received an excellent rating in teaching quality assessments and offers a number of career-related postgraduate courses.

The Faculty of Human Sciences runs courses in business and financial economics as well as its full range of modular courses.

In the Faculty of Health and Social Care Sciences, students of radiography, nursing and midwifery and physiotherapy, are taught alongside medical students at St George's Hospital Medical School.

The Faculty of Art and Design covers fields such as architecture, urban estate management, surveying, fashion, graphic design, fine art and music.

International students often start on courses tailored to their individual needs which lead to degree study at the appropriate entry level.

Student life

Although Kingston takes large numbers of students, each campus aims to have a smaller community feel with its own library, bar, shop and student restaurant. There is a fully-equipped gymnasium and fitness centre and the university has its own sports ground nearby. A large health centre on the main campus caters for students' medical needs.

International students follow an orientation programme to help adjust to life in the UK. Most first-year students live in Kingston's modern, self-catering halls of residence. International students are encouraged to join free English language and study skills classes.

Each student is allocated a personal tutor and some courses also offer peer-assisted learning where the older students take care of new arrivals. An international student adviser is available to provide guidance and support. The students' union offers a varied sports and social programme.

Lampeter

The University of Wales, Lampeter

Write to: Admissions Office
The University of Wales,
Lampeter, Ceredigion
Wales SA48 7ED

Tel: +44 (0)1570 423530

Fax: +44 (0)1570 423530

Email: admissions@lamp.ac.uk

Website: www.lamp.ac.uk

Accommodation: room-only basis
£40.50 a week (term time only);
room in typical hall with shared
kitchen facilities £38.70; room with
en-suite and shared kitchen £45.90.

Entrance requirements: IELTS 6.5;
Cambridge Proficiency grade B or C;
TOEFL 600 to 800; International
Baccalaureate or equivalent overseas
qualifications.

Fees: information is available from
the student financial service on
+44 (0)1570 422351, extension 479.

The University of Wales, Lampeter campus

Student profile

"I come from a big hectic city so I thought that moving to Lampeter would be a huge culture shock. When I arrived, everything appeared to be different from the environment I came from but after just a short time I realised that, in fact, nearly everything was similar to what I was already used to. I spent one year in another university before coming here, and because of the huge number of students there I felt anonymous, more like a number. Here at Lampeter, there is genuine interest  in me as an individual, and staff and students are friendly and very keen to help you if you are in need of any kind of support."

Thomas Dahl Jensen, Denmark

The University of Wales, Lampeter is a compact and intimate campus university. Lampeter is one of the oldest degree-awarding institutions in Britain after Oxford and Cambridge. The university is in the market town of Lampeter, west Wales, surrounded by countryside full of myths and legends. The university has been awarded a Queen's Anniversary Prize for the Certificate in Interpersonal Skills for Volunteers. The prizes, awarded biannually, are given in recognition of excellence in further and higher education that make a contribution to the life of the nation.

Academic strengths

The main library holds 180,000 volumes and subscribes to over 1,000 journals, periodicals and serials. The Founders Library is the original college library and houses some 24,000 books along with periodicals printed between 1470 and 1850. Even older materials include a *Vulgate Bible* dating from 1279, a manuscript of the *Qur'an* and a Buddhist text in Pali inscribed on palm leaves. The university bookshop is a key local source of textbooks and stationery, with a next-day ordering service for anything which is out of stock.

The Centre for Media allows access to video conferencing on WelshNet and the internet. It has video facilities including equipment for sub-titling and editing, so students from any course can learn to make their own videos. One of the main academic advantages of Lampeter is its size. Small group teaching and a personal tutor system ensure a friendly, positive and supportive atmosphere, enabling students to get the most out of their course.

Student life

A president, three sabbatical officers and an entertainments officer represent the interests of students. Students can choose from over 70 clubs and societies, from the Pagan Society to the Drama Society, or create their own if their particular interest is not covered. The union bar has recently been extended and a new nightclub venue added to host comedy nights, cover bands and live acts. Lampeter has a range of live music to suit virtually all tastes. If your music taste is more classically inclined, there is free admission to the Lampeter Music Club's concerts between October and March.

There are over 20 halls of residence, ranging in size from three to 111 rooms and there is a choice of either 'pay-as-you-eat' or self catering accommodation.

The campus sports centre has a multigym, badminton, squash and tennis courts. Most of the sports clubs compete in local leagues and inter-university competitions. Lampeter is one of the few universities in the country to host its own festival held in early June. The Drovers Arts Festival brings together the talents of the university and its local community in a celebration of life and creativity.

There are specific meeting spaces on campus for various religions, including Anglican, Greek Orthodox, Islam and Roman Catholic. Orientation programmes which are specifically designed for overseas students are held to welcome them to both the country and the university and an overseas co-ordinator is available to discuss any concerns that students may have.

L E E D S   M E T R O P O L I T A N   U N I V E R S I T Y

Leeds

Leeds Metropolitan University

Write to: The International Office, City Campus, Leeds Metropolitan University, Leeds LS1 3HE

Tel: +44 (0)113 283 6765

Fax: +44 (0)113 283 3129

Email: international@lmu.ac.uk

Website: www.lmu.ac.uk

Students: approximately 36,000 (full and part time) in 2000/01 (600 from overseas).

Accommodation: university residences from £40 to £65 a week self-catering (en suite available).

Entrance requirements: all types of qualifications and work experience considered.

EFL: IELTS 6.0, TOEFL 550 or the equivalent.

Foundation: one-year international foundation programme guaranteeing entry to many undergraduate courses. One-year pre-master's programme.

Fees: in 2001/02, classroom based £6,650; workshop based £7,150; MBA £7,950.

Leeds Metropolitan University

Student profile

"I gained a first-class degree in my BSc (Hons) Applied Computing at Leeds Metropolitan University. After completing a higher diploma in Malaysia, I chose to top up my qualification to a degree in one year. This is an option available within several subject areas at the university, including business, hospitality management, electronic engineering and computing. My course was very flexible and allowed me to pursue my own interests by choosing different subjects which suited me. I selected my own dissertation title which was concerned

with educational computing. The lecturers at the university were very supportive and the standard is very high. I'm thrilled to gain a first."

Arokia Mekala Soosay Manickam, Malaysia

Leeds is mid way between London and Edinburgh. By train, London is just over two hours away and there are direct flights from the Leeds/Bradford Airport to many international destinations. Leeds was recently voted best university city and a survey of 6,000 students voted Leeds Metropolitan University (LMU) as the best for university accommodation. Students can enjoy a wide variety of international cuisine and multicultural events in an exciting environment which combines the best of historical and contemporary Britain. The cost of living remains relatively low. Leeds is the most important financial centre outside of London and the home of major businesses for which West Yorkshire is famous.

Academic strengths

Leeds Metropolitan University combines a long tradition of quality and excellence with the latest teaching methods, vocational subject choices and state-of-the-art facilities. The university has always focused on professional and vocational education and has excellent graduate employment. Recent departments to be awarded top scores for teaching quality include the School of Economics and Human Resource Management (including MBA), the School of Business Strategy and the School of Tourism and Hospitality Management.

Facilities include multimillion pound Learning Centres and one of the finest sports complexes in British higher education with a swimming pool and facilities for weight training, gymnastics, tennis, rugby league, football and volleyball.

Diplomas, first degrees and postgraduate courses, as well as research degrees are offered in most disciplines. There is also a wide choice of English language courses of varying duration with flexible entry points throughout the year.

Master's programmes are usually completed in one year and some offer a February intake. The International Foundation Programme offers students guaranteed progression onto a wide range of undergraduate programmes and the pre-master's programmes prepare students for entry onto LMU master's programmes.

Student life

There are two campuses at LMU. The City campus is situated in the city centre and the Beckett Park campus is set in beautiful parkland a short bus ride from the city centre. The wide choice of university accommodation includes an award-winning student village development as well as city centre and on-campus housing which is in easy reach of both campuses.

Prior to the start of their course, students are invited to attend the international students induction programme. A full-time international student development officer is available to help students with any queries or advice they may need during the course of their study at LMU.

LMU runs a thriving Job Shop, providing well-paid temporary work for students (often within the university), designed to fit in around study timetables. The students' union runs numerous student societies covering leisure pursuits and interests, including a Malaysian Society and a Chinese Society. The union also has a student advice centre providing support on matters such as finance, housing, health and legal matters. A safety bus operates from the Beckett Park campus and City campus to north and central Leeds.

Universities and colleges
of higher education

University *of* Leicester

Leicester

University of Leicester

Write to: International Office, University of Leicester, University Road, Leicester LE1 7RH

Tel: +44 (0)116 252 2296

Fax: +44 (0)116 252 5127

Email: international.office@le.ac.uk

Website: www.le.ac.uk

Students: 8,200 full time (1,479 postgraduate, 776 international from 100 countries); 50:50 male:female.

Accommodation: single sex, married/family, vacation, en suite. University catered residences from £60 to £95 a week; self-catering accommodation £38 to £67 a week.

Entrance requirements: three A levels or equivalent. Wide range of international qualifications accepted. Please refer to prospectus/website.

EFL: IELTS 6.0 to 6.5 or TOEFL 575 to 600/233 to 250 depending on course. Certain local qualifications accepted. Please refer to prospectus/website.

Foundation: engineering, science (including computer science and biological sciences), social sciences.

Fees: 2002/3: classroom-based courses £7,470, laboratory-based (including Engineering) £9,660, MBChB (years three, four and five) £18,285 MBA £9,735.

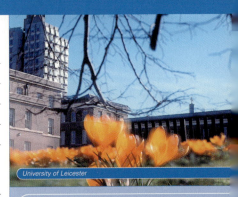

University of Leicester

Student profile

"I took a master's degree in the UK and my professors advised me where I could take a PhD in my subject. I applied to three or four universities but only had a week to decide and Leicester understood what I wanted. I had to go back to Mexico to arrange my scholarship, so I started in January. Some of my professors in Mexico had taken a PhD in the UK and advised me how to apply to the different UK universities. I applied through the internet, friends helped me and student associations on the internet supported me. Student life here is completely different from what I expected,

but everyone is really friendly. There is no need to worry about feeling strange at first. Also, you don't expect this level of support."

Rebeca Muñoz Torres, Mexico

The University of Leicester was founded in 1921 and gained its Royal Charter in 1957. The university is internationally renowned for pioneering DNA genetic fingerprinting and has the biggest university-based space science research centre in Europe. Research underpins teaching in all five faculties, creating a superb learning environment, coupled with a consistently excellent track record in independent assessments of teaching quality.

The university is only 75 minutes from London by train, at the centre of air, road and rail transport networks. As the UK's first Environment City it is an exceptionally pleasant and safe place in which to study and is home to the UK National Space Centre. A lively, cosmopolitan city with a population of 300,000, Leicester has excellent shopping, restaurants and cultural life and is famous for sport. The university lies 1.5 kilometres from the city centre on a compact campus surrounded by parkland.

Academic strengths

Excellent ratings have been awarded to the following subjects: American studies, biological sciences, economics, education, history of art, law, mathematics and statistics, medicine, museum studies, physics and astronomy, politics and psychology. The 2001 research assessment exercise saw a grade 5*/5 awarded to archaeology, biochemistry, biology, economics, engineering, English, history, law, applied mathematics, pure mathematics, pharmacology and physics. A total of 12 subject areas were awarded a grade 4. A wide range of programmes is available, including English language and foundation programmes, study abroad, undergraduate and postgraduate degrees, distance learning and research degrees.

The university has several specialist libraries in addition to the main library, offering 1,100 study spaces and more than 1,000,000 volumes. The university was the first educational institution in the world to base its student computing on the Microsoft Windows 2000 platform.

Open access computer laboratories are provided throughout the university. The Department of Physics and Astronomy hosts the UKAFF national supercomputer for astrophysics research. The Language Services Unit includes three language laboratories and a self-access centre.

Student life

The students' union provides services including shops, bars, clubs, a laundrette and travel agency. There are more than 100 clubs and societies catering for all interests. There is a thriving International Students' Society with over 700 members whose activities include weekends away and an annual cultural evening.

The university has an international welfare officer and is one of only five UK universities to have a vice president for international students within the union. Practical, financial and personal advice are thus available throughout the year, as is a campus medical centre. An airport pick-up service and orientation programme are available at the beginning of the year and a re-orientation programme at the end. A range of university accommodation is available, both catered and self-catering. It is guaranteed to international students.

Liverpool

Liverpool Hope

Write to: Admissions, Liverpool Hope, Hope Park, Liverpool L16 9JD

Tel: +44 (0)151 291 3295

Fax: +44 (0)151 291 2050

Email: admission@hope.ac.uk

Website: www.hope.ac.uk

Students: 6,000 students in 2000/01 (697 postgraduates, four per cent from overseas from over 40 countries), 30:70 male:female.

Accommodation: mixed and single-sex halls of residence on Hope's campuses from £69 to £80 a week. Private accommodation in Liverpool from £45 a week.

Entrance requirements: generally C grades in two A levels or equivalent.

EFL: Cambridge Advanced or Proficiency. IELTS 6.0, TOEFL 560.

Fees: English language studies £3,600 a year, all undergraduate and postgraduate courses £4,200 a year for tuition and £6,700 a year including accommodation.

Students at Liverpool Hope

Student profile

"I attended English classes at Liverpool Hope with 10 students from different countries such as Korea, the Czech Republic, Poland, France and more. We often discussed our cultural differences in class, which benefited my work for my course in sociology and European studies. This course has just started and it is much more interesting than I had expected. I'm looking forward to doing community-based work experience. I stay in off-campus accommodation with 11 other students from all over the UK. I usually go out at the weekend and my favourite place is a new jazz café in

the Albert Dock. I am enjoying studying and living here and am really glad that I can spend three more years at this really friendly college."

Mariko Yamada, Japan

Universities and colleges of higher education

Liverpool Hope was established 150 years ago, providing education for the mind, body and spirit. Today, over 6,000 students study at Hope – the only fully ecumenical higher education institution in the UK. There are currently over 300 international students from over 40 countries studying alongside 6,000 UK students.

A wide range of qualifications are available, with courses from BA, BSc and BEd to PGCE, MA, MPhil and PhD. Degrees are awarded by The University of Liverpool.

Academic strengths

Hope welcomes students from across the UK and throughout the world. It thrives on its multicultural diversity, and students benefit greatly from the opportunity to meet people from across the globe.

Courses are delivered at Hope Park, Childwall and Hope at Everton, a new £19.5 million development in Liverpool city centre. Students also study at numerous Network of Hope locations across the northwest, including Bury, Blackburn, Orrell, Stockport, Manchester and Wigan.

Hope has four deaneries which aim to fulfil the college's mission. The Foundation Deanery reflects Hope's religious roots, while the Education Deanery is grounded in teacher training. The Deanery of Arts and Sciences offers a range of degree courses across numerous academic disciplines. The Centre for English Language Studies (CELS), for example, offers full-time English language tuition for international students.

Since 1995, Hope Park has seen major investment across the campus. The 'World of Difference' lecture theatre complex offers three state-of-the-art lecture rooms with full audiovisual support to aid the lectures and presentations. The campus also features a nursery for students, staff and the local community, a new sports hall and fitness centre, an astroturf pitch, refectory, café bar, and The Sheppard-Worlock Library.

The Cornerstone, a grade II listed building at Hope at Everton, is a winner in the Merseyside Awards for Architecture and Design 2000. It is part of Hope's £19.5 million regeneration project, which has become the new home of Hope's fine art, design and music teams. It is also the headquarters of Hope in the Community, which aims to open up access to education. It includes the 'REACHOut® to Parents Project', with the intent of offering access to lifelong learning to all.

Student life

Hope Park lies in 30 acres of landscaped grounds, five miles from Liverpool centre. The facilities ensure that students have plenty of opportunities to work and play. The students' union is the ideal place to meet with friends and become involved in the various sporting clubs and societies.

Hope's outdoor education centre in Wales, Plas Caerdeon, is set in 20 acres of woodland in Snowdonia. This Victorian mansion offers an ideal base for academic and other activities. Field trips, study weekends and social events are held here.

Plas Caerdeon offers adventure activities such as canoeing, mountaineering, climbing and orienteering. Mountain biking, riding, dry slope skiing and dinghy sailing are also possible nearby. International students enjoy trips to Plas Caerdeon as part of the International Social Programme.

LONDON GUILDHALL
UNIVERSITY

London

London Guildhall University

Write to: Course Enquiries
(Hotcourses), London Guildhall University,
133 Whitechapel High Street,
London E1 7QA

Tel: +44 (0)20 7320 1616

Fax: +44 (0)20 7320 1163

Email: intprogs@lgu.ac.uk

Website: www.lgu.ac.uk/international

Students: 14,356 in 2000/01,
(1,538 postgraduate, 1,290 international
from 84 countries outside the EU).
49:51 male:female.

Entrance requirements: two
A level passes or international
equivalent. Contact admissions office
for detailed course requirements.

EFL: IELTS 6.0, TOEFL 550, Cambridge
Advanced, Cambridge Proficiency or
equivalent.

Foundation: September or January
start. English language centre offers
foundation course (successful completion
guarantees entry onto modular degree
programme), International Business
Diploma (two terms) and Business
English Certificate (one term).

Fees: foundation diploma £5,845, HND
BA/BSc £6,750, most postgraduate
courses £6,750 a year.

Jewry Street, London Guildhall University

Student profile

"I came to the UK six years ago because
of family connections and to improve my
English skills. I studied my A levels at a
boarding school in Cambridge where I had
a good time. When it came to choosing a
university, I wanted to be based in a big-
ger commercial city and I wanted to study
accountancy. London Guildhall University
was my first choice. The accounting and
finance courses have been developed in
conjunction with the accounting profession. The course was challenging at first,

but it has always been
very interesting and
practical. It's different
in the UK, but I've had
a really good time and
I have acclimatised
quite quickly."

Sarah Wong, Hong Kong

London is truly a world city and London Guildhall University's unique location in the City of London makes it an ideal base from which to take advantage of the benefits of studying in London. The roots of the university go back to 1848 when the Bishop of London called for education to improve the moral, intellectual and spiritual condition of young men in the metropolis. Between then and the end of the 19th century, commercial and technical subjects were introduced. This tradition has been continued with the university now offering courses in areas relevant to the City of London, such as banking, business, computing, finance, insurance and law, and to the Greater London area such as art and design, civil aviation, politics, social policy, psychology and shipping.

The university's six teaching sites are within walking distance of each other and include historical sites such as Jewry Street, built on the foundations of the original Roman city walls that protected Londinium, as well as modern, purpose-built buildings around Aldgate and next to the Tower of London.

Academic strengths

London Guildhall University offers courses at three levels: further education (including a wide range of art and design courses), undergraduate and finally postgraduate. Additionally, the Business School offers students a large selection of professional courses.

The degree structure enables students to study what really interests them, allowing them to combine subjects.

The university maintains close links with employers to ensure its courses are up to date and career orientated. Many lecturers have worked, or are still employed, in relevant professions and industries, bringing real-world expertise. Links have also been made with City Livery companies – ancient trade associations – which provide the university with prizes, bursaries, equipment and grants to benefit students.

Student life

Due to its location, the university is well positioned to enable students to enjoy London. There are many markets, shops, theatres, museums and art galleries within easy reach of the university as well as clubs and pubs for those of more nocturnal habits. The university has an active students' union offering a host of different societies together with international student support activities.

International students are invited to attend a three-day residential orientation course to welcome them when they arrive. The course includes an introduction to the university and its many services as well as providing an opportunity to meet both staff and students. During their course of studies, international students enjoy the support of both the university and the student union international student services. These include counselling and advice, study support, an accommodation office and a buddies scheme. International students have automatic membership of International Student House – a special club in London offering social events, a gym, a travel club and general interest classes. There is also a university health service. Religious needs are fulfilled by chaplains who will listen in confidence to any student. There are also separate Muslim prayer rooms.

London

London School of Economics and Political Science (University of London)

Write to: Student Recruitment Office, London School of Economics and Political Science, Houghton Street, London WC2A 2AE

Tel: +44 (0)20 7955 6613

Fax: +44 (0)20 7955 7421

Email: stu.rec@lse.ac.uk

Website: www.lse.ac.uk

Students: 7,218 in 2000/01 (3,518 undergraduates, 3,698 postgraduates, 4,477 international from over 135 countries), 53:47 male:female.

Accommodation: single sex, married, vacation, storage facilities. University residences £47 to £107 a week self-catered/catered; room in town from £75 a week.

Entrance requirements: for undergraduates, AAB to BBB at A level. International Baccalaureate 35 to 39. For postgraduates, upper second class honours degree from good university.

EFL: for undergraduate IELTS 7.0, TOEFL 627; for postgraduate IELTS 6.5/7.0, TOEFL 603/627.

Foundation: not applicable.

Fees: undergraduate courses £9,859 a year; postgraduate courses £10,575 a year.

London School of Economics and Political Science (University of London)

Student profile

"LSE's and London's international dimension allows you to meet, learn and share experiences with people from all over the world. I recommend staying in halls for at least one year; it allows you to integrate and experience student life. Lecture and class hours tend to be minimal, leaving a lot up to the student, so lots of reading is essential. I also try to attend LSE's public lectures which provide a very interesting view on issues such as globalisation. The BSc Management degree at LSE has provided me  with significant business knowledge and also access to management-based careers where I can use my skills."

Gursheen Khandari, Kenya

Universities and colleges of higher education

London School of Economics and Political Science (LSE) is unique in the UK in its concentration on teaching and research across the full range of the social, political and economic sciences. It was founded in 1895 by Beatrice and Sidney Webb, founding members of the Fabian Society, and became part of the federal University of London (UL) in 1900. Today, the London School of Ecomomics is one of the largest institutions within UL. With over half of LSE's students coming from overseas, it has a large international student community. Alumni include MPs and members of the House of Lords, 26 current or former heads of government around the world and figures such as George Soros, Romano Prodi and Mick Jagger.

The London School of Economics is located in Holborn, central London, between the West End and the City. The British Library, the UL Senate House library and smaller specialist libraries are within easy reach of LSE. Students naturally benefit from London's considerable social and cultural opportunities as well as its excellent travel connections.

Academic strengths

LSE teaches much more than just economics and political science. Teaching and research is carried out in 18 academic departments and 30 centres and institutes. While degrees are awarded through the University of London, the London School of Economics has total autonomy over the content and structure of its degrees, some of which involve intercollegiate collaboration within the federal university.

In teaching quality assessments, LSE has been rated excellent in anthropology, economic history, information systems, international history, law, management, operational research and social policy. In the 2001 research assessment exercise, LSE achieved the rating of either 5 or 5* in over 20 subject areas including accounting, economics and international relations.

There are a range of study facilities at the London School of Economics. The library has recently undergone a multimillion pound re-development. It also serves as a national collection of material for research and is one of the largest libraries in the world devoted to the economic and social sciences. LSE is committed to ensuring that staff and students have access to necessary IT tools and support.

Student life

LSE has various support networks for its students. For both academic and personal advice, students consult personal tutors. There is pre- and in-sessional English language support and ongoing academic support and students can find three chaplains – Roman Catholic, Church of England and Free Church – and a Rabbi on campus. There is also an Islamic prayer room and societies for all major religions.

The London School of Economics offers more than £3 million a year in financial support to its students. Scholarships are available for students from particular countries or taking certain courses.

As members of the UL union, students have access to all the university's facilities including counselling services, health and dental care and the students' union itself, which has bars, cafés, a gym and a swimming pool. Of its three newly refurbished bars, the Three Tuns is the most popular venue to relax and socialise.

Loughborough

Loughborough University

Write to: International Office, Student Recruitment and Admissions, Loughborough University, Loughborough, Leicestershire LE11 3TU

Tel: +44 (0)1509 222499

Fax: +44 (0)1509 223905

Email: international-office@lboro.ac.uk

Website: www.lboro.ac.uk

Students: 12,527 in 2000/01 (2,867 postgraduates, 885 international from over 100 countries), 1.7:1 male:female.

Accommodation: single sex, married/family, vacation, storage facilities. University residences from £47 to £64 a week self-catered, £75 to £95 catered. Room in town from £37 to £48 a week.

Entrance requirements: for undergraduates, a combination of GCSE and A level passes either in five subjects, with two at A level, or in four subjects with three at A level or international equivalent.

EFL: for undergraduates Cambridge Proficiency grade C, Advanced grade B, GCSE English grade C, IELTS 6.5, TOEFL 550; for postgraduates GCSE English, IELTS 6.5, TOEFL 570.

Foundation: one year, full time or two years, part time for science and engineering or art and design.

Fees: classroom courses £7,400 a year; laboratory courses £9,650 a year (2002 entry).

Loughborough University

Student profile

"I chose Loughborough because of its good reputation. The opportunity to do an industrial placement confirmed my choice. The course is well structured and has the right balance between theoretical studies and coursework. The lecturers are approachable and the tutor system means there is always help on academic and personal matters. I spent a year on placement working as a research and development engineer. I was involved in key projects and developed skills I would not be able to learn from a lecture. My confidence soared and it has definitely prepared me for a graduate job. I will

 graduate this summer and I know that I will then have a good degree with plenty of good memories to cherish and to bring home with me."

Kim Yen Chia, Malaysia

Loughborough University dates from 1909, when a small technical institute was established at Loughborough in the East Midlands. Since 1966, Loughborough has held university status. The town of Loughborough is about half an hour by car or 20 minutes by train from three major cities – Derby, Nottingham and Leicester. Loughborough is very well served by public transport, with East Midlands Airport nearby and London an hour and a half train journey away. Loughborough is a thriving market town, surrounded by Charnwood Forest.

Academic strengths

The university is divided into the three faculties of engineering, science and social sciences and humanities. It achieved 11th place in the 2001 *Sunday Times* league table of UK universities and was rated excellent in 11 subjects. The university boasts its status as the winner of three Queen's Anniversary prizes in the past six years. Many UK and worldwide sandwich placements are available for home and international students and there have been zero unemployment levels in more than 60 per cent of Loughborough's recent undergraduate programmes.

The large library gives direct access to more than six million printed items and electronic access to many other resources. Computing services are available to all students free of charge, 24 hours a day through a networked system that includes every hall of residence.

Student life

Everything you need can be found on the single-site campus, from shops to medical care. The National Union of Students has identified Loughborough's self-catering facilities as one of the top three value-for-money deals in the UK. University accommodation is guaranteed to all first-year international students.

A handbook advising travel preparations and a free coach service to Loughborough University on arrival at Heathrow Airport are provided for all new students. Pre-sessional courses are held to provide English language teaching and practical help and advice regarding living and studying in the UK.

There are free, on-campus support systems for all, including the medical centre, year-round English language support, the student advice centre, the employment exchange, various groups and facilities for worship, international student officers and advisers, as well as an International Students Association providing social life support. Overall, there are some 112 clubs and societies, run by and for students, and one of the most active student unions in the country.

The students' union is a huge provider of professional entertainment catering for a wide range of tastes. Each week there are discos, big-screen films and live comedy nights, as well as end-of-term parties. The new £1.4 million media centre houses facilities including a radio station, *LCR*, the student magazine, *Label*, and a TV and video suite, all of which students are encouraged to make use of.

The university is known for having some of the most extensive sports facilities in Britain, helping to produce many international sporting personalities. There are a number of sports scholarships and bursaries which are available specifically for international students.

Manchester

The Manchester Metropolitan University

Write to : The International Office,
The Manchester Metropolitan University,
All Saints, Manchester M15 6BH

Tel: +44 (0)161 247 1022

Fax: +44 (0)161 247 6310

Email: intoff@mmu.ac.uk

Website: www.mmu.ac.uk

Students: 31,000 in 2000/01 (5 per cent
international), 44:55 male:female.

Accommodation: single rooms –
catered/self-catered. En suite available.
University residences £46 to £74 a week
self-catered and £72 to £76 a week
catered. Private rented accommodation
from £35 a week.

Location: seven campuses located in
Manchester, Crewe and Alsager.

Entrance requirements: depending
on course.

EFL: courses of 20 and 10 weeks and a
two-month intensive pre-sessional
English course in the summer. Minimum
entry for courses: GCSE English grade C,
IELTS 6,0, TOEFL, 550 (paper based) and
213 (computer based).

Foundation: foundation year is year '0'
for over 80 courses across the university.
Art and design foundation courses lead to
most degrees in art and design.

Fees: 2001/02 undergraduate: classroom
£6,760; lab £7310. Postgraduate classroom
£7,310; lab £7,880.

The Manchester Metropolitan University campus

Student profile

"Leaving Kenya to study business in
Manchester was one of the hardest
decisions I've had to make. I believe in
taking every opportunity as it comes,
and my degree has offered me many. In
my second year, I went to Flinders
University, South Australia. I travelled
around Adelaide and visited Melbourne
and Sydney. MMU also provided a
student work placement. This involved
a marketing role at Siemens, a large
company in Manchester. This placement
has given me the advantage of having a
whole year's valuable work experience.
Living so far away from home has made

me more independent
and responsible and
I have made many
friends. I am glad I
was strong enough to
leave home and my
mum's cooking."

Natasha Montet, Kenya

Manchester, with its 2.5 million inhabitants, is a cosmopolitan city with over 70,000 students. Manchester is hosting the Commonwealth Games in 2002. A major construction initiative is providing the city with some of the best sporting facilities in the country. The city centre ensures easy access to facilities and amenities, and the city isn't far from the Peak District, Pennines, Yorkshire Dales, Lake District and North Wales.

Manchester is also known as being a city of entertainment. Its large student population has a wide choice of clubs, comedy and music venues. With regard to musical talent, The Smiths, The Stone Roses, Take That, Oasis, Simply Red and the Bee Gees all started out in Manchester.

The city houses many cinemas, theatres, galleries and Britain's first African and Caribbean Arts Centre. The university is spread out over seven campuses, five in the Manchester area and two in Cheshire.

Academic strengths

The Manchester Metropolitan University offers over 400 courses, many of which are practical, equipping students with transferable skills valued by employers. The university has links with industry, business and professional bodies – many staff members are involved in applied research and have business backgrounds. The range of courses that are popular with international students include accounting, law, art and design, marketing, tourism, librarianship, hospitality, clothing, sports and exercise science. Students have the opportunity to study in the USA, Canada and Europe or Australia in year two.

The university works to improve its facilities for students. There has recently been extensive refurbishment and new building on the university's campuses. This includes split-level library facilities, lecture theatres, seminar rooms, new laboratories, design studios for the art and design faculty and a purpose-built Faculty of Humanities and Social Science.

Seven site libraries and language labs hold over a million print and electronic materials. Students can reserve and renew books online and search bibliographic databases either from the drop-in centres or from home. The full text of many of the articles referenced are also online.

Student life

The students' union hosts a range of services for the students. In addition to providing a busy entertainment schedule for students including comedy nights, live music and club nights, the union also offers a welfare service, a minibus service for women and several bars and shops.

The union also organises over 80 different clubs and societies. The Athletic Union, together with the University Sport and Recreational Unit, co-ordinates over 45 sports clubs ranging from water polo to badminton. On arrival, international students are welcomed to the university with airport and station pick-ups and an international orientation course at the beginning of term. Pre-sessional and general English language courses are offered to international students.

The university provides a meeting and prayer space for Jewish, Muslim and Christian students. The city of Manchester itself is a multicultural, multifaith society where students of other religions will, more than likely, be able to contact members for worship.

Manchester

THE UNIVERSITY
of MANCHESTER

Manchester

The University of Manchester

Write to: Kate Cohoon,
International Office, Beyer Building,
The University of Manchester, Oxford
Road, Manchester M13 9PL

Tel: +44 (0)161 275 2196

Fax: +44 (0)161 275 2058

Email: international.unit@man.ac.uk

Website: www.man.ac.uk

Students: 24,415 in 2000/01
(5,435 postgraduate, 2,498
international from more than 130
countries), 48:52 male:female.

Accommodation: single sex,
married, vacation – sometimes extra
charge. Storage facilities. University
residences from £43 to £57 a week
self-catered, from £75 a week catered.

Entrance requirements: vary
according to subject, generally
three high grades at A level.

EFL: Cambridge Proficiency grade C,
GCSE English Language grade C, IELTS
minimum 6.0, TOEFL minimum 550,
computer-based TOEFL minimum 213
(variable according to subject).

Foundation: none on campus.
Two available at City College,
Manchester for entry to science
and engineering programmes or
economics and social studies.

Fees: classroom courses £7,650 a year;
laboratory courses £9,950 a year; clinical
courses £18,150 a year.

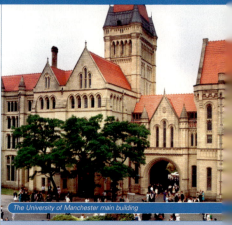

The University of Manchester main building

Student profile

"The University of Manchester is one of
the best places to get a good education.
I heard about my course from my
brother who graduated with a BA (Econ)
from here. He has gone on to become a
successful chartered accountant back
home. My course is very demanding. It
is difficult to stay on top of things but
everyone gets a lot of assistance from
the academic personnel whose greatest
concern is about the students' progress.
Combining the above with the campus

facilities, the people
and the city itself,
I would say that
The University of
Manchester was the
best choice I could
have made."

Apollo Athanasiades, Greece

The University of Manchester, founded in 1851, was one of the first 'red brick' or civic universities in England. Over the years, several major scientific and technological advances have been made here including the world's first working prototypes of the computer in 1948 and Sir Ernest Rutherford's work leading to the splitting of the atom. The university occupies a compact campus site, half a mile to the south of the centre of Manchester.

The city itself is large and cosmopolitan (it has a population of over 500,000). Manchester is particularly renowned for its club and music scene. However, other tastes are catered for; it is home to two symphony orchestras – the Hallé and the BBC Philharmonic. Recently, Manchester has undergone rejuvenation through public and private projects such as the Bridgewater Concert Hall and the Metrolink tram system. This cultural and economic revival has been recognised internationally by the city being given the opportunity to host the Commonwealth Games in 2002.

Academic strengths

The university is divided into seven academic areas: the faculties of Arts, Biological Sciences, Business Administration, Education, Medicine, (including Dentistry, Nursing and Pharmacy), Science and Engineering and Social Science and Law. In teaching quality assessments during 1999/2000 and 2000/01, the following grades were attained: religions and theology 24, classics and ancient history 24, philosophy 24, archaeology 23, economics 24, pharmacy 24, nursing 23, audiology 22, dentistry 24, medicine 24, all out of a possible 24.

Among the university's study facilities is the John Rylands university library. This is the third largest university library in the country and houses more than 3.5 million books. The library distributes electronic information resources across the campus via the computer networks which are available 24 hours a day.

Student life

Manchester has a number of services in place for international students. Before the start of term, students can be picked up at airports and railway stations. A four-day residential course for new students is then available to help students settle in and meet people. The international student welfare officer and adviser also organise a welcome desk for the first two weeks of the term and then later host a welcome reception event for all new international students. The international society runs a hospitality scheme, giving international students the opportunity to meet and briefly stay with local families.

The University of Manchester's student union has welfare and advice services and organises a variety of social events through its societies which number over 100. Societies include religious and national groups. Students have access to two chapels (Roman Catholic and Protestant) and a Muslim prayer room. Two large, indoor sports centres include gymnasia, tennis, badminton and squash courts and indoor football pitches. There are also two outdoor sports centres as well as an Olympic-standard swimming pool. The university has student health and dental provision and a counselling service.

NAPIER UNIVERSITY
EDINBURGH

Edinburgh

Napier University

Write to: The International Recruitment Officer, Old Craig, Craighouse Campus, Napier University, Edinburgh EH10 5LG

Tel: +44 (0)131 455 6277

Fax: +44 (0)131 455 6261

Email: intoffice@napier.ac.uk

Website: www.napier.ac.uk

Students: 12,000 in 1999/2000 (1,484 postgraduate, 8.5 per cent international from 80 countries), 51:49 male:female.

Accommodation: mainly single-sex flats. University residences from £56 to £57 a week. Room in town from £45 to £55 a week.

Entrance requirements: generally two or three A levels in appropriate subjects. 24 points at International Baccalaureate.

EFL: IELTS 5.5, TOEFL 550 (computer-based test 215).

Fees: (2001/02) fees for undergraduate: classroom £6,600; laboratory £7,350. Postgraduate: classroom £6,900; business £7,200; laboratory £8,200 to £8,750.

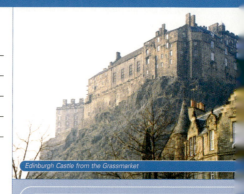

Edinburgh Castle from the Grassmarket

Student profile

In 1998, Napier University was granted a joint scholarship with the British Trade and Cultural Office (BTCO) Taiwan, for students applying for the MSc Information Technology (Multimedia Technology) degree. This covered full tuition fees for the master's programme and a pre-sessional English language course.

"I was the first successful applicant for the joint scholarship and joined the course for 1998/99. The scholarship helped me fulfil my dream to study in the UK. I received a lot of support from BTCO and Napier University when I  needed it, not just in terms of the tuition fees, but also from the people around me. I appreciate the scholarship, especially as Edinburgh is a very good place to study."

Jack Chu, Taiwan

Napier University is named after the 16th-century philosopher and mathematician, John Napier, one of Scotland's most illustrious sons and the man who developed the concept of logarithms. In the last three decades, Napier has progressed from polytechnic to university status and, in *The Times Good University Guide 1999*, was rated as one of the top two new universities in the UK.

The university is based on 11 sites in Edinburgh, Scotland's capital. Edinburgh is a relatively small city and students may move around easily and cheaply. Architecturally, the city centre is full of beautiful, historic buildings, ranging from the 16th-century Royal Mile to the 18th and 19th-century New Town. The main campuses are at Craiglockhart, Merchiston, Sighthill, Craighouse and Canaan Lane. The Merchiston campus incorporates Napier Tower, the castle where John Napier was born in 1550.

Academic strengths

The university is divided into the four faculties of Arts and Social Sciences, Engineering and Computing, Life Sciences and the Napier Business School.

Napier University Business School is the largest in Scotland and the engineering faculty is the biggest in eastern Scotland. The university produces more graduates of mathematics than any other institution in Scotland. Napier's School of Communication Arts offers programmes including communication, journalism, publishing, design, photography, film and television. The university careers advisory service provides a series of seminars and workshops to assist with careers preparation and planning. *The Financial Times* league table of the top 100 universities in the UK has placed Napier amongst the top 10 in terms of students finding jobs once they graduate.

Student life

All of the university sites in southwest Edinburgh have their own libraries. These are open seven days a week during term time and have extensive collections of books and printed, audiovisual, CD-Rom and self-instructional materials. Both individual and group study rooms are available, the latter accommodating between three and eight people and offering students the opportunity to work together on projects.

Computing facilities are available at each campus and students are given their own email address on enrolment. The university computer services unit provides expertise and support to all the campuses, while help desks are available to answer questions and offer advice on computer usage. Media units, providing both audio and visual services, are available at each of the main campuses. These offer a range of support services from graphics to photography, as well as facilities for in-house video production and editing.

Achievements in sport include the university football team winning the Scottish Universities League and the badminton club winning the Scottish Universities Badminton Championship.

Every student who enrols for a course at Napier University automatically becomes a member of the Napier students' association (NSA), membership to which entitles students to a range of services, including welfare support, clubs and societies and social events.

New College Nottingham

Nottingham

New College Nottingham

Write to: Sue Griffin HC,
The International Office,
New College Nottingham, The Adams
Building, The Lace Market,
Nottingham NG1 1LJ

Tel: +44 (0)115 910 4612

Fax: +44 (0)115 910 4611

Email: internat@ncn.ac.uk
EFL enquiries: english.enquiries@ncn.ac.uk

Website: www.ncn.ac.uk

Students: 14,000 full time and 30,000
part time in 2000/01 (1,000 international
students from over 50 countries),
40: 60 male:female.

Accommodation: single, married,
single sex, vacation. Homestay £80 a week
half board/full board at weekends. Also
homestay self-catering for £50 a week.

Entrance requirements: depending
on course. Equivalent of five GCSEs for
most but A level equivalent for higher
level courses with IELTS/ TOEFL score of
5.5/500 respectively.

EFL : at all levels except beginners.
Flexible enrolment throughout year.

Foundation courses: one-year courses
provide access to higher education in
business, IT, computing, travel and
tourism management, art and design.

Fees: further education £3,990;
international access to higher education
£4,400; HND £5,500. Discounts if fees
paid at start of each course.

New College Nottingham

Student profile

"This is my second year of the GNVQ
Advanced Leisure and Tourism course
which is a vocational A level. It covers
subjects such as business, marketing,
customer service, health and safety
and travel management. I do coursework
and have exams for each unit of study.
When I finish I can apply to university or
study for an HND here at the college.
British qualifications are recognised all
over the world so it will be easier for me
to find a job in my own country. The
International Office is brilliant at New
College too. If you have any problems
about your visas or accommodation,

or need some friendly
advice and guidance
on your course or
indeed, anything else,
they will always wel-
come you and help
you. I made a good
choice coming here."

Yong Fang,

People's Republic of China

Nottingham has been voted the most popular student city on a number of occasions. This lively city, situated in the centre of Britain has a population of 300,000 and it takes less than two hours by train to London. Nottingham is famous for the legend of Robin Hood and Sherwood Forest. Four million tourists explore its heritage every year. Other famous visitor attractions are within easy reach and include the historic cities of York, Cambridge, and Stratford-upon-Avon.

Nottingham values culture and loves learning. Over 400 artists create original artwork here and around 100,000 students attend its colleges and two universities. New College has grown to offer a broad range of academic and professional courses for both local and international students.

Students can work towards qualifications in such subjects as fashion, art, music, building and construction crafts, dance and drama, languages, business, media, leisure and tourism, beauty and complementary therapies, child and healthcare and IT.

Academic strengths

New College Nottingham is a state college of further education with an educational history that goes back 300 years. It is one of Europe's largest colleges and has over 30 years' experience of English language teaching. Its courses have been inspected and accredited by the British Council for more than 16 years.

The college has an excellent reputation and has achieved an ISO 9001 for business standards and a government Chartermark for its outstanding customer services.

College learning centres are equipped with computers, internet access, CD-Roms, satellite and cable television and video conferencing. Two training restaurants are open to students, as are two theatres in the arts centre, a dance studio, gym and fitness suite, hair and beauty salons, quiet study areas and a prayer room.

Student life

Nottingham offers numerous attractions for students including a lively nightlife. There are theatres, an international concert hall, cinemas, nightclubs and an excellent choice of restaurants. There are outstanding leisure facilities too with 16 multisport centres and nine swimming pools to choose from.

For those interested in water sports, racket sports, skating and ice-hockey, Nottingham has three national sports and international events complexes, namely the National Water Sports Centre, Tennis Centre and newly opened £40 million National Ice Centre which also holds regular pop and orchestral concerts. Nottingham also plays host to the world famous Trent Bridge Cricket Ground for county and international matches.

The college has an active students' union and overseas students have often been represented on the committee. New College Nottingham has a friendly and dedicated International Office which offers support services including such matters as pre-arrival information and college induction. Comprehensive advice and guidance on important issues like courses, welfare, health, finance and visa concerns is available.

The team can also arrange homestay accommodation with an English family. The international office has a well-established network of host families.

London

University of North London

Write to: Mark Bickerton, Director, International Office, University of North London, Holloway Road, London N7 8DB

Tel: +44 (0)20 7753 3314

Fax: +44 (0)20 7753 5015

Email: oncourse@unl.ac.uk

Website: www.unl.ac.uk/international

Students:
17,000 including 2,400 international.

Accommodation: guaranteed to international students who book by 9 August each year. £68 to £83 a week.

Entrance requirements: good year-12 results for foundation year. A level equivalent for degree. Good bachelor's degree or PGDip for master's. Mature students and those with professional qualifications accepted. Huge number of worldwide qualifications recognised.

EFL: IELTS, TOEFL, Cambridge and many others accepted. Foundation year IELTS 4.5, bachelor's IELTS 5.5, pre-master's IELTS 5.5, master's IELTS 6.0. One, three, six and nine-month English courses available on campus.

Fees: foundation £4,800; degree £6,600; pre-master's £3,300; master's £3,600 to £7,200; MBA £9,000.

University of North London

Student profile

"I am now on the second year of BA (Hons) Business Economics and Finance. I originally came to the UK in 1998 to take my A levels at a school here. It was hard to orientate to the UK system at first but I worked hard and gained four As and one B. My school was in the countryside, so I chose to take my degree in London because I wanted to be near to the financial district. Also, there are lots of good part-time jobs in London; this helps both

to pay for my social life and to help me match theory and practice. I live in International Students House in central London, which is brilliant."

Dat Hoang, Vietnam

The University of North London is over 100 years old and located in the centre of London. The university is located about 10 minutes from Piccadilly Circus and about one hour from London Heathrow Airport.

Academic strengths

The University of North London offers over 200 degree courses in more than 80 subjects including accounting, design, architecture, fine art, chemistry, mass communications, biology, health, business administration, economics, pharmaceutical science, computing, education, electronics, languages, law, mathematics, polymers, psychology, sociology, sports science, tourism, hotel management, e-commerce and forensic science.

The one-year International Foundation Programme (IFP) provides academic study and English preparation. Completion of the IFP leads to an undergraduate pathway in one of the following subjects: biology and chemistry, architecture and interior design, computing and electronics, business studies (including hospitality management), humanities or law and social science.

There is also a year-round programme offering one, three six and nine-month full-time academic English courses and a Junior Year Abroad (JYA) which includes English language tuition, classes on British culture and academic study. The university also offers bachelor's degrees, pre-master's, pre-MBA, master's degrees, PhDs and there are September and February intakes for the most popular courses.

Student life

The university has three gyms, a dance studio, performance spaces, video suites, an outdoor sports centre and a host of bars, cafés and restaurants.

North London's student complex, the Rocket, has won awards for being the Best Student Venue in London, and second best across the whole of the UK at the 1999 Live Slow awards. There are regular discos and bands on campus.

The University of North London offers a wide range of support services for students including accommodation, religious support, counselling, placements, careers advice, visa advice and also English language testing.

The university's unique Technology Tower provides free access to networks and the internet through 700 Pentium computers, coupled with spectacular views over London. The institution also has a Language Centre offering nine languages and well-equipped science and specialist IT facilities for its students.

The Learning Centre hosts a well-stocked library, areas for group work, individual quiet study spaces and a language lab. Students are able to take a language module as part of their studies and can choose from a range of European languages including English.

The university strives to be both friendly and welcoming for its students with a focus on their welfare, education and personal development.

The International Office provides advice and information, visits most countries around the world and organises a week-long orientation and cultural programme for new students. It also has an airport welcome service on arrival and helps international students from their first enquiry through to when they have completed their degree.

Northampton

University College Northampton

Write to: International Office, Park Campus, University College Northampton, Boughton Green Road, Northampton NN2 7AL

Tel: +44 (0)1604 735500

Fax: +44 (0)1604 710703

Email: international@northampton.ac.uk

Website: www.northampton.ac.uk

Students: 9,000 (500 international students from 80 countries).

Accommodation: university residences from £35 to £60 a week self-catering. Room in town from £30 to £50 a week.

Entrance requirements: qualifications from all countries are considered. Certain courses have specific subject requirements.

EFL: IELTS 6.5 to 7.5 depending on course. TOEFL or Cambridge Advanced equivalent.

Foundation: art and design, business and computing.

Fees: between £3,750 and £7,000 depending on the course.

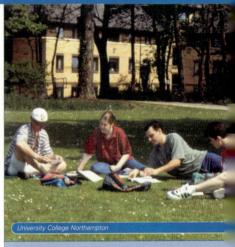
University College Northampton

Student profile

"It has been a wonderful experience studying at UCN. I have met people with various backgrounds, lecturers who are ever willing to help students and very efficient staff from the International Office who make international students feel very much at home. I am really grateful for the opportunity given me to study at UCN. With a master's in Environmental Management I hope

to be able to help improve upon environmental conditions in my country. Thanks to everyone at UCN for making me what I am today."

Sandra Kesse, Kenya

University College Northampton (UCN) is based on two campuses. Park campus is set in 80 acres surrounded by woodland. Avenue campus is two miles from Park campus and occupies 24 acres overlooking a large park. UCN is large enough to offer top-quality modern facilities yet it retains a friendly and relaxed environment which encourages students to enjoy their time there while extending their knowledge and talents and developing as individuals. This, of course, is accompanied by the aim to attain the highest possible academic standards.

Northampton is a thriving town with one of the fastest-growing economies in the UK. Much of the surrounding countryside is rural and typically English. It is centrally located and within easy travelling distance of many cultural and historic sites. London, with its many attractions, is less than an hour away.

The university college is easily accessible from Heathrow, Gatwick, Stansted, Luton and Birmingham International airports.

Academic strengths

UCN is divided into three faculties: Arts and Social Sciences, Applied Sciences and the Northampton Business School. They offer a range of relevant and up-to-date courses in over 100 subjects. The university college has received excellent ratings in its most recent QAA reviews in art and design, nursing and midwifery and materials technology.

Student life

University College Northampton offers over 1,600 rooms in halls of residence in single-study bedrooms. Much of the accomodation has en-suite facilities in shared self-catering flats.

UCN has invested £65 million in recent years in student facilities which include new teaching buildings, library extensions, computing facilities, the students' union, student services and sports facilities. The town centre, with its range of shops, banks, pubs, clubs, theatres, museums and an art gallery, is easily accessible. University College Northampton offers a diverse recreational, sporting and cultural experience for students. Northampton's central location can enable frequent visits to theatrical presentations, concerts and exhibitions in London, Birmingham, Stratford-upon-Avon and Oxford.

The university has up to 50 different clubs and societies covering a wide range of interests. The sports hall, dance studio and playing fields are extensively used and there are successful teams for both men and women covering football, rugby, basketball, hockey and cricket.

UCN has a dedicated international office to assist students through the application process, providing support and advice on visa/immagration issues, scholarships, travel arrangements and accommodation, as well as on-going advice and support during your stay at UCN.

The international office staff organise induction programmes and events with the international student society to help overseas students integrate more readily into British life. These include a cultural programme with opportunities for students to visit places of interest, host family visits and much more.

Worthing

Northbrook College

Write to: International Office,
Northbrook College,
Union Place, Worthing,
West Sussex BN11 1LG

Tel: +44 (0)1903 606107

Fax: +44 (0)1903 606113

Email: international@nbcol.ac.uk

Website:
www.northbrook.ac.uk/international

Students: there are approximately 300
international students at the college on
many different courses studying with
approximately 3,000 students from the UK.

Accommodation: there is an excellent
homestay network in Worthing and new
halls of residence are being planned.

Entrance requirements: for college
courses, appropriate qualifications from
your country and the following:
Cambridge First Certificate; TOEFL 450;
IELTS 4.5. For higher education courses
(undergraduate), appropriate qualifications
from your country as well as: Cambridge
First Certificate; (passed at C or higher);
TOEFL 500; IELTS score of 5.5.

Foundation: programmes in business,
IT, art and design, music, media,
engineering and hospitality.

Northbrook College

Student profiles

"I am taking an art and design course
as well as English which will help me
find a good job when I return to the
Czech Republic. I have passed the First
Certificate as well as the Advanced and
am now studying for Proficiency."
Zlatica Zacheloya, Czech Republic

"I have passed the PET examination and
am making good progress. I would like to
be a car mechanic so I am planning on
studying mechanical engineering at
Northbrook College. The qualifications I
get will help me find a good job when I
return home."
Sukit Pechasiri, Thailand

"I love the greenery around the college
very much. We can use the canteen,
library and sports facilities. Worthing is
situated by the sea, so it's wonderful.
Also the teachers are excellent. I hope I
can use English for my future career."
Yanoi Inoue, Japan

Northbrook College students

Northbrook College has a strong international student population who come from over 60 countries in Europe and further overseas to study everything from basic English to higher courses like degrees. The combination of English, undergraduate and college courses makes Northbrook unique different from other colleges and universities in England.

As a college of both further and higher education, Northbrook offers courses at access or intermediate levels; those courses which will give students a foundation for progression to university courses as well as offering its own undergraduate degrees and diplomas.

Northbrook also offers personal and individual treatment to its students. Class sizes are small, usually about 15 to 20 students, and there is a tutorial system that gives students one-to-one contact with their tutors. The college builds strong relationships with all of its students and especially so with international students who often begin with English classes and go on to higher level courses.

Northbrook is a large college and has five campuses. A large, modern institution, the college has all the normal facilities expected of a college of Northbrook's size, including IT and computing resources.

Students also study on the south coast of England. Worthing is a traditional town of just under 100,000 people and is a holiday resort with a reputation for being clean and friendly. It is only 75 kilometres from London and its airports.

Academic strengths

With over 100 college courses and 50 university courses, Northbrook is one of the largest colleges in the south of England. It is possible to study degrees, foundation degrees, Higher National Diplomas, foundation courses and also college diplomas.

Northbrook has all the traditional areas one would expect from a large college. It is one of the largest colleges in the UK for art, design, media, music and performing arts. Its unique range of aeronautical engineering courses is based at the Shoreham Airport campus. In the 1999/2000 (former) Further Education Funding Council inspection, Northbrook received a grade 1 for its hospitality and catering courses at college level – one of only five colleges in the country to receive such recognition. It is also an accredited college of the Open University and its degree courses are indeed both validated and awarded by the Open University.

In recent inspections by the government, the college received some excellent grades (such as 21 out of 24) for its work, demonstrating its quality in higher education work.

The School of English has been operating for over 15 years as part of the college and has helped many hundreds of students from all over the world to improve their English and gain access to educational and career opportunities in the UK and their home countries. Courses that follow the Cambridge Examination syllabus and IELTS testing are also on offer and the college can provide individual tuition.

Northbrook College offers small classes at all levels, all year round. This means that students can join at any level, for as long as they like, including during the summer.

Newcastle

northumbria
UNIVERSITY

Northumbria University

Write to: The International Office, Northumbria University, Ellison Place, Newcastle upon Tyne NE1 8ST

Tel: +44 (0)191 227 4271

Fax: +44 (0)191 261 1264

Email: er.intoff@unn.ac.uk

Website: www.northumbria.ac.uk

Students: 24,000 in 2000/01 (2,600 postgraduate, 2,500 international from about 80 countries), 45:55 male:female.

Accommodation: single sex, married, vacation. University residences from £45 a week. Room in town from £42 a week.

Entrance requirements: qualifications from all countries considered. Certain courses have specific subject requirements.

EFL: Cambridge Advanced, IELTS 5.5 to 7.0 depending on course, TOEFL 550 minimum.

Foundation: art and design, engineering, science, technology and general foundation.

Fees: classroom courses from £6,600; laboratory courses from £7,200.

Longhirst

Student profile

"I graduated from Northumbria University with a first class honours degree in transportation design, and have recently gained a prestigious work placement with the Alfa Romeo motor company in Milan. My language skills will help because in this field you often have to work with different nationalities. Having a British degree will definitely  work in my favour and Northumbria's outstanding reputation for teaching will hopefully put me ahead of the competition."

Matteo Conti, Italy

Northumbria University is one of the largest universities in Britain, with approximately 25,000 students including 2,000 from outside the UK. The largest campus is based in the centre of Newcastle, a popular university city. Known as the capital of England's northeast, Newcastle lies on the river Tyne near the east coast of England, at the centre of one of Britain's most beautiful and historic regions. Newcastle is ideal for students, with its low cost of living and lively atmosphere. It is also known for its great social life and has a busy calendar of entertainments, arts and musical events.

mathematics, education, engineering, health, humanities, information studies, law, MBA, modern languages, nursing, psychology, social sciences, social work, and travel and tourism.

The range of English language courses at Northumbria offer expert tuition in a campus environment. Courses cater for different levels of ability and some are intended for students preparing for academic study. Popular courses include general English, Spring School and the Summer School. The undergraduate and postgraduate foundation courses allow you to start in February or September.

Academic strengths

The university's reputation for high standards has been recognised by some of Britain's leading newspapers. It has been named Best New University by the *Sunday Times University Guide* for three successive years. (New universities are those which specialise in practical, career-oriented courses).

In official assessments carried out by the UK higher education Quality Assurance Agency, the university has been judged excellent in art and design, dance, built environment, business management, drama, economics, education, English, electrical and electronic engineering, information management, law, modern languages, nursing, physics, politics, psychology and subjects allied to medicine.

Over 300 courses and many research programmes are offered in the following subject areas: accountancy and finance, applied and molecular sciences, arts, business and management, design, built environment, English, EFL, combined honours, economics, computing and

Student life

Northumbria has a long tradition of welcoming international students and a special effort is made to support them in their studies. There is a good choice of accommodation and numerous free facilities and specialist services, such as the meet and greet service, an induction programme, in-sessional English language tuition and support with study skills. There is also an international student adviser who is there to help students throughout their time at the university.

All Northumbria University students automatically become members of the students' union. Run by students for students, the union provides a wide range of facilities, entertainment and services. On the City campus, the union is the hub of student social life with discos, concerts, cafés, clubs and societies. As well as housing a ballroom and theatre, the City campus union has three bars, a full service travel agent, a bookshop, sandwich and stationery shops, lounges and TV rooms.

Universities and colleges
of higher education

Nottingham

The Nottingham Trent University

Write to: International Officer, International Student Recruitment Office, Registry, Dryden Centre, The Nottingham Trent University, Nottingham NG1 4BU

Tel: +44 (0)115 848 6153

Fax: +44 (0)115 848 6063

Email: international@ntu.ac.uk

Website: www.ntu.ac.uk

Students: 23,581 in 2001 (4,792 postgraduates, EU 764, 1,092 international, from over 80 countries), 50:50 male:female.

Accommodation: single sex, mostly en-suite. University residences from £50 to £58 a week self-catered. Room in town from £40 to £60 a week.

Entrance requirements: normally two A levels or equivalent overseas qualification, 24 points at International Baccalaureate.

EFL: IELTS 6.5, TOEFL 550, computer-based TOEFL 213.

Foundation: the university offers a foundation programme directly linked to the undergraduate programmes in The Nottingham Trent School of Art and Design. Foundation programmes for other subjects are offered by local partner further education colleges.

Fees: (2002/03 entry) undergraduate classroom £6,840, laboratory £7,710; postgraduate classroom £7,040, laboratory £7,770; study abroad programme £2,690 per semester.

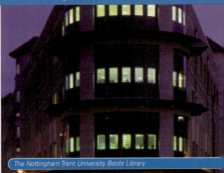
The Nottingham Trent University Boots Library

Student profile

"Everything is different in England: the culture, food and the language. The British people smile a lot, which makes you feel at ease, and they have always been nice to me. Teaching methods are different; it is more in-depth and there's lots of access to information. I had heard about the reputation of Nottingham Law School, which is one of the best in the country. The course more than met my expectations. The lecturers are very good – professional, encouraging and supportive. The international student support is brilliant. The orientation week is a real ice-breaker and I was able to help out

with it this year. There are events every weekend. My aim is to do a BVC, and then a pupillage, either in the UK or in Ghana."

Irene Dodoo, Ghana

Nottingham is a vibrant city situated in the centre of England, just two hours away from London. With over 50,000 students, the city has proved to be a popular choice for prospective undergraduates. The Nottingham Trent University, which attained university status in 1992, has some 23,000 students studying a variety of undergraduate, professional and postgraduate programmes and research, making it one of the largest universities in the UK. It consists of three campuses, one in the city centre, one in a greenbelt campus alongside the River Trent just outside the centre, and a third in a rural market town near Southwell.

Academic strengths

The university offers many programmes that are designed to be both flexible and to prepare students for the world of work.

They are grouped into nine faculties: Nottingham Business School, Nottingham Law School, Nottingham School of Art and Design, Computing and Technology, Economics and Social Sciences, School of Property and Construction, Science, Humanities and Education. Teaching and learning at Nottingham Trent is of a high standard. In recent Quality Assurance Agency subject reviews, eight out of nine subjects were graded excellent.

Students can take advantage of the university's new £13 million electronic library and education resource centre which holds over 800 study spaces and more than 500,000 books. IT services comprise student resource rooms with access to PCs, email and CD-Roms. There are over 5,000 workstations in total. The university has many links with local and international businesses and institutions, and statistics show that, within six months of their graduation, 98 per cent of students are either settled in employment or in postgraduate education.

The study abroad programme enables students already doing a degree in their home country to study for one semester or one year at the university.

Student life

The university has committed some £30 million to refurbishment and new buildings in its aim to provide high-quality student residences. There are over 3,000 bed spaces available in university-owned and managed residences, and international students are given priority during their first year of study.

The university's sheer size means that it provides for a vast range of interests and activities. The students' union offers a variety of facilities and more than 90 clubs and societies from Bushido to the Hellenic Society. The city students' union offers a bank, insurance and travel agents, a general shop and a specialist shop as well as a nightclub and bar. It also has its own radio station which offers many opportunities for students to get involved and receive both experience and training.

International students also benefit from a free, five-day orientation programme on their arrival in the UK. Religious and cultural advisers are available to offer support and advice and there are Muslim prayer room facilities. The university's Language Centre provides English language support prior to and throughout students' studies, and undergraduates on registered programmes are also eligible for free English language classes.

Nottingham

The University of Nottingham

Write to: International Office,
The University of Nottingham,
University Park, Nottingham NG7 2RD

Tel: +44 (0)115 951 5247

Fax: +44 (0)115 951 5155

Email: international-office@
nottingham.ac.uk

Website: www.nott.ac.uk

Students: 15,725 full time (4,336
postgraduates, 4,500 international
students from 125 countries),
50:50 male:female.

Accommodation: single sex,
married/family, vacation. University
residences from £82 to £85. Self-
catering flats from £42 to £50.

Entrance requirements: three good
A levels or equivalent. European/
International Baccalaureate 28
to 34 points.

EFL: IELTS 6, TOEFL 550 for
engineering and science; IELTS 6.5,
TOEFL 600 for social science and
business; IELTS 7.5, TOEFL 650 for
medicine and others.

Foundation: architecture, computer
sciences, management, engineering,
science and psychology.

Fees: 2002 (to be confirmed):
Arts (BA, MA) £7,519; science (BSc,
MSc) £9,900; clinical medicine
£18,000; MBA £15,000. Candidates
are advised to refer to specific fee
sheets for details (available from the
International Office).

The University of Nottingham

Student profile

"My brother graduated from Nottingham
with a first class degree in chemical
engineering, so I already knew that
Nottingham had a very good reputation
and I also knew what the university and
the city had to offer. I think it's a fabulous
place to be and there's an interesting mix
of people here from all over the world. I
enjoy the course and the new Jubilee
campus very much. It helps living on
campus, just two minutes away from
where I study. I got a scholarship to do a
BSc in E-commerce and the faculty has
been extremely helpful. I've been back
to my school in Delhi to help students

 wanting to study
abroad. It's a different
culture but if they
keep an open mind
and are committed to
studying, they'll have
no problems at all."

Poornima Narayanan, India

The University of Nottingham has made a significant contribution to higher education in Britain for 120 years. The forerunner of today's university was University College, Nottingham, established in 1881 on a site in Nottingham city centre.

Today Nottingham is a multicampus university, with major sites at University Park, Sutton Bonington, Jubilee campus – which has regenerated a former inner-city industrial site – and a new campus in Kuala Lumpur, Malaysia. The Medical School is linked to University Hospital and other facilities at the Queen's Medical School, adjacent to University Park. The School of Nursing has sites throughout the East Midlands.

Academic strengths

The university has an outstanding record in the independent assessments of teaching quality undertaken with only Cambridge University having more subjects rated excellent than the 27 at Nottingham (including agriculture and food sciences, anatomy and physiology, architecture, business and management, economics, engineering, classics and ancient history, education, English, geography, German, history of art, architecture and design, law, statistics and operational research, music, nursing, physics and astronomy, pharmacology and pharmacy, psychology and landscape).

Teaching success is backed up by a strong research record, with a number of world-class research departments. Scientific breakthroughs at the university have included the use of nuclear magnetic resonance imaging (MRI), the development of genetic engineering for the food industry and trials for a vaccine for bowel cancer.

Extensive support facilities include five major libraries providing services with collections for arts, social sciences and education, science and engineering, medicine and health sciences and agricultural and food sciences. The Cripps Computing Centre houses extensive computing facilities for students as well as providing public access areas at a number of departments throughout the campuses. The Language Centre houses teaching laboratories, satellite dishes, TV, computer and audio facilities and video work stations. The university has a purpose-built arts centre equipped with an art gallery, music department, café and recital hall.

Student life

The students' union provides welfare, advice, information and a programme of entertainment. Students can join any of the 120 societies that cater to cultural, political, recreational or religious interests, or start their own. There is a chaplaincy available for Anglican, Roman Catholic, Methodist, United Reformed Church and Baptist practitioners which can offer information on nearby Muslim, Jewish, Hindu, Sikh and Buddhist groups. The university houses meeting rooms within the Christian chapel and a prayer room for Muslim students.

A free welcome programme is offered to international students, with coach pick-up from Heathrow airport. Families are given support and help in finding schools for children and English language courses for spouses. Students are put in touch with national societies near the university. In 2001, the university won the Queen's Award for Enterprise: International Trade, for its international activities.

OXFORD BROOKES UNIVERSITY

Oxford

Oxford Brookes University

Write to: Student Liaison Office, Oxford Brookes University, Headington Campus, Oxford OX3 0BP

Tel: +44 (0)1865 484848

Fax: +44 (0)1865 483616

Email: query@brookes.ac.uk

Students: 17,703 in 2000/01 (4,741 postgraduate and research, 3,606 international and EU from over 100 countries), 41:59 male:female.

Accommodation: some all-female and vacation (except summer) accommodation. University residences from £53 to £66 a week self-catered, from £80 (approx) a week catered (2001/02 figures).

Entrance requirements: two A levels for undergraduates, International Baccalaureate or equivalent 28+ points.

EFL: for undergraduates IELTS 6.0 to 6.5; TOEFL 213 to 232.

Foundation: International Foundation Diploma (study skills and English language tuition); Foundation Diploma in Liberal Arts (study skills, no language tuition); foundation programmes in art and design, building, civil engineering, engineering and science.

Oxford Brookes University Sports Bar

Student profile

"Having completed the appropriate English language courses, I went on to study a Master of Business Administration (MBA) at Oxford Brookes. Before I came to Oxford, I worked for the head office of Mitsubishi Motors Corporation in Japan and was in charge of the recruitment and training of staff. The MBA course consists of people from 31 countries, so I have not only gained academic knowledge but also a broader view through interactions with my classmates who have various cultural backgrounds. The course is difficult and involves a high degree of commitment

and dedicated study; however, the MBA degree is of great value, and my two years here have been both worthwhile and rewarding for me."

Junko Noguchi, Japan

Universities and colleges of higher education

Oxford has a long academic tradition dating back over eight centuries. During this time the city has gained many historic buildings of great splendour, while the rivers Thames and Cherwell add to its beauty. Student life is well catered for, with restaurants, bars, nightclubs, cinemas and theatres. The city is also noted for its publishing, car manufacturing and new technology industries. Public transport is reliable and cheap but Oxford is compact enough to walk or cycle around. It is located just an hour away from London and its international airports.

Oxford Brookes University originates from 1865 when it was a School of Art. Today it has a large international community of students and staff, with a warm welcome and support for those from other countries.

Academic strengths

Oxford Brookes' reputation has been endorsed by high ratings in UK government teaching quality assessments. Business and management, economics and town planning have achieved maximum ratings of 24 out of 24. Other subject areas achieving excellent ratings include biology, building, environmental sciences, fine art, history of art, psychology and real estate management at 23; French, hotel and restaurant management, Italian, mathematical sciences and Spanish at 22; and civil engineering, education, publishing and sociology at 21. Every subject assessed achieved top marks in the student support and guidance category.

The modular degree programme, based on credit accumulation and transfer, provides opportunities for overseas exchanges and admission with credit. The range of courses offers flexibility to create programmes that suit students' individual interests and strengths.

Modern learning resources include libraries and networked computers in open access rooms and halls of residence. Use of the internet and email is free, so you can keep in touch with home.

Student life

Oxford Brookes students' union has a custom-built 1,200 capacity venue with state-of-the-art lighting and sound equipment. Club nights, live music, comedy acts, film nights and guest lectures take place here. In addition, there are more than 65 student-run societies covering a wide range of interests.

The interdenominational Christian chaplaincy has a lively and diverse programme of worship and there are two Muslim prayer rooms on campus.

The university encourages its students to take part in sport. It has a fine centre for sport with a fitness suite, badminton, basketball and squash courts, climbing room and heavy weights training room. The university's sports of excellence are basketball, climbing, cricket, hockey, rowing and rugby.

The International Student Advisory Service offers support with financial, personal and immigration matters. It also provides students with newsletters and social events, including weekend trips to places of interest in the UK. Also on offer is an airport meet-and-greet service and an induction programme when students arrive. Students can take English language modules to support their studies, which can sometimes count towards their final degree mark.

Oxford

Oxford University

Write to: Oxford Colleges Admissions Office (undergraduates) or Graduate Admissions Office, Oxford University, University Offices, Wellington Square, Oxford OX1 2JD

Tel:
undergraduates: +44 (0)1865 270207
graduates: +44 (0)1865 270059

Fax: 44 (0)1865 270708

Email: undergraduate.admissions@admin.ox.ac.uk or graduate.admissions@admin.ox.ac.uk

Website: www.ox.ac.uk

Students: 16,411 (2000/01) (4,931 postgraduates, 3,942 international from over 130 countries), male:female 56:44.

Accommodation: varies from college to college. St Hilda's is female only. University residence from £60 a week self-catered; some married and family accommodation available. Room in town from £58 a week plus heating etc.

Entrance requirements: typically AAA or AAB at A level or at least 39 in the International Baccalaureate with 6 to 7 in one or more specified subjects at higher level. Postgraduate study requires an upper second class honours degree or equivalent.

EFL: IELTS 7.0 or 600 TOEFL (250 in computer-based tests) required for postgraduate study.

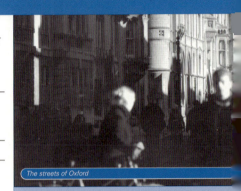

The streets of Oxford

Student profile

"Studying at Oxford is an immensely rewarding and inspiring experience, and I don't mean just academically. I fell in love with the place the first time I came here. It had this unique almost magic air you'd expect from the city of dreaming spires, but, as I soon discovered, it was very friendly and informal. The tutorial system means that you meet once a week with your tutor, giving you direct contact with leading experts in their fields. The emphasis is on helping you gain self confidence. Being responsible for planning my own work, I soon developed time management skills. I am in my second

year studying physics and philosophy. The courses leave room for pursuing your own interests. There are clubs and societies for every interest."

Daniel Pytlik, Poland

Oxford is the oldest university in the English-speaking world and has welcomed international scholars and students for more than 800 years. It is made up of 39 colleges (30 of which accept undergraduates) and six permanent private halls. Oxford offers the advantage of studying in a large international university whilst still living in a smaller college community.

Colleges provide tutorial teaching for undergraduates as well as pastoral support, accommodation, social facilities and sports. The university organises lectures, laboratory teaching, examinations and awards degrees. All colleges provide accommodation for undergraduates in their first year and many can offer this throughout the student's course. Most college accommodation is situated in and around the city centre.

Academic strengths

Oxford consistently achieves top marks in research and teaching assessment exercises. It has leading science and medical departments, in addition to its long tradition in the arts. It has recently opened a business school.

All courses have a core element but also offer scope for students to follow their own interests. An important aspect of undergraduate teaching is the tutorial, a weekly meeting of one or two students with their college tutor to discuss the week's work.

Oxford students have access to some of the best laboratories, libraries and museums in the world, including the Bodleian which, as a copyright library, can claim a copy of every book published in the UK and Ireland.

Student life

Oxford boasts a youthful and cosmopolitan atmosphere, with all the main high street shops and amenities. Its beautiful and historic architecture is world renowned; less known are the green spaces in and around the centre, including the parks and gardens.

There are some 300 university clubs and societies ranging from aikido to water polo, debating and media, including two student newspapers and a radio station.

The Oxford union also runs a number of voluntary student societies, including Oxford Union Amnesty International, the Oxford Conservation group and the Oxford Union Life Saving Club.

Most colleges provide sports grounds, squash courts and boat houses for inter-college rowing competitions. The university has a multigym, all-weather track, artificial hockey pitch, rowing tank and small rugby stadium. A swimming pool should be completed in 2002. The university has student orchestras of professional calibre and several well known choirs. College music societies cater for other levels of accomplishment. There are two university opera societies and other organisations catering for interests from soul to jazz, and from Indian to contemporary.

In addition to college drama societies, there are three Oxford theatres available for student use, one of which is owned by the university. Many famous actors began their careers here, including Imogen Stubbs, Hugh Grant and Rowan Atkinson.

Oxford is a good base for exploring other parts of the UK and is 90 minutes by coach from central London. It has direct coach links to Heathrow and Gatwick airports.

Universities and colleges
of higher education

Plymouth

University of Plymouth

Write to: The International Office, University of Plymouth, Drake Circus, Plymouth, Devon PL4 8AA

Tel: +44 (0)1752 233345

Fax: +44 (0)1752 232014

Email: intoff@plymouth.ac.uk

Website: www.plym.ac.uk

Students: 24,000 in 2000/01 (3,226 postgraduate, 1,876 international from over 100 countries), 41:59 male:female.

Accommodation: single sex, vacation. University residence from £45 to £92 a week. Room in town from £40 to £50 a week, flat from £60 to £75 a week.

Entrance requirements: CCC at A level or equivalent (Bs and Cs for media, economics, social sciences, art, English, business and related subjects, biology, languages, geography, law). European or International Baccalaureate and other overseas qualifications accepted.

EFL: IELTS 6.0, TOEFL 600 (6.5 for postgraduate).

Foundation: courses available.

Fees: (2002) classroom courses £6,500 a year undergraduate, £7,750 a year postgraduate; laboratory courses £7,250 a year undergraduate, £8,000 a year postgraduate.

University of Plymouth - the Plymouth campus

Student profile

"I am an Egyptian postgraduate student and worked as an assistant lecturer at the Suez Canal University in Egypt. I completed my master's in genetic plant studies, after which my government offered me a fellowship to study for a PhD in the UK. I am now at the Seale-Hayne Faculty of Agriculture, Food and Land Use which is located in an attractive setting with nice views of the countryside. Although the campus is small, it has good resources including a library and computing service which includes email and the internet. Teaching staff maintain a high research and consultancy profile and have excellent contacts in the UK and overseas.

All these factors have helped and encouraged me to overcome my homesickness as well as to continue with my course of study and enjoy my life in the UK."

Manal Hassan Eid, Egypt

The University of Plymouth is based on four main campuses in Devon, and provides a pleasant location for learning and leisure – here students can both study in and enjoy an area of wonderful scenery. The largest campus is in Plymouth, a historic city set between the sea and Dartmoor, providing many opportunities for outdoor and cultural activities. The Exeter campus is one of the bases for the Faculty of Arts and Education, the other being at Exmouth. Exeter is one of England's oldest and most graceful cities and has a lively cultural environment. The small town of Exmouth is the seaside campus with bracing sea air, miles of beach and cliff walks. The Seale-Hayne campus is in a rural setting close to the market town of Newton Abbot.

Academic strengths

The University of Plymouth was founded in 1970 but its roots go back nearly 200 years when it provided a range of education and training for all kinds of maritime activities. Since those days, the university has grown into one of the UK's largest universities, offering modular programmes within six faculties.

The Faculty of Science, on the Plymouth campus, built when the university was founded, is still one of its main strengths, along with human sciences, technology and business. The new Peninsula Medical School is due to admit its very first students in 2002.

The university has six sites in the south-west of England and a network of regional partner colleges. There is an active research programme which supports teaching carried out there. The university received excellent ratings in 12 of the areas most recently assessed, including the overall top score in the United Kingdom for civil engineering.

The university has libraries, computing laboratories and media workshops on their sites to support students' work.

These facilities are well staffed and advice is readily available. Most courses include the development of IT skills and an increasing number of tutors are using technology to deliver teaching materials. Students have both email and access to the university's software libraries and internet.

Student life

With campuses on or near the coast, each with its own students' union at Plymouth, Exeter, Exmouth and Newton Abbot, virtually every imaginable coastal and river sport is open to students, including a Diving and Sailing Centre at Plymouth with a sports diving course. Students can join winning teams for national student yachting, waterski and surfing events, or lounge on a beach on warm summer days.

In addition to water sports, there is a host of clubs and societies run by the university. Drama, political and cultural groups and an international students society are on offer.

Students can also join the orchestra or sing with the choral society. The students' union is the university's base for entertainments and tries to provide something to suit every taste.

The university arranges approved accommodation for all international students in their first year. There is an international office with the specific responsibility of advising and supporting all international students throughout their time at university.

Portsmouth

University of Portsmouth

Write to: Karen Arnold, International Recruitment Office, University of Portsmouth, Nuffield Centre, St Michaels Road, Portsmouth PO1 2ED

Tel: +44 (0)23 9284 5118

Fax: +44 (0)23 9284 3538

Email: karen.arnold@port.ac.uk

Website: www.port.ac.uk/international

Students: 20,000 in 2000/01 (3,000 postgraduates, 2,000 international from 80 countries), 50:50 male:female.

Accommodation: vacation – extra charge. University residences from £60 to £78 a week self-catered. Room in town from £50 to £70 a week.

Entrance requirements: 12 to 22 points in two A levels. Minimum 24 points at International Baccalaureate.

EFL: IELTS 6, TOEFL 550 (undergraduate); some postgraduate business courses require IELTS 6.5, TOEFL 580.

Foundation: courses available in engineering, business, science, art, design and media.

Fees: classroom courses £6,700 a year (some business courses mark up fees by £200 to £400), laboratory courses £7,750.

University of Portsmouth students

Student profile

"I come from Istanbul in Turkey. I studied for the MA in Marketing at the University of Portsmouth. This was a one-year, full-time course. During this time, I had the chance to meet some students from many different cultures. This was something which I found fantastically interesting. The tutors were also very helpful. For the rest of my life, I will never forget my time in Portsmouth and will always remember it with a smile. I now have my own insurance agency business and I am honestly very happy

there. I use the skills and the background gained from my marketing studies at university in my own business, which is very exciting."

Esra Kulan, Turkey

University of Portsmouth, an educational institution for 129 years, was made a university in 1992. It is based on two campuses, the main one situated in the city centre around Guildhall Square. The Business School is based on the Milton campus three miles to the east, home to both sports fields and seaside accommodation. The university sites vary from modern to lovely listed buildings.

Some halls of residence overlook the sea and one appealing aspect of Portsmouth is that it is a southern coastal town. This gives it one of the warmest climates in Britain with average temperatures of 20 degrees in summer months. It is well positioned for water sports and close to the rest of Europe. Portsmouth is good for cyclists as Portsea (the island that Portsmouth and Southsea are built on) is flat. Trains and coaches both run from Portsmouth to London which is one hour and 20 minutes away.

Academic strengths

The first degree from the University of Portsmouth was awarded in 1900 from the Faculty of Technology. Today the university is divided into five faculties that are all continually developing new courses and research.

The Faculty of Technology is divided into five areas: computer science, electrical and electronic engineering, information systems, mechanical and manufacturing engineering and mathematics. The Faculty of Science's teaching areas include biology, earth science, geology and pharmacy. The Business School has become one of the largest in Britain with 180 academic research staff and 2,400 students on award-bearing courses. The school's four departments are quality management, accounting and management science, business and management and economics and project. The largest department in the university, with over 400 members of staff, is the Faculty of Humanities and Social Science. The School of Language and Area Studies has achieved high ratings in both research and teaching, with a top grade 5 in Russian. Finally, the Faculty of the Environment covers a broad mix of disciplines concerned with the operation, interpretation, design, construction and management of the environment. Portsmouth offers courses that lead to jobs. As such, it is able to boast 97 per cent graduate employment.

Student life

There are over 200 clubs and societies at the university. Some of these, such as the Latin American Society and the Malaysian Society, have a distinct multicultural feel. There are university chaplains who have links with all faiths. International students can also benefit from free language classes, as well as pre-sessional English and English for academic purposes.

Upon arrival at Portsmouth, airport pick-ups are arranged for international students. Also laid on is a free four-day induction period to welcome them to the university. First-year students are guaranteed university accommodation (providing it is booked prior to 2 September) and most halls of residence are within walking distance of teaching blocks. Competitive bursaries of £1,000 are available for international students.

Portsmouth is known as being both welcoming and supportive.

London

Queen Mary, University of London

Write to: Mrs Jackie Saito, International Office, Queen Mary, University of London, Mile End Road, London E1 4NS

Tel: + 44 (0)20 7882 3066

Fax: + 44 (0)20 7882 5556

Email international-office@qmul.ac.uk

Web: www.qmul.ac.uk

Student: 8,617 (1,614 postgraduate, 15 per cent international from over 100 countries), male:female 1:1.

Accommodation: single and mixed sex, vacation; college residences £55 to £85. House share in private sector £65 or above.

Entrance requirements: please see website or prospectus.

EFL: foundation IELTS 5, TOEFL 510; undergraduate IELTS 6.5, TOEFL 580; postgraduate IELTS 6.5, TOEFL 580. Free English language support during study, pre-sessional English courses available up to three months.

Foundation: international foundation course for business, economics, law and the arts; science and engineering foundation programme.

Fees: arts, social studies and law £7,950 a year; engineering and sciences £9,950 a year; pre-clinical medicine and dentistry (year one) £10,700 a year.

Queen Mary, University of London

Student profile

"The engineering department at Queen Mary is very well known. That's why I chose to come here. It's the complete package. Because it is a campus university, the facilities are excellent when compared with other colleges in London. The library, for example, is just a short

walk away and the lecturers are always open to see you and are willing to help. The course is great. It is hard work but really interesting."

Gunn Hultin, Thailand

540

Queen Mary is one of the four largest Colleges of the University of London alongside Kings College, Imperial College and University College London. Its strong performance in quality assessments has led to Queen Mary's international recognition as a leading teaching and research institution. Queen Mary offers a wide range of undergraduate and postgraduate courses with extensive research opportunities. The college incorporates the world famous Barts and The London School of Medicine and Dentistry, a major centre for medical and dental teaching and research. International students from over 100 countries each year add to the diversity of the college.

Queen Mary is the only University of London college to have an integrated teaching, research and residential campus in central London. The Mile End campus is located between the financial area of London and the Docklands development. Getting to other parts of London is easy with two underground stations within five minutes' walk. The college has three other sites for medical and dental students: Whitechapel, West Smithfield and Charter House Square, all of which are located in central London.

Academic strengths

Queen Mary is a leading research university, which ranks in the top 25 per cent of all UK universities. Particular strengths are medicine and dentistry, law, electronic engineering, computer science and economics. Over 90 per cent of Queen Mary's departments scored four or five in research assessment exercises (2001), with several leading international research units such as the Centre for Commercial Law Studies and the Interdisciplinary Research Centre in Biomedical Materials. The college offers two foundation courses preparing students for undergraduate entry.

Facilities

The college has invested heavily in new buildings and upgrading existing facilities, boasting excellent academic, housing and social facilities on campus. A central focus on campus is the modern library, with study space for 1,000 students. Students also have access to the collections of the University of London library. All students have free email and internet access, and the student to computer ratio is one of the highest in Britain. Workstations can be found throughout the departments of the college.

The Advice and Counselling Service and on-campus health centre offer a range of advice and support services to all students. The college also runs a two-day orientation programme for international students.

Student life

Queen Mary's student union is located on the main Mile End campus. It is one of the most active unions in the University of London and forms an important part of college life. It provides bars, cafés, shops and E1, recently voted the best student union club venue in London (*Time Out*). Other facilities include squash courts, a multipurpose sports hall, and approximately 75 clubs and societies are offered. Some of the university's most popular annual events include the Freshers' Ball, Rag Week and the Summer Ball.

Belfast

Queen's University Belfast

Write to: S M Wisener, The Admissions Office, Queen's University Belfast, Belfast, Northern Ireland BT7 1NN

Tel: +44 (0)28 9033 5081

Fax: +44 (0)28 9024 7895

Email: admissions@qub.ac.uk

Website: www.qub.ac.uk

Students: 14,000 in 2000/01 (2,000 postgraduates, 1,750 international from over 60 countries including the rest of Europe), 48:52 male:female.

Accommodation: single sex, vacation, storage facilities. University residences from £41 to £62 a week. Room in town from £36 a week.

Entrance requirements: CCC to AAB (for medicine). Other qualifications also considered.

EFL: IELTS 6.0 to 6.5, TOEFL 550 minimum.

Foundation: science, engineering, agriculture and food science have two levels of entry, level 0 (for students with qualifications which would normally require a foundation course) and level 1.

Fees: (2001/02) undergraduate a year: classroom £6,115, laboratory £7,935, medicine and dentistry pre-clinical £9,580; clinical £17,650. Postgraduate a year: £7,315; clinical, medical and dental £11,540.

Queen's University Belfast

Student profile

"I decided to come to Queen's because it is a well-known traditional university and also because its fees for my course were reasonable. Also, my university in China, Shenzhen University, has a connection with Queen's. I really enjoy being at the university. The environment is enjoyable and the library facilities are good. I would recommend Queen's to other students from overseas. People here are very friendly and there are lots of clubs to join. Belfast is a quiet  place to live and study and summer here is lovely. When I leave Queen's, I am going to apply for jobs in the areas of finance or management."

Zhang Ye, People's Republic of China

Queen's University Belfast recently celebrated its 150th anniversary. Established in 1845, it became a full university in 1908. It has a long history but is modern in its outlook, with four major library complexes and computerised study facilities. While it is not a campus university, everything is compact and within easy walking distance, including the main accommodation complex. For two and a half weeks each November, it organises the Belfast Festival during which over 200 performances cater for all tastes. The university is near the Ulster museum and city art gallery. Former students include Seamus Heaney, who was recently awarded the Nobel Prize for literature, as well as Mary McAleese, the current president of Ireland.

Academic strengths

Last year, Queen's Chancellor, Senator George Mitchell, led a team from one of the university's world-class research centres to receive the prestigious Queen's Anniversary Prize at Buckingham Palace. The prize was awarded to the university's Palaeoecology Centre – a flagship research facility which uses nature's markers to measure time.

Queen's has received a £24 million funding package which will help pay for research projects in a number of fields. In the university's last assessment, a number of subject areas were assessed highly for teaching, all receiving a score of at least 75 per cent of the total available.

Queen's has established a multimedia language centre, with a CAN-8 VirtuLab system. Courses incorporate audio material, video images and text and can be used to improve pronunciation, conversation, grammar and comprehension skills.

Student life

Queen's is a mile from the city centre and a major part of Belfast's social and cultural scene. Over 150 sporting clubs and societies are recognised by the students' union and are eligible to apply for an annual grant from the university. The students' union and the students' union building are at the centre of student social life. The union's entertainments programme covers a large number of events to suit most interests. There are two bars in the students' union building with different atmospheres on different nights of the week. There are comedy nights, folk nights, quiz nights, local bands and so on. There are discos up to six nights a week with music to suit most tastes. The union also arranges balls, starting with the Freshers' Ball in the first week of the first semester.

There are thriving societies for international students, including those from Hong Kong, Malaysia and Singapore as well as a society for Islamic students. These societies cover a range of interests – sporting, cultural and community-oriented. The main sporting venues are the Malone Playing Fields, the Physical Education Centre, the students' union, the Malone Golf Club, the River Lagan and the Mourne Mountains. International students are offered a meet and greet service at the airport and halls of residence.

The playing fields are three kilometres from the main site. There are a number of pitches to accommodate most outdoor sports in which the university has a tradition of competing. There are two synthetic pitches, one full-size hockey pitch and one full-size ball pitch.

The University of Reading

Reading

The University of Reading

Write to: International and Study Abroad Office, The University of Reading, Whiteknights, PO Box 217, Reading RG6 6AH

Tel: +44 (0)118 987 5123

Fax: +44 (0)118 975 2252

Email: intoff@reading.ac.uk

Website: www.rdg.ac.uk

Students: 12,524 in 2001/02 (4,483 postgraduates, 2,532 international from 118 countries), 47:53 male:female.

Accommodation: single room, married/family, vacation storage facilities. University residences from £45 to £68 a week. Self-catered from £69 to £103 catered. Room in town from £55 a week.

Entrance requirements: range from CDD to BBB to ABC at A level, 27 to 33 points in International Baccalaureate. Postgraduate applications are made directly to the university and are welcomed from qualified graduates from recognised institutions.

EFL: IELTS 6.5, TOEFL 575 (for linguistically-demanding courses IELTS 7.0, TOEFL 590).

Foundation: preparatory course on campus includes English language and three subject options relevant to intended degree. Success in exam guarantees place on degree course. Foundation members are full members of the university. The course is also recognised by other universities.

Fees: classroom courses £7,098 a year; laboratory courses £9,198 a year.

Whiteknights campus

Student profile

"After completing an English language course at the university, I thought I wanted to study linguistics. However, having studied psychology in the first two terms of my degree course, I enjoyed it so much that I changed my mind. I am now grateful to this system which gives flexibility in degree choice. My policy as a student is 'play hard, study hard'. I am involved in Focus International – an organisation run by students and local people for English and international students to build friendships. I enjoy meeting people from a wide variety of countries. I believe we are fortunate to have an international atmosphere here – I sometimes feel I am seeing a miniature world while being on campus."

Maki Yasui, Japan

The University of Reading is situated in Britain's dynamic 'silicon valley', 60 kilometres west of London. Though its main buildings are modern, the university was first set up as a university college in the 19th century. It was granted its Royal Charter in 1926. Some of the beautiful 18th century landscape parkland of the Marquis of Blandford is still in evidence in the lake, woods and gardens of the Whiteknights campus. At the centre of the campus is the library, which is surrounded by the academic buildings and the students' union. Most of the 15 halls of residence and the student village lie within walking distance around the northern perimeter and in the nearby residential streets. The university also has two other sites; Bulmershe Court, housing the Faculty of Education and Community Studies, and London Road.

Academic strengths

The University of Reading is divided into four faculties, namely agriculture and food, education and communication studies, letters and social sciences, science with urban and regional studies standing separately. Almost 60 per cent of the staff are now in departments rated 5 or 5* for research– the top for international quality. The departments of Archaeology, English, Italian, Meteorology and Psychology now rank 5*, and 15 research areas earned grade 5 ranking (2001). The university also scored excellent in the 1994/95 teaching quality assessments for geography, geology, and mechanical engineering, 24 out of 24 in the 1998 assessment for film and drama and physics and 21 or more for 14 out of 15

subjects assessed in the last three years. The university has a range of facilities to aid academic study. The library offers over one million books, periodicals and special collections. Students have 24 hour use of PCs linked to the university network.

Student life

The university has a long history of international activity – the first ever international student graduated in 1901. All new international students joining the university can attend the university's week-long welcome programme and support is continued for the duration of their course.

The university's Centre for Applied Language Studies provides full-time, pre-entry English courses from October to September. In-session English language tuition is also provided free of charge for students paying full international fees.

Other support services and facilities include a medical practice and counselling service, a university chaplaincy catering for Protestant, Roman Catholic and Jewish students, and for Islamic students there is a Muslim centre. Students holding an International Baccalaureate may be eligible to apply for one of the three scholarships that are available for undergraduates. Other scholarships are also available.

More than 100 university clubs and societies with extensive sports facilities on campus and on the river provide for a varied and active social life. The student union has five bars which are at the heart of the student scene. They provide an excellent atmosphere so all students can enjoy a great social life.

Universities and colleges of higher education

THE
**ROBERT GORDON
UNIVERSITY**
ABERDEEN

Aberdeen

The Robert Gordon University

Write to: The International Office, The Robert Gordon University, Schoolhill, Aberdeen AB10 1FR

Tel: +44 (0)1224 262208/9

Fax: +44 (0)1224 262202

Email: international@rgu.ac.uk

Website: www.rgu.ac.uk

Students: nearly 10,000 in 1999/2000 (900 international, including 350 from outside European Union).

Accommodation: on-campus accommodation is guaranteed for all single, international students.

Entrance requirements: examples of undergraduate entry requirements include foundation programmes, A levels, BTEC National Diplomas, International Baccalaureate, Malaysian or Hong Kong Advanced Level, MARA diplomas, Australian Matriculation and American School Diploma.

EFL: IELTS 6.0 (6.5 for MBA) TOEFL 550 to 600, Cambridge UCLES, GCSE grade C, AEB test grade 3, or Cambridge or Michigan Proficiency pass.

Foundation: courses available. Successful completion of these leads to degree course entry.

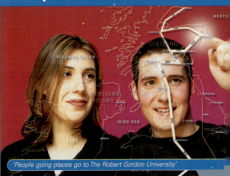

'People going places go to The Robert Gordon University'

Student profile

Trishul Baxi, from West Bengal, came to The Robert Gordon University in 1997. The course he chose, covering internet technology, information strategy, software development and systems analysis, enabled Trishul to study business methods and enterprise and develop a high degree of computing expertise. He graduated in July 2001 with a BSc (Hons) in Business Computing and is now employed by the university as a junior systems and network engineer. A keen sportsman and self-confessed extrovert, Trishul now has friends in almost every country in Europe. He values the qualifications he has acquired but

says the overall learning experience at RGU, meeting new people and living in Scotland will provide him with happy memories.

Trishul Baxi, West Bengal

The Robert Gordon University has an educational heritage going back to 1750 with university status being granted in 1992. Since then, the university has established itself as one of the UK's premier vocational universities, with an outstanding record for graduate employment. It enjoys strong links with industry and the professions and in recent years has received more industry funding per student than any other UK university (*Financial Times*, April 2001). This has been wisely invested to provide a modern, supportive learning environment. A new state-of-the art building for the Faculty of Health and Social Care is to be opened in September 2002, on the same riverside site as the award-winning (RIBA Regional Architecture Award 1999) Faculty of Management building and the Faculty of Design and Technology.

The university is situated in Aberdeen – the third largest city in Scotland. Aberdeen has become the commercial and cultural capital of the northeast of Scotland. The city has an abundance of leisure facilities, fitness gyms, traditional pubs and wine bars, clubs and restaurants and splendid shopping malls. It also has a fine theatre, museums and art galleries. For those who wish to escape city life, the nearby mountains, countryside and wide sweeping beaches provide ideal retreats.

Academic strengths

The Robert Gordon University has approximately 10,000 undergraduate and postgraduate students with more than 300 courses. These cover a wide range of subjects including art and design, built environment, business, management and finance, IT and computing, communica-tion and media studies, engineering, legal studies, life sciences, nursing, pharmacy, the professions allied to medicine, social studies and tourism management.

Many of the courses carry professional accreditation and the success of the university's practice-based approach to learning is reflected in an outstanding record for graduate employment, currently at 98 per cent. Language opportunities exist in many courses and the universities belief and investment in open and distance learning, including the RGU Virtual Campus, means that provided you have access to the internet, you can become a student at RGU. Students don't have to be physically at the university in order to study there.

The university has a first rate student learning support facility, access courses, excellent student computing facilities – on and off line – and well-stocked libraries. Plans are currently in progress to develop a comprehensive sporting complex for students on the riverside site at Garthdee.

Student life

The student association, housed in the student union building, is run by the students. Situated in the centre of the city, it is an ideal place to meet new people and make new friends. It offers entertainment, relaxation and a common place to eat, drink and chat. The union is a great source of information on such matters as student discounts, travel deals and even job opportunities.

Studying abroad is a big commitment but it should also be exciting and fun. The Robert Gordon University has support facilities in place that will make students' stay at the university a fulfilling, enjoyable and rewarding experience.

Universities and colleges
of higher education

Rose Bruford College

Rose Bruford College

Write to: Sue McTavish, Registrar, The Admissions Office, Rose Bruford College, Lamorbey Park, Sidcup, Kent DA15 9DF

Tel: +44 (0)20 8300 3024

Fax: +44 (0)20 8308 0542

Email: admiss@bruford.ac.uk

Website: www.bruford.ac.uk

Students: 601 in 2000/01, plus 274 distance learners (107 international from 23 countries), 40:60 male:female.

Accommodation: college residences from £70 a week self-catered. Room in town from £65 to £70 a week.

Entrance requirements: two A levels or equivalent.

EFL: for BA degrees IELTS 6.5; for foundation course IELTS 5.5.

Foundation: one-year course to bring students to entry requirement standard for degree courses at Rose Bruford and other UK universities. International Summer School students study acting and technical subjects. English language classes are taught through role-play and improvisation.

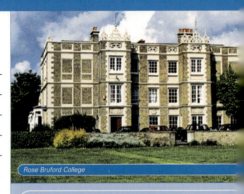
Rose Bruford College

Student profile

"I come from Singapore and I first heard about Rose Bruford College when I went to an exhibition of British universities. The reputation of theatre in Britain is very good and that is why I wanted to study here. On the course, I am learning about all areas of theatre and gaining the technical knowledge I need with the help and support of good tutors. I enjoy being so involved in the shows we put on, which give me the experience I need. When I first came to Britain, I found it difficult to find my way but I soon had friends who helped me discover London. Before I came to Britain, I worked as a

production assistant in theatre and television in Singapore. When I finish, I want to stay in the UK and work in stage management on West End musicals."

Joy Lee, Singapore

Rose Bruford, a former teacher of speech and drama at the Royal Academy of Dramatic Art, founded the college in 1950 by setting up a course that combined both acting and teacher training. Recognised by the then Department of Education and Science in 1951, it has remained in the public sector ever since.

Today the college is very different – a university sector institution operating internationally to offer a range of degree courses in all areas of theatre and related arts. The college is set in a landscaped park in the London Borough of Bexley, about 30 minutes from central London. The city naturally has much to offer students interested in the theatre, from large scale West End shows to small, innovative productions in fringe venues.

theatre arts and American theatre arts. The college also offers an MA in Theatre Practices. The college offers distance learning BA (Hons) degrees in Opera Studies and Theatre Studies and MAs in Theatre and Performance Studies. The college has links with institutions in Japan, the USA, Estonia and Spain.

Performances take place in the college's own theatres and studios. These include a proscenium theatre and also a 330-seat theatre-in-the-round. The college also has lighting studios, a MIDI laboratory and recording and rehearsal studios. An £8.75 million building programme, which is to be completed in July 2002, will provide students with the most comprehensive theatre training facilities in the UK.

Academic strengths

The college is known for its pioneering work in the field of theatre training; for example it offered the UK's first degree in acting in 1976. Courses range from an international foundation course, summer schools, BA (Hons) and MA degrees, through to MPhil and PhD. All degrees at Rose Bruford are validated by The University of Manchester and accredited, where appropriate, by the National Council for Drama Training. The college was awarded 20 out of 24 in the teaching quality assessment for drama in 1997.

Full-time BA (Hons) degrees in all major aspects of the theatre are available, including acting, directing, music technology, actor-musicianship, sound and image design, stage management, lighting design, costume production, scenic arts, theatre design, European

Student life

Rose Bruford has facilities to take care of most aspects of student life. The students' union arranges social events including concerts, cabarets, outings and theatre visits. There are meetings and social evenings organised for international students who are also granted free membership of the London International Student House – a centre in the West End offering facilities such as bars, restaurants, study rooms, a disco, nightclub and sports amenities.

The college's adviser helps students to find accommodation and helps with any problems that might arise. In addition, the college provides purpose-built residences to a limited number of students. Some bursaries are also available to international students. Please contact the university for further information.

London

Royal Holloway, University of London

Write to: Educational and International Liaison Office, Royal Holloway, University of London, Egham, Surrey TW20 0EX

Tel: +44 (0)1784 443399

Fax: +44 (0)1784 471381

Email: liaison-office@rhul.ac.uk

Website: www.rhul.ac.uk

Students: 5,766 in 1998/99 (1,106 postgraduate, 24 per cent international from 90 countries), 45:55 male:female.

Accommodation: single, married/family. College residences from £41 to £75 a week. Room in town from £60 a week.

Entrance requirements: BCC to ABB at A level. 28 to 34 points in International Baccalaureate.

EFL: IELTS 6.5 (some courses 6.0), TOEFL 570 to 550 (230 to 213 in computer-based tests). Postgraduate: IELTS 7.0 (some courses 6.5), TOEFL 600 to 570 (250 to 230 in computer-based test).

Fees: foundation £7,020 a year; undergraduate £8,160 to £9,800 a year; postgraduate £8,168 to £10,000 a year.

The Founder's Building

Student profile

"I did my first degree in Moscow and chose Royal Holloway for my computer science PhD as it was recommended by my tutors. I have found the staff to be supportive and approachable. Learning a foreign language in your home country and using this language in everyday life are completely different things. A couple of years ago, I couldn't have imagined that I would have friends from countries all over the world. The sort of experience I am getting here is unique. Our beautiful location has to be mentioned and the campus is close to Heathrow and central London where you can see places like  Westminster Abbey, Trafalgar Square... everything you read about in books. You can only benefit from being an overseas student here!"

Yuri Kalnishkan, Russia

Founded in 1886, Royal Holloway celebrated 100 years as a member college of the University of London in the year 2000. Although part of the University of London, Royal Holloway is situated in Egham, Surrey, 19 miles from the centre of the capital. The location of the college is quite rural and relatively peaceful compared with London. The campus covers over 120 acres, with modern academic, residential and recreational facilities located alongside the Founder's Building. However, London does play a significant part in the lives of most students and travel to the centre is easy – four trains an hour take you to London Waterloo. It is also conveniently situated for Heathrow Airport, which is just eight miles away.

Academic strengths

The college comprises 21 departments covering the humanities, performing arts, social sciences and sciences. In addition to single honours degrees, a variety of joint honours and major-minor courses are offered. In the 1996 research assessment exercise, Royal Holloway was ranked 13th overall in the UK, coming third in the arts. The following subjects scored ratings of 5 and 5*: psychology, geography, French, classics, Italian, music, drama and theatre, media arts and history. In teaching quality assessments, the university gained 23 out of 24 for physics, drama and theatre and media arts, and 24 out of 24 for biology and psychology.

The main library stocks over half a million volumes and subscribes to 1,700 periodical titles. The majority of stock is housed in three separate buildings: the Bedford Library for history, social science and science texts; the Founder's library for modern and classical languages and literature; and the music library, which is alongside the Music Department. Students using the library can access a variety of equipment, from microfilm, audio and video cassettes to CD-Rom databases, the internet and computer-based literature catalogues. The college's proximity to London means that all of the capital's academic facilities and services, including national, university and specialist libraries are within easy reach.

Student life

There is an orientation and welcome programme at the beginning of each year for all international students. There is also in-sessional as well as pre-sessional language support for non-native English speakers.

The students' union can be found in the centre of the campus. Facilities include three bars, a function space and a coffee bar. A number of clubs and societies are available for international students (mostly run by the students themselves and supported by the union). There are sports societies covering rugby to skydiving, as well as fun societies from the James Bond Society down to the Battle Re-enactment Society. There is some form of entertainment on campus most nights of the week including discos, cabaret, live bands, stand-up comedy and theme nights. London also offers a variety of alternative activities.

Religious amenities include both an interdenominational chaplaincy and a Muslim prayer room. The University of London union (ULU) has hailed Royal Holloway as the best sporting college in London and most tastes are catered for.

Manchester

The University of Salford

Write to: The International Office,
The University of Salford,
Salford M5 4WT

Tel: +44 (0)161 295 5543

Fax: +44 (0)161 295 5256

Email: intoff@salford.ac.uk

Website: www.salford.ac.uk

Students: 18,616 in 1999 (2,389 postgraduate, 999 international), 51:49 male:female.

Accommodation: single, single sex, married, vacation. University residence from £40 a week self-catering, £65 a week with all meals. Room in town from £35 to £43 a week.

Entrance requirements: generally high. A minimum CCC in A levels or equivalent for most subjects. European Baccalaureate pass; International Baccalaureate full diploma (minimum 28 points).

EFL: Cambridge Proficiency grade C; GCSE English grade C; IELTS 6.0; TOEFL 550, computer-based 215.

Fees: science preliminary year £6,500; arts £6,000 a year; undergraduate classroom-based subjects £7,900 a year (science and engineering); £9,050 a year (arts).

The University of Salford

Student profile

"When I arrived in Salford, I thought I could speak and understand English. I'd been studying it since school and I am reading for a degree in English at Fukuoka University in Japan. Salford has an exchange scheme with Fukuoka. I arranged to arrive early and spend the summer doing an intensive course in London. I've been surprised at the difference in teaching. In Japan, I hardly had to speak but at Salford I have to give opinions. I've realised how important it is to live in England among the people. I've discovered all sorts of new things like musicals, Chinatown and I've joined an aerobics club. At the weekends, I travel to places with a friend. So far, we've been to Liverpool, Edinburgh and the Lake District."

Naoko Ogawa, Japan

Universities and colleges of higher education

Manchester United Football Ground is about one mile (1.6 kilometres) from The University of Salford and Old Trafford Cricket Ground is approximately two miles (three kilometres) away. Transport links to the university are excellent – the university has its own railway station and the international airport is only six miles away.

Manchester is a cosmopolitan and dynamic city, home to Europe's largest student population. It's an important, lively, attractive city with four universities, two football teams, its own orchestra and a reputation for musical innovation. Manchester is an international city with its own Chinatown. It is conveniently located for the Lake District, the Pennine hills and Welsh mountains.

Academic strengths

Work placements and partnerships with industry and the arts are built into many courses. The range of courses offered by the university span across four faculties.

Information sciences, which includes IT and data networking, has been awarded 5* rating in the 2001 research assessment exercise. This adds to additional 5 and 5* ratings in built environment, statistics and operational research and European studies. Many engineering courses are available including audio engineering, acoustics and environmental engineering. Science programmes include information technology, computing, mathematics and futuristic courses such as physics with optoelectronics or space technology.

Accounting and business courses are particularly liked by international students. Health courses are also popular at the university and include podiatry,

nursing, midwifery, radiography, sports rehabilitation, occupational therapy, physiotherapy, prosthetics, orthotics and social work.

Music has been graded excellent and biological sciences obtained a maximum 24 points for teaching quality. The research teams in all academic disciplines gained good ratings in the recent research exercise. The School of Art and Design is housed in a new hi-tech building which won the first Sterling Prize for Architectural Design. The university also runs an extensive range of English language progress for its international students. All English language courses are accredited by the British Council.

Student life

All first-year students are guaranteed accommodation if they apply early enough. International students can usually remain in university residences or flats throughout their course. The residences are well planned and all within walking distance of the campus and there are flats for postgraduate students and also for married students with children.

The students' union runs about 80 clubs and societies. Discos, concerts, cabarets and balls are held at various times throughout the year. There are regular film shows and other special events such as the popular international students evening. The university has a great variety of sports facilities open to all students including a new swimming pool.

The academic year is organised around two semesters, starting in September and February. Most degree courses last three years but there are one-year foundation courses in some subjects.

SOAS

University of London

London

School of Oriental and African Studies (University of London)

Write to: Student Recruitment Office, School of Oriental and African Studies (SOAS), University of London, Russell Square, London WC1H 0XG

Tel: +44 (0)20 7898 4034

Fax: +44 (0)20 7898 4039

Email: study@soas.ac.uk

Website: www.soas.ac.uk

Students: approx 3,000 (1,500 post-graduate, 29 per cent international from over 80 countries), 40:60 male:female.

Accommodation: single sex, married, vacation. University residences from £85 a week self-catered. Room in town prices vary enormously.

Entrance requirements: generally BBB at A level, 30 to 32 points at International Baccalaureate.

EFL: IELTS 7.0 overall and minimum or 5.5 in each sub test; TOEFL minimum of 640.

Foundation: several available. Intermediate Certificate Course (ICC) one-year, full-time for prospective undergraduates offers help with English; includes modules in business, international relations and European culture. The Diploma in English for Academic Purposes helps students improve their language skills. Diploma for prospective postgraduates includes independent study project. Both recognised by UK universities.

Fees: £8,350 a year (2001/02).

Students at SOAS

Student profile

"I have always been interested in development economics, and enrolled on an MSc in Development at SOAS because of its reputation for expertise in matters to do with African and Asian countries. Although I was daunted before starting, it was in fact not as difficult as I feared, and the highlight was the environmental development course which had an extremely interesting set of guest lecturers. SOAS is also

very cosmopolitan – I made friends from all over Europe and Asia, not just from Britain. And of course living in London was a big highlight."

Yoko Hashimoto, Japan

Housed in attractive buildings on Russell Square, the School of Oriental and African Studies (SOAS) is one of the world's major centres for the study of Africa and Asia. It was founded in 1916 and is part of the University of London. There are five regional, departments (Africa, East Asia, Near and Middle East, South Asia and Southeast Asia), which teach the languages and cultures of these areas. There are also 11 subject or discipline departments (art and archaeology, anthropology and sociology, development studies, economics, law, geography, history, linguistics, music, political studies and the study of religion). In addition, the school provides a range of English and foundation preparatory courses for overseas students, ranging from three weeks to one year.

Academic strengths

SOAS has been awarded high research ratings (5 or 5*) in anthropology, religious studies linguistics, music, history and archaeology (1996). All of the departments assessed in the last three years have been awarded maximum or near-maximum teaching ratings. Students can choose from over 400 undergraduate degree combinations including law, economics, history, politics, geography, linguistics, art and archaeology, music and one of more than 40 non-European languages. Graduate students can take an intensive one-year master's degree or a three-year PhD programme. The school specialises in the social sciences, humanities and languages of Asia and Africa and its alumni are found in many institutions around the world.

SOAS has a library of almost a million volumes in 1,000 languages. It has language teaching facilities that include computerised language learning facilities and a language laboratory that uses a Sony digital system. The library also plays a national role and is used by readers from industry and government. In 1995, SOAS opened the Brunei gallery. It has been designed to provide two distinct areas: a teaching block and a gallery. There is space for a small permanent art collection as well as facilities for visiting exhibitions.

Student life

SOAS is centrally located, very near to the British Museum, the West End and Covent Garden. Despite being right at the heart of London, the school itself is set in a leafy and peaceful location. SOAS has long had an international community and caters for students' many different religions. There are two single-sex prayer rooms, a number of religious communities and five Anglican chaplaincies.

The students' union runs its own student newspaper and organises entertainment from all over the world through its twice-weekly discos. There are over 30 registered societies within the union, many of which represent a region or country.

SOAS can offer modern accommodation with en suite study bedrooms 15 minutes' walk from the main building. Students are also eligible to apply for University of London accommodation.

International students take part in a welcome session on arrival and can study English for up to four hours a week in the English language centre. In addition to this, every student is allocated a personal tutor for academic advice.

**School of Pharmacy
University of London**

London

The School of Pharmacy, University of London

Write to: The Registry, The School of Pharmacy, University of London, 29-39 Brunswick Square, London WC1N 1AX

Tel: +44 (0)20 7753 5831

Fax: +44 (0)20 7753 5829

Email: registry@cua.ulsop.ac.uk

Website: www.ulsop.ac.uk

Students: 800 in 2000 (270 postgraduates, 150 international from 30 countries), 40:60 male:female.

Accommodation: housing in London is often more expensive than elsewhere but nearly everything else is cheaper and part-time pharmacy work is much easier to find than in any other English city.

Entrance requirements: a good academic record is needed, particularly in chemistry and at least some other science, as well as a general interest in science and pharmacy and the will to succeed. Students need good English, a pass in GCSE/O level English are the kinds of levels you need. Details are in the prospectus.

EFL: 6.0 or equivalent (240 computer based).

Fees: MPharm £10,000; MSc £10,000; PhD £10,000 plus bench fee. All fees are provisional.

Laboratory work at The School of Pharmacy, University of London

Student profile

"I had an English education in Singapore and received a government scholarship, enabling me to study in the UK. Chemistry was my favourite subject but because I didn't want to do it on its own, I chose pharmacy which has better job prospects. I wanted to come to the SOP because of its reputation. I also liked the idea of studying in London. One of the best things about the course is the emphasis on understanding and applying rather than memorising facts. I'm living in a university residence where life is busy and exciting. Making friends has been easy, and with other Singaporeans

I have helped to set up a Singaporean Society. I haven't been very homesick, partly because the registry staff are around to make sure all is well."

Sheila Rankin, Singapore

The School of Pharmacy (SOP) has been central to the London education system for 150 years, contributing to the city's continuing success as the largest scientific community in the world. The school's research quality rating would, as *The Sunday Times* scales, put it fourth of some 200 universities. It is the first British institution to have contributed to the complete mapping of a human chromosome. The school is a small, friendly, co-operative and close-knit community of 800 scientists in a multi-ethnic international city.

The school's small size and strong social support mechanisms provide an environment that is coherent, co-operative and focused where students, administrators and teachers work together. In turn, the school expects its students to work hard and honestly.

Academic strengths

The School of Pharmacy draws practising professional pharmacists from governments, community pharmacies, hospitals and pharmaceutical companies from around the world. The UK Quality Assurance Agency (which rated the school's teaching as excellent in 2000) noted the care with which academic and administrative staff look after students' needs and encourage their ambitions, as well the high level and availability of up-to-date scientific equipment.

The four-year undergraduate MPharm integrates the teaching, learning and understanding of pharmaceutical science with pharmacy practice in all its different forms. Alongside the science of drug action and the discovery, synthesis and analysis of medicines, the school also teaches the social and behavioural needs and skills needed by a responsible professional. Following graduation, students can do a year's internship and take the examinations of the Royal Pharmaceutical Society for registration as a pharmacist, valid in 32 countries and territories.

The school's curriculum is acclaimed for its small group teaching, applying science to problems in pharmacy and drug use through regular tutor groups of five to six students, as well as lectures, seminars and laboratory classes. The school emphasises self-directed and problem-based learning. Undergraduates can apply to spend three months studying abroad in their third year in a university, hospital or research laboratory.

Student life

The international campus officer describes The School of Pharmacy as a campus without walls, as it has a clear academic base (the Brunswick Square building), yet its students live in the same residences as those from other colleges of the University of London. International Hall is one of six residences within a five or 10 minute walk of SOP. SOP students become members of the University of London students' union, ULU, which is conveniently located around the corner.

London is not expensive for students. Housing costs are high but almost everything else is cheaper and part-time jobs are easy to come by for pharmacy students (London has some 800 pharmacies).

Whilst many SOP students become community pharmacists, substantial numbers enter hospital pharmacy, the pharmaceutical industry, government scientific services and universities and rise to senior administrative posts in health services.

Universities and colleges of higher education

Sheffield

The University of Sheffield

Write to: International Office,
The University of Sheffield,
4 Palmerston Road,
Sheffield S10 2TE

Tel: +44 (0)114 222 1255

Fax: +44 (0)114 272 9145

Email: international@sheffield.ac.uk

Website: www.shef.ac.uk/international

Students: (2000/01) 21,425
(3,465 international from over
106 countries), 48:52 male:female.

Accommodation: (2000/01) university
residences from £73 a week, self-catering
flats £47 a week, off-campus self-catering
£36 a week. International undergraduates
guaranteed university accommodation
and international postgraduates given
priority if they apply early.

Entrance requirements:
undergraduates A level AAB to BBC
or international equivalent (see the
prospectus for details); postgraduates
normally the equivalent of a higher
second class British degree.

EFL: IELTS 6.0 to 6.5, TOEFL 550 to 650,
depending on the degree subject (see
prospectus for further details).

Foundation: available for degrees in
science and engineering.

Fees: £7,450 to £9,900;
clinical degrees £18,290.

The University of Sheffield

Student profile

"I chose Sheffield for two reasons.
Firstly because of its reputation as a
research university and also because
of the excellent rating the psychology
department received. Secondly, the idea
of a university in a city which is close
to a national park appealed to me.

It's an exciting and
friendly place to live.
Sheffield offers so
much more than I
expected, it's a great
place to live and
study."

Terence Quek, Singapore

The University of Sheffield was founded in 1905 and is now one of the leading UK higher education institutions. Its reputation for excellence in teaching and research is one of the key reasons why Sheffield attracts more applications per place than nearly all other UK universities.

Located 160 miles north of London, Sheffield is surrounded by the Peak District National Park. The university is a city-based campus, which means students can access student accommodation, the departments and the city centre.

Academic strengths

The university's academic strengths span a range of disciplines and place Sheffield in the premier league of institutions for teaching quality and research. The independent government assessments of the quality of teaching in UK universities resulted in ratings of excellent for the following subjects: architecture, animal and plant sciences, automatic control and systems engineering, biomedical science, dentistry, education, English, electronic and electrical engineering, East Asian studies, engineering materials, geography, landscape, law, linguistics, mechanical engineering, molecular biology and biotechnology, music, philosophy, psychology, sociology and town and regional planning. The university also has a very strong Department of Computer Science and Management School.

The university's impressive research profile sees 75 per cent of departments having been awarded the top 5 or 5* in the 2001 government assessment of the quality of research. Outstanding research departments include Electronic and Electrical Engineering, Engineering Materials, Animal and Plant Sciences, Molecular Biology and Biotechnology, Information Management and Politics.

Four Nobel Prizes have been awarded to graduates and staff of the university, including Sir Hans Krebs, professor of biochemistry. Two of the prizes were awarded to Richard Roberts for medicine/physiology in 1993, and Sir Harry Kroto, who was awarded a share of the Nobel Prize for Chemistry in 1996.

Student life

Sheffield was placed top of the league in the *Virgin Alternative Guide* to UK universities, testament to the quality of facilities and social life. The students' union funds over 140 societies, reflecting the wide range of interests shared by students, with over 60 different sports clubs. The university and city sports facilities are among the finest in the country. The city has an Olympic-sized stadium and pool, which are the venue for international athletics and swimming events. The university has its own pool, as well as floodlit artificial turf pitches, an all-weather jogging track, tennis courts and playing fields.

Services to students are wide-ranging and include, among other things, a meet and greet scheme for students arriving at Manchester International Airport, as well as a week-long orientation programme. Free English language support is also available to students throughout their time at Sheffield.

In fact the overall provision offered by Sheffield was so impressive that it won the coveted title of UK University of the Year (*The Sunday Times*).

Southampton

Southampton Institute

Write to: International Marketing Officer, Southampton Institute, East Park Terrace, Southampton SO14 0RB

Tel: +44 (0)23 8031 9422

Fax: +44 (0)23 8031 9412

Email: international@solent.ac.uk

Website: www.solent.ac.uk

Students: around 11,500 in 2001 (797 postgraduate, around 1,000 international from nearly 50 countries) 70:30 male:female.

Accommodation: institute residences from £71 to £78 a week self-catering.

Entrance requirements: two or three A levels in appropriate subjects or equivalent.

EFL: Cambridge Advanced or Proficiency depending on course, IELTS 6.0 to 6.5, TOEFL 550 to 600.

Foundation: International Foundation Programme.

Fees: £5,700 a year, plus £50 annual studio fees for some courses or £100 registration fees for BTEC courses.

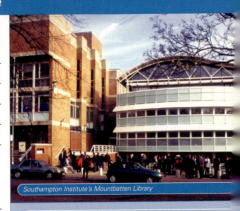
Southampton Institute's Mountbatten Library

Student profile

"Although I am from the USA, I was actually brought up in Germany. I chose Southampton Institute because it is one of the top five institutions in the UK for film studies. Southampton is also ideal for student life as nothing is further than 15 minutes' walk away. The only surprise to me has been the amount of coursework we have to do. Staff at the International Affairs Office provide all-year-round support for international students, which is important because it's often hard to make friends with British students. I have been involved in the

institute's meet and greet service for the last couple of years. I think it's a very important first point of contact for all new arrivals."

Michael Deming, USA

Southampton is located on the south coast of England with excellent connections to Europe and the rest of the world by road, rail, sea and air. London is only an hour away by train whilst Gatwick and Heathrow airports are both within two hours' travelling. Southampton Institute is surrounded by parks, shopping centres and many leisure attractions. The climate in Southampton is milder than most other parts of the British Isles.

Academic strengths

Southampton's college of higher education was founded in 1969 and merged with the Southampton College of Art in 1981. Southampton Institute was founded in 1984 with the incorporation of the College of Nautical Studies at Warsash. This heritage is reflected in the strengths of the institute's maritime and design courses. Courses in maritime include the BSc (Hons) Shipping Operations and the BEng (Hons) Yacht and Powercraft Design. The institute also offers degrees in fine art, fashion, graphic design, multimedia design and the more unusual degrees in fine arts valuation and antiques (history and collecting), in which students are able to handle real art objects from the unique Study Collection.

Southampton Institute's mission is to provide "courses for careers, research for results". Vocational, practical and innovative courses offered by the institute include a four-year sandwich BA (Hons) in Financial Services and a BSc (Hons) Business Information Technology course, both of which include a placement year in industry. The institute is well equipped with two TV studios with control room, film studios, several video editing suites, a 32-track recording studio and a multi-media suite equipped with Apple Macs.

Southampton Business School (with over 4,000 students) offers numerous degree courses in various disciplines such as marketing, international business, business management, human resource management, tourism management and also sports studies with business. Each of the degrees offered by Southampton Institute are validated by The Nottingham Trent University.

Student life

The institute has well-developed student support systems including full-time counselling, study assistance, information services and careers services, backed up by modern IT systems and easy access to computers, software and networks. There are six new student residences providing 2,300 rooms (over 1,000 with en suite facilities) within walking distance of the main campus.

Facilities on the campus include a bookshop, general shops, cashpoints, a sports hall and a library. There is also a fitness suite and swimming pool, and saunas and solariums are available to all. Southampton itself can offer all kinds of entertainments including bowling, a multiscreen cinema as well as many pubs, clubs, bars and restaurants.

An induction programme prior to enrolment and social events throughout the year are organised for international students. The institute is committed to ensuring that students from all other countries settle in to Southampton Institute well; as such, it provides support services to deal with any difficulties that may arise.

University
of Southampton

Southampton

University of Southampton

Write to: Siân Williams, Academic Registrar's, University of Southampton, Highfield, Southampton SO17 1BJ

Tel: +44 (0)23 8059 6808

Fax: +44 (0)23 8059 5789

Email: ednfairs@soton.ac.uk

Website: www.soton.ac.uk

Students: 18,935 in 2000/01 (3,530 postgraduates, 1,965 international students from over 100 countries).

Accommodation: catered, self-catered, limited family facilities. Vacation facilities. University residences from £45 to £100 a week. Rooms in town from £40 a week.

Entrance requirements: vary according to subject, please refer to the prospectus for details.

EFL: IELTS 6.5, TOEFL 600, minimum. Lower qualifications for pre-sessional English courses.

Foundation: engineering, art and design. Successful completion of foundation courses leads to degree course entry.

Fees: classroom courses £7,300 a year; laboratory courses £9,600 a year; clinical medicine £18,060 a year (2001/02 rates). A small number of courses have non-standard fees, please check prospectus for details.

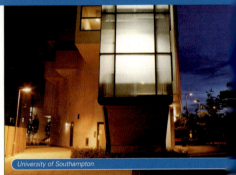

University of Southampton

Student profile

"I am in my second year at the University of Southampton. I have a particular interest in the subject of accounting, so I chose to pursue a degree in accounting and finance in the Management Department. I chose the university as the Management Department has been graded excellent for its teaching. There is also a wide range of facilities at the university which provide its students with a good environment for studying. I have taken part in many extracurricular activities during my leisure time. There are over 100 clubs and societies offered by the students' union. I have joined

the Chinese Students' Society so I have the opportunity to meet other students from Hong Kong and China. This helps to make me feel at home here."

Carine Chan, Hong Kong

Universities and colleges of higher education

The University of Southampton has its roots in the Hartley Institute, founded in 1862. It was granted its Royal Charter in 1952. Since then, it has had some notable, international alumni including John Hyde, who played a part in designing the Intel Pentium Processor.

The main campus at Southampton is at Highfield, just two miles from the city centre. The Avenue campus is home to the Faculty of Arts while the School of Ocean and Earth Science is based at the dockside Southampton Oceanography Centre. Art and design are both taught in the nearby town of Winchester, at the Winchester School of Art.

Southampton has a population of 200,000 including 40,000 students. It is situated on the south coast – a ferry ride away from France and the rest of Europe. The marina, Ocean Village, regularly plays host to international sailing events such as the Whitbread Round-the-World yacht race. The city also has a number of cinemas and two large theatres, plus several concert halls and art galleries.

Academic strengths

The University of Southampton has seven faculties which cover most academic disciplines. All departments which have been assessed scored over 18 out of 24 in teaching quality assessments. The Economics, Politics, and Electronics and Computer Science Departments have all obtained 24 out of 24 – the highest possible rating.

The university prides itself on its research and 24 out of 34 subject areas assessed in the last research assessment exercise (2001) obtained ratings of 5 or 5*. This makes the University of Southampton one of the UK's top 10 research universities.

There are seven libraries affiliated to the university, the largest of which is the Hartley Library housing over one million books on the main campus. Networked computer work stations can be found throughout the campus and may be accessed by all students.

Student life

The student scene is based around the Highfield campus although students are sufficiently near the town to take advantage of the facilities there. The students' union supports over one hundred clubs and societies covering such broad areas as massage, windsurfing and jazz. Many of these have an international dimension such as the Chinese, Singapore and Turkish societies. Furthermore, there are religious societies including the Buddhist society and the Islamic society. The Christian chaplaincy caters for all denominations and there is a Muslim prayer room on the campus.

The university has an international students' welfare adviser and offers many English language courses both before courses start and during term time. All international students are invited to attend a welcome conference. The Student Advice and Information Centre is there to offer assistance on practical issues which may be of concern to students, such as finance and immigration.

A limited number of scholarships exist in a range of departments. Please refer to the website for details.

Stoke-on-Trent

Staffordshire University

Write to: International Office, Staffordshire University, College Road, Stoke-on-Trent ST4 2DE

Tel: +44 (0)1782 292718

Fax: +44 (0)1782 292796

Email: international@staffs.ac.uk

Website: www.staffs.ac.uk/international

Students: (2000/01) 17,763 (1,993 postgraduate, 1,194 international from 77 countries), male:female 51:49.

Accommodation: single or twin rooms, vacation. University residences approximately £31 to £58 a week self-catering. Some en suite rooms.

Entrance requirements: vary across courses. Applicants with a wide variety of educational experience and international qualifications are welcomed.

EFL: Cambridge Proficiency grade C, IELTS 6, TOEFL 550/213.

Foundation: English language foundation programmes. For details of other subjects, please contact the International Office.

Fees: 2002/03 undergraduate courses £6,500; postgraduate courses £7,000; MBA £7,800. Scholarships available.

The Law School

Student profile

"It was through a friend of mine that I heard about Staffordshire University. The first time I came here from Taiwan, it felt like a great place to study and I was impressed with the staff and lecturers who are so friendly and helpful. I love my course (MSc Global Marketing) and it has given me the chance to visit other countries and undertake research overseas. This year we went to the Czech Republic and had a great time experiencing a different environment. As part of my research, I got the chance to interview our vice chancellor about overseas students choosing to study in

the UK. Apart from university life, there is lots to do in Stoke-on-Trent, and I have made many good friends in the church that I have joined."

Emily Liao Yuan Ying, Taiwan

Universities and colleges of higher education

Staffordshire is located in central England between Birmingham and Manchester, in a region known as the Midlands. The area is famous for the adventure theme park, Alton Towers, the beautiful Staffordshire moorlands and an internationally-renowned ceramic industry. A network of roads and railways enables easy access to major cities in England and London is only one hour 45 minutes away by train.

Staffordshire University began as an assortment of technical and art colleges in the early part of this century and has grown into a modern thriving institution. Based at two campuses, the university offers a mix of city and country, with one campus located at a greenfield site at Stafford and one in the centre of the busy city of Stoke-on-Trent.

Academic strengths

The university has eight academic schools and has received excellent ratings in its most recent QAA reviews for art and design, psychology, nursing, economics, sport and philosophy. The university is continually reviewing and updating its courses so that they are relevant to the needs of its students and their future employers.

New courses in design, media and e-commerce are available including design technology for mobile communications, e-commerce, interactive multimedia and internet commerce.

The School of Art and Design now offers 14 specialist degree courses including multimedia or electronic graphics, animation, media production and product design. The computing degree scheme offers a general award, more focused awards such as software engineering or specialist routes such as internet technology or intelligent systems. Media courses are supported by a digital production centre with television and music studios.

Computer facilities are available to all students and the university houses the third biggest higher education computing centre in Europe. All students have email and most halls of residence have telephone and internet access.

Student life

The students' union provides bars, shops and catering outlets, along with a range of clubs and societies. The international society welcomes students from all over the world and arranges social events. The Film Theatre shows popular films on campus during term time.

The university sports facilities are extensive and include a new sports centre at the Stafford campus. Both sites have all-weather floodlit pitches and fitness suites, plus provision for sports ranging from trampolining to t'ai chi and indoor climbing to hockey.

International students are welcomed with an induction week at the beginning of the year including orientation and social activities. Coach transfers from Heathrow airport are arranged for specific days. Students are offered a wide choice in English language provision including an international foundation course, an intensive summer school and a two-week, pre-sessional course in addition to free modules that can be taken as part of a degree.

Stirling

The University of Stirling

Write to: Student Recruitment and Admissions Service, The University of Stirling, Stirling FK9 4LA

Tel: +44 (0)1786 467046

Fax: +44 (0)1786 466800

Email: international@stir.ac.uk

Website: www.stir.ac.uk

Students: 8,000 in 2000/01 (1,200 postgraduates, 600 to 900 international from over 70 countries), 49:51 male:female.

Accommodation: single, married, single sex, vacation. University residences from £45 a week. Room in town from £45 to £50 a week.

Entrance requirements: Bs and Cs in Scottish Highers, A levels or equivalent required for most subjects (BBC for business, English, film and media, human resource management, marketing and Scottish studies).

EFL: Cambridge Advanced grade A, Cambridge Proficiency grade C, IELTS 5.5 to 7.0, TOEFL 550.

Fees: classroom courses £6,250 a year; laboratory courses £8,250 a year; taught MA, some MSc and MBA £8,900 a year; postgraduate, please contact the International Office for details.

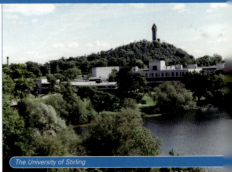

The University of Stirling

Student profile

"I came to Stirling at the beginning of the autumn semester to read for an MPhil in Publishing Studies. I graduated in English from the University of Beijing four years ago, then joined a publishing company. I work with English clients like Longmans, Oxford University Press and BBC Books, so they sent me on this course to improve my knowledge of publishing. At the British Council in Beijing, I found out that Stirling's media studies courses are famous internationally. I'm learning lots about publishing – editing, electronic publishing, printing, production and even marketing. Stirling is peaceful. I live in a  university flat and it's very comfortable but there's no TV. I wish I had known – I was really looking forward to watching TV in English."

Sheng Chiang, People's Republic of (

Stirling's Bridge of Allan campus is built around a lake, Airthrey Loch, and is surrounded by the steep, wooded Ochil Hills. The stark, white university buildings rising through the tree tops have a certain grandeur, although those who decry modern architecture compare them unfavourably with the beautiful green, landscaped grounds and the area's solid, typically Scottish stone houses.

This region preserves sacred monuments of Scottish history so it isn't surprising that Stirling is a very popular choice for history students. The Wallace Monument looms over the campus, commemorating one of Scotland's most famous fighters for independence, William Wallace, who won a victory there in the 13th century. The university lies just outside the town of Stirling, whose castle was the home of Scottish kings. Close by is Bannockburn, site of the battle of 1314 where Robert the Bruce defeated an English army three times larger than his own.

Frequent buses connect the university with Stirling, whose railway service is prompt, clean and efficient and serves Glasgow and Edinburgh respectively. It also has direct services to London, Perth and Aberdeen. Not bad for a small town, considering that students make up 10 per cent of the population.

Academic strengths

Stirling is one of Scotland's smaller universities and in fact one of its most modern, having been founded as recently as 1967. It is also one of its most innovative – it was the first in the UK to introduce a semester system of two terms of 15 weeks each, from September and February, with a short summer semester from late June to mid August. It puts a higher value on teaching standards than on research. The country's teaching quality assessors recently awarded excellent ratings in economics, environmental science, religious studies and sociology. The university has four faculties, namely arts, human sciences, management and natural sciences. Many attractive and unusual courses are on offer. The Faculty of Management offers the widest range, including sports studies with management.

Stirling is the Scottish centre for Japanese studies and has strong courses in film and media, an aquaculture course in its Environmental Science Department as well as a degree in English as a foreign language. Flexibility is the keyword at Stirling – there are many routes through the curriculum, and combined degrees in many subjects are offered by each different faculty.

Student life

The campus is the focus of university life. There is enough accommodation for all first-year students, and amenities include cafés, shops and the McRobert Arts Centre, which provides a venue for film showings, concerts and theatre. All students have an adviser to help plan coursework and achieve goals and deadlines. English language classes are available for international students (at a cost).

The Student Information and Support Service also offers specialist assistance and advice. It is staffed by workers who are professionally trained to give confidential support to students during their time at The University of Stirling.

Strathclyde

The University of Strathclyde

Write to: International Office, The University of Strathclyde, Graham Hills Building, 50 George Street, Glasgow G1 1QE

Tel: +44 (0)141 548 4793

Fax: +44 (0)141 552 7493

Email: international@mis.strath.ac.uk

Website: www.strath.ac.uk

Students: 14,000 students (11,000 of which are undergraduate, 1,500 international students from over 100 countries).

Accommodation: ranging from shared furnished flats in the campus village to single and shared rooms in traditional residences elsewhere in the city centre. En suite accommodation is available. Student accommodation has been designed to provide a secure home at an affordable price. All accommodation is networked for free internet access and phone lines are installed in each room.

Entrance requirements: good grades at A level or equivalent qualifications. Good undergraduate degree for postgraduate study. A foundation route is also available via the Scottish International Foundation Programme (SIFP).

EFL: generally 6.5 at IELTS or 600 TOEFL (250 computer-based test).

Fees: arts and social sciences £7,100; science and engineering £9,300; business £7,100.

The University of Strathclyde students

Student profile

"Before I arrived in Glasgow, I knew what I wanted to study next but not what I wanted to do with my career. The course at Strathclyde has given me the maturity to look at environmental issues from a wider perspective, involving several other related areas. This is crucial, since more and more global and local problems are intricately linked with social, economic and political factors. Further, due to the broad nature of the environmental studies course, I have been exposed to different areas of the environment and have been able to choose my areas of specific interest

from this exposure. This, I think, has been extremely useful to me in deciding the kind of jobs I want and the type of career that I would like."

Mahua Acharya, India

Glasgow, the largest city in Scotland, is a tourist, financial and commercial centre. The city is ideally located for easy access to London and other major European cities. Glasgow is host to some of the most exciting arts and cultural events in the world and is identified with innovative architecture and design, as demonstrated by its award of the prestigious title City of Architecture and Design of 1999.

The University of Strathclyde has a very strong reputation not only in teaching and research but also for its links with industry and business. The University of Strathclyde has been cited by the Cabinet Office as being one of only two universities in the UK that have been the most successful at working with industry in developing academic research into commercial applications.

Academic strengths

The university provides a stimulating environment for study in a wide range of subjects at undergraduate and postgraduate levels. There are five faculties, namely Arts and Social Sciences, Education, Engineering, Science and the Strathclyde Business School. The university is the largest provider of postgraduate courses in the UK, and no fewer than nine subject areas have achieved the very highest ratings in the last two UK-wide research assessment exercises.

There is a range of opportunities for undergraduate and postgraduate study and research across the faculties in many departments. These include subjects such as accounting and finance, architecture, bioscience, bioengineering, chemical engineering, chemistry, civil engineering, computer science, design manufacture and engineering management, economics, education, English studies, electronic and electrical engineering, human resource management, law, environmental studies, immunology, information science, management science, marketing, mathematics, mechanical engineering, pharmaceutical sciences, physics, physiology and pharmacology, ship and marine technology, as well as those offered by the Strathclyde Graduate School of Business and the Scottish Hotel School.

Student life

An international student adviser is available to assist with any difficulties experienced by international students and to organise social activities. The university also provides a welcome programme for international students aiming to assist them on their arrival in Glasgow. Pre-sessional and in-sessional English courses are available and four weeks of pre-sessional English is also offered free of charge to overseas students.

The international students club meets regularly. This provides an informal forum for students to meet and get to know each other in a relaxed atmosphere. A programme of social and cultural events is planned every three months. These often include day and weekend tours to other parts of Scotland, ceilidhs (Scottish dancing), theatres or concerts and national and international food evenings. In addition to this, the students union offers a variety of entertainment in many different venues.

THE SURREY INSTITUTE OF ART & DESIGN
UNIVERSITY COLLEGE

Farnham

Surrey Institute of Art and Design, University College

Write to: The Registry,
Surrey Institute of Art and Design,
University College, Falkner Road,
Farnham Campus, Surrey GU9 7DS

Tel: +44 (0)1252 722441

Fax: +44 (0)1252 892616

Email: registry@surrart.ac.uk

Website: www.surrart.ac.uk

Students: 3,383 (including 2,716
undergraduates, 46 postgraduates
and 216 international students from 63
countries), 45:55 male:female.

Accommodation: single sex,
summer vacation extra charge. Institute
residences from £33 to £55 a week
self-catered (Farnham only). Room in
town from £45 to £70 a week.

Entrance requirements: A levels
in appropriate subjects or Foundation
Diploma in Art and Design. International
Baccalaureate accepted. IELTS 6,
TOEFL 575 (undergraduate).

Fees: undergraduate £7,400;
postgraduate £6,300 (2001 fees);
Foundation Studies £4,700; Foundation
Studies with English £5,950.

Surrey Institute of Art and Design, University College

Student profile

"After graduating from high school, I did a Foundation course in European Studies and it was then I first became attracted to fashion and communication. I heard about the degree in fashion promotion and illustration at The Surrey Institute of Art and Design from an English friend. A year later, I found myself at Heathrow Airport ready to start a new life. Having spent almost three years here, it has been the best experience of my life so far. Apart from learning how to become more independent, I have cultivated all of the intellectual and practical skills I will need to enter

the fashion industry. I have found it very interesting to study a foreign fashion industry that is so different from that of my own culture."

Harris Spyropoulou, Greece

The Surrey Institute of Art and Design, situated in picturesque Surrey, has two purpose-built campuses in Epsom and Farnham – small market towns half an hour from London by train. Both towns are pleasant and rather genteel, set in attractive countryside but close enough to get to London easily for shopping or clubbing.

The Farnham campus is set in 16 acres of grounds beneath Farnham castle and has a spectacular entrance building that doubles as a gallery. The Epsom campus has just opened a new library and learning resource centre

Academic strengths

The institute is one of the largest independent university colleges in the UK specialising in art, design and media communication in Europe. It has over 30 programmes, offering progression routes from the foundation diploma right through to undergraduate and postgraduate degrees as well as short courses. All courses have a professional practice element in each year of the programme. Many of the lecturers are also professional practitioners and there is a strong emphasis on developing practical, employable skills.

Popular with international students is the one-year Foundation Diploma in Art and Design, which can be taken at both the Epsom and Farnham campuses. For this, you need one A level and three GCSE passes or the international equivalent. This programme is also offered with an English language component.

Epsom offers degrees in graphic design, graphic design and new media, fashion, fashion journalism and fashion promotion and illustration. Animation is a popular area and the Farnham campus offers degrees in this as well as fine art, three-dimensional design, film and video, graphic design and photography.

It also offers journalism, design management, packaging design, product design, advertising, interior design and textiles courses.

Student life

Much of the social life of students is based around the busy students' union (SU). It hosts a number of clubs and societies and organises bands, dances and films. As well as Epsom's famous racecourse, both towns have a number of pubs, bars, restaurants and sporting facilities. The towns are close to London so students can benefit from all of the cultural and entertainment opportunities the capital has to offer.

There is an international welfare officer with the specific responsibility to look after international students and advice is also available for health matters and careers. International students have priority in booking accommodation in the student village in Farnham. There is also a meet and greet programme and induction course for international students on arrival. English language and specialist short courses are available throughout the summer.

Student advisers are on hand to give all students advice and information on anything from finance and money management to personal problems and practical issues such as immigration, visas and course problems.

Brighton

University of Sussex

Write to: Dr Philip Baker,
International and Study Abroad Office,
Arts B, University of Sussex,
Falmer, Brighton BN1 9QN

Tel: +44 (0)1273 678422

Fax: +44 (0)1273 678640

Email: international@sussex.ac.uk

Website: www.sussex.ac.uk

Students: 9,515 in 2000/01
(2,634 postgraduate, 2,298
international from 116 countries),
45:55 male:female.

Accommodation: single sex (female),
family, vacation. University residences
from £48 a week self-catered. Room in
town £55 a week (2001 figures).

Entrance requirements: vary
according to subject, generally BBB to
BCD. Overall pass in International
Baccalaureate, including 14 to 17 in
the three appropriate highers.

EFL: for undergraduate IELTS 6.5, TOEFL
paper-based test 600 and TWE 4,
computer-based test 250; for
postgraduate IELTS 6.0 to 7.0, TOEFL
550 and TWE 4 or 600 and TWE 5,
computer-based test 213 to 250.

Foundation: courses are currently
available at Sussex and local colleges
in most subjects in the arts and
sciences. Please contact the university
for further details.

Fees: classroom courses £7,290 a
year; laboratory courses £9,580 a
year (2001/02 figures).

Sussex campus

Student profile

"I studied sociology at Universidad Complutense in Madrid and spent my last year as an Erasmus student at the University of Sussex. I chose to stay on for my MA in Migration Studies because of the excellent resources this university offers and its brilliant teachers. At first, it was difficult to get used to a different academic system, especially when participating in seminars with few students and having to write essays in English. But everybody is very helpful. Brighton is also a great place to live. Its location and the young and cosmopolitan nature of its inhabitants make it

an ideal place to spend a year abroad. Definitely, this is one of the best (if not the best) places to choose to study. Enjoy it."

Maira Vergara, Spain

The University of Sussex is a campus university and most of its residences, lecture theatres, seminar rooms, bars, laboratories, restaurants and sports facilities are within close proximity to each other in the university's parkland. Sussex is the only university in England which has the whole of its academic campus situated in a designated area of outstanding natural beauty. The South Downs countryside, consisting of historic villages, hills and open farmland, is very popular with day trippers, hikers and mountain bikers.

A few minutes' train journey from the university is the seaside city of Brighton. Students form a large proportion of the town's population – over 10 per cent – and many of the local bars and clubs have nights geared towards student entertainment. The atmosphere of the town is liberal and cosmopolitan. One major cultural attraction is the annual Brighton Festival. For three weeks in May, international musicians, dancers and performers come to the town for England's biggest arts festival.

Academic strengths

The University of Sussex offers nearly 200 undergraduate degrees and over 120 taught postgraduate programmes. In the 1996 research assessment exercise, Sussex was awarded 5 or 5* in the following subjects: American studies, biological sciences, chemistry, computer science, English, history, history of art, pure mathematics, French, German, media studies and the science policy research unit. A total of 83 per cent of academic staff at the university work in subject areas which have received a rating of 4 or 5. 15 of the 17 subjects assessed under the current teaching quality assessment scheme have scored 21 or more points out of a possible 24, with philosophy and sociology achieving the maximum score of 24.

The university library has a collection of over 750,000 books. It also has special collections which include the papers of Leonard and Virginia Woolf, Rudyard Kipling and the archive of the *New Statesman* journal.

Student life

To ease international students into the start of their courses, a welcome and information programme takes place before the start of the autumn term. Pre-sessional English language courses are available and, during term time, there are classes in English for academic purposes for those who should require them. Students can take Cambridge exams in English at the university.

The International and Study Abroad Office organises day trips to places of interest, social events and trips for students. There is also the HOST scheme, in which students can stay with a British family for a weekend.

The students' union is the focus of many activities at Sussex. As well as over 100 clubs and societies, it runs a newspaper, a radio station that won BBC Radio One best student radio station (1997) and *The Pulse* – a Guardian Student Media winner for best campus magazine (1996). The Gardner Arts Centre hosts contemporary plays and dance, has a cinema and exhibition galleries. The university's sports facilities include 14 acres of playing fields, sports halls and squash courts.

Middlesbrough

University of Teesside

Write to: Academic Registry, University of Teesside, Middlesbrough TS1 3BA

Tel: +44 (0)1642 218121

Fax: +44 (0)1642 342067

Email: reg@tees.ac.uk

Website: www.tees.ac.uk

Students: 14,788 undergraduates (1,577 postgraduates, around 700 international from 62 countries).

Accommodation: priority given to international students, with 776 places available in halls and 561 in university-managed private housing in and around Middlesbrough. Prices from £30 to £54 a week. Private rented accommodation ranges from £29 to £33 a week.

Entrance requirements: international students are evaluated on an individual basis.

Foundation: an international foundation course is available.

Fees: from £6,000 a year plus supplements for health-related courses. Scholarships are available. Contact the International Office for further information.

Learning Resource Centre

Student profile

"I came to England from Australia with my parents. I chose Teesside after coming to an open day and seeing the facilities. I was impressed by the Virtual Reality Centre and Learning Resource Centre. I have been particularly impressed by the amount of labs the university has; it seems way ahead of other universities. The technical support is good and we are also encouraged to learn by ourselves. I would recommend the Computer Animation course. My career expectations are excellent so when I graduate I will be in a good position to find employment. The campus and surrounding areas are

student friendly and the shopping and entertainment facilities are very good. I'm really enjoying the student experience in Middlesbrough."

Caroline Delengaigne, Australia

Universities and colleges of higher education

574

Located on a single campus in the centre of Middlesbrough, the University of Teesside offers more than 220 full-time courses from HND through to degree and postgraduate qualifications. Middlesbrough is in the Teesside region of northeast England, which has undergone somewhat of a renaissance in recent years with a number of new developments. For students, one of the big benefits is that this is one of the least expensive places to live in the UK, as well as being near some beautiful coastline and countryside. Other attractions include the multimillion pound Riverside Stadium – home to Middlesbrough Football Club – and the international-standard water sports facility on the Tees Barrage.

Academic strengths

The university is divided into six schools: Teesside Business School, Computing and Mathematics, Arts and Media, Health and Social Care, Science and Technology, Social Sciences and Law. The university's principal strengths are in computing, design, nursing and health-related areas which all have an excellent teaching quality rating. It also offers courses in business, social sciences, law, engineering, media, forensic investigation, life sciences and humanities. Many of the programmes are run in a flexible modular form and students may tailor their studies to meet their own needs or interests. Many of the undergraduate programmes are professionally oriented, with opportunities to undertake work placements with relevant organisations.

The Learning Resource Centre is a combined IT and library centre with over 1,300 specially designed study places, 400 open access computer workstations with email and internet software and video viewing stations.

Student life

The university has spent over £50 million on new buildings and improvements to existing facilities, much of which has been carried out recently. This includes student accommodation, an Innovation and Virtual Reality Centre and a new School of Health and Social Care.

The students' union puts on a varied programme of events. Features include theme nights, live bands, DJs, comedy and big screen coverage of sporting events. Social events are focused around the union's three bars, Union Central, Central Café and Club One, a 1,000 capacity venue. The union building is fully accessible to students with disabilities, with lifts running to each floor. There is a chaplaincy, nursery, health service, advice centre and a counselling service. The university also has its own cinema.

North Yorkshire's coastline and moors provide opportunities for a wide range of outdoor activities. Sporting strengths include rugby league, canoeing, martial arts, women's rugby, cycling, athletics and soccer. International trips are arranged for skiing, squash, basketball, soccer and watersports. The university also plans to invest in a new indoor sports facility.

The Student Support Unit provides welfare and advice to help international students adjust to the environment, as well as practical assistance with accommodation, immigration procedures and healthcare. Subject to availability, the university also provides English language courses for international students.

London

Thames Valley University

Write to: Learning Advice Centre,
Thames Valley University,
18-22 Bond Street, Ealing,
London W5 5RF

Tel: +44 (0)20 8579 5000

Fax: +44 (0)20 8231 2056

Email: learning.advice@tvu.ac.uk

Website: www.tvu.ac.uk

Students: 26,739 in 2000/01 (3,991
postgraduates, students from over 70
countries, 7 per cent outside the UK),
male:female 1:2.

Accommodation: university
accommodation service available.
Room in town from £55 to £116
a week in private/rented accommodation.

Entrance requirements: two
A levels or international equivalent.

EFL: IELTS 5.5, TOEFL 550.

Foundation: one-year International
Foundation Programme at the
university available.

Fees: undergraduate £6,000 a year;
postgraduate £1,450 to £9,270 a year.
International Student Scholarship Scheme
available in the form of bursaries.

The Paul Hamlyn Learning Resource Centre

Student profile

"I was a little nervous about going to
university at first, especially in a different
country. I decided to do a degree at TVU
in order to acquire a firm foundation for a
master's degree. I was keen to improve
my future prospects. My lecturers are
great and the course is enjoyable and
stimulating. Studying here is giving me a
much broader perspective on life. The
apprehension I felt coming to study in a
foreign land was allayed by the
International Centre who are there to
support overseas students. Through the
centre, I have met other international
students who share similar experiences.

Studying in a different
country can be very
daunting but TVU is
friendly, so it's easy to
settle in. Everyone
I've met has made me
feel very welcome."

Urvasi Santokhee, Malaysia

Universities and colleges of higher education

Thames Valley University (TVU) aims to be innovative, forward-looking and is a mixture of old and new. Its roots trace back some 130 years yet its courses are designed to prepare students for the 21st century.

TVU goes back a long way to a school founded in 1860 on the main site in St Mary's Road, Ealing. Since 1966, when it became a higher education institution, it has taught international students. There are currently students from 77 different countries studying at TVU. The student population at the university represents the cultural diversity of London.

The main university campus is in Ealing, West London, 20 minutes by train from central London. Heathrow Airport is within easy access, just 20 minutes by tube. The university campus at Slough is near Windsor Castle to the west of London. There is a university shuttle service between Slough and Ealing, which is free to TVU students.

Academic strengths

The range of relevant and up-to-date courses, facilities, professional staff and the London location makes TVU a good choice for hundreds of international students who study each year in the UK.

The university's strengths lie in music, media, nursing, midwifery, hospitality and leisure, tourism, psychology, business, accountancy and law, all of which are recognised nationally and internationally.

The university runs a large selection of courses ranging from foundation level to the MBA. These programmes include innovative courses like entrepreneurship, web and e-business, new media journalism, sport and health and fitness manage-ment degrees. TVU also offers the pre-sessional course and a semester abroad programme.

Students are encouraged to become independent learners with the support of over 600 fully-networked computers, open-access workstations, scanners, colour printers, CD-Roms, video and audio playback, internet and remote database access, as well as an extensive stock of specialist books and journals.

Student life

There is a dedicated accommodation service with extensive networks in the local area. The service helps students to find family accommodation, lodgings, rooms, flats and houses reasonably near the campuses.

TVU students' union supplements all of the theatre, cinema, club and music entertainment to be found in west London with its own entertainment programme and with a student sports card you can use at the university and local sports facilities at low prices.

London may be large but the university's international office and student support services are geared to ensure that all international students have a source of help and information throughout their years of study.

The university offers free English language support to assist its international students in writing essays and preparing presentations. TVU also runs an induction programme at the start of the course to introduce its international students to the university as well as the local area. A free meet and greet service is available upon request for those students arriving in the country at either Gatwick or Heathrow airports.

Coventry

The University of Warwick

Write to: The International Office,
The University of Warwick,
Coventry CV4 7AL

Tel: +44 (0)2476 523706

Fax: +44 (0)2476 524337

Email: int.office@warwick.ac.uk

Website: www.warwick.ac.uk

Students: 16,869 (6,439 postgraduate, 8,995 undergraduate, including 2,502 international students from over 100 countries), 54:46 male:female.

Accommodation: single, married or family accommodation, 30, 39 and 50-week let. University residences £48 to £70 a week self-catered, from £65 catered, room off campus £40 to £65 a week. All on-campus rooms with internet access point, many postgraduate rooms with telephone.

Entrance requirements: as a guide, the university requires 18 to 20 units of study at AS/A2 level with at least two subjects studied to A2 level, (grades equivalent to ABB at A level). International Baccalaureate accepted and equivalent qualifications also considered.

Foundation course: one of the UK's longest running International Higher Education Foundation Programmes (HEFP). Courses run in law, social science, business studies, science and engineering.

Fees: band one £7,530. Band two £9,700.

The University of Warwick

Student profile

"I joined the MA in Organisation Studies at The University of Warwick after having worked for IBM for five years following my graduation from Keio University in 1995. I am sponsored by my employer to study on this programme. I arrived at Warwick before the course started in order to attend the pre-sessional English language course. This prepared me with the academic English skills I would need for my course. I have now been here for six months and enjoy the opportunity to prepare and make presentations to my seminar group. Students are very keen to

express their views and there is generally more opportunity for discussion compared to a Japanese seminar group. This is a very refreshing change."

Nanako Komiyama, Japan

The University of Warwick received its Royal Charter in 1965 when it admitted 450 students. The campus has since spread across three neighbouring sites and is now home to over 16,000 students. Warwick is a lively, modern campus which provides accommodation for over 5,000 students. The university is located about three miles from Coventry – a city whose cathedral is famous as a centre for international peace and reconciliation.

In 1984, the university established the Science Park to foster the growth of new technology. It is now home to over 65 technology-based companies and is strategically placed in one of the UK's major business regions. The surrounding countryside has plenty of historic attractions such as Warwick Castle and Shakespeare's birthplace in Stratford-Upon-Avon.

Academic strengths

The university is divided into three main faculties: Arts, Science and Social Studies. The Faculty of Medicine was also recently added with the introduction of the Leicester-Warwick Medical School in partnership with the University of Leicester.

Warwick is one of the UK's leading research universities and was awarded consistently high scores in recent research assessments carried out by the government (2001). To date, 21 out of 23 departments have been awarded excellent for the quality of teaching in assessments carried out by the Quality Assurance Agency.

The main campus library is centrally located and is open seven days a week during term time. There is an extensive network of PCs as well as a computer room, which is open for student use 24 hours a day.

The university's Centre for English Language Teacher Education (CELTE) offers pre-sessional English courses for international students, as well as English lessons which run throughout the term. For students wanting to learn another language other than English, the university has a well-equipped language centre.

Student life

Warwick students' union is one of the most active in the UK and provides all the facilities required for student life. The union building, located in the centre of campus, houses several large bars, a club, a radio station (where BBC DJ Simon Mayo began his career), snack bars, restaurant, pharmacy, hairdressers, travel agents and three high street banks. The student union also runs over 160 clubs and societies.

Around 70 sports clubs at Warwick are recognised by the sports federation and the campus provides a good range of sporting facilities for their use, including two swimming pools, 60 acres of playing fields and an indoor climbing centre.

Cultural life at Warwick is among the best in the country, as the university campus is also home to the Warwick Arts Centre, the largest venue of its kind outside London. The Arts Centre houses a concert hall, theatres, art gallery, restaurant, music centre, cinema and university bookshop.

The international office organises the orientation programme for students, which takes place before the start of the autumn term. A regular programme of events runs throughout the year. The office also arranges homestay programmes for students wanting to experience life with a British family.

UNIVERSITY OF WESTMINSTER

London

University of Westminster

Write to: International Education Office, University of Westminster, 16 Little Titchfield Street, London W1W 7UW

Tel: +44 (0)20 7911 5769

Fax: +44 (0)20 7911 5132

Email: international-office@wmin.ac.uk

Website: www.wmin.ac.uk/international

Students: 22,000 in 2001 (6,000 postgraduate, 16,000 undergraduate, 4,000 international from over 130 countries), 49:51 male:female.

Accommodation: single sex, married, vacation. University residences averaging £75 a week self-catering.

Entrance requirements: two or three A levels at grade C (BBC for business, law or media) or international equivalent. International Baccalaureate 28 or more points.

EFL: foundation 500 TOEFL, IELTS 5.5; undergraduate 550 TOEFL, IELTS 6; postgraduate 600 TOEFL, IELTS 6.5.

Fees: undergraduate courses from £6,700 to £7,300.

University of Westminster entrance

Student profile

"Before I came here, I was studying in Kuala Lumpur, working in a travel agency in order to gain experience in tourism. I managed to get sponsorship from my government and I decided to come to Westminster because I'd heard it did a good degree in business studies with tourism. It was also because they offered me a place on the spot. The international office has been helpful and I use it a lot. Since I've been here, I've set up a Malaysian Student Society and last year, I set up the International Student Society. This aims to provide a meeting place for international students and

members are from all over the world. We feel it is important to mix with students from other countries, as well as British students."

Shazly Bashah, Malaysia

Universities and colleges of higher education

580

Located in the centre of London, the University of Westminster is a gateway to professional life. For more than 160 years, the university has led the development of education in emerging technologies and modern professional practice, designing programmes to meet the needs of the international economy. The university endeavours to offer companies highly trained and capable graduates, while giving students a rare combination of practical, relevant knowledge honed by transferable skills – teamwork, communication and leadership – that they will need in their career. The relevance of its programmes was endorsed in May 2000 when the university won the prestigious Queen's Award for Enterprise for its success in international markets.

Academic strengths

In the demanding environment of the global economy, quality is paramount. Of the 25 subject areas recently assessed for teaching standards, more than half were considered excellent. The university's research profile also demonstrates its status. In 2001, Asian studies, communication and media, law and linguistics all achieved a 5. Art and design, electronic engineering and politics and international studies received 4.

In particular, they have one of the UK's leading communication and media teaching and research centres. From assessing the impact of the Jubilee Line extension on London's underground, to the development of a Hypertrans communication system for Europe's hauliers, Westminster researchers are at the cutting edge of applied knowledge. It is understandable, therefore, that the majority of Westminster graduates go straight into work.

Student life

It is the emphasis on skills development, the cosmopolitan mix of students and the atmosphere of London which should make studying at Westminster different. The campuses are a short distance from London landmarks such as the Houses of Parliament and Big Ben, the BBC and the British Library.

Accommodation is provided for international students in halls of residence. An international student adviser is on hand to advise on all matters relevant to international students and to organise social events. The orientation programme helps students find out more about London and the university. English language support is provided for all those who require it and the university offers pre-sessional English courses lasting from two weeks to one year.

The information systems and library services provide library, computer and network services and give teaching, research and administrative support to staff and students. In addition, Westminster offers extensive sporting facilities including a large sports ground on the bank of the River Thames and on-campus sports halls and fitness suites.

During July and August, as part of the university's summer school programme, more than 600 international students take part in a wide variety of short courses in business, arts and English, some of which may be taken for credit.

For those students from overseas that are already studying at a university in another country, there is the option of enrolling at Westminster for a semester or a year, and then transferring the credits earned towards their degree back at home.

WIMBLEDON | SCHOOL OF ART

London

Wimbledon School of Art

Write to: The Academic Registrar, Wimbledon School of Art, Merton Hall Road, London SW19 3QA

Tel: +44 (0)20 8408 5000

Fax: +44 (0)20 8408 5050

Email: registry@wimbledon.ac.uk

Website: www.wimbledon.ac.uk

Students: 225 full-time foundation students, 3:7 male to female. 428 full-time and 15 part-time undergraduates, 3:7 male to female. 37 full-time and 64 part-time postgraduates, 1:4 male to female. International students: 28 undergraduate and 13 postgraduate.

Accommodation: the welfare officer advises students on accommodation problems they may have. £55 to £100 a week self-catering. Most accommodation with families.

Entrance requirements: all applications should be supported by slides/photos of your work. Interviews not always necessary for international students. Basic IELTS requirement 5.0.

Foundation: full-time and part-time foundation course. Orientation courses run for six weeks during the summer for international students as a lead into the foundation course.

Fees: (2001/02) foundation £4,700. Other courses £7,510 a year.

'Sat with a clock on my head' by Scott Griffiths

Student profile

"I have been studying in England for two years after learning basic techniques and processes in fine art in Japan. As I am interested in the combination of European and Japanese cultures, I decided that England, where many international artists live and work, was an ideal place for me to study. I chose the BA Fine Art Sculpture at Wimbledon School of Art because it is flexible in allowing me to work across many kinds of contemporary practice. The school has five specialist theatre courses, which are an exciting influence on my work. I have the opportunity to exhibit my work in locations such as

Cannizaro Park or installation spaces in the school. Every tutor is a professional practising artist and they are accessible to me on a regular basis."

Kei Hosaka, Japan

Founded in 1890, Wimbledon School of Art is one of London's major art schools. The school has good transport links into the centre of London and to the main national and international station, Waterloo, via the underground, overland train, tram and London buses. London, 20 minutes by rail, is a major centre for fine art and theatre, and students are encouraged to use it as a resource.

Academic strengths

All staff are practising artists or designers in their own fields. The school has eight subject areas: foundation studies, painting, sculpture, print, theatre design, costume, technical arts and history of art and contextual studies. The school was awarded 23 out of 24 in Quality Agency assessments in 1999. Foundation studies offers a one-year, diagnostic, full-time course, in which students are introduced to specialisms such as graphics, theatre, costume, fine art and ceramics. The course has a wide range of studio space and workshop facilities for the range of art and design disciplines it teaches.

The full-time undergraduate fine art course specialises in painting or sculpture and lasts for three years, leading to the award of BA (Hons). Both specialist areas encourage students to explore processes in contemporary practice such as installation, photography, drawing, film and video, performance, traditional and digital print. The theatre courses available include theatre design, costume design or costume interpretation, technical arts design or technical arts interpretation. All five courses lead to the award Diploma of Higher Education (Dip HE) after two years study, or BA (Hons) on the successful completion of three years study. The part-time undergraduate course, BA (Hons) Practice and Theory in Art and Design, is of a five year duration.

The school also offers postgraduate research degrees and taught MA courses in subjects such as fine art (specialising in painting, drawing, sculpture and print), theatre: the visual language of performance or art, and performance theory. These courses are full time over one year or part time over two years.

All of the courses are supported by lectures, tutorials, seminars in history of art and contextual studies, a specialist art library, IT centre and workshops run by skilled technicians. All Wimbledon School of Art degree courses are accredited by The University of Surrey.

The Integrated Learning Resources Centre consists of a book library, slide library and an information technology centre. The computers are equipped with professional levels of software, including programmes such as Adobe Photoshop, 3D Max, Macromedia Director and Freehand and Microsoft Word.

Student life

Wimbledon School of Art provides support for international students through the welfare and accommodation officer and TEFL classes. The school also has a careers consultant. There is a strong student community at the school and all students are encouraged to participate in and organise exhibitions, collaborations, sponsorship, work experience and also degree shows.

Universities and colleges
of higher education

Wolverhampton

University of Wolverhampton

Write to: International Relations Office, University of Wolverhampton, Wulfruna Street, Wolverhampton WV1 1SB

Tel: +44 (0)1902 322332

Fax: +44 (0)1902 322488

Email: international@wlv.ac.uk

Website: www.wlv.ac.uk

Students: 22,084 in 2000/01 (3,296 postgraduate, 1,512 international from 89 countries), 5:7 male:female.

Accommodation: university residences from £41 a week. Room in town from £28 per week plus bills.

Entrance requirements: each course has different requirements. Maturity and experience are taken into account as well as international qualifications.

EFL: Cambridge Advanced or Proficiency. IELTS 6.0, TOEFL 550 (or 213 computer based). GCSE/GCE O level grade C.

Foundation: flexible routes including the international Student Foundation Course, English Plus and pre-sessional study skills courses.

Fees: classroom, laboratory, undergraduate and postgraduate £6,050 (2000/01) a year; MBA £6,300 a year; MSc Development Training and Education, MSc Forestry £8,125 a year. Extra fees for materials may be payable on some art and design courses.

The main entrance to the University of Wolverhampton

Student profile

"When I was looking for a course in business, I decided to look abroad and chose the centrally located University of Wolverhampton in England. Studying abroad was important to me as I wanted to have an international degree and travel the world. I combined both by studying the business administration course at Wolverhampton. I enjoyed my time at one of the biggest universities in the UK and especially enjoyed meeting new people and experiencing different cultures. I would recommend studying abroad to anyone and would say enjoy  your time as much as you can while studying in England. Make the most of meeting loads of new friends and discovering new cultures."

Beatriz Aguilar, Spain

Universities and colleges of higher education

584

The University of Wolverhampton is a regional university with a particular commitment to widening access to higher education in the West Midlands. It gained university status in 1992 and has since added two new learning centres, the Wolverhampton Science Park and a whole new purpose-built campus at Telford in Shropshire.

Wolverhampton students study over 100 different subjects. The university combines traditional areas, such as history and English literature, with the latest disciplines including virtual reality and interactive multimedia design and e-commerce. The flexible and modular structure of its undergraduate courses make it possible to design individual programmes of study, for example including English language tuition at all levels up to degree standard.

The university is one of only two in the United Kingdom to have been awarded the government's Charter Mark for the high quality of services it offers to students. An international student unit and an international student counsellor ensure that special attention is paid to the needs of international students.

Academic strengths

The University of Wolverhampton has 10 schools: Applied Sciences, Art and Design, Business, Computing and Information Technology, Engineering and the Built Environment, Education, Health, Humanities, Languages and Social Sciences, Legal Studies, Sport, Performing Arts and Leisure. The Schools of Applied Sciences, Business and Education have all received excellent ratings in recent Quality Assurance Agency reviews.

The university learning centres combine access to IT and electronic information resources with traditional university library services to make hi-tech, flexible and user-friendly learning environments.

Student life

Wolverhampton has a students' union and an international student association. The university provides a limited airport pick-up service for students arriving from abroad, special short English language and study skills courses, a full orientation programme and specialised counselling and advice.

The university also provides some 20 scholarships for students from outside the EU (all subjects) and for students from inside the EU (for sport and for science and technology). Wolverhampton has a specific committee that considers all applications for fee reductions in cases of exceptional hardship.

For the benefit of international students, the university runs the English Plus course: an intensive, one-year programme which includes English and one other subject, designed to allow students to reach the entry standard required by the university. Shorter English language preparatory courses are also provided.

The Wolverhampton International Student Foundation Programme began in September 2001. The course combines English language with academic study and prepares students with senior high school leaving certificates from a number of different countries around the world to the standard required for entry to any of the university's undergraduate degree programmes.

Writtle COLLEGE

Chelmsford

Writtle College

Write to: International Office, Writtle College, Chelmsford, Essex CM1 3RR

Tel: +44 (0)1245 424200

Fax: +44 (0)1245 420456

Email: internationaloffice@writtle.ac.uk

Website: www.writtle.ac.uk

Students: 3,000 students, of which 1,600 are full time. There are international students from over 40 nations.

Accommodation: accommodation with main meals between £877 and £1,062 a term. Hall fees include vouchers for 10 meals a week during term time.

Entrance requirements: vary according to subject. Please contact the International Office for details.

EFL: IELTS 5.5 or 6, TOEFL 550 to 580 (200 to 220 computer-tested).

Foundation: certificate and diploma programmes in vocational subjects with progression opportunities.

Fees: 2001/02 undergraduate £6,990 a year; postgraduate £8,145 a year; HND £6,990 a year; further education £4,125 a year.

Writtle College

Student profile

"I was sent to Writtle College by the Bermudan government to further my training because I had been promoted to the post of trainee superintendent in the parks department. I enjoyed my classes, especially the hands-on training. The quality of the teaching is excellent and standards are very high. Living on campus was like a home from home. When I went back to Bermuda, I continued working for the government but at the higher level of superintendent. I received such an excellent grounding in horticulture that I started this new job with real confidence. What's more, I was able to teach the skills I'd learnt to my crews, which helped me to gain their confidence and respect. Make the most of your time, because it goes quickly. Mine certainly did."

Lisa-Dawn Johnston, Bermuda

Writtle College is situated within a landscaped campus in a 220-hectare estate, three kilometers from the university town of Chelmsford and 40 minutes by rail from London. Founded in 1893, Writtle is Britain's largest, oldest university sector college for those aiming towards a career in the natural environment and with plants, animals and related industries. Because of the specialist nature of a land-based college, the courses are geared towards the needs of industry, mixing practical experience with a theory base. Writtle's undergraduate and postgraduate degrees are awarded by its partner, The University of Essex.

Academic strengths

All programmes have a practical focus and include diplomas and degrees in such subjects as landscape and garden design, amenity horticulture, floristry, business management, environmental management and animal science. Educational facilities include a library, computer suites, a design centre, CAD workshop, floristry centre, science complex, project gardens, a garden centre shop, farms, a vineyard, orchards and a glasshouse unit. The college library is a bright, spacious building, housing one of the leading specialist book and information collections in the country. 50,000 volumes and 500 periodicals, international databases and internet access on selected PCs make the library a busy area of the college.

An official inspection (HEFCE) particularly cited the excellence of the college's learning resources, curriculum provision and teaching; where 82 per cent of classes were graded excellent or good. There is a consistently high post-education employ-

ment record. Writtle's Postgraduate School offers a number of postgraduate programmes including PhDs plus a growing range of master's degrees including one in international horticulture run jointly with its Dutch partners. Somewhat uniquely the college has a separate Further Education Department offering certificate and diploma programmes with progression opportunities to higher diploma and higher education degree programmes. This department also has a well-established and renowned Floristry School.

Writtle's growing international community currently is represented by over 40 nations including students from Asia, Africa, North America and Europe. English as a Foreign Language (EFL) support is provided free of charge.

Student life

All international students at Writtle have priority for offers of accommodation on campus, and most bedrooms have their own private facilities. There are plenty of recreational facilities on campus and in nearby Chelmsford. The college has a strong international support system, catering not only for specific religious, cultural and dietary requirements but also providing counselling and help with issues such as homesickness.

The college also provides social activities co-ordinated by the international student support officer. The Overseas Students' Club organises quiz evenings, day trips, ethnic theme parties and other activities such as trips to the local bowling alley. The support system also extends to vacation periods as it is recognised that it may be impractical for some overseas students to return home in the holidays.

YORK ST JOHN
COLLEGE OF THE UNIVERSITY OF LEEDS

York

York St John

Write to: International Office, York St John, Lord Mayor's Walk, York YO31 7EX

Tel: +44 (0)1904 716942

Fax: +44 (0)1904 716928

Email: m.williams@yorksj.ac.uk

Students: 5,175 in 2001 (849 postgraduate, 253 international from 15 countries), 26:74 male:female.

Accommodation: university residences from £49 a week self-catered and £69.25 a week catered.

Entrance requirements: normally two A levels plus 3 GCSE passes at grade C or equivalent; pass in European Baccalaureate; 20 points in International Baccalaureate.

EFL: Cambridge Certificate of Proficiency in English, GCSE English, IELTS 6.0, TOEFL 550.

Foundation: in marketing management, humanities, social science, creative and performing arts. Entrance requirements: IELTS 4.5, TOEFL 475.

Fees: classroom courses £5,700 a year; combined classroom and practical/workshop courses £7,020; foundation £4,500.

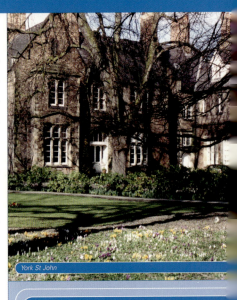

York St John

Student profile

"York is a lovely city with a historic charm. York St John College is next to the old city walls, so you can easily make your way round the city on foot. The international office staff help you with everything, inviting you to regard their office as a second home.

The lecturers are all committed to both their subjects and their students. In conclusion, I think York St John and York itself are well worth a visit."

Doris Puchberger, Germany

York St John is located in one of northern England's most beautiful, unspoilt cathedral cities. York's 13th-century Minster, ringed by narrow streets, overlooks the surrounding medieval buildings and the city's Roman walls.

The college was founded in the mid 19th century as a teacher-training college. The college occupies sites around the city centre and the international office is located in a medieval building beside the Minster. The office will look after students' welfare and deal with any queries they may have. It also gives advice on travel in the UK and Europe as well as on the rich programme of social and cultural events in the North Yorkshire region.

The college's main campus, Lord Mayor's Walk, is a compact eight-acre site. The campus contains teaching accommodation for a wide range of degree subjects plus bar areas, a refectory, a shop, halls of residence, drama, music, dance and television studios, a library, a health centre and the students' union building. London is just two hours away by train.

Academic strengths

The college offers a range of modular degree programmes validated by the University of Leeds. There is a wide choice of subject combinations together with a range of specialist degrees. Many of the degrees have an international slant; they include American studies and English studies. The college places emphasis on vocational courses leading to specific careers including management studies, film, television and theatre studies, communication arts, with options in music, dance and drama, physical education, sport and exercise science, counselling and occupational therapy. The college also has a strong tradition and reputation in teacher education. Other options include community studies, psychology, theology and religious studies, art and design and history.

The International Short Course Centre offers a variety of EFL programmes including a one-year foundation course in English with options available in marketing and management, creative and performing arts, humanities and social science.

Student life

York St John places great emphasis on international contact. It organised its first exchange programme with a college in New Hampshire, USA, 25 years ago. Students can study abroad in North America and Europe and every year students from North America, Europe and East and Southeast Asia come to York St John to study. All international students are warmly welcomed to the campus with its international tradition and they are guaranteed accommodation on campus. English tuition and help in developing study skills are readily available.

York is a small, lively city. There are pubs with jazz and folk music, theatres, cinemas and an art museum plus over 50 social and sports clubs supported by the students union. York city centre is very compact with all major shops within easy walking distance of each other. Parliament Street in the centre offers various forms of live street entertainment such as juggling, classical string trios and the usual collection of buskers.

York

York

The University of York

Write to: Simon Willis, International Office, The University of York, York YO10 5DD

Tel: +44 (0)1904 433534

Fax: +44 (0)1904 434268

Email: international@york.ac.uk

Website: www.york.ac.uk

Students: 8,966 in 2000/01 (2,039 postgraduate, 1,292 international from 99 countries), 51:49 male:female.

Accommodation: guaranteed for single overseas students. Some family and vacation. University residences from £48 a week self-catered. Room in town about £40 a week.

Entrance requirements: three A level passes or international equivalent, see prospectus for grade requirements.

EFL: IELTS 6.0, TOEFL paper-based 550, computer-based 213, Cambridge Proficiency grade C.

Foundation: six-month English Language Foundation programme, one-year York International Foundation programme at local college for entrance to undergraduate courses at York or elsewhere.

Fees: (2001/02) classroom courses £7,362 a year, laboratory courses £9,696 a year.

Universities and colleges of higher education

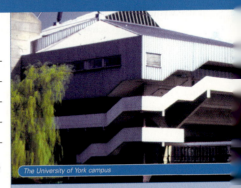
The University of York campus

Student profile

"I came to York from Singapore to read an undergraduate degree in English language and linguistics. The main reasons I chose York were the glowing reports I had heard from friends and relatives who had studied here and its excellent academic reputation. I have to say that I have not been disappointed – if anything, my expectations have been surpassed! I have been encouraged to flourish academically and personally with the staff providing guidance as and when I needed it. I spent a year studying in America as part of my course – that was an amazing experience. After graduation,

I wanted to come back, so I'm studying for a PhD. Everyone I know who has come to York has found it both a rewarding and fulfilling experience."

Dinesh Vaswani, Singapore

The University of York is proud of its national and international reputation for teaching and research which place the university consistently in the top 10 in UK university league tables. The university is based on two sites: one a 200-acre campus at Heslington on the edge of the city, the other in the city centre. The Heslington campus is quiet and relatively traffic free. There is a regular bus service to the city centre from the campus. The Kings Manor, the city campus, houses the Department of History of Art and parts of the English and history departments. This is a historic building dating back to the medieval period.

York is an ancient city that has been an important political, cultural, religious and trading centre since Roman times. This rich heritage is visible in the ancient city walls, medieval lanes, Georgian terraced townhouses and York Minster – the largest medieval cathedral in Europe.

Academic strengths

The university's 24 departments offer a wide range of courses across subjects in the arts, sciences and social sciences. As the university's performance in the teaching quality and research assessment exercise demonstrates, York has strengths in all these areas. Departments which have received excellent ratings include archaeology, biology, computer science, economics, education, electronics, English, history, language and linguistics, management, mathematics, music, physics, philosophy, politics, psychology, social policy and sociology.

International students are found in all subject areas at York. Particularly popular are undergraduate courses in computer science, economics, electronics, English, history, music, psychology and combined courses in the School of Politics, Economics and Philosophy.

The main library provides for all the information needs of undergraduate students. There are over 800 PCs around the campus. These are available 24 hours a day, giving students access to word processing, database and spreadsheet programmes as well as email and the internet. English language support is available for international students through the EFL unit.

Student life

Single, full-time international students are guaranteed accommodation and the university provides most other students with accommodation. This large resident population generates a varied and lively social life with over 60 clubs and societies.

International students form a sizeable proportion of the university community – about 15 per cent in 2000/01. For many, the focus is the Overseas Students' Association (OSA), which represents specific interests of the international population. As well as providing advice and guidance on a range of issues, the OSA arranges a programme of social events throughout the year.

The International Office provides support for students on various issues and acts as a focal point for enquiries. On arrival, students can take part in an orientation and welcome programme, which complements freshers' activities on campus. All international students are assigned a supervisor who is responsible for progress during their time at York. Supervisors form part of a welfare network which is designed to give students maximum support.

The British Council
You will find that the British Council has offices all over the world. Telephone and fax numbers are written as if dialled internationally. You can also try their information centre on +44 (0)161 957 7755 or at www.britishcouncil.org

ALBANIA
British Information Centre
c/o British Embassy
Rruga Skenderbeg 12 Tirana
Tel: + 355 (42) 40856
Fax: + 355 (42) 40858
Email: evis@jcc.al.eu.org
Website: www.britishcouncil.org/albania

ALGERIA
c/o British Embassy
6 Avenue Soudani Boudiemaa
BP 08 Alger-Gare, 1600 Algiers
Tel: +213 (21) 230068
Fax: +213 (21) 230751
Email:
Hafida.Gabouze@algiers.mail.fco.gov.uk
Website: www.britishcouncil.org/algeria

ARGENTINA
The British Council
Marcelo T de Alvear 590
4th floor, C1058AAF, Buenos Aires
Tel: +54 (0) 11 4311 9814
Fax: +54 (0) 11 4311 7747
Email: info@britishcouncil.org.ar
Website: www.britishcouncil.org.ar

AUSTRALIA
Suite 401, Level 4
The Edgecliff Centre
203-233 New South
Head Road, Edgecliff
Sydney NSW 2027
Tel: +61 (2) 9326 2022
Fax: +61 (2) 9327 4868
Email: enquiries@britishcouncil.org.au
Website: www.britishcouncil.org/australia

AUSTRIA
The British Council
Schenkenstrasse 4, 1010 Vienna
Tel: +43 (0) 1533 261684
Fax: +43 (0) 1533 261685
Email: bc.vienna@britishcouncil.at
Website: www.britishcouncil.at

AZERBAIJAN
The British Council
1 Vali Mammadov Street
Ichari Shahar, Baku 370004
Tel: +994 (12) 972013/971593
Fax: +994 (12) 989236
Email: enquiries@britishcouncil.az

BAHRAIN
AMA Centre
146 Shaikh Salman Highway
PO Box 452 Manama 356
Tel: +973 261 555
Fax: +973 241272
Email: amanda.burrell@britishcouncil.org.bh
Website: www.britishcouncil.org/bahrain

BANGLADESH
5 Fuller Road
Dhaka 1000 PO Box 161
Tel: +88 (02) 861 89057/88678
Fax: +88 (02) 861 3375
Email: Dhaka.Enquiries@
bd.britishcouncil.org
Website: www.britishcouncil.org/bangladesh

BELGIUM
The British Council, 15 Rue de la Charité
Liefdadigheidstraat 15, 1210 Brussels
Tel: +32 (2) 227 0841
Fax: +32 (2) 227 0849
Email: enquiries@britishcouncil.be
Website: www.britishcouncil.org/belgium

BOLIVIA
The British Council, Avenida Arce 2708
(esq. Campos) La Paz
Tel: +591 (2) 431240
Fax: +591 (2) 431377
Email: information@britishcouncil.org.bo
Website: www.britishcouncil.org/bolivia

BOSNIA-HERZEGOVINA
Obala Kulina Bana 4
2nd floor, 71 000 Sarajevo
Bosnia-Herzegovina
Tel: +(00) 387 (33) 200895/207836
Fax: +(00) 387 (33) 200890
Email: British.Council@britishcouncil.ba
Website: www.britishcouncil.org/
bosniaherzegovina

BOTSWANA
The British Council High Commission
Building, PO Box 439, Gaborone
Tel: +(010) 267 353602
Fax: +(010) 267 356643
Email:general.enquiries@bc.bw
Website: www.britishcouncil.org/botswana

BRAZIL
Ed. Centro Empresarial Varig
SCN.Quadra 04 Bloco B
Torre Oeste conjunto 202
Brasilia – DF 70710-926 Brazil
Tel: +55 (0) 61 327 7230
Fax: +55 (0) 61 326 8917
Email: brasilia@britishcouncil.org.br
Website: www.britishcouncil.org/brazil

BRUNEI
2.01, 2nd Floor, Block D
Kompleks Bangunan Yayasan Sultan Haji
Jalan Pretty, Bandar Seri Begawan BS8711
Tel: +359 (0) 29 424344
Fax: +359 (0) 87 424344
Email: all.enquiries@bn.britishcouncil.org
Website: www.britishcouncil.org/brunei

BULGARIA
The British Council
7 Krakra Street, 1504 Sofia
Tel: +359 (2) 946 0098/0099
Fax: +359 (2) 946 0102
Email: bc.sofia@britishcouncil.bg
Website: www.britishcouncil.org/bulgaria

BURMA
The British Council
78 Kanna Road, (PO Box 638)
Yangon, Myanmar
Tel: +95 (0) 1 254658/256290/256291
Fax: +95 (0) 1 245345
Email: enquiries@britishcouncil.org.mm
Website: www.britishcouncil.org/burma

CAMEROON
Immeuble Christo
Avenue Charles de Gaulle
BP 818, Yaoundé
Tel: +237 211696/203172
Fax: +237 215691
Email:
general.enquiries@bc-yaounde.iccnet.cm
Website: www.britishcouncil.org/cameroon

CANADA
British High Commission
80 Elgin Street Ottawa
Ontario KIP 5K7
Tel: +1 613 237 1542
Fax: +1 613 232 2533
Email: ottawa.enquiries@
ca.britishcouncil.org
Website: www.britishcouncil.org/canada

CHILE
Eliodoro Yáñez Óez 832
Providencia Santiago
Tel: +56 (2) 4106900
Fax: +56 (2) 4106929
Email: info@britcouncil.cl
Website: www.britishcouncil.org.chile

PEOPLE'S REPUBLIC OF CHINA
British Embassy
3/4 Floor Landmark Building
Tower 1, 8 Dongsanhuan Beilu
Beijing 100004
Tel: +86 (10) 6590 6903
Fax: +86 (10) 6590 0977
Email: bc.beijing@britishcouncil.org.cn
Website: www.britishcouncil.org.cn

COLOMBIA
Calle 87 No 12-79 Bogotá
Tel: +57 (1) 618 7680
Fax: +57 (1) 218 7754
Email: info@britishcouncil.org.co
Website: www.britishcouncil.org.co

CROATIA
Illica 12, pp 55
10001 Zagreb
Tel: +385 (0) 1 481 3700
Fax: +385 (0) 1 483 3955
Email: zagreb.info@britishcouncil.hr
Website: www.britshcouncil.org/croatia

CUBA
The British Embassy
Calle 34 No 702, esq 7ma
Avenida Miramar C Habana
Tel: +53 (0) 7 241 771
Fax: +53 (0) 7 249 214
Email: britcoun@ip.etecsa.cu
Website: www.britishcouncil.org/cuba

CYPRUS
The British Council
3 Museum Street
CY-1097 Nicosia
(Postal address:
PO Box 25654
CY-1387 Nicosia)
Tel: +357 (2) 665152
Fax: +357(2) 677257
Email: Enquiries@britishcouncil.org.cy
Website: www.britishcouncil.org/cyprus

CZECH REPUBLIC
Národní 10, 12501 Praga 1
Tel: 420 (0) 2 2199 1111
Fax: 420 (0) 2 2199 3839
Email: info@britishcouncil.cz
Website: www.britishcouncil.org/czechrepublic

DENMARK
denmark
Gammel Mont 12
1117 Copenhagen K
Tel: +45 (33) 369 400
Fax: +45 (33) 359 406
Email: british.council@britishcouncil.dk
Website: www.britishcouncil.org/

EAST JERUSALEM
WEST BANK and GAZA
Al-Nuzha Building
4 Abu Obeida Street
PO Box 19136 Jerusalem
Tel: +972 (0) 2 628 2545
Fax: +972 (0) 2 628 3021
Email: omar.hathieh@ej.britishcouncil.org
Website: www.ej.britishcouncil.org

ECUADOR
British Embassy
Piso 14, Edificio Citiplaza
Avienda Naciones
Unidas y Republica de El Salvador
PO Box 17-17-830 Quito
Tel: +593 (2) 970 800/970 801
Fax: +593 (2) 970 809
Email: britembq@interactive.net.ec
Website: www.britishcouncil.org/ecuador

EGYPT
The British Council
192 El Nil St, Agouza, Cairo
Tel: + 20 (2) 3031514
Fax: +20 (2) 3443076
Email: british.council@britishcouncil.org.eg
Website: www.britishcouncil.org/egypt

ERITREA
Lorenzo Tazaz Street No 23
PO Box 997 Asmara
Tel: +291 (1) 123415/120529
Fax: +29 (1) 127230
Email: britcoun@eol.com.er
Website: www.britishcouncil.org/eritrea

ESTONIA
British Council Vana Posti 7
Tallinn 10146
Tel: +372 (6) 314010
Fax: +372 (6) 313111
Email: british.council@britishcouncil.ee
Website: www.britishcouncil.org/estonia

ETHIOPIA
PO Box 1043
Artistic Building
Adwa Avenue
Addis Ababa
Tel: +251 (1) 550 022
Fax: +251 (1) 552 544
Email: britcoun@telecom.net.et
Website: www.britishcouncil.org/ethiopia

FINLAND
Hakaniemenkatu 2
00530 Helsinki
Tel: +358 (9) 774 3330
Fax: +358 (9) 701 8725
Email: info@britishcouncil.fi
Website: www.britishcouncil.org/finland

FRANCE
The British Council
9 rue de Constantine
75340 Paris Cedex 07
Tel: +33 (0) 1 4955 7300
Fax: +33 (0) 1 4705 7702
Email: information@britishcouncil.fr
Website: www.britishcouncil.org/france

GEORGIA
University Building 8
13 Chavchavadze Avenue
2nd floor Tbilisi 380079
Tel: +995 (32) 252360
Fax: +995 (32) 250 409
Email: office@britishcouncil.org.ge
Website: www.britishcouncil.org/georgia

GERMANY
The British Council
Hackescher Markt 1, 10178 Berlin
Tel: +49 (30) 311 099
Fax: +49 (30) 311 099
Email: bc.berlin@britcoun.de
Website: www.britishcouncil.org/germany

GHANA
The British Council, 11 Liberia Road
PO Box GP 771 Accra
Tel: +233 (21) 244744
Fax: +233 (21) 240330
Email: derek.nikoi@britishcouncil.org.gh
Website: www.britishcouncil.org/ghana

GREECE
The British Council
17 Kolonaki Square, GR10673 Athens
Tel: +30 (1) 369 2333
Fax: +30 (1) 363 4769
Email: general.enquiries@britishcouncil.gr
Website: www.britishcouncil.org/greece

HONG KONG
3 Supreme Court Road, Admiralty
Tel: +852 291 35100
Fax: +852 291 35102
Email: info@britishcouncil.org.hk
Website: www.britishcouncil.org/hongkong

HUNGARY
The British Council
Benezúr u. 26, 1068 Budapest
Tel: +361 4784700
Fax: +361 3425728
Email: information@britishcouncil.hu
Website: www.britishcouncil.org/hungary

INDIA
British Council Division
British High Commission
17 Kasturba Gandhi Marg
New Delhi 110 001
Tel: +91 (11) 3711401/3710111/3710555
Fax: +91 (11) 3710717/3719616
Email: delhi.enquiry@in.britishcouncil.org
Website: www.britishcouncil.org/india

INDONESIA
The British Council
S Widjojo Centre, Jalan Jenderal Sudirman
Kav 71, Jakarta 12190
Tel: +62 (21) 252 4115
Fax: +62 (21) 252 4129
Email: information@britishcouncil.or.id
Website: www.britcoun.or.id

IRISH REPUBLIC
The British Council
Newmount House
22/24 Lower Mount Street, Dublin 2
Tel: +3531 676 4088/676 6943
Fax: +3531 676 6945
Email: bcdublin@iol.ie
Website: www.britishcouncil.org/ireland

ISRAEL
The British Council
140 Hayarkon Street
PO Box 3302, Tel Aviv 61032
Tel: +972 (0) 3 5222194/
Fax: +972 (0) 3 5221229
Email: bcta@britishcouncil.org.il
Website: www.britishcouncil.org/israel

ITALY
The British Council
Via Quattro Fontane 20
00184 Rome
Tel: +39 (06) 478141
Fax: + 39 (06) 4814296
Website: www.britishcouncil.org/italy

JAMAICA
The British High Commission
28 Trafalgar Road Kingston 10.
Tel: +1 876 296915/9297049
Fax: +1 876 9603030
Email: bcjamaica@britishcouncil.org.jm
Website: www.britishcouncil.org/caribbean

JAPAN
The British Council
1-2 Kagurazaka, Shinjuku-ku
Tokyo 162-0825
Tel: +81 (0) 3 3235 8031
Tel: +81 (0) 3 3235 8011
Email: bctokyo@britishcouncil.or.jp
Website: www.britishcouncil.org/japan

JORDAN
First Circle, Jebel Amman
PO Box 634 Amman 11118
Tel: +962 (6) 4636147
Fax: +962 (6) 4656413
Email: bcamman@britishcouncil.org.jo
Website: www.britishcouncil.org/jordan

KAZAKHSTAN
13 Republic Square
Almaty 480013, Kazakhstan

Tel: +7 (3272) 63339
Fax: +7 (3272) 633443
Email: general@kz.britishcouncil.org
Website: www.britishcouncil.org/kazakhstan

KENYA
The British Council, ICEA Building, Kenyatta
Avenue, PO Box 40751 Nairobi
Tel: +254 (0) 2 334855
Fax: +254 (0) 2 339854
Email: information@britishcouncil.or.ke
Website: www.britishcouncil.org/kenya

KUWAIT
The British Council, 2 Al Arabi Street
Mansouriya Kuwait
Tel: +965 252 0067/0068
Fax: +965 252 0069
Email: bc.kuwait@kw.britishcouncil.org
Website: www.britishcouncil.org/kuwait

KYRGYZSTAN
Hotel of the Bishkek Business School
The British Council Information Point
237 Panfilov Street, Room
202b, 720000 Bishkek
Tel/Fax: +996 3312 220324
Email: bc@britcoun.elcat.kg
Website: www.britishcouncil.org/kyrgyzstan

LESOTHO
The British Council, Hobson's Square
PO Box 429 Maseru 100
Tel: + 266 312609
Fax: +266 310363
Website: www.britishcouncil.org/lesotho

LIBYA
British Embassy
24th Floor Bourj al Fateh
PO Box 4206 Tripoli
Tel: +218 21 335 1473/5
Fax: +218 21 335 1471
Email: british.council@lttnet.net

LEBANON
The British Council
Sidani Street
Azar Building Ras Beirut
Tel: +961 (1) 740123
Fax: +961 (1) 739461
Email: general.enquiries@
lb.britishcouncil.org
Website: www.britishcouncil.org/lebanon

LITHUANIA
The British Council
Vilnius 39/6 LT001 Vilnius
Tel: +370 (2) 616607/222615
Fax: +370 (2) 221602
Email: mail@britishcouncil.lt
Website: www.britishcouncil.org/lithuania

MACEDONIA
British Information Centre
Bulevar Goce Delcev 6
PO Box 562, 1000 Skopje
Tel: +389 02 1 35035
Fax: +389 02 1 35036

MALAYSIA
Jalan Bukit Aman
PO Box 10539
50916 Kuala Lumpur
Tel: +60 (0) 3 2698 7555
Fax: +60 (0) 3 2693 72 14
Email: Kualalumpur@britishcouncil.org.
Website: www.britishcouncil.org/malaysia

MALTA
The British Council Education and
Information Centre, c/o British High
Commission, 7 St Anne St
Floriana VLT 15
Tel: +(00) 356 226 227
Fax: +(00) 356 226 207
Email: ronnie.micallef@britishcouncil.org.mt
Website: www.britishcouncil.org/malta

MAURITIUS
36 Rue de Tanger, BP 427 Rabat
Tel: +212 (0) 3776 0836
Fax: +212 (0) 3776 0850
Email:
britcoun.morocco@britishcouncil.org.ma
Website: www.britishcouncil.org/morocco

MEXICO
The British Council
Lope de Vega 316
CP 11570 Mexico DF
Tel: +52 (5) 263 1900
Email: bcmexico@britishcouncil.org.mx
Website: www.britishcouncil.org/mexico

MOROCCO
The British Council
PO Box 111, Royal Road
Rose Hill
Tel: +230 4549550/1/2
Fax: +230 4549553
Email:
general.enquiries@mu.britishcouncil.org
Website: www.britishcouncil.org/mauritius

MOZAMBIQUE
Rua John Issa, 226
PO Box 4178 Maputo
Tel: +258 (1) 310 921/925
Fax: +258 (1) 421577
Email: General.enquiries@
britishcouncil.org.mz
Website: www.britishcouncil.org/mozambique

NAMIBIA
British Council, 1-5 Peter Muller Street
Private Bag 13392 Windhoek
Tel: +264 (61) 226776
Fax: + 264 (61) 227530
Email: general.enquiries@britcoun.org.na
Website: www.britishcouncil.org/namibia

NEPAL
PO Box 640
Lainchaur Kathmandu
Tel: +977 (1) 410798
Fax: +977 (1) 410545
Email: general.enquiry@
britishcouncil.org.np
Website: www.britishcouncil.org/nepal

NETHERLANDS
The British Council
Keizersgracht 269
1016 ED Amsterdam
Tel: +31 (20) 550 6060
Fax: +31 (20) 620 7389
Email: education.info@britishcouncil.nl
Website: www.britishcouncil.org/netherlands

NEW ZEALAND
44 Hill Street
PO Box 1812 Wellington 6001
Tel: +64 (0) 9373 4545
Fax: +64 (0) 4473 6261
Email: enquiries@britishcouncil.org.nz
Website: www.britishcouncil.org.nz

NIGERIA
Abuja Centre, Plot 2965, IBB Way
Maitama PMB 550 Garki
Abuja Nigeria
Tel: +413 7870/7
Fax: +413 0902
Email: info.abuja@ng.britishcouncil.org
Website: www.britishcouncil.org/nigeria

NORWAY
The British Council
Fridtjof Nansens Plass 5
0160 Oslo
Tel: +47 22396 195
Fax: +47 22424 039
Email: british.council@britishcouncil.no
Website: www.britishcouncil.org/nigeria

OMAN
The British Council
Road One Madinat al Sultan, Qaboos
West, Muscat
PO Box 73 Postal Code 115
Tel: +968 600548
Fax: +968 699613
Email: bc.muscat@om.britishcouncil.org
Website: www.britishcouncil.org/oman

PAKISTAN
Block14, Civic Centre G 6
PO Box 1135 Islamabad 44000
Tel: +92 (51)1111 424 424
Fax: +92 (51) 111 425 425
Email: bc.islamabad@britishcouncil.org.pk
Website: www.britishcouncil.org/pakistan

PERU
Calle Alberto Lynch 110
San Isidro, Lima 27, Perú
Tel: +51 (1) 2217552
Fax: +51 (1) 4215215
Email: postmaster@britishcouncil.org.pe
Website: www.britishcouncil.org/peru

PHILIPPINES
10th Floor
Taipan Place
Emerald Avenue
Ortigas Centre Pasig City 1605
Tel: +63 (2) 914 1011-14
Fax: +63 (2) 914 1020
Email: britishcouncil@britishcouncil.org.ph
Website: www.britishcouncil.org/philippines

POLAND
The British Council
Al. Jerozolimskie 59
00 697 Warsaw
Tel: +48 (22) 695 5900
Fax: +49 (22) 621 9955
Website: www.britishcouncil.org/poland

PORTUGAL
The British Council
Rua de Sao Marcal, 174
1249 062 Lisbon
Tel: +351 (21) 347 6141
Fax: +351 (21) 347 6151
Website: www.britishcouncil.org/portugal

QATAR
93 Al Sadd Street
PO Box 2992 Doha
Tel: +974 4426193/4
Fax: +974 423315
Email: Alan Smart@qa.britishcouncil.org
Website: www.britishcouncil.org/qatar

ROMANIA
The British Council
Calea Dorobantilor 14
71132 Bucharest
Tel: +40 (0) 1 210 0314
Fax: +40 (0) 1 2100310
Email: bc.romania@
bc-bucharest.bcouncil.org
Website: www.britishcouncil.org/romania

RUSSIA
The British Council
VGBIL Ulitsa Nikoloyamskaya 1
Moscow 109189
Tel: + (095) 234 0201
Fax: + (095) 234 0205
Email: bc.moscow@britishcouncil.ru
Website: www.britishcouncil.org/russia

SAUDI ARABIA
The British Council, Tower B
2nd floor, Al Mousa Centre
Olaya Street, PO Box 58012
Riyadh 11594
Tel: +966 (0) 1 4621818
Fax: + 966 (0) 1 4620663
Email: Enquiry.riyadh@
sa.britishcouncil.org
Website: www.britishcouncil.org/saudiarabia

SENEGAL
The British Council
34-36 Boulevard, de la Republique
BP 6232 Dakar
Tel: +221 822 2015
Fax: +221 821 8136
Email: bcdakar@sonatel.senet.net
Website: www.britishcouncil.org/senegal

SIERRA LEONE
The British Council
Tower Hill PO Box 124, Freetown
Tel: +232 (22) 222223
Fax: +232 (22) 224123
Email: bcouncil@sierratel.sl
Website: www.britishcouncil.org/sierraleone

SINGAPORE
The British Council
30 Napier Road 258509
Tel: +65 4731111
Fax: +65 4721010
Email:britcoun@britishcouncil.org.sg
Website: www.britishcouncil.org/singapore

SLOVAKIA
The British Council
Panska 17
PO Box 68
814 99 Bratislava 01
Tel: +421 (2) 54431074
Website: www.britishcouncil.org/slovakia

SLOVENIA
The British Council
Cankarjevo Nabrezje 27
1000 Ljubljana
Tel: +386 (0) 12000130
Fax: +386 (0) 11264446
Email: info@britishcouncil.si

SOUTH AFRICA
The British Council
76 Juta Street
Braamfontein 2017
Johannesburg PO Box 30637
Tel: +27 (0) 11 403 3316
Fax: +27 (0) 11 339 7806/3715
Website: www.britishcouncil.org/southafrica

SPAIN
The British Council
Paseo del General Martinez
Campos 31 28010 Madrid
Tel: +34 (91) 337 3500
Fax: +34 (91) 337 3573
Email: madrid@britishcouncil.es
Website: www.britishcouncil.org/spain

SRI LANKA
49 Alfred House Gardens
PO Box 753, Colombo 3
Tel: +94 1 581171
Fax: +94 1 587079
Email: enquiries@britishcouncil.lk
Website: www.britishcouncil.lk

SUDAN
14 Abu Sin Street
PO Box 1253, Central Khartoum
Tel: + 249 (11) 780817
Fax: +249 (11) 774935
Email: paul.doubleday@sd.britishcouncil.org
Website: www.britishcouncil.org/sudan

SWAZILAND
The British Council
Ground Floor, Lilunga House
Gilfillan Street, Mbabane
Tel: +268 (40) 44605
Fax: +268 (40) 43101
Email: info@britishcouncil.sz
Website: www.britishcouncil.org/swaziland

SWEDEN
The British Council
c/o British Embassy, PO Box 27819
S-115 93 Stockholm
Tel: + 46 (0) 8 663 6004
Fax: + 46 (0) 8 663 7271
Email: info@britishcouncil.se
Website: www.britishcouncil.org/sweden

SWITZERLAND
The British Council
Box 532 Sennweg 2, PO 3000 Beme 11
Tel: + (031) 301 1473
Fax: + (031) 301 1459
Email: caroline.morrissey@britishcouncil.ch
Website: www.britishcouncil.org/switzerland

SYRIA
The BritisH Council
Maysaloun Street, Shalaan
PO Box 33105, Damascus
Tel: +963 (11) 3310631
Fax: +963 (11) 3321467
Email: general.enquiries@
bc-damascus.bcouncil.org
Website: www.britishcouncil.org/syria

TAIWAN
British Trade and Cultural Office
Education and Cultural Section
7F-1, Fu Key Building
No 99 Jen Ai Road
Section 2, Taipei 100
Tel: +886 (2) 2396 2238
Fax: +886 (2) 2341 5749
Email: inquiries@britishcouncil.org.tw
Website: www.britishcouncil.org.tw

TANZANIA
The British Council, Samora Avenue/Ohio
Street, PO Box 9100, Dar Es Salaam
Tel: +255 (22) 2116574
Fax: +255 (22) 2112669
Email: info@britishcouncil.or.tz.or.th
Website: www.britishcouncil.org/tanzania

THAILAND
254 Chulalongkorn 64
Siam Square, Phayathai Road
Pathumwan, Bangkok 10330
Tel: + 66 (2) 652 5480/9
Fax: +66 (2) 2535312
Email: info@britishcouncil.org.tn
Website: www.britishcouncil.org/thailand

TRINIDAD (Caribbean)
c/o British High Commission
19 St Clair Avenue, St Clair, PO Box 778
Port of Spain, Trinidad
Tel: +1 868 628 0565
Fax: +1 868 622 2853
Email: Magella.Moreau@britishcouncil.org.tt

TUNISIA
c/o British Embassy
5 Place de la Victoire
BP 229 Tunis 1015 RP
Tel: +216 (1) 259053/351754
Fax: +216 (1) 353411
Email: info@britishcouncil.org.tn
Website: www.britishcouncil.org/tunisia

TURKEY
The British Council
Esat Caddesi No 41
Kucukesat
06660 Ankara
Tel: +90 (312) 424 1644
Fax: +90 (312) 427 6182
Email: bc.ankara@britishcouncil.org.tr
Website: www.britishcouncil.org.tr

UGANDA
Ground Floor, Rwenzori Courts
Plot 2 and 4a, Nakasero Road
PO Box 7070 Kampala
Tel: +256 (041) 234 725/730
Fax: +256 (041) 254853
Email: info@britishcouncil.org.ug
Website: www.britishcouncil.org/uganda

UKRAINE
4/12 Vul Hryhoriya Skovorody
Kyiv 04070
Tel:+380 (44) 490 5600
Fax: +380 (44) 490 5602
Email: enquiry@britishcouncil.org.ua
Website: www.britishcouncil.org/ukraine

UNITED ARAB EMIRATES
The British Council
illa no 7, Al Nasr Street, Khalidiya
Abu Dhabi, PO Box 46523
Tel: +971 (2) 659300
Fax:+971 (2) 664340
Email: information@britishcouncil.org.ae
Website: www.britishcouncil.org/uae

USA
The British Council, Cultural Department
The British Embassy
3100 Massachusetts Avenue NW
Washington DC 20008-3600
Tel: +1 800 488 2235
Fax: +1 202 588 7918
Email: studyintheuk@us.britishcouncil.org
Website: www.studyintheuk.org

UZBEKISTAN
British Council Information Centre
11 D. Kounaev Street
Tashkent 700031
Tel: +998 (71) 120 6752
Fax: +998 (71) 1206371
Email: bc-tashkent@britishcouncil.uz
Website: www.britishcouncil.org/uzbekistan

VENEZUELA
The British Council, Piso 3 Av. Principal de
El Bosque Chacaito, Caracas 1065
Tel: +58 (212) 952 9965/9757
Fax: +58 (212) 952 9691
Email: bc-venezuela@britishcouncil.org.ve
Website: www.britishcouncil.org/venezuela

VIETNAM
The British Council
40 Cat Linh Street, Hanoi
Tel: +84 (0) 4 8436780
Fax: +84 (0) 4 8434962
Email: bchanoi@britishcouncil.org.vn
Website: www.britishcouncil.org/vietnam

YEMEN
The British Council
3rd Floor, Administrative Tower
Sana'a Trade Centre, Algiers Street
PO Box 2157 Sana'a
Tel: +967 (1) 215000/215006/215816
Fax: +967 (1) 215009
Email: britishcouncil@
britishcouncil.org.ye
Website: www.britishcouncil.org/yemen

YUGOSLAVIA
Generala Zdanova 34
(Mezanin) Belgrade
Tel: +381 (11) 3232 441/2
Fax: +381 (11) 631664
Email: bcyu@britcoun.org.yu

ZAMBIA
Heroes Place, Cairo Road
(PO Box 34571) Lusaka, Zambia
Tel: +260 (1) 223602/228332/3/4
Fax: +260 (1) 224124
Email: info@britishcouncil.org.zm
Website: www.britishcouncil.org/zambia

ZIMBABWE
The British Council
Corner House Samora
Machel Avenue
PO Box 664 Harare
Tel: + 263 (4) 775313
Fax: +263 (4) 756661
Email: general.enquiries@britishcouncil.org.zw
Website: www.britishcouncil.org.zw

ENGLAND
Birmingham
The British Council
1st Floor, Guild of Students
The University of Birmingham
Edgbaston Park Road
Birmingham B15 2TU
Tel: +44 (0)121 693 3345
Fax: +44 (0)121 693 3346
Email: chris.gately@britishcouncil.org

Brighton
Room 156 Arts B Building, University of
Sussex, Falmer, East Sussex BN I 9RH
Tel: +44 (0)1273 678363
Fax: +44 (0)1273 689562
Email: reena.johl@britishcouncil.org

Bristol
Berkeley House, 7 Richmond Hill Avenue
Clifton, Bristol BS8 1BG
Tel: +44 (0)117 970 8466
Fax: +44 (0)117 970 6638

Cambridge
5/7 New Park Street, Cambridge CB5 8AT
Tel: +44 (0)1223 354786
Fax: +44 (0)1223 361432
Email: ian.marvin@britishcouncil.org

Canterbury
PO Box 602, Canterbury
Kent CT1 2GZ
Tel: +44 (0)1227 760374
Fax: +44 (0)1227 760370
Email: anita.selwood@britishcouncil.org

Coventry
Room 232, International
Manufacturing Centre
The University of Warwick
Coventry CV4 7AL
Tel: +44 (0)24 7657 2515
Fax: +44 (0)24 7657 2529
Email: helen.fearn@britishcouncil.org

Leeds
Room B01, 18 Blenheim Terrace
University of Leeds, Leeds LS2 9HD
Tel: +44 (0)113 2439502
Fax: +44 (0)113 2432294
Email: lisa.firth@britishcouncil.org

Liverpool
PO Box 140
New Ferry CH63 8WE
Tel: +44 (0)151 644 6390
Fax: +44 (0)151 644 6820
Email: Sarah.Kiaer@britishcouncil.org

London
10 Spring Gardens
London SW1A 2BN
Tel: +44 (0) 20 7930 8466
Fax: +44 (0) 20 7839 6347

Loughborough
Room X1.12
Pilkington Library
Loughborough University
Loughborough
Leicestershire LE11 3TU
Tel: +44 (0)1509 228090
Fax: +44 (0)1509 218065
Email: ellen.alcock@britishcouncil.org

Manchester
Bridgewater House
58 Whitworth Street
Manchester M1 6BB
Tel: +44 (0)161 957 7000
Fax: +44 (0)161 957 7111
Email: general.enquiries@
britishcouncil.org

Newcastle-upon-Tyne
13 Windsor Terrace
Jesmond
Newcastle-upon-Tyne NE2 4HE
Tel: +44 (0)191 281 4366
Fax: +44 (0)191 281 6919
Email: judith.elliot@britishcouncil.org

Nottingham
Room C18
C20 Old Engineering Building
Cherry Tree Hill
The University of Nottingham
Nottingham NG7 2RD
Tel: +44 (0)115 951 6116
Fax: +44 (0)115 951 4644
Email: katy.manns@britishcouncil.org

Oxford
1 Beaumont Place
Oxford OX1 2PJ
Tel: +44 (0)1865 316636
Fax: +44 (0)1865 557368/516590
Email: anjum.masood@britishcouncil.org

Reading
Agriculture Building
Room 1L 32
The University of Reading
Earley Gate
PO Box 237
Reading RG6 6AR
Tel: +44 (0)118 931 6980
Fax: +44 (0)118 921 0578
Email: maureen.kirk@britishcouncil.org

SCOTLAND
Edinburgh
3 Bruntsfield Crescent
Edinburgh EH10 4HD
Tel: +44 (0)131 447 4716
Fax: +44 (0)131 452 8487
Email: eunice.crook@britishcouncil.org
Website: www.britishcouncil.org/scotland

WALES
Cardiff
28 Park Place
Cardiff CF1 3QE
Tel: +44 (0)29 2039 7346
Fax: +44 (0)29 2023 7494
Email: tony.deyes@britishcouncil.org
Website: www.britishcouncil.org/wales

NORTHERN IRELAND
Belfast
The British Council
Norwich Union House
7 Fountain Street
Belfast BT1 5 EG
Tel: +44 (0)28 9023 3440
Fax: +44 (0)28 9024 0341
Email: peter.lyner@britishcouncil.org
Website: www.britishcouncil.org/nireland

Abberley Hall
Head: J G W Walker
Worcester, WR6 6DD
Tel: +44 (0)1299 896275
Fax: +44 (0)1299 896875
Email: postmaster@abberleyhall.co.uk
Website: www.abberleyhall.co.uk

Abbey School
Head: J H Milton
Church Street, Tewkesbury GL20 5PD
Tel: +44 (0)1684 294460
Fax: +44 (0)1684 290797
Email: abbeyschtewks@ukonline.co.uk

Abbot's Hill
Head: Mrs Kerstin Lewis
Bunkers Lane, Hemel Hempstead HP3 8RP
Tel: +44 (0)1442 240333
Fax: +44 (0)1442 269981
Email: klewis@abbotshill.herts.sch.uk

Abbotsholme School
Head: Dr Stephen Tommis
Rocester, Uttoxeter ST14 5BS
Tel: +44 (0)1889 590217
Fax: +44 (0)1889 591001
Email: headabbotshome@btconnect.com

Aberlour House
Head: N W Gardner
Aberlour AB38 9LJ
Tel: +44 (0)1340 871267
Fax: +44 (0)1340 872925
Email: admissions@aberlourhouse.org.uk
Website: www.aberlourhouse.org.uk

Abingdon School
Head: M St John Parker
Park Road, Abingdon OX14 1DE
Tel: +44 (0)1235 521563
Fax: +44 (0)1235 849085
Email: registrar@abingdon.org.uk
Website: www.abingdon.org.uk

Ackworth School
Head: M J Dickinson
Ackworth, Pontefract WF7 7LT
Tel: +44 (0)1977 611401
Fax: +44 (0)1977 616225
Email: Ackworthq@aol.com
Website: www.Ackworth.w-yorks.sch.uk

Adcote School for Girls
Head: Mrs A E Read
Little Ness, Shrewsbury SY4 2JY
Tel: +44 (0)1939 260202
Fax: +44 (0)1939 261300
Email: headmistress@adcoteschool.co.uk

Aldenham School
Head: Richard Harman
Elstree, Borehamwood WD6 3AJ
Tel: +44 (0)1923 858122
Fax: +44 (0)1923 854410
Email: enquiries@aldenham.com
Website: www.aldenham.com

Aldro
Head: D W N Aston
Shackleford, Godalming, GU8 6AS
Tel: +44 (0)1483 810266
Fax: +44 (0)1483 409010
Email: hm@aldro.demon.co.uk
Website: www.aldro.surrey.sch.uk

Aldwickbury School
Head: P H Jeffery
Wheathampstead Road
Harpenden AL5 1AE
Tel: +44 (0)1582 713022
Fax: +44 (0)1582 767696
Email: Head@aldwickbury.herts.sch.uk

All Hallows School
Head: C J Bird
Cranmore Hall, East Cranmore
Shepton Mallet BA4 4SF
Tel: +44 (0)1749 880227
Fax: +44 (0)1749 880709
Email: info@allhallows.somerset.sch.uk
Website: ww.allhallows.somerset.sch.uk

American Community School
Head: T Lehman
Heywood, Portsmouth Road
Cobham KT11 1BL
Tel: +44 (0)1932 867251
Fax: +44 (0)1932 869790
Email: tlehman@acs-england.co.uk
Website: www.acs-england.co.uk

Amesbury
Head: N G Taylor
Hindhead GU26 6BL
Tel: +44 (0)1428 604322
Fax: +44 (0)1428 607715

Ampleforth College
Head: The Rev G F L Chamberlain OSB
York YO62 4ER
Tel: +44 (0)1439 766000
Fax: +44 (0)1439 788330
Email: admin@ampleforth.org.uk
Website: www.ampleforthcollege.york.sch.uk

Appleford School
Head: P Stanley
Shrewton, Salisbury SP3 4HL
Tel: +44 (0)1980 621020
Fax: +44 (0)1980 621366
Email: secretary@appleford.demon.co.uk

Aravon Preparatory School
Head: Kevin Allwright
Old Conna House, Bray, Eire
Tel: +353 1282 1355
Fax: +353 1282 1242
Email: aravon@indigo.ie

Ardingly College
Head: John R Franklin
Haywards Heath
RH17 6SQ
Tel: +44 (0)1444 892577
Fax: +44 (0)1444 892266
Email: registrar@ardingly.com
Website: www.ardingly.com

Ardingly College Junior School
Head: Mrs J L Robinson
Haywards Heath, RH17 6SQ
Tel: +44 (0)1444 892279
Fax: +44 (0)1444 892169
Email: registrar@ardingly.com
Website: www.ardingly.com

Ardvreck School
Head: P G Watson
Perthshire
Crieff PH7 4EX
Tel: +44 (0)1764 653112
Fax: +44 (0)1764 654920
Email: ardvreck@bosinternet.com
Website: www.ardvreck.co.uk

Arts Educational School
Head: Mrs J D Billing
Tring Park, Tring HP23 5LX
Tel: +44 (0)1442 824255
Fax: +44 (0)1442 891069
Email: info@aes-tring.com
Website: www.aes-tring.com

Ashdown House
Head: AJ Fowler-Watt
Forest Row RH18 5JY
Tel: +44 (0)134 282 2574
Fax: +44 (0)134 282 4380
Email: bursar@ashdown-house.e-sussex.sch.uk
Website: www.ashdownhouse.co.uk

Ashfold
Head: M O M Chitty
Dorton, Aylesbury HP18 9NG
Tel: +44 (0)1844 238237
Fax: +44 (0)1844 238505
Email: ashfold@rmplc.co.uk
Website: www.ashfold.bucks.sch.uk

Ashford School
Head: Mrs Paula Holloway
East Hill, Ashford TN24 8PB
Tel: +44 (0)1233 625171
Fax: +44 (0)1233 647185
Email: registrar@ashfordschool.co.uk
Website: www.ashfordschool.co.uk

Ashville College
Head: M H Crosby, Harrogate HG2 9JP
Tel: +44 (0)1423 566358
Fax: +44 (0)1423 505142
Email: ashville@ashville.co.uk
Website: www.ashville.co.uk

Aysgarth School Trust Ltd
Head: J C Hodgkinson and P J Southall
Bedale DL8 1TF
Tel: +44 (0)1677 450240
Fax: +44 (0)1677 450736
Email: enquiries@aysgarthschool.co.uk

Badminton Junior School
Head: Mrs A Lloyd
Westbury-on-Trym, Bristol BS9 3BA
Tel: +44 (0)117 905 5222
Fax: +44 (0)117 962 8963
Email: juniorhead@badminton.bristol.sch.uk
Website: www.badminton.bristol.sch.uk

Badminton School
Head: Mrs J Scarrow
Westbury-on-Trym, Bristol BS9 3BA
Tel: +44 (0)117 905 5200
Fax: +44 (0)117 962 8963
Email: registrar@badminton.bristol.sch.uk
Website: www.badminton.bristol.sch.uk

Barnard Castle School
Head: M D Featherstone
Barnard Castle DL12 8UN
Tel: +44 (0)1833 690222
Fax: +44 (0)1833 638985
Email: secretary@barneyschool.org.uk
Website: www.barneyschool.org.uk

Barnardiston Hall Preparatory School
Head: Lt Col K A Boulter
Barnardiston, Haverhill CB9 7TG
Tel: +44 (0)1440 786316
Fax: +44 (0)1440 786355

Battle Abbey School
Head: R C Clark
Battle TN33 0AD
Tel: +44 (0)1424 772385
Fax: +44 (0)1424 773573
Email: office@
battleabbeyschool.btinternet.com
Website: www.battleabbeyschool.com

Beachborough School
Head: A J L Boardman
Westbury, Brackley NN13 5LB
Tel: +44 (0)1280 700071
Fax: +44 (0)1280 704839
Email: tonyhead@aol.com

Bearwood College
Head: S G G Aiano
Bearwood Wokingham RG41 5BG
Tel: +44 (0)118 978 6915
Fax: +44 (0)118 977 3186
Email: headmaster@
bearwoodcollege.berks.sch.uk

Beaudesert Park
Head: J P R Womersley
Minchinhampton, Stroud GL6 9AF
Tel: +44 (0)1453 832072
Fax: +44 (0)1453 836040
Email: office@beaudesert.gloucs.sch.uk
Website: www.beaudesert.gloucs.sch.uk

Bedales School
Head: K Budge
Petersfield GU32 2DG
Tel: +44 (0)1730 300100
Fax: +44 (0)1730 300500
Email: registra@bedales.org.uk
Website: www.bedales.org.uk

Bedford High School
Head: Mrs G Piotrowska
Bromham Road, Bedford MK40 2BS
Tel: +44 (0)1234 360221
Fax: +44 (0)1234 353552
Email: admissions@bedfordhigh.co.uk
Website: www.bedfordhigh.co.uk

Bedford Modern School
Head: Stephen Smith
Manton Lane, Bedford MK41 7NT
Tel: +44 (0)1234 332500
Fax: +44 (0)1234 332550
Email: info@bedmod.co.uk

Bedford Preparatory School
Head: C Godwin
De Parys Avenue, Bedford MK40 2TU
Tel: +44 (0)1234 362271
Fax: +44 (0)1234 362285
Email: prepinfo@bedfordschool.org.uk
Website: www.bedfordschool.org.uk

Bedford School
Head: Dr I P Evans OBE
De Parys Avenue, Bedford MK40 2TU
Tel: +44 (0)1234 362200
Fax: +44 (0)1234 362283
Email: triseborough@bedfordschool.org.uk
Website: www.bedfordschool.org.uk

Bedgebury School
Head: Mrs H Moriarty
Goudhurst, Cranbrook TN17 2SH
Tel: +44 (0)1580 211221
Fax: +44 (0)1580 212252
Email: info@bedgeburyschool.co.uk
Website: www.bedgeburyschool.co.uk

Bedstone College
Head: M S Symonds
Bucknell SY7 0BG
Tel: +44 (0)1547 530303
Fax: +44 (0)1547 530740
Email: headmaster@bedstone.demon.co.uk
Website: www.bedstone.org

Beechwood Park
Head: D S Macpherson
Markyate, St Albans AL3 8AW
Tel: +44 (0)1582 840333
Fax: +44 (0)1582 842372
Email: admissions@beechwoodpark.herts.sch.uk
Website: www.beechwoodpark.herts.sch.uk

Beechwood Sacred Heart
Head: N R Beesley
Pembury Road, Tunbridge Wells TN2 3QD
Tel: +44 (0)1892 532747
Fax: +44 (0)1892 536164
Email: bsh@beechwood.org.uk
Website: www.beechwood.org.uk

Beeston Hall
Head: I K MacAskill
West Runton, Cromer NR27 9NQ
Tel: +44 (0)1263 837324
Fax: +44 (0)1263 838177
Email: office@beestonhall.co.uk
Website: www.beestonhall.co.uk

Belhaven Hill
Head: I M Osborne
Dunbar EH42 1NN
Tel: +44 (0)1368 862785
Fax: +44 (0)1368 865225
Email: belhavenhill@learnfree.co.uk

Belmont Grosvenor School
Head: Mrs R H Innocent
Swarcliffe Hall, Birstwith
Harrogate HG3 2JG
Tel: +44 (0)1423 771029
Fax: +44 (0)1423 772600
Email: bbirklands@aol.com

Belmont School
Head: D Gainer
Feldemore, Holmbury St Mary
Dorking RH5 6LQ
Tel: +44 (0)1306 730852
Fax: +44 (0)1306 731220
Email: enquiries@belmont-school.org
Website: www.belmont-school.org

Benenden School
Head: Mrs C M Oulton
Cranbrook TN17 4AA
Tel: +44 (0)1580 240592
Fax: +44 (0)1580 240280
Email: registry@benenden.kent.sch.uk

Bentham Grammar School
Head: Ruth E Colman
Low Bentham, Lancaster LA2 7DB
Tel: +44 (0)15242 61275
Fax: +44 (0)15242 62944
Email: secretary@
benthamschool.demon.co.uk
Website: www.benthamschool.demon.co.uk

Berkhamsted Collegiate School
Head: Dr P Chadwick
Overton, 131 High Street
Berkhamsted HP4 2DJ
Tel: +44 (0)1442 358002
Fax: +44 (0)1442 358003
Email: berkhamcoll@porthill.com
Website: berkhamstedcollegiateschool.org.uk

Bethany School
Head: N D B Dorey
Goudhurst, Cranbrook TN17 1LB
Tel: +44 (0)1580 211273
Fax: +44 (0)1580 211151
Email: admin@bethany.demon.co.uk
Website: www.bethany.demon.co.uk

Bilton Grange
Head: Q G Edwards
Dunchurch, Rugby CV22 6QU
Tel: +44 (0)1788 810217
Fax: +44 (0)1788 816922
Email: enquiry@biltongrange.co.uk
Website: www.biltongrange.co.uk

Birchfield School
Head: R P Merriman
Albrighton, Wolverhampton WV7 3AF
Tel: +44 (0)1902 372534
Fax: +44 (0)1902 373516
Email: birchfieldschool@aol.com

Bishop's Stortford College
Head: John Trotman
Maze Green Road CM23 2PJ
Tel: +44 (0)1279 838575
Fax: +44 (0)1279 836570
Email: admissions@bsc.biblio.net
Website:
www.bishops_stortford_college.herts.sch.uk

Bishop's Stortford College Junior School
Head: J A Greathead
Maze Green Road
Bishop's Stortford CM23 2PH
Tel: +44 (0)1279 838607
Fax: +44 (0)1279 306110
Email: jsadmissions@bsc.biblio.net

Bishopsgate School
Head: M Dunning
Englefield Green, Egham TW20 0YJ
Tel: +44 (0)1784 432109
Fax: +44 (0)1784 430460
Email: headmaster@Bishopsgate.surrey.sch.uk

Bloxham School
Head: D K Exham
Banbury OX15 4PE
Tel: +44 (0)1295 720206
Fax: +44 (0)1295 721897
Email: registrar@bloxhamschool.co.uk
Website: www.bloxhamschool.com

The Blue Coat School
Head: A D J Browning
Somerset Road, Edgbaston
Birmingham B17 0HR

Tel: +44 (0)121 454 1425
Fax: +44 (0)121 454 7757
Email: admissions@bluecoat.bham.sch.uk
Website: www.bluecoat.bham.sch.uk

Blundell's School
Head: J Leigh
Tiverton EX16 4DN
Tel: +44 (0)1884 252543
Fax: +44 (0)1884 243232
Email: registrars@blundells.org
Website: www.blundells.org

The Bolitho School
Head: N P Johnson
Penzance TR18 4JR
Tel: +44 (0)1736 363271
Fax: +44 (0)1736 330960
Email: enquiries@bolitho.cornwall.sch.uk

Bootham School
Head: I M Small
York YO30 7BU
Tel: +44 (0)1904 623261
Fax: +44 (0)1904 652106
Email: office@bootham.york.sch.uk
Website: www.bootham.york.sch.uk

Boundary Oak School
Head: R B Bliss
Roche Court, Fareham PO17 5BL
Tel: +44 (0)1329 280955
Fax: +44 (0)1329 827 656
Email: rbliss@boundaryoak.freeserve.co.uk
Website: www.boundaryoak.co.uk

Box Hill School
Head: Dr R A S Atwood
Mickleham, Dorking RH5 6EA
Tel: +44 (0)1372 373382
Fax: +44 (0)1372 363942
Email: registrar@boxhillschool.org.uk
Website: www.boxhillschool.org.uk

Bradfield College
Head: P B Smith
Reading RG7 6AU
Tel: +44 (0)118 964 4510
Fax: +44 (0)118 964 4511
Email: headmaster@bradfieldcollege.org.uk
Website: www.bradfieldcollege.org.uk

Brambletye
Head: H D Cocke
East Grinstead RH19 3PD
Tel: +44 (0)1342 321004
Fax: +44 (0)1342 317562
Email: brambletye@brambletye.rmplc.co.uk
Website: www.brambletye.com

Bramcote Lorne School
Head: J H Gibson
Gamston, Retford DN22 0QQ
Tel: +44 (0)1777 838636
Fax: +44 (0)1777 838633
Email: headmaster@
bramcote-lorne.notts.sch.uk
Website: www.bramcotelorne.com

Bramcote School
Head: J P Kirk
Filey Road, Scarborough YO11 2TT
Tel: +44 (0)1723 373086
Fax: +44 (0)1723 364186
Email: bramcote.school@talk21.com
Website: www.bramcoteschool.com

Bredon School
Head: Mike Newby
Pull Court, Bushley
Tewkesbury GL20 6AH
Tel: +44 (0)1684 293156
Fax: +44 (0)1684 298008
Email: enquiries@bredonschool.worcs.sch.uk

Brentwood School
Head: J A B Kelsall
Brentwood CM15 8AS
Tel: +44 (0)1277 243243
Fax: +44 (0)1277 243299
Email: headmaster@brentwood.essex.sch.uk
Website: www.brentwoodschool.com

Brighton College
Head: Dr A F Seldon
Eastern Road
Brighton BN2 2AL
Tel: +44 (0)1273 704200
Fax: +44 (0)1273 704204
Email: head@brightoncollege.net
Website: www.brightoncollege.net

Brighton College Prep School
Head: B Melia
Walpole Lodge, Walpole Road
Brighton BN2 2EU
Tel: +44 (0)1273 704210
Fax: +44 (0)1273 704286
Email: prepsch@brightoncollege.org.uk

Brockhurst and Marlston House
Head: D J W Fleming and Mrs C Riley
Marlston Hermitage, Newbury RG18 9UL
Tel: +44 (0)1635 200293
Fax: +44 (0)1635 200190
Email: brocksch@rmplc.co.uk
Website: www.brockmarl.org.uk

Bromsgrove Lower School
Head: Peter Lee-Smith
Cobham House, Conway Road
Bromsgrove B60 2AD
Tel: +44 (0)1527 579600
Fax: +44 (0)1527 579571
Email: admissions.lower@
bromsgrove-school.co.uk

Bromsgrove School
Head: T M Taylor
Bromsgrove B61 7DU
Tel: +44 (0)1527 579679
Fax: +44 (0)1527 576177
Email: admissions.upper@
bromsgrove-school.co.uk
Website: www.bromsgrove-school.co.uk

Bronte House
Head: C B F Hall
(Woodhouse Grove Preparatory School)
Apperley Bridge, Bradford BD10 0PQ
Tel: +44 (0)113 250 2811
Fax: +44 (0)113 250 0666

Bruton School for Girls
Head: Mrs B C Bates
Sunny Hill, Bruton BA10 0NT
Tel: +44 (0)1749 812277
Fax: +44 (0)1749 812537
Email: brutonschoolforgirls@btinternet.com

Bryanston School
Head: T D Wheare
Blandford DT11 0PX
Tel: +44 (0)1258 452411
Fax: +44 (0)1258 484661
Email: headmaster@bryanston.co.uk

Burgess Hill School
Head: Mrs Susan Gorham
Keymer Road, Burgess Hill RH15 0EG
Tel: +44 (0)1444 241050
Fax: +44 (0)1444 870314
Email: registrar@burgesshill-school.co.uk
Website: www.burgesshill-school.com

Butterstone School
Head: M and B Whitten
Arthurstone, Meigle
Blairgowrie PH12 8QY
Tel: +44 (0)1828 640528
Fax: +44 (0)1828 640640
Email: heads@butterstone.freeserve.co.uk
Website:
www.users.zetnet.co.uk/butterstone/

Cabin Hill
Head: N I Kendrick
562-594 Upper Newtownards Road
Belfast BT4 3HJ
Tel: +44 (0)28 9065 3368
Fax: +44 (0)28 9065 1966
Email: tbell@cabinhill.belfast.ni.sch.uk

Caldicott
Head: S J G Doggart
Farnham, Royal Slough SL2 3SL
Tel: +44 (0)1753 644457
Fax: +44 (0)1753 649325
Email: office@caldicott.com
Website: www.caldicott.com

**Cambridge Arts and Sciences
Sixth Form College**
Head: Peter McLaughlin and Elizabeth Armstrong
13-14 Round Church Street
Cambridge CB5 8AD
Tel: +44 (0)1223 314431
Fax: +44 (0)1223 467773
Email: cats@dial.pipex.com

Cambridge Centre for Sixth-form Studies
Head: P Redhead
1 Salisbury Villas, Station Road

Cambridge CB1 2JF
Tel: +44 (0)1223 716890
Fax: +44 (0)1223 517530
Email: office@ccss.co.uk
Website: www.ccss.co.uk

Campbell College
Head: Dr R J I Pollock
Belmont, Belfast BT4 2ND
Tel: +44 (0)28 9076 3076
Fax: +44 (0)28 9076 1894
Website: www.campbellcollege.co.uk

Canford School
Head: J D Lever
Wimborne BH21 3AD
Tel: +44 (0)1202 841254
Fax: +44 (0)1202 881009
Email: canford.admissions@dial.pipex.com
Website: www.canford.com

Cargilfield
Head: Mark Seymour
Barnton Avenue West, Edinburgh EH4 6HU
Tel: +44 (0)131 336 2207
Fax: +44 (0)131 336 3179
Email: secretary@cargilfield.edin.sch.uk

Casterton School
Head: A F Thomas
Kirkby Lonsdale LA6 2SG
Tel: +44 (0)15242 79200
Fax: +44 (0)15242 79208
Email: headmaster@castertonschool.co.uk
Website: www.castertonschool.co.uk

Caterham School
Head: R A E Davey
Harestone Valley, Caterham CR3 6YA
Tel: +44 (0)1883 343028
Fax: +44 (0)1883 347795
Email: caterhamschool@caterham.rmplc.co.uk
Website: www.caterhamschool.com

Catteral Hall
Head: R D Hunter
Giggleswick, Settle BD24 0DG
Tel: +44 (0)1729 893100
Fax: +44 (0)1729 893158
Email: rdhunter@giggleswick.n-yorks.sch.uk
Website: www.giggleswick.n-yorks.sch.uk

Chafyn Grove School
Head: James E A Barnes
Salisbury SP1 1LR
Tel: +44 (0)1722 333423
Fax: +44 (0)1722 323114
Email: officecgs@lineone.net
Website: www.chafyngrove.co.uk

Charterhouse
Head: Rev J S Witheridge
Godalming GU7 2DJ
Tel: +44 (0)1483 291500
Fax: +44 (0)1483 291507
Email: admissions@charterhouse.org.uk
Website: www.charterhouse.org.uk

Chase Academy
Head: M D Ellse
Lyncroft House, St John's Road
Cannock WS11 3UR
Tel: +44 (0)1543 501800
Fax: +44 (0)1543 501801
Email: info@chaseacademy.com
Website: www.chaseacademy.com

Cheam School
Head: M R Johnson
Headley, Newbury RG19 8LD
Tel: +44 (0)1635 268381
Fax: +44 (0)1635 269345
Email: office@cheamschool.co.uk
Website: www.cheamschool.co.uk

Cheltenham College
Head: P A Chamberlain
Bath Road, Cheltenham GL53 7LD
Tel: +44 (0)1242 513540
Fax: +44 (0)1242 265630
Email: registrar@cheltcoll.gloucs.sch.uk
Website: www.cheltcoll.gloucs.sch.uk

Cheltenham College Junior School
Head: N I Archdale
Thirlestaine Road, Cheltenham GL53 7AB
Tel: +44 (0)1242 522697
Fax: +44 (0)1242 265620
Email: ccjs@cheltcoll.gloucs.sch.uk
Website: www.cheltcoll.gloucs.S/web/
college/junior/intro.html

The Cheltenham Ladies' College
Head: Mrs V Tuck
Cheltenham GL50 3EP
Tel: +44 (0)1242 520691
Fax: +44 (0)1242 227882
Email: enquiries@cheltladiescollege.org
Website: www.cheltladiescollege.org

Cherry Trees School
Head: Mrs W E S Compson
Flempton Road, Bury St Edmunds IP28 6QJ
Tel: +44 (0)1284 760531
Fax: +44 (0)1284 750177

Chetham's School of Music
Head: Claire Moreland
Long Millgate, Manchester M3 1SB
Tel: +44 (0)161 834 9644
Fax: +44 (0)161 839 3609
Email: chets@chethams.com
Website: www.chethams.com

Chigwell Junior School
Head: P R Bowden
Chigwell IG7 6QF
Tel: +44 (0)20 8501 5720
Fax: +44 (0)20 8501 5723
Email: pbowden@chigwell-school.org
Website: www.chigwell-school.org

Chigwell School
Head: D F Gibbs
Chigwell IG7 6QF
Tel: +44 (0)20 8501 5700
Fax: +44 (0)20 8500 6232
Email: hm@chigwell-school.org
Website: www.chigwell-school.org

The Chorister School
Head: C S S Drew
Durham DH1 3EL
Tel: +44 (0)191 3842935
Fax: +44 (0)191 3839261
Email: head@choristers.durham.sch.uk
Website: www.choristers.durham.sch.uk

Christ's Hospital
Head: P C D Southern
Horsham RH13 7YP
Tel: +44 (0)1403 211293
Fax: +44 (0)1403 211580
Email: adoff@christs-hospital.org.uk
Website: www.christs-hospital.org.uk

Christ Church Cathedral School
Head: J R Smith
3 Brewer Street, Oxford OX1 1QW
Tel: +44 (0)1865 242561
Fax: +44 (0)1865 202945
Email: admin@cccs.org.uk
Website: www.cccs.org.uk

Christ College
Head: Phillip Jones
Brecon LD3 8AG
Tel: +44 (0)1874 623359
Fax: +44 (0)1874 611478
Email: christcolbrecon@clara.net
Website: www.christcollegebrecon.com

City of London Freemen's School
Head: D C Haywood
Ashtead Park, Ashtead KT21 1ET
Tel: +44 (0)1372 277933
Fax: +44 (0)1372 276165
Email: david.haywood@corpoflondon.gov.uk
Website: www.clfs.surrey.sch.uk

Claremont Fan Court School
Head: Mrs P B Farrar
Claremont Drive, Esher KT10 9LY
Tel: +44 (0)1372 467841
Fax: +44 (0)1372 471109
Email: admissions@claremont.surrey.sch.uk
Website: www.claremont-school.co.uk

Clayesmore Prep School
Head: A P Roberts-Wray
Iverne Minster, Blandford DT11 8PH
Tel: +44 (0)1747 811707
Fax: +44 (0)1747 811692
Email: clayesmore@aol.com
Website: www.clayesmore.co.uk

Clayesmore School
Head: M G Cooke
Iverne Minster, Blandford DT11 8LL
Tel: +44 (0)1747 812122
Fax: +44 (0)1747 811343
Email: hmsec@clayesmore.co.uk
Website: www.clayesmore.co.uk

Clifton College
Head: Dr M S Spurr
Clifton, Bristol BS8 3JH
Tel: +44 (0)117 315 7000
Fax: +44 (0)117 315 7101
Email: admissions@
clifton-college.avon.sch.uk
Website: cliftoncollegeuk.com

Clifton College Prep School
Head: Dr R J Acheson
The Avenue, Bristol BS8 3HE
Tel: +44 (0)117 315 7501
Fax: +44 (0)117 315 7504
Email: admissions@cliftoncollegepre.com
Website: www.cliftoncollegepre.com

Clifton High School
Head: Mrs M C Culligan
College Road, Clifton, Bristol BS8 3JD
Tel: +44 (0)117 973 0201
Fax: +44 (0)117 923 8962
Email: enquiries@chs.bristol.sch.uk
Website: www.chs.bristol.sch.uk

Cobham Hall School
Head: Mrs R J McCarthy
Cobham, Gravesend DA12 3BL
Tel: +44 (0)1474 823371
Fax: +44 (0)1474 825906
Email: cobhamhall@aol.com
Website: www.cobhamhall.com

Cokethorpe School
Head: P J S Cantwell
Witney OX8 7PU
Tel: +44 (0)1993 703921
Fax: +44 (0)1993 773499
Email: admin@cokethorpe.org

Colston's Collegiate School
Head: D G Crawford
Stapleton, Bristol BS16 1BJ
Tel: +44 (0)117 965 5207
Fax: +44 (0)117 958 5652
Email: enquiries@colstons.bristol.sch.uk

Copthorne School Trust Ltd
Head: G C Allen
Effingham Lane, Copthorne
Crawley RH10 3HR
Tel: +44 (0)1342 712311
Fax: +44 (0)1342 714014
Email: office@copthorneprep.co.uk
Website: www.copthorneprep.co.uk

Cothill House
Head: A D Richardson
Cothill, Abingdon OX13 6JL
Tel: +44 (0)1865 390800
Fax: +44 (0)1865 390205
Email: office@cothill.oxon.sch.uk

Cottesmore School
Head: M A Rogerson
Buchan Hill
Pease Pottage RH11 9AU
Tel: +44 (0)1293 520648
Fax: +44 (0)1293 614784
Website: cottesmore@compuserve.com

Cranleigh Preparatory School
Head: M W Roulston
Cranleigh GU8 8QH
Tel: +44 (0)1483 274199
Fax: +44 (0)1483 277136
Email: TheMaster@cranprep.demon.co.uk

Cranleigh School
Head: Guy de W Waller
Cranleigh GU6 8QQ
Tel: +44 (0)1483 273666
Fax: +44 (0)1483 267398
Email: jeh@Cranleigh.org

Culford School
Head: J S Richardson
Bury St Edmunds IP28 6TX
Tel: +44 (0)1284 728615
Fax: +44 (0)1284 728631
Email: culfordschool@culford.co.uk
Website: www.culford.co.uk

Cumnor House School
Head: C S Heinrich
Danehill
Haywards Heath RH17 7HT
Tel: +44 (0)1825 790347
Fax: +44 (0)1825 790910
Email: office@cumnor.co.uk
Website: www.cumnor.co.uk

Cundall Manor
Head: Peter Phillips
Helperby, York YO61 2RW
Tel: +44 (0)1423 360200
Fax: +44 (0)1423 360754
Email: headmaster@cundallmanor.co.uk
Website: www.cundallmanor.n-yorks.sch.uk

D'Overbroeck's College
Head: S N Cohen and R M Knowles
Beechlawn House, 1 Park Town
Oxford OX2 6SN
Tel: +44 (0)1865 310000
Fax: +44 (0)1865 552296
Email: mail@doverbroecks.com
Website: www.doverbroecks.com

Dauntsey's School
Head: S B Roberts
West Lavington, Devizes SN10 4HE
Tel: +44 (0)1380 814500
Fax: +44 (0)1380 814501
Email: information@dauntseys.wilts.sch.uk
Website: www.dauntseys.wilts.sch.uk

Dean Close Preparatory School
Head: S W Baird
Cheltenham GL51 6QS
Tel: +44 (0)1242 512217
Fax: +44 (0)1242 258005
Email: office@deancloseprep.gloucs.sch.uk

Dean Close School
Head: Rev Timothy Hastie-Smith
Shelburne Road, Cheltenham GL51 6HE
Tel: +44 (0)1242 522640
Fax: +44 (0)1242 258003
Email: dean@epinet.co.uk
Website: www.deanclose.org.uk

Denstone College
Head: David M Derbyshire
Uttoxeter ST14 5HN
Tel: +44 (0)1889 590484
Fax: +44 (0)1889 591295
Email: tracy.wedgwood@denstone.staffs.sch.uk
Website: www.denstone.staffs.sch.uk

Dollar Academy
Head: J S Robertson
Dollar FK14 7DU
Tel: +44 (0)1259 742511
Fax: +44 (0)1259 742867
Email: rector@dollaracademy.org.uk
Website: www.dollaracademy.org.uk

Dorset House
Head: A L James
The Manor, Bury, Pulborough RH20 1PB
Tel: +44 (0)1798 831456
Fax: +44 (0)1798 831141
Email: headmaster@
dorsethouse.w-sussex.sch.uk

Dover College
Head: H W Blackett
Dover CT17 9RH
Tel: +44 (0)1304 205969
Fax: +44 (0)1304 242208
Email: registrar@dovercollege.demon.co.uk
Website: www.dover-college.kent.sch.uk

Downe House
Head: Mrs E McKendrick
Cold Ash
Thatcham RG18 9JJ
Tel: +44 (0)1635 200286
Fax: +44 (0)1635 202026
Email: correspondence@
downehouse.berks.sch.uk
Website: www.downehouse.net

Downside School
Head: Dom Antony Sutch
Stratton-on-the-Fosse, Radstock BA3 4RJ
Tel: +44 (0)1761 235100
Fax: +44 (0)1761 235105
Email: admin@downside.co.uk
Website: www.downside.co.uk

The Downs School
Head: A A J Williams
Charlton House, Wraxall, Bristol BS48 1PF
Tel: +44 (0)1275 852008
Fax: +44 (0)1275 855840
Email: theoffice@thedowns.biblio.net
Website: www.thedowns.avon.sch.uk

The Downs School
Head: A P Ramsey
Colwall, Malvern WR13 6EY

Tel: +44 (0)1684 540277
Fax: +44 (0)1684 540094
Email: downsHM@aol.com
Website: www.thedowns.org.uk

Dragon School
Head: R S Trafford
Bardwell Road Oxford OX2 6SS
Tel: +44 (0)1865 315400
Fax: +44 (0)1865 311664
Email: secretary@dragonschool.org
Website: www.dragonschool.org

Duke of Kent School
Head: A D Cameron
Peaslake Road, Ewhurst GU6 7NS
Tel: +44 (0)1483 277 313
Fax: +44 (0)1483 273 862
Email: dok.school@virgin.net

Duke of York's Royal Military School
Head: J A Cummings
Dover CT15 5EQ
Tel: +44 (0)1304 245024
Fax: +44 (0)1304 245019
Email: duke@easynet.co.uk

Dulwich College
Head: G G Able
London SE21 7LD
Tel: +44 (0)20 8693 3601
Fax: +44 (0)20 8693 6319
Email: the.registrar@dulwich.org.uk
Website: www.dulwich.org.uk

Dulwich College Prep School
Head: G Marsh
42 Alleyn Park, Dulwich SE21 7AA
Tel: +44 (0)20 8670 3217
Fax: +44 (0)20 8766 7586
Email: headmaster@dcpslondon.org

Dulwich Prep School
Head: M C Wagstaffe
Coursehorn, Cranbrook TN17 3NP
Tel: +44 (0)1580 712179
Fax: +44 (0)1580 715322
Email: registrar@dcpskent.org
Website: www.dcpskent.org

Dumpton School
Head: A G M Watson
Wimborne BH21 7AF
Tel: +44 (0)1202 883818
Fax: +44 (0)1202 848760
Email: secretary@dumpton.com

Dunhurst (Bedales Junior School)
Head: M R Piercy
Petersfield GU32 2DP
Tel: +44 (0)1730 300200
Fax: +44 (0)1730 300600
Email: dunhurst@bedales.org.uk

Durham School
Head: N G Kern
Durham DH1 4SZ
Tel: +44 (0)191 384 7977
Fax: +44 (0)191 386 9400
Website: www.durhamschool.co.uk

Eagle House
Head: S J Carder
Sandhurst GU47 8PH
Tel: +44 (0)1344 772134
Fax: +44 (0)1344 779039
Email: info@eaglehouseschool.com
Website: www.eaglehouseschool.com

Eastbourne College
Head: C M P Bush
Old Wish Road
Eastbourne BN21 4JX
Tel: +44 (0)1323 452320
Fax: +44 (0)1323 452327
Email: hmsec@eastbourne-college.co.uk
Website: www.eastbourne-college.co.uk

Edgeborough
Head: R A Jackson and Mrs M A Jackson
Frensham, Farnham GU10 3AH
Tel: +44 (0)1252 792495
Fax: +44 (0)1252 795156
Email: office@edgeborough.co.uk
Website: www.edgeborough.co.uk

Edge Grove
Head: J R Baugh
Aldenham, Watford WD25 8NL
Tel: +44 (0)1923 855724
Fax: +44 (0)1923 859920

Email: headmaster@edgegrove.indschools.co.uk
Website: www.edgegrove.co.uk

Edgehill College
Head: Mrs E M Burton
Bideford EX39 3LY
Tel: +44 (0)1237 471701
Fax: +44 (0)1237 425981
Email: edgehill@btconnect.com
Website: www.edgecoll.clara.net

The Edinburgh Academy
Head: J V Light
42 Henderson Row, Edinburgh EH3 5BL
Tel: +44 (0)131 556 4603
Fax: +44 (0)131 624 4994
Email: rector@edinburghacademy.org.uk
Website: www.edinburghac.demon.co.uk

Edington and Shapwick School
Head: D C Walker and J P Whittock
Mark Road, Burtle, Bridgwater TA7 8NJ
Tel: +44 (0)1278 722012
Fax: +44 (0)1278 723312
Email: burtle@globalnet.co.uk
Website: www.edingtonshapwick.co.uk

Ellesmere College
Head: B J Wignall
Ellesmere SY12 9AB
Tel: +44 (0)1691 622321
Fax: +44 (0)1691 623286
Email: admin@ellesmere.biblio.net

**Elmhurst the School for Dance
and Performing Arts**
Head: J McNamara
Heathcote Road, Camberley GU15 2EU
Tel: +44 (0)1276 65301
Fax: +44 (0)1276 670320
Email: elmhurst@cableol.co.uk
Website: www.elmhurstdance.co.uk

The Elms
Head: L A C Ashby
Colwall, Malvern WR13 6EF
Tel: +44 (0)1684 540344
Fax: +44 (0)1684 541174
Email: office@elmsschool.co.uk

Elstree School
Head: S M Hill
Woolhampton, Reading RG7 5TD
Tel: +44 (0)118 971 3302
Fax: +44 (0)118 971 4280
Email: postmaster@
elstreeschool.demon.co.uk
Website: www.elstreeschool.demon.co.uk

Eltham College
Head: P J Henderson
Grove Park Road, Mottingham
London SE9 4QF
Tel: +44 (0)20 8857 1455
Fax: +44 (0)20 8857 1913
Email: mail@eltham-college.org.uk
Website: www.eltham-college.org.uk

Embley Park School
Head: David Chapman
Romsey SO51 6ZE
Tel: +44 (0)1794 512206
Fax: +44 (0)1794 518737
Email: embley.park.school@virgin.net
Website:
www.city2000.com/ed/embleyparkschoool

Epsom College
Head: Stephen Borthwick
Epsom KT17 4JQ
Tel: +44 (0)1372 821000
Fax: +44 (0)1372 821005
Email: postmaster@epsomcollege.org.uk
Website: www.epsomcollege.sch.uk

Eton College
Head: J E Lewis
Windsor SL4 6DW
Tel: +44 (0)1753 671000
Fax: +44 (0)1753 671248
Email: admissions@etoncollege.org.uk

Exeter Cathedral School
Head: C I S Dickinson
The Chantry, Palace Gate, Exeter EX1 1HX
Tel: +44 (0)1392 255298
Fax: +44 (0)1392 422718
Email: ExeterCS@aol.com

Farleigh School
Head: J A Allcott
Red Rice, Andover SP11 7PW

Tel: +44 (0)1264 710766
Fax: +44 (0)1264 710070
Email: office@farleighschool.co.uk

Farlington School
Head: Mrs P Mawer
Strood Park, Horsham RH12 3PN
Tel: +44 (0)1403 254967
Fax: +44 (0)1403 272258
Email: TheOffice@
farlington.w-sussex.sch.uk
Website: www.farlington.w-sussex.sch.uk

Farringtons and Stratford House
Head: Mrs C E James
Chislehurst BR7 6LR
Tel: +44 (0)20 8467 0256
Fax: +44 (0)20 8467 5442
Email: head@farringtons.kent.sch.uk
Website: www.farringtons.org.uk

Felsted Preparatory School
Head: E J Newton, Felsted
Dunmow CM6 3JL
Tel: +44 (0)1371 820252
Fax: +44 (0)1371 821443
Website: www.felsted.org

Felsted School
Head: S C Roberts
Dunmow CM6 3LL
Tel: +44 (0)1371 820258
Fax: +44 (0)1371 821232
Email: hms@felsted.essex.sch.uk
Website: www.felsted.org

Feltonfleet School
Head: P C Ward
Cobham KT11 1DR
Tel: +44 (0)1932 862264
Fax: +44 (0)1932 860280
Email: pcw@feltonfleet.co.uk

Fettes College
Head: M C B Spens
Carrington Road, Edinburgh EH4 1QX
Tel: +44 (0)131 332 2281
Fax: +44 (0)131 332 3081
Email: enquiries@fettes.com
Website: www.fettes.com

Finborough School
Head: J Sinclair
The Hall, Great Finborough
Stowmarket IP14 3EF
Tel: +44 (0)1449 773600
Fax: +44 (0)1449 773601
Email: anything@finborough.suffolk.sch.uk
Website: www.finborough.suffolk.sch.uk

Forest School
Head: A G Boggis
Nr Snaresbrook, London E17 3PY
Tel: +44 (0)20 8520 1744
Fax: +44 (0)20 8520 3656
Email: warden@forest.org.uk
Website: www.forest.org.uk

Forres Sandle Manor
Head: R P J Moore
Fordingbridge SP6 1NS
Tel: +44 (0)1425 653181
Fax: +44 (0)1425 655676
Email: fsmsch@globalnet.co.uk

Framlingham College
Head: Mrs G M Randall
Framlingham, Woodbridge IP13 9EY
Tel: +44 (0)1728 723789
Fax: +44 (0)1728 724546
Email: info@framlingham.suffolk.sch.uk
Website: www.framlingham.suffolk.sch.uk

Framlingham College Junior School
Head: S Player
Brandeston Hall, Brandeston
Woodbridge IP13 7AH
Tel: +44 (0)1728 685331
Fax: +44 (0)1728 685437

Frensham Heights
Head: P M de Voil
Rowledge Farnham GU10 4EA
Tel: +44 (0)1252 792134
Fax: +44 (0)1252 794335
Email: headmaster@frensham-heights.org.uk
Website: www.demon.co.uk/
frensham-heights

Frewen College
Head: S C Horsley
Brickwall, Northiam, Rye TN31 6NL

Tel: +44 (0)1797 252494
Fax: +44 (0)1797 252567
Email: post@frewcoll.demon.co.uk

Friars School
Head: P M Ashley
Great Chart, Ashford TN23 3DJ
Tel: +44 (0)1233 620493
Fax: +44 (0)1233 636579
Email: friarsschool@btconnect.com

Friends School
Head: Andy Waters
Saffron Walden CB11 3EB
Tel: +44 (0)1799 525351
Fax: +44 (0)1799 523808
Email: fsswmain@aol.com
Website: www.friends.org.uk

Fulneck School
Head: Mrs Honoree S Gordon
Pudsey LS28 8DS
Tel: +44 (0)113 257 0235
Fax: +44 (0)113 255 7316
Email: general@fulneckschool.co.uk
Website: www.fulneckschool.co.uk

Fyling Hall School
Head: Michael Bayes
Robin Hood's Bay, Whitby YO22 4QD
Tel: +44 (0)1947 880353
Fax: +44 (0)1947 880919
Email: fylinghall@clara.co.uk
Website: www.fylinghall.clara.net

George Watson's College
Head: G H Edwards
Colinton Road, Edinburgh EH10 5EG
Tel: +44 (0)131 447 7931
Fax: +44 (0)131 452 8594
Email: g.edwards@watsons.edin.sch.uk
Website: www.watsons.edin.sch.uk

Giggleswick School
Head: G P Boult
Settle BD24 0DE
Tel: +44 (0)1729 893000
Fax: +44 (0)1729 893150
Email: headmaster@giggleswick.org.uk
Website: www.giggleswick.org.uk

Glebe House
Head: R E Crosley
2 Cromer Road, Hunstanton PE36 6HW
Tel: +44 (0)1485 532809
Fax: +44 (0)1485 533900
Email: enquiries@glebehouseschool.co.uk

Glenalmond College
Head: I G Templeton
Perth PH1 3RY
Tel: +44 (0)1738 842061
Fax: +44 (0)1738 842063
Email: registrar@glenalmondcollege.co.uk
Website: www.glenalmondcollege.co.uk

The Godolphin School
Head: Miss M J Horsburgh
Milford Hill, Salisbury SP1 2RA
Tel: +44 (0)1722 430500
Fax: +44 (0)1722 430501
Email: admissions@godolphin.wilts.sch.uk
Website: www.godolphin.org

Godstowe Prep School
Head: Mrs F Henson
High Wycombe HP13 6PR
Tel: +44 (0)1494 529273
Fax: +44 (0)1494 429009
Email: headmistress@godstowe.org

Gordonstoun School
Head: M C S-R Pyper
Elgin IV30 5RF
Tel: +44 (0)1343 837837
Fax: +44 (0)1343 837808
Email: admin@gordonstoun.org.uk
Website: www.gordonstoun.org.uk

Gosfield School
Head: Ian Clews
Halstead Road, Gosfield
Halstead CO9 1PF
Tel: +44 (0)1787 474040
Fax: +44 (0)1787 478228

Great Ballard
Head: R E T Jennings
Eartham, Chichester PO18 0LR
Tel: +44 (0)1243 814236
Fax: +44 (0)1243 814586
Email: GBSchool@breathemail.net

Great Walstead
Head: H J Lowries
Lindfield, Haywards Heath RH16 2QL
Tel: +44 (0)1444 483528
Fax: +44 (0)1444 482122
Email: admin@greatwalstead.co.uk
Website: www.greatwalstead.co.uk

Greenfields School
M McQuade
Priory Road, Forest Row RH18 5JD
Tel: +44 (0)1342 822189
Fax: +44 (0)1342 825289
Email: grnflds@aol.com
Website: www.greenfieldsschool.com

Grenville College
Head: M C V Cane
Bideford EX39 3JR
Tel: +44 (0)1237 472212
Fax: +44 (0)1237 477020
Email: info@grenville.devon.sch.uk
Website: www.grenville.devon.sch.uk

Grenville Coll Jnr Sch (Stella Maris)
Head: Mrs L Maggs-Wellings
Moreton House, Abbotsham Road
Bideford EX39 3QN
Tel: +44 (0)1237 472208
Fax: +44 (0)1237 477020
Email: info@grenville.devon.sch.uk
Website: www.grenville.devon.sch.uk

Gresham's Preparatory School
Head: A H Cuff
Holt NR25 6EY
Tel: +44 (0)1263 712227
Fax: +44 (0)1263 714060
Website: www.greshams.com

Gresham's School
Head: J H Arkell
Holt NR25 6EA
Tel: +44 (0)1263 713271
Fax: +44 (0)1263 712028
Email: headmaster@greshams-school.co.uk
Website: www.greshams.com

**Haberdashers' Monmouth
School for Girls**
Head: Dr B Despontin
Hereford Road, Monmouth NP25 3XT
Tel: +44 (0)1600 711100
Fax: +44 (0)1600 711233
Email: admissions@hmsg.gwent.sch.uk
Website: www.habs-monmouth.org

Haileybury
Head: S A Westley
Hertford SG13 7NU
Tel: +44 (0)1992 706222
Fax: +44 (0)1992 467603
Email: stuartaw@haileybury.herts.sch.uk
Website: www.haileybury.herts.sch.uk

Hall Grove
Head: A R Graham
London Road, Bagshot GU19 5HZ
Tel: +44 (0)1276 473059
Fax: +44 (0)1276 452003
Email: registrar@hallgrove.surrey.sch.uk
Website: www.hallgrove.surrey.sch.uk

Hammond School
Head: Mrs M P Dangerfield
Hoole Bank House
Mannings Lane
Chester CH2 4ES
Tel: +44 (0)1244 328542
Fax: +44 (0)1244 315845
Email: info@thehammondschool.co.uk
Website: www.thehammondschool.co.uk

Handcross Park School
Head: W J Hilton
Handcross, Haywards Heath RH17 6HF
Tel: +44 (0)1444 400526
Fax: +44 (0)1444 400527
Email: head@handxpark.demon.co.uk
Website: www.handxpark.com

Hanford School
Head: Miss S Canning and Mr and
Mrs R A McKenzie Johnston
Childe Okeford, Blandford DT11 8HL
Tel: +44 (0)1258 860219
Fax: +44 (0)1258 861255
Email: hanfordsch@aol.com
Website: www.hanford.dorset.sch.uk

Harecroft School
Head: D G Hoddy

Gosforth, Seascale CA20 1HS
Tel: +44 (0)19467 25220
Fax: +44 (0)19467 25885

Harrogate Ladies' College
Head: Dr Margaret J Hustler
Clarence Drive, Harrogate HG1 2QG
Tel: +44 (0)1423 504543
Fax: +44 (0)1423 568893
Email: enquire@hlc.org.uk
Website: www.hlc.org.uk

Harrow School
Head: B J Lenon
Harrow on the Hill, Harrow HA1 3HW
Tel: +44 (0)20 8872 8000
Fax: +44 (0)20 8423 3112
Email: harrow@harrowschool.org.uk
Website: www.harrowschool.org.uk

Hatherop Castle Preparatory School
Head: P Easterbrook
Cirencester GL7 3NB
Tel: +44 (0)1285 750206
Fax: +44 (0)1285 750430

**Hazlegrove (King's Bruton
Preparatory School)**
Head: Revd B A Bearcroft
Hazlegrove House, Sparkford
Yeovil BA22 7JA
Tel: +44 (0)1963 440314
Fax: +44 (0)1963 440569
Email: office@hazlegrove.somerset.sch.uk
Website: www.hazlegrove.somerset.sch.uk

Headfort School
Head: W L W Goulding
Kells, Co Meath, Eire
Tel: +44 (0)46 40065
Fax: +44 (0)46 41842
Email: headfort@iol.ie
Website: www.iol.ie/~headfort

Headington School
Head: Mrs H A Fender
Oxford OX3 7TD
Tel: +44 (0)1865 759100
Fax: +44 (0)1865 760268
Email: enquiries@headington.org
Website: www.headington.org

Heathfield School
Head: Mrs Helen Wright
Ascot SL5 8BQ
Tel: +44 (0)1344 898343
Fax: +44 (0)1344 890689
Email: admin@heathfield.ascot.sch.uk

Heath Mount School
Head: The Revd H J Matthews
Woodhall Park, Watton-at-Stone
Hertford SG14 3NG
Tel: +44 (0)1920 830 230
Fax: +44 (0)1920 830 357

Hethersett Old Hall School
Head: Mrs J M Mark
Hethersett, Norwich NR9 3DW
Tel: +44 (0)1603 810390
Fax: +44 (0)1603 812094
Email: prospectus@hohs.co.uk
Website: www.hohs.co.uk

Highfield School
Head: P G S Evitt
Liphook GU30 7LQ
Tel: +44 (0)1428 728000
Fax: +44 (0)1428 728001
Email: office@highfieldschool.org.uk
Website: www.highfieldschool.org.uk

Hillstone
Head: P H Moody
Malvern College, Abbey Road
Malvern WR14 3HF
Tel: +44 (0)1684 571600
Fax: +44 (0)1684 571601
Email: hillstone@malcol.org
Website: www.malcol.org/web/hillstone

Holmewood House
Head: A S R Corbett
Langton Green, Tunbridge Wells TN3 0EB
Tel: +44 (0)1892 860000
Fax: +44 (0)1892 863570
Email: admin@holmewood.kent.sch.uk
Website: www.holmewood.kent.sch.uk

Holmwood House
Head: H S Thackrah
Lexden, Colchester CO3 5ST

Tel: +44 (0)1206 574305
Fax: +44 (0)1206 768269
Email: hst@holmwood.essex.sch.uk
Website: www.holmwood.essex.sch.uk

Homefield School
Head: A C Partridge
Salisbury Road, Winkton
Christchurch BH23 7AR
Tel: +44 (0)1202 476644
Fax: +44 (0)1202 477923
Email: admin@homefieldschool.co.uk
Website: www.homefieldschool.co.uk

Hordle Walhampton School
Henry Phillips
Lymington SO41 5ZG
Tel: +44 (0)1590 672013
Fax: +44 (0)1590 678498
Email: jb@walhamp.demon.co.uk
Website: www.walhamp.demon.co.uk

Horris Hill
Head: N J Chapman
Newtown, Newbury RG20 9DJ
Tel: +44 (0)1635 40594
Fax: +44 (0)1635 35241
Email: enquiries@horrishill.demon.co.uk
Website: www.horrishill.com

Howell's Preparatory School
Head: Mrs L A Robinson
Park Street, Denbigh LL16 3DD
Tel: +44 (0)1745 816001
Fax: +44 (0)1745 816010
Email: webmaster@howells.org

Howell's School
Head: Mrs L A Robinson
Denbigh LL16 3EN
Tel: +44 (0)1745 813631
Fax: +44 (0)1745 814443
Email: howells@cix.co.uk
Website: www.howells.org

Howsham Hall
Head: S Knock
York YO60 7PJ
Tel: +44 (0)1653 618374
Fax: +44 (0)1653 618295
Email: Howsham@simonknock.freeserve.co.uk
Website: www.howshamhall.co.uk

Hull Grammar School
Head: R Haworth
Cottingham Road, Kingston upon Hull HU5 2DL
Tel: +44 (0)1482 440144
Fax: +44 (0)1482 441312
Email: info@hullgrammarsch.karoo.co.uk
Website: www.hullgrammarsch.karoo.net

Hurst Lodge School
Head: Mrs A M Smit
Bagshot Road, Ascot SL5 9JU
Tel: +44 (0)1344 622154
Fax: +44 (0)1344 627049
Email: admissionshurstlodge@supanet.com
Website: www.hurstlodge.freeserve.co.uk

Hurstpierpoint College
Head: S D A Meek
Hassocks BN6 9JS
Tel: +44 (0)1273 833636
Fax: +44 (0)1273 835257
Email: info@hppc.co.uk
Website: www.hppc.co.uk

Hurstpierpoint College Preparatory School
Head: S J Andrews
Hassocks BN6 9JS
Tel: +44 (0)1273 834975
Fax: +44 (0)1273 833957
Email: hurstprep@hppc.co.uk

Hurtwood House
Head: K R B Jackson
Holmbury St Mary, Dorking RH5 6NU
Tel: +44 (0)1483 277416
Fax: +44 (0)1483 267586
Email: hurtwood2@aol.com
Website: www.hurtwood-house.co.uk

Ipswich School
Head: Ian Galbraith
Ipswich IP1 3SG
Tel: +44 (0)1473 408300
Fax: +44 (0)1473 400058
Email: registrar@ipswich.suffolk.sch.uk
Website: www.ipswich.suffolk.sch.uk

Junior King's School
Head: P M Wells

Milner Court, Sturry
Canterbury CT2 0AY
Tel: +44 (0)1227 714000
Fax: +44 (0)1227 713171
Email: head@junior-kings.co.uk
Website: www.junior-kings.co.uk

Kelly College
Head: M S Steed
Tavistock PL19 0HZ
Tel: +44 (0)1822 813100
Fax: +44 (0)1822 813110
Email: admin@kellycollege.com
Website: www.kellycollege.com

Kelly College Junior School
Head: R P Jeynes
Hazeldon, Parkwood Road
Tavistock PL19 0JS
Tel: +44 (0)1822 612919
Fax: +44 (0)1822 612919
Email: admin@kellyjunior.freeserve.co.uk
Website: www.clickable.co.uk/kcjs

Kent College
Head: E B Halse
Canterbury CT2 9DT
Tel: +44 (0)1227 763231
Fax: +44 (0)1227 764777
Email: hm@kentcollege.co.uk
Website: www.kentcollege.co.uk

Kent College Infant and Junior School
Head: A J Carter
Vernon Holme, Harbledown
Canterbury CT2 9AQ
Tel: +44 (0)1227 762436
Fax: +44 (0)1227 763880
Email: hmkcollege@rmplc.co.uk

Kent College Junior School
Head: Mrs D C Dunham
Aultmore House, Old Church Road
Tunbridge Wells TN2 4AX
Tel: +44 (0)1892 820204
Fax: +44 (0)1892 820214
Email: JuniorSchool@kentcollege.kent.sch.uk
Website: www.kent-college.co.uk

Kent College Pembury
Head: Miss B J Crompton
Tunbridge Wells TN2 4AX
Tel: +44 (0)1892 822006
Fax: +44 (0)1892 820221
Email: admissions@kentcollege.kent.sch.uk
Website: www.kent-college.co.uk

Kilgraston (A Sacred Heart School)
Head: Mrs Juliet L Austin
Bridge of Earn, Perth PH2 9BQ
Tel: +44 (0)1738 812257
Fax: +44 (0)1738 813410
Email: mkeay@kilgraston.pkc.sch.uk
Website: www.kilgraston.pkc.sch.uk

Kimbolton School
Head: R V Peel
Kimbolton, Huntingdon PE28 0EA
Tel: +44 (0)1480 860505
Fax: +44 (0)1480 860386
Email: headmaster@
kimboltonschool.demon.co.uk
Website: www.kimbolton.cambs.sch.uk

King's College
Head: R S Funnell
Taunton TA1 3DX
Tel: +44 (0)1823 328204
Fax: +44 (0)1823 328202
Email: kingscol@aol.com
Website: www.kings-taunton.co.uk

King's College School
Head: N J Robinson
West Road, Cambridge CB3 9DN
Tel: +44 (0)1223 365814
Fax: +44 (0)1223 461388
Email: office@kingscam.demon.co.uk
Website: www.kcs.cambs.sch.uk

King's Hall
Head: J K Macpherson
Kingston Road, Taunton TA2 8AA
Tel: +44 (0)1823 285920
Fax: +44 (0)1823 285922
Email: kingshall@aol.com

King's Hospital
Head: H Meyer
Palmerstown, Dublin, 20, Eire
Tel: +353 1626 5933
Fax: +353 1623 0349

King's Junior School
Head: A G Duncan
Ely CB7 4DB
Tel: +44 (0)1353 660732
Fax: +44 (0)1353 665281
Email: admissions@kings-ely.cambs.sch.uk

King's Preparatory School
Head: C J Nickless
St Nicholas House, King Edward Road
Rochester ME1 1UB
Tel: +44 (0)1634 843657
Fax: +44 (0)1634 840569
Email: walker@kings-school-rochester.co.uk
Website: www.kings-school-rochester.co.uk

King's School
Head: R H Youdale
Ely CB7 4DB
Tel: +44 (0)1353 660702
Fax: +44 (0)1353 662187
Email: admissions@kings-ely.cambs.sch.uk
Website: www.kings-ely.cambs.sch.uk

King's School
Head: R I Smyth
Bruton BA10 0ED
Tel: +44 (0)1749 814200
Fax: +44 (0)1749 813426
Email: kingshm@kingsbruton.somerset.sch.uk
Website: www.kingsbruton.com

King's School
Head: The Revd Canon Keith Wilkinson
Canterbury CT1 2ES
Tel: +44 (0)1227 595579
Fax: +44 (0)1227 595595
Email: headmaster@kings-school.co.uk
Website: www.kings-school.co.uk

King's School
Head: P R Lacey
Pitt Street, Gloucester GL1 2BG
Tel: +44 (0)1452 337337
Fax: +44 (0)1452 337319
Email: headmaster@thekingsschool.co.uk
Website: www.thekingsschool.co.uk

King's School Rochester
Head: Dr I R Walker
Satis House, Boley Hill, Rochester ME1 1TE
Tel: +44 (0)1634 843913
Fax: +44 (0)1634 832493
Email: walker@kings-school-rochester.co.uk
Website: www.kings-school-rochester.co.uk

King Edward's School
Head: P K Fulton-Peebles
Witley, Godalming GU8 5SG
Tel: +44 (0)1428 686700
Fax: +44 (0)1428 685260
Email: hmsec@kesw.surrey.sch.uk

Kingham Hill School
Head: Martin J Morris
Kingham, Chipping Norton OX7 6TH
Tel: +44 (0)1608 658999
Fax: +44 (0)1608 658658
Email: secretary@kinghamhill.org.uk
Website: www.kinghamhill.org.uk

Kingsmead School
Head: E H Bradby
Bertram Drive, Hoylake CH47 0LL
Tel: +44 (0)151 632 3156
Fax: +44 (0)151 632 0302
Email: KingsmeadSchool@compuserve.com
Website: www.kingsmead.wirral.sch.uk

Kingswood Preparatory School
Head: Miss A Gleave
College Road, Lansdown
Bath BA1 5SD
Tel: +44 (0)1225 310468
Fax: +44 (0)1225 464434
Email: mjecornah@aol.com

Kingswood School
Head: G M Best
Lansdown, Bath BA1 5RG
Tel: +44 (0)1225 734200
Fax: +44 (0)1225 734205
Email: registrar@kingswoodschool.org.uk
Website: www.kingswood.bath.sch.uk

King William's College
Head: P John
Castletown, Isle of Man IM9 1TP
Tel: +44 (0)1624 822551
Fax: +44 (0)1624 824287
Email: Principal@kwc.sch.im
Website: www.kwc.sch.im

Kirkham Grammar School
Head: B Stacey
Ribby Road, Kirkham, Preston PR4 2BH
Tel: +44 (0)1772 671079
Fax: +44 (0)1772 672747
Email: info@kgs.lancs.sch.uk
Website: www.kgs.lancs.sch.uk

Knighton House
Head: Mrs Heath
Durweston, Blandford DT11 0PY
Tel: +44 (0)1258 452065
Fax: +44 (0)1258 450744
Email: Knighton@durweston.freeserve.co.uk
Website: www.knightonhouse.co.uk

Lambrook Haileybury
Head: R Deighton
Winkfield Row, Bracknell RG42 6LU
Tel: +44 (0)1344 882717
Fax: +44 (0)1344 891114
Email: info@lambrook.berks.sch.uk

Lancing College
Head: P M Tinniswood, Lancing BN15 0RW
Tel: +44 (0)1273 452213
Fax: +44 (0)1273 464720
Email: admin@lancing.dialnet.com
Website: www.lancing.org.uk

Langley School
Head: J G Malcolm
Langley Park, Norwich NR14 6BJ
Tel: +44 (0)1508 520210
Fax: +44 (0)1508 528058
Email: administration@langleyschool.co.uk
Website: www.langleyschool.co.uk

Lathallan School
Head: P Platts-Martin
Montrose DD10 0HN
Tel: +44 (0)1561 362220
Fax: +44 (0)1561 361695
Email: office@lathallan.com
Website: www.lathallan.com

Lavant House Rosemead
Head: Mrs Marian Scott
Chichester PO18 9AB
Tel: +44 (0)1243 527211
Fax: +44 (0)1243 530490
Email: office@lhr.org.uk
Website: www.lhr.org.uk

Leaden Hall School
Head: Mrs D E Watkins
70 The Close, Salisbury SP1 2EP
Tel: +44 (0)1722 334700
Fax: +44 (0)1722 410575
Email: leaden.hall@virgin.net

Leighton Park School
Head: John Dunston
Shinfield Road, Reading RG2 7ED
Tel: +44 (0)118 987 9600
Fax: +44 (0)118 987 9625
Email: info@leightonpark.reading.sch.uk
Website: www.leightonpark.reading.sch.uk

The Leys School
Head: The Rev Dr J C A Barrett
Cambridge CB2 2AD
Tel: +44 (0)1223 508900
Fax: +44 (0)1223 505303
Email: office@theleys.cambs.sch.uk
Website: www.theleys.cambs.sch.uk

Licensed Victuallers' School
Head: Ian Mullins
London Road, Ascot SL5 8DR
Tel: +44 (0)1344 882770
Fax: +44 (0)1344 890648
Email: Catrin.Miller-Smith@lvsascot.org.uk

Lichfield Cathedral Sch (St Chad's)
Head: Peter Allwood
The Palace, Lichfield WS13 7LH
Tel: +44 (0)1543 306170
Fax: +44 (0)1543 306170

Lime House School
Head: Nigel A Rice
Holm Hill, Dalston, Carlisle CA5 7BX
Tel: +44 (0)1228 710225
Fax: +44 (0)1228 710508
Email: NRice51711@aol.com
Website: www.limehouseschool.co.uk

Lincoln Minster Preparatory School
Head: Mrs K Maltby
Eastgate, Lincoln LN2 1QG
Tel: +44 (0)1522 523769

Fax: +44 (0)1522 514778
Email: lms@lincolnminsterschool.co.uk

Lincoln Minster School
Head: Clive Rickart
Hillside, Lindum Terrace, Lincoln LN2 5RW
Tel: +44 (0)1522 543764
Fax: +44 (0)1522 537938
Email: admin@lincolnminsterschool.co.uk
Website: www.lincolnminsterschool.co.uk

**Lisvane – Scarborough
College Junior School**
Head: G S Twist
Filey Road, Scarborough YO11 3BA
Tel: +44 (0)1723 380606
Fax: +44 (0)1723 380607
Email: lisvane@scarboroughcoll.co.uk

Llandovery College
Head: Peter A Hogan
Llandovery SA20 0EE
Tel: +44 (0)1550 723000
Fax: +44 (0)1550 723049
Email: mail@llandoverycollege.com
Website: www.llandoverycollege.com

Lockers Park School
Head: D R Lees-Jones
Hemel Hempstead HP1 1TL
Tel: +44 (0)1442 251712
Fax: +44 (0)1442 234150
Email: secretary@lockerspark.herts.sch.uk

Lomond School
Head: A D Macdonald
Stafford Street, Helensburgh G84 9JX
Tel: +44 (0)1436 672476
Fax: +44 (0)1436 678320
Email: admin@lomond-school.demon.co.uk
Website: www.lomond-school.org

Longridge Towers School
Head: Dr M J Barron
Berwick-upon-Tweed TD15 2XQ
Tel: +44 (0)1289 307584
Fax: +44 (0)1289 302581
Email: pupilsadmissions@lts.org.uk
Website: www.lts.org.uk

Lord Wandsworth College
Head: Ian Power
Long Sutton, Hook RG29 1TB
Tel: +44 (0)1256 862482
Fax: +44 (0)1256 862563
Email: igp@lord-wandsworth.hants.sch.uk

Loretto Junior School
Head: Andrew G W Lewin
North Esk Lodge, Musselburgh EH21 6JA
Tel: +44 (0)131 653 4570
Fax: +44 (0)131 653 4571
Email: agwlewin@loretto.lothian.sch.uk

Loretto School
Head: Michael Mavor
Musselburgh EH21 7RE
Tel: +44 (0)131 653 4455
Fax: +44 (0)131 653 4456
Email: admissions@loretto.lothian.sch.uk
Website: www.loretto.com

Loughborough Grammar School
Head: Paul Fisher
Burton Walks, Loughborough LE11 2DU
Tel: +44 (0)1509 233233
Fax: +44 (0)1509 218436
Email: admin@loughgs.co.uk
Website: www.loughgs.leics.sch.uk

Luckley-Oakfield School
Head: R C Blake
Wokingham RG40 3EU
Tel: +44 (0)118 9784175
Fax: +44 (0)118 9770305
Email: registrar@luckley.wokingham.sch.uk
Website: www.luckley.wokingham.sch.uk

Ludgrove
Head: G W P Barber and C N J Marston
Wixenford, Wokingham RG40 3AB
Tel: +44 (0)118 978 9881
Fax: +44 (0)118 979 2973

Maidwell Hall
Head: R A Lankester
Northampton NN6 9JG
Tel: +44 (0)1604 686234
Fax: +44 (0)1604 686659
Email: TheHeadmaster@
maidwellhall.northants.sch.uk

Malsis School
Head: J Elder
Cross Hills BD20 8DT
Tel: +44 (0)1535 633027
Fax: +44 (0)1535 630571
Email: admin@malsis.fsnet.co.uk

Malvern College
Head: H C K Carson
Malvern WR14 3DF
Tel: +44 (0)1684 581500
Fax: +44 (0)1684 581617
Email: enquiry@malcol.org
Website: www.malcol.org

Malvern Girls' College
Head: Mrs Philippa M C Leggate
Malvern WR14 3BA
Tel: +44 (0)1684 892288
Fax: +44 (0)1684 566204
Email: registrar@mgc.worcs.sch.uk
Website: www.mgc.worcs.sch.uk

Manor House School
Head: Mrs Alison Morris
Manor House Lane, Little Bookham KT23 4EN
Tel: +44 (0)1372 458538
Fax: +44 (0)1372 450514

Maple Hayes Hall School for Dyslexics
Head: Dr E N Brown
Abnalls Lane, Lichfield WS13 8BL
Tel: +44 (0)1543 264387
Fax: +44 (0)1543 262022
Email: office@dyslexia-gb.com

Mark College
Head: Mrs J Y Kay
Mark, Highbridge TA9 4NP
Tel: +44 (0)1278 641632
Fax: +44 (0)1278 641426
Email: post@markcollege.somerset.sch.uk
Website: www.markcollege.somerset.sch.uk

Marlborough College
Head: E J H Gould
Marlborough SN8 1PA
Tel: +44 (0)1672 892300
Fax: +44 (0)1672 892307
Email: admissions@
marlboroughcollege.wilts.sch.uk
Website: www.marlboroughcollege.org

Marlborough House School
Head: D N Hopkins
Hawkhurst TN18 4PY
Tel: +44 (0)1580 753555
Fax: +44 (0)1580 754281
Email: registrar@marlbhouse.demon.co.uk
Website: www.marlbhouse.demon.co.uk

**The Mary Erskine and Stewart's
Melville Junior School**
Head: Bryan Lewis
Queensferry Road, Edinburgh EH4 3EZ
Tel: +44 (0)131 332 0888
Fax: +44 (0)131 332 0831
Email: jssecretary@mesmjuniorschool.edin.sch.uk
Website: www.mesmjuniorschool.edin.sch.uk

The Mary Erskine School
Head: J N D Gray
Ravelston, Edinburgh EH4 3NT
Tel: +44 (0)131 337 2391
Fax: +44 (0)131 346 1137
Email: schoolsecretary@maryerskine.edin.sch.uk
Website: www.maryerskine.edin.sch.uk

Marymount International School
Head: Sister Rosaleen Sheridan RSHM
George Road, Kingston-upon-Thames KT2 7PE
Tel: +44 (0)20 8949 0571
Fax: +44 (0)20 8336 2485
Email: info@marymount.kingston.sch.uk
Website: www.marymount.kingston.sch.uk

Merchiston Castle School
Head: Andrew Hunter
Colinton, Edinburgh EH13 0PU
Tel: +44 (0)131 312 2200
Fax: +44 (0)131 441 6060
Email: headmaster@merchiston.co.uk
Website: www.merchiston.co.uk

Methodist College
Head: Dr T W Mulryne
1 Malone Road, Belfast BT9 6BY
Tel: +44 (0)28 9020 5205
Fax: +44 (0)28 9020 5230
Email: school@methody.org
Website: www.methody.org

Millfield Preparatory
Head: K A Cheney
Glastonbury BA6 8LD
Tel: +44 (0)1458 832446
Fax: +44 (0)1458 833679
Email: office@millfieldprep.somerset.sch.uk
Website: www.millfield.co.uk/prep

Millfield School
P M Johnson
Street BA16 0YD
Tel: +44 (0)1458 442291
Fax: +44 (0)1458 447276
Email: postmaster@millfield.somerset.sch.uk
Website: www.millfield.co.uk

Mill Hill School
Head: W R Winfield
The Ridgeway, London NW7 1QS
Tel: +44 (0)20 8959 1176
Fax: +44 (0)20 8201 0663
Email: headmaster@millhill.org.uk

Milton Abbey School
Head: W J Hughes-D'Aeth
Blandford DT11 0BZ
Tel: +44 (0)1258 880 484
Fax: +44 (0)1258 881250
Email: info@miltonabbey.co.uk
Website: www.miltonabbey.co.uk

Moffats School
Head: M and A Daborn
Kinlet Hall, Bewdley DY12 3AY
Tel: +44 (0)1299 841230
Fax: +44 (0)1299 841444
Email: office@moffats.co.uk
Website: www.moffats.co.uk

Moira House Girls School
Head: Ann Harris
Upper Carlisle Road, Eastbourne BN20 7TE
Tel: +44 (0)1323 644144
Fax: +44 (0)1323 649720
Email: head@moirahouse.co.uk
Website: www.moirahouse.e-sussex.sch.uk

Monkton Combe Junior School
Head: C J Stafford
Combe Down, Bath BA2 7ET
Tel: +44 (0)1225 837912
Fax: +44 (0)1225 840312
Email: admin@monktonjunior.org.uk
Website: www.monktoncombeschool.com

Monkton Combe School
Head: M J Cuthbertson
Bath BA2 7HG
Tel: +44 (0)1225 721102
Fax: +44 (0)1225 721181
Email: harriska@monkton.org.uk
Website: www.monktoncombeschool.com

Monmouth School
Head: T H P Haynes
Monmouth NP5 3XP
Tel: +44 (0)1600 713143
Fax: +44 (0)1600 772701
Email: admissions@monmouth.monm.sch.uk

Moon Hall School
Head: Mrs J Lovett
Feldemore, Pasturewood Lane
Dorking RH5 6LQ
Tel: +44 (0)1306 731464
Fax: +44 (0)1306 731504
Email: enquiries@moonhall.surrey.sch.uk
Website: www.moonhall.surrey.sch.uk

Moor Park
Head: N R Colquhoun
Ludlow SY8 4DZ
Tel: +44 (0)1584 876061
Fax: +44 (0)1584 877311
Email: moorpark.staff@netmatters.co.uk
Website: www.moorpark.shropshire.sch.uk

More House School
Head: B G Huggett
Frensham, Farnham GU10 3AP
Tel: +44 (0)1252 792303
Fax: +44 (0)1252 797601
Email: MoreHouseSchool@hotmail.com

Moreton Hall Preparatory School
Head: N Higham
Mount Road, Bury St Edmunds IP32 7BJ
Tel: +44 (0)1284 753532
Fax: +44 (0)1284 769197
Email: moretonh2@aol.com
Website: www.moretonhall.suffolk.sch.uk

Moreton Hall School
Head: J Forster
Weston Rhyn, Oswestry SY11 3EW
Tel: +44 (0)1691 773 671
Fax: +44 (0)1691 778 552
Email: jfmhall@aol.com

Morrison's Academy
Head: I Bendall
Crieff PH7 3AN
Tel: +44 (0)1764 653885
Fax: +44 (0)1764 655411
Email: principal@morrisons.pkc.sch.uk
Website: www.morrisons.pkc.sch.uk

Moulsford Preparatory School
Head: M J Higham
Moulsford, Wallingford OX10 9HR
Tel: +44 (0)1491 651438
Fax: +44 (0)1491 651868

Mount House School
Head: C D Price
Tavistock PL19 9JL
Tel: +44 (0)1822 612244
Fax: +44 (0)1822 610042
Email: mounthouse@aol.com
Website: www.mounthouse.devon.sch.uk

The Mount School
Head: Mrs Diana Gant
Dalton Terrace, York YO24 4DD
Tel: +44 (0)1904 667500
Fax: +44 (0)1904 667524
Email: registrar@mount.n-yorks.sch.uk
Website: www.mount.n-yorks.sch.uk

Mount St Mary's College
Head: Philip MacDonald
Spinkhill, Sheffield S21 3YL
Tel: +44 (0)1246 433388
Fax: +44 (0)1246 435511
Email: headmaster@msmcollege.com
Website: www.msmcollege.com

Mowden Hall School
Head: A P Lewis
Stocksfield NE43 7TP
Tel: +44 (0)1661 842147
Fax: +44 (0)1661 842529

Mowden School
Head: C E M Snell
The Droveway, Hove BN3 6LU
Tel: +44 (0)1273 503452
Fax: +44 (0)1273 503457
Email: mowden@freenet.co.uk

Moyles Court School
Head: R A Dean
Moyles Court, Ringwood BH24 3NF
Tel: +44 (0)1425 472856
Fax: +44 (0)1425 474715
Email: moylescourt@btinternet.com
Website: www.moylescourt.co.uk

The New Beacon
Head: R Constantine
Brittains Lane, Sevenoaks TN13 2PB
Tel: +44 (0)1732 452131
Fax: +44 (0)1732 459509

The New Eccles Hall School
Head: R Allard
Quidenham, Norwich NR16 2NZ
Tel: +44 (0)1953 887217
Fax: +44 (0)1953 887397
Email: nehs@quidenham.freeserve.co.uk
Website: www.quidenham.freeserve.co.uk

New Hall School
Head: Sister Anne-Marie Brister CRSS
Chelmsford CM3 3HT
Tel: +44 (0)1245 467588
Fax: +44 (0)1245 464348
Email: admin@newhallschool.co.uk
Website: www.newhallschool.co.uk

Newlands Manor School
Head: O T Price
Sutton Place, Seaford BN25 3PL
Tel: +44 (0)1323 892334
Fax: +44 (0)1323 898420
Email: Newlands1@msn.com

Newlands Preparatory School
Head: O T Price
Eastbourne Road
Seaford BN25 4NP
Tel: +44 (0)1323 892334
Fax: +44 (0)1323 898420
Email: newlands1@msn.com

Norman Court Preparatory School
Head: K N Foyle
West Tytherley, Salisbury SP5 1NH
Tel: +44 (0)1980 862345
Fax: +44 (0)1980 862082
Email: office@normancourt.co.uk
Website: www.normancourt.co.uk

Northbourne Park
Head: S Sides
Betteshanger, Deal CT14 0NW
Tel: +44 (0)1304 611215
Fax: +44 (0)1304 619020
Email: office@northbourne.kent.sch.uk
Website: www.northbourne.kent.sch.uk

North Foreland Lodge
Head: Miss S R Cameron
Sherfield-on-Loddon, Hook RG27 0HT
Tel: +44 (0)1256 884800
Fax: +44 (0)1256 884803
Email: postmaster@northforelandlodge.org.uk

Nunnykirk Centre for Dyslexia
Head: S Dalby-Ball
Netherwitton, Morpeth NE61 4PB
Tel: +44 (0)1670 772685
Fax: +44 (0)1670 772434
Email: secretary@nkirk.freeserve.co.uk

Oakham School
Head: Anthony Little
Chapel Close, Oakham LE15 6DT
Tel: +44 (0)1572 758500
Fax: +44 (0)1572 755786
Email: admissions@oakham.rutland.sch.uk
Website: www.oakham.org.uk

Oakwood
Head: A H Cowell
Chichester, PO18 9AN
Tel: +44 (0)1243 575209
Fax: +44 (0)1243 575433
Email: Oakwood.Office@qick.com
Website: www.OakwoodSchool.co.uk

Ockbrook School
Head: Denise P Bolland
The Settlement, Ockbrook DE72 3RJ
Tel: +44 (0)1332 673532
Fax: +44 (0)1332 665184
Website: www.ockbrook.derby.sch.uk

Old Buckenham Hall School
Head: M A Ives
Brettenham Park, Ipswich IP7 7PH
Tel: +44 (0)1449 740252
Fax: +44 (0)1449 740955
Email: office@obh.co.uk
Website: www.obh.co.uk

Old Hall School
Head: R J Ward
Wellington, Telford TF1 2DN
Tel: +44 (0)1952 223117
Fax: +44 (0)1952 222674
Email: ohs@btinternet.com

The Old Malthouse
Head: J H L Phillips
Langton Matravers, Swanage BH19 3HB
Tel: +44 (0)1929 422302
Fax: +44 (0)1929 422154
Email: office@oldmalthouseschool.co.uk
Website: www.oldmalthouseschool.co.uk

Oratory Prep School
Head: D L Sexon
Great Oaks, Goring Heath, Reading RG8 7SF
Tel: +44 (0)118 984 4511
Fax: +44 (0)118 984 4806
Email: office@oratoryprep.co.uk

The Oratory School
Head: C I Dytor
Woodcote, Reading RG8 0PJ
Tel: +44 (0)1491 680207
Fax: +44 (0)1491 680020
Email: enquiries@oratory.co.uk
Website: www.oratory.co.uk

Orwell Park School
Head: A H Auster
Nacton, Ipswich IP10 0ER
Tel: +44 (0)1473 659225
Fax: +44 (0)1473 659822
Email: headmaster@orwellpark.co.uk
Website: www.orwellpark.co.uk

Oswestry School
Head: P D Stockdale
Upper Brook Street, Oswestry SY11 2TL

Tel: +44 (0)1691 655711
Fax: +44 (0)1691 671194
Email: osschoolhm@aol.com
Website: www.oswestryschool.org.uk

Oundle School
Head: Dr R D Townsend
Oundle, Peterborough PE8 4EN
Tel: +44 (0)1832 277122
Fax: +44 (0)1832 277123
Email: headmaster@oundle.co.uk
Website: www.oundleschool.org.uk

Packwood Haugh
N T Westlake, Ruyton-XI-Towns
Shrewsbury SY4 1HX
Tel: +44 (0)1939 260217
Fax: +44 (0)1939 260051
Email: enquiries@packwood-haugh.co.uk
Website: www.packwood-haugh.co.uk

Pangbourne College
Head: Dr Kenneth Greig
Pangbourne, Reading RG8 8LA
Tel: +44 (0)118 984 2101
Fax: +44 (0)118 984 1239
Email: registrar@pangcoll.co.uk
Website: www.pangbournecollege.com

Papplewick
Head: D R Llewellyn
Ascot SL5 7LH
Tel: +44 (0)1344 621488
Fax: +44 (0)1344 874639
Email: Saraht@papplewick.org.uk

The Park School
Head: Paul W Bate
Yeovil BA20 1DH
Tel: +44 (0)1935 423514
Fax: +44 (0)1935 411257
Email: admin.parkschool@ukonline.co.uk
Website: www.parkschool.com

Parkside School
Head: David Aylward
The Manor, Stoke d'Abernon
Cobham KT11 3PX
Tel: +44 (0)1932 862749
Fax: +44 (0)1932 860251

Parsons Mead School
Head: Mrs P Taylor
Ottways Lane, Ashtead KT21 2PE
Tel: +44 (0)1372 276401
Fax: +44 (0)1372 278796
Email: parsonsmead@parsonsmead.co.uk

Perrott Hill School
Head: M J Davies
North Perrott, Crewkerne TA18 7SL
Tel: +44 (0)1460 72051
Fax: +44 (0)1460 78246
Email: headmaster@perrott-hill.sch.uk
Website: www.perrott-hill.sch.uk

Peterborough High School
Head: Mrs S A Dixon
Westwood House, Thorpe Road
Peterborough PE3 6JF
Tel: +44 (0)1733 343357
Fax: +44 (0)1733 355710
Email: phs@
peterboroughhigh.peterborough.sch.uk
Website:
www.peterboroughhigh.peterborough.sch.uk

Pilgrims' School
Head: The Rev Dr B A Rees
Winchester SO23 9LT
Tel: +44 (0)1962 854189
Fax: +44 (0)1962 843610
Email: pilgrimshead@btinternet.com

Pinewood School
Head: J S Croysdale
Bourton, Swindon SN6 8HZ
Tel: +44 (0)1793 782205
Fax: +44 (0)1793 783476
Email: jimcroysdale@pinewood.biblio.net
Website: www.pinewood.oxon.sch.uk

Pipers Corner School
Head: Mrs V M Stattersfield
Great Kingshill, High Wycombe HP15 6LP
Tel: +44 (0)1494 718255
Fax: +44 (0)1494 719806
Email: pipers@enterprise.net

Plymouth College
Head: A J Morsley
Ford Park, Plymouth PL4 6RN

Tel: +44 (0)1752 203300
Fax: +44 (0)1752 203246
Email: admin@plymouthcollege.com
Website: www.plymouthcollege.com

Pocklington School
Head: N Clements
West Green, Pocklington, York YO42 2NJ
Tel: +44 (0)1759 303125
Fax: +44 (0)1759 306366
Email: mainoffice@
pocklington.e-yorks.sch.uk
Website: www.pocklington.e-yorks.sch.uk

Polam Hall School
Head: Mrs H C Hamilton
Grange Road, Darlington DL1 5PA
Tel: +44 (0)1325 463383
Fax: +44 (0)1325 383539
Email: information@polamhall.com
Website: www.polamhall.com

Polwhele House School
Head: Mr and Mrs R I White
Truro TR4 9AE
Tel: +44 (0)1872 273011
Fax: +44 (0)1872 273011
Email: polwhele@talk21.com
Website: www.polwhelehouse.co.uk

Port Regis
Head: P A E Dix
Motcombe Park, Shaftesbury SP7 9QA
Tel: +44 (0)1747 852566
Fax: +44 (0)1747 854684
Email: office@portregis.com
Website: www.portregis.com

Prebendal School
Head: The Revd Canon G C Hall
Chichester PO19 1RT
Tel: +44 (0)1243 782026
Fax: +44 (0)1243 771821
Email: postmaster@prebendal.w-sussex.sch.uk
Website: www.prebendal.w-sussex.sch.uk

Prestfelde
Head: J R Bridgeland
Shrewsbury SY2 6NZ
Tel: +44 (0)1743 245400
Fax: +44 (0)1743 241434
Email: office@prestfelde.net
Website: www.prestfelde.net

The Princess Helena College
Head: Mrs Anne-Marie Hodgkiss
Preston, Hitchin SG4 7RT
Tel: +44 (0)1462 432100
Fax: +44 (0)1462 431497
Email: head@phc.herts.sch.uk
Website: www.phc.herts.sch.uk

Princethorpe College
Head: J M Shinkwin
Leamington Road, Princethorpe
Rugby CV23 9PX
Tel: +44 (0)1926 634200
Fax: +44 (0)1926 633365
Email: post@princethorpe.co.uk
Website: www.princethorpe.co.uk

Prior's Field
Head: Mrs J C Dwyer
Godalming GU7 2RH
Tel: +44 (0)1483 810551
Fax: +44 (0)1483 810180
Email: admin@priorsfield.demon.co.uk
Website: www.priorsfield.demon.co.uk

Prior Park College
Head: Dr R G G Mercer
Bath BA2 5AH
Tel: +44 (0)1225 831000
Fax: +44 (0)1225 835753
Email: admissions@priorpark.co.uk
Website: www.priorpark.co.uk

Prior Park Preparatory School
Head: G B Hobern
Cricklade SN6 6BB
Tel: +44 (0)1793 750275
Fax: +44 (0)1793 750910
Email: prior.park.prep@ukonline.co.uk

Purcell School of Music
Head: J N Tolputt
Aldenham Road, Bushey
Watford WD2 3TS
Tel: +44 (0)1923 331100
Fax: +44 (0)1923 331166
Email: info@purcell-school.org
Website: www.purcell-school.org

Queen's College
Head: Christopher J Alcock
Taunton TA1 4QS
Tel: +44 (0)1823 272559
Fax: +44 (0)1823 338430
Email: headmaster.sec@
queenscollege.org.uk
Website: www.queenscollege.org.uk

Queen's College Junior School
Trull Road, Taunton TA1 4QP
Tel: +44 (0)1823 272990
Fax: +44 (0)1823 323811
Email: junior.head@queenscollege.org.uk
Website:
www.queens-college-taunton.org.uk

Queen Anne's School
Head: Mrs D Forbes
Caversham, Reading RG4 6DX
Tel: +44 (0)118 918 7300
Fax: +44 (0)118 918 7310
Email: ssec@queenannes.reading.sch.uk

Queen Elizabeth's Hospital
Head: S W Holliday
Berkeley Place, Clifton, Bristol BS8 1JX
Tel: +44 (0)117 929 1856
Fax: +44 (0)117 929 3106
Email: headmaster@qehbristol.co.uk

Queen Ethelburga's College
Head: Peter Dass
Thorpe Underwood Hall
Thorpe Underwood, York YO26 9SS
Tel: +44 (0)870 742 3300
Fax: +44 (0)870 742 3310
Email: enquiries@queenethelburgas.edu
Website: www.queenethelburgas.edu

Queen Margaret's School
Head: Dr G A H Chapman
Escrick Park, York YO19 6EU
Tel: +44 (0)1904 728261
Fax: +44 (0)1904 728150
Email: enquiries@qmyork.force9.co.uk
Website: www.queenmargarets.org.uk

Queen Mary's School
Head: Mr and Mrs I H Angus
Baldersby Park, Topcliffe, Thirsk YO7 3BZ
Tel: +44 (0)1845 575000
Fax: +44 (0)1845 575001
Email: admin@queenmarys.org

Queenswood
Head: Ms C M Farr
Shepherds Way, Brookmans Park
Hatfield AL9 6NS
Tel: +44 (0)1707 602500
Fax: +44 (0)1707 602597
Email: registry@queenswood.herts.sch.uk
Website: www.queenswood.herts.sch.uk

RNIB New College Worcester
Head: Mr Nick Ratcliffe
Whittington Road, Worcester WR5 2JX
Tel: +44 (0)1905 763933
Fax: +44 (0)1905 763277
Email: hodgetts@rnibncw.demon.co.uk

Radley College
Head: A W McPhail
Abingdon OX14 2HR
Tel: +44 (0)1235 543000
Fax: +44 (0)1235 543106
Email: warden@radley.org.uk
Website: www.radley.org.uk

Ramillies Hall
Head: Mrs A L Poole and Miss D M
Patterson, Cheadle Hulme SK8 7AJ
Tel: +44 (0)161 485 3804
Fax: +44 (0)161 486 6021
Email: ramillies@btinternet.com

Ranby House
Head: A C Morris
Retford DN22 8HX
Tel: +44 (0)1777 703138
Fax: +44 (0)1777 702813
Email: office@
ranbyhouse.u-net.com
Website: www.ranbyhouseschool.co.uk

Rannoch School
Head: Arthur Andrews
Rannoch, By Pitlochry PH17 2QQ
Tel: +44 (0)1882 632332
Fax: +44 (0)1882 632443
Email: headmaster@rannoch.co.uk
Website: www.rannoch.co.uk

Ratcliffe College
Head: Peter Farrar
Fosse Way, Ratcliffe on the Wreake
Leicester LE7 4SG
Tel: +44 (0)1509 817000
Fax: +44 (0)1509 817004
Email: registrar@ratcliffe.leics.sch.uk
Website: www.ratcliffecollege.com

Reading Blue Coat School
Head: S J W McArthur
Holme Park, Sonning, Reading RG4 6SU
Tel: +44 (0)118 944 1005
Fax: +44 (0)118 944 2690
Email: headsec@blue-coat.reading.sch.uk

Read School
Head: R A Hadfield
Drax, Selby YO8 8NL
Tel: +44 (0)1757 618248
Fax: +44 (0)1757 617432
Email: richard.hadfield@virgin.net
Website: www.readdrax.demon.co.uk

Red Maids' School
Head: Mrs I Tobias
Westbury-on-Trym, Bristol BS9 3AW
Tel: +44 (0)117 962 2641
Fax: +44 (0)117 962 1687
Email: admin@redmaids.bristol.sch.uk
Website: www.redmaids.bristol.sch.uk

Reed's School
Head: David Jarrett
Cobham KT11 2ES
Tel: +44 (0)1932 869044
Fax: +44 (0)1932 869046
Email: hm@reeds.surrey.sch.uk
Website: www.reeds.surrey.sch.uk

Rendcomb College
Head: Gerry Holden
Cirencester GL7 7HA
Tel: +44 (0)1285 831213
Fax: +44 (0)1285 831331
Email: info@rendcomb.gloucs.sch.uk
Website: www.rendcomb.dircon.co.uk

Repton Prep School
Head: P H Brewster
Foremarke Hall, Milton, Derby DE65 6EJ
Tel: +44 (0)1283 703269
Fax: +44 (0)1283 701185
Email: office@foremarke.org.uk
Website: www.foremarke.org.uk

Repton School
Head: G E Jones
Repton, Derby DE65 6FH
Tel: +44 (0)1283 559220
Fax: +44 (0)1283 559223
Email: registrar@repton.org.uk
Website: www.repton.org.uk

Riddlesworth Hall Prep School
Head: C Campbell
Diss IP22 2TA
Tel: +44 (0)195 368 1246
Fax: +44 (0)195 368 8124
Email: riddlseworthhall@pobox.com

Ripon Cathedral Choir School
Ripon HG4 2LA
Tel: +44 (0)1765 602134
Fax: +44 (0)1765 608760
Email: admin@choirschool.demon.co.uk
Website: www.choirschool.demon.co.uk

Rishworth School
Head: Richard Baker
Rishworth, Sowerby Bridge HX6 4QA
Tel: +44 (0)1422 822217
Fax: +44 (0)1422 820911
Email: admin@rishworth-school.co.uk
Website: www.rishworth-school.co.uk

Rockport
Head: Mrs H G Pentland
Craigavad, Holywood BT18 0DD
Tel: +44 (0)28 9042 8372
Fax: +44 (0)28 9042 2608
Email: info@rockportschool.com
Website: www.rockportschool.com

Rodney School
Head: Miss G R T Howe
Kirklington,
Newark NG22 8NB
Tel: +44 (0)1636 813281
Fax: +44 (0)1636 813281
Email: rodney@proweb.co.uk
Website: www.rodney-school.co.uk

Roedean School
Head: Mrs P Metham
Roedean Way, Brighton BN2 5RQ
Tel: +44 (0)1273 603181
Fax: +44 (0)1273 676722
Email: admissions@roedean.co.uk
Website: www.roedean.co.uk

Rookesbury Park School
Head: Mrs S Cook
Wickham PO17 6HT
Tel: +44 (0)1329 833108
Fax: +44 (0)1329 835090
Email: rookesbury.park@ukonline.co.uk
Website: www.rookesburypark.co.uk

Rookwood School
Head: Mrs M P Langley
Weyhill Road, Andover SP10 3AL
Tel: +44 (0)1264 325900
Fax: +44 (0)1264 325909
Email: office@rookwood.hants.sch.uk
Website: www.rookwood.hants.sch.uk

Rose Hill School
Head: R C G Lyne-Pirkis
Alderley, Wotton-under-Edge GL12 7QT
Tel: +44 (0)1453 843196
Fax: +44 (0)1453 846126
Email: rosehillschool.glos@btinternet.com
Website: www.rosehillschoolglos.co.uk

Rossall Preparatory School
Head: D Mitchell
Broadway, Fleetwood FY7 8JW
Tel: +44 (0)1253 774222
Fax: +44 (0)1253 774222
Email: dmitchell.hmrps@virgin.net

Rossall School
Head: T J Wilbur
Fleetwood, FY7 8JW
Tel: +44 (0)1253 774263
Fax: +44 (0)1253 772052
Email: RRhodesHMRossall@compuserve.com

The Royal High School
Head: James Graham-Brown
Lansdown Road, Bath BA1 5SZ
Tel: +44 (0)1225 313877
Fax: +44 (0)1225 420338
Email: royalhigh@bat.gdst.net
Website: www.gdst.net/royalhighbath

Royal Hospital School
Head: N K D Ward
Holbrook, Ipswich IP9 2RX
Tel: +44 (0)1473 326200
Fax: +44 (0)1473 326213
Email: reception@royalhospitalschool.org
Website: www.royalhospitalschool.org

The Royal Masonic School
Head: Mrs I M Andrews
Rickmansworth Park WD3 4HF
Tel: +44 (0)1923 773168
Fax: +44 (0)1923 896729
Email: enquiries@royalmasonic.herts.sch.uk
Website: www.royalmasonic.herts.sch.uk

Royal Russell School
Head: Dr J R Jennings
Coombe Lane, Croydon CR9 5BX
Tel: +44 (0)20 8657 3669
Fax: +44 (0)20 8657 9555
Email: admissions@royalrussell.co.uk

The Royal School
Head: Mrs L Taylor-Gooby
Haslemere GU27 1HQ
Tel: +44 (0)1428 605805
Fax: +44 (0)1428 607451
Email: admissions@royal.surrey.sch.uk
Website: www.royal.surrey.sch.uk

The Royal School
Head: Mrs C A Sibson
65 Rosslyn Hill, London NW3 5UD
Tel: +44 (0)20 7794 7708
Fax: +44 (0)20 7431 6741
Email: royschham@aol.com
Website: www.royalschoolhampstead.net

The Royal School
Head: P D Hewitt
Northland Row, Dungannon BT71 6AP
Tel: +44 (0)28 8772 2710
Fax: +44 (0)28 8775 2506
Email: info@rsd.dungannon.ni.sch.uk

Royal Wolverhampton Junior School
Head: Mrs M Saunders

Penn Road, Wolverhampton WV3 0EF
Tel: +44 (0)1902 349100
Fax: +44 (0)1902 344496
Email: sjs@royal.wolverhampton.sch.uk

Royal Wolverhampton School
Head: T Brooker
Penn Road, Wolverhampton WV3 0EG
Tel: +44 (0)1902 341230
Fax: +44 (0)1902 344496
Email: mo@royal.wolverhampton.sch.uk
Website: www.theroyalschool.co.uk

Rugby School
Head: P Derham, Rugby CV22 5EH
Tel: +44 (0)1788 556274
Fax: +44 (0)1788 556277
Email: registry@rugby-school.warwks.sch.uk
Website: www.rugby-school.warwks.sch.uk

Ruthin School
Head: John Rowlands
Ruthin LL15 1EE
Tel: +44 (0)1824 702543
Fax: +44 (0)1824 707141
Email: secretary@ruthinschool.co.uk
Website: www.ruthinschool.co.uk

Rydal Penrhos Preparatory School
Head: Simon Beavan
Pwllycrochan Avenue,
Colwyn Bay LL29 7BP
Tel: +44 (0)1492 530381
Fax: +44 (0)1492 533983
Email: rydalpenrhosprep@rmplc.co.uk

Rydal Penrhos Senior School
Head: M S James
Colwyn Bay LL29 7BT
Tel: +44 (0)1492 530155
Fax: +44 (0)1492 531872
Email: info@rydal-penrhos.com
Website: www.rydal-penrhos.com

Ryde Junior School
Head: H Edwards
Queen's Road, Ryde PO33 3BE
Tel: +44 (0)1983 612901
Fax: +44 (0)1983 614973
Email: juniorhead@rydeschool.org.uk

Ryde School
Head: Dr N J England
Queen's Road, Ryde PO33 3BE
Tel: +44 (0)1983 562229
Fax: +44 (0)1983 564714
Email: headmaster@rydeschool.org.uk
Website: www.rydeschool.org.uk

Rye St Antony School
Head: Miss A M Jones
Pullen's Lane, Oxford OX3 0BY
Tel: +44 (0)1865 762802
Fax: +44 (0)1865 763611
Email: ryestantony@btconnect.com
Website: home.btconnect.com/ryestantony

The Ryleys
Head: P G Barrett
Alderley Edge SK9 7UY
Tel: +44 (0)1625 583241
Fax: +44 (0)1625 581900
Email: headmaster@ryleys.cheshire.sch.uk

Sacred Heart Convent School
Head: Sister Francis Ridler FDC
17 Mangate Street, Swaffham PE37 7QW
Tel: +44 (0)1760 721330
Fax: +44 (0)1760 725557
Email: info@sacredheartschool.co.uk

Saint Andrew's School
Head: J M Snow
Buckhold, Pangbourne Reading RG8 8QA
Tel: +44 (0)118 974 4276
Fax: +44 (0)118 974 5049
Email: admin@standrews.reading.sch.uk

Saint Andrews School
Head: F Roche
Meads, Eastbourne BN20 7RP
Tel: +44 (0)1323 733203
Fax: +44 (0)1323 646860
Email: office@androvian.co.uk
Website: www.androvian.co.uk

Saint Anselm's School
Head: R J Foster
Bakewell DE45 1DP
Tel: +44 (0)1629 812 734
Fax: +44 (0)1629 814742
Email: headmaster@s.anselms.btinternet.com

Saint Antony's-Leweston School
Head: H J MacDonald
Sherborne DT9 6EN
Tel: +44 (0)1963 210691
Fax: +44 (0)1963 210786
Email: st.antony@virgin.net

Saint Antony's Preparatory School
Head: Mrs L M Walker
Leweston, Sherborne DT9 6EN
Tel: +44 (0)1963 210790
Fax: +44 (0)1963 210648
Email: enquiries@stantonysprep.co.uk

Saint Aubyn's School
Head: B J McDowell
Milestones House
Blundell's Road
Tiverton EX16 4NA
Tel: +44 (0)1884 252393
Fax: +44 (0)1884 232333
Email: staubyns@blundells.org

Saint Aubyns
Head: A G Gobat
Rottingdean, Brighton BN2 7JN
Tel: +44 (0)1273 302170
Fax: +44 (0)1273 304004
Email: office@st-aubyns.brighton-hove.sch.uk

Saint Bede's School
Head: A H and H C Stafford Northcote
Bishton Hall, Wolseley Bridge
Stafford ST17 0XN
Tel: +44 (0)1889 881277
Fax: +44 (0)1889 882749
Email: st.bedes.bishton@which.net

Saint Bede's School – Eastbourne
Head: C P Pyemont
Eastbourne BN20 7XL
Tel: +44 (0)1323 734222
Fax: +44 (0)1323 746438
Email: prep.school@stbedesschool.org
Website: www.stbedesschool.org

Saint Bede's School – The Dicker
Head: R Perrin
Hailsham BN27 3QH
Tel: +44 (0)1323 843252
Fax: +44 (0)1323 442628
Email: school.office@stbedes.e-sussex.sch.uk
Website: www.stbedes.e-sussex.sch.uk

Saint Bees School
Head: Philip Capes
St Bees CA27 0DU
Tel: +44 (0)1946 822 263
Fax: +44 (0)1946 823657
Email: mailbox@st-bees-school.co.uk
Website: www.st-bees-school.co.uk

Saint Catherine's School
Head: Mrs A M Phillips
Bramley
Guildford GU5 0DF
Tel: +44 (0)1483 893363
Fax: +44 (0)1483 899608
Email: schooloffice@st-catherines.surrey.sch.uk
Website: www.st-catherines.surrey.sch.uk

Saint Christopher School
Head: Colin Reid
Letchworth SG6 3JZ
Tel: +44 (0)1462 679301
Fax: +44 (0)1462 481578
Email: stchris.admin@rmplc.co.uk
Website: www.stchris.co.uk

Saint Columba's College
Head: Dr Lindsay Haslett
Whitechurch, Dublin 16, Eire
Tel: +353 1490 6791
Fax: +353 1493 6655
Email: admin@stcolumbas.ie
Website: www.stcolumbas.ie

Saint David's College
Head: W G Seymour
Llandudno LL30 1RD
Tel: +44 (0)1492 875974
Fax: +44 (0)1492 870383
Email: headmaster@stdavidscollege.co.uk
Website: www.stdavidscollege.co.uk

Saint David's School
Head: Ms P Bristow
Ashford TW15 3DZ
Tel: +44 (0)1784 252494
Fax: +44 (0)1784 248652
Email: office@st-davids.demon.co.uk
Website: www.st-davids.demon.co.uk

Saint Dunstan's Abbey School
Head: Mrs T Smith
The Millfields, Plymouth PL1 3JL
Tel: +44 (0)1752 201350
Fax: +44 (0)1752 201351
Email: info@sda.org.uk
Website: www.sda.org.uk

Saint Edmund's College
Head: D J J McEwen
Old Hall Green, Ware SG11 1DS
Tel: +44 (0)1920 821504
Fax: +44 (0)1920 823011
Email: admissions@stedmundscollege.org
Website: www.stedmundscollege.org

Saint Edmund's Junior School
Head: R G Bacon
Canterbury CT2 8HU
Tel: +44 (0)1227 475600
Fax: +44 (0)1227 471083
Email: junsch@stedmunds.org.uk
Website: www.stedmunds.org.uk

Saint Edmund's School
Head: A N Ridley
Canterbury CT2 8HU
Tel: +44 (0)1227 475600
Fax: +44 (0)1227 471083
Email: headmaster@stedmunds.org.uk
Website: www.stedmunds.org.uk

Saint Edmund's School
Head: A J Walliker
Hindhead GU26 6BH
Tel: +44 (0)1428 604808
Fax: +44 (0)1428 607898
Email: StEds1874@aol.com

Saint Edward's School
Head: D Christie
Woodstock Road
Oxford OX2 7NN
Tel: +44 (0)1865 319200
Fax: +44 (0)1865 319202
Email: mrsannebrooks@stedward.oxon.sch.uk
Website: www.stedward.oxon.sch.uk

Saint Elphin's School
Head: Mrs E Taylor
Darley Dale, Matlock DE4 2HA
Tel: +44 (0)1629 733263
Fax: +44 (0)1629 733956
Email: admin@st-elphins.co.uk
Website: www.st-elphins.co.uk

Saint Felix School
Head: R Williams
Southwold IP18 6SD
Tel: +44 (0)1502 722175
Fax: +44 (0)1502 722641
Email: schooladmin@stfelix.suffolk.sch.uk
Website: www.stfelix.co.uk

Saint Francis' College
Head: Miss M Hegarty
Broadway, Letchworth SG6 3PJ
Tel: +44 (0)1462 670511
Fax: +44 (0)1462 682361
Email: stfran@rmplc.co.uk
Website: www.st-francis.herts.sch.uk

Saint George's School
Head: J R Jones
Windsor Castle, Windsor SL4 1QF
Tel: +44 (0)1753 865553
Fax: +44 (0)1753 842093
Email: enqs@stgwindsor.co.uk

Saint George's School – Ascot
Head: Mrs J Grant Peterkin
Ascot SL5 7DZ
Tel: +44 (0)1344 629900
Fax: +44 (0)1344 629901
Email: office@stgeorges-ascot.org.uk

Saint George's School for Girls
Head: Dr J McClure
Garscube Terrace
Edinburgh EH12 6BG
Tel: +44 (0)131 332 4575
Fax: +44 (0)131 315 2035
Email: head@st.georges.edin.sch.uk
Website: www.st.georges.edin.sch.uk

Saint Helen's School
Head: Mrs Mary Morris
Eastbury Road, Northwood HA6 3AS
Tel: +44 (0)1923 843210
Fax: +44 (0)1923 843211
Email: StHelensNorthwood.co.uk

Saint Hugh's
Head: S G C Greenish
Woodhall Spa LN10 6TQ
Tel: +44 (0)1526 352169
Fax: +44 (0)1526 353153
Email: office@sthughs.biblio.net
Website: www.st-hughs.lincs.sch.uk

Saint Hugh's School
Head: D Cannon
Carswell Manor, Faringdon SN7 8PT
Tel: +44 (0)1367 870 223
Fax: +44 (0)1367 870 376
Email: headmaster@st-hughs.co.uk

Saint James's
Head: Mrs S Kershaw
West Malvern WR14 4DF
Tel: +44 (0)1684 560851
Fax: +44 (0)1684 569252
Email: kershawwm@aol.com
Website: www.st-james-school.co.uk

**Saint James Independent
School for Boys (Senior)**
Head: N Debenham
Popes Villa, 19 Cross Deep TW1 4QG
Tel: +44 (0)20 8892 2002
Fax: +44 (0)20 8892 4442
Email: stjames@boysschool.wordonline.co.uk
Website: www.stjamesschools.co.uk

Saint James School
Head: Susan M Isaac
22 Bargate, Grimsby DN34 4SY
Tel: +44 (0)1472 503260
Fax: +44 (0)1472 503275
Email: enquiries@
saintjamesschool.freeserve.co.uk
Website: www.saintjamesschool.freeserve.co.uk

Saint John's-on-the-Hill
Head: I K Etchells
Chepstow NP16 7LE
Tel: +44 (0)1291 622045
Fax: +44 (0)1291 623932
Email: st.johns.chepstow@dial.pipex.com

Saint John's Beaumont
Head: D St J Gogarty
Old Windsor, Windsor SL4 2JN
Tel: +44 (0)1784 432428
Fax: +44 (0)1784 494048
Email: admissions@stjohnsbeaumont.co.uk
Website: www.stjohnsbeaumont.org.uk

Saint John's College
Head: Mrs S M Bell
Grove Road South, Southsea PO5 3QW
Tel: +44 (0)23 9281 5118
Fax: +44 (0)23 9281 8603
Email: sjc.southsea@lineone.net
Website: www.stjohnscollege.co.uk

Saint John's College School
Head: K L Jones
73 Grange Road, Cambridge CB3 9AB
Tel: +44 (0)1223 353532
Fax: +44 (0)1223 315535
Email: shoffice@sjcs.co.uk
Website: www.sjcs.co.uk

Saint John's School
Head: C H Tongue, Leatherhead KT22 8SP
Tel: +44 (0)1372 372021
Fax: +44 (0)1372 386606
Email: secretary@stjohns.surrey.sch.uk
Website: www.stjohns.surrey.sch.uk

Saint John's School
Head: N Pockett, Sidmouth EX10 8RG
Tel: +44 (0)1395 513984
Fax: +44 (0)1395 514539
Email: nrp@stjohndevon.demon.co.uk
Website: www.st-johns.devon.sch.uk

Saint Joseph's College
Birkfield, Ipswich IP2 9DR
Tel: +44 (0)1473 690281
Fax: +44 (0)1473 602409
Email: hmsjcjm@aol.co
Website: www.stjos.co.uk

Saint Joseph's School
Head: P S Larkman
15 St Stephen's Hill, Launceston PL15 8HN
Tel: +44 (0)1566 772580
Fax: +44 (0)1566 775902
Email: bursar@stjosephslaunceston-
cornwall.schoolzone.co.uk
Website: www.st.josephs.schoolzone.co.uk

Saint Katharines School
Head: Mrs J Gibson
The Pends, St Andrews KY16 9RB
Tel: +44 (0)1334 460470
Fax: +44 (0)1334 479196
Email: info@stleonards-fife.org
Website: www.stleonards-fife.org

Saint Lawrence College
Head: M Slater
Ramsgate CT11 7AE
Tel: +44 (0)1843 592680
Fax: +44 (0)1843 851123
Email: headmaster.slc@dial.pipex.com
Website: www.st-lawrence-college.com

Saint Lawrence College Junior School
Head: R Tunnicliffe
Ramsgate CT11 7AF
Tel: +44 (0)1843 591788
Fax: +44 (0)1843 853271

Saint Leonards and Sixth Form College
Head: Mrs Wendy A Bellars
St Andrews KY16 9QJ
Tel: +44 (0)1334 472126
Fax: +44 (0)1334 476152
Email: info@stleonards-fife.org
Website: www.stleonards-fife.org

Saint Leonards-Mayfield School
Head: Mrs Julia Dalton
The Old Palace, Mayfield TN20 6PH
Tel: +44 (0)1435 874600
Fax: +44 (0)1435 872627
Email: enquiry@stlm.e-sussex.sch.uk
Website: www.stlm.e-sussex.sch.uk

Saint Margaret's School
Head: Miss M de Villiers
Bushey, Watford WD23 1DT
Tel: +44 (0)20 8901 0870
Fax: +44 (0)20 8950 1677
Email: schooloffice@stmargarets.herts.sch.uk

Saint Margaret's School
Head: Mrs Elaine Davis
East Suffolk Road, Edinburgh EH16 5PJ
Tel: +44 (0)131 668 1986
Fax: +44 (0)131 662 0957
Email: contact@stmargaretsschool.net

Saint Martin's Ampleforth
Head: S Mullen
The Castle, Gilling East, York YO62 4HP
Tel: +44 (0)1439 766600
Fax: +44 (0)1439 788538
Email: headmaster@stmartins.ampleforth.org.uk

Saint Mary's Hall
Head: Mrs Susan M Meek
Eastern Road, Brighton BN2 5JF
Tel: +44 (0)1273 606061
Fax: +44 (0)1273 620782
Email: Communicate@stmaryshall.co.uk
Website: www.stmaryshall.co.uk

Saint Mary's Hall
Head: M Higgins, Stonyhurst BB7 9PU
Tel: +44 (0)1254 826 242
Fax: +44 (0)1254 826 382
Email: Stmaryshall@aol.com

Saint Mary's School
Head: Mrs Jayne Triffitt
Bateman Street, Cambridge CB2 1LY
Tel: +44 (0)1223 353253
Fax: +44 (0)1223 357451
Email: enquiries@stmarys.cambs.sch.uk
Website: www.stmarys.cambs.sch.uk

Saint Mary's School
Head: Mrs Sue Pennington
Shaftesbury SP7 9LP
Tel: +44 (0)1747 854005
Fax: +44 (0)1747 851557
Email: head@st-marys-shaftesbury.co.uk

Saint Mary's School
Head: J A Brett
Abbey Park, Melrose TD6 9LN
Tel: +44 (0)189 682 2517
Fax: +44 (0)189 682 3550

Saint Mary's School Ascot
Head: Mrs Mary Breen
St Mary's Road, South Ascot, Ascot SL5 9JF
Tel: +44 (0)1344 623721
Fax: +44 (0)1344 873281
Email: admissions@st-marys-ascot.co.uk
Website: www.st-marys-ascot.co.uk

Saint Mary's School Calne
Head: Mrs Carolyn J Shaw
Calne SN11 0DF
Tel: +44 (0)1249 857200
Fax: +44 (0)1249 857207
Email: sms@stmaryscalne.wilts.sch.uk
Website: www.stmaryscalne.wilts.sch.uk

Saint Mary's School
with St Andrews Prep School
Head: Mrs S Sowden
Newbury Street, Wantage OX12 8BZ
Tel: +44 (0)1235 763571
Fax: +44 (0)1235 760467
Email: stmarysw@rmplc.co.uk
Website: www.stmarys.oxon.sch.uk

Saint Mary's Westbrook
Head: Mrs L A Watson
Ravenlea Road, Folkestone CT20 2JU
Tel: +44 (0)1303 854006
Fax: +44 (0)1303 249901
Email: hm@st-marys-westbrook.co.uk
Website: www.st-marys-westbrook.co.uk

Saint Michael's
Head: J W Pratt
Tawstock Court, Barnstaple EX31 3HY
Tel: +44 (0)1271 343242
Fax: +44 (0)1271 346771
Email: admin@st-michaels-school.com
Website: www.st-michaels-school.com

Saint Neots
Head: R J Thorp
Eversley, Hook RG27 0PN
Tel: +44 (0)118 973 2118
Fax: +44 (0)118 973 7404
Email: st.neots@talk21.com

Saint Olave's School
Head: T Mulryne
The Junior School of St Peter's, York YO30 6AB
Tel: +44 (0)1904 623269
Fax: +44 (0)1904 640975
Email: enquiries@saint-olaves.york.sch.uk

Saint Paul's Cathedral School
Head: Andrew Dobbin
2 New Change, London EC4M 9AD
Tel: +44 (0)20 7248 5156
Fax: +44 (0)20 7329 6568
Email: admissions@spcs.city-of-london.sch.uk

Saint Paul's Prep School
Head: G J Thompson
Colet Court, Lonsdale Road SW13 9JT
Tel: +44 (0)20 8748 3461
Fax: +44 (0)20 8563 7361
Website: www.stpaulsschool.org.uk/coletcourt

Saint Paul's School
Head: R S Baldock
Lonsdale Road, Barnes, London SW13 9JT
Tel: +44 (0)20 8748 9162
Fax: +44 (0)20 8748 9557
Email: HMSec@stpaulsschool.org.uk
Website: www.stpaulsschool.org.uk

Saint Peter's School
Head: C N C Abram
Lympstone, Exmouth EX8 5AU
Tel: +44 (0)1395 272148
Fax: +44 (0)1395 274410
Email: st.peters@eclipse.co.uk
Website: www.stpetersprep.devon.sch.uk

Saint Peter's School
Head: A F Trotman
York YO30 6AB
Tel: +44 (0)1904 623213
Fax: +44 (0)1904 640974
Email: enquiry@admin.saintpeters.york.sch.uk
Website: www.rmplc.co.uk/
eduweb/sites/stpyork/index.html

Saint Richard's
Head: R E H Coghlan
Bredenbury Court, Bromyard HR7 4TD
Tel: +44 (0)1885 482491
Fax: +44 (0)1885 488982
Email: st.dix@virgin.net
Website: www.st-richards.co.uk

Saint Ronan's
Head: Edward Yeats-Brown
Hawkhurst TN18 5DJ
Tel: +44 (0)1580 752271
Fax: +44 (0)1580 754882
Email: info@stronans.kent.sch.uk
Website: www.stronans.kent.sch.uk

Saint Swithun's School
Head: Dr H L Harvey
Winchester SO21 1HA
Tel: +44 (0)1962 835700
Fax: +44 (0)1962 835779
Email: headmistress@
st-swithuns.hants.sch.uk

Saint Teresa's Preparatory School
Head: Mrs A Stewart
Grove House, Guildford Road KT24 5QA
Tel: +44 (0)1372 453456
Fax: +44 (0)1372 451562
Email: prep@st-teresas.demon.co.uk

Saint Teresa's School
Head: Mrs M E Prescott
Effingham Hill, Dorking RH5 6ST
Tel: +44 (0)1372 452037
Fax: +44 (0)1372 450311
Email: info@stteresas.surrey.sch.uk
Website: www.stteresas.surrey.sch.uk

Salisbury Cathedral School
Head: R M Thackray
1 The Close, Salisbury SP1 2EQ
Tel: +44 (0)1722 555300
Fax: +44 (0)1722 410910
Email: aspire@salisbury.enterprise-plc.com
Website: www.eluk.co.uk/scs

Sandroyd School
Head: Michael J Hatch
Tollard Royal, Salisbury SP5 5QD
Tel: +44 (0)1725 516264
Fax: +44 (0)1725 516441
Email: sandroyd@dial.pipex.com
Website: www.sandroyd.co.uk

Scarborough College
Head: T L Kirkup
Filey Road, Scarborough YO11 3BA
Tel: +44 (0)1723 360620
Fax: +44 (0)1723 377265
Email: admin@scarboroughcollege.co.uk
Website: www.scarboroughcollege.co.uk

School of St Mary and St Anne
Head: Mrs M Steel
Abbots Bromley
Rugeley WS15 3BW
Tel: +44 (0)1283 840232
Fax: +44 (0)1283 840988
Email: info@abbotsbromley.staffs.sch.uk

Seaford College
Head: T J Mullins
Petworth GU28 0NB
Tel: +44 (0)1798 867392
Fax: +44 (0)1798 867606
Email: seaford@freeuk.com
Website: www.seaford.org

Sedbergh School
Head: C H Hirst
Sedbergh LA10 5HG
Tel: +44 (0)15396 20535
Fax: +44 (0)15396 21301
Email: HMSedbergh@aol.com
Website: www.sedbergh.co.uk

Sevenoaks School
Head: T R Cookson
Sevenoaks TN13 1HU
Tel: +44 (0)1732 455133
Fax: +44 (0)1732 456143
Email: regist@admin.soaks.kent.sch.uk

Shebbear College
Head: L Clark
Beaworthy EX21 5HJ
Tel: +44 (0)1409 281228
Fax: +44 (0)1409 281784
Email: info@shebbearcollege.co.uk
Website: www.shebbearcollege.co.uk

Sherborne Preparatory School
Head: P S Tait
Acreman Street
Sherborne DT9 3NY
Tel: +44 (0)1935 812097
Fax: +44 (0)1935 813948
Email: sherborneprep@hotmail.com
Website: www.sherborneprep.com

Sherborne School
Head: S F Eliot
Sherborne DT9 3AP
Tel: +44 (0)1935 812249
Fax: +44 (0)1935 810426
Email: enquiries@sherborne.org
Website: www.sherborne.org

Sherborne School for Girls
Head: Mrs G B Kerton-Johnson
Sherborne DT9 3QN
Tel: +44 (0)1935 812245
Fax: +44 (0)1935 818290
Email: enquiry@sherborne.com
Website: www.sherborne.com

Sherborne School International College
Head: Dr C Greenfield
Newell Grange, Sherborne DT9 4EZ
Tel: +44 (0)1935 814743
Fax: +44 (0)1935 816863
Email: reception@sherborne-ic.net
Website: www.sherborne-ic.net

Shiplake College
Head: N V Bevan
Henley-on-Thames RG9 4BW
Tel: +44 (0)118 940 2455
Fax: +44 (0)118 940 5204

Shrewsbury School
Head: Jeremy Goulding
The Schools, Shrewsbury SY3 7BA
Tel: +44 (0)1743 280525
Fax: +44 (0)1743 340048
Email: headmaster@shrewsbury.org.uk
Website: www.shrewsbury.org.uk

Sibford School
Head: Susan Freestone
Sibford Ferris
Banbury OX15 5QL
Tel: +44 (0)1295 781200
Fax: +44 (0)1295 781204
Email: sibford.school@dial.pipex.com
Website: www.sibford.oxon.sch.uk

Sidcot School
Head: A Slesser
Winscombe BS25 1PD
Tel: +44 (0)193 484 3102
Fax: +44 (0)1934 844 181
Email: sidcotad@aol.com

Slindon College
Head: I Graham
Slindon, Arundel BN18 0RH
Tel: +44 (0)1243 814320
Fax: +44 (0)1243 814702
Email: registrar@slindoncollege.fsnet.co.uk
Website:
www.slindoncollege.w-sussex.sch.uk

Sompting Abbotts
Head: R M Johnson
Lancing BN15 0AZ
Tel: +44 (0)1903 235960
Fax: +44 (0)1903 210045
Email: office@
somptingabbotts-prep-school.co.uk
Website:
www.somptingabbotts-prep-school.co.uk

Stamford High School for Girls
Head: Dr P R Mason
St Martin's, Stamford PE9 2LJ
Tel: +44 (0)1780 750310
Fax: +44 (0)1780 750397
Email: ses@stamfordschool.lincs.sch.uk
Website: www.ses.lincs.sch.uk

Stamford Junior School
Head: Miss E M Craig
Kettering Road
Stamford PE9 2LR
Tel: +44 (0)1780 484400
Fax: +44 (0)1780 484401
Email: headjs@shs.lincs.sch.uk

Stamford School
Head: Dr P R Mason
Stamford PE9 2BS
Tel: +44 (0)1780 750310
Fax: +44 (0)1780 750397
Email: ses@stamfordschool.lincs.sch.uk
Website: www.ses.lincs.sch.uk

Stanborough School
Head: Steve Rivers
Stanborough Park, Garston
Watford WD25 9JT
Tel: +44 (0)1923 673268
Fax: +44 (0)1923 893943

Stanbridge Earls School
Head: H Moxon
Romsey SO51 0ZS
Tel: +44 (0)1794 516777
Fax: +44 (0)1794 511201
Email: Stanbridgesec@aol.com

Stancliffe Hall
Head: Andrew Lamb
Darley Dale, Matlock 608DE4 2HJ
Tel: +44 (0)1629 732310
Fax: +44 (0)1629 734509
Email: stanclif@globalnet.co.uk
Website: www.stancliffe.co.uk

Stewart's Melville College
Head: J N D Gray
Queensferry Road, Edinburgh EH4 3EZ
Tel: +44 (0)131 332 7925
Fax: +44 (0)131 343 2432
Email: principal@stewartsmelville.edin.sch.uk
Website: www.stewartsmelville.edin.sch.uk

Stoke Brunswick
Head: W M Ellerton
Ashurst Wood, East Grinstead RH19 3PF
Tel: +44 (0)1342 828200
Fax: +44 (0)1342 828201
Email: headmaster@stokebrunswick.co.uk
Website: www.stokebrunswick.co.uk

Stoke College
Head: J Gibson
Stoke-by-Clare, Sudbury CO10 8JE
Tel: +44 (0)1787 278141
Fax: +44 (0)1787 277904
Email: stoke.college@btinternet.com

Stonar School
Head: Mrs S Hopkinson
Cottles Park, Atworth SN12 8NT
Tel: +44 (0)1225 702309
Fax: +44 (0)1225 790830
Email: office@stonar.wilts.sch.uk
Website: www.stonar.wilts.sch.uk

Stonyhurst College
Head: A J F Aylward
Stonyhurst, Clitheroe BB7 9PZ
Tel: +44 (0)1254 827093
Fax: +44 (0)1254 826370
Email: admissions@stonyhurst.ac.uk
Website: www.stonyhurst.ac.uk

Stover School for Girls
Head: P E Bujak
Newton Abbot TQ12 6QG
Tel: +44 (0)1626 354505
Fax: +44 (0)1626 361475
Email: mail@stover.co.uk
Website: www.stover.co.uk

Stowe School
Head: J G L Nichols
Stowe, Buckingham MK18 5EH
Tel: +44 (0)1280 818000
Fax: +44 (0)1280 818181
Email: enquiries@stowe.co.uk
Website: www.stowe.co.uk

Strathallan School
Head: B K Thompson
Forgandenny, Perth PH2 9EG
Tel: +44 (0)1738 812546
Fax: +44 (0)1738 812549
Email: admissions@strathallan.pkc.sch.uk
Website: www.strathallan.co.uk

Summer Fields
Head: R Badham-Thornhill
Mayfield Road, Oxford OX2 7EN
Tel: +44 (0)1865 454433
Fax: +44 (0)1865 459200

Sunningdale School
Head: A J N Dawson and T M E Dawson
Sunningdale SL5 9PY
Tel: +44 (0)1344 620159
Fax: +44 (0)1344 873304
Email: headmaster@sunningdaleschool.co.uk

Sutton Valence School
Head: J S Davies
Sutton Valence, Maidstone ME17 3HN
Tel: +44 (0)1622 842281
Fax: +44 (0)1622 844093
Email: enquiries@svs.org.uk
Website: www.svs.org.uk

Swanbourne House
Head: Mr S Goodhart and Mrs J Goodhart
Swanbourne MK17 0HZ
Tel: +44 (0)129 672 0264
Fax: +44 (0)129 672 8089
Email: office@swanbourne.org

Sylvia Young Theatre School
Head: Colin Townsend
Rossmore Road, London NW1 6NJ

Tel: +44 (0)20 7402 0673
Fax: +44 (0)20 7723 1040
Email: sylviayoung@freeuk.com

Talbot Heath School
Head: Mrs C Dipple
Rothesay Road
Bournemouth BH4 9NJ
Tel: +44 (0)1202 761881
Fax: +44 (0)1202 768155
Email: admissions.secretary@
talbot-heath.dorset.sch.uk
Website: www.talbotheath.org.uk

Taunton Preparatory School
Head: M Anderson
Staplegrove Road, Taunton TA2 6AE
Tel: +44 (0)1823 349250
Fax: +44 (0)1823 349202
Email: enquiries@tauntonschool.co.uk
Website: www.tauntonschool.co.uk

Taunton School
Head: Julian Whiteley
Taunton TA2 6AD
Tel: +44 (0)1823 349200
Fax: +44 (0)1823 349201
Email: enquiries@tauntonschool.co.uk
Website: www.tauntonschool.co.uk

Taverham Hall School
W D Lawton
Norwich NR8 6HU
Tel: +44 (0)1603 868206
Fax: +44 (0)1603 861061
Email: enquire@taverhamhall.co.uk
Website: www.taverhamhall.co.uk

Temple Grove
Head: M H Kneath
Heron's Ghyll, Uckfield TN22 4DA
Tel: +44 (0)182 571 2112
Fax: +44 (0)182 571 3432
Email: office@templegrove.e-sussex.sch.uk

Terra Nova
Head: N Johnson
Jodrell Bank, Holmes Chapel CW4 8BT
Tel: +44 (0)1477 571251
Fax: +44 (0)1477 571646
Email: terranova@argonet.co.uk
Website: www.tnschool.demon.co.uk

Terrington Hall
Head: M Jon Glen
York YO60 6PR
Tel: +44 (0)1653 648227
Fax: +44 (0)1653 648458
Email: jglen@thps.demon.co.uk

Tettenhall College
Head: P C Bodkin
Wolverhampton WV6 8QX
Tel: +44 (0)1902 751119
Fax: +44 (0)1902 741940
Email: head@tettcoll.wolverhants.sch.uk
Website: www.tettcoll.co.uk

Thornton College – Convent of Jesus and Mary
Head: Miss A Williams
Thornton, Milton Keynes MK17 0HJ
Tel: +44 (0)1280 812610
Fax: +44 (0)1280 824042
Email: thorntoncl@aol.com

Tockington Manor
Head: R G Tovey
Tockington, Bristol BS32 4NY
Tel: +44 (0)1454 613229
Fax: +44 (0)1454 615776
Email: Tock63974@aol.com
Website: www.tockington.bristol.sch.uk

Tonbridge School
Head: J M Hammond
Tonbridge TN9 1JP
Tel: +44 (0)1732 365555
Fax: +44 (0)1732 363424
Email: hmsec@tonbridge-school.org
Website: www.tonbridge-school.co.uk

The Towers Convent School
Head: Sister Mary Andrew Fulgoney
Upper Beeding, Steyning BN44 3TF
Tel: +44 (0)1903 812185
Fax: +44 (0)1903 812188
Bursar.Towers@virgin.net

Town Close House Prep School
Head: R Gordon
14 Ipswich Road, Norwich NR2 2LR

Tel: +44 (0)1603 620180
Fax: +44 (0)1603 618256
Email: head@towncose.com

Treliske Preparatory School
Head: R L Hollins
Truro TR1 3QN
Tel: +44 (0)1872 272616
Fax: +44 (0)1872 222377
Email: enquiries@treliske.cornwall.sch.uk
Website: www.treliske.cornwall.sch.uk

Trent College
Head: J S Lee
Long Eaton, Nottingham NG10 4AD
Tel: +44 (0)115 849 4949
Fax: +44 (0)115 849 4997
Email: enquiry@trentcollege.nott.sch.uk
Website: www.trentcollege.nott.sch.uk

Trinity School
Head: C J Ashby
Buckeridge Road, Teignmouth TQ14 8LY
Tel: +44 (0)1626 774138
Fax: +44 (0)1626 771541
Email: Trinsc123@aol.com
Website: www.trinityschool.co.uk

Truro High School for Girls
Head: Michael McDowell
Falmouth Road, Truro TR1 2HU
Tel: +44 (0)1872 272830
Fax: +44 (0)1872 279393
Email: admin@trurohigh.co.uk

Truro School
Head: Paul Smith
Trennick Lane, Truro TR1 1TH
Tel: +44 (0)1872 272763
Fax: +44 (0)1872 223431
Email: enquiries@truro-school.cornwall.sch.uk

Tudor Hall School
Head: Miss N Godfrey
Banbury OX16 9UR
Tel: +44 (0)1295 263434
Fax: +44 (0)1295 253264
Email: tudorhall@rmplc.co.uk
Website: atschool.eduweb.co.uk/tudorsch

Twyford School
Head: P F Fawkes
Winchester SO21 1NW
Tel: +44 (0)1962 712269
Fax: +44 (0)1962 712100
Email: registrar@twyfordschool.com
Website: www.twyfordschool.com

Uppingham School
Head: Dr S C Winkley
Uppingham LE15 9QE
Tel: +44 (0)157 282 2216
Fax: +44 (0)157 282 2332
Email: headmaster@uppingham.co.uk
Website: www.uppingham.co.uk

Vinehall
Head: D C Chaplin
Robertsbridge TN32 5JL
Tel: +44 (0)1580 880413
Fax: +44 (0)1580 882119
Email: office@vinehall.e-sussex.sch.uk
Website: www.vinehall.e-sussex.sch.uk

Walthamstow Hall
Head: Mrs J S Lang
Hollybush Lane, Sevenoaks TN13 3UL
Tel: +44 (0)1732 451334
Fax: +44 (0)1732 740439
Email: headmistress@walthamstow-hall.co.uk
Website: www.walthamstow-hall.co.uk

Warminster Preparatory School
Head: C J Jones
11 Vicarage Street, Warminster BA12 8JG
Tel: +44 (0)1985 210152
Fax: +44 (0)1985 218850
Email: prep@warminsterschool.org.uk

Warminster School
Head: D Dowdles
Warminster BA12 8PJ
Tel: +44 (0)1985 210100
Fax: +44 (0)1985 214129
Email: admin@warminsterschool.org.uk
Website: ourworld.compuserve.com/
homepages/warminsterschool

Warwick School
Head: P J Cheshire
Warwick CV34 6PP
Tel: +44 (0)1926 776400

Fax: +44 (0)1926 401259
Email: enquiries@warwick.warwks.sch.uk
Website: www.warwick.warwks.sch.uk

Wellesley House
Head: R R Steel
Broadstairs CT10 2DG
Tel: +44 (0)1843 862991
Fax: +44 (0)1843 602068
Email: wellesley.office@lineone.net
Website: www.wellesley.kent.sch.uk

Wellington College
Head: A H Monro
Crowthorne RG45 7PU
Tel: +44 (0)1344 444010
Fax: +44 (0)1344 444004

Wellington School
Head: A J Rogers
Wellington TA21 8NT
Tel: +44 (0)1823 668800
Fax: +44 (0)1823 668844
Email: admin@wellington-school.org.uk
Website: www.wellington-school.org.uk

Wellow House School
Head: Dr Malcolm Tozer
Wellow
Near Newark NG22 0EA
Tel: +44 (0)1623 861054
Fax: +44 (0)1623 836665
Email: wellowhouse@btinternet.com

Wells Cathedral Junior School
Head: N M Wilson
8 New Street
Wells BA5 2LQ
Tel: +44 (0)1749 672291
Fax: +44 (0)1749 671940
Email: headmaster@wcjs80.fsnet.co.uk
Website: members.tripod.co.uk/wcjs

Wells Cathedral School
Head: Mrs E C Cairncross
Wells BA5 2ST
Tel: +44 (0)1749 672117
Fax: +44 (0)1749 673639
Email: admissions@
wells-cathedral-school.com
Website: www.wells-cathedral-school.com

Wentworth College
Head: Miss S Coe
College Road, Boscombe
Bournemouth BH5 2DY
Tel: +44 (0)1202 423266
Fax: +44 (0)1202 418030
Email: wentcolleg@aol.com
Website: www.wentworthcollege.org.uk

Westbourne House
Head: S L Rigby
Shopwyke
Chichester PO20 6BH
Tel: +44 (0)1243 782739
Fax: +44 (0)1243 770759
Email: whousestaff@rmplc.co.uk

Westbrook Hay Prep School
Head: Keith Young
London Road
Hemel Hempstead HP1 2RF
Tel: +44 (0)1442 256143
Fax: +44 (0)1442 232076
Email: headmaster@westbrookhay.co.uk
Website: www.westbrookhay.co.uk

West Buckland School
Head: J F Vick
Barnstaple EX32 0SX
Tel: +44 (0)1598 760281
Fax: +44 (0)1598 760546
Email: headmaster@
westbuckland.devon.sch.uk
Website: www.westbuckland.devon.sch.uk

West Hill Park
Head: E P K Hudson
Titchfield
Fareham PO14 4BS
Tel: +44 (0)1329 842356
Fax: +44 (0)1329 842911
Email: westhill@rmplc.co.uk
Website: www.westhill.hants.sch.uk

Westminster Abbey Choir School
Deans Yard
London SW1P 3NY

Tel: +44 (0)20 7222 6151
Fax: +44 (0)20 7222 1548
Email: headmaster@westminster-abbey.org

Westminster Cathedral Choir School
Head: C Foulds
Ambrosden Avenue
London SW1P 1QH
Tel: +44 (0)20 7798 9081
Fax: +44 (0)20 7630 7209
Email: emailwccs@aol.com

Westminster School
Head: T Jones-Parry
17 Dean's Yard
London SW1P 3PB
Tel: +44 (0)20 7963 1003
Fax: +44 (0)20 7963 1006
Email: headmaster@westminster.org.uk
Website: www.westminster.org.uk

Westonbirt School
Head: Mrs M Henderson
Tetbury GL8 8QG
Tel: +44 (0)1666 880333
Fax: +44 (0)1666 880364
Email: office@westonbirt.gloucs.sch.uk
Website: www.westonbirt.gloucs.sch.uk

Winchester College
Head: E N Tate
College Street
Winchester SO23 9NA
Tel: +44 (0)1962 621100
Fax: +44 (0)1962 621106
Email: information@wincoll.ac.uk
Website: www.wincoll.ac.uk

Winchester House School
Head: J R G Griffith
Brackley NN13 7AZ
Tel: +44 (0)1280 702483
Fax: +44 (0)1280 706400
Email: head@winchester-house.org
Website: www.winchester-house.org

Windermere St Anne's School
Head: Miss W A Ellis
Windermere LA23 1NW
Tel: +44 (0)15394 46164
Fax: +44 (0)15394 88414
Email: win@windermerest-annes.
cumbria.sch.uk
Website:
www.windermerest-annes.cumbria.sch.uk

Windlesham House School
Head: Philip Lough
Washington
Pulborough RH20 4AY
Tel: +44 (0)1903 8734700
Fax: +44 (0)1903 8734702
Email: office@windlesham.com
Website: www.windlesham.com

Wispers School
Head: L H Beltran
High Lane Haslemere GU27 1AD
Tel: +44 (0)1428 643646
Fax: +44 (0)1428 641120
Email: head@wispers.prestel.co.uk

Witham Hall
Head: D Telfer and Mrs S Telfer
Bourne PE10 0JJ
Tel: +44 (0)1778 590222
Fax: +44 (0)1778 590606
Email: withamhall@hotmail.com
Website: www.withamhall.com

Woldingham School
Head: Miss Diana Vernon
Marden Park, Woldingham
Caterham CR3 7YA
Tel: +44 (0)1883 349431
Fax: +44 (0)1883 348 653
Email: registrar@
woldingham.surrey.sch.uk
Website: www.woldingham.surrey.sch.uk

Woodbridge School
Head: S H Cole
Woodbridge IP12 4JH
Tel: +44 (0)1394 385547
Fax: +44 (0)1394 380944
Email: e-mail@
woodbridge.suffolk.sch.uk
Website: www.woodbridge.
suffolk.sch.uk

Woodcote House School
Head: N H K Paterson
Windlesham GU20 6PF
Tel: +44 (0)1276 472115
Fax: +44 (0)1276 472890
Email: N.H.K.P@btinternet.com
Website: www.woodcote.cjb.net

Woodhouse Grove School
Head: David Humphreys
Apperley Bridge
West Yorkshire BD10 0NR
Tel: +44 (0)113 250 2477
Fax: +44 (0)113 250 5290
Email: enquiries@woodhouse-grove.demon.co.uk
Website: www.woodhouse-grove.demon.co.uk

Woodleigh School
Head: D M England
Langton, Malton YO17 9QN
Tel: +44 (0)1653 658215
Fax: +44 (0)1653 658423
Email: woodleighschool@bigfoot.com

Worksop College
Head: R A Collard
Worksop
Nottinghamshire S80 3AP
Tel: +44 (0)1909 537100
Fax: +44 (0)1909 537102
Email: headmaster@worksopcollege.notts.sch.uk
Website: www.worksopcollege.notts.sch.uk

Worth School
Head: Fr Christopher Jamison
Paddockhurst Road
Turners Hill
Crawley RH10 4SD
Tel: +44 (0)1342 710200
Fax: +44 (0)1342 710201
Email: office@worth.org.uk
Website: www.worth.org.uk

Wrekin College
Head: S G Drew
Wellington, Telford TF1 3BG
Tel: +44 (0)1952 240131
Fax: +44 (0)1952 415068
Email: headmaster@wrekincollege.ac.uk

Wychwood School
Head: Mrs S Wingfield Digby
74 Banbury Road
Oxford OX2 6JR
Tel: +44 (0)1865 557976
Fax: +44 (0)1865 556806
Email: admin@wychwood-school.org.uk
Website: www.oxfordcity.co.uk/
education/wychwood

Wycliffe College
Head: Dr R A Collins
Stonehouse, Gloucestershire GL10 2JQ
Tel: +44 (0)1453 822432
Fax: +44 (0)1453 827634
Email: senior@wycliffe.co.uk
Website: www.wycliffe.co.uk

Wycliffe College Jnr School
Head: K Melber
Ryeford Hall, Stonehouse
Gloucestershire GL10 2LD
Tel: +44 (0)1453 823233
Fax: +44 (0)1453 825604
Email: junior@wycliffe.co.uk
Website: www.ik.org

Wycombe Abbey School
Head: Mrs P E Davies
High Wycombe HP11 1PE
Tel: +44 (0)1494 520381
Fax: +44 (0)1494 473836
Website: www.wycombeabbey.com

Yarlet School
Head: R S Plant
Yarlet, Stafford ST18 9SU
Tel: +44 (0)1785 286568
Fax: +44 (0)1785 286569
Email: enquiries@yarletschool.co.uk
Website: www.yarletschool.co.uk

Yehudi Menuhin School
Head: N Chisholm
Stoke d'Abernon, Cobham, Surrey KT11 3QQ
Tel: +44 (0)1932 864739
Fax: +44 (0)1932 864633
Email: admin@yehudimenuhinschool.co.uk
Website: www.yehudimenuhinschool.co.uk

**Aspect International
Language Academies**
Heliting House
Richmond Hill
Bournemouth BH2 6HT
Tel: +44 (0)1202 638100
Fax: +44 (0)1202 438900

Bell International
Hillscross, Red Cross Lane
Cambridge CB2 2QX
Tel: +44 (0)1223 212333
Fax: +44 (0)1223 410282
Email: info@bell-centres.com
Website: www.bell-centres.com

Birkbeck, University of London
Malet Street
London WC1E 7HX
Tel: +44 (0)845 601 0174
Fax: +44 (0)20 7631 6270
Email: admissions@bbk.ac.uk
Website: www.bbk.ac.uk

Blake College
162 New Cavendish Street
London W1W 6YF
Tel: +44 (0)20 7636 0658
Fax: +44 (0)20 7436 0049
Email: study@blake.ac.uk
Website: www.blake.ac.uk

Cambridge School of English
7-11 Stukeley Street
Covent Garden, London WC2B 5LT
Tel: +44 (0)20 7242 3787
Fax: +44 (0)20 7242 3626

Chelsea College of Art and Design
Manresa Road, London SW3 6LS
Tel: +44 (0)20 7514 7750
Fax: +44 (0)20 7514 7777
Email: enquiries@chelsea.linst.ac.uk
Website: www.chelsea.linst.ac.uk

City College
University House, 55 East Road
London N1 6AH
Tel: +44 (0)20 7253 1133
Fax: +44 (0)20 7251 6610
Email: admin@citycollege.ac.uk
Website: www.citycollege.ac.uk

City of London College
The Registry
71 Whitechapel High Street
London E1 7PL
Tel: +44 (0)20 7247 2166
Fax: +44 (0)20 7247 1226
Email: registry@clc-london.ac.uk
Website: www.clc-london.ac.uk

**The Chippendale International
School of Furniture**
Gifford, East Lothian EH41 4JA
Tel: +44 (0)1620 810680
Fax: +44 (0)1620 810701
Email: info@chippendale.co.uk
Website: www.chippendale.co.uk

Christie's Education
5 King Street, St James's
London SW1Y 6QS
Tel: +44 (0)20 7747 6800
Fax: +44 (0)20 7747 6801
Email: education@christies.com
Website: www.christies.com

City Business College
178 Goswell Road, London EC1V 7DT
Tel: +44 (0)20 7251 6473/0427
Fax: +44 (0)20 7251 9410
Email: info@cbcenglish.bdx.co.uk
Website: www.citybusinesscollege.com

City of Westminster College
25 Paddington Green
London W12 1NB
Tel: +44 (0)20 7723 8826
Fax: +44 (0)20 7258 7200
Email: customer.services@cwc.ac.uk
Website: www.cwc.ac.uk

David Game College
David Game House
69 Notting Hill Gate
London W11 3JS
Tel: +44 (0)20 7221 6665
Fax: +44 (0)20 7243 1730
Email: david-game@easynet.co.uk
Website: www.davidgame-group.com

EF International Language Schools
EF House, 1-3 Farmam Street
Hove, East Sussex BN3 1AL
Tel: +44 (0)1273 201410
Fax: +44 (0)1273 748566
Website: www.ef.com

The Hampstead School of Art
19-21 Kidderpore Avenue
London NW3 7ST
Tel: +44 (0)20 7431 1292
Fax: +44 (0)20 7431 1292
Email: hsanw3@aol.com

Heatherley's School of Fine Art
80 Upcerne Road,
Chelsea, London SW10 0SH
Tel: +44 (0)20 7351 4190
Fax: +44 (0)20 7351 6945
Email: info@heatherleys.org
Website: www.heatherleys.org

Huron University USA in London
58 Princes Gate
London SW7 2PG
Tel: +44 (0)20 7584 9696
Fax: +44 (0)20 7589 9406
Email: admissions@huron.ac.uk
Website: www.huron.ac.uk

Kensington College of Business
Wesley House
4 Wild Court
London WC2B 4AU
Tel: +44 (0)20 7404 6330
Fax: +44 (0)20 7404 6708
Email: kcb@kensingtoncoll.ac.uk
Website: www.kensingtoncoll.ac.uk

King Street College
4 Hammersmith Broadway
London W6 7AL
Tel: +44 (0)20 8748 0971
Fax: +44 (0)20 8741 1098
Email: info@kingstreet.co.uk
Website: www.kingstreet.co.uk

KLC School of Design
Unit 503, 5th Floor (North Entrance)
The Chambers, Chelsea Harbour
London SW10 0XF
Tel: +44 (0)20 7376 3377
Fax: +44 (0)20 7376 7807
Email: info@klc.co.uk
Website: www.klc.co.uk

Leith's School of Food and Wine
21 St Alban's Grove
Kensington, London W8 5BP
Tel: +44 (0)20 7229 0177
Fax: +44 (0)20 7937 5257
Email: info@leiths.com
Website: www.leiths.com

London Business School
Regent's Park, Sussex Place
London NW1 4SA
Tel: +44 (0)20 7262 5050
Fax: +44 (0)20 7724 7875
Website: www.lbs.lon.ac.uk

London Capital Computer College
38 King Street, Covent Garden
London WC2E 7BB
Tel: +44 (0)20 7240 2124
Fax: +44 (0)20 7240 1991
Email: info@london-college.com

London Centre for Fashion Studies
Bradley Close
White Lion Street
London N1 9PF
Tel: +44 (0)20 7713 1991
Fax: +44 (0)20 7713 1997
Email: Learnf@shion.demon.co.uk
Website: www.fashionstudies.com

London City College
51-55 Waterloo Road
London SE1 8TX
Tel: +44 (0)20 7928 0029
Fax: +44 (0)20 7401 2231
Email: office@londoncitycollege.com
Website: www.londoncitycollege.com

London College of English
354 Goswell Road, London EC1V 7LQ
Tel: +44 (0)20 7713 9393
Fax: +44 (0)20 7251 9410
Email: info@cbc.english.bdx.co.uk
Website: www.londoncollegeofenglish.com

**London College of International
Business Studies**
14 Southampton Place
London WC1A 2AJ
Tel: +44 (0)20 7242 1004
Fax: +44 (0)20 7242 1005
Email: lcibs@compuserve.com
Website: www.lcibs.co.uk

London Executive Schools
The Administration Officer
5 Westminster Bridge Road
London SE1 7XM
Tel: +44 (0)20 7620 0334
Fax: +44 (0)20 7620 0092
Email: info@esbca.co.uk
Website:www.esbca.co.uk

London Hotel School
Springvale Terrace
London W14 0AE
Tel: +44 (0)20 7665 0000
Fax: +44 (0)20 7665 0001
Email: Registrar@londonhotelschool.com
Website: www.londonhotelschool.com

**London Institute of
Technology and English (LITE)**
1 Sherwood Street
Piccadilly Street
London WIV 7RA
Tel: +44 (0)20 7439 2226
Fax: +44 (0)20 7439 2240

London School of Beauty and Make-up
75-77 Margaret Street
London W1W 8SY
Tel: +44 (0)20 7636 1893
Fax: +44 (0)20 7323 1805
Email: info@lond-est.com
Website: www.beauty-school.co.uk

**London School of
Business Administration**
10 Cleveland Way
London E1 4TR
Tel: +44 (0)20 7423 9000
Fax: +44 (0)20 7790 6363
Email: lsba@clara.co.uk
Website: www.lsba.clara.net

London Tower College
151 Rye Lane, Peckham
London SE15
Tel: +44 (0)20 635 7717
Fax: +44 (0)20 7732 3887
Email: itc@londontowercollege.co.uk
Website: www.londontowercollege.co.uk

Lucie Clayton College
4 Cornwall Gardens
London SW7 4AJ
Tel: +44 (0)20 7581 0024
Fax: +44 (0)20 7589 9693

Malvern House
29 John Adam Street
London WC2N 6HX
Tel: +44 (0)20 7930 8080
Fax: +44 (0)20 7930 8079
Email: Malvern@malvernhouse.com
Website: www.malvernhouse.com

**The Northern School
of Contemporary Dance**
98 Chapeltown Road, Leeds
West Yorkshire LS7 4BH
Iel: +44 (0)113 219 3000
Fax: +44 (0)113 219 3030
Website: www.nscd.ac.uk

The Norwich School of Art and Design
St George Street
Norwich NR3 1BB
Tel: +44 (0)1603 610561
Fax: +44 (0)1603 615728
Email: info@nsad.ac.uk
Website: www.nsad.ac.uk

Oxford House College
28 Market Place
London W1W 8AW
Tel: +44 (0)20 7436 4214
Fax: +44 (0)20 7323 4582
Email: english@oxfordhouse.co.uk
Website: www.oxford-house-college.ac.uk

Oxford Media and Business School
Rose Place, St Aldates
Oxford OX1 1SB
Tel: +44 (0)1865 240963
Fax: +44 (0)1865 242783
Email: courses@oxfordbusiness.co.uk
Website: www.oxfordbusiness.co.uk

The Prince's Foundation
19-22 Charlotte Street
London EC2A 3SG
Tel: +44 (0)20 7613 8500
Fax: +44 (0)20 7613 8599
Email: enquiry@princes-foundation.org
Website: www.princes-foundation.org

**Purley Secretarial
and Language College**
14 Brighton Road, Purley CR8 3AB
Tel: +44 (0)20 8660 5060
Fax: +44 (0)20 8668 4022
Email: purleycollege@compuserve.com

**Queen's Business
and Secretarial College**
24 Queensbury Place
London SW7 2DS
Tel: +44 (0)20 7589 8583
Fax: +44 (0)20 7823 9915
Email: info@qbsc.ac.uk
Website: www.qbsc.ac.uk

The Ray Cochrane Beauty School
118 Baker Street, London W1U 6TT
Tel: +44 (0)20 7486 6291
Fax: +44 (0)20 7935 3405
Email: beauty@raycochrane.co.uk
Website: www.raycochrane.co.uk

The Royal Ballet School
155 Talgarth Road
Barons Court, London W14 9DE
Tel: +44 (0)20 8237 7128
Fax: +44 (0)20 8237 7127
Website: www.royal-ballet-school.org.uk

**The Royal Scottish Academy
of Music and Drama**
100 Renfrew Street
Glasgow G2 3DB
Tel: +44 (0)141 332 4101
Fax: +44 (0)141 332 8901
Email: registry@rsamd.ac.uk
Website: www.rsamd.ac.uk

St Patrick's International College
24 Great Chapel Street
London W1F 8FS
Tel: +44 (0)20 7734 2156
Fax: +44 (0)20 7287 6282
Email: info@st-patrick.ac.uk
Website: www.st-patrick.ac.uk

Sels College London
64-65 Longacre
Covent Garden
London WC2E 9SX
Tel: +44 (0)20 7240 2581
Fax: +44 (0)20 7379 5793
Email: english@sels.co.uk
Website: www.sels.co.uk

Skola
12 Porchester Place
London W2 2BS
Tel: +44 (0)20 7706 7676
Fax: +44 (0)20 7706 8171
Email: info@skola.co.uk
Website: www.skola.co.uk

Student Placement Services
29 Bristol Street, Brighton
East Sussex BN2 5JT
Tel: +44 (0)1273 670412
Fax: +44 (0)1273 570663
Email: c.lay@btinternet.com
Website: www.members.aol.com/spser

Study UK
PO Box 758, Maidstone
Kent ME16 8SZ
Tel: +44 (0)1622 687934
Fax: +44 (0)1622 757209
Email: enq@studyuk.org.uk
Website: www.studyuk.org.uk

Tate Britain
Interpretation and Education
Millbank
London SW1P 4RG
Tel: +44 (0)20 7887 8888
Fax: +44 (0)20 7887 8762
Email: tate.ticketing@tate.org.uk
Website: www.tate.org.uk

Tante Marie School of Cookery
Woodham House
Carlton Road, Woking
Surrey GU21 4HF
Tel: +44 (0)1483 726957
Fax: +44 (0)1483 724173
Email: info@tantemarie.co.uk
Website: www.tantemarie.co.uk

Thames Valley College
Principal, Celeveland Way
London E1 4TR
Tel: +44 (0)20 7423 9898
Fax: +44 (0)20 7790 3407
Email: Admissions@
thamesvalleycollege.org.uk
Website: www.thamesvalleycollege.org.uk

United International College
Woodstock House
10-12 James Street
London W1M 5HN
Tel: +44 (0)20 7495 6667
Fax: +44 (0)20 7495 6668
Email: registrar@uiclondon.com
Website: www.uiclondon.com

West London College
Parliament House
35 North Row, Mayfair
London W1K 6DB
Tel: +44 (0)20 7491 1841
Fax: +44 (0)20 7499 5853
Email: courses@w-l-c.co.uk
Website: www.w-l-c.co.uk

Westminster College of Computing
12 Hatton Gardens
London EC1N 8AN
Tel: +44 (0)20 7269 7960
Fax: +44 (0)20 7242 8361

Further education

Boston College
Skirbeck Road
Boston
Lincolnshire PE21 6JF
Tel: +44 (0)1205 365701
Fax: +44 (0)1205 313252
Email: enquiry@boston.ac.uk
Website: www.boston.ac.uk

Brighton and Hove College
Medina House, Medina Villas
Hove, East Sussex BN3 2RP
Tel: +44 (0)1273 772577
Fax: +44 (0)1273 208401
Email: courses@brightonhovecollege.org
Website: www.brightonhovecollege.org

**Bromley College of Further
& Higher Education**
International Office
Rookery Lane, Bromley BR2 8HE
Tel: +44 (0)20 8295 7031
Fax: +44 (0)20 8295 7051
Email: international@bromley.ac.uk
Website: www.bromley.ac.uk

Cardonald College Glasgow
690 Mosspark Drive
Glasgow G52 3AY
Tel: +44 (0)141 272 3333
Fax: +44 (0)141 272 3444
Email: enquiries@cardonald.ac.uk
Website: www.cardonald.ac.uk

Chelmsford College
Moulsham Street
Chelmsford CM2 0JQ
Tel: +44 (0)1245 265611
Fax: +44 (0)1245 266908
Website: www.chelmsford-college.ac.uk

City & Guilds of London Art School
124 Kennington Park Road
London SE11 4DJ
Tel: +44 (0)20 7735 2306
Fax: +44 (0)20 7582 5361
Email: info@cityandguildsartschool.ac.uk
Website: www.cityandguildsartschool.ac.uk

Harrogate College
Hornbeam Park Avenue
Harrogate HG2 8QT
Tel: +44 (0)1423 879466
Fax: +44 (0)1423 879829
Website: www.lmu.ac.uk/harrogate

Hartpury College
Hartpury House, Hartpury
Gloucester, GL19 3BE
Tel: +44 (0)1452 702132
Fax: +44 (0)1452 700629
Website: www.hartpury.ac.uk

Hastings College
The International Department
Hastings College of Arts and Technology,
80 St Saviours Road, St Leonards-on-Sea
East Sussex TN38 0AR
Tel: +44 (0)1424 445400
Fax: +44 (0)1424 424804
Wesbite: www.hastings.ac.uk

Le Cordon Bleu
114 Marylebone Lane, London W1U 6HH
Tel: +44 (0)20 7935 3503
Fax: +44 (0)20 7935 7621
Email: london@cordonbleu.net
Website: www.cordonbleu.net

**The London Academy of Music
and Dramatic Art (LAMDA)**
Tower House, 226 Cromwell Road
London SW5 0SR
Tel: +44 (0)20 7373 9883
Fax: +44 (0)20 7370 4739
Email: enquiries@lamda.org.uk
Website: www.lamda.org.uk

Newham College of Further Education
Admissions Officer, East Ham Campus
High Street South, London E6 4ER
Tel: +44 (0)20 8257 4000
Fax: +44 (0)20 8257 4325
Email: admissions@newham.ac.uk
Website: www.newham.ac.uk

**North East Institute of Further
and Higher Education**
Admissions Office, Trostan Avenue Building
Ballymena, Co Antrim
Northern Ireland BT43 7BN
Tel: +44 (0)28 2565 2871
Fax: +44 (0)28 2565 9245
Email: admissions@nei.ac.uk
Website: www.nei.ac.uk

North Nottinghamshire College
Carlton Road, Worksop
Nottinghamshire S81 7HP
Tel: +44 (0)1909 504500
Fax: +44 (0)1909 504505
Email: tslater@nnc.ac.uk
Website: www.nnc.ac.uk

**Oxford College of
Further Education**
City Centre Campus, Oxford OX1 1SA
Tel: +44 (0)1865 245871
Fax: +44 (0)1865 248871
Email: oxford@oxfe.ac.uk
Website: www.oxfe.ac.ukc.uk

The Royal Academy of Dance
36 Battersea Square, London SW11 3RA
Tel: +44 (0)20 7326 8000
Fax: +44 (0)20 7924 3129
Email: info@rad.org.uk
Website: www.rad.org.uk

Royal Academy of Dramatic Art (RADA)
62-64 Gower Street
London WC1E 6ED
Tel: +44 (0)20 7636 7076
Fax: +44 (0)20 7323 3865
Email: enquiries@rada.ac.uk
Website: www.rada.org

Royal College of Music
Prince Consort Road
London SW7 2BS
Tel: +44 (0)20 7589 3643
Fax: +44 (0)20 7589 7740
Email: dharpham@rcm.ac.uk
Website: www.rcm.ac.uk

St Austell College
Trevarthian Road
St Austell PL25 4BU
Tel: +44 (0)1726 67911
Fax: +44 (0)1726 68499
Email: info@st-austell.ac.uk
Website: www.st-austell.ac.uk

Telford College of Arts and Technology
Overseas Admissions
Student Services
Haybridge Road, Wellington
Telford, Shropshire
Tel: +44 (0)1952 642237
Fax: +44 (0)1952 642293
Email: studserv@tcat.ac.uk
Website: www.tcat.ac.uk

Walsall College of Arts and Technology
Susan Stokes
International Officer
St Pauls Street, Walsall WS1 1XN
Tel: 44 (0)1922 657000
Fax: 44 (0)1922 657083
Email: sstokes@walcat.ac.uk
Website: www.walcat.ac.uk

UCAS institutions

The University of Aberdeen
Student Recruitment
and Admissions Office
King's College, Aberdeen AB24 3FX
Tel: +44 (0)1224 272090
Fax: +44 (0)1224 272031
Email: sras@abdn.ac.uk
Website: www.abdn.ac.uk

University of Abertay Dundee
International Office, Bell Street
Dundee DD1 1HG
Tel: +44 (0)1382 308080
Fax: +44 (0)1382 308081
Email: iro@abertay.ac.uk
Website: www.abertay.ac.uk

Aberystwyth: United Theological College and College of Welsh Independents
King Street
Aberystwyth SY23 2LT
Tel: +44 (0)1970 624574
Fax: +44 (0)1970 626 350
Email: esl998@aber.ac.uk
Website: www.ebcpcw.org.uk

The University of Wales, Aberystwyth
Old College, King Street
Aberystwyth, Ceredigion SY23 2AX
Tel: +44 (0)1970 623111
Fax: +44 (0)1970 611446
Email: ug-admissions@aber.ac.uk
Website: www.aber.ac.uk

Anglia Polytechnic University
International Office
East Road, Cambridge CB1 1PT
Tel: +44 (0)1223 363271
Fax: +44 (0)1223 417712
Email: international@apu.ac.uk
Website: www.apu.ac.uk

Askham Bryan College
Central Admissions Manager
Askham Bryan, York YO23 3FR
Tel: +44 (0)1904 772211
Fax: +44 (0)1904 772288
Email: myra@tla.askham-bryan.ac.uk
Website: www.askham-bryan.ac.uk

Aston University
International Office
Aston Triangle
Birmingham B4 7ET
Tel: +44 (0)121 359 7046
Fax: +44 (0)121 333 6350
Email: international@aston.ac.uk
Website: www.aston.ac.uk

Aylesbury College
Customer Services, Oxford Road
Aylesbury HP21 8PD
Tel: +44 (0)1296 588588
Fax: +44 (0)1296 588589
Email: customerservices@aylesbury.ac.uk
Website: www.aylesbury.ac.uk

University of Wales, Bangor
Bangor, Gwynedd LL57 2DG
Tel: +44 (0)1248 382028
Fax: +44 (0)1248 383268
Email: international@bangor. ac.uk
Website: www.bangor.ac.uk

Barking College
Admissions Office, Dagenham Road
Romford, Essex RM7 0XU
Tel: +44 (0)1708 770000
Fax: +44 (0)1708 770007
Email: admissions@barking-coll.ac.uk
Website: www.barking-coll.ac.uk

Barnet College
Grahame Park Way, Collindale
London NW9 5RA
Tel: +44 (0)20 8200 8300
Fax: +44 (0)20 8205 7177
Website: www.barnet.ac.uk

Barnfield College, Luton
New Bedford Road, Luton
Bedfordshire LU2 7BF
Tel: +44 (0)1582 569607
Fax: +44 (0)1582 572264
Email: brianc@nbr.barnfield.ac.uk

Barnsley College
Central Registry, PO Box 266
Church Street, Barnsley S70 2YW
Tel: +44 (0)1226 216171
Fax: +44 (0)1226 216613
Email: programme.enquiries@barnsley.ac.uk
Website: www.barnsley.ac.uk

Basingstoke College of Technology
Student Administration
Worting Road, Basingstoke
Hampshire RG21 8TN
Tel: +44 (0)1256 354141
Fax: +44 (0)1256 306444
Email: information@bcot.ac.uk
Website: www.bcot.ac.uk

University of Bath
Admissions Office
Claverton Down, Bath BA2 7AY
Tel: +44 (0)1225 826832
Fax: +44 (0)1225 826366
Email: international-office@bath.ac.uk
Website: www.bath.ac.uk

Bath Spa University College
The International Office
Newton Park, Newton St Loe
Bath BA2 9BN
Tel: +44 (0)1225 875577
Fax: +44 (0)1225 875501
Email: international-enquiries
@bathspa.ac.uk
Website:www.bathspa.ac.uk

Bedford College
Cauldwell Street, Bedford MK42 9AH
Tel: +44 (0)1234 291000
Fax: +44 (0)1234 342674
Email: info@bedford.ac.uk
Website: www.bedford.ac.uk

Bell College of Technology
Registry Admissions
Almada Street, Hamilton
Lanarkshire, Scotland ML3 OJB
Tel: +44 (0)1698 283100
Fax: +44 (0)1698 282131
Email: enquiries@bell.ac.uk
Website: www.bell.ac.uk

The University of Birmingham
International Office
Edgbaston
Birmingham B15 2TT
Tel: +44 (0)121 414 7167
Fax: +44 (0)121 414 3850
Email: international@bham.ac.uk
Website: www.birmingham.ac.uk

Birmingham College of Food, Tourism and Creative Studies
International Admissions Officer
Summer Row
Birmingham B3 1JB
Tel: +44 (0)121 604 1000
Fax: +44 (0)121 200 1376
Email: admissions@bcftcs.ac.uk
Website: www.bcftcs.ac.uk

Bishop Burton College
Bishop Burton, Beverley
East Yorkshire HU17 8QG
Tel: +44 (0)1964 553000
Fax: +44 (0)1964 553101
Email: enquiries@bishopb-college.ac.uk
Website: www.bishopb-college.ac.uk

Bishop Grosseteste College
College Registry
Newport, Lincoln LN1 3DY
Tel: +44 (0)1522 527347
Fax: +44 (0)1522 530243
Email: registry@bgc.ac.uk
Website: www.bgc.ac.uk

Blackburn College
Student Services, Feilden Street
Blackburn, Lancashire BB2 1LH
Tel: +44 (0)1254 551440
Fax: +44 (0)1254 682700
Website: www.blackburn.ac.uk

Blackpool and The Fylde College
Admissions Office
Ashfield Road
Bispham, Blackpool
Lancashire FY2 0HB
Tel: +44 (0)1253 352352
Fax: +44 (0)1253 356127
Email: visitors@blackpool.ac.uk
Website: www.blackpool.ac.uk

Bolton Institute of Higher Education
Senior Assistant Registrar
Deane Road, Bolton BL3 5AB
Tel: +44 (0)1204 900600
Fax: +44 (0)1204 399074
Email: mar1@bolton.ac.uk
Website: www.bolton.ac.uk

Bournemouth University
The International Office
Poole House, Talbot Campus
Fern Barrow, Poole
Dorset BH12 5BB
Tel: +44 (0)1202 595470
Fax: +44 (0)1202 595287
Email: inta@bournemouth.ac.uk
Website: www.bournemouth.ac.uk

The Arts Institute at Bournemouth
Admissions, Wallisdown, Poole
Dorset BH12 5HH
Tel: +44 (0)1202 533011
Fax: +44 (0)1202 537729
Email: general@arts-inst-bournemouth.ac.uk
Website: www.arts-inst-bournemouth.ac.uk

The University of Bradford
International Office
Richmond Road, Bradford
West Yorkshire BD7 1DP
Tel: +44 (0)1274 233080
Fax: +44 (0)1274 235950
Email: international-office@bradford.ac.uk
Website: www.brad.ac.uk

Bradford College (an associate college of The University of Bradford)
International Office, Westbrook Building
Great Horton Road, Bradford
West Yorkshire BD7 1AY
Tel: +44 (0)1274 753004
Fax: +44 (0)1274 753241
Email: admissions@bradfordcollege.ac.uk
Website: www.bradfordcollege.ac.uk

Bridgwater College
Information and Guidance
Bath Road, Bridgwater, Somerset TA6 4PZ
Tel: +44 (0)1278 441234
Fax: +44 (0)1278 44363
Email: information@bridgwater.ac.uk
Website: www.bridgwater.ac.uk

University of Brighton
Admissions, Mithras House
Lewes Road, Brighton
East Sussex BN2 4AT
Tel: +44 (0)1273 600900
Fax: +44 (0)1273 642825
Email: intrel@brighton.ac.uk
Website: www.brighton.ac.uk

University of Bristol
International Centre, University
of Bristol Union, Queen's Road
Clifton, Bristol BS8 1LN
Tel: +44 (0)117 9545788
Fax: +44 (0)117 9545851
Email: orlo@bristol.ac.uk
Website: www.bris.ac.uk

University of the West of England, Bristol
Enquiry and Admissions Service
Frenchay Campus
Coldharbour Lane
Bristol BS16 1QY
Tel: +44 (0)117 344 3333
Fax: +44 (0)117 344 2810
Email: admissions@uwe.ac.uk
Website: www.uwe.ac.uk

British College of Naturopathy and Osteopathy
Academic Registry
Lief House
120/122 Finchley Road
London NW3 5HR
Tel: +44 (0)20 7435 6464
Fax: +44 (0)20 7431 3630
Email: bcd@bcno.ac.uk
Website: www.bcno.ac.uk

The British Institute in Paris (University of London)
Department d'Etudes Françaises
Institut Britannique de Paris
11 rue de Constantine
75340 Paris Cedex 07, France
Tel: +33 1 441173 83/84
Fax: +33 1 4550 315
Email: campos@ext.jussieu.fr
Website: www.bip.lon.ac.uk

British School of Osteopathy
Admissions Office
275 Borough High Street
London SE1 1JE
Tel: +44 (0)20 7407 0222
Fax: +44 (0)20 7089 5300
Email: admissions@bso.ac.uk
Website: www.bso.ac.uk

Brockenhurst College
Admissions
Lyndhurst Road, Brockenhurst
Hampshire SO42 7ZE
Tel: +44 (0)1590 625540
Fax: +44 (0)1590 625526
Email: enquiries@brock.ac.uk
Website: www.brock.ac.uk

Broxtowe College, Nottingham
HE Administrator
High Road, Chilwell, Beeston
Nottingham NG9 4AH
Tel: +44 (0)115 917 5252
Fax: +44 (0)115 917 5200
Email: attles@broxtowe.ac.uk
Website: www.broxtowe.ac.uk

Brunel University
International Office, Uxbridge
Middlesex UB8 3PH
Tel: +44 (0)1895 27400
Fax: +44 (0)1895 203084
Email: international-office@brunel.ac.uk
Website: www.brunel.ac.uk

The University of Buckingham
Admissions Office, Hunter Street
Buckingham MK18 1EG
Tel: +44 (0)1280 814080
Fax: +44 (0)1280 824081
Email: admissions@buckingham.ac.uk
Website: www.buckingham.ac.uk

Buckinghamshire Chilterns University College
Admissions Office
Queen Alexandra Road, High Wycombe
Buckinghamshire HP11 2JZ
Tel: +44 (0)1494 522141
Fax: +44 (0)1494 524392
Email: postmaster@bcuc.ac.uk
Website: www.bcuc.ac.uk

Burton College
Student Services
Lichfield Street, Burton-on-Trent
Staffordshire DE14 3RL
Tel: +44 (0)1283 494411
Fax: +44 (0)1283 494800
Email: studserv@burton-college.ac.uk
Website: www.burton-college.ac.uk

Cambridge University
Intercollegiate Applications Office
Kellet Lodge, Tennis Court Road
Cambridge CB2 1QJ
Tel: +44 (0)1223 333308
Fax: +44 (0)1223 366383
Email: ucam-undergraduate-admissions
@lists.cam.ac.uk
Website: www.cam.ac.uk

Cannington College
Enquiries, Cannington, Bridgwater
Somerset TA5 2LS
Tel: +44 (0)1278 655000
Fax: +44 (0)1278 655055
Email: enquiries@cannington.ac.uk
Website: www.cannington.ac.uk

Canterbury Christ Church University College
Admissions Office, North Holmes Road
Canterbury, Kent CT1 1QU
Tel: +44 (0)1227 458459
Fax: +44 (0)1227 781558
Email: ipo@cant.ac.uk
Website: www.cant.ac.uk

Canterbury College
Admissions Office
New Dover Road
Canterbury, Kent CT1 3AJ
Tel: +44 (0)1227 811188
Fax: +44 (0)1227 811101
Email: admissions@cant-col.ac.uk
Website: www.cant-col.ac.uk

Capel Manor College
Bullsmoor Lane, Enfield
Middlesex EN1 4RQ
Tel: +44 (0)20 8366 4442
Fax: +44 (0)1992 717544
Email: ruth.barber@capel.ac.uk
Website: www.capel.ac.uk

Cardiff University
International Office
42 Park Place, Cardiff CF10 3BB
Tel: +44 (0)29 2087 4432
Fax: +44 (0)29 2087 4622
Email: international@cf.ac.uk
Website: www.cf.ac.uk

University of Wales Institute, Cardiff
International Office
PO Box 377, Western Avenue
Cardiff CF5 2SG
Tel: +44 (0)29 2041 6045
Fax: +44 (0)29 2041 6928
Email: international@uwic.ac.uk
Website: www.uwic.ac.uk

Carmarthenshire College
Admissions Unit, Graig Campus
Sand Road, Llanelli
Dyfed SA15 4DN
Tel: +44 (0)1554 748000
Fax: +44 (0)1554 756088
Website: www.ccta.ac.uk

Carshalton College
Customer Services
Nightingale Road
Carshalton, Surrey SM5 2EJ
Tel: +44 (0)20 8770 6800
Fax: +44 (0)20 8770 6899
Email: tds@carshalton.ac.uk
Website: www.carshalton.ac.uk

University of Central England in Birmingham
Academic Registry, Perry Barr
Birmingham B42 2SU
Tel: +44 (0)121 331 5389
Fax: +44 (0)121 331 6706
Email: international.office@uce.ac.uk
Website: www.uce.ac.uk

University of Central Lancashire
Course Enquiries, Preston
Lancashire PR1 2HE
Tel: +44 (0)1772 894954
Fax: +44 (0)1772 892911
Email cenquiries@uclan.ac.uk
Website: www.uclan.ac.uk

Central Saint Martins College of Art and Design
Information Office, Southampton Row
London WC1B 4AP
Tel: +44 (0)20 7514 7000
Fax: +44 (0)20 7514 7024
Email: applications@csm.linst.ac.uk
Website: www.csm.linst.ac.uk

The Central School of Speech and Drama
Embassy Theatre
64 Eton Avenue
London NW3 3HY
Tel: +44 (0)20 7722 8183
Fax: +44 (0)20 7722 4132
Website: www.cssd.ac.uk

Chester, A College of The University of Liverpool
Assistant Registrar
Parkgate Road, Chester CH1 4BJ
Tel: +44 (0)1244 375444
Fax: +44 (0)1244 392821
Email: enquiries@chester.ac.uk
Website: www.chester.ac.uk

Chesterfield College
Information Office, Infirmary Road
Chesterfield, Derbyshire S41 7NG
Tel: +44 (0)1246 500562
Fax: +44 (0)1246 500587
Email: advice@chesterfield.ac.uk
Website: www.chesterfield.ac.uk/
chesterfield-college

Chichester College of Arts, Science and Technology
Westgate Fields, Chichester
West Sussex PO19 1SB
Tel: +44 (0)1243 536196
Fax: +44 (0)1243 539481
Email: info@chichester.ac.uk
Website: www.chichester.ac.uk

University College Chichester
Admissions Office, Bishop Otter Campus
College Lane, Chichester
West Sussex PO19 4PE
Tel: +44 (0)1243 816001
Fax: +44 (0)1243 816078
Email: admissions@ucc.ac.uk
Website: www.ucc.ac.uk

City and Islington College
Admissions, The Marlborough Building
383 Holloway Road, London N7 0RN
Tel: +44 (0)20 7700 9200
Fax: +44 (0)20 7700 9222
Email: courseinfo@candi.ac.uk
Website: www.candi.ac.uk

City College, Birmingham
47a George Street
Birmingham B3 1QA
Tel: +44 (0)121 236 4725
Fax: +44 (0)121 236 4726
Email: enquiries@citycol.ac.uk
Website: www.citycol.ac.uk

City College Manchester
International Office, Fielden Centre
141 Barlow Moor Road
West Didsbury
Manchester M20 2PQ
Tel: +44 (0)161 957 16500
Fax: +44 (0)161 434 0443
Email: admissions@ccm.ac.uk
Website: www.ccm.ac.uk

City College, Tile Hill Centre
Tile Hill Lane, Tile Hill
Coventry CV4 9SU
Tel: +44 (0)24 7679 1000
Fax: +44 (0)24 7646 4903
Email: info@tilehill.ac.uk
Website: www.tilehill.ac.uk

City of Bristol College
Brunel Centre, Ashley Down
Bristol BS7 9BU
Tel: +44 (0)117 904 5000
Fax: +44 (0)117 904 5050
Email: enquiries@cityofbristol.ac.uk
Website: www.cityofbristol.ac.uk

City of Sunderland College
Vice Principal's Office
Hylton Centre
North Hylton Road
Sunderland SR5 5DB
Tel: +44 (0)191 511 6201
Fax: +44 (0)191 511 6233
Email: he.admissions@citysun.ac.uk
Website: www.citysun.ac.uk

City University
International Office
Northampton Square
London EC1V 0HB
Tel: +44 (0)20 7040 8019
Fax: +44 (0)20 7040 8322
Email: international@city.ac.uk
Website: www.city.ac.uk/international

Cleveland College of Art and Design
Student Recruitment Office
Green Lane, Linthorpe
Middlesbrough TS5 7RJ
Tel: +44 (0)1642 288888
Fax: +44 (0)1642 288828
Email: admissions@ccad.ac.uk
Website: www.ccad.ac.uk

Colchester Institute
Assistant Registrar/Admissions
Sheepen Road, Colchester
Essex CO3 3LL
Tel: +44 (0)1206 518000
Fax: +44 (0)1206 763041
Email: info@colch-inst.ac.uk
Website: www.colch-inst.ac.uk

Cornwall College
Student Services,
Pool, Redruth
Cornwall TR15 3RD
Tel: +44 (0)1209 611611
Fax: +44 (0)1209 611612
Email: enquiries@cornwall.ac.uk
website: www.cornwall.ac.uk

**Courtauld Institute of Art
(University of London)**
Somerset House, Strand
London WC2R 0RN
Tel: +44 (0)20 7848 2645
Fax: +44 (0)20 7848 2410
Email: ugadmissions@courtauld.ac.uk
Website: www.courtauld.ac.uk

Coventry Technical College
Butts, Coventry CV1 3GD
Tel: +44 (0)24 7652 6700
Fax: +44 (0)24 7652 6789
Email: info@covcollege.ac.uk
Website: www.covcollege.ac.uk

Coventry University
International Office
Priory Street
Coventry CV1 5FB
Tel: +44 (0)24 7688 7688
Fax: +44 (0)24 7688 8793
Email: interlink@coventry.ac.uk
Website: www.coventry.ac.uk

Cranfield University
Cranfield
Bedfordshire MK43 0AL
Tel: +44 (0)1234 750111
Fax: +44 (0)1234 750875
Email: international@cranfield.ac.uk
Website: www.cranfield.ac.uk

Crawley College
College Road, Crawley
West Sussex RH10 1NR
Tel: +44 (0)1293 442205
Fax: +44 (0)1293 442399
Email: information@crawley-college.ac.uk
Website: www.crawley-college.ac.uk

Croydon College
College Road, Croydon CR9 1DX
Tel: +44 (0)20 8760 5999
Fax: +44 (0)20 8760 5880
Email: info@croydon.ac.uk
Website: www.croydon.ac.uk

Cumbria College of Art and Design
Admissions Officer
Brampton Road Carlisle
Cumbria CA3 9AY
Tel: +44 (0)1228 400300
Fax: +44 (0)1228 514491
Email: admissions@cumbriacad.ac.uk
Website: www.cumbriacad.ac.uk

Darlington College of Technology
Cleveland Avenue, Darlington DL3 7BB
Tel: +44 (0)1325 503050
Fax: +44 (0)1325 503000
Email: enquire@darlington.ac.uk
Website: www.darlington.ac.uk

Dartington College of Arts
Totnes, Devon TQ9 6EJ
Tel: +44 (0)1803 862224
Fax: +44 (0)1803 861666
Email: registry@dartington.ac.uk
Website: www.dartington.ac.uk

Dearne Valley College
Higher Education Office
Manvers Park, Wath-upon-Dearne
Rotherham, South Yorkshire S63 7EW
Tel: +44 (0)1709 513101
Fax: +44 (0)1709 513110
Email: probinson@dearne-coll.ac.uk
Website: www.dearne-coll.ac.uk

De Montfort University
International Office
The Gateway
Leicester LE1 9BH
Tel: +44 (0)116 250 6086
Fax: +44 (0)116 257 7353
Email: intoff@dmu.ac.uk
Website: www.dmu.ac.uk

University of Derby
Kedleston Road, Derby DE22 1GB
Tel: +44 (0)1332 621327
Fax: +44 (0)1332 597749
Email: international@derby.ac.uk
Website: www.derby.ac.uk

Dewsbury College
Halifax Road, Dewsbury
West Yorkshire WF13 2AS
Tel: +44 (0)1924 436229
Fax: +44 (0)1924 457047
Email: info@dewsbury.ac.uk
Website: www.dewsbury.ac.uk

Doncaster College
Waterdale, Doncaster,
South Yorkshire DN1 3EX
Tel: +44 (0)1302 553610
Fax: +44 (0)1302 553766
Email: he@don.ac.uk
Website: www.don.ac.uk

Dudley College of Technology
International Office, The Broadway
Dudley DY1 4AS
Tel: +44 (0)1384 363000
Fax: +44 (0)1384 363311
Email: international@dudleycol.ac.uk
Website: www.dudleycol.ac.uk

University of Dundee
Admissions, Dundee DD1 4HN
Tel: +44 (0)1382 344160
Fax: +44 (0)1382 348150
Email: srs@dundee.ac.uk
Website: www.dundee.ac.uk/

The University of Durham
International Office
Old Shire Hall, Durham DH1 3HP
Tel: +44 (0)191 374 4694
Fax: +44 (0)191 374 7216
Email: international.office@durham.ac.uk
Website: www.dur.ac.uk

University of East Anglia
Norwich, Norfolk NR4 7TJ
Tel: +44 (0)1603 456161
Fax: +44 (0)1603 458553
Email: intl.office@uea.ac.uk
Website: www.uea.ac.uk

**East Durham & Houghall
Community College**
Burnhope Way Centre, Burnhope Way
Peterlee, Co Durham SR8 1NU
Tel: +44 (0)191 518 2000
Fax: +44 (0)191 586 7125
Email: enquiry@edhcc.ac.uk
Website: www.edhcc.ac.uk

University of East London
International Office, Barking Campus,
Longbridge Road, Essex RM8 2AS
Tel: +44 (0)20 8223 2835
Fax: +44 (0)20 8223 2978
Email: admiss@uel.ac.uk
Website: www.uel.ac.uk

Eastleigh College
Chestnut Avenue, Eastleigh SO50 5HT
Tel: +44 (0)23 8091 1006
Fax: +44 (0)23 8032 2133
Email: rmatthews@eastleigh.ac.uk
Website: www.eastleigh.ac.uk

Easton College
Easton, Norwich, Norfolk NR9 5DX
Tel: +44 (0)1603 731200
Fax: +44 (0)1603 741438
Email: registry@easton-college.ac.uk
Website: www.easton-college.ac.uk

**East Surrey College (incorporating
Reigate School of Art and Design)**
Admissions Office, 127 Blackborough Road
Reigate, Surrey RH2 7DE
Tel: +44 (0)1737 772611
Fax: +44 (0)1737 768643
Website: www.esc.org.uk

**Edge Hill College of Higher Education
(a higher education institution
accredited by Lancaster University)**
St Helens Road, Ormskirk
Lancashire L39 4QP
Tel: +44 (0)1695 584274
Fax: +44 (0)1695 579997
Email: enquiries@edgehill.ac.uk
Website: www.edgehill.ac.uk

The University of Edinburgh
The International Office
57 George Square, Edinburgh FH8 9JU
Tel: +44 (0)131 650 4296
Fax: +44 (0)131 668 4565
Email: enquiries.international@ed.ac.uk
Website: www.ed.ac.uk

**The University of Edinburgh Faculty of
Education at Moray House**
Old Moray House, Holyrood Road
Edinburgh EH8 8AQ
Tel: +44 (0)131 651 6138
Fax: +44 (0)131 651 6052
Email: education.faculty@ed.ac.uk
Website: www.education.ed.ac.uk

The University of Essex
Wivenhoe Park, Colchester
Essex CO4 3SQ
Tel: +44 (0)1206 873666
Fax: +44 (0)1206 873423
Email: admit@essex.ac.uk
Website: www.essex.ac.uk

European Business School, London
Regent's College, Inner Circle
Regent's Park, London NW1 4NS
Tel: +44 (0)20 7487 7400
Fax: +44 (0)20 7487 7465
Email: ebslondon@regents.ac.uk
Website: www.ebslondon.ac.uk

European School of Osteopathy
Boxley House, The Street
Boxley, Kent ME14 3DZ
Tel: +44 (0)1622 671558
Fax: +44 (0)1622 662165
Email: kellyrose@eso.ac.uk
Website: www.eso.ac.uk

Exeter College
Business School, Brittany House
New North Road, Exeter EX4 4EP
Tel: +44 (0)1392 205581
Fax: +44 (0)1392 279972
Email: busschool@exe-coll.ac.uk
Website: www.exe-coll.ac.uk

University of Exeter
International Office, Northcote House
The Queen's Drive, Exeter EX4 4QJ
Tel: +44 (0)1392 263041
Fax: +44 (0)1392 263039
Email: intoff@exeter.ac.uk
Website: www.ex.ac.uk

Falmouth College of Arts
International Office, 27 Woodlane
Falmouth, Cornwall TR11 4RH
Tel: +44 (0)1326 211077
Fax: +44 (0)1326 212261
Email: international@falmouth.ac.uk
Website: www.falmouth.ac.uk

Fareham College
Bishopsfield Road, Fareham
Hampshire PO14 1NH
Tel: +44 (0)1329 815200
Fax: +44 (0)1329 822483
Email: careers@fareham.ac.uk
Website: www.fareham.ac.uk

Farnborough College of Technology
Boundary Road, Farnborough
Hampshire GU14 6SB
Tel: +44 (0)1252 407028
Fax: +44 (0)1252 407041
Email: information@farn-ct.ac.uk
Website: www.farn-ct.ac.uk

University of Glamorgan
Treforest, Pontypridd
Mid Glamorgan CF37 1DL
Tel: +44 (0)1443 828812
Fax: +44 (0)1443 822055
Email: enquiries@glam.ac.uk
Website: www.glam.ac.uk

**Glamorgan Centre for
Art and Design Technology**
Glyntaff Road, Pontypridd
Glamorgan CF37 4AT
Tel: +44 (0)1443 663309
Fax: +44 (0)1443 663313
Email: info@gcadt.ac.uk
Website: www.gcadt.ac.uk

University of Glasgow
Glasgow G12 8QQ
Tel: +44 (0)141 330 4575
Fax: +44 (0)141 330 4413
Email: admissions@gla.ac.uk
Website: www.gla.ac.uk

Glasgow Caledonian University
City Campus, 70 Cowcaddens Road
Glasgow G4 0BA
Tel: +44 (0)141 331 8673
Fax: +44 (0)141 331 8676
Email: international@gcal.ac.uk
Website: www.caledonian.ac.uk

University of Gloucestershire
Admissions Office
PO Box 220
The Park, Cheltenham
Gloucestershire GL50 2QF
Tel: +44 (0)1242 532825
Fax: +44 (0)1242 543334
Email: admissions@glos.ac.uk
Website: www.glos.ac.uk

**Gloucestershire College of Arts
and Technology**
Brunswick Road, Gloucester
Gloucestershire GL1 1HU
Tel: +44 (0)1452 426549
Fax: +44 (0)1452 426531
Email: info@gloscat.ac.uk
Website: www.gloscat.ac.uk

**Goldsmiths College
(University of London)**
International Office
Lewisham Way
New Cross
London SE14 6NW
Tel: +44 (0)20 7919 7700
Fax: +44 (0)20 7919 7704
Email: international-office@gold.ac.uk
Website: www.goldmiths.ac.uk

Great Yarmouth College
Southtown, Great Yarmouth
Norfolk NR31 0ED
Tel: +44 (0)1493 655261
Fax: +44 (0)1493 653423
Email: info@gyc.ac.uk
Website: www.gyc.ac.uk

Greenmount and Enniskillen Colleges
22 Greenmount Road
Antrim BT41 4PU
Tel: +44 (0)28 9442 6700
Fax: +44 (0)28 94 426606
Email: enquiries@dardni.gov.uk
Website: www.greenmount.ac.uk

University of Greenwich
Enquiry Unit, Bank House
Wellington Street
Woolwich SE18 6PF
Tel: +44 (0)20 8331 8590
Fax: +44 (0)20 8331 8145
Email: courseinfo@gre.ac.uk
Website: www.gre.ac.uk

Greenwich School of Management
Meridian House
Royal Hill, Greenwich
London SE10 8RD
Tel: +44 (0)20 8516 7800
Fax: +44 (0)20 8516 7801
Website: www.greenwich-college.ac.uk

Grimsby College
Nuns Corner, Grimsby
Lincolnshire DN34 5BQ
Tel: +44 (0)1472 311222
Fax: +44 (0)1472 879924
Website: www.grimsby.ac.uk

**Guildford College of Further
and Higher Education**
Stoke Park, Guildford
Surrey GU1 1EZ
Tel: +44 (0)1483 448500
Fax: +44 (0)1483 448600
Email: hnd@guildford.ac.uk
Website: www.guildford.ac.uk

Gyosei International College
London Road
Reading
Berkshire RG1 5AQ
Tel: +44 (0)118 931 0152
Fax: +44 (0)118 931 0137
Email: ba.admin@gyosei.ac.uk or
ma.admin@gyosei.ac.uk
Website: www.gyosei.ac.uk

Halesowen College
Whittingham Road
Halesowen, West Midlands B63 3NA
Tel: +44 (0)121 602 7777
Fax: +44 (0)121 585 0369
Website: www.halesowen.ac.uk

Halton College
Kingsway, Widness, Cheshire WA8 7QQ
Tel: +44 (0)151 423 1391
Fax: +44 (0)151 420 2408
Email: studentservices@haltoncollege.ac.uk
Website: www.haltoncollege.ac.uk

Hammersmith & West London College
Gliddon Road, Barons Court
London W14 9BL
Tel: +44 (0)20 8741 1688
Fax: +44 (0)20 8741 2491
Email: cic@hwlc.ac.uk
Website: www.hwlc.ac.uk

Harper Adams University College
Admissions Secretary
Newport, Shropshire TF10 8NB
Tel: +44 (0)1952 815000
Fax: +44 (0)1952 813210
Email: admissions@harper-adams.ac.uk
Website: www.harper-adams.ac.uk

**Havering College of Further
and Higher Education**
Ardleigh Green Road
Hornchurch, Essex RM11 2LL
Tel: +44 (0)1708 462801
Fax: +44 (0)1708 462788
Email: ciac@havering-college.ac.uk
Website: www.havering-college.ac.uk

Henley College Coventry
Henley Road
Bell Green
Coventry CV2 1ED
Tel: +44 (0)24 7662 6300
Fax: +44 (0)24 7661 1837
Email: info@henley-cov.ac.uk
Website: www.henley-cov.ac.uk

Herefordshire College of Technology
Folly Lane, Hereford
Herefordshire HR1 1LS
Tel: +44 (0)1432 365376
Fax: +44 (0)1432 353449
Email: enquiries@hereford-tech.ac.uk
Website: www.hereford-tech.ac.uk

Herefordshire College of Art and Design
Folly Lane
Hereford
Herefordshire HR1 1LT
Tel: +44 (0)1432 273359
Fax: +44 (0)1432 341099
Email: hcad@hereford-art-col.ac.uk
Website: www.hereford-art-col.ac.uk

Heriot-Watt University, Edinburgh
International Recruitment Office
Riccarton, Edinburgh EH14 4AS
Tel: +44 (0)131 451 3633
Fax: +44 (0)131 451 3630
Email: admissions@hw.ac.uk
Website: www.hw.ac.uk

University of Hertfordshire
International Office, College Lane
Hatfield, Hertfordshire AL10 9AB
Tel: +44 (0)1707 284800
Fax: +44 (0)1707 284870
Email: admissions@herts.ac.uk
Website: www.herts.ac.uk

Hertford Regional College
Admissions, Broxbourne Centre
Turnford, Broxbourne
Hertfordshire EN10 6AE
Tel: +44 (0)1992 411411
Fax: +44 (0)1992 411885
Website: www.hertreg.ac.uk

Heythrop College (University of London)
Kensington Square, London W8 5HQ
Tel: +44 (0)20 7795 6600
Fax: +44 (0)20 7795 4200
Email: r.bolland@heythrop.ac.uk

Highbury College
The Admissions Team, Dovercourt Road
Cosham, Portsmouth PO6 2SA
Tel: +44 (0)23 9231 3281
Fax: +44 (0)23 9232 5551
Email: student.services@highbury.ac.uk
Website: www.highbury.ac.uk

Hillcroft College
Student Admissions
South Bank, Surbiton
Surrey KT6 6DF
Tel: +44 (0)20 8399 2688
Fax: +44 (0)20 8390 9171
Email: enquiry@hillcroft.ac.uk
Website: www.hillcroft.ac.uk

UHI Millennium Institute
Admissions Service
Caledonia House
63 Academy Street
Inverness IV1 1BB
Tel: +44 (0)1463 279000
Email: eo@uhi.ac.uk
Website: www.uhi.ac.uk

Holborn College
Admissions Office
200 Greyhound Road
London W14 9RY
Tel: +44 (0)20 7385 3377
Fax: +44 (0)20 7381 3377
Email: hlt@holborncollege.ac.uk
Website: www.holborncollege.ac.uk

Hopwood Hall College
St Mary's Gate, Rochdale
Lancashire OL12 6RY
Tel: +44 (0)1706 345346
Fax: +44 (0)1706 641426
Email: irene.sweetman@hopwood.ac.uk
Website: www.hopwood.ac.uk

Huddersfield Technical College
New North Road
Huddersfield
West Yorkshire HD1 5NN
Tel: +44 (0)1484 536521
Fax: +44 (0)1484 511885
Email: info@huddcoll.ac.uk
Website: www.huddcoll.ac.uk

The University of Huddersfield
International and European Office
Central Services Building
Queensgate, Huddersfield
West Yorkshire HD1 3DH
Tel: +44 (0)1484 472219
Fax: +44 (0)1484 450408
Email: international.office@hud.ac.uk
Website: www.hud.ac.uk

Hull College
Queen's Gardens
Hull HU1 3DG
Tel: 01482 598744
Fax: 10482 598851
Email: tbarber@hull-college.ac.uk
Website: www.hull-college.ac.uk

The University of Hull
International Office
Cottingham Road, Hull HU6 7RX
Tel: +44 (0)1482 466904
Fax: +44 (0)1482 466554
Email: international@hull.ac.uk
Website: www.hull.ac.uk

Imperial College of Science, Technology and Medicine (University of London)
Admissions Office, Registrar's Division
London SW7 2AZ
Tel: +44 (0)20 7594 8014
Fax: +44 (0)20 7594 8004
Email: admissions@ic.ac.uk
Website: www.ic.ac.uk/

Institute of Education, University of London
20 Bedford Way
London WC1H 0AL
Tel: +44 (0)20 7612 6000
Fax: +44 (0)20 7612 6097
Email: ma.enquiries@ioe.ac.uk
Website: www.ioe.ac.uk

The Isle of Wight College
Medina Way, Newport
Isle of Wight PO30 5TA
Tel: +44 (0)1983 526631
Fax: +44 (0)1983 522803
Email: info@iwightc.ac.uk
Website: www.iwightc.ac.uk

Keele University
Admissions Office, Keele
Staffordshire ST5 5BG
Tel: +44 (0)1782 584005
Fax: +44 (0)1782 632343
Email: aaa14@admin.keele.ac.uk
Website: www.keele.ac.uk

The University of Kent
Recruitment and Admissions Office
The Registry, Canterbury
Kent CT2 7NZ
Tel: +44 (0)1227 827272
Fax: +44 (0)1227 827077
Email: admissions@ukc.ac.uk
Website: www.ukc.ac.uk

Kent Institute of Art and Design
Registry Office
Oakwood Park, Maidstone
Kent ME16 8AG
Tel: +44 (0)1622 757286
Fax: +44 (0)1622 621100
Email: dnorman@kiad.ac.uk
Website: www.kiad.ac.uk

Kidderminster College
Student Admissions
Hoo Road, Kidderminster
Worcestershire DY10 1LX
Tel: +44 (0)1562 820811/7322222
Fax: +44 (0)1562 748504
Email: glittle@kidderminster.ac.uk
Website: www.kidderminster.ac.uk

King Alfred's Winchester
Winchester, Hampshire
SO22 4NR
Tel: +44 (0)1962 827235
Fax: +44 (0)1962 827406
Email: srobinson1@wkac.ac.uk
Website: www.wkac.ac.uk

King's College London (University of London)
Strand, London WC2 2LS
Tel: +44 (0)20 7836 5454
Fax: +44 (0)20 7836 1799
Email: ucas.enquiries@kcl.ac.uk
Website: www.kcl.ac.uk

Kingston University
Student Enquiry and Applicant Services
Cooper House
40-46 Surbiton Road
Kingston upon Thames
Surrey KT1 2HX
Tel: +44 (0)20 8547 7053
Fax: +44 (0)20 8547 7080
Email: int.recruit@kingston.ac.uk
Website: www.kingston.ac.uk

Lakes College West Cumbria
Hallwood Road
Lillyhall Business Park
Workington CA14 4JN
Tel: +44 (0)1946 839300
Fax: +44 (0)1946 839302
Email: enquiries@lcwc.ac.uk
Website: www.lakescollegewestcumbria.ac.uk

The University of Wales, Lampeter
Recruitment, Marketing and Admissions
Lampeter, Ceredigion SA48 7ED
Tel: +44 (0)1570 422351
Fax: +44 (0)1570 423423
Email: admissions@lampeter.ac.uk
Website: www.lamp.ac.uk

Lancaster University
Undergraduate Admissions Office
University House
Lancaster LA1 4YW
Tel: +44 (0)1524 65201
Fax: +44 (0)1524 846243
Email: ugadmissions@lancaster.ac.uk
Website: www.lancs.ac.uk/

Lancaster & Morecambe College
Morecambe Road
Lancaster LA1 2TY
Tel: +44 (0)1524 66215
Fax: +44 (0)1524 843078
Email: info@lanmore.ac.uk
Website: www.lanmore.ac.uk

Lansdowne College
40/44 Bark Place
London W2 4AT
Tel: +44 (0)20 7616 4400
Fax: +44 (0)20 7616 4401
Email: education@landsdownecollege.com
Website: www.landsdownecollege.com

University of Leeds
International Office
Leeds LS2 9JT
Tel: +44 (0)113 233 4023
Fax: +44 (0)113 233 4056
Email: international@leeds.ac.uk
Website: www.leeds.ac.uk/

Leeds College of Art and Design
Student Services
Jacob Kramer Building
Blenheim Walk
Leeds LS2 9AQ
Tel: +44 (0)113 202 8000
Fax: +44 (0)113 202 8001
Email: info@leeds-art.ac.uk
Website: www.leeds-art.ac.uk

Leeds College of Music
Admissions Tutor
3 Quarry Hill, Leeds
West Yorkshire LS2 7PD
Tel: +44 (0)113 222 3400
Fax: +44 (0)113 243 8798
Email: enquiries@lcm.ac.uk
Website: www.lcm.ac.uk

Leeds Metropolitan University
International Office
City Campus
Leeds LS1 3HE
Tel: +44 (0)113 283 6737
Fax: +44 (0)113 283 3129
Email: international@lmu.ac.uk
Website: www.lmu.ac.uk

Leeds: Park Lane College
Leeds, LS3 1AA
Tel: +44 (0)113 216 2000
Email: course.enquiry@
mail.parklanecoll.ac.uk
Website: www.parklanecoll.ac.uk

University of Leicester
Admissions and Student
Recruitment Office
University Road
Leicester LE1 7RH
Tel: +44 (0)116 252 5281
Fax: +44 (0)116 252 2447
Email: admissions@le.ac.uk
Website: www.le.ac.uk

Leicester College
Freemens Park Campus
Aylestone Road
Leicester LE2 7LW
Tel: +44 (0)116 224 2000
Fax: +44 (0)116 224 2190
Email: info@leicestercollege.ac.uk
Website: www.leicestercollege.ac.uk

Leo Baeck College
Admissions Office
80 East End Road
London N3 2SY
Tel: +44 (0)20 8349 5600
Fax: +44 (0)20 8343 2558
Email: info@lbc.ac.uk
Website: www.lbc.ac.uk

Lewisham College
Information Unit
Lewisham Way
London SE4 1UT
Tel: +44 (0)20 8694 3240
Email: info@lewisham.ac.uk
Website: www.lewisham.ac.uk

University of Lincoln
Central Admissions Unit
Cottingham Road
Kingston-upon-Hull HU6 7RT
Tel: +44 (0)1482 440550
Fax: +44 (0)1482 463052
Email: admissions@lincoln.ac.uk
Website: www.lincoln.ac.uk

The University of Liverpool
International Recruitment and
Relations Office, Senate House
Abercromby Square, Liverpool L69 3BX
Tel: +44 (0)151 794 6730
Fax: +44 (0)151 794 6733
Email: irro@liv.ac.uk
Website: www.liv.ac.uk

Liverpool Community College
Karen Finlay, English Language Centre
Riversdale Site, Riversdale Road
Aigeurth, Liverpool L19 3QK
Tel: +44 (0)151 2524711
Email: karen-finlay@liv-coll.ac.uk
Website: www.liv-coll.ac.uk

Liverpool Hope
International Office, Hope Park
Liverpool L16 9JD
Tel: +44 (0)151 291 3431
Fax: +44 (0)151 291 3116
Email: patersk@hope.ac.uk
Website: www.hope.ac.uk

**The Liverpool Institute for
Performing Arts**
Admissions Office, Mount Street
Liverpool L1 9HF
Tel: +44 (0)151 330 3084
Fax: +44 (0)151 330 3131
Email: reception@lipa.ac.uk
Website: www.lipa.ac.uk

Liverpool John Moores University
International Office, John Foster Building
98 Mount Crescent
Liverpool L3 5UZ
Tel: +44 (0)151 231 3522
Fax: +44 (0)151 707 0199
Email: international@livjm.ac.uk
Website: www.livjm.ac.uk

Llandrillo College, North Wales
Admissions Office, Llandrillo College
Llandudno Road, Rhos-on-Sea, Colwyn Bay
North Wales LL28 4HZ
Tel: +44 (0)1492 542338
Email: admissions@llandrillo.ac.uk
Website: www.llandrillo.ac.uk

London Guildhall University
Course Enquiries
133 Whitechapel High Street
London E1 7QA
Tel: +44 (0)20 7320 1616
Fax: +44 (0)20 7320 1163
Email: enqs@lgu.ac.uk
Website: www.lgu.ac.uk

The London Institute
65 Davies Street
London W1K 5DA
Tel: +44 (0)20 7514 6000
Fax: +44 (0)20 7514 6131
Email: c.anderson@linst.ac.uk
Website: www.linst.ac.uk

**London School of Economics
and Political Science
(University of London)**
Student Recruitment Office
Clare Market Building
Houghton Street
London WC2A 2AE
Tel: +44 (0)20 7955 6143
Fax: +44 (0)20 7955 7421
Email: stu.rec@lse.ac.uk
Website: www.lse.ac.uk

Loughborough College
Information Centre, Radmoor Road
Loughborough LE11 3BT
Tel: +44 (0)1509 618375
Fax: +44 (0)1509 618109
Email: info@loucoll.ac.uk
Website: www.loucoll.ac.uk

Loughborough University
International Office
Student Recruitment and Admissions
Loughborough, Leicestershire LE11 3TU
Tel: +44 (0)1509 223522
Email: international-office@lboro.ac.uk
Website: www.lboro.ac.uk

Lowestoft College
St Peters Street, Lowestoft
Suffolk NR32 2NB
Tel: +44 (0)1502 583521
Fax: +44 (0)1502 500031
Email: info@lowestoft.ac.uk
Website: www.lowestoft.ac.uk

University of Luton
Park Square, Luton
Bedfordshire LU1 3JU
Tel: +44 (0)1582 489319
Fax: +44 (0)1582 486260
Email: international-office@luton.ac.uk
Website: www.luton.ac.uk/

Macclesfield College
Park Lane, Macclesfield
Cheshire SK11 8LF
Tel: +44 (0)1625 410000
Fax: +44 (0)1625 410001
Email: info@macclesfield.ac.uk
Website: www.macclesfield.ac.uk

**Manchester College of Arts
and Technology**
City Centre Campus
Lower Hardman Street
Manchester M3 3ER
Tel: +44 (0)161 455 2434
Fax: +44 (0)161 953 2259
Email: international@mancat.ac.uk
Website: www.mancat.ac.uk

The University of Manchester
International Office
Beyer Building, Oxford Road
Manchester M13 9PL
Tel: +44 (0)161 275 2161
Fax: +44 (0)161 275 2058
Email: international.unit@man.ac.uk
Website: www.man.ac.uk

**The University of Manchester
Institute of Science and
Technology (UMIST)**
International Office, PO Box 88
Manchester M60 1QD
Tel: +44 (0)161 200 4+44 (0)20
Fax: +44 (0)161 200 4337
Email: intoff@umist.ac.uk
Website: www.umist.ac.uk

The Manchester Metropolitan University
International Office
All Saints Building, Oxford Road
Manchester M15 6BH
Tel: +44 (0)161 247 1017
Fax: +44 (0)161 247 6310
Email: intoff@mmu.ac.uk
Website: www.mmu.ac.uk

**Matthew Boulton College of
Further and Higher Education**
College Admissions Unit, Sherlock Street
Birmingham B5 7DB
Tel: +44 (0)121 446 4545
Fax: +44 (0)121 446 3105
Email: ask@matthew-boulton.ac.uk
Website: www.matthew-boulton.ac.uk

Coleg Menai
Friddoedd Road, Gwynnedd LL57 2TP
Tel: +44 (0)1248 370125
Fax: +44 (0)1248 370052
Email: student.services@menai.ac.uk
Website: www.menai.ac.uk

Mid-Cheshire College
Admissions Office, Hartford Campus
Chester Road, Northwich
Cheshire CW8 1LJ
Tel: +44 (0)1606 74444
Fax: +44 (0)1606 720700
Email: info@midchesh.ac.uk
Website: www.midchesh.ac.uk

Middlesex University
Admissions Enquiries
White Hart Lane
London N17 8HR
Tel: +44 (0)20 8411 5000
Fax: +44 (0)20 8411 5649
Email: admissions@mdx.ac.uk
Website: www.mdx.ac.uk

Napier University
International Student Recruitment Office
Old Craig, Craighouse Campus
Edinburgh EH10 5LG
Tel: +44 (0)131 455 6277
Email: intoffice@napier.ac.uk
Website: www.napier.ac.uk

Neath Port Talbot College
Admissions Unit
Neath Campus
Dwr-y-Felin Road
Neath SA10 7RF
Tel: +44 (0)1639 648000
Fax: +44 (0)1639 648009
Email: admissions@nptc.ac.uk
Website: www.nptc.ac.uk

NESCOT
Admissions Unit
Reigate Road, Ewell
Surrey KT17 3DS
Tel: +44 (0)20 8394 3038
Fax: +44 (0)20 8394 3030
Email: info@nescot.ac.uk
Website: www.nescot.ac.uk

University of Newcastle upon Tyne
International Office
10 Kensington Terrace
Newcastle-upon-Tyne NE1 7RU
Tel: +44 (0)191 222 8152
Fax: +44 (0)191 222 5212
Email: international.office@ncl.ac.uk
Website: www.ncl.ac.uk

Newcastle College
Rye Hill Campus, Scotswood Road
Newcastle-upon-Tyne NE4 7SA
Tel: +44 (0)191 200 4000
Fax: +44 (0)191 200 4517
Email: enquiries@ncl-coll.ac.uk
Website: www.ncl-coll.ac.uk

Newcastle-under-Lyme College
Liverpool Road
Newcastle-under-Lyme
Staffordshire ST5 2DF
Tel: +44 (0)1782 715111
Fax: +44 (0)1782 717396
Email: enquiries@nulc.ac.uk
Website: www.nulc.ac.uk

New College Durham
Admissions Officer, Framwellgate Moor
Durham DH1 5ES
Tel: +44 (0)191 375 4210
Fax: +44 (0)191 375 4222
Email: admissions@newdur.ac.uk
Website: www.newdur.ac.uk

New College Nottingham
The International Office
The Adams Building, Stoney Street
Nottingham NG1 1LJ
Tel: +44 (0)115 910 4610
Fax: +44 (0)115 910 4611
Email: internat@ncn.ac.uk
Website: www.ncn.ac.uk

Newman College of Higher Education
Admissions Registry
Genners Lane, Bartley Green
Birmingham B32 3NT
Tel: +44 (0)121 476 1181
Fax: +44 (0)121 476 1196
Email: registry@newman.ac.uk
Website: www.newman.ac.uk

University of Wales College, Newport
University Information Centre
Caerleon Campus, PO Box 101
Newport NP18 3YH
Tel: +44 (0)1633 432432
Fax: +44 (0)1633 432850
Email: uic@newport.ac.uk
Website: www.newport.ac.uk

Northbrook College Sussex
Admissions Office, Littlehampton Road
Worthing, West Sussex BN12 6NU
Tel: +44 (0)1903 606060
Fax: +44 (0)1903 606007
Email: admissions@nbcol.ac.uk
Website: www.nbcol.ac.uk

The Northern College of Education
Aberdeen Campus
Hilton Place
Aberdeen AB24 4FA
Tel: +44 (0)1224 283500
Fax: +44 (0)1224 283900
Website: www.norcol.ac.uk

**The North East Wales Institute
of Higher Education**
Admissions, Plas Coch
Mold Road
Wrexham LL11 2AW
Tel: +44 (0)1978 293045
Fax: +44 (0)1978 290008
Email: k.mitchell@newi.ac.uk
Website: www.newi.ac.uk

North East Worcestershire College
Admissions
Blackwood Road, Bromsgrove
Worcestershire B60 1PQ
Tel: +44 (0)1527 570020
Fax: +44 (0)1527 572900
Email: info@ne-worcs.ac.uk
Website: www.ne-worcs.ac.uk

North Highland College
Admissions, Dornoch Centre
Grange Road Dornoch
Scotland IV25 3LE
Tel: +44 (0)1862 811855
Fax: +44 (0)1862 811853
Website: www.nhdornoch.com

North Lincolnshire College
Registry, Monks Road
Lincoln LN2 5HQ
Tel: +44 (0)1522 876000
Fax: +44 (0)1522 876200
Email: nlc@nlincs-coll.ac.uk
Website: www.nlincs-coll.ac.uk

University of North London
The International Office
The Learning Centre
166-220 Holloway Road
London N7 8DB
Tel: +44 (0)20 7753 3314
Fax: +44 (0)20 7753 5015
Email: international@unl.ac.uk
Website: www.unl.ac.uk

North Tyneside College
Admissions Office
Embleton Avenue, Wallsend
Tyne and Wear NE28 9NJ
Tel: +44 (0)191 229 5000
Fax: +44 (0)191 229 0301
Email: admissions@ntyneside.ac.uk
Website: www.ntyneside.ac.uk

University College Northampton
The Academic Registrar
Park Campus, Boughton Green Road
Northampton NN2 7AL
Tel: +44 (0)1604 735500
Fax: +44 (0)1604 /22083
Email: admissions@northampton.ac.uk
Website: www.northampton.ac.uk

Northumbria University
The International Office
21 Ellison Place
Newcastle upon Tyne NE1 8ST
Tel: +44 (0)191 227 4271
Fax: +44 (0)191 261 1264
Email: er.intoff@unn.ac.uk
Website: www.unn.ac.uk

Northumberland College
Advice Centre, College Road
Ashington Northumberland NE63 9RG
Tel: +44 (0)1670 841200
Fax: +44 (0)1670 841201
Email: advice.centre@northland.ac.uk
Website: www.northland.ac.uk

North Radstock College
Admissions, South Hill Park
Radstock, BA3 3RW
Tel: +44 (0)1761 433161
Fax: +44 (0)1761 436173
Email: courses@nortcoll.ac.uk
Website: www.nortcoll.ac.uk

**North Warwickshire and
Hinckley College**
Admissions, Student Services
Hinckley Road, Nuneaton
Warwickshire CV11 6BH
Tel: +44 (0)2476 243000
Fax: +44 (0)2476 329056
Email:
admissions@nwarks-hinckley.ac.uk
Website: www.nwarks.hinckley.ac.uk

Norwich: City College
Registry, Ipswich Road
Norwich, Norfolk NR2 2LJ
Tel: +44 (0)1603 773311
Fax: +44 (0)1603 773301
Email: registry@ccn.ac.uk
Website: www.ccn.ac.uk

The University of Nottingham
International Office
University Park
Nottingham NG7 2RD
Tel: +44 (0)115 951 5247
Fax: +44 (0)115 951 5155
Email: international-office@
nottingham.ac.uk
Website: www.nott.ac.uk

The Nottingham Trent University
Burton Street
Nottingham NG1 4BU
Tel: +44 (0)115 941 8418
Fax: +44 (0)115 848 6063
Email: admissions@ntu.ac.uk
Website: www.ntu.ac.uk

The Oldham College
Rochdale Road
Oldham OL9 6AA
Tel: +44 (0)161 624 5214
Fax: +44 (0)161 785 4234
Email: info@oldham.ac.uk
Website: www.oldham.ac.uk

Oxford Brookes University
The International Office
Gipsy Lane Campus
Headington
Oxford OX3 0BP
Tel: +44 (0)1865 484880
Fax: +44 (0)1865 483616
Email: international@brookes.ac.uk
Website: www.brookes.ac.uk

Oxford University
Oxford Colleges Admissions Office
Wellington Square
Oxford OX1 2JD
Tel: +44 (0)1865 270207
Fax: +44 (0)1865 270708
Email: undergraduate.admissions@
admin.ox.ac.uk
Website: www.ox.ac.uk

Oxfordshire School of Art and Design
Administrator, Broughton Road Banbury
Oxfordshire OX16 9QA
Tel: +44 (0)1295 257979
Fax: +44 (0)1295 279623
Email: enquiries@northox.ac.uk

University of Paisley
Overseas Marketing, High Street
Paisley PA1 2BE
Tel: +44 (0)141 848 3000
Fax: +44 (0)141 848 3333
Email: overseas@paisley.ac.uk
Website: www.paisley.ac.uk

Pembrokeshire College
Admissions Unit, Haverfordwest
Pembrokeshire SA61 1SZ
Tel: +44 (0)1437 765247
Fax: +44 (0)1437 767279
Email: info@pembrokeshire.ac.uk
Website: www.pembrokeshire.ac.uk

Peninsula Medical School
Tamar Science Park, Davy Road
Derriford, Plymouth PL6 8BX
Tel: +44 (0)1752 764261
Fax: +44 (0)1752 764226
Email: medadmissions@pms.ac.uk
Website: www.pms.ac.uk

The People's College Nottingham
Student Services
Maid Marian Way
Nottingham NG1 6AB
Tel: +44 (0)115 912 3500
Fax: +44 (0)115 912 8600
Email: admissions@peoples.ac.uk
Website: www.peoples.ac.uk

Pershore Group of Colleges
Admissions Office
Avonbank, Pershore
Worcestershire WR10 3JP
Tel: +44 (0)1386 552443
Fax: +44 (0)1386 556528
Email: admissions-pershore@
pershore.ac.uk
Website: www.pershore.ac.uk

Peterborough Regional College
Park Crescent
Peterborough PE1 4DZ
Tel: +44 (0)1733 762400
Fax: +44 (0)1733 767986
Email: information@peterborough.ac.uk
Website: www.peterborough.ac.uk

University of Plymouth
The International Office
Drake Circus, Plymouth
Devon PL4 8AA
Tel: +44 (0)1752 233345
Fax: +44 (0)1752 232014
Email: intoff@plymouth.ac.uk
Website: www.plymouth.ac.uk

Plymouth College of Art and Design
Tavistock Place, Plymouth
Devon PL4 8AT
Tel: +44 (0)1752 203434
Fax: +44 (0)1752 203444
Email: enquiries@pcad.ac.uk
Website: www.pcad.ac.uk

University of Portsmouth
International Office, Nuffield Centre
St Michael's Road
Portsmouth PO1 2ED
Tel: +44 (0)23 9284 5118
Fax: +44 (0)23 9284 3538
Email: karen.arnold@port.ac.uk
Website: www.port.ac.uk

**Queen Margaret University
College, Edinburgh**
Admissions Office
Clerwood Terrace
Edinburgh EH12 8TS
Tel: +44 (0)131 317 3240
Fax: +44 (0)131 317 3248
Email: admissions@qmuc.ac.uk
Website: www.qmuc.ac.uk

Queen Mary, University of London
Mile End Road, London E1 4NS
Tel: +44 (0)20 7882 3066
Fax: i 44 (0)20 7882 5556
Email: international-office@qmul.ac.uk
Website: www.qmul.ac.uk

Queen's University Belfast
The Admissions Office
Belfast BT7 1NN
Tel: +44 (0)28 9033 5081
Fax: +44 (0)28 9068 7895
Email: admissions@qub.ac.uk
Website: www.qub.ac.uk

**Ravensbourne College of Design
and Communication**
Walden Road, Chislehurst
Kent BR7 5SN
Tel: +44 (0)20 8289 4900
Fax: +44 (0)20 8325 8320
Email: info@rave.ac.uk
Website: www.rave.ac.uk

**Reading College and School
of Arts and Design**
Crescent Road, Reading
Berkshire RG1 5RQ
Tel: +44 (0)118 967 5000
Fax: +44 (0)118 967 5301
Email: enquiries@reading-college.ac.uk
Website: www.reading-college.ac.uk

The University of Reading
The International Office
Whiteknights House
PO Box 217, Reading RG6 6AH
Tel: +44 (0)118 987 8111
Fax: +44 (0)118 975 2252
Email: intoff@reading.ac.uk
Website: www.rdg.ac.uk

Regents Business School London
External Relations
Regent's College
Regent's Park, London NW1 4NS
Tel: +44 (0)20 7487 7654
Fax: +44 (0)20 7487 7425
Email: rbs@regents.ac.uk
Website: www.regents.ac.uk

Richmond, The American International University in London
Queens Road
Richmond Upon Thames TW10 6JP
Tel: +44 (0)20 8332 8203
Fax: +44 (0)20 8332 1596
Email: enroll@richmond.ac.uk
Website: www.richmond.ac.uk

The Robert Gordon University
The International Office
Schoolhill, Aberdeen AB10 1FR
Tel: +44 (0)1224 262209
Fax: +44 (0)1224 262202
Email: international@rgu.ac.uk
Website: www.rgu.ac.uk

Rose Bruford College
Lamorbey Park
Sidcup, Kent DA15 9DF
Tel: +44 (0)20 8300 3024
Fax: +44 (0)20 8308 0542
Email: admiss@bruford.ac.uk
Website: www.bruford.ac.uk

Rotherham College of Arts and Technology
Eastwood Lane
Rotherham S65 1EG
Tel: +44 (0)1709 362111
Fax: +44 (0)1709 373053

Royal Agricultural College
Cirencester, Gloucestershire GL7 6JS
Tel: +44 (0)1285 652531
Fax: +44 (0)1285 650219
Email: admissions@royagcol.ac.uk
Website: www.royagcol.ac.uk

Royal Holloway, University of London
Educational and International
Liaison Office
Egham, Surrey TW20 0EX
Tel: +44 (0)1784 443957
Fax: +44 (0)1784 471381
Email: liaison-office@rhul.ac.uk
Website: www.rhul.ac.uk

Royal Veterinary College, University of London
Royal College Street
London NW1 0TU
Tel: +44 (0)20 7468 5148
Fax: +44 (0)20 7388 2342
Website: www.rvc.ac.uk

Ruskin College Oxford
Student Enquiry Office
Walton Street
Oxford OX1 2HE
Tel: +44 (0)1865 310713
Fax: +44 (0)1865 554372
Email: enquiries@ruskin.ac.uk
Website: www.ruskin.ac.uk

The Rutland College
Barleythorpe Road
Oakham, Rutland LE15 6QH
Tel: +44 (0)1572 722863

Rycotewood College
Priest End, Thame
Oxfordshire OX9 2AF
Tel: +44 (0)1844 212501
Fax: +44 (0)1844 218809
Email: enquiries@rycote.ac.uk
Website: www.rycote.ac.uk

University of St Andrews
Old Union Building
79 North Street, St Andrews
Fife KY16 9AJ
Tel: +44 (0)1334 462150
Fax: +44 (0)1334 463388
Email: admissions@st-and.ac.uk
Website: www.st-and.ac.uk

St George's Hospital Medical School (University of London)
Cranmer Terrace, London SW17 0RE
Tel: +44 (0)20 8725 5992
Fax: +44 (0)20 8725 3426
Email: c.persaud@sghms.ac.uk
Website: www.sghms.ac.uk

St Helens College
Brook Street, St Helens WA10 1PZ
Tel: +44 (0)1744 6733766
Fax: +44 (0)1744 623 400
Email: enquiries@sthelens.ac.uk
Website: www.sthelens.ac.uk

St Loye's School of Health Medicine
Millbrook House, Millbrook Lane
Topsham Road, Exeter EX2 6ES
Tel: +44 (0)1392 219774
Fax: +44 (0)1392 435357
Email: stloyes@exr.ac.uk
Website: www.ex.ac.uk/affiliate/stloyes

The College of St Mark and St John
Derriford Road
Plymouth, Devon PL6 8BH
Tel: +44 (0)1752 636700
Fax: +44 (0)1752 636751
Email: admissions@marjon.ac.uk
Website: www.marjon.ac.uk

St Martin's College, Lancaster: Ambleside: Carlisle
Bowerham Road
Lancaster, Lancashire LA1 3JD
Tel: +44 (0)1524 384444
Fax: +44 (0)1524 384567
Email: admissions@ucsm.ac.uk
Website: www.ucsm.ac.uk

St Mary's College
Waldegrave Road, Strawberry Hill
Twickenham TW1 4SX
Tel: +44 (0)20 8240 4029
Fax: +44 (0)20 8240 4255
Website: www.smuc.ac.uk

The University of Salford
Faraday Building, Salford
Greater Manchester M5 4WT
Tel: +44 (0)161 295 3251
Fax: +44 (0)161 295 5256
Email: intoff@salford.ac.uk
Website: www.salford.ac.uk

Salford College
Worsley Campus, Walkden Road
WorsleyManchester M28 7GD
Tel: +44 (0)161 702 8272
Fax: +44 (0)161 295 5256

SAE Institute
United House, North Road
Islington, London N7 9DP
Tel: +44 (0)20 7609 2653
Fax: +44 (0)20 7609 6944
Email: saelondon@sael.demon.co.uk
Website: www.sae.edu

Salisbury College
Southampton Road
Salisbury, Wiltshire SP1 2LW
Tel: +44 (0)1722 344344
Fax: +44 (0)1722 344345
Email: enquiries@salisbury.com
Website: www.salisbury.ac.uk

Sandwell College
Wednesbury Campus
Woden Road South, Wednesbury
West Midlands WS10 0PE
Tel: +44 (0)121 556 6000
Fax: +44 (0)121 253 6104
Email: enquiries@sandwell.ac.uk
Website: www.sandwell.ac.uk

School of Oriental and African Studies (University of London)
Thornaugh Street
Russell Square
London WC1H 0XG
Tel: +44 (0)20 7637 2388
Fax: +44 (0)20 7436 3944
Email: study@soas.ac.uk
Website: www.soas.ac.uk

The School of Pharmacy (University of London)
29-39 Brunswick Square
London WC1N 1AX
Tel: +44 (0)20 7753 5831
Fax: +44 (0)20 7753 5829
Email: registry@ulsop.ac.uk
Website: www.ulsop.ac.uk

Scottish Agricultural College
Auchincruive
Ayr KA6 5HW
Tel: +44 (0)1292 525350
Fax: +44 (0)1292 525349
Email: etsu@au.sac.ac.uk
Website: www.sac.ac.uk

The University of Sheffield
International Office
4 Palmerston Road
Sheffield S10 2TE
Tel: +44 (0)114 222 1255
Fax: +44 (0)114 272 9145
Email: international@sheffield.ac.uk
Website: www.shef.ac.uk

Sheffield Hallam University
International Office
Room 5111, Surrey Building
City Campus, Howard Street
Sheffield S1 1WB
Tel: +44 (0)114 225 3880
Fax: +44 (0)114 225 4768
Email: international@shu.ac.uk
Website: www.shu.ac.uk

Sheffield College
PO Box 730, Sheffield S6 5YF
Tel: +44 (0)114 260 2216
Fax: +44 (0)114 260 2282
Email: heunit@sheffcol.ac.uk
Website: www.sheffcol.ac.uk

Shrewsbury College of Arts and Technology
London Road, Shrewsbury
Shropshire SY2 6PR
Tel: +44 (0)1743 342342
Fax: +44 (0)1743 342343
Email: prospects@shrewsbury.ac.uk
Website: www.shrewsbury.ac.uk

Solihull College
Blossomfield Road
Solihull B91 1SB
Tel: +44 (0)121 678 7000
Fax: +44 (0)121 678 7200
Email: enquiries@staff.solihull.ac.uk
Website: www.solihull.ac.uk

Somerset College of Arts and Technology
Wellington Road, Taunton
Somerset TA1 5AX
Tel: +44 (0)1823 366366
Fax: +44 (0)1823 366418
Email: enquiries@somerset.ac.uk
Website: www.somerset.ac.uk

Southampton City College
St Mary Street
Southampton SO14 1AR
Tel: +44 (0)23 8048 4848
Fax: +44 (0)23 8057 7473
Email: information@southampton-city.ac.uk
Website: www.southampton-city.ac.uk

Southampton Institute
External Relations Service
East Park Terrace
Southampton
Hampshire SO14 0RB
Tel: +44 (0)23 8031 9422
Fax: +44 (0)23 8031 9412
Email: international@solent.ac.uk
Website: www.solent.ac.uk

University of Southampton
International Office
Southampton SO17 1BJ
Tel: +44 (0)23 8059 6808
Fax: +44 (0)23 8059 3037
Email: ednfairs@soton.ac.uk
Website: www.soton.ac.uk

South Bank University
Admissions Office, 103 Borough Road
London SE1 0AA
Tel: +44 (0)20 7815 7815
Fax: +44 (0)20 7815 8273
Email: internat@sbu.ac.uk
Website: www.sbu.ac.uk/

South Birmingham College
Hall Green Campus, Cole Bank Road
Hall Green, Birmingham B28 8ES
Tel: +44 (0)121 694 5002
Fax: +44 (0)121 694 6290
Email: davidh@sbirm.ac.uk
Website: www.sbirm.ac.uk

South Cheshire College
Dane Bank Avenue
Crewe CW2 8AB
Tel: +44 (0)1270 654654
Fax: +44 (0)1270 651515
Email: admissions@s-cheshire.ac.uk
Website: www.s-cheshire.ac.uk

South Devon College
Newton Road
Torquay, Devon TQ2 5BY
Tel: +44 (0)1803 406406
Fax: +44 (0)1803 400701
Email: courses@s-devon.ac.uk
Website: www.s-devon.ac.uk

South Downs College
College Road
Waterlooville, Hampshire PO7 8AA
Tel: +44 (0)23 9279 7979
Fax: +44 (0)23 9279 7940
Email: college@southdowns.ac.uk
Website: www.southdowns.ac.uk

South East Essex College
Carnarvon Road, Southend-on-Sea
Essex SS2 6LS
Tel: +44 (0)1702 220400
Fax: +44 (0)1702 432320
Email: admissions@
se-essex-college.ac.uk
Website: www.se-essex-college.ac.uk

South Nottingham College
West Bridgford Centre
Greythorn Drive, West Bridgford
Nottingham NG2 7GA
Tel: +44 (0)115 914 6400
Fax: +44 (0)115 914 6444
Email: enquiries@
south-nottingham.ac.uk
Wesite: www.south-nottingham.ac.uk

South Trafford College
Manchester Road, West Timperley
Cheshire WA14 5PQ
Tel: +44 (0)161 952 4600
Fax: +44 (0)161 952 4672
Website: www.stcoll.ac.uk

South Tyneside College
St George's Avenue
South Shields
Tyne and Wear NE34 6ET
Email: info@stc.ac.uk
Website: www.stc.ac.uk

Southport College
Mornington Road, Southport PR9 0TT
Tel: +44 (0)1704 500606
Fax: +44 (0)1704 546240
Website: www.southport.mernet.org.uk

Southwark College
The Bermondsey Centre
Drummond Road
London SE16 4EE
Tel: +44 (0)20 7815 1526
Fax: +44 (0)20 7815 1525
Email: info@southwark.ac.uk
Website: www.southwark.ac.uk

Sparsholt College Hampshire
Sparsholt, Winchester SO21 2NF
Tel: +44 (0)1962 797280
Fax: +44 (0)1962 776587
Email: enquiry@sparsholt.ac.uk
Website: www.sparsholt.ac.uk

Stafford College
Earl Street
Stafford ST16 2QR
Tel: +44 (0)1785 223800
Fax: +44 (0)1785 259953
Website: www.staffordcoll.ac.uk

Staffordshire University
International Office
College Road
Stoke-on-Trent ST4 2DE
Tel: +44 (0)1782 292718
Fax: +44 (0)1782 292796
Email: international@staffs.ac.uk
Website: www.staffs.ac.uk

Stamford College
Drift Road, Stamford PE9 1XA
Tel: +44 (0)1780 484300
Fax: +44 (0)1780 484301
Email: enquiries@stamford.ac.uk
Website: www.stamford.ac.uk

Stephenson College Coalville
Bridge Road, Coalville
Leicestershire LE67 3PW
Tel: +44 (0)1530 836136
Fax: +44 (0)1530 814253
Email: services@stephensoncoll.ac.uk
Website: www.stephensoncoll.ac.uk

The University of Stirling
Student Recruitment and
Admissions Service
Stirling FK9 4LA
Tel: +44 (0)1786 467046
Fax: +44 (0)1786 466800
Email: international@stir.ac.uk
Website: www.stir.ac.uk

**Stockport College of Further
and Higher Education**
Wellington Road South
Stockport SK1 3UQ
Tel: +44 (0)161 958 3417
Fax: +44 (0)161 958 3305
Email: belinda.hinds@stockport.ac.uk
Website: www.stockport.ac.uk/

Stoke on Trent College
Stoke Road, Shelton
Stoke-on-Trent ST4 2DG
Tel: +44 (0)1782 208208
Fax: +44 (0)1782 603504
Email: info@stokecoll.ac.uk
Website: www.stokecoll.ac.uk

Stratford upon Avon College
The Willows North
Stratford upon Avon
Warwickshire CV37 9QR
Tel: +44 (0)1789 266245
Fax: +44 (0)1789 267524
Email: college@strat-avon.ac.uk
Website: www.strat-avon.ac.uk

The University of Strathclyde
International Office
Graham Hills Building
50 George Street, Glasgow G1 1QE
Tel: +44 (0)141 548 2912
Fax: +44 (0)141 552 7493
Email: international@mis.strath.ac.uk
Website: www.strath.ac.uk

Stranmillis University College
Stranmillis Road
Belfast BT9 5DY
Tel: +44 (0)28 9038 1271
Fax: +44 (0)28 9066 4423
Email: info@stran.ni.ac.uk
Website: www.stran.ni.ac.uk

Suffolk College
Ipswich IP4 1BR
lel: +44 (0)1473 296369
Fax: +44 (0)1473 343628
Website: www.suffolk.ac.uk

University of Sunderland
Centre of International Education
North Sands Business Centre
Liberty Way, Sunderland SR6 0QA
Tel: +44 (0)191 515 2648
Fax: +44 (0)191 515 2960
Email: international@sunderland.ac.uk
Website: www.sunderland.ac.uk

The University of Surrey
The Registry, Guildford
Surrey GU2 7XH
Tel: +44 (0)1483 689005
Fax: +44 (0)1483 689525
Email: g.brown@surrey.ac.uk
Website: www.surrey.ac.uk

Roehampton University of Surrey
International Centre
Roehampton Lane, London SW15 5PU
Tel: +44 (0)20 8392 3192
Fax: +44 (0)20 8392 3031
Email: international@roehampton.ac.uk
Website: www.roehampton.ac.uk

**Surrey Institute of Art
and Design, University College**
Falkner Road, Farnham
Surrey GU9 7DS
Tel: +44 (0)1252 722441
Fax: +44 (0)1252 892616
Email: registry@surrart.ac.uk
Website: www.surrart.ac.uk

University of Sussex
International and Study Abroad Office
Falmer, Brighton
Sussex BN1 9QN
Tel: +44 (0)1273 678422
Fax: +44 (0)1273 678640
Email: international@sussex.ac.uk
Website: www.sussex.ac.uk

Sutton Coldfield College
Lichfield Road, Sutton Coldfield
West Midlands B74 2NW
Tel: +44 (0)121 355 5671
Fax: +44 (0)121 355 0799
Email: cnewman@sutcol.ac.uk
Website: www.sutcol.ac.uk

University of Wales, Swansea
The Admissions Office
Singleton Park, Swansea SA2 8PP
Tel: +44 (0)1792 295111
Fax: +44 (0)1792 295110
Email: admissions@swan.ac.uk
Website: www.swan.ac.uk

Swansea College
Tycoch Road, Sketty, Swansea SA2 9EB
Tel: +44 (0)1792 284000
Fax: +44 (0)1792 284074
Email: recovery@swancoll.ac.uk
Website: www.swancoll.ac.uk

Swansea Institute of Higher Education
Mount Pleasant, Swansea SA1 6ED
Tel: +44 (0)1792 481259
Fax: +44 (0)1792 297876
Email: enquiry@sihe.ac.uk
Website: www.sihe.ac.uk

Swindon College
Regent Circus, Swindon SN1 1PT
Tel: +44 (0)1793 498308
Fax: +44 (0)1793 641794
Email: admissions@swindon-college.ac.uk
Website: www.swindon-college.ac.uk

Tameside College
Ashton Campus, Beaufort Road
Ashton-under-Lyne, Lancashire OL6 6NX
Tel: +44 (0)161 908 6600
Fax: +44 (0)161 908 6611
Email: info@tamesidecollege.ac.uk
Website: www.tameside.ac.uk

University of Teesside
Academic Registry
Middlesbrough TS1 3BA
Tel: +44 (0)1642 218121
Fax: +44 (0)1642 342067
Email: reg@tees.ac.uk
Website: www.tees.ac.uk

Thomas Danby College
Roundhay Road
Leeds LS7 3BG
Tel: +44 (0)113 249 4912
Fax: +44 (0)113 240 1967
Email: info@thomasdanby.ac.uk
Website: www.thomasdanby.ac.uk

Thames Valley University
Learning Advice Centre
18-22 Bond Street
Ealing, London W5 5AA
Tel: +44 (0)20 8579 5000
Fax: +44 (0)20 8231 2900
Email: learning.advice@tvu.ac.uk
Website: www.tvu.ac.uk

Totton College
Water Lane, Totton
Southampton SO40 3ZX
Tel: +44 (0)23 8087 4874
Fax: +44 (0)23 8087 4879
Email: admissions@totton.ac.uk
Website: www.totton.ac.uk

**Trinity and All Saints College
(accredited college of the
University of Leeds)**
Brownberrie Lane
Horsforth
Leeds LS18 5HD
Tel: +44 (0)113 283 7123
Fax: +44 (0)113 283 7321
Email: admissions@tasc.ac.uk
Website: www.tasc.ac.uk

Trinity College Carmarthen
College Road, Carmarthen
Carmarthenshire SA31 3EP
Tel: +44 (0)1267 676767
Fax: +44 (0)1267 676766

**University College London
(University of London)**
The International Office
Gower Street
London WC1E 6BT
Tel: +44 (0)20 7679 7765
Fax: +44 (0)20 7679 3001
Email: international@ucl.ac.uk
Website: www.ucl.ac.uk

University of Ulster
International Office
Cromore Park, Coleraine
County Londonderry BT52 1SA
Tel: +44 (0)28 9032 8515
Fax: +44 (0)28 7032 4930
Email: ep.simpson@ulst.ac.uk
Website: www.ulst.ac.uk

Uxbridge College
Park Road, Uxbridge
Middlesex UB8 1NQ
Tel: +44 (0)1895 853 333
Website: www.uxbridgecollege.ac.uk

Wakefield College
Margaret Street
Wakefield WF1 2DH
Tel: +44 (0)1924 789789
Fax: +44 (0)1924 789340

University of Wales College of Medicine
Heath Park
Cardiff CF14 4XN
Tel: +44 (0)29 2074 2027
Fax: +44 (0)29 2074 2914
Website: www.uwcm.ac.uk/

Warrington Collegiate Institution
Padgate Campus
Crab Lane, Warrington WA2 0DB
Tel: +44 (0)1925 494494
Fax: +44 (0)1925 494289
Email: registry.he@warr.ac.uk
Website: www.warr.ac.uk/unicoll

The University of Warwick
The International Office
Coventry CV4 7AL
Tel: +44 (0)24 7652 3706
Fax: +44 (0)24 7652 4337
Email: int.office@warwick.ac.uk
Website: www.warwick.ac.uk

**Warwickshire College, Royal Leamington
Spa and Moreton Morrell**
Warwick New Road
Leamington Spa
Warwickshire CV32 5JE
Tel: +44 (0)1926 318000
Fax: +44 (0)1926 318111
Email: enquiries@warkscol.ac.uk

Welsh College of Music and Drama
Cathays Park
Cardiff CF10 3ER
Tel: +44 (0)29 2034 2854
Fax: +44 (0)29 2039 1304
Email: robertskt@wcmd.ac.uk
Website: www.wcmd.ac.uk/

College of West Anglia
Tennyson Avenue
King's Lynn PE30 2QW
Tel: +44 (0)1553 761144
Fax: +44 (0)1553 764902
Email: enquiries@col-westanglia.ac.uk
Website: www.col-westanglia.ac.uk

West Herts College, Watford
Hempstead Road, Watford
Hertfordshire WD1 3EZ
Tel: +44 (0)1923 812565
Fax: +44 (0)1923 812556
Email: admissions@westherts.ac.uk

West Nottingham College
Derby Road
Mansfield NG18 5BH
Tel: +44 (0)1623 627191
Fax: +44 (0)1623 623063

Weston College
Knightstone Road
Weston-Super-Mare BS23 2AL
Tel: +44 (0)1934 411411
Fax: +44 (0)1934 411410
Website: www.weston.ac.uk

University of Westminster
16 Little Titchfield Street
London W1W 7UW
Tel: +44 (0)20 7911 5769
Fax: +44 (0)20 7911 5132
Email: international-office@wmin.ac.uk
Website: www.wmin.ac.uk/international

Westminster Kingsway College
Battersea Park Road
London SW11 4JR
Tel: +44 (0)20 7556 8068
Fax: +44 (0)20 7498 4765
Email: tony.tucker@westking.ac.uk
Website: www.westking.ac.uk

West Thames College
London Road, Isleworth
Middlesex TW7 4HS
Tel: +44 (0)20 8568 0244
Fax: +44 (0)20 8569 7787
Email: admissions@west-thames.ac.uk
Website: www.west-thames.ac.uk

Weymouth College
Cranford Avenue
Weymouth DT4 7LQ
Tel: +44 (0)1305 208808
Fax: +44 (0)1305 208892
Email: igs@weymouth.ac.uk
Website: www.weymouth.ac.uk

Wigan and Leigh College
PO Box 53, Parsons Walk
Wigan, Lancashire WN1 1RS
Tel: +44 (0)1942 761601
Fax: +44 (0)1942 501533

Wigston College of Further Education
Station Road, Wigston
Leicestershire LE18 2DW
Tel: +44 (0)116 288 5051
Fax: +44 (0)116 288 0823

Wiltshire College, Lackham
Registrar, Lacock, Chippenham
Wiltshire SN15 2NY
Tel: +44 (0)1249 466800
Fax: +44 (0)1249 444474
Website: www.wiltscoll.ac.uk

Wimbledon School of Art
Merton Hall Road
London SW19 3QA
Tel: +44 (0)20 8408 5000
Fax: +44 (0)20 8408 5050
Email: art@wimbledon.ac.uk
Website: www.wimbledon.ac.uk

Wirral Metropolitan College
Borough Road
Birkenhead, Wirral
Merseyside CH42 9QD
Tel: +44 (0)151 551 7777
Fax: +44 (0)151 551 7401
Email: h.e.enquiries@wmc.ac.uk
Website: www.wmc.ac.uk

University of Wolverhampton
Compton Park Campus
Wolverhampton WV3 9DX
Tel: +44 (0)1902 322332
Fax: +44 (0)1902 323755
Email: international@wlv.ac.uk
Website: www.wlv.ac.uk

University College Worcester
Henwick Grove
Worcester WR2 6AJ
Tel: +44 (0)1905 855111
Fax: +44 (0) 01905 855132
Website: www.worc.ac.uk

Worcester College of Technology
Deansway
Worcester WR1 2JF
Tel: +44 (0)1905 725563
Fax: +44 (0)1905 28906
Email: tad@wortech.ac.uk
Website: www.wortech.ac.uk

Writtle College
Lordship Road, Writtle
Chelmsford
Essex CM1 3RR
Tel: +44 (0)1245 424200
Fax: +44 (0)1245 420456
Email: postmaster@writtle.ac.uk
Website: www.writtle.ac.uk/

Yeovil College
Joint University Centre
Mudford Road
Yeovil BA21 4DR
Tel: +44 (0)1935 423921
Fax: +44 (0)1935 415483

The University of York
International Office
The Stables Building
Heslington
York YO1 5DD
Tel: +44 (0)1904 433534
Fax: +44 (0)1904 434268
Email: international@york.ac.uk
Website: www.york.ac.uk

York College
Tadcaster Road
York YO24 1UA
Tel: +44 (0)1904 770398
Fax: +44 (0)1904 770499

York St John College
Director, School of
International Education
Lord Mayor's Walk, York YO31 7EX
Tel: +44 (0)1904 716942
Fax: +44 (0)1904 716928
Email: d.moulds@yorksj.ac.uk
Website: www.yorksj.ac.uk

**Yorkshire Coast College
of Further and Higher Education**
Lady Edith's Drive
Scarborough
North Yorkshire YO12 5RN
Tel: +44 (0)1723 372105
Fax: +44 (0)1723 501918
Email: admissions@ycoastco.ac.uk
Website: www.ycoastco.ac.uk

Ystrad Mynach College
Twyn Road
Ystrad Mynach CF82 7XR
Tel: +44 (0)1443 816888

This chapter is a summary of the institutions offering undergraduate degrees in the main subject areas. A comprehensive listing can be found in the *UCAS Directory* available from UCAS on +44 (0)1242 544610.

Accountancy and finance
A20, A30, A40, A60, A80, B06, B26, B32, B40, B44, B50, B56, B60, B72, B78, B80, B84, B90, B94, C10, C15, C20, C25, C30, C50, C56, C60, C84, C85, C92, D26, D39, D65, D86, E14, E28, E56, E70, E81, E84, F66, G14, G28, G42, G64, G70, G90, H06, H16, H24, H36, H49, H50, H54, H60, H72, K12, K24, K84, L14, L21, L23, L27, L34, L39, L41, L51, L55, L72, L79, L93, M20, M25, M40, M77, M80, N07, N21, N28, N37, N38, N56, N63, N77, N81, N82, N84, N91, O10, O66, P20, P60, P80, Q75, R10, R12, R18, R36, R54, S03, S18, S21, S27, S29, S30, S33, S51, S72, S75, S78, S81, S84, S85, S93, S94, S96, T20, T40, U20, W12, W20, W37, W40, W50, W60, W75

Agriculture and forestry
A20, A40, A60, A70, B06, B16, B37, B44, B50, B72, B78, B80, B94, C08, C10, C13, C30, C50, C55, C58, C78, C85, D26, D39, E14, E26, E28, E56, G14, G67, G70, H12, H24, H36, H49, H54, H72, I50, K24, K48, L21, L23, L41, M40, N07, N21, N38, n49, N63, N84, N91, O66, p50, P60, Q75, R12, R48, R54, S01, S03, S26, S34, S75, S81, T20, T80, W25, W35, W74, W75, W80, W85

American studies
A40, B06, B32, B84, C10, C30, C50, D26, D39, D65, E14, E28, E56, E70, E84, G14, G56, G64, G70, H72, K12, K24, K48, K60, l07, L14, L34, L41, l46, L51, L55, L79, M20, M25, M40, M80, N38, N84, P60, Q75, R12, S18, S84, S90, S93, U20, W20, W75, Y75

Anatomy/physiology/genetics
A20, A30, A40, A60, A80, B13, B32, B50, B56, B78, B80, B84, c05, C15, C30, C50, C85, D26, D39, D65, E28, E56, F66, G14, G28, G42, G70, H06, H12, H36, H49, H60, K12, K24, K60, L14, L23, L27, L34, L39, L41, l46, L51, L79, L93, M20, M25, M40, M80, N21, N38, N63, N77, N91, O10, O33, O66, P60, P80, Q50, Q75, R12, R36, R72, S03, S18, S21, S27, S33, S36, S64, S72, S78, S81, S84, S85, S90, S93, T20, U80, W50, W74, W75, Y50

Archaeology
A20, B06, B32, B50, B56, B78, C05, C15, C55, C95, D26, D86, E14, E56, E84, G14, G28, H72, K24, K48, K60, l07, L34, L41, M20, N21, N37, N38, N84, O33, Q75, R12, S09, S18, S27, S33, S36, S93, T80, U80, W20, W80, Y50

Architecture
A60, B16, B41, B72, B80, C05, C08, C15, C20, C25, C50, C60, C75, D26, D39, D65, E28, E56, F66, G14, G28, G42, G70, H14, H24, H60, K24, k36, K84, L27, L39, L41, L51, L93, M20, M25, M40, N07, N21, N23, N56, N63, N77, N84, N91, O66, P35, P60, P80, Q75, R06, R36, S18, S21, S27, S30, S33, S43, S78, U20, U80, W50, W66, W78

Art and design
A30, A40, A60, A70, A80, B06, B09, B11, B13, B15, B20, B23, B26, B32, B37, B38, B40, B41, B44, B50, B53, B56, B60, B72, B78, B80, B84, B88, B90, B94, B95, C08, C10, C13, C15, C20, C22, C24, C25, C30, C35, C50, C55, C56, C58, C60, C62, C63, C66, C63, C65, C66, C71, C75, C78, C84, C85, C92, C95, D13, D26, D39, D45, D52, D58, D65, E28, E32, E42, E56, F33, F66, G14, G20, G28, G42, G45, G56, G64,

G70, H04, H06, H18, H24, H36, H37, H47, H49, H54, H60, H72, H73, K12, K24, k36, K48, K84, L14, L16, L23, L27, L28, L36, L39, L43, l46, l48, L51, L53, L55, L65, L79, L82, L93, M05, M10, M25, M40, M77, M80, N07, N21, N23, N24, N28, N30, N31, N37, N38, N39, N41, N56, N58, N63, N72, N77, N78, N79, N82, N91, O10, O30, O33, O66, O80, P20, P35, P55, P60, P65, P80, R06, R10, R12, R20, R36, R48, R51, R95, S03, S05, S07, S21, S22, S23, S24, S26, S27, S28, S29, S30, S32, S33, S35, S38, S39, S43, S46, S51, S59, S68, S72, S76, S78, S79, S81, S84, S88, S90, S91, S94, S96, S98, T10, T20, T40, T80, U20, U80, W12, W17, W25, W35, W40, W45, W47, W50, W65, W66, W67, W69, W73, W75, W80, W81, W85, Y25, Y70, Y75, Y80

Biochemistry/biophysics/biotechnology
A20, A30, A40, A60, A80, B06, B13, B16, B32, B56, B78, B80, B84, C05, C15, C30, C55, C85, D26, D65, D86, E14, E28, E56, E70, E84, G28, G42, G70, H06, H12, H24, H36, H49, H60, H72, I50, K12, K24, K60, K84, L14, L23, L34, L41, L51, L93, M20, M25, M40, N21, n49, N56, N63, N77, N84, N91, O33, O66, P20, P80, Q50, Q75, R12, R36, R72, S03, S18, S21, S27, S33, S36, S72, S75, S78, S85, S90, S93, U20, U80, W20, W50, W75, Y50

Biology
A20, A30, A40, A60, A80, B06, B13, B16, B20, B26, B32, B37, B44, B56, B72, B78, B80, B84, B95, C05, C08, C10, C15, C20, C30, C55, C78, C85, D26, D39, D65, D86, E14, E28, E42, E56, E70, E84, G14, G28, G42, G70, H06, H24, H36, H49, H60, H72, I50, K12, K24, K48, K60, K84, L14, L22, L23, L27, L34, L39, L41, l46, L51, L93, M20, M25, M40, M80, N07, N21, N30, N36, N38, N41, N49, N56, N63, N77, N82, N84, N91, O33, O66, P20, P40, P60, P80, Q25, Q50, Q75, R12, R36, R48, R72, S01, S03, S18, S21, S24, S27, S33, S34, S36, S51, S64, S71, S72, S74, S75, S78, S81, S84, S90, S93, T80, U20, U80, W20, W50, W74, W75, W80, W85, Y50

Botany
A20, A40, B06, B13, B32, B78, C05, C08, D86, E14, E56, G28, I50, L23, L34, L41, M20, M40, N84, N91, P60, Q75, R12, R72, S18, S27, S36, W74, W75, W85

Building and surveying
A30, A60, A80, B26, B40, B41, B44, B60, B72, B80, B84, B95, C20, C25, C30, C75, C85, C91, D39, D52, D58, E56, G14, G42, G45, G70, H24, H49, H60, K24, k36, K84, L27, L36, L39, L51, L79, M25, M65, N07, N30, N37, N38, N49, N56, N63, N77, N84, N91, O10, O66, P20, P35, P60, P80, R10, R12, R36, R52, S03, S21, S29, S30, S32, S33, S43, S51, S71, S72, S78, S96, T20, U20, U80, W37, W50, W67, W73, W75, W81

Business and management
A20, A30, A40, A60, A70, A80, B06, B11, B13, B15, B16, B20, B26, B32, B35, B40, B41, B44, B50, B53, B56, B60, B70, B72, B78, B80, B84, B88, B90, B94, B95, C08, C10, C13, C15, C20, C22, C24, C25, C30, C50, C55, C56, C58, C60, C62, C63, C66, C69, C75, C78, C84, C85, C90, C91, C92, C95, D22, D26, D39, D52, D58, D65, D86, E14, E27, E28, E42, E56, E70, E77, E81, E84, F50, F66, G14, G28, G42, G45, G56,

G64, G70, G74, G80, G90, G96, H06, H10, H12, H14, H16, H24, H36, H49, H50, H54, H60, H72, H73, I50, K12, K24, K48, K60, K84, l07, L14, L21, L23, L24, L27, L28, L34, L39, L41, L43, l46, L51, L53, L55, L65, L72, L77, L79, L82, L93, M05, M10, M20, M25, M40, M60, M77, M80, N07, N13, N21, N23, N28, N30, N31, N37, N38, N41, N49, N56, N58, N63, N72, N77, N81, N82, N84, N91, O10, O30, O33, O66, P20, P35, P40, P55, P60, P80, Q25, Q50, Q75, R10, R12, R18, R20, R36, R48, R52, R54, R72, S01, S03, S08, S09, S18, S21, S22, S23, S24, S26, S27, S28, S29, S30, S32, S33, S34, S36, S43, S47, S51, S59, S64, S65, S69, S71, S72, S75, S76, S78, S79, S81, S84, S85, S90, S91, S93, S94, S96, S98, T10, T20, T40, T45, T65, T80, U20, U80, U95, W08, W12, W17, W20, W25, W35, W37, W40, W45, W50, W52, W60, W65, W67, W71, W73, W74, W75, W80, W81, W85, Y50, Y70, Y75, Y80

Chemistry
A20, A60, A80, B06, B13, B16, B26, B32, B56, B72, B78, B80, C05, C15, C30, C85, D26, D39, D65, D86, E14, E56, E84, G14, G28, G42, G70, H06, H24, H60, H72, I50, K12, K24, K60, K84, L14, L23, L34, L41, L51, L79, M20, M25, M40, N21, N38, N56, N63, N77, N84, N91, O10, O33, O66, P20, P40, P60, Q50, Q75, R12, R36, R48, S03, S18, S21, S27, S36, S75, S78, S84, S85, S90, S93, T20, U80, W20, W73, Y50

Cinematics – film, TV, photography
A20, A40, A60, B06, B40, B41, B44, B50, B53, B56, B60, B72, B80, B84, B94, C10, C22, C25, C30, C50, C55, C63, C65, C66, C69, C71, C92, C95, D26, D39, D52, E14, E28, E32, E42, E70, E84, F33, G14, G20, G28, G42, G70, G80, H18, H24, H36, H49, K24, k36, K48, K60, K84, l07, L27, L28, L34, L36, L39, L41, L43, L51, L55, L65, L93, M20, M40, M77, M80, N07, N21, N23, N37, N38, N41, N49, N56, N63, N77, N78, N84, N91, O66, O80, P20, P60, P65, P80, Q50, Q75, R06, R10, R12, R48, R72, S05, S07, S08, S21, S22, S24, S26, S27, S30, S43, S46, S51, S71, S72, S76, S84, S88, S90, S96, T10, T20, T40, T45, T80, W12, W17, W20, W25, W40, W50, W66, W75, Y75, Y80

Computer sciences and engineering
A20, A30, A40, A60, A80, B06, B09, B13, B15, B16, B20, B23, B26, B32, B40, B41, B44, B50, B56, B60, B70, B72, B78, B80, B84, B90, B94, B95, C05, C10, C13, C15, C20, C22, C24, C25, C30, C50, C55, C57, C58, C60, C62, C63, C66, C69, C75, C78, C84, C85, C90, C91, C92, D22, D26, D39, D52, D58, D65, D86, E14, E26, E27, E28, E42, E56, E70, E84, F50, F66, G14, G28, G42, G45, G56, G64, G67, G70, G74, G80, H06, H16, H24, H36, H49, H54, H60, H72, H73, I50, K12, K24, K60, K84, l07, L14, L21, L23, L24, L27, L28, L34, L39, L41, L43, l46, L51, L53, L55, L65, L77, L79, L93, M05, M10, M20, M25, M40, M77, M80, N07, N13, N21, N23, N28, N30, N31, N36, N37, N38, N41, N49, N56, N58, N62, N63, N72, N77, N81, N82, N84, N91, O10, O33, O66, O80, P20, P35, P40, P55, P60, P80, Q50, Q75, R06, R10, R12, R20, R36, R48, R52, R72, S03, S08, S18, S21, S23, S24, S26, S27, S28, S29, S30, S32, S33, S35, S36, S40, S43, S51, S59, S65, S68, S69, S71, S72, S74, S75, S76, S78, S79, S81, S84, S85, S90, S93, S94, S96, S98, T10, T20, T40, T45, T80, U20, U80, U95, W08, W12, W17,

W20, W25, W35, W37, W40, W45, W47, W50, W52, W60, W64, W66, W67, W73, W75, W80, W81, Y50, Y70, Y75, Y80

Dentistry
B32, B78, D65, G28, K60, L23, L41, M20, N21, Q50, Q75, S18, W10

Drama, dance and performance arts
A40, A60, A80, B06, B13, B20, B32, B38, B41, B44, B50, B53, B60, B72, B78, B80, B84, B94, B95, C05, C20, C24, C25, C30, C35, C50, C55, C58, C62, C63, C66, C71, C75, C85, C91, C92, C95, D13, D26, D39, D52, D58, E14, E27, E28, E42, E70, E84, F50, G14, G28, G45, G56, G64, G70, H10, H24, H36, H49, H60, H72, H73, K12, K24, K42, K48, K84, L14, L21, L23, L36, L79, L82, L93, M20, M40, M60, M80, N07, N23, N30, N36, N38, N41, N49, N56, N63, N72, N77, N91, O10, O30, O66, P55, P60, P80, Q25, Q50, Q75, R10, R12, R20, R48, R51, R55, R72, S03, S07, S23, S24, S28, S29, S30, S32, S33, S38, S39, S43, S51, S59, S64, S71, S72, S74, S79, S81, S84, S85, S90, S91, S96, T10, T20, T80, U20, W08, W12, W17, W20, W30, W35, W40, W45, W47, W52, W65, W66, W69, W75, W80, W81, Y25, Y75, Y80

Economics
A20, A30, A40, A60, A80, B06, B16, B32, B56, B78, B80, B84, B90, C05, C15, C20, C25, C30, C60, C85, D39, D52, D65, D86, E14, E28, E42, E56, E70, E84, G14, G28, G42, G56, G70, H24, H36, H60, H72, K12, K24, K84, L14, L23, L27, L34, L39, L41, L51, L55, L72, L79, M20, M40, M80, N07, N21, N38, N63, N77, N84, N91, O33, O66, P20, P60, P80, Q50, Q75, R12, R20, R36, R72, S03, S09, S18, S27, S33, S36, S72, S75, S78, S81, S84, S85, S90, S93, S96, T20, U20, W20, W50, W75, Y50

Education studies
A20, A30, A40, A60, A80, B06, B13, B16, B20, B26, B32, B35, B40, B41, B44, B60, B70, B78, B80, B84, B90, C05, C10, C15, C20, C25, C30, C35, C50, C55, C58, C63, C75, C84, C92, D22, D26, D39, D52, D86, E28, E42, E56, E70, E84, G14, G28, G70, G80, G90, H04, H24, H36, H37, H49, H54, H60, H73, K12, K48, K60, K84, L14, L23, L27, L39, L41, L43, I46, L51, L53, L79, L93, M20, M40, M80, N21, N23, N24, N36, N38, N41, N56, N58, N60, N63, N72, N77, N82, N91, O10, O66, P20, P60, R48, R55, S21, S22, S23, S28, S29, S36, S43, S51, S59, S64, S72, S75, S76, S78, S79, S81, S84, S93, T10, T80, W12, W17, W20, W25, W35, W40, W45, W74, W75, W80, Y50, Y80

Engineering – aeronautical
A60, B16, B72, B78, B80, B84, C60, C63, C78, C85, C90, F66, G28, H36, H49, I50, K84, L23, L39, L41, L55, L79, M20, M25, N41, N56, Q50, Q75, S03, S18, S26, S27, S72, S76, S78, S84, S85

Engineering – chemical
A80, B16, B32, B56, C05, C30, D58, E28, E56, H24, H60, I50, K12, L23, L79, M25, N21, N49, N84, O33, P20, P60, Q75, S18, S33, S78, S85, S93, T20, U80, W37

Engineering – civil
A20, A30, A60, A80, B16, B26, B32, B44, B56, B72, B78, B84, B95, C15, C60, C85, C90, D52, D65, D86, E28, E56, E84, G14,

G28, G42, G45, G70, H24, H49, H60, I50, K84, L23, L27, L41, L51, L55, L79, M20, M25, M65, N07, N21, N37, N84, N91, O33, O66, P20, P60, P80, Q75, R36, R52, S03, S18, S21, S27, S30, S33, S51, S78, S85, S93, S96, T20, U20, U80, W20, W67, W74, W75

Engineering – electrical and electronic
A20, A30, A60, A80, B06, B16, B23, B26, B32, B40, B41, B44, B50, B56, B72, B78, B80, B84, B95, C10, C15, C20, C22, C25, C56, C57, C60, C75, C84, C85, C90, D26, D39, D52, D58, D65, D86, E14, E28, E56, E70, E84, F66, G14, G28, G42, G70, G80, H24, H36, H49, H54, H60, H72, I50, K24, K60, K84, L14, L23, L27, L34, L39, L41, L43, L48, L51, L53, L55, L77, L79, L93, M20, M25, M40, M80, N07, N21, N37, N41, N49, N56, N62, N63, N77, N82, N84, N91, O10, O33, O66, P20, P40, P60, P80, Q50, Q75, R06, R10, R12, R36, R52, S03, S08, S18, S21, S23, S24, S26, S27, S30, S33, S36, S51, S71, S72, S78, S81, S84, S85, S90, S93, S96, T20, T40, U20, U80, U95, W12, W20, W25, W37, W50, W60, W67, W75, Y50, Y80

Engineering – general
A20, A30, A60, A80, B16, B32, B40, B41, B44, B50, B56, B60, B72, B78, B80, B84, B94, C05, C10, C15, C22, C25, C30, C60, C62, C85, C91, D26, D39, D52, D86, E28, E56, E84, G14, G28, G42, G64, G70, H24, H36, H49, H60, H72, I50, K48, K84, L14, L23, L27, L34, L39, L41, L51, L53, L55, L65, L79, L93, M05, M20, M25, M40, M77, M80, N07, N37, N38, N56, N77, N82, N84, N91, O33, O66, P20, P40, P55, P60, P80, Q50, R10, R12, R36, R48, R54, S03, S08, S18, S21, S26, S28, S30, S33, S43, S72, S78, S81, S84, S85, S90, S93, T10, T20, T40, T80, U20, U80, U95, W12, W17, W20, W25, W37, W50, W60, W74, W75, W81

Engineering – mechanical and production
A20, A30, A60, A80, B06, B11, B16, B23, B26, B32, B41, B44, B50, B56, B72, B78, B80, B84, B94, B95, C10, C15, C20, C22, C30, C56, C57, C60, C75, C84, C85, C90, C95, D26, D39, D58, D65, D86, E28, E56, E84, F66, G14, G28, G42, G45, G70, G80, H12, H24, H36, H49, H60, H72, I50, K24, K48, K60, K84, L14, L23, L27, L34, L39, L41, L43, L51, L53, L55, L77, L79, L93, M20, M25, M40, M80, N07, N21, N23, N31, N37, N38, N41, N49, N56, N77, N82, N84, N91, O10, O30, O33, O66, P20, P40, P60, P80, Q50, Q75, R10, R12, R36, S03, S18, S21, S23, S27, S28, S30, S33, S51, S71, S72, S76, S78, S81, S84, S85, S88, S90, S93, S96, T20, U20, U80, U95, W12, W20, W25, W37, W50, W60, W67, W74, W75, W85

English
A20, A40, A60, B06, B13, B20, B32, B38, B40, B41, B44, B56, B72, B78, B80, B84, B90, B94, C05, C10, C15, C25, C30, C50, C55, C58, C84, C85, C95, D13, D26, D39, D52, D65, D86, E14, E28, E42, E56, E70, E84, F33, G14, G28, G56, G70, G80, H24, H36, H60, H72, K12, K24, K48, K60, K84, I07, L14, L23, L24, L27, L34, L41, L39, L41, I46, L51, L55, L79, L93, M20, M40, M80, N21, N36, N37, N38, N56, N63, N77, N82, N84, N91, O33, O66, P60, P80, Q25, Q50, Q75, R12, R48, R72, S03, S09, S18, S21, S24, S26, S27,

S33, S36, S59, S64, S72, S75, S78, S79, S84, S90, S93, S96, T20, T80, U20, U80, W20, W50, W75, W80, Y50, Y75

Environmental studies, technology and oceanography
A20, A30, A40, A60, A70, A80, B06, B13, B20, B26, B32, B41, B44, B50, B53, B56, B72, B80, B84, B94, C05, C08, C10, C13, C15, C20, C22, C25, C30, C50, C55, C58, C60, C78, C85, D26, D39, D65, D86, E14, E28, E42, E56, E84, F66, G14, G28, G42, G70, H12, H24, H36, H49, H60, H72, I50, I70, K12, K60, K84, I07, L14, L21, L23, L27, L34, L39, L41, I46, L51, L72, L79, M20, M25, M40, M80, N21, N31, N37, N38, N56, N63, N77, N84, N91, O66, P20, P35, P60, P80, Q50, R10, R12, R48, S01, S03, S18, S21, S24, S26, S27, S30, S33, S43, S51, S72, S75, S78, S81, S84, S90, S96, T20, T80, U20, W50, W67, W74, W75, W80, W85, Y50

European studies and languages
A20, A30, A40, A80, B06, B16, B26, B32, B35, B44, B50, B56, B60, B72, B78, B80, C05, C15, C30, C50, C78, C85, D39, D52, D65, D86, E14, E28, E42, E56, E70, E77, G28, G42, G56, G70, G96, H24, H36, H49, H60, H72, K12, K24, K60, K84, L14, L23, L27, L34, L39, L41, I46, L51, L55, L79, M20, M25, M40, M77, M80, N07, N21, N37, N38, N41, N56, N63, N77, N84, N91, O33, O66, P20, P60, P80, Q50, Q75, R12, R36, R48, R54, R72, S03, S09, S18, S21, S27, S30, S33, S36, S64, S72, S75, S78, S81, S85, S90, S93, S96, T40, U20, U80, W50, W75, W80, Y50

Food science/technology and nutrition
A20, A30, B20, B35, B41, B50, C08, C13, C20, C30, C55, C58, C78, C85, G28, G42, G70, H12, H60, I50, K60, K84, L22, L23, L24, L27, L39, L51, L93, M40, N21, N63, N77, N84, N91, O66, P60, P80, Q25, Q75, R12, R36, R48, S01, S03, S21, S27, S33, S64, S81, S85, T20, U20, W35, W50, W75, W80

Geography
A20, A40, A60, A80, B06, B13, B20, B32, B38, B50, B56, B60, B72, B78, B80, B84, C05, C08, C10, C15, C25, C30, C50, C55, C58, C60, C75, D26, D39, D65, D86, E14, E28, E42, E56, E84, G14, G28, G70, H36, H60, H72, K12, K48, K60, K84, I07, L14, L23, L27, L34, L41, I46, L51, L72, L79, M20, M25, M40, M80, N21, N36, N37, N38, N56, N63, N77, N84, N91, O33, O66, P20, P60, P80, Q50, Q75, R12, R48, R72, S03, S09, S18, S21, S24, S27, S28, S30, S36, S59, S64, S72, S75, S78, S79, S84, S90, S93, T20, T70, T80, U20, U80, W50, W75, W80

Geological sciences
A20, A40, B06, B20, B32, B50, B56, B72, B78, C05, C15, C25, C50, D39, D86, E14, E42, E56, E84, G14, G28, G70, H36, H60, I50, K12, K84, L14, L23, L34, L41, L51, M20, N38, N91, O33, O66, P20, P60, P80, Q75, R12, R72, S27, S36, S72, U80, W75

Healthcare and therapies
A20, A30, A40, A80, B06, B13, B32, B35, B40, B41, B44, B50, B56, B60, B72, B80, B81, B84, B87, B88, B94, C10, C15, C20, C22, C25, C30, C50, C55, C57, C58, C60, C66, C75, C78, C84, C85, C90, C91, C95, D26, D39, D58, D86, E14, E28, E70, E80, G14, G28, G42, G45, G70, H10, H12,

H36, H47, H49, H60, H72, I50, K12, K24, K60, K84, L14, L23, L27, L36, L39, L41, I46, L51, L53, L65, L93, M20, M25, M40, M60, M80, N07, N21, N23, N28, N30, N38, N49, N56, N63, N77, N82, N84, N91, O66, P20, P60, P80, Q25, Q50, Q75, R10, R12, R36, R48, S03, S03, S18, S21, S24, S26, S27, S28, S29, S30, S32, S33, S42, S43, S49, S51, S54, S59, S64, S67, S68, S72, S76, S78, S81, S84, S93, S96, T20, T40, T80, U20, U80, W10, W12, W25, W35, W40, W50, W75, W80, Y50, Y75

History

A20, A40, A60, B06, B13, B20, B32, B38, B44, B56, B60, B72, B78, B80, B84, B90, C05, C10, C15, C20, C30, C50, C55, C58, C85, C95, D26, D39, D65, D86, E14, E28, E42, E56, E70, E84, G14, G28, G56, G70, G80, G96, H36, H60, H72, K12, K24, K48, K60, K84, I07, L14, L23, L24, L27, L34, L39, L41, I46, L51, L55, L65, L72, M20, M40, M80, N21, N36, N37, N38, N56, N63, N77, N82, N84, N91, O10, O33, O66, P60, P80, Q50, Q75, R12, R20, R48, R72, S03, S09, S18, S21, S24, S27, S33, S36, S59, S64, S72, S75, S78, S79, S81, S84, S90, S93, T20, T80, U20, U80, W20, W50, W75, W80, Y50, Y75

History of art

A20, A40, A60, B32, B44, B72, B78, B90, B94, C05, C25, C55, C80, C95, D26, D39, E14, E28, E56, E70, F33, G14, G28, G56, H72, K24, K84, L14, L23, L34, L41, L51, L55, L65, L79, M20, M40, M80, N21, N30, N38, N39, N77, N84, O66, O80, P60, P80, Q75, R12, R20, R48, R72, S09, S21, S27, S30, S36, S72, S81, S84, S90, U80, W20, Y50

Hotel, institutional and recreation management

A20, A30, A60, B06, B11, B13, B15, B16, B26, B35, B37, B40, B41, B44, B50, B60, B72, B80, B88, B89, B90, B94, C10, C20, C30, C45, C50, C55, C57, C58, C66, C69, C75, C78, C85, C91, C92, D10, D22, D26, D39, D52, E42, E56, E84, F50, F66, G14, G42, G45, G64, G70, G80, G90, H16, H36, H39, H49, H60, H72, I70, K24, K48, K84, I07, L16, L21, L22, L27, L36, L39, L41, L43, L46, L51, L53, L55, L65, L77, L79, L93, M20, M40, M65, M77, M80, N07, N13, N21, N23, N28, N30, N41, N49, N56, N58, N63, N77, N82, N91, O10, O30, O66, P35, P55, P60, P80, Q25, R10, R12, R36, R48, S01, S03, S07, S21, S22, S23, S24, S26, S27, S28, S30, S32, S34, S38, S43, S51, S64, S67, S71, S72, S74, S78, S81, S85, S94, S96, T10, T20, T40, T70, U20, W08, W12, W17, W25, W35, W37, W40, W50, W52, W60, W65, W67, W73, W74, W75, W80, W81, W85, Y25, Y70, Y75, Y80

Languages – African, Asian and Oriental

B32, B60, C05, C15, C30, D86, E28, E56, E77, H72, K12, L23, L41, L51, L55, M20, M80, N21, N63, N84, O33, O66, R12, R72, S03, S09, S18, S75, U20, U80, W50

Languages – Celtic

A20, A40, B06, C15, C20, E56, G14, G28, H49, I07, L41, N63, Q75, S64, S93, T80, U20, W50

Languages – classical and ancient

A20, B32, B78, C05, D86, E56, E84, G28, K60, I07, L23, L38, L41, I46, M20, N21, N84, O33, Q75, R12, R48, R72, S09, S27, S36, S84, S93, U80, W20

Languages – East European

B78, G28, H72, N84, S18, U80, W50

Languages – French

A20, A40, A60, A80, B06, B16, B32, B56, B72, B78, B80, B82, B84, B90, B94, C08, C10, C15, C20, C30, C50, C55, C85, D26, D39, D52, D65, D86, E14, E28, E56, E70, E77, E84, G28, G70, G96, H24, H36, H60, H72, K12, K24, K60, K84, L14, L23, L24, L27, L34, L41, L51, L55, L79, M20, M25, M40, M80, N21, N38, N63, N77, N84, N91, O66, P20, P35, P60, P80, Q50, Q75, R12, R36, R48, R72, S03, S18, S21, S27, S36, S59, S72, S75, S78, S85, S90, S93, T20, U20, U80, W20, W50, W74, W75, Y50

Languages – German

A20, A40, A60, A80, B06, B16, B32, B56, B72, B78, B80, B84, B94, C10, C15, C20, C30, C55, C85, D26, D39, D52, D65, D86, E14, E28, E56, E70, E77, E84, G28, G70, G96, H24, H36, H60, H72, K12, K24, K60, K84, L14, L23, L27, L34, L41, L51, L55, L79, M20, M25, M40, M80, N21, N38, N77, N84, N91, O66, P20, P60, P80, Q50, Q75, R12, R36, R72, S03, S18, S27, S36, S72, S75, S78, S85, S90, S93, T20, U20, U80, W20, W50, W75, Y50

Languages – Italian

A40, A60, B06, B16, B32, B78, B88, B94, C15, C30, C85, D86, E28, E56, E77, E84, G28, G70, H72, K24, L14, L23, L34, L41, L51, L55, M20, M40, N84, N91, O66, P60, P80, R12, R72, S03, S21, S36, S78, S90, S93, U80, W20, W50, W75, W80

Languages – Middle Eastern

B32, D86, E56, E84, G28, I07, L23, M20, N21, O33, S03, S09, S36, U80, W50

Languages – Russian

B16, B32, B78, C85, D86, E56, E77, E84, G28, H24, K12, L23, M20, N84, P80, Q50, S18, S36, S78, S85, S90, S93, U80, W75

Languages – Scandinavian

B16, E14, E56, G28, H72, U80

Languages – Spanish/Latin American

A20, A40, A60, B06, B16, B32, B56, B78, B80, B90, B94, C15, C20, C30, C55, C85, D26, D39, D65, D86, E14, E28, E56, E70, E77, E84, G28, G56, G70, H24, H36, H72, K12, K24, K60, K84, L14, L23, L24, I27, L34, L39, L41, L51, L55, L79, M20, M40, M80, N21, N63, N77, N84, N91, O66, P20, P60, P80, Q50, Q75, R12, R48, R72, S03, S18, S21, S27, S30, S36, S72, S75, S78, S90, S93, U20, U80, W20, W50, W75

Law

A20, A30, A40, A60, B06, B26, B32, B40, B41, B44, B50, B56, B60, B72, B78, B80, B84, B90, B94, C05, C10, C15, C25, C30, C58, C60, C85, C92, D26, D39, D52, D65, D86, E14, E28, E42, E56, E70, E84, G14, G28, G42, G70, H24, H36, H50, H60, H72, K12, K24, K60, K84, L14, L20, L23, L27, L34, L39, L41, L51, L55, L72, L79, M20, M40, M80, N07, N21, N37, N38, N56, N63, N77, N84, N91, O10, O33, O66, P20, P55, P60, P80, Q50, Q75, R12, R36, S09, S18, S21, S27, S29, S30, S33, S72, S75, S78, S81, S84, S85, S90, S93, S96, T20, T40, U20, U80, W20, W50, W75, W80, W81

Librarianship and information studies

A30, A40, B26, B72, C25, E70, H49, I07, L27, L39, I46, L51, L65, L79, L93, M40, N07, N63, N77, P20, P60, Q25, S18, U80, W75

Linguistics and literature

A20, A40, A60, B06, B13, B32, B41, B44, B72, B80, B90, C10, C15, C30, C95, D39, D86, E14, E28, E42, E56, E70, G14, G28, G70, H36, H72, K24, K60, K84, L14, L23, L27, I46, L93, M20, M80, N21, N77, N91, O33, P55, P80, Q50, R12, R20, S03, S09, S18, S36, S59, S72, S75, S78, S81, S84, S90, S93, U20, U80, W20, W50, W75, Y50, Y75

Marine sciences and technologies

B41, C15, C78, G28, H24, H72, L41, L51, N21, P35, P60, P80, S27, S30, S75, S78, U80

Materials/minerals sciences and technologies

A20, B11, B32, B44, B56, B60, B78, B94, B95, C05, C10, C13, C25, C30, C60, C78, C85, C92, D26, D52, D65, E14, E28, E84, G14, H24, H60, H72, I50, L23, L28, L41, L55, L65, L79, M10, M20, M25, M40, N07, N21, N38, N41, N63, N79, N84, O33, P40, P60, Q50, Q75, R52, S18, S22, S23, S26, S28, S78, S85, S88, S91, S93, S98, U80, W40, W50, W75

Mathematics and statistics

A20, A40, A60, A80, B06, B13, B16, B32, B38, B44, B60, B72, B78, B80, B84, C05, C10, C15, C30, C50, C55, C60, C85, D26, D39, D65, D86, E14, E27, E42, E56, E70, E84, G14, G28, G42, G56, G70, H24, H36, H54, H60, H72, I50, K12, K24, K48, K60, K84, L14, L23, L24, L34, L41, I46, L51, L55, L72, L79, M20, M25, M40, M80, N07, N21, N37, N38, N63, N77, N81, N84, N91, O33, O66, P20, P60, P80, Q50, Q75, R12, R72, S03, S08, S18, S21, S24, S27, S36, S59, S72, S75, S78, S79, S84, S85, S90, S93, T20, T80, U20, U80, W20, W50, W75, Y50, Y75

Media studies – communications, journalism, publishing

A30, A40, A60, B06, B11, B13, B15, B16, B20, B26, B40, B41, B50, B56, B60, B72, B80, B84, B88, B90, B94, C10, C15, C20, C22, C25, C30, C50, C55, C58, C60, C71, C75, C78, C85, C91, C92, C95, D26, D39, D52, D58, E14, E28, E42, E70, F33, F66, G14, G42, G56, G70, G80, G90, H10, H36, H39, I149, H54, H60, H73, K12, K48, K60, K84, I07, L14, L23, L24, L27, L34, L39, L41, L51, L53, L55, L65, L79, L93, M40, M80, N07, N13, N21, N23, N30, N38, N49, N56, N58, N63, N72, N77, N78, N79, N82, N91, O66, O80, P20, P55, P60, P80, Q25, Q50, R06, R10, R20, R36, R48, R72, S03, S18, S21, S26, S27, S28, S29, S30, S32, S33, S43, S46, S51, S59, S64, S71, S72, S74, S75, S76, S81, S84, S85, S88, S90, S91, S93, S96, T20, T40, T45, T80, U20, W08, W17, W20, W25, W40, W50, W65, W66, W73, W75, W80, Y75

Medicine

A20, B06, B32, B78, C05, D65, E14, E56, G28, I50, K60, L23, L34, L41, M20, N21, N84, O33, P37, Q50, Q75, R12, S18, S27, S36, S49, U80, W10, W20

Microbiology

A20, A40, A60, A80, B13, B32, B56, B78, B80, B94, C15, C30, D65, E14, E28, E56, G14, G28, G42, H24, H36, H49, H60,

I50, K24, K60, L23, L34, L39, L41, L51, L93, M20, M40, N07, N21, N49, N63, N84, N91, P20, P60, P80, Q50, Q75, R12, S03, S18, S33, S72, S78, S85, S90, T20, W20, W50, W75, W80

Music
A20, A60, B06, B13, B20, B32, B38, B41, B50, B72, B78, B80, B84, B94, C05, C10, C15, C20, C22, C24, C25, C30, C58, C60, C62, C66, C75, C85, C95, D13, D26, D39, D52, D86, E14, E27, E28, E56, E84, F66, G14, G28, G42, G56, G64, G70, H36, H49, H60, H72, H73, I50, K12, K24, K42, K48, K60, K84, L14, L23, L27, L30, L39, L41, L43, I46, L48, L51, L53, L55, L65, L82, L93, M20, M40, M80, N07, N13, N21, N23, N30, N31, N38, N41, N56, N60, N63, N84, O33, O66, P20, P60, P80, Q75, R10, R12, R48, R51, R72, S03, S08, S09, S18, S24, S27, S30, S42, S43, S51, S71, S72, S78, S79, S84, S85, S90, S96, T20, T40, T45, T80, U20, W08, W12, W17, W30, W50, W60, W67, W75, W81, Y50, Y75

Nursing
A30, A60, B06, B32, B50, B56, B72, B80, B94, C10, C25, C30, C50, C60, C85, D26, E14, E56, G14, G28, G42, G70, H36, H60, H72, K12, K60, K84, L14, L23, L27, L41, L51, L93, M20, M40, N07, N38, N56, N77, N84, O66, P60, Q25, R12, R36, S03, S21, S24, S27, S33, S72, S75, S81, S84, S85, S93, T20, T40, U20, W10, W37, W75, W80

Pharmacy and pharmacology
A20, A60, A80, B13, B16, B56, B60, B72, B78, B80, C05, C15, C20, C30, C50, C85, D26, D39, D65, E28, E56, E56, G28, G70, H36, H60, K60, K84, L23, L41, L51, L93, M20, M40, M80, N07, N21, N49, N63, N84, N91, O66, P40, P80, Q75, R36, S03, S12, S18, S21, S27, S29, S36, S76, S78, S84, S85, U80, W50, W75

Philosophy
A20, A60, A70, B20, B32, B44, B56, B60, B72, B78, B94, C05, C15, C30, C55, D39, D65, D86, E14, E28, E56, E70, E84, G14, G28, G70, H36, H48, H49, H72, K12, K24, K48, K60, K84, I07, L14, L23, L41, L55, L72, M20, M40, M77, M80, N21, N36, N37, N38, N63, N84, N91, O33, O66, P60, Q75, R12, R48, S18, S24, S27, S36, S59, S72, S75, S90, S93, U20, U80, W20, W50, W75, Y50

Physical science
A20, A40, B13, B16, B32, B78, C05, C15, C30, D65, D86, E14, E56, E84, G14, G28, G42, G67, H24, H36, H72, I50, K12, K24, K60, L14, L23, L24, L34, L41, L51, L77, L79, M20, M25, N21, N84, N91, O33, O66, P20, P40, P60, Q50, Q75, R12, R72, S03, S18, S21, S24, S27, S36, S59, S78, S85, S90, S93, T20, U80, W20, Y50

Planning – town and country
A20, A60, A80, B06, B32, B56, B72, B80, C05, C15, C20, C25, C50, C85, D26, D52, D65, G14, G70, H24, K24, K84, L21, L27, L41, L51, M20, M40, M80, N07, N21, N56, N77, N84, N91, O66, Q50, Q75, R12, S03, S18, S21, S33, S78, U20, U80, W50, W75

Politics
A20, A40, A60, A80, B06, B13, B16, B32, B56, B72, B78, B80, B84, B90, C05, C08, C15, C20, C25, C30, C50, C85, D26,

D39, D65, D86, E14, E28, E56, E70, E84, G14, G28, G42, G56, G70, H60, H72, K12, K24, K84, I07, L14, L23, L27, L34, L39, L41, L51, L55, L72, L79, M20, M40, M80, N21, N38, N63, N77, N84, N91, O33, O66, P20, P35, P60, P80, Q50, Q75, R12, R20, R36, R48, R72, S03, S09, S18, S21, S27, S33, S36, S64, S72, S75, S78, S84, S90, S93, T20, T70, U20, U80, W08, W20, W50, W74, W75, W81, Y50

Psychology
A20, A30, A40, A60, A70, A80, B06, B16, B20, B32, B41, B44, B50, B56, B60, B78, B80, B84, B90, B94, C05, C10, C15, C20, C25, C30, C50, C55, C60, C85, D26, D39, D65, D86, E14, E28, E42, E56, E70, E84, G14, G28, G42, G56, G70, G96, H06, H24, H36, H60, H72, K12, K24, K48, K84, L14, L22, L23, L24, L27, L34, L39, L41, I46, L51, L55, L72, L79, L93, M20, M40, M80, N07, N21, N36, N38, N56, N63, N77, N82, N84, N91, O30, O33, O66, P20, P55, P60, P80, Q25, Q75, R12, R20, R48, R72, S03, S18, S21, S24, S27, S28, S30, S33, S36, S59, S64, S72, S75, S78, S81, S84, S85, S90, S93, S72, T40, U20, U80, W20, W25, W35, W50, W60, W75, W80, Y50, Y75

Sociology and anthropology
A20, A30, A40, A60, A80, B06, B13, B15, B16, B20, B26, B32, B40, B41, B44, B56, B60, B72, B78, B80, B84, B88, B94, C05, C10, C15, C20, C25, C30, C50, C55, C58, C60, C85, C95, D26, D39, D52, D86, E14, E28, E42, E56, E70, E84, G14, G28, G42, G56, G70, G80, G96, H14, H47, H49, H60, H72, K12, K24, K48, K60, K84, I07, L14, L22, L23, L24, L27, L34, L39, L41, I46, L51, L55, L72, L79, L93, M20, M40, M80, N07, N21, N38, N41, N56, N77, N82, N84, N91, O10, O30, O33, O66, P20, P60, P80, Q25, Q75, R12, R20, R36, R48, R72, S03, S09, S18, S21, S24, S26, S27, S30, S33, S35, S36, S43, S51, S59, S64, S72, S75, S78, S81, S84, S85, S90, S93, T20, U20, U80, W20, W50, W75, W80, Y50, Y75

Social policy, social work and administration
A30, A60, A80, B06, B13, B15, B16, B20, B26, B32, B37, B40, B41, B44, B50, B56, B60, B72, B78, B80, B84, B94, B95, C10, C15, C20, C22, C25, C30, C50, C85, D26, D27, E28, E42, E56, E70, G14, G28, G42, G45, G56, G70, G80, G90, H14, H16, H24, H36, H47, H49, H60, H72, K12, K24, K48, K84, L14, L21, L23, L27, L34, L39, L41, L43, I46, L51, L53, L55, L72, L79, L93, M20, M40, M80, N07, N13, N21, N23, N30, N37, N38, N56, N58, N60, N63, N72, N77, N84, N91, O10, O33, O66, P20, P40, P55, P60, P80, Q25, S22, S27, S28, S29, S30, S33, S35, S43, S51, S59, S64, S69, S72, S75, S76, S78, S79, S81, S84, S85, S93, S94, S96, T20, T80, U20, U95, W12, W17, W20, W25, W45, W60, W67, W75, W80, W81, Y50, Y75, Y80

Sport science/studies
A20, A30, A60, B06, B13, B15, B16, B26, B32, B35, B40, B41, B44, B50, B56, B60, B70, B72, B80, B84, B94, C08, C10, C20, C22, C30, C45, C50, C55, C58, C75, C78, C85, C92, D26, D39, D52, D86, E28, E42, E56, E70, E84, G14, G28, G70, G80, G90, H06, H24, H36, H49, H60, H72, K24, K48, K84, L16, L21, L23, L24, L27, L39,

I46, L51, L53, L77, L79, L93, M20, M40, M77, M80, N07, N13, N23, N28, N30, N37, N38, N56, N58, N63, N77, N91, O66, P35, P60, P80, R12, R36, R48, S03, S08, S21, S22, S23, S24, S26, S27, S28, S29, S30, S32, S33, S36, S38, S43, S46, S51, S59, S64, S65, S68, S71, S72, S75, S76, S78, S79, S81, S84, S91, S93, S96, T10, T20, T40, T80, U20, W08, W17, W25, W35, W45, W50, W60, W67, W74, W75, W80, W81, W85, Y25, Y70, Y75, Y80

Teacher training
A60, B06, B16, B38, B40, B44, B60, B70, B72, B80, B84, C05, C10, C15, C20, C25, C50, C55, C58, C75, D26, D39, D86, E42, E56, G14, G28, G56, G70, G80, H36, H54, H60, H72, H73, K48, K84, N36, N37, N38, N56, N60, N63, N77, N91, O66, P20, P60, R12, R48, S21, S24, S51, S59, S64, S75, S78, S79, S94, S96, T80, W20, W75, W80, Y75

Theology
A20, B06, B20, B32, B38, B60, B72, B78, C05, C10, C15, C50, C55, C58, D39, D86, E56, E84, G28, G70, H36, H48, H49, H50, H72, K24, K48, K60, I07, L14, L23, L24, L38, I46, M20, M77, N21, N36, N84, O33, O66, Q75, R48, S09, S18, S24, S36, S59, S64, S72, S75, S79, S84, T80, W75, Y75

Tourism
A30, A40, A60, B06, B11, B13, B15, B16, B20, B26, B35, B40, B41, B44, B50, B60, B70, B72, B80, B88, B89, B90, B94, C10, C20, C30, C45, C50, C55, C58, C66, C69, C75, C78, C84, C85, C92, D22, D39, D52, D58, E28, E50, F66, G14, G42, G45, G70, G74, G80, G90, H10, H14, H16, H24, H36, H39, H49, H60, H72, I70, K24, K48, L21, L27, L36, L39, I46, L51, L53, L55, L65, L77, L93, M40, M77, M80, N07, N23, N30, N41, N56, N58, N63, N72, N77, N79, N82, O10, O66, P20, P35, P60, P80, Q25, R10, R36, S01, S03, S07, S21, S22, S23, S24, S26, S28, S30, S32, S33, S35, S41, S42, S43, S51, S59, S71, S72, S74, S75, S76, S78, S81, S84, S85, S91, S94, S96, T20, T40, T70, T80, U20, W08, W17, W40, W50, W52, W60, W67, W73, W75, W80, W81, W85, Y70, Y80

Veterinary science
B78, B80, C05, C30, C78, E56, G14, G28, L41, M80, R84, S26, S51

Zoology
A20, A40, A60, B06, B13, B32, B37, B78, C05, C13, C15, C78, D39, D65, D86, E28, E56, G28, H58, H72, I50, L23, L34, L41, L51, M20, N21, N84, P60, P80, Q50, Q75, R12, R48, R72, S18, S27, S75, S84, S93, W74, W80, W85

Combined programmes
A20, A40, A60, B06, B13, B16, B32, B38, B40, B56, B60, B72, B80, B84, B90, B95, C05, C10, C30, C50, C78, C90, D39, D52, D65, D86, E14, E28, E42, E56, E70, E84, G14, G28, G42, G70, H06, H24, H36, H49, H60, H72, K12, K60, K84, I07, L14, L23, L27, L34, L41, I46, L51, L55, L72, L93, M20, M40, M80, N07, N21, N36, N37, N38, N56, N63, N77, N91, O33, O66, P20, P40, P55, P60, Q25, Q50, R36, R48, R72, R90, S03, S09, S18, S21, S24, S27, S28, S30, S32, S33, S35, S36, S42, S64, S72, S75, S78, S79, S81, S84, S90, S93, S96, T20, U20, U80, W20, W25, W35, W50, W73, W75, Y25, Y50, Y90

Course directory

Index